The Partings of the Ways

JAMES D. G. DUNN

The Partings of the Ways

*Between Christianity and Judaism
and their Significance for the
Character of Christianity*

Second Edition

scm press

First published 1991
Second impression 1996
Second edition 2006

British Library Cataloguing in Publication data

A catalogue record for this book is available
from the British Library

0 334 02999 6 / 9780 334 02990 1

Published in 2006 by SCM Press
9–17 St Alban's Place
London N1 0NX

www.scm-canterburypress.co.uk

SCM Press is a division of
SCM-Canterbury Press Ltd

Typeset by Rowland Phototypesetting Ltd,
Bury St Edmunds, Suffolk
Printed and bound in Great Britain by
William Clowes Ltd, Beccles, Suffolk

To
the Staff and Students of
THE VENERABLE ENGLISH COLLEGE,
ROME
in grateful thanks for hospitality
and fellowship

and
in memory of
JOSEPH GREGORY MCCARTHY
under whose name these lectures
were first delivered at
The Gregorian Pontifical University,
Rome, 1990

Contents

Preface to the Second Edition

The reason for entitling this volume, 'The *Partings* (plural) of the Ways', was and is, of course, to make the point that the separation of Christianity from rabbinic Judaism cannot neatly be identified as taking place at a particular point in time or place, as though there was only one 'parting of the ways'.[1] The separation from each other of what are now two quite independent religions was much more of a process, and took much longer to become clear-cut and final than most people realize.[2] To be sure, there were various points at which the tear(s), or pulling apart, was more evident than at others; there were various events and confrontations in particular locations which markedly accelerated the process. And with hindsight several 'tipping points', starting with the crucifixion and resurrection (or the earliest claims that Jesus had been raised from the dead), are said by some to have been decisive more or less from the first.[3] Indeed, those who

---

1. B. Wander's title makes the same point – *Trennungsprozesse zwischen frühen Christentum und Judentum im 1. Jahrhundert n. Chr.*, Tübingen: Mohr Siebeck 1994; see particularly pp. 2 and 289.

2. The main thesis of A. H. Becker and A. Y. Reed (eds), *The Ways that Never Parted*, TSAJ 95; Tübingen: Mohr Siebeck 2003, is obvious from the title, but unfortunately the editors see their task as dispelling 'the notion of a single and simple "Parting of the Ways" in the first or second century CE' (p. 22); but 'single and simple' is too much of a straw man. Becker himself concludes that 'There were, in fact, many "partings", and they happened in different places at different times in different ways' (p. 392). Becker and Reed also press the case for 'convergences' subsequent to partings (pp. 22–3), but I question whether resort to the Hebrew Bible by Origen and Jerome is well described as a 'convergence' of the ways, as A. Salvesen argues in a subsequent essay – 'A Convergence of the Ways?', pp. 233–58 – or that such use is well described as 'the judaizing of Christian Scripture' (the article's subtitle; the title of the final diagram, 'The "Hebraization" of Greek and Latin Scripture', p. 258, is more appropriate).

3. E.g., C. A. Evans, 'Root Causes of the Jewish–Christian Rift from Jesus to Justin', in *Christian-Jewish Relations through the Centuries*, ed. S. E. Porter and B. W. R. Pearson, JSNTS 192; Sheffield Academic 2000 pp. 20–35, argues that 'the fundamental sticking points for many Jewish people were the simple facts that Jesus had been put to death and the kingdom of God had failed to materialize' (p. 23). P. Fredriksen, 'What "Parting of the Ways"?', in Becker and Reed (eds), *The Ways that Never Parted*, pp. 35–63, thinks that I undermine my case, and 'by opining that Jesus, in rejecting distinctions between the

emphasize the apocalyptic dimension of the first claims for Jesus' resurrection would seem to imply thereby that Christianity was seen from the beginning to have emerged on a quite different plane, without any *heilsgeschichtlich* continuity with Israel of old except as a claim made by Paul's Jewish-Christian opponents.[4] But most accept that Christianity functioned initially as a sect within second Temple Judaism, 'the sect of the Nazarenes' (Acts 24.5, 14), so that the question whether the ways would or should part was by no means an obvious conclusion to be drawn during the first generation and beyond.

In the fifteen years since I wrote *Partings*, however, I have come to recognize that the process was still more complex than I first envisaged. I accept Judith Lieu's critique that the imagery of 'ways' parting is too simple:[5] it can too easily imply two embryonic religions as two homogeneous (or even monolithic) entities each pursuing a single path, with developments in each case marching forward uniformly across the diverse contexts of the Mediterranean and Middle East;[6] whereas the sociological reality might be better depicted as 'a criss-crossing of muddy tracks'.[7] In some defence, it could be observed that the second plural in the title ('The Partings of the *Ways*') need (or should) not be taken to imply that there were only two ways in view,

---

righteous and sinners [*not* the way I would put it], thereby implicitly rejected the social and ethnic boundary between Jews and Gentiles' (pp. 35–6, n. 1). But she fails to take my process point and forgets that there was good Jewish precedent for Jesus' questioning of boundaries drawn by the 'righteous', not least in Jonah and John the Baptist.

4. Particularly J. L. Martyn, *Galatians*, AB 33 A; New York: Doubleday 1997; also *Theological Issues in the Letters of Paul*, Edinburgh: T. & T. Clark 1997.

5. J. Lieu, ' "The Parting of the Ways": Theological Construct or Historic Reality?', *JSNT* 56 (1994), pp. 101–19, reprinted in *Neither Jew nor Greek? Constructing Christian Identity*, Edinburgh: T. & T. Clark 2003, pp. 11–29.

6. 'The problem with the model of the "parting of the ways" is that . . . it operates essentially with the abstract or universal conception of each religion, Judaism and Christianity, when what we know about is the specific and local' (Lieu, 'Parting', p. 108/18). Other weaknesses are noted in Becker and Reed (eds), *The Ways that Never Parted*, pp. 19–22; but also strengths (pp. 15–16, 18–19)!

7. Lieu, 'Parting', p. 119/29. Lieu returns to the theme in *Christian Identity in the Jewish and Graeco-Roman World*, Oxford University 2004. Observing that debate on the relationship between Christianity and Judaism has largely failed to achieve a consensus as to how, when and why the two parted, she continues: 'There are two key reasons for this failure: first, because it is never clear whether the objects of that question are ideas, or people, or systems; and secondly, because much depends on whether the respondent is a hypothetical Jew, Christian, or pagan of the time, or is the contemporary scholar, or even the believer, both the latter having the benefits . . . of hindsight and of subsequent history' (p. 305, and further pp. 305–10). In correspondence Lieu adds the further complicating factor of 'the filter of literary genre'; I am grateful to Judith for commenting on a first draft of this new introduction.

as though both rabbinic Judaism and Christianity each travelled a single well-defined path which diverged into two similarly single and well-defined paths.[8] To change the metaphor, there were various currents within the broader streams which became rabbinic Judaism and Christianity. But I still prefer the imagery of 'ways' or 'paths'. The alternative of 'trajectories' which became popular in the 1970s[9] implies pre-determined 'flight-paths' for the entities in view. And 'stream' suffers somewhat from the same defect, as implying an irresistable force carving out its own channel. Whereas the imagery of 'ways' or 'paths' need not imply directness and can include a landscape of moor or hillside criss-crossed by several or many paths, whose directions are not always clear and which ramblers or fellwalkers may follow without a clear sense of where they are headed; the path actually travelled is always clearer looking back![10]

The principal fact remains, however, that 'Judaism' and 'Christianity' have been quite distinct religions for many centuries. So the question how that came about, given their common beginnings within second Temple Judaism, is one which cannot be avoided, whatever imagery we use. And the task of exploring how the ways parted is one of looking back, to discern the paths actually travelled – why it was that Judaism and Christianity became separate religions – rather than to assume that the two embryonic religions travelled predetermined paths whose parting was inevitable or unavoidable.[11] Moreover, the imagery picks up a motif present in the heritage of both religions, of religious practice as a 'way' of living,[12] and not only a matter of doctrines to be believed. This is one of the principal reasons why I continue to think that 'the four pillars of second Temple

---

8. This is also the weakness of the various models diagramed by M. Goodman, 'Modeling the "Parting of the Ways"', in Becker and Reed (eds), *The Ways that Never Parted*, pp. 119–29, which mostly have to rely on single, one-dimensional lines, when at least two-dimensional breadth is surely necessary to model complex social phenomena such as diverse religious movements.

9. J. M. Robinson and H. Koester, *Trajectories through Earliest Christianity*, Philadelphia: Fortress 1971.

10. For other models see D. Boyarin, 'Semantic Differences; or, "Judaism"/"Christianity"', in Becker and Reed (eds), *The Ways that Never Parted*, pp. 74–7: the familiar family tree, or, adapted to languages (the emergence of families of languages or dialects which continue to interact even when they have become largely distinct), or Boyarin's own 'wave-theory' ('innovations disseminate and interact like waves caused by stones thrown in a pond').

11. But to argue that 'the ways *never* parted' (Becker and Reed (eds), *The Ways that Never Parted*) is surely an over-reaction. As one of the essayists, R. A. Kraft, 'The Weighing of the Parts', pp. 87–94) observes, 'It is quite obvious that the "ways" that led to classical Christianity and rabbinic Judaism did indeed "part" by the fourth century CE' (p. 87).

12. See the thorough study by W. Michaelis, *hodos*, *TDNT* 5.42–96.

Judaism' are the obvious areas to be examined for traces of early divergences among the heirs of second Temple Judaism which were to deepen in due course into the clear and often sharp divisions and separations between Judaism and Christianity.[13] For the four 'pillars' include, of course, credal assertions (principally the Shema), but Temple[14] and Law are also very much about praxis.[15] So despite its inadequacies I continue to work with the imagery of 'ways' parting, indeed of many 'partings', in the hope that the imagery is helpfully eirenic and not too misleading.

All that being said, however, I soon realized that in particular the early phase and latter phase of the messy process of 'parting' do need more careful statement. In what sense can we speak of 'Judaism' in the first century of the common era? What was a 'Jew'? And when did 'Christian' and 'Christianity' emerge as clear referents? How pluriform was second Temple Judaism, and how hospitable to the developments which saw the emergence of both rabbinic Judaism and Christianity? And if the beginning of the process makes greater demands on the language we use, if it is adequately to reflect the realities of the first century, the latter phase of the process certainly requires substantial revision in terms of when a final parting can be said to have happened.

Who or what parted?

Fundamental in this whole discussion is the recognition that the categories 'Jew' and 'Judaism', 'Christian' and 'Christianity' were only in process of emerging and gaining definition in the latter stages of second Temple Judaism[16] and the early years of the second century.[17]

---

13. Cf. Wander's list of what have been identified as factors making for the separation (*Trennungsprozesse*, pp. 36-7).

14. R. Bauckham, 'The Parting of the Ways: What Happened and Why', *St. Th.* 47 (1993), pp. 135-51, thinks that the Temple was the real issue (as also with both Qumran and the Samaritans) and that I do not give sufficient recognition to this fact (pp. 142-4 and n. 32).

15. This in reference to M. Zetterholm, *The Formation of Christianity in Antioch: A Social-Scientific Approach to the Separation between Judaism and Christianity*, London: Routledge 2003, who criticizes my 'theoretical outlook and analytical tools' as 'almost exclusively focused on ideological aspects' (p. 4).

16. Of course, the description 'second Temple Judaism' also begs a few questions; see e.g. my *Jesus Remembered*, Grand Rapids: Eerdmans 2003, pp. 255-92. But some referential term has to be used!

17. I began to explore this dimension of the problem in the essay which now appears as an appendix; see below, pp. 339-65 (=107-13).

The term 'Jew' (*Ioudaios*) began, of course, as a way of identifying someone from Judaea (*Ioudaia*). So initially *Ioudaios* is better translated 'Judaean'. And just when it was that the referent 'Judaean' broadened to the referent 'Jew' is a matter of some dispute;[18] whenever it happened, of course, it would not have happened uniformly and everywhere at the same time. The ambiguity highlights the tension which ran through late second Temple Judaism, and which was critical in the attempts of the first Christians to identify themselves: whether Israel's heritage was ethnically or religiously determined. Since it is only at the end of the first century CE that Graeco-Roman writers begin to use *Ioudaios* as a religious referent ('Jew'),[19] the ambiguity was both in self-identification and in the eye of the observer.[20]

'Christian' first appears in Acts 11.26 as a reference to the believers in Messiah Jesus and followers of his 'way'. Luke evidently did not intend to imply by the usage that 'Christians' were thus early distinguished from 'Jews', for he goes out of his way to stress that the disputes between local Jews and Paul's converts were an internal matter – 'questions about words and names and their own (Jewish) law' (Acts 18.15).[21] So 'Christians' was first coined as an alternative to 'the sect of the Nazarenes', one of the 'ways' practised within second Temple Judaism. This inference is borne out by the fact that *Christianoi* is a Latinism (*Christiani*), on the model of *Hērōdianoi* (Herodians), or *Kaisarianoi* (Caesareans)[22] – that is, supporters of or members of the faction which regarded the one named as their leader. This suggests that the title was coined by the Roman authorities in Antioch, who recognized the growing body of followers of the one known as 'Christ' as a significant faction within the melting-pot of Jews and Jewish adherents in Antioch.[23] Here too, it is only with

---

18. The third English edition of Bauer's lexicon advocates that *Ioudaios* in the NT should consistently be translated 'Judaean' (BDAG, pp. 478–9). But S. J. D. Cohen, *The Beginnings of Jewishness: Boundaries, Varieties, Uncertainties*, Berkeley: University of California 1999, ch. 3, argues that the transition began at the end of the first century BCE, from an ethno-geographical term to one of religious significance.

19. Cohen, *Beginnings* 96.

20. The re-emergence of the state of Israel in 1948 has revived the ambiguity – whether 'Jew' is primarily an ethnic or a religious identifier.

21. See further, e.g., Acts 3.22–6; 15.13–18; 28.20; and the arguments put forward by J. Jervell in a number of publications – most recently, *The Theology of the Acts of the Apostles*, Cambridge University 1996.

22. BAGD, p. 1090; see also below, p. 352.

23. Josephus reports that in Antioch many Greeks and God-fearers or 'judaizers' were during this period attracted to Jewish ways and mixed themselves with the Jewish community (*War* 2.462–3; 7.45).

Graeco-Roman writers early in the second century that the name 'Christian' begins to appear (Tacitus, Suetonius, the younger Pliny).[24]

As already indicated in the first edition of *Partings*,[25] the term 'Judaism' (*Ioudaismos*) first appears in literature in 2 Maccabees (2.21; 8.1; 14.38). These passages clearly indicate the emergence of a self-understanding determined by and expressive of the Maccabean resistance to Syrian oppression. The term itself was evidently coined as a counter to 'Hellenism' (*hellēnismos* – 2 Macc. 4.13) and 'foreignness' (*allophylismos* – 2 Macc. 4.13; 6.24). That is to say, for the author of 2 Maccabees, 'Judaism' was the summary term for that national and religious identity which was marked from the first by its unyielding insistence on maintaining distinctive and defining Torah practices like circumcision and food laws (1 Macc. 1.60–3; 2.46; 2 Macc. 6). This indicates that 'Judaism' was initially a narrower term than in its normal use today – as expressing a strongly nationalistic self-understanding ('Judaean') and a religious identity defined precisely as a sharply defined and resolutely defended distinctiveness from other religions.[26] All this should be remembered when we consider the only occurrence of the term in the NT, in Gal. 1.13–14, where Paul speaks of his former way of life 'in Judaism'. Here particularly to be avoided is the anachronism of concluding that Paul thereby signalled that he had abandoned what we today regard as 'Judaism', or even its first-century equivalent (what *we* call 'second Temple Judaism'). For the 'Judaism' Paul had in view is marked precisely by the same 'zeal' as distinguished the Maccabees (1 Macc. 2.26–7, 50, 58; 2 Macc. 4.2), a zeal which caused Paul to seek the destruction of 'the church of God (*qahal Yahweh*)' (Gal. 1.13; Phil. 3.6). It would be more accurate, then, to say that the converted Paul turned away from the more specific and tightly defined understanding of Judaism espoused by the zealous among the sect of the Pharisees;[27] that is, the 'Judaism' of Gal. 1.13–14 was one of the varieties of second Temple Judaism and not the whole of second Temple Judaism, even if, of

---

24. BDAG, p. 1090.

25. *Partings*, p. 22 (= 30 below).

26. *Ioudaismos* 'meant something else than what we call Judaism'; it meant 'remaining loyal to the ways of the Judeans and the political cause of Jerusalem' (Boyarin, 'Semantic Differences', pp. 67–8). Boyarin goes on to argue that 'religion', which he understands as 'a discrete category of human experience', 'disembeddable from the culture as a whole' (p. 70), was a Christian invention; but he does not deal with Cohen's argument (n. 18 above), and is hard put to make sense of what happened to Paul as a 'conversion' (p. 68, n. 15) – a telling admission.

27. A. F. Segal, *Paul the Convert: The Apostolate and Apostasy of Saul the Pharisee*, New Haven: Yale University 1990.

course, the zealous would want their (form of) 'Judaism' to be regarded as the only legitimate expression of Judaism (they would have preferred to use the term 'Israel').[28] Within that broader stream of late second Temple Judaism, the Jesus messianists became an increasingly stronger current.[29]

Somewhat curiously the term 'Christianity' emerged in a somewhat similar way. It first appears in our sources once again in the early second century, that is, in the Apostolic Fathers (Ignatius, *Magn.* 10.1–3; *Rom.* 3.3; *Phil.* 6.1; *Mart. Pol.* 10.1). In two of these references 'Christianity' is set over against 'Judaism', as two distinct entities, to be defined in large part by their distinctiveness from each other. As 'Judaism' was initially defined by way of contrast or antithesis to 'Hellenism', so 'Christianity' was initially defined by way of contrast or antithesis to 'Judaism'.[30] But does the parallel extend further? I have just noted that 'Judaism' as used by Paul (Gal. 1.13–14) should be seen as a factional or sectarian understanding of the more diverse reality of second Temple Judaism. The question which *Partings* poses is whether Ignatius' initial definition of 'Christianity' has to be qualified in the same or in an equivalent way. That is to say, was Ignatius espousing an understanding of the movement stemming from Jesus (to use as nondescript a referent as possible) which was equivalently narrow, or rigorous (or sectarian!) as Paul's use of 'Judaism'? Was the attempt to define 'Christianity' in contrast to 'Judaism' only one current within the broader stream of emerging Christianity, only one track within the more diverse but properly called 'Christian' ways emerging from the first century? The alternative, of maintaining Ignatius' contrast with Judaism as integral to Christianity's self-understanding, forces us into a situation where Jewish–Christian dialogue can go forward only from two sides of quite a wide gulf of separation from the 'other'. But just as second Temple Judaism is a larger and more diverse entity than 2 Maccabees' or Paul's 'Judaism', perhaps we should recognize a larger and more

---

28. See particularly P. Tomson, 'The Names Israel and Jew in Ancient Judaism and in the New Testament', *Bijdragen* 47 (1986), pp. 120–40, 266–89; also J. Neusner, 'Was Rabbinic Judaism Really "Ethnic"?', *CBQ* 57 (1995), pp. 281–305 (here 285–301).

29. Bauckham justifiably warns against a too simplistic model of many 'Judaisms' for the period: 'common Judaism' could embrace a substantial range of diversity; 'somewhat differing interpretations of a religion can easily coexist within a single, even a strongly unified community'; variety (as embracing Pharisees and Sadducees) is not the same as separation (as between Jews and Samaritans) ('The Parting of the Ways', pp. 137–41).

30. See also K.-W. Niebuhr, ' "Judentum" und "Christentum" bei Paulus und Ignatius von Antiochien', *ZNW* 85 (1994), pp. 218–33 (here 224–33). For this section cf. also Lieu, *Christian Identity*, ch. 8.

diverse Christianity emerging from the first century than Ignatius seems to imply.[31]

Even such a cursory review of the main terms to describe who and what parted (Jews, Christians; Judaism, Christianity) should be a sufficient indication of how complex were the initial stages of the process of parting. The difficulty of defining the terms is a salutary reminder that such definition comes more clearly with hindsight, and that to retroject the subsequently clearer definitions into the early days runs the risk of imposing a pseudo-clarity on a much less clear situation. If we want to see things as first-century writers like Paul saw them, and not just with the twenty-twenty vision of hindsight, then anachronistic clarifications should be regarded with the greatest caution. And if the still fuzzy notions of a Paul on matters of Jew/ Christian self-identity[32] continue to have force for Christians as one of Christianity's canonical voices, then perhaps such lack of sharpness in identity should be given a fuller hearing than is usually the case. In this case, *The Partings of the Ways* may have increasing rather than decreasing relevance to Christianity's seeking for fresh self-understanding and identity in the twenty-first century.

When did they part?

In the first edition of *Partings* I made bold to draw the conclusion that a final 'parting' can be discerned in the second century – with the second Jewish revolt against Rome, and certainly by the end of the second century.[33] Further study soon made it clearer to me that these were but

---

31. J. G. Gager, 'Did Jewish Christians See the Rise of Islam?', in Becker and Reed (eds), *The Ways that Never Parted*, pp. 361–72: 'we simply cannot speak of "Judaism" and "Christianity" as uniform entities; we must speak, rather, of Jews and Christians at different times and in different places' (p. 369).

32. See my 'Who Did Paul Think He was? A Study of Jewish Christian Identity', *NTS* 45 (1999), pp. 174–93.

33. *Partings*, p. 243 (= p. 318 below). Qualified support, and on the basis of a much fuller treatment of second-century texts, is given by S. G. Wilson, *Related Strangers: Jews and Christians 70–170 CE*, Minneapolis: Fortress 1995, particularly pp. 285–8; also 306 n.37. Bauckham also thinks the non-participation of Christians in the Bar Kokhba revolt 'probably sealed their exclusion from common Judaism and removed the rabbis' main rivals for dominance in Palestinian Judaism' ('The Parting of the Ways', pp. 145–6). And similarly the essays by P. J. Tomson and S. Schoon, in *The Image of the Judaeo-Christians in Ancient Jewish and Christian Literature*, ed. P. J. Tomson and D. Lambers-Petry, WUNT 158; Tübingen: Mohr Siebeck 2003, consider the decisive factors to be the political and social upheavals caused by the two Jewish revolts (here 22–7 and 309–11). This is the consensus view (Becker and Reed (eds), *The Ways that Never Parted*, p. 1; with a good statement of the 'master narrative', pp. 4–5). In some contrast, E. A. Judge, 'Judaism and the Rise of Christianity: A Roman Perspective', *TynB* 45 (1994), pp. 355–68, points out

further partings, of great significance for some, but perhaps no more significant than the expulsions from the synagogue (of which the Fourth Gospel speaks)[34] for others. Indeed, already the first conclusion to the 1989 Durham/Tübingen Research Symposium on 'The Parting of the Ways, AD 70–135', pointed to a less clear-cut process: '"The parting of the ways", properly speaking, was very "bitty", long drawn out and influenced by a range of social, geographical, and political, as well as theological factors.'[35] What I began to see more clearly, however, is that if the beginning of the process of the partings of the ways was much less clear-cut, then the outcome of the process was even less clear-cut and the final parting a lot longer delayed than I had allowed.

Some basic data is assembled in the essay which forms the new appendix to this edition.[36] There in particular I draw attention to

---

that Romans 'seem to have been unaware of the links between Jews and Christians', and deduces that 'a socially clear-cut separation from an early stage must be assumed' (366), though the fact that the Roman authorities perceived the early Christians as a distinct body may tell us little about many/most early Christians' sense of identity. William Horbury, *Jews and Christians in Contact and Controversy*, Edinburgh: T. & T. Clark 1998, observes that 'a Christian sense of accepted separation from the Jewish community seems first clearly detectable in writings from about the end of the first century onwards, notably the Epistle of Barnabas'. He also notes that concerns to maintain Jewish unity put limits on communal tolerance from an early period (Paul's persecution, 2 Cor. 11.24; John 9.22) and argues that the *Birkat ha-minim* would have been consistent with that (pp. 11–13). Wander observes that most NT research sees the break between Judaism and Christianity as effectively documented in the *Birkat ha-minim* (*Trennungsprozesse*, p. 3). But see the next note.

34. The *Birkat ha-minim* (the cursing of heretics) has been fruitful of much confusion at this point, especially since the influential study of John's Gospel by J. L. Martyn, *History and Theology in the Fourth Gospel*, Nashville: Abingdon[2]1979, postulated it as the background to John 9.22. Subsequent discussion, however, has made it likely that the *Birkat ha-minim* did not emerge till later, and that any explicit reference to Christians is unlikely to have been part of its original formulation. See now D. Boyarin, *Border Lines: The Partition of Judaeo-Christianity*, Philadelphia: University of Pennsylvania 2004, pp. 67–73, and further bibliography there, including particularly P. W. van der Horst, 'The Birkat ha-minim in Recent Research', in *Hellenism-Judaism-Christianity: Essays on their Interaction*, Kampen: Pharos 1994, pp. 99–111; also Horbury, *Jews and Christians*, ch. 2 and pp. 240–2.

35. J. D. G. Dunn (ed.), *Jews and Christians: The Parting of the Ways AD 70 to 135*, Tübingen: Mohr Siebeck 1992; Grand Rapids: Eerdmans 1999, p. 367; also §21.1e below.

36. See below, pp. 343–6 (= 100–3). In that essay I draw particularly on J. Parkes, *The Conflict of the Church and the Synagogue*, Jewish Publication Society 1934; reprinted New York: Macmillan; and M. Simon, *Verus Israel: A Study of the Relations between Christians and Jews in the Roman Empire (AD 152–425)*, 1948, 1964; Oxford University 1989. See further Lieu, 'Parting', pp. 110–18/20–9; also 'History and Theology in Christian Views of Judaism', in *Neither Jew nor Greek?*, pp. 117–34 (here 126–31); summaries in Becker and Reed (eds), *The Ways that Never Parted*, p. 6 n. 17 (bibliography, p. 2 n.7), and Fredriksen, 'What "Parting of the Ways"?', pp. 60 n.79, 61 n.82. J. T. Sanders, *Schismatics, Sectarians, Dissidents, Deviants: The First One Hundred Years of Jewish–Christian Relations*, London: SCM Press 1993, reaches different conclusions – 'little

the fact that Christian leaders, as late as the fourth century, had to continually rebuke and warn their congregations against attending synagogues and observing Jewish feasts and customs.[37] This clearly indicates that throughout the first three to four centuries what we might call 'ordinary Christians' did *not* see Christianity and Judaism as two separate far less opposed religions. Rather the position was more like what is common in the days of denominational Christianity; that is, where 'ordinary Christians' feel free to attend the services of different denominations without thinking that they are being untrue to their more specific Christian heritage. The two ways were evidently seen by very many as (still) overlapping, so that participation in the synagogue could be seen as entirely consistent with their ecclesial commitment. The fact that such rebukes and warnings are to be found so frequently through this period tells us two things. One is that such a perception of the continuing overlap of Judaism and Christianity was widespread among Christians of the period. The other is that it was the Christian leadership which considered it necessary to press for a much clearer and sharper divide between the ways of Christianity and Judaism.[38] An appropriate question, however, is whether it was the Christian leadership or the 'ordinary Christians' who were being truer to the heritage of first-century Christianity.

In the appended essay I also draw attention to two further aspects of the complex picture.[39] One is the much less clear indications that the rabbis had a rather similar problem with Jews who believed in Jesus as Messiah but who wished nevertheless to continue practising as Jews.[40] 'Jewish Christianity' – 'Christians (who) still want to live according to the law of the Jews like the multitude of the Jews' (Origen, *contra Celsum* 5.61) – has had a 'bad press' in both Christ-

---

evidence of relations between Christians of any stripe and non-Christian Jews' in the diaspora (231) – but does not extend his study far enough beyond the first hundred years. Wander, *Trennungsprozesse*, also limits his discussion to the first century and focuses solely on Palestine.

37. See now also D. S. Ben Ezra, ' "Christians" observing "Jewish" Festivals of Autumn', in Tomson and Lambers-Petry (eds), *The Image of the Judaeo-Christians*, pp. 53–73; also 'Whose Fast Is It? The Ember Day of September and Yom Kippur', in Becker and Reed (eds), *The Ways that Never Parted*, pp. 259–82.

38. Becker and Reed put forward the proposition 'that Jews and Christians (or at least the elites among them) may have been engaged in the task of "parting" throughout Late Antiquity and the early Middle Ages, *precisely because* the two never really "parted" during that period with the degree of decisiveness or finality needed to render either tradition irrelevant to the self-definition of the other, or even to make participation in both an unattractive or inconceivable option' (*The Ways that Never Parted*, p. 23).

39. See below, pp. 346–50.

40. See also Wilson, *Related Strangers*, ch. 6; Horbury, *Jews and Christians*, ch. 5.

ianity and Judaism, as a heresy unacceptable to both sides.[41] That is unfortunate, since Jewish Christianity largely filled the middle-ground which was opening up between the two diverging ways.[42] It is no surprise that the disappearance of 'Jewish Christianity' more or less coincides with a final 'parting' between Christianity and Judaism in the latter half of the fourth century,[43] as, presumably, the remnants of Jewish-Christian groups were absorbed into the now two quite distinct religions. A salutary reminder of the poignancy of that disappearance and of the possibilities which 'Jewish Christianity' represented is the reappearance of Messianic Jews ('Jews for Jesus') in the last thirty or so years. It should occasion no surprise, either, that such Messianic Jews seem to be disowned equally by Christian and Jewish leadership today.[44] Evidently the challenge to identities which were formed by contrast (or antithesis) is as sensitive today as it was in the early centuries of the common era.

The other aspect to which I draw attention in the appended essay is that it was Christians, and not the rabbis, who preserved much of the Jewish literature of the late second Temple period and beyond.[45] Indeed, rather than assuming that documents like the *Ascension of Isaiah* and the *Testaments of the Twelve Patriarchs* are 'Christian' redactions of originally 'Jewish' documents, perhaps they should be seen more appropriately as Jewish-Christian writings, manifesting a

41. Often quoted are the comments of Jerome on the Nazarenes: 'While they want to be both Jews and Christians, they are neither Jews nor Christians' (*Ep.* 112.13). A valuable overview is provided by J. Carleton Paget, 'Jewish Christianity', in W. Horbury *et al.*, *The Cambridge History of Judaism*, vol. 3: *The Early Roman Period*, Cambridge University 1999, pp. 731–75.

42. See again Wilson, *Related Strangers*, pp. 143–59; and further the essays in Tomson and Lambers-Petry (eds), *The Image of the Judaeo-Christians*.

43. Cf. especially A. Y. Reed, ' "Jewish Christianity" after the "Parting of the Ways" ', in Becker and Reed (eds), *The Ways that Never Parted*, pp. 189–231. A. H. Becker, 'Beyond the Spatial and Temporal *Limes*', in the same volume (pp. 373–92) justly notes that 'parting of the ways' scholarship has focused too narrowly on the west (the Constantinian settlement) and has failed to examine the relationship between Jews and Christians not living under a Christian empire. Indeed, in Arabia, Mesopotamia and Syria the Christians initially encountered by burgeoning Islam may fairly (and most accurately) be described as Jewish-Christians. See further Gager, 'Did Jewish Christians See the Rise of Islam?', pp. 361–5.

44. Observed by D. Cohn-Sherbok, 'Modern Hebrew Christianity and Messianic Judaism', in Tomson and Lambers-Petry (eds), *The Image of the Judaeo-Christians*, pp. 287–98.

45. J. H. Charlesworth, 'Christian and Jewish Self-Definition in Light of the Christian Additions to the Apocryphal Writings', in vol. 2: *Aspects of Judaism in the Graeco-Roman Period*, ed. E. P. Sanders, London: SCM Press 1981, pp. 27–55, already referred to in §12.1d below; M. A. Knibb, 'Christian Adoption and Transmission of Jewish-Pseudepigrapha: The Case of 1 Enoch', *JSJ* 32 (2001), pp. 396–415.

Jesus-devotion within a Jewish self-definition.[46] This reminds us that such Christians saw themselves in continuity with the more diverse strands of second Temple Judaism; thus the points made in the last two paragraphs are reinforced. But it also reminds us that rabbinic Judaism was itself a narrower current within the broader stream which flowed from second Temple Judaism. Here we should underline a point which demands greater attention in all this: that second Temple Judaism was not transformed into rabbinic Judaism overnight. In contrast to the older, simplistic and anachronistic view that Judaism became rabbinic Judaism when it was reconstituted at Yavneh following the destruction of Jerusalem in 70, the growing consensus today is that the rabbis did not succeed in winning over or imposing their interpretation of Israel's heritage until much later[47] – probably, indeed, at about the same period, in the latter half of the fourth century, when Christianity's state recognition presumably hastened the final parting. The corollary to this is that the great mass of Jews in the western diaspora during the first two or three centuries of the common era should not in the strict sense be regarded as part of rabbinic Judaism. In other words, the lack of clear boundaries between Jew, Messiah-Jesus-believing Jew and Christian in these early centuries becomes still more evident, and we gain a further reminder that the partings of the ways took a lot longer to become clear and effective than has usually been thought.

At this point special mention should be made of the most recent contribution of Daniel Boyarin, one of the most stimulating of contributors to the current debate.[48] His basic thesis elaborates the above perception that 'Judaism and Christianity were not separate entities until very late in late antiquity'.[49] His particular argument is that both Christian

---

46. So argued by D. Frankfurter, 'Beyond "Jewish Christianity"', in Becker and Reed (eds), *The Ways that Never Parted*, pp. 131–43, who warns more generally about the tendency 'to retroject modern anxieties about religious clarity and orthodoxy onto a period of blur and flux in religious boundaries' (p. 131).

47. See e.g. the essays by P. S. Alexander, '"The Parting of the Ways" from the Perspective of Rabbinic Judaism', and M. Goodman, 'Diaspora Reactions to the Destruction of the Temple', in Dunn (ed.), *Jews and Christians*, pp. 1–25 and 27–38 respectively.

48. Boyarin, *Border Lines*; see also his earlier *Dying for God: Martyrdom and the Making of Judaism and Christianity*, Stanford: Stanford University 1999; cf. also M. S. Taylor, *Anti-Judaism and Early Christian Identity: A Critique of the Scholarly Consensus*, Leiden: Brill 1995.

49. In almost the same breath Boyarin observes that 'There is no reason to imagine . . . that "rabbinic Judaism" ever became the popular hegemonic form of Jewish religiosity among the "People of the Land", and there is good reason to believe the opposite'; and that 'In the earliest stages of their development – indeed I suggest until the end of the fourth century, if we consider all of their varieties and not just the nascent "orthodox" ones –

writers and the rabbis developed the model of orthodoxy/heresy precisely as a means of establishing their respective self-identities, that
in both cases there was a major transition from a sectarian structure
to one of orthodoxy and heresy which began to take place in the
first half of the second century, 'the transformation of both nascent
Christianity and nascent Judaism from groups of sects ... into
orthodox churches with their heretical others'.[50] The observation is
salutary, partly because the categories of 'orthodoxy' and 'heresy'
have usually been reckoned as Christian terms. More important, however, is the fact that since Walter Bauer's epochal study[51] they have
been somewhat controversial and contested terms of Christian self-
definition – Bauer's claim being that 'orthodoxy' was the creed of the
winners of a contested identity, and 'heresy' the creed of the losers,
the categorization, of course, being the language of the winners. The
point being made by Boyarin, is that very similar processes were
taking place within both emergent Christianity and emergent Judaism.
In terms of the imagery used here, both Christianity and Judaism
defined themselves as narrower paths within the broader ways which
emerged from the first century, a process which included the 'orthodox' designation of the overlap areas between the two ways as
'heresy'. So the question I posed tentatively in my earlier *Unity and
Diversity in the New Testament*[52] still stands: given that other
responses to Jesus and the gospel were recognized to produce too
extreme expressions, would it not be wise to recognize that orthodoxy
too could have its too extreme aspects? Is the failure of overscrupulous
restrictiveness any worse than the failure of overgenerous hospitality
to diverging ideas and practices?

In short, then, in response to the question, When did the ways

Judaism and Christianity were phenomenologically indistinguishable as entities . . .' (*Border
Lines*, p. 89).

50. Boyarin, *Border Lines*, pp. 21, 28, 30; see particularly his ch. 2, with the telling
quotation from J. Lieu, ' "I am a Christian": Martyrdom and the Beginning of "Christian
Identity" ', in *Neither Jew nor Greek?*: 'It is in opposition that Christianity gains its true
identity, so all identity becomes articulated, perhaps for the first time, in the face of "the
other", as well as in face of attempts by the "other" to deny its existence' (72). See further
Lieu, *Christian Identity* ch. 4 ('Boundaries') and ch. 9 ('The Other'); also several essays in
G. N. Stanton and G. G. Stroumsa (eds.), *Tolerance and Intolerance in Early Judaism and
Christianity*, Cambridge University, 1998.

51. W. Bauer, *Rechtgläubigkeit und Ketzerei im ältesten Christentum*, Tübingen: Mohr
Siebeck 1934; ET *Orthodoxy and Heresy in Earliest Christianity*, Philadelphia: Fortress
1971.

52. *Unity and Diversity in the New Testament: An Inquiry into the Character of
Earliest Christianity*, London: SCM Press 1977, [2]1990, [3]2006; already taken up in *Partings*,
pp. 253–4 (= 331–2 below). I develop the reflections on 'scripture and tradition' (*Partings*,
§12.5) in the Foreword to the third edition of *Unity and Diversity*.

part?, the answer has to be: Over a lengthy period, at different times and places, and as judged by different people differently, depending on what was regarded as a non-negotiable boundary marker and by whom. So, early for some, or demanded by a leadership seeking clarity of self-definition, but for many ordinary believers and practitioners there was a long lingering embrace which was broken finally only after the Constantinian settlement.[53]

Once more, the four pillars of Judaism

On the other question asked above, at the end of the first section – How hospitable was second Temple Judaism to the developments which saw the emergence of Christianity as well as rabbinic Judaism? – I need simply draw attention to some of the further discussion which suggests that a very positive answer is appropriate. As regards what I treated as the first pillar of Judaism (the Temple), two points should be made. One is in reference to Richard Bauckham's insistence that the key factor in the separation of Christianity, as of the Samaritans (and the Qumran Essenes) was the Temple. Bauckham notes that the early Jerusalem church did not withdraw from the Temple or regard the Temple services as invalid (cf. Matt. 5.23–4; Acts 3.1), and so remained fully part of 'common Judaism', even though the Jerusalem church seems to have regarded itself as *the* eschatological Temple – a more radical relativism of the Jerusalem Temple than the Qumran view![54] That being the case, more attention should be given to the more radical critique of the Temple (already *in* Jerusalem!) associated with Stephen (Acts 6.14; 7.48) than Bauckham allows.[55] The other is to recall the observations made in §12.6: that rabbinic Judaism as well as Christianity was able to flourish despite the destruction of the Temple; and that it was rabbinic Judaism rather than Christianity which drew the consequences of that loss more consistently than Christianity. That observation deserves more attention than it has thus far attracted.

So far as the law is concerned, what becomes evident, and probably crucial, is a tension between theology and praxis. So far as the former

---

53. A. D. Crown, 'Judaism and Christianity: The Parting of the Ways', in A. J. Avery-Peck *et al.* (eds), *When Judaism and Christianity Began*, Leiden: Brill 2004, 2.545–62, concludes that 'the work of the Council of Nicaea must be seen as the parting of the ways for Judaism and Christianity' (561).

54. Bauckham, 'The Parting of the Ways' pp. 143–5.

55. Wander thinks that the confrontation of Acts 6.1 already 'decisively prefigures' the later separation of Jews and Christians (*Trennungsprozesse*, p. 130).

is concerned, the debate following on from 'the new perspective on Paul' has served as much to highlight the similarity between Judaism's 'covenantal nomism' and Paul's call for the obedience of faith and for a faith which works through love (Rom. 1.5; Gal. 5.6), as to bring out the differences.[56] As early Judaism's soteriology revolved round the double foci of election and law, so Paul's theology similarly revolved round the double foci of grace and obedience. Paul no less than his Jewish forebears expected a judgement according to works, for Christians as well (Rom. 2.6–16; 14.10–12; 2 Cor. 5.10) and envisaged the possibility of believers being disqualified in the race to which they had committed themselves, himself included (1 Cor. 9.24–27; Phil. 3.11–14). So, theologically we have to recognize a substantial overlap between the two soteriologies. The more decisive factor, evidently, was the degree to which Jewish self-identity was bound up with the law – 'the circumcision' = Jews, laws of clean and unclean as constitutive of covenant identity. This was a cultural matter, a matter of deep psychological self-understanding, which, following the Temple's destruction, became even more vital for the survival of the Jews as a people despite their dispersion, for the flourishing of their religious as well as their ethnic identity. It was not so much a theological knife which sliced Jewish-Christian into the separate entities of Jew and Christian; diaspora Judaism embraced a wide range of practical devices which enabled socializing between Jew and Gentile,[57] and the so-called 'apostolic decree' of Acts 15.28–9 indicates similar willingness for compromise from the Christian side. But rather as the twentieth-century ecumenical movement found – that initial reconciliations at the level of common formulae often conceal much deeper differences at a cultural and psychological level (deeply rooted perspectives and long-established praxis) – so the possibility of theological rapprochement was wrecked precisely on the sense of doctor and rabbi that Christian and Jewish identity depended on the

---

56. See my *The New Perspective on Paul*, WUNT 185; Tübingen: Mohr Siebeck 2005; but already earlier, e.g., M. Hooker, 'Paul and "Covenantal Nomism" ' (1982), in *From Adam to Christ: Essays on Paul*, Cambridge: Cambridge University 1990, pp. 155–64. So while it is true that faith in Christ is the unifying centre for Paul, the antithesis of faith/ grace versus law, or Christ versus law, is much too simple to serve adequately as an analytical key to Paul's soteriology or teaching on social responsibility – in some contrast to Zetterholm, *Formation*.

57. See E. P. Sanders, 'Jewish Association with Gentiles and Galatians ii. 11–14', in *Studies in Paul and John*, ed. R. T. Fortna and B. R. Gaventa, J. L. Martyn FS, Nashville: Abingdon 1990, pp. 170–88; Cohen, *Beginnings*, pp. 140–74; and further J. M. G. Barclay, *Jews in the Mediterranean Diaspora from Alexander to Trajan (323 BCE–117 CE)*, Edinburgh: T. & T. Clark 1996.

establishment and maintenance of their respective distinctives rather on how they could live in harmony.[58]

In the first edition of *Partings* I concluded that christology has been seen as a, if not the, decisive factor in the partings of the ways: the attempt to understand Jesus as on the God side of the God/human divide in the event proved totally unacceptable to Jewish monotheism. Christian insistence that Christianity is a monotheistic faith still cuts little ice with Jew and Muslim, who continue to find the Christian doctrine of the Trinity incomprehensible. In the face of that stark reality I have argued in *Partings* that in the first two generations of Christianity Christian attempts to express the significance of Jesus stayed within the more diverse reflections of second Temple Judaism on the varied ways in which the one God interacts with his human creation and his chosen people. Nor do I see any need now to revise substantially that assessment. It is true that some want to see a very large tear already beginning to separate earliest Christianity from that wider Jewish reflection about God's revelation and redemption, particularly in the worship given to Jesus by the first Christians (1 Cor. 8.4–6; Phil. 2.10–11).[59] But I still think that more weight should be given to the fact that Paul seems (deliberately) to avoid using certain worship and prayer language in reference to Jesus, to Paul's continuing recognition of God as '*the God* and Father *of our Lord* Jesus Christ' (Rom. 15.6; 2 Cor. 1.3; 11.31; Col. 1.3; Eph. 1.3, 17), and to the only place where he spells out the relation he conceives to pertain between God and the exalted Jesus (1 Cor. 15.24–8).[60]

In addition, Boyarin now makes a substantial case that Christianity's developing Logos Christology should be seen as closely parallel to Judaism's (the Targums') Memra theology. He argues, indeed, that 'Logos theology (and hence trinitarianism) emerges as a difference between Judaism and Christianity only through the activities of heresiologists on both sides of the divide'. Rabbinic theology chose to name what had been the traditional Logos (or Memra) doctrine of God as a heresy, indeed, *the* heresy, the archetypal 'two powers in heaven' heresy, and thus in effect labelled Christianity a heresy. The Christian heresoiologists for their part named Monarchianism and

---

58. Zetterholm argues that this crisis of identity was a crisis *within* early Christianity: 'the parting of the ways in Antioch was primarily between Jesus-believing Jews and Jesus-believing Gentiles' (*Formation*, p. 233).

59. See particularly L. W. Hurtado, *Lord Jesus Christ: Devotion to Jesus in Earliest Christianity*, Grand Rapids: Eerdmans 2003.

60. See my *The Theology of Paul the Apostle*, Grand Rapids: Eerdmans; Edinburgh: T. & T. Clark 1998, pp. 252–60.

Modalism a heresy by calling it 'Judaism'![61] The claim is provocative, but it makes good sense of the rather confusing christological controversies of the early centuries,[62] and it reinforces the continuing strong impression that the overlap between the more diverse expressions of Judaism and Christianity in the earliest centuries of the common era would repay closer attention.[63]

As for the fourth of 'the pillars of Judaism', the election of Israel, I confess that in the end of the day I still find myself identifying most closely with Paul. By that I mean Paul in his conflictual state, wanting to remain faithful to his heritage, but also (and primarily) to the revelation which had been given him in Christ. His resolution of the conflict, if it can be described as such, is the classic treatment of Romans 9–11, with its climax in the not distinctively (certainly not emphasized as distinctively) Christian expectation that all Israel will be saved by the deliverer to come from Zion (11.26), and the wonderment expressed in the final monotheistic doxology (11.33–6). Indeed, perhaps my own conflictual position is well indicated by the degree to which I resonate fully with both the Christ-directed paean of praise at the end of Romans 8 and the monotheistic doxology at the end of Romans 11. The point here, however, is that in these chapters (Romans 9–11) Paul shifts the focus from the contrasted categories of Jew and Greek/Gentile and focuses rather on 'Israel'. And the point is that without abandoning the ethnic character of the people of Israel (11.25–6), he nevertheless insists that Israel is to find its identity as 'Israel' not in ethnic descent or a distinctive way of living, but in God's call (9.6–13). It is God's call which makes Israel 'Israel', and that call, he goes on to argue, has been extended to embrace Gentiles as well as Jews (9.24–6).[64] That remains a controversial (and unacceptable) argument in most Jewish ears.[65] But it is the argument of a Jew seeking

---

61. Boyarin, *Border Lines*, pp. 92, 145–6. His response to Hurtado is noteworthy: 'I believe that the binitarianism is not specifically Christian; only its association with Jesus is' (p. 283 n.97).

62. Cf. my undeveloped reflections in the Foreword to *Christology in the Making*, London: SCM Press² 1989 = Grand Rapids: Eerdmans 1996, pp. xxx–xxxi.

63. For an alternative view, using (in my view) more clear-cut 'identity-markers' than is historically justified, see M. Casey, *From Jewish Prophet to Gentile God*, Cambridge: James Clarke 1991.

64. See further below, pp. 354–7; also *Theology of Paul*, §19.

65. But see the very different responses of Neusner, 'Was Rabbinic Judaism Really "Ethnic"?', and D. Boyarin, *A Radical Jew: Paul and the Politics of Identity*, Berkeley: University of California 1994. Of course, there is no call here to revive the old contrast between Jewish 'particularism' and Christian 'universalism'; see e.g. my 'Was Judaism Particularist or Universalist?', in *Judaism in Late Antiquity*, part III: *Where We Stand: Issues and Debates in Ancient Judaism*, vol. 2, ed. J. Neusner and A. J. Avery-Peck, Handbuch der Orientalisk, Leiden: Brill 1999, pp. 57–73.

to be true to his scriptures and his heritage, and to fulfil God's call for Israel to be a light to the nations.[66] And as a Jewish argument emerging from the diversity of second Temple Judaism it deserves more attention than it has received from both Christians and Jews, including, somewhat disappointingly, from those engaged in Jewish–Christian dialogue, for whom Paul seems to be more of an embarrassment than a resource.[67]

The Way(s) ahead

The most disappointing reviews of *Partings* (from my perspective) came from Jewish writers who saw the published lectures as an expression of Christian 'triumphalism'.[68] Postmodern hermeneutics, of course, remind us that a text may be read legitimately or 'authentically' in ways different from the author's intention. But I still found the critiques depressing since they were so seriously at odds with my hopes and intention in the volume. The disappointment focused on two aspects. One was that a principal part of my endeavour was to demonstrate the common roots in first-century or late second Temple Judaism shared by both Christianity and rabbinic Judaism, in the hope that a fuller appreciation of our common heritage would help forward the process of mutual understanding and genuine dialogue. Alan Segal had earlier used the helpful, if mutually challenging imagery of Judaism and Christianity as two siblings from the same mother.[69] And Boyarin's thesis that Christianity and Judaism engaged in a similar process of each defining itself over against the other, drawing 'border lines' between them, indicates that failure ('apostasy'?) or success ('triumphalism'?) were processes and attitudes to be found on both sides of the lines, inevitable concomitants (rationalizations) of the very process of 'partitioning Judaeo-Christianity'.[70] My

---

66. The allusion is to Paul's description of his conversion as a calling in Gal. 1.15–16 in language which clearly and no doubt deliberately echoes Jer. 1.5 and Isa. 49.1–6.

67. See further below, pp. 357–65, also my 'The Jew Paul and his Meaning for Israel', in *Paulinische Christologie: Exegetische Beiträge*, ed. U. Schnelle and T. Söding, H. Hübner FS, Göttingen: Vandenhoeck & Ruprecht 2000, pp. 32–46, reprinted in *A Shadow of Glory: Reading the New Testament after the Holocaust*, ed. T. Linafelt, New York: Routledge, 2002, pp. 201–15.

68. Rabbi A. M. Bayfield, *The Church Times*, 14.2.92; Josephine Knopp, *Journal of Ecumenical Studies* 29 (1992), p. 485. Cf. the warmer welcome from A. F. Segal, *Theology* (March 1993), pp. 150–2.

69. A. F. Segal, *Rebecca's Children: Judaism and Christianity in the Roman World*, Harvard University 1986. More strongly Boyarin: 'Judaism is not the "mother" of Christianity; they are twins, joined at the hip' (*Border Lines*, p. 5).

70. I echo Boyarin's subtitle: *The Partition of Judaeo-Christianity*.

own particular contribution, referred to in the preceding paragraph, is the endeavour to reinstate Paul into the dialogue, as an apostle of the Gentiles on behalf of Israel, but not yet justifiably described as an 'apostate' from Israel, whose teaching should be considered more carefully on both sides of the dialogue, as an authentically second Temple Jewish voice.[71]

Also disappointing was the failure to recognize the importance of the subtitle of *Partings: their significance for the Character of Christianity*. My intention in so subtitling the volume was to indicate that in demonstrating the various factors involved in the partings and the process character of the separating, I was attempting primarily to address my fellow-Christians, the majority at any rate of whom tend to take the Christianity/Judaism distinction (antithesis!) for granted as pertaining from the first. (One only needs to listen to some Christian sermons which work from a surface reading of John's Gospel to see the point.) My concern was, and still is, that Christians should realize the extent to which Christianity has been shaped by its Jewish heritage, the extent to which Christianity emerged as one strand out of the rich diversity of second Temple Judaism, and how that Jewishness of Christianity continues to be integral to its identity. A religion, two-thirds of whose scriptures (the OT) are the scriptures of another religion (the Hebrew Bible), can only properly understand itself when it takes that fact fully into account.[72] To recognize the OT/Tanach as scripture is to affirm Christianity's Jewishness (or Israel-ness, but the re-establishment of the nation 'Israel' makes it more difficult to make the theological point in 'Israel' terms). A Christianity which has formulated its identity by distinguishing and distancing itself from Judaism has always run the risk of losing (sight of) an important aspect of its own identity – the very overlap with Judaism which was disowned and discounted as heresy in the early centuries. My suggestion, therefore, is that an important task before us, Christians certainly but also Jews, is the fuller (and mutual) exploration of that lost overlap. For such mutual exploration to have any chance of success, it will have to be accompanied by a willingness to hold in suspense that aspect of mutual identity which was formulated by heresiologists, rabbis and Christian teachers who could only see the

---

71. See also my 'Paul: Apostate or Apostle of Israel?', *ZNW* 89 (1998), pp. 256–71.

72. Horbury observes that 'the Christians, recognizing their biblical inheritance as Jewish, wanted to share the Jewish Bible in the canonical form recognized by Jews ... recognition of a biblical canon was a fundamental common presupposition, and both communities shared a biblical culture focused on what can properly be called a common Bible' (*Jews and Christians*, pp. 25–6, and further 26–35 and ch. 8).

other as a threat to their own identity; and a willingness rather to see Judaism and Christianity as siblings who have grown apart over many years, but for whom reconciliation may well hold out prospects of unexpected blessing, not least in the *self*-discoveries which such reconciliation might prompt.

Lieu also criticizes *Partings* for its theological agenda.[73] I do not deny the charge: I never intended a sociologically descriptive exercise. But neither do I recoil from it. Of course it is a theological concern for Christians to understand better where Christianity came from and how its identity took shape. It was precisely Israel's theological heritage (not least belief in God as one, and in God as revealer and redeemer) which Christianity 'took over' from Judaism; so it remains a legitimate concern (call it 'theological' if you will) to understand better how this 'take over' came about and what it says about Christianity and still says to twenty-first-century Christians. The point can be made by reference to the two earlier terms in which the 'take over' was understood – apostasy and supersession.[74] These latter, of course, are a truer echo of the dominant Christian voices of the early centuries. But the theological agenda pursued in *Partings* is intended precisely to question these voices and to ask whether the gains of a sharper identity for Christianity (over against Judaism) were not made at too great expense, particularly in the horrific history of Christian anti-Judaism (and latterly anti-Semitism). The ways parted, that is true; but is there nothing to be said in favour of Paul's hope that the ways will again finally merge at the coming of Messiah?

JAMES D. G. DUNN
University of Durham
August 2005

---

73. Lieu, 'Parting', pp. 107–10/17–20.
74. Lieu, 'Parting', pp. 105–6/15–16.

Preface to the First Edition

One of my besetting sins as a scholar (but perhaps it's a strength!) is the desire to see the large picture, to gain the (so far as possible) comprehensive overview. As a student of the New Testament and of Christian beginnings I want to see how it all fits together. It's not that I am unwilling to engage in the fine detailed work necessary in the analysis of particular texts. Far from it. But all the time I want to step back and see how my findings cohere with the rest of our information (not just the New Testament, but the New Testament writings within their historical contexts). Like a painter on a large canvas, I need to step back time and again to check how the fine detail of particular parts blends into the whole. As a reviewer of others' writing, I must confess that one of the things which irritates me most is the essay or monograph where a conclusion is driven through or drawn forth from one of the NT texts without, apparently, any questioning as to how that conclusion fits with the rest of the picture.

This is the underlying rationale behind the following chapters. Over the 1980s it had become increasingly clear to me that Christianity's origins within second Temple Judaism and its emergence from within that matrix was the central issue for our understanding of the beginnings of Christianity and is still a major issue for understanding the character of Christianity itself. It cannot be otherwise for a religion which numbers the sacred writings of the Jews as part of its own scripture, and which focusses its faith on and through the first-century Jew, Jesus.

The conclusion was by no means mine alone, as witness the flood of literature on aspects of the theme in recent years. But the very volume of individual studies was daunting, few had attempted to pull the threads together, and those who had attempted to do so had left something to be desired. As part of my own long-term project to gain as clear as possible an understanding of the beginnings of Christianity, the challenge was one I could not ignore. The invitation to lecture at the Gregorian Pontifical University in Rome from February to April in 1990 seemed to me the obvious opportunity to attempt my own gathering of the threads to see what sort of pattern emerged.

The lecture format dictated the style. I had to lecture twice a week, two lectures a day, for six weeks. The material proved reasonably adaptable to a twelve chapter structure and I have felt comfortable in retaining it. Such a structure does, however, impose its own constraints. There was no way I could take proper, documented account of all views expressed on the topics covered. The range of bibliography in such a wide-ranging discussion is immense. I have attempted therefore to deal with representative views or those which I have perceived as posing specific issues most sharply. It seemed appropriate, in particular, that I should continue my debate with E. P. Sanders. The need to compress and summarize should also help explain the extent to which I have had to refer to my own earlier and fuller treatment of individual points (a degree of self-indulgence for which I apologize). As already indicated, however, the lectures are my attempt to step back and fit my own detailed work, as well as that of others into the broader picture.

With more (or fewer) lectures in play, a different scheme would have been appropriate. The compression of the discussion of election and Torah into a single sequence (chs 6–8) is probably the weakest feature, and in a different scheme I would have been able to give more consideration to the old covenant/new covenant question. In chapter 8, however, the issue of anti-semitism/anti-Judaism seemed the more pressing and took over the whole chapter. Fuller treatment of the second century, especially of Barnabas, Justin, Melito and the pseudo-Clementines would also have been desirable, but not practicable in the circumstances, and the more dispensable when the final 'parting of the ways' is dated to the second Jewish revolt (132–135 CE: §12.2). The simple fact is that no scheme is going to be wholly satisfactory.

Since I see these lectures as part of my larger project to gain as full as possible an understanding of Christianity's beginnings, I put them forward in the hope that reviewers and fellow students of the period and of the issues will offer constructive criticism, which in turn should sharpen up my own perception for future work in the area. This is what the collegial character of scholarship and the dialogical nature of inquiry into the past means for me.

The lectures were also delivered in full in summer school at Fuller Theological Seminary, Pasadena, in the summer of 1990, and subsequently in briefer version in New College, Berkeley. And again, in a still briefer and revamped version to the Exeter and Plymouth Methodist District study conference in January 1991. I am grateful to all who contributed in class, in open session and in personal conversation. Such contributions help to mature content and refine presentation.

Professors Graham Stanton and Ed Sanders also kindly read parts of the first draft and made helpful comments, though, of course, they should not be held responsible for any of the views expressed in the following pages.

Meta (my wife) and I are particularly grateful to Gerry O'Collins, Dean of the Faculty of Theology at the Gregorian, for being responsible for the original invitation to Rome, and to Mgr Jack Kennedy, Rector of the Venerable English College, to his staff and students, for making our six weeks in Rome such a memorable time – one of the highlights of our whole life. Also to Eugene and Maureen McCarthy who have generously funded the Visiting Professorship in memory of their son, and whose friendship has become one of the uncovenanted blessings of the whole experience. We are grateful too for memories of hospitality and warm friendships in Pasadena, Berkeley and Exeter, which are bound up with this book, and for confirmation that the issues discussed therein are of interest and concern beyond the confines of academe. Above all, how can I express enough gratitude to Meta for her support and encouragement throughout the round of gestation, lecture-writing, delivery, writing-up, proof-reading and indexing? The passages on priesthood and women have her particularly in mind.

Since, in my view at least, the Jewishness of Christianity is so important, my hope is that the following pages will contribute to the further growth of mutual understanding between Judaism and Christianity, of Jew and Christian.

James D. G. Dunn
University of Durham
July 1991

Abbreviations

AB	Anchor Bible
AGAJU	Arbeiten zur Geschichte des Spätjudentums und Urchristentums
AJA	*American Journal of Archaeology*
AnBib	Analecta Biblica
ANRW	*Aufstieg und Niedergang des römische Welt*, ed. H. Temparini and W. Haase (Berlin, 1972–)
BAGD	W. Bauer, *A Greek-English Lexicon of the New Testament and Other Early Christian Literature*, ET ed. W. F. Arndt and F. W. Gingrich, ²F. W. Gingrich and F. W. Danker (University of Chicago 1979)
BCE	Before the Common Era
BDAG	3rd edn of BAGD, ed. F. W. Danger (1999)
BDB	E. Brown, S. R. Driver and C. A. Briggs, *Hebrew and English Lexicon of the Old Testament* (Oxford: Clarendon 1907)
BETL	Bibliotheca ephemeridum theologicum
BJRL	*Bulletin of the John Rylands University Library of Manchester*
BJS	Brown Judaic Studies
BZ	*Biblische Zeitschrift*
CBQ	*Catholic Biblical Quarterly*
CD	Damascus Document
CE	Common Era
CIJ	*Corpus Inscriptionum Judaicorum*
ConB	Coniectanea biblica
EJMI	*Early Judaism and Its Modern Interpreters*, ed. R. A. Kraft and G. W. E. Nickelsburg (Atlanta: Scholars 1986)
EKK	Evangelisch-katholischer Kommentar zum Neuen Testament
ET	English translation
EvTh	*Evangelische Theologie*

ExpT	*Expository Times*
FRLANT	Forschungen zur Religion und Literatur des Alten und Neuen Testaments
FS	Festschrift
GLAJJ	M. Stern, *Greek and Latin Authors on Jews and Judaism*, 3 vols. (Jerusalem: Israel Academy of Sciences and Humanities, 1976, 1980, 1984)
HBT	*Horizons in Biblical Theology*
HE	Eusebius, *Historia Ecclesiastica*
HNT	Handbuch zum Neuen Testament
HTR	*Harvard Theological Review*
HUCA	*Hebrew Union College Annual*
ICC	International Critical Commentary
IDB	G. A. Buttrick (ed.), *Interpreter's Dictionary of the Bible* (4 vols, Nashville: Abingdon 1962)
IDBS	Supplementary volume to *IDB*
JBL	*Journal of Biblical Literature*
JCSD	E. P. Sanders (ed.), *Jewish and Christian Self-Definition*, Vol. 2 (London: SCM Press/ Philadelphia: Fortress 1981)
JJS	*Journal of Jewish Studies*
JRS	*Journal of Roman Studies*
JSJ	*Journal for the Study of Judaism*
JSNT	*Journal for the Study of the New Testament*
JSNTSupp	*JSNT* Supplement Series
JSOT	*Journal for the Study of the Old Testament*
JTS	*Journal of Theological Studies*
Lampe	G. W. H. Lampe, *A Patristic Greek Lexicon* (Oxford: Clarendon 1961).
LCL	Loeb Classical Library
LSJ	H. G. Liddell and R. Scott, *A Greek-English Lexicon*, rev. H. J. Jones (Oxford: Clarendon ^{9}1940; with supplement, 1968)
NCB	New Century Bible
NICNT	New International Commentary on the New Testament
NIGTC	New International Greek Testament Commentary
NovT	*Novum Testamentum*
NovT Supp	Supplement to *NovT*
NTS	*New Testament Studies*
OCD	N. G. L. Hammond and H. N. Scullard, *Oxford Classical Dictionary* (Oxford: Clarendon 1970)
PG	Patrologia Graeca

SANT	Studien zum Alten und Neuen Testament
SBL	Society of Biblical Literature
SBLDS	SBL Dissertation Series
SBLMS	SBL Monograph Series
Schürer	E. Schürer, *The History of the Jewish People in the Age of Jesus Christ*, rev. and ed. G. Vermes et al. (4 vols., Edinburgh: T. & T. Clark 1973, 1979, 1986, 1987)
SR	*Studies in Religion/Sciences religieuses*
SJT	*Scottish Journal of Theology*
SNTSMS	Society for New Testament Studies Monograph Series
St. Th.	*Studia Theologica*
SUNT	Studien zur Umwelt des Neuen Testaments
TDNT	G. Kittel and G. Friedrich (eds), *Theological Dictionary of the New Testament*, 10 vols (ET Grand Rapids, Eerdmans 1964–76)
TS	*Theological Studies*
TSAJ	Texts and Studies in Ancient Judaism
TynB	*Tyndale Bulletin*
TübZth	*Tübinger Zeitschrift für Theologie*
TZ	*Theologische Zeitschrift*
VC	*Vigiliae christianae*
WBC	Word Biblical Commentary
WMANT	Wissenschaftliche Menographien zum Aten und Neuen Testament
WUNT	Wissenschaftliche Untersuchungen zum Neuen Testament
ZNW	*Zeitschrift für die neutestamentliche Wissenschaft*

Introduction: From Baur to Sanders

Christianity is a movement which emerged from within first-century Judaism. That simple, uncontestable fact is crucial to our understanding of the beginnings of Christianity. But its significance has not been adequately appreciated. The same fact continues to be determinative of Christianity's character. But its implications have not been thought through with sufficient care. Such is the basic concern behind these chapters.

It is bound up with an equally simple line of questions. Rabbinic Judaism and Christianity, two of the world's great religions, emerged from the same matrix – second Temple Judaism.[1] Why did they pull apart? Given the thoroughly Jewish character of Christianity's beginnings, why did it become a separate religion? What were, and are, the distinctive emphases of Christianity which caused the parting of the ways? How soon did it take place? Can we indeed speak of a single parting? And was it inevitable from the first, or could it, should it have been avoided? Such are the issues which motivate these chapters.

1.1 Baur and Lightfoot

In the last two centuries the importance of these issues was brought to the fore particularly by the work of F. C. Baur. Thus Baur writes at the beginning of his *Paul*:

> . . . how Christianity, instead of remaining a mere form of Judaism . . . asserted itself as a separate, independent principle, broke loose from it, and took its stand as a new enfranchised form of religious thought and life, essentially different from all the national

---

1. 'Second Temple Judaism' is the simplest and most acceptable way of speaking of the Judaism within which Jesus and the first Christians functioned. The title distinguishes it from the Judaism which became most characteristic after 70 CE (rabbinic Judaism), and it is much preferable to a more slanted description like 'pre-Christian Judaism'.

peculiarities of Judaism is the ultimate, most important point of the primitive history of Christianity.[2]

Baur had begun to develop his own explanation of Christian origins several years earlier in his article on the Christ party in the Corinthian congregation. His central thesis is already clear in the second part of the title of that article – 'the opposition between Petrine and Pauline Christianity in the earliest church'.[3] That is to say, earliest Christianity was characterized by a conflict between two factions, one with marked Jewish tendencies, and the other, Pauline Christianity. From this initial observation Baur's reconstruction of earliest Christian history evolved inexorably. For example, the historical value of Acts could not be defended, since it shows Paul and Peter as closely similar in message and conviction, that is, a Paul who is manifestly different from the Paul of the Epistles. The Acts of the Apostles must derive, therefore, from a later period at which attempts were being made to reconcile the conflicting views of the Petrine and Pauline factions.[4] And the epistles of Ignatius and Polycarp could not be authentic simply because a date for them in the second decade of the second century did not fit within this paradigm of a sustained conflict between these factions which was reconciled only later in the century.

Baur's overarching schema is most clearly articulated in his *Church History*.[5] In its simplest terms, Christianity for Baur was the highest expression of the religious consciousness of mankind, because its spirituality, expressed quintessentially in the first beatitude, is far more free than any other religion from everything merely external, sensuous, or material. The characteristic feature of the Christian principle is that 'it looks beyond the outward, the accidental, the particular, and rises to the universal, the unconditioned, the essential'. This refusal to regard true religion as a thing bound down to special ordinances and localities is at the heart of its universalism. The dispute between the Petrine and Pauline parties was thus a dispute between *Jewish particularism* and *Christian universalism*. The problem was that this absolute moral and spiritual insight could only enter the

---

2. F. C. Baur, *Paul: the Apostle of Jesus Christ*, 1845; ET London: Williams & Norgate; vol. 1, 1873, p. 3.

3. F. C. Baur, 'Die Christuspartei in der Korinthischen Gemeinde, der Gegensatz des petrinischen und paulinischen Christentums in der ältesten Kirche, der Apostel Petrus in Rom', *TübZTh*, V:4 (1831), pp. 61–206.

4. See particularly the Introduction to Baur's *Paul*.

5. F. C. Baur, *The Church History of the First Three Centuries*, 1853; ET London: Williams & Norgate 1878–79.

stream of history in a particular form – the cramping and narrowing form of the Jewish National Messianic idea. It was not surprising then that one set of Jesus' followers should hold to the national aspect of his appearance and miss the moral and spiritual universalism of the morality and spirituality which he inculcated. But Paul must have the credit for delivering Christianity from the status of a mere Jewish sect and liberating 'the all-commanding universalism of its spirit and aims'.[6] This analysis also enabled Baur to make a point of more contemporary polemical application: the Catholicism which became the compromise between the Petrine and Pauline factions is like Judaism in its attachment to the formal and external; whereas Protestantism is like Pauline Christianity in its attachment to the inner and spiritual![7]

That Baur saw the issue as crucial for Christianity's own self-understanding is clear when in his *Church History* he affirms:

> there can be no question that the purely moral element which lies at its first source has ever been (Christianity's) unchangeable and substantial foundation. Christianity has never been removed from this foundation without denying its true and proper character.[8]

In English speaking scholarship the one who did most to undermine Baur's portrayal of Christian beginnings was J. B. Lightfoot. He was equally convinced of the seriousness of the issues at stake:

> If the primitive Gospel was, as some have represented it, merely one of many phases of Judaism, if those cherished beliefs which have been the life and light of many generations were afterthoughts, progressive accretions, having no foundation in the Person and Teaching of Christ, then indeed St Paul's preaching was vain and our faith is vain also.[9]

Lightfoot also accepted that there was a vigorous antagonism between Paul and Jewish Christianity. Thus in reading Gal. 2.3ff., Paul's report of how Titus was not compelled to be circumcised on his visit to

---

6. See Baur, *Church History*, pp. 5–6, 9, 27–9, 33, 38–9, 43, 49–50, etc.

7. B. N. Kaye, 'Lightfoot and Baur on Early Christianity', *NovT* 26 (1984), pp. 193–224, here p. 201.

8. Baur, *Church History*, p. 37.

9. J. B. Lightfoot, *Saint's Paul's Epistle to the Galatians*, London: Macmillan 1865, p. xi; see also p. 293.

Jerusalem even though a Greek, Lightfoot does not resist an implication in Paul's language that the pillar apostles (James, Peter and John)
were sympathetic to the conservative or judaizing 'false brothers'.

> On the whole it seems probable that they (the pillar apostles)
> recommended St Paul to yield the point . . . The counsels of the
> Apostles of the Circumcision are the hidden rock on which the
> grammar of the sentence is wrecked.[10]

And in his essay on 'St Paul and the Three' Lightfoot does not hesitate
to speak of 'The systematic hatred of St Paul (as) an important fact,
which we are too apt to overlook, but without which the whole
history of the Apostolic ages will be misread and misunderstood.[11]
'Pharisaic Ebionism' (as he calls it) 'was a disease in the Church of
the Circumcision from the first'.[12]

Where Lightfoot differed from Baur was in his application of historical critical method. Baur began with the, to him, clear evidence
of the undisputed Pauline letters and extrapolated the conflict revealed
therein to the whole history of Christian beginnings, read through
the lenses of an overarching *philosophical* schema. Lightfoot replied
with a rigorous *historical* analysis of the language and context of the
key texts, drawing on his unrivalled knowledge of ancient languages
and writings. And particularly in his massive three volume study of
Ignatius and Polycarp he undermined completely the Baurian attempt
to date these documents late in the second century in order to fit his
schema.[13] What emerged, however, was not a complete destruction
of Baur, but what C. K. Barrett speaks of as Lightfoot's 'modified
Baurian position' whose effect was the destruction of the *chronology*
of the Tübingen school.[14] As Lightfoot himself claimed:

---

10. Lightfoot, *Galatians*, pp. 105–6; similarly p. 350– 'St Paul's language leaves the
impression (though the inference cannot be regarded as certain), that they (the pillar
apostles) had not offered a prompt resistance to the Judaizers in the first instance, hoping
perhaps to conciliate them . . .'

11. Lightfoot, *Galatians*, p. 311.

12. Lightfoot, *Galatians*, pp. 322–3. Lightfoot ends the same essay with the sobering
conclusion: 'However great may be the theological differences and religious animosities of
our own time, they are far surpassed in magnitude by the distractions of an age which,
closing our eyes to facts, we are apt to invest with an ideal excellence. In the early Church
was fulfilled, in its inward dissensions no less than in its outward sufferings, the Master's
sad warning that He came "not to send peace on earth, but a sword"' (*Galatians*, p. 374).

13. Lightfoot, *The Apostolic Fathers. Part I: S. Clement of Rome* (2 vols. London: Macmillan 1869, ²1890); *Part II: S. Ignatius, S. Polycarp* (3 vols. London: Macmillan 1885,
²1889).

14. C. K. Barrett, 'Quomodo historia conscribenda sit', *NTS* 28 (1982) pp. 303–20,
here pp. 310, 313–14. In an earlier essay Barrett had noted that the frank picture in the

The great battle with this form of error [Ebionism] seems to have been fought out at an early date, in the lifetime of the Apostles themselves and in the age [by which I presume he means the generation] immediately following.[15]

On the German front the reaction was more complex. But the result was to swing the focus of the discussion steadily *away* from the issue of Christianity's emergence from Judaism.

The earliest, most influential reaction to Baur was expressed by A. Ritschl, in the second edition of his *Die Entstehung der altkatholischen Kirche*.[16] In this he demonstrated that early Christian history was not simply the case of two monolithic blocks grinding against each other. Peter (and the original apostles) were to be distinguished from the opponents of Paul (the judaizers); and there was also a Gentile Christianity distinct from Paul and little influenced by him. The resulting qualification of Baur's too simple schema can be easily illustrated:

THE SPECTRUM OF EARLIEST CHRISTIANITY

	Gentile Christianity		*Primitive Church*	
Gentile Christians		Paul	Peter and the Twelve	judaizers

The elaboration of this schema has been one of the most important trends in the hundred years since Ritschl. Most notably by the History of Religions School, who were the first in the modern period to highlight the existence of another expression of Christianity *between* the primitive church and Paul – viz. *Hellenistic* Christianity.[17] Thus the spectrum of earliest Christianity is seen to be still further extended:

THE SPECTRUM OF EARLIEST CHRISTIANITY

Gentile Christianity		*Hellenistic Christianity*	*Primitive Church*	
Gentile Christians	Paul		Peter and the Twelve	judaizers

---

immediately preceding quotation from Lightfoot is not easy to parallel in English writers of the period, and sums up: 'It might not be too inaccurate to say that Baur asked the right questions, and that Lightfoot set them in the right historical context' – 'Joseph Barber Lightfoot', *Durham University Journal* 64 (1972) pp. 193–204, here p. 203.

15. Lightfoot, *Galatians*, p. 336.

16. Bonn [2]1857.

17. W. Heitmüller, 'Zum Problem Paulus und Jesus', *ZNW* 13 (1912), pp. 320–37, particularly pp. 329ff.; reprinted in K. H. Rengstorf, (ed.), *Das Paulusbild in der neuren deutschen Forschung* Darmstadt: WB, 1964, pp. 124–43, particularly pp. 135ff.; W. Bousset, *Kyrios Christos*, 1913; [2]1921; ET Nashville: Abingdon 1970, ch. 3. See R. Bultmann's Introduction to Bousset in the 5th edition and ET.

In the twentieth century the same trend continued – partly in terms of a regularly recurring but never fully convincing thesis of a Galilean Christianity independent of Jerusalem.[18] More influential were the studies of christology which sought to explain the developments in christology by discerning a still further complexity within the spectrum of earliest Christianity by subdividing Hellenistic Christianity into Hellenistic Jewish Christianity and Hellenistic Gentile Christianity. Thus:

THE SPECTRUM OF EARLIEST CHRISTIANITY

Gentile Christianity		*Hellenistic Christianity*		*Primitive Church*	
Gentile	Paul	Hellenistic	Hellenistic	Peter and	judaizers
Christians		Gentiles	Jews	the Twelve	

The value of all this has been to bring home to twentieth-century students of Christian origins the *diversity* of first-century Christianity. Earliest Christianity is not to be seen simply in terms of distinct warring factions. A closer approximation to first-century reality is to see it as a more or less unbroken spectrum across a wide front from conservative judaizers at one end to radical Gentile Christians at the other. *The effect, however, has been to obscure the key issue of Christianity's emergence from the Judaism of the second Temple period* and the importance of the continuing Jewish character of Christianity.

1.2 The Jesus of History and the Christ of Faith

The issue is probably seen most starkly in the way in which the whole debate since Baur has opened up a *gulf between Jesus and subsequent Christianity*, in which the Jewish matrix of both has been very largely marginalized or effectively ignored. This can be readily documented from either side of this gulf.

(a) Jesus. In the Liberal Protestantism which followed Baur, the Liberal Protestantism of Ritschl and his pupil A. Harnack, Jesus was effectively removed from his Jewish matrix. In the tradition of Baur's idealism, Jesus was presented as a timeless moralist – his ethical teaching detachable from its Jewish context, so as to be easily transportable across the centuries. In terms of an evolutionary world-view,

---

18. E. Lohmeyer, *Galiläa und Jerusalem*, Göttingen: Vandenhoeck & Ruprecht 1936; L. E. Elliot-Binns, *Galilean Christianity*, London: SCM Press 1956; W. Schmithals, *Paul and James*, 1963; ET London: SCM Press 1965.

moral evolution was too readily assumed to be continuous with and the climax of physiological evolution; with the convenient consequence that Jesus could be portrayed as the moral climax of humanity's evolution.

Thus Ritschl could define the central category of Jesus' message, the kingdom of God, in purely ethical terms:

> The kingdom of God consists of those who believe in Christ, inasmuch as they treat one another with love without regard to differences of sex, rank or race, thereby bringing about a fellowship of moral attitude and moral properties extending through the whole range of human life in every possible variation.[19]

And Harnack, looking for the kernel within the husk, the essential and permanent within the transitory, found it in Jesus' teaching on God as the Father of all men, and on each human soul as of infinite value. True faith in Jesus was not a matter of credal orthodoxy, but of 'doing as he did'.[20]

The effect, of course, was to remove Jesus from his Jewish context. The Jewish complexion of his ministry could be stripped off and thrown away as irrelevant and of no lasting significance or worth. Jesus, the timeless ideal, whether seen in terms of Jesus himself[21] or in terms of his message,[22] transcended his social historical context. What is of continuing value in his message is quite unaffected by his Jewishness. In effect a kind of Docetism emerged – a Jesus himself, or his message, independent of history. Also to be noted is the still less savoury implication that the Jewishness of Jesus is something undesirable, primitive, needing to be stripped off to reach the matter of real value, with Jewish apocalypticism in Harnack's view a religion of miserabilism, the religion of the wretched[23] – all this reflecting an uncomfortable antipathy to things Jewish which was to bear its fearful fruit within another four decades.

The reaction to this was equally striking, as expressed with greatest

---

19. *Rechtfertigung und Versöhnung*, III p. 271; cited by G. Lundström, *The Kingdom of God in the Teaching of Jesus. A History of Interpretation from the Last Decades of the Nineteenth Century to the Present Day*, 1947; ET Edinburgh: Oliver & Boyd 1963, p. 5.

20. A. Harnack, *What is Christianity?*, London: Williams & Norgate 1901; 5th edition, London: Benn 1958, p. 110.

21. As in the idealism of D. F. Strauss, *The Life of Jesus Critically Examined*, ⁴1840; ET 1846; reprinted ed. P. C. Hodgson; Philadelphia: Fortress 1972; London: SCM Press 1973, 'Concluding Dissertation: the dogmatic import of the life of Jesus' (pp. 757ff.).

22. So Harnack.

23. Harnack, *Christianity*, pp. 23–4.

effect by J. Weiss and A. Schweitzer.[24] They began by criticizing such de-historicizing, de-judaizing of Jesus. They set Jesus within the tradition of Jewish apocalyptic. Against Ritschl's portrayal of the kingdom of God in this-worldly, ethical terms, Weiss showed the kingdom to be *other*-worldly – not something brought about by human means, but dependent on divine intervention; and *eschatological* – not a developing, ethically pure society, but the end of the present order; and *future* – not yet and not in the society of the disciples; in short, an *event*, which *God* would bring about in the near *future*. Against Harnack's portrayal of Jesus as a preacher of a timeless ethic, Schweitzer portrayed Jesus as an apocalyptic fanatic, consumed by expectation of the imminent final intervention of God, his ethic only an *interim* ethic for life in the short period before the end, and destroyed by his attempt to create the eschatological conditions which would climax in God's intervention.

The result was of no little interest for our study. Weiss and Schweitzer located Jesus and his message firmly within the tradition of Jewish apocalypticism. The effect was to distance Jesus immeasurably from the present; for Schweitzer Jesus comes to us as 'a stranger and an enigma', 'one unknown'.[25] But neither of them found it possible to live with that conclusion, and both of them sprang with surprising equanimity back to the older categories of Liberal Protestantism which they themselves had so effectively undermined. Unashamedly Weiss concludes his famous study:

> That which is unreservedly valid in Jesus' preaching, which should form the kernel of our systematic theology is not his idea of the kingdom of God, but that of the religious and ethical fellowship of the children of God.[26]

And Schweitzer ends with a Christian variation of his subsequent 'reverence for life' philosophy or mysticism:

> He comes to us as one Unknown, without a name, as of old, by the lake-side, He came to those men who knew him not. He speaks to us in the same word: 'Follow thou me!' and sets us the tasks

---

24. J. Weiss, *Jesus' Proclamation of the Kingdom of God*, 1892; ET Philadelphia: Fortress/London: SCM Press 1971; A. Schweitzer, *The Quest of the Historical Jesus*, ET London: A. & C. Black 1910, particularly pp. 348ff. = Schweitzer's own interpretation in terms of 'thoroughgoing eschatology'.

25. Schweitzer, *Quest*, pp. 397, 401.

26. Weiss, *Proclamation*, p. 135.

which He has to fulfil in our time. He commands. And to those who obey Him, whether they be wise or simple, He will reveal Himself in the toils, the conflicts, the sufferings which they shall pass through in His fellowship, and, as an ineffable mystery, they shall learn in their own experience who He is.[27]

What is striking here is the fact that *the attempt to locate Jesus firmly within a first-century Jewish context* (Jewish apocalypticism) *proved to be so unnerving that its results had effectively to be ignored or disowned.* The historical Jesus could be understood only within the context of Jewish eschatology, as an exponent of it. But that simply succeeded in distancing Jesus from the present and in a portrayal of him as irrelevant. The only way his continuing significance could be maintained was by stripping away this Jewish framework and clothing, to leave, once again, the Jesus of Liberal Protestantism, the timeless moralist or ideal. His Jewish context and character remained a puzzle[28] and an embarrassment.

(*b*) *Earliest Christianity*. At the same time the gap between Jesus and earliest Christianity was being opened more and more widely on the other side.

For Harnack the whole process following on from Jesus could be described in terms of the 'hellenization' of Jesus' message. That meant the rendering of the simple message of Jesus into the ever more complex and philosophical categories of Hellenism; in particular, the transformation of the simple profundity of Jesus' message of love of God and love of brother, into a *religion* of redemption, God requiring propitiation by means of bloody sacrifice, etc., where christology, the doctrine of Christ, supplants Jesus' own message, the doctrine of the divine Son of God supplants the teaching of the Galilean prophet, the doctrine of the cross supplants his proclamation of God's love and forgiveness.[29] The process began already with Paul!

Looked at from another angle, the same process could be described, again in terms of the old idealism which Baur would have recognized,

---

27. Schweitzer, *Quest*, p. 401.

28. Hence the title of K. Koch's monograph, *Ratlos vor der Apokalyptik* – lost in the ET which was given the quite different title, *The Rediscovery of Apocalyptic*, London: SCM Press 1972. Consider, e.g., his challenging claim: 'Apocalyptic serves as a touchstone for the extent to which exegetes work consistently historically, i.e., how far they really transpose themselves into the spirit of the age which they profess to be talking about' (p. 11).

29. Harnack, *Christianity*, pp. 132ff.

as a stripping the *husk* away from Jesus' message and giving it universal significance.[30] And again it is Paul who deserves the credit!

The criteria of judgment in such an analysis are clear: to have
removed the Jewish character of Jesus' message was something good;
to have transformed it into the categories of Greek philosophy was
something bad. But the effect was to widen the gulf between the
historical Jesus and Paul's Christ of faith: the historical Jesus belongs
to Judaism; Paul's Christ of faith belongs to Hellenism. And the
significance of both could be maintained only by ignoring these historical contexts and by abstracting the timeless kernel from *both*.

With the History of Religions School emerged, by way of reaction,
the laudable concern to locate Christianity within its historical context, that is, within the context of the other religions of the day,
particularly those of the Graeco-Roman world. In practice this meant,
for Heitmüller and Bousset, that Christianity could be considered as
itself a kind of mystery cult – drawing in and increasingly shaped by
influences from that wider environment. The process was clearest in
the case of the sacraments and christology. Heitmüller argued strongly
that baptism and Lord's Supper are to be seen as strongly influenced
by the sacramental ideas of the cults, their initiation rites and sacral
means.[31] And Bousset provided the first full exploration of the development of christology – through the idea of Christ as Kyrios of the
Christ (mystery) cult to the full scale Gnostic redeemer.[32]

Here again the effect was to drive an ever broadening wedge
between Jesus and the Christianity which followed, and between
Christianity's original Jewish matrix and the Hellenistic categories
which quickly took over and dominated Christianity, shaping it deter-
minatively for all time *as Hellenistic and no longer Jewish*. No wonder
W. Wrede could hail Paul as 'the second founder of Christianity',
who has 'exercised beyond all doubt the stronger – not the better –
influence' than the first (Jesus).[33]

(c) *Rudolf Bultmann*. The trends on both sides of the gulf in the
middle decades of the twentieth century were summed up in the
leading Protestant NT scholar of the period – Rudolf Bultmann.

On the Jesus side of the gulf Bultmann was very ready to recognize
the Jewishness of Jesus, at least in the terms provided by Weiss (Jewish

30. Harnack, *Christianity*, pp. 131–2.

31. W. Heitmüller, *Taufe und Abendmahl bei Paulus. Darstellung und religionsgeschichtliche Beleuchtung*, Göttingen: Vandenhoeck & Ruprecht 1903.

32. See above n. 17.

33. W. Wrede. *Paul*, 1904; ET Boston: Beacon 1908 p. 180.

apocalypticism). But what was the consequence? On the one hand it meant that Jesus belonged to the Jewish prolegomenon of NT theology, indeed of Christianity itself; consequently his message could be treated in a mere thirty pages in a two volume *New Testament Theology* (more than six hundred pages in length).[34] On the other, it meant that Jesus' continuing significance could only be appreciated by means of and in terms of existentialist philosophy. Jesus' proclamation of and expectation regarding the kingdom of God belonged to the mythological categories in which Jesus spoke and framed his message. And for Bultmann 'myth' meant something primitive, a form of primitive conceptuality outmoded in a modern scientific world.[35] He rejected the Liberal Protestant idea that the eschatology of Jesus' message was a husk which could be stripped away. On the contrary, it was *inseparable* from that message; the message was mythical through and through. Consequently, it could be appropriated only by *de*-mythologizing it. Which for Bultmann meant demythologizing into the categories of existentialist philosophy. Bultmann's critique of Liberal Protestantism was subtle and sharp. In the end, however, the effect was the same. An existentialist Jesus had replaced Jesus the moralist of Liberal Protestantism. But the Jewish context, or framework, or myth was still something to be abandoned. *Jesus could be appropriated only insofar as he could be disentangled from his Jewishness.*

On the early Christian side of the gulf Bultmann opened it still wider by arguing that the Gnosticizing of the gospel took place very early. In Bultmann we see the quest for a *pre*-Christian Gnostic Redeemer myth in full cry. The only way he could make sense of the developing categories of christology, particularly in Paul and John, was to hypothesize Christian dependence on an *already* shaped and widespread myth of a heavenly redeemer figure, understood *already* in characteristic Gnostic terms, 'a cosmic figure, the pre-existent divine being, Son of the Father, who came down from heaven and assumed human form'. Thus in the chapter of his *New Testament Theology* on the kerygma of the Hellenistic church, aside from (that is, already

---

34. *Theology of the New Testament*, ET London: SCM Press 1952, 1955. In Bultmann's *Primitive Christianity in its Contemporary Setting*, ET London: Thames & Hudson 1956, Jesus is included in the section entitled 'Judaism'.

35. R. Bultmann, 'The New Testament and Mythology', 1941; ET H. W. Bartsch (ed.), *Kerygma and Myth* Vol. 1, London: SPCK 1953, pp. 1–44. Bultmann's too casual definition of 'myth', however, left him open to serious criticism; see e.g. my 'Demythologizing – the Problem of Myth in the New Testament', in I. H. Marshall (ed.), *New Testament Interpretation*, Exeter: Paternoster 1977, pp. 285–307, here pp. 296–300.

before Paul), he could even sketch out a full-blown Gnostic redeemer myth, which he believed must have been in existence before Paul and which must have influenced the christology of the Hellenistic churches.[36] Even if this pre-Christian myth may well have influenced Hellenistic Jewish Wisdom thinking (as Bultmann had also earlier maintained),[37] the effect of the overall thesis is clear: *Christianity very quickly distanced itself from its distinctively Jewish matrix and from a characteristically Jewish Jesus*; and it is in this distanced form that Christianity developed and became what it is.

1.3 The end of a parenthesis

This last phase has largely drained away into the sand – for several reasons.

(*a*) On the Jesus side of the gulf, Bultmann's existentialist re-interpretation has been unable to outlast the influence of its parent philosophy. The new quest of the historical Jesus which began in reaction against Bultmann's dehistoricizing of Jesus' significance,[38] has itself broken down in a confused welter of unanswered methodological questions (particularly the failure to achieve an agreed set of criteria for recognizing 'authentic' words of Jesus, and for distinguishing Markan redaction), part of a much larger crisis affecting the whole historical critical method of studying the NT texts. The consequence being that many scholars in effect despair of knowing anything with confidence regarding the historical Jesus.[39]

(*b*) The gulf itself between Jesus and early Christianity presupposed to a considerable and unconscious extent that Judaism and Hellenism were two distinct entities, so that *Hellenistic* meant in effect *non-*Jewish, and Hellenistic influence denoted in reality a leaving behind of things Jewish. Such a distinction between Judaism and Hellenism

---

36. Bultmann, *Theology*, pp. 166–7.

37. 'Der religionsgeschichtliche Hintergrund des Prologs zum Johannes-Evangelium', 1923 *Exegetica*, Tübingen: Mohr-Siebeck 1967, pp. 10–35.

38. See particularly the critique of Bultmann by his leading pupil, E. Käsemann, which is generally credited with launching 'the new quest' – 'The Problem of the Historical Jesus', 1954, ET in his *Essays on New Testament Themes*, London: SCM Press 1964, pp. 15–47.

39. D. E. Nineham expresses the point most forcibly; see e.g. his 'Epilogue' in J. Hick (ed.), *The Myth of God Incarnate*, London: SCM Press/Philadelphia: Westminster 1977. For another influential expression of the same pessimism see W. Wink, *The Bible in Human Transformation*, Philadelphia: Fortress 1973. The same issue is repeatedly raised by J. Bowden, *Jesus: The Unanswered Questions*, London: SCM Press/Nashville: Abingdon 1988.

can no longer be held. Particularly influential here has been the work of Martin Hengel, especially his massive study of the same title.[40] The basic point which he makes is that Hellenistic influences had penetrated into Palestine for centuries before Jesus – from Alexander the Great onwards in particular, but even before then. So, for example, for the time of Jesus we can say with confidence that Greek would have been widely known and used in Palestine. We know from inscriptions that people in Jerusalem could be expected to read and appreciate public announcements in Greek; a good one-third of the ossuary inscriptions from around Jerusalem are written in Greek; even the bar Kochba (Kosiba) letters from the second Jewish revolt against Rome in the 130s, which might be expected to be so fiercely nationalistic as to avoid any hint of 'Hellenism', contain two letters written in Greek, which also show that bar Kochba (Kosiba) himself was more comfortable in Greek than in Hebrew.[41] Strictly speaking, then, for the time of Jesus there was no such thing as a non-Hellenistic Judaism.

Hengel has also been quick to remind us that in Jerusalem, from very early on, perhaps from the earliest days of Christianity, there was a group of Hellenistic, that is, Greek-speaking believers.[42] That is to say, the transition from an Aramaic 'stage' to a 'Greek' stage of Christianity should not and cannot be conceived of as only happening well on in the sequence of events in the evolution of Christianity, as a stage only achieved when Christianity spread beyond Palestine in the 40s and 50s. Already in Jerusalem the gospel was being expressed in Greek, in 'Hellenistic' terms; already from the beginning the tradition of Jesus' teaching was being translated from Aramaic to Greek. Indeed, if Greek was so widespread in Palestine, especially in the cities, we may suppose that there were Greek versions of sayings of

---

40. M. Hengel, *Judaism and Hellenism*, 2 vols., ET London: SCM Press/Philadelphia: Fortress 1974; see now also his *The 'Hellenization' of Judaea in the First Century after Christ*, ET London: SCM Press/Philadelphia: TPI 1989. 'The new scholarly consensus suggests that the issue during the early Hasmonean era was not Hellenism per se; rather, the issue must have been to determine exactly when one had become *too* hellenized' (G. G. Porton, 'Diversity in Postbiblical Judaism', *EJMI*, pp. 57–80, here p. 58).

41. See further E. M. Meyers and J. F. Strange, *Archaeology, the Rabbis and Early Christianity*, Nashville: Abingdon, London: SCM Press 1981, ch. 4; Hengel, 'Hellenization', ch. 2.

42. Particularly Hengel's essay in his volume of the same title, *Between Jesus and Paul*, ET London: SCM Press/Philadelphia: Fortress 1984. See further below ch. 4. In 'Hellenization' Hengel reckons that about 10–20% of the population of Jerusalem probably used Greek as their vernacular or mother tongue – i.e. about 8,000–16,000 people (p. 10).

and stories about Jesus already *before* Good Friday and the first Easter. Why not?[43]

In the face of such evidence, *talk of Hellenizing in the sense of de-judaizing, or as implying a gulf between a Jewish Jesus and a Greek-speaking Christianity is undermined.* Differences there will be (and to that subject we must return); but not because we can label neatly one stage as 'Jewish' and the other, later stage as 'Hellenistic'.

(c) On the other side of the gulf from Jesus the hunt for the pre-Christian Gnostic Redeemer myth has proved increasingly to be a wild goose chase. Bultmann's reconstruction of the pre-Christian myth had in fact been largely drawn from the discourses of the Fourth Gospel, on the assumption that the Fourth Evangelist had taken them over from a (Gnostic) source.[44] But that, of course, is a completely circular argument which cannot stand without external support; and such support is quite lacking. There is no real evidence of such a myth prior to Christianity. On the contrary, all the indications are of a *post*-Christian (second-century) development, in which the *already* formulated Christian belief regarding *Jesus* was one of the crucial building blocks. It is only from the second century onwards that we find Gnostic systems emerging which include a redeemer figure. And it is most likely that Christian belief in Jesus provided the model – the ingredient, we may say, which Christianity added to the melting pot of ideas from which the syncretistic Gnostic systems developed.[45]

It is true that several scholars see evidence in the Nag Hammadi literature which they think may imply a non-Christian and therefore pre-Christian myth. But *non*-Christian does *not* signify *pre*-Christian in the melting pot of second-century religious philosophy. The date and developed character of the Nag Hammadi beliefs all point to a period of second century onwards for the Nag Hammadi texts, and there is nothing of substance in these texts to shake that conclusion so far as the hints and inferences which some have drawn out in support of a pre-Christian myth are concerned. The Nag Hammadi fever which has afflicted some NT scholars is like the Mandean fever

---

43. Since Greek was so widespread in Palestine we may suppose that Jesus himself could speak some Greek. Since Jewish coins of the period used Greek inscriptions, part at least of the interchange recalled in Mark 12.13–17 pars. may well have used Greek. We could also ask in what language such encounters as those between Jesus and Pilate (Mark 15.2–5 pars.), or between Peter and Cornelius (Acts 10) took place.

44. According to R. H. Fuller, Bultmann readily admitted as much – *The New Testament in Current Study*, London: SCM Press 1963, p. 136 and n. 1.

45. For this and what follows see further J. D. G. Dunn, *Christology in the Making*, London: SCM Press/Philadelphia: Westminster ²1989, pp. 99–100, 215–6; also *Romans*, WBC 38; Dallas: Word 1988, pp. 277–9. For full discussion see S. Pétrement, *Le Dieu séparé: les origines du gnosticisme*, Paris: Cerf 1984.

of an earlier generation. It is a persistent virus, but we may entertain a good hope that the healthy body of historical criticism will shake it off in due course.

The same is true of attempts to find the myth behind Philo and the figure of heavenly Wisdom. Philo's treatment, for example of Gen. 1.27, can be explained entirely from the combined influences of earlier Jewish Wisdom, of the Stoic belief in the *logos* as the rational power which sustains the cosmos, and of the Platonic view of the heavenly world as the realm of eternal realities. And the earlier Jewish Wisdom tradition is a classic expression of poetic Hebrew's vivid style of personification.[46] A pre-Christian Gnostic Redeemer myth or Urmensch myth is simply an unnecessary hypothesis. Rather than see these as fragments of an earlier unpreserved but now broken myth, the evidence much more strongly suggests that they are elements which *subsequently* became the building blocks out of which the later myth was constructed.

In short, *the attempt to find either a historical Jesus lacking signifi-cance for faith, or a Jesus significant for faith apart from his Jewish-ness, and distinct from a hellenized Christ of faith, has broken down in irretrievable ruin.*

1.4 The re-emergence of the issue of Jesus' Jewishness and Christianity's Jewish matrix

At the same time, as old lines of inquiry were running into the sand, over the past twenty years or so, there has been a tremendous renewal of interest in the Jewish context of earliest Christianity and second Temple Judaism. A number of factors have been of particular signifi-cance here.[47]

(*a*) *The Dead Sea Scrolls.* Discovered more than forty years ago, their impact is only now reaching through the whole of NT and early Christian scholarship. This is partly because not all of them have yet been published,[48] but partly also because the full ramifications of the

---

46. See further ch. 10 below.

47. For a complementary review of recent scholarship on early Judaism see the Introduc-tion to *EJMI*, pp. 1–30, with bibliography.

48. The failure to publish some of the Dead Sea Scrolls has been one of the most shameful episodes in modern scholarship. Some scholars are still sitting on texts for which they were given responsibility nearly forty years ago; with the consequence that there are other scholars of the period who have gone through their whole career without the opportu-nity to read and check primary sources to whose interpretation they might have been able to contribute important insights.

discovery have taken a long time to be appreciated. The key point for us is that we now have documents from the time of Jesus and immediately before which we can relate directly to one of the groups within the Judaism of that period. Not that we lacked documents from this period; the trouble is that with documents like Jubilees and Psalms of Solomon, we simply cannot be sure who wrote them or what group within second Temple Judaism they represent or speak for. But with the Dead Sea Scrolls we can have strong confidence that they include documents written by Essenes and expressive of their views.[49] That is to say, for the *first* time we have clear first-hand testimony as to the views of one of the main sub-groups within the Judaism of Jesus' time – something we do *not* have with any of the other main sub-groups identified by Josephus – Pharisees, Sadducees, or Zealots.[50]

Moreover, what these documents illustrate vividly is the *diversity* of second Temple Judaism. Prior to the discovery of the Dead Sea Scrolls it was easy to assume that there was a normative Judaism dominant during the period, and that the other writings of the period were exceptional, the expressions of small minority groups. But now, suddenly, with one of these groups able to speak for itself, the whole picture has changed. Now it begins to become clear that second Temple Judaism was made up of a number of more fragmented and diverse interest groups. They all shared a common heritage, as we shall go on to note,[51] but they expressed that common heritage in different ways.[52]

(*b*) The discovery of the Dead Sea Scrolls sparked off a renewed interest in the study of so-called '*intertestamental*' *Judaism*, that is, in the Jewish apocrypha and pseudepigrapha. There had been an earlier wave of interest a hundred years ago, at the turn of the century,

---

49. Despite the misgivings of some, the closeness of the 'fit' between the evidence of the elder Pliny as to the presence of an Essene community on the (north-)west side of the Dead Sea (*Naturalis Historia* V.73; in *GLAJJ*, 1.472; commentary at 1.480–1), the archaeological discoveries at Qumran, and the scrolls found nearby makes the identification of Qumran and the Dead Sea Scrolls as 'Essene' as probable as most 'facts' from ancient history can be; 'the identification of the people of the scrolls with the Essenes is virtually certain' and 'commands unanimous (sic!) assent' (J. Murphy-O'Connor, 'The Judean Desert', *EJMI*, pp. 119–56, here pp. 124–5).

50. The last two named seem to have perished as coherent groupings with the destruction of the political system and of the nation state in the suppression of the first Jewish revolt (66–73 CE). Or at least their continuing influence was not such as to ensure that any documentation from their hands survived; whereas some Jewish apocalypses did survive. On the issue see below ch. 12. On the Pharisees see below ch. 6.

51. See below ch. 2.

52. See e.g. Porton, and further below ch. 6.

climaxing in the massive two volumes edited by R. H. Charles.[53] Then
for half a century not much concentrated fresh work was done. But
in the last twenty years or so interest has revived with a flood of new
introductions to the texts,[54] and fresh editions of the texts themselves.[55] The importance of all this is not always fully appreciated.
But the fact is that these documents come closest in time, together
with the writings of Philo and Josephus and the Dead Sea Scrolls, to
the writings of the first Christians. They are not simply convenient
sources of information to fill in the gap between the Old and New
Testaments, as the unfortunate title 'intertestamental' might imply.
They, more than any other, together with the Dead Sea Scrolls, give
us an insight into the context out of which Jesus and his contemporaries came, which we cannot gain anywhere else. So long as we
thought there was a normative Judaism, beside which such texts were
'heterodox', the views of small, insignificant minorities, they could be
largely ignored. But now they can be recognized as alternative and
competing understandings of Judaism – alongside the further alternative, that of the movement sparked off by Jesus of Nazareth. And
thus we gain a much clearer perspective on and grasp of what was
involved in the emergence of that movement.

(c) A further factor was the development of a *tradition-historical
analysis of the rabbinic traditions.* For which we stand hugely indebted to one man – Jacob Neusner.[56] Before Neusner made his
impact, scholars of this period, both Jews and Christians, had tended
to assume that the rabbinic traditions in Mishnah, Tosefta, Talmud,
Midrash, etc., could be freely used to build up a picture of first-
century Judaism, which was then simply assumed to be the *de facto*
normative Judaism. J. Jeremias was one who, despite the eminence of

---

53. R. H. Charles, *The Apocrypha and Pseudepigrapha of the Old Testament*, 2 vols.,
Oxford: Clarendon 1913.
54. See particularly J. H. Charlesworth, *The Pseudepigrapha and Modern Research
with a Supplement*, Chico: Scholars 1981; G. W. E. Nickelsburg, *Jewish Literature Between
the Bible and the Mishnah*, Philadelphia: Fortress/London: SCM Press 1981; M. E. Stone,
Jewish Writings of the Second Temple Period, Assen: Van Gorcum 1984; E. Schürer, *The
History of the Jewish People in the Age of Jesus Christ*, revised by G. Vermes, F. Millar
and M. Goodman, Edinburgh: T. & T. Clark; vol. 3.1, 1986; R. A. Kraft and G. W. E.
Nickelsburg, *Early Judaism and its Modern Interpreters*, Atlanta: Scholars, 1986.
55. Particularly J. H. Charlesworth (ed.), *The Old Testament Pseudepigrapha*, 2 vols.,
New York: Doubleday/London: Darton, Longman & Todd 1983, 1985; H. F. D. Sparks
(ed.), *The Apocryphal Old Testament*, Oxford: Clarendon 1984.
56. Particularly his *The Rabbinic Traditions about the Pharisees before AD 70*, Leiden:
Brill 1971, and in many publications thereafter.

his scholarship, fell into this trap.[57] On the Jewish side H. Maccoby is still open to the same criticism.[58] The mistake is twofold. First, to read documents and traditions which are often clearly dated to the third and fourth centuries[59] as though they bore immediate witness to the views and conditions of the first century; and second, to do so largely in disregard for the documents which we *know do* stem from that period (those referred to under (*b*) above). The mistake is not a little astonishing, of course. Understandable in the case of Jewish scholars, for whose whole tradition rabbinic Judaism has been Judaism for (now) nearly 1900 years. But astonishing for Christian scholars who would have criticized unmercifully any patristic scholar who attempted in the same way to read Christian texts of the third and fourth centuries back in to the first.[60]

Neusner, however, has taken the logical step of applying the source-, form-, and tradition-history critical techniques of analysis, developed particularly in the study of the Christian texts themselves, to the rabbinic texts, and has thus succeeded in documenting beyond doubt the fact that these traditions have been built up, often layer upon layer over many decades and generations, before reaching their present state in the Mishnah and subsequent rabbinic writings. There is a temptation, of course, to react in the same way that some have reacted to the tradition-historical analysis of the Jesus-tradition: now we can be sure of nothing; we cannot be confident that any particular tradition goes back to the time of Jesus.[61] That is much too extreme a conclusion, as Neusner has also argued – and as we shall see. All we need note here, however, is that Neusner's work, when taken together with (*a*) and (*b*), has succeeded in exposing and exploding the old assumption that there was a single, normative Judaism prior to 70 CE, or that rabbinic or Pharisaic Judaism was already so strongly established as to constitute that normative Judaism.

---

57. E.g. J. Jeremias, *Jerusalem at the Time of Jesus*, ET London: SCM Press 1969.

58. H. Maccoby, *Judaism in the First Century*, London: Sheldon 1989.

59. Not least by H. L. Strack and P. Billerbeck, *Kommentar zum Neuen Testament aus Talmud und Midrasch*, München: C. H. Beck, 4 vols., 1922–28, who have been unjustly blamed at this point for the misuse made of the materials which they, or more accurately Billerbeck put together.

60. See also the justified criticisms at this point of P. S. Alexander, 'Rabbinic Judaism and the New Testament', *ZNW* 74 (1983), pp. 237–46; similarly by A. J. Saldarini, 'Reconstructions of Rabbinic Judaism', *EJMI*, pp. 437–77, here pp. 454–7; and *Pharisees Scribes and Sadducees*, Wilmington: Glazier, 1988/Edinburgh: T. & T. Clark 1989, pp. 7–9, 199ff.

61. See above n. 39. Something of this over-reaction is evident in E. P. Sanders, *Jesus and Judaism*, London: SCM Press/Philadelphia: Fortress 1985, though he does also show how much of the Jesus tradition stands up well to the strictest historical scrutiny.

(*d*) A fourth factor is the recent significant *reappraisal of the charac-ter of the Judaism* of the period. For centuries it had been assumed, particularly in Protestant circles, that Judaism, or Pharisaic Judaism in particular, was a narrow, legalistic religion. Pharisees taught a religion of 'works-righteousness', of salvation earned by merit – so the argument would run – thus providing a stark foil for the gospel of Jesus and of Paul who, in contrast, brought a religion of forgiveness and grace. For long enough Jewish scholars had protested against this portrayal, caricature as they saw it, of Pharisees and of Judaism. Apart from anything else, the Judaism they knew emphasized repentence, forgiveness, atonement. A Jesus or Paul who seemed to ignore or deny these characteristic emphases of Judaism they could not understand. Some Christian scholars protested too, particularly G. F. Moore, R. T. Herford, and J. Parkes.[62] But it was not until E. P. Sanders' *Paul and Palestinian Judaism*, that the point seems to have got through, especially to English-speaking scholarship.[63]

The point which emerged was this: that the traditional Protestant view of Paul's gospel was derived more from the Lutheran interpret-ation of Paul than from Paul himself. Luther had reacted against the mediaeval church's doctrine of merit, and had found peace with God at last through rediscovering Paul's teaching on justification by faith – that God accepts the individual freely and not by virtue of any merit of his own. The trouble was that Luther had read his own experience back into Paul. He assumed that Paul too must have been confronted by a dominant tradition which taught justification by works, that is, by merit-earning good works, and that his doctrine of justification by faith, the insight which had brought such relief to Luther himself, was the same insight that Paul had discovered in his conversion.[64] The obvious corollary was that the Judaism of Paul's day must have taught the equivalent of the Catholicism of Luther's day – Judaism as a religion of legalism, with no place for grace and free pardon. In

---

62. G. F. Moore, 'Christian Writers on Judaism', *HTR* 14 (1921), pp. 197–254; R. T. Herford, *Judaism in the New Testament*, London: Lindsey 1928; J. Parkes, *The Conflict of the Church and the Synagogue. A Study in the Origins of Antisemitism*, 1934; New York: Athaneum, Macmillan.

63. London: SCM Press 1977, particularly pp. 1–12, 33–59. S. Sandmel, *The First Christian Century in Judaism and Christianity. Certainties and Uncertainties*, New York: Oxford University 1969, regarded the work of G. F. Moore as a still more important watershed: 'prior to Moore's time, there was almost no effort to be fair to Judaism' (p. 66).

64. In the light of Sanders' work the earlier contribution by K. Stendahl has gained fresh significance and weight – 'The Apostle Paul and the Introspective Conscience of the West', *HTR* 56 (1963), pp. 199–215; reprinted in his *Paul Among Jews and Gentiles*, London: SCM Press 1977, pp. 78–96.

short, Luther read Paul and the situation confronting Paul through the grid of his own experience.[65]

Unfortunately the grid remained firmly in place for Protestant scholarship thereafter. Consequently in studies of Paul by, for example, Bultmann, or E. Käsemann, or H. Ridderbos, or C. E. B. Cranfield, the basic paradigm has not really shifted – Pharisees and Pharisaic Judaism being portrayed consistently as proponents of a joyless, narrowly legalistic religion.[66] Now, however, in the light of Sanders' contribution the scales have fallen from many eyes, and we can see, as never before, given also (*a*) to (*c*), the degree to which early Judaism was in fact a religion of grace and forgiveness.[67]

The paradigm shift which all this calls for is enormous, and raises fundamental questions which are still subject to fierce debate. For example, if Pharisees were not all legalistic bigots, what do we make of the Gospel traditions regarding the conflicts between Jesus and the Pharisees? What was there to be in conflict over? *Were* they in fact in conflict at all, or is the Gospel tradition at this point the result of early Christians reading back their own conflicts? Again, if Paul was not protesting against a concept of merit-earning good-works right-eousness, to what was he objecting? Was the puzzlement of so many Jewish scholars at the Protestant Paul a puzzlement caused by the *Protestant* interpreted Paul, or caused by Paul himself? To such questions we must return. Suffice it simply to note here that we are in the midst of a reassessment of many points regarding earliest Christianity, and that a fresh reassessment of earliest Christianity's relationship with Judaism and emergence from Judaism must be one of our highest priorities. What was the Judaism within which Jesus grew up, and from which earliest Christianity emerged? And why did it break away from that Judaism and become distinct and separate? Our thematic questions thus re-emerge with still greater force and urgency.

(*e*) One other factor should not be ignored – that is, the continuing reaction within Christian scholarship against the Holocaust and the recognition of *Christian anti-semitism* within Christian history and potentially at least within the NT itself. Particularly significant here has been Vatican II's *Declaration on the Relationship of the Church to Non-Christian Religions* – including the following passage:

---

65. See further my 'The Justice of God. A Renewed Perspective on Justification by Faith', *JTS* 43 (1992) reprinted in *The New Perspective on Paul* (WUNT 185; Mohr Siebeck, 2005), ch. 7.

66. Fuller details can be found in my *Romans*; see e.g. pp. lxv, 185, 587. See further my *Jesus, Paul and the Law*, London: SPCK 1990.

67. See further below, ch. 7.

Although the Church is the new people of God, the Jews should not be presented as repudiated or cursed by God, as if such views followed from the holy Scriptures ... The Church repudiates all persecutions against any man ... she deplores the hatred, persecution, and displays of anti-Semitism directed against the Jews at any time and from any source (§4).[68]

Noteworthy too has been the World Council of Churches' more recent recognition that the relationship between the church and the Jewish people is an essential part of the apostolic faith and must therefore form part of the current *ecumenical* agenda.[69]

However, the stakes have been raised over the past fifteen years and the issues posed with a fresh sharpness, particularly by R. Ruether.[70] Her challenge, echoed by others, is straightforward. Antisemitism is endemic to Christianity, an inevitable corollary to the church's proclamation of Jesus as Messiah. To take over Israel's Messiah so completely, to take over the concepts of 'Israel' and 'the people of God' so completely, is anti-semitic, or at least anti-Jewish. By clear implication, Christians are anti-semitic because they are Christians. Christian anti-semitism grows inevitably out of and is already contained in the NT characterization of the Jews as the enemies of Jesus (John's Gospel) and of the early Christian mission (Acts), as the murderers of Jesus (Matt. 27.25), and children of Satan (John 8.44).[71]

In the face of such a challenge a re-examination of earliest Christianity's relationship to its parent faith is undoubtedly essential.

1.5 The need for a fresh study

It is important to take a fresh look at Christian beginnings in the light of all this.

(*a*) There is a temptation to abandon such historical questing because of the difficulties already mentioned and the lack of any widespread agreement on historical questions. Today, in fact, many scholars prefer to concentrate their efforts instead on a literary study of the NT texts. And certainly the recognition and appreciation of

---

68. W. Abbott, *The Documents of Vatican II*, America Press 1966, pp. 666–7, notes that the last sentence was weakened in the course of the Council by the dropping of the phrase 'and condemns' from the earlier draft.

69. H. G. Link (ed.) *Apostolic Faith Today*, Geneva: WCC 1985, pp. 259–60, 265.

70. R. R. Ruether, *Faith and Fratricide. The Theological Roots of Anti-Semitism*, New York: Seabury 1974.

71. See further below, ch. 8.

the literary and rhetorical character of these texts is essential and can be very valuable for our understanding and use of these texts today. But *not* as an *alternative* to historical study. The literary study of the NT texts has been most valuable when treated as a supplement to historical study (historical literary criticism); the value diminishes in proportion to the degree that the historical character of the text is ignored or devalued; a text freed ('liberated'!) from its native context is a text much more readily abused and subjected to the reader's will.

(*b*) It is a natural human curiosity to wish to inquire into the historical actuality of Jesus and of the beginnings of a movement so formative and influential in our European history and culture – a curiosity which the historical difficulties only arouse further and do nothing to diminish. This endless fascination with Jesus and the beginnings of Christianity is well reflected in a seemingly non-stop flow of films, plays, musicals and documentaries on these themes. We have responsibility to ensure that such curiosity of the 'person in the street' is met with well researched answers – otherwise it will be the imaginative story lines of the merely curious, or the tendentious portrayals of those with an axe to grind, or the fantasizing of the sensation-mongers which will set the images for a generation addicted to the television screen.

(*c*) A fresh inquiry is essential not least for theological reasons – two at least. First, if Jesus is the incarnation of God in history, then that man in all his historical particularity is an essential definition for us of God, essential to our understanding of God and of God's will for humankind. And second, the Christian canon makes the documents from that period (the first two generations of Christianity) of constitutional importance. Consequently, an understanding of these documents and of the impact they made from the beginning must be central to any attempt to define Christianity. They more than any other writings tell us what Christianity *is*.

It is hardly surprising that all these factors have given rise to what is often now referred to as 'the third quest of the historical Jesus'[72] – where it is *precisely the readiness to recognize and give weight to the Jewish context and character of Jesus and his ministry* which has provided the fresh stimulus and the new angle of entry into the Jesus-tradition, just at the time when the older questers had lost their way and their successors were ready to give up any idea of a continuing

---

72. See particularly S. Neill and T. Wright, *The Interpretation of the New Testament 1861–1986*, Oxford University [2]1988, pp. 379–403.

quest, but with an increased danger of opening up once again the gulf between (a Jewish) Jesus and (a Christian) Paul.[73]

In these chapters we do not join that quest as such, though what we attempt can be taken as a contribution to it. Our concern, however, is broader. In particular, the question which motivates this inquiry can be posed thus: Since Jesus was a Jew, since Christianity emerged from within second Temple Judaism, and since the Jewish scriptures are still part of the Christian Bible, what does all *this* tell us about Christianity – not only about its beginnings, but also about its enduring character? Or to focus our question still more precisely in the terms used at the beginning of the chapter: the end of the first century of the common era saw the emergence of two great world religions – (rabbinic) Judaism and Christianity. They emerged from the *same* matrix. Why did they pull apart and become so distinct? How did it come about? Was there any single event or factor which made the rupture inevitable, impossible to avoid, irretrievable? Or was it a longer, slower pulling apart at the seams, where a re-stitching might have been possible for several decades, given sufficient good will on both sides? What does this 'parting of the ways' tell us about both of these great religions? And what does it say to us about their continuing inter-relationship?

But first we must attempt to gain a clearer picture of this matrix, of second Temple Judaism in the period prior to 70 CE.

---

73. Evident to a grotesque degree in H. Maccoby, *The Mythmaker. Paul and the Invention of Christianity*, London: Weidenfeld & Nicolson 1986; but the danger is present also in E. P. Sanders' characterization of Judaism and Christianity as two distinct forms or patterns of religion.

2

The Four Pillars of
second Temple Judaism

As already indicated in ch. 1, it is now widely recognized that there was no single, uniform type of Judaism in the first century of the common era, certainly for the period we have primarily in view – prior to 70 CE. The older working assumption that rabbinic Judaism was already normative in first-century Palestine at the time of Jesus has to be abandoned. Jewish scholars of the period such as Jacob Neusner and Alan Segal are leading the way in speaking of Judaisms (plural).[1] Another way to put the point is that second Temple Judaism to a large extent, latterly at least, consisted of a range of different interest groups. Josephus speaks of four 'sects' (*haireseis*) or 'schools of thought' – Pharisees, Sadducees, Essenes and Zealots (particularly *Ant.* 13.171; *War* 2.118).[2] In addition, most of the Jewish pseude-pigrapha of the period are properly to be described as 'sectarian' documents.[3] Not to mention the mass of people, the people(s) of the land (*'am[me] ha'arets*) (Ezra 10.2, 11; Neh. 10.30–31; cf.Jer. 39.10;

---

1. J. Neusner, et al. (ed.), *Judaisms and their Messiahs at the Turn of the Christian Era*, Cambridge University 1987; A. F. Segal, *The Other Judaisms of Late Antiquity*, BJS 127; Atlanta: Scholars 1987. R. T. Herford, *Judaism in the New Testament Period*, London: Lindsey 1928, notes that C. G. Montefiore had already spoken of 'many Judaisms', pp. 14–15.

2. Josephus calls the Zealots a 'sect' in *War* 2.118, and later a 'fourth philosophy' (*Ant.* 18.9, 23) alongside the three-fold philosophy of Pharisee, Sadducee and Essene (*War* 2.119). See discussion in M. Hengel, *The Zealots*, 1961, ²1976; ET Edinburgh: T. & T. Clark, 1989, ch. 3; Schürer 2.598–606. 'Sect' is not entirely a satisfactory term; elsewhere I use the almost as unsatisfactory 'faction' (see further below ch. 6). For present purposes I am content with the definition offered by S. J. D. Cohen, *From Maccabees to the Mishnah*, Philadelphia: Westminster 1987, p. 125 – 'A sect is a small, organized group that separates itself from a larger religious body and asserts that it alone embodies the ideals of the larger group because it alone understands God's will.' But there are, of course, different degrees of sectarianism and different kinds of sect. On a narrow definition perhaps only the Qumran community should be called a 'sect'; on a broader definition the movement spawned by Jesus should certainly be included. See further Saldarini, *Pharisees*, particularly pp. 70–3, 123–7.

3. See further below ch. 6.

John 7.49),[4] and the large proportion of Jews who lived outside the land of Israel, that is, the diaspora.[5] In short, the concept of an orthodox or normative Judaism for the period prior to 70 CE is, to say the least, very questionable.[6]

Nevertheless, all that being said, we can still speak of a common and unifying core for second Temple Judaism, a fourfold foundation on which all these more diverse forms of Judaism built, a common heritage which they all interpreted in their own ways. We cannot say that the four common elements *were* Judaism, since each group or 'sect' differed in emphasis and understanding and in the way it brought the common core to expression. Even when *Ioudaismos* ('Judaism') is used in texts of the time, it may well have included something at least of a sectarian understanding of the term.[7] Nevertheless, the fact remains that the word could be used; there was something recognizable as 'Judaism', something common to these various diverse expressions of second Temple Judaism(s). And it is that common element which we seek to clarify here, the family resemblance in the different siblings of pre-70 Judaism.

In focussing on what seem to me to be 'the four pillars' of early Judaism,[8] I am not, of course, attempting a complete taxonomy or even characterization of early Judaism. Many will want to bring other elements to the fore – particularly, perhaps, the Jewish scriptures. And a fuller treatment of law than is possible here (§2.3) would have to deal with that issue more fully, though the discussion of subsequent chapters does attempt to bear in mind the broader reference of 'the law'. I am encouraged, however, by other studies of Judaism which suggest that an analysis of early Judaism in these terms is not entirely idiosyncratic.[9] And, as will become apparent, it is precisely on these

---

4. See further *IDB*, 1.106–7; and particularly A. Oppenheimer, *The Am Ha-aretz: a Study in the Social History of the Jewish People in the Hellenistic-Roman Period*, Leiden: Brill 1977.

5. See e.g. the estimates cited by M. Simon, *Verus Israel. A study of the relations between Christians and Jews in the Roman Empire (AD 135–425)*, Littman library: Oxford University 1986, pp. 33–4. For details of the geographical dispersion see the geographical survey in Schürer 3.1–86.

6. See e.g. N. J. McEleney, 'Orthodoxy in Judaism of the first Christian Century', *JSJ* 4 (1973), pp. 19–42; L. L. Grabbe, 'Orthodoxy in First Century Judaism. What are the Issues?' *JSJ* 8 (1977), pp. 149–53; as well as those mentioned in n. 1 above. See also §1.4a–b.

7. See further below §8.2.

8. The imagery is drawn, of course, from the more familiar idea of 'the five pillars of Islam'.

9. I have in mind, e.g., H. R. Greenstein, *Judaism – An Eternal Covenant*, Philadelphia: Fortress 1983, with its analysis of 'the components' as 1. God, 2–3. Torah, 4. Israel: the

fundamental matters that the differences in interpretation began to pull Christianity apart from the rest of the Judaisms of the period.

2.1 Monotheism: God is one

Monotheism was absolutely fundamental for the Jew of Jesus' day.[10] Every day every Jew had been taught to say the *Shema*: 'Hear O Israel: The Lord our God is one Lord'; or, '. . . the Lord our God, the Lord is one' (Deut. 6.4); indeed, on the basis of Deut. 6.7 a devout Jew would say the *Shema* twice a day. So, without doubt, Jesus would have been taught. Similarly, the basic statement of Jewish obligation, the ten commandments, begins with the clear charge: 'You shall have no other gods besides (or before) me' (Ex. 20.3). According to *m. Tamid* 5.1 these too were to be recited daily, in public worship; and even if that reflects later practice, we need not doubt that the first of the ten commandments was deeply ingrained in Jewish faith and praxis. Such deductions are borne out by the contemporary Jewish literature. Josephus, for example, notes that the acknowledgment of 'God as one is common to all the Hebrews' (*Ant.* 5.1, 27, 112); Philo climaxes his exposition of the first commandment thus –

> Let us, then, engrave deep in our hearts this as the first and most sacred of commandments, to acknowledge and honour one God who is above all, and let the idea that gods are many never even reach the ears of the man whose rule of life is to seek for truth in purity and goodness (*Decal.* 65);

People, and 5. Israel: the Land; and S. Nigosian, *Judaism. The way of Holiness*, Crucible 1986, with its five main chapters, 1. Holy God, 2. Holy People, 3. Holy Land, 4. Holy Book, and 5. Holy Observances. E. L. Fackenheim, *What is Judaism?*, New York: Summit 1987, begins his answer by citing the much-quoted saying in the Zohar: 'God, Torah and Israel are one' (p. 43). Similarly Herford, *Judaism*, pp. 16–21, 30, 36–7; Cohen, *Maccabees to Mishnah*, pp. 103, 105; M. R. Wilson, *Our Father Abraham. Jewish Roots of the Christian Faith*, Grand Rapids: Eerdmans 1989, p. 259 – 'four foundational pillars: God, Torah, People, and land'; P. M. van Buren, *A Theology of the Jewish—Christian Reality. Part 2. A Christian Theology of the People of Israel*, San Francisco: Harper & Row 1983, chs 2–7.

10. 'The founding axiom of the Mosaic law is that expressing the reality of God' – L. E. Goodman, *Monotheism*, Allanheld, Osmun & Co. 1981, p. 113; 'The belief common to all Jews at the beginning of the first century was that their God was the only God and their religion the only true religion' – E. E. Urbach, 'Self-Isolation or Self-Affirmation in Judaism in the First Three Centuries: Theory and Practice', *JCSD*. 2.269–98, here p. 273.

and the Jewish Sibyl, despite prophesying in Gentile guise, states forth-rightly, 'He alone is God and there is no other' (*Sib. Or.* 3.629).[11]

We need not explore here the early history of Jewish monotheism. For us it is enough that in the post-exilic period it became (or had already become) a fundamental dogma of Judaism. Pre-exilic syncretism was recalled as the main cause of the exile (as in Amos 5.25–7; Jer. 19.13; taken up in Acts 7.42–3), and Second Isaiah's bold reaffirmation that Israel's God is the only God (note especially Isa. 45.20–25) must have provided a powerful rallying point for the Jews of the exile. Typical of Judaism's self-affirmation and apologetic thereafter was precisely a fierce antipathy to syncretism and virulent hostility to anything which smacked of idolatry. Characteristic is the claim of Judith 8.18; 'For never in our generation, nor in these present days, has there been any tribe or family or people or city of ours which worshipped gods made with hands, as was done in days gone by.' And scathing attacks on pagan idolatry are a feature of Jewish literature from then on (Isa. 44.9–20; Wisd. Sol. 11–15; Ep. Jer.; *Sib. Or.* 3.8–45).

All this is in marked contrast to the spirit of Hellenistic religion generally. There the tendency was precisely towards syncretism, to see different local or national gods as but manifestations of one and the same divine being. As Hengel notes: 'The universal religious attitude of learned men which developed in the Hellenistic period . . . regarded the different religions as in the end only manifestations of the one deity.'[12] For example, the Greek Zeus and the Roman Jupiter were clearly one and the same; at Bath in England there is a statue to Minerva-Sulis – Minerva the Roman goddess, regularly identified with the Greek Athena, Sulis the local equivalent; in the great hymns to (the originally Egyptian goddess) Isis, she is addressed as 'Thou of countless names', because she was identified with so many other deities.[13]

This was the theology, we may say, which underlay the policy of both Alexander the Great and the Romans by which they sought to incorporate defeated nations – that is by absorbing the local religions

---

11. See further G. F. Moore, *Judaism in the First Centuries of the Christian Era*, Cambridge: Harvard University 1927, 1.360–2.372; also F. Mussner, *Tractate on the Jews. The Significance of Judaism for Christian Faith*, 1979; ET Philadelphia: Fortress 1984, p. 52; both of whom also cite Philo, *Opif.* 171, where he numbers the confession of God's unity as the second great teaching of Moses (the first being the eternity of the Deity).

12. Hengel, *Judaism*, 1.261; see further pp. 26–7; R. M. Grant, *Gods and the One God*, Philadelphia: Westminster/London: SPCK 1986, ch. 6.

13. *OCD* 'Isis'.

into the larger syncretistic whole of the empire – religion being used cleverly as a means to unify the diverse nations, and thus prevented from becoming a rallying point for nationalist sentiment. Hence the attempt by Antiochus Epiphanes to set up a cult of Olympian Zeus in the Jerusalem Temple (II Macc. 6.1–2); for a Hellenist, Yahweh was simply the local manifestation of Zeus. The attitude is well expressed in the Letter of Aristeas, by the Alexandrian Jew, Aristeas, himself: 'These people (the Jews of Alexandria) worship God the overseer and creator of all, whom all men worship including our-selves, O King, except that we have a different name. Their name for him is Zeus and Jove' (*Ep. Arist.* 16). As is well known, however, the policy backfired badly; the Maccabeans and their successors would have none of it. Hence the widespread belief among cultured Hellen-ists in the Graeco-Roman world that Jews (and subsequently Christ-ians) were *atheists* – not because they were monotheists as such, but because they were *exclusive* monotheists, whereas the cultured Hellenists were typically *syncretistic* monotheists (Josephus, *Ap.* 2.148; *Mart. Pol.* 3.2; Justin, *Apol.* 1.13.1).[14] Hengel cites Celsus appositely in his subsequent attack on this attitude: '(They) thought that there was one God called the Most High, or Adonai, or the Heavenly One, or Sabbaoth, or however they like to call this world; and they acknowledged nothing more'; whereas in Celsus' own view, 'it makes no difference whether one calls the supreme God by the name used among the Greeks, or by that, for example, used among the Indians, or by that among the Egyptians' (*c. Celsum* 1.24).

Israel solved the problem of other gods chiefly in two ways. One was by means of *subordination*. The gods of other nations were simply angels appointed by Yahweh to rule over these nations (e.g. Deut. 32.8–9; Sir. 17.17; *Jub.* 15.31). In other words, they could be portrayed as Yahweh's court retinue (as in Job 1–2), thereby greatly enhancing the majesty of the king who had so many attendants. Another way was by *absorption*, or domestication. Thus divine Wis-dom in other religions and cults could be depicted as a distinct divine being. But, as we shall see, Jewish Wisdom writers used the figure of Wisdom rather as a way of expressing the self-revelation of Yahweh. So, for example, in Sir. 24.4 Wisdom identifies herself as having her throne 'in a pillar of cloud'; that is, Wisdom is identified with the presence or angel of the Lord as in Ex. 14.19–20,24. And in Wisd. Sol. 10ff. Wisdom is portrayed as Yahweh's care for the patriarchs

---

14. E. Stauffer, *TDNT*, 3.121. Such monotheism (belief in a single supreme being) was maintained by many on philosophic grounds, though Graeco-Roman and middle-Eastern religion was characteristically polytheistic, but including a hierarchy of gods.

and Israel.[15] In such ways, concerned Jews could remain in dialogue with their neighbours without abandoning their monotheism.

We need not press the point any further. It is sufficient simply to note that subsequently in rabbinic Judaism blasphemy was regarded as the most serious crime, blasphemy being defined as whatever violated the unique majesty of God, with breach of the first commandment regarded as the fundamental sin.[16] So fundamental was the issue for the rabbis, indeed, that he who disavowed (belief in) the One God was called *kofer ba-'Iqqar*, that is, 'one who denies the primary principle of the faith'.[17]

2.2 Election – a covenant people, a promised land

Equally fundamental to Israel's self-understanding was its conviction that it had been specially chosen by Yahweh, that the one God had bound himself to Israel and Israel to himself by a special contract, or *covenant*.[18] If anything this is even more deeply rooted (than monotheism) already in the pre-exilic period, in the ancient stories and credal summaries which recall and reaffirm the choice of Abraham and the promise of the land. Thus in Genesis the initial choice of and promise to Abraham in 12.1–3 and 15.1–6 is filled out in more explicitly covenant terms and with explicit reference to the land in 15.17–21 and 17.1–8. In Deuteronomy we might simply note the powerful statement of 7.6ff., with its preceding commission to clear the land completely of other nations and avoid any entanglements with them (7.1–7), and the central place given to the divine initiative in rescuing Israel from Egypt and to his commitment to give Israel the land promised to the fathers (6.20–25; 26.5–10).[19]

As with the other pillars of second Temple Judaism, these convictions were re-established in the post-exilic period: we need only think again of the influence of Second Isaiah (Isa. 41.8–9 and 44.1), and of the importance of the Ezra reforms, the enforced abandonment of mixed marriages to cleanse people and land of just such entanglements. Israel was to be a people separated to and for the Lord. The strength of the Maccabean resistance against cultural and national assimilation (second century BCE) was motivated precisely by this

---

15. See further below ch. 10.

16. E.g. H. W. Beyer, *TDNT*, 1.622; Moore, *Judaism*, 1.465–7

17. E. E. Urbach, *The Sages*, Jerusalem: Magnes 1979, p. 26.

18. 'The root metaphor underlying Hebrew society is expressed in the word *covenant*' – A. F. Segal, *Rebecca's Children. Judaism and Christianity in the Roman World*, Cambridge: Harvard University 1986, p. 4.

19. See further Mussner, *Tractate*, pp. 11–13, with further literature.

conviction that Israel, both land and people, was not simply one among so many others, but was the special choice of the one God. The word 'Judaism' (*Ioudaismos*) first meets us in literature at this time (II Macc. 2.21; 8.1; 14.38), and in each case the talk is of the zeal for and faithfulness to 'Judaism' shown by the heroes of the Maccabean resistance. The implication is clear: that the word was coined precisely in opposition to 'Hellenism', precisely to express the reaffirmation of covenant faith by the natives of Judaea ('Jews')[20] in their resistance against 'Hellenizing' assimilation. Consequently the word bears a clear overtone from its first usage of a fierce nationalistic assertion of Israel's election and of divine right to religious (if not national) freedom in the land given it by God.

The same emphases come through consistently in the Jewish writings which stretch down to our period. For example, *Jub.* 15.31–32 –

> ... He chose Israel that they might be a people for himself. And he sanctified them and gathered them from all the sons of man because (there are) many nations and many people, and they all belong to him, but over all of them he caused spirits to rule so that they might lead them astray from following him. But over Israel he did not cause any angel or spirit to rule because he alone is their ruler and he will protect them ...

Similarly, *Pss. Sol.* 9.8–9 –

> And now, you are God and we are the people whom you have loved; look and be compassionate, O God of Israel, for we are yours, and do not take away your mercy from us, lest they set upon us.
> For you chose the descendants of Abraham above all the nations, and you put your name upon us, Lord, and it will not cease forever.

It is probably unnecessary to document the point in more detail, since the thought of Israel as *God's* inheritance can be traced through many strands of Jewish literature.[21] So too in the Dead Sea Scrolls and

---

20. See further below ch. 8.

21. Deut. 32.9; I Kings 8.51, 53; II Kings 21.14; Ps. 33.12; 74.2; Isa. 63.17; Jer. 10.16; Micah 7.18; Judith 13.5; Sir. 24.8, 12; *Jub.* 1.19–21; 22.9–10, 15; 33.20; *III Macc.* 6.3; *II Bar.* 5.1; *Ps. Philo* 12.9; 21.10; 27.7; 28.2; 39.7; 49.6. See also my *Romans* on Rom. 4.13 and 9.4.

rabbinic traditions the conviction that Israel is God's elect, chosen, God's vineyard is absolutely axiomatic.[22] And in the diaspora we can tell from not a few allusions to Deut. 30.1–10 that hope of return to the land of promise was one which sustained many diaspora Jews.[23]

All this would no doubt have been familiar to Jesus. In the Eighteen Benedictions (*Shemoneh 'Esreh*), an early version of which he would probably have been taught to pray daily, God is addressed as 'God of our fathers, God of Abraham, God of Isaac and God of Jacob . . .' (First Benediction). A subsequent prayer is for the gathering in of the Jews of the dispersion (Tenth Benediction). The Fourteenth Benediction asks, 'Be merciful, Lord our God, with your great mercies, to Israel your people and to Jerusalem your city; and to Zion, the dwelling-place of your glory . . .' And the final petition is: 'Bring your peace over Israel, your people, and over your city and over your inheritance . . .' (Eighteenth Benediction).[24]

In this connection it may also be significant that we never hear of Jesus going into either of the Hellenistic cities in Galilee – Sepphoris and Tiberias – a silence all the more eloquent, perhaps, in the case of the former, since it was the provincial capital of Galilee in the time of Jesus and since it lay just over the hill from Nazareth. We must beware of reading too much into the silences of the Gospel traditions, of course.[25] But there were no doubt many in Galilee who resented these foreign establishments, intruded into the promised land by its conquerors and so antipathetic to Israel's history, culture and religion. And Jesus would surely be aware, we can say no more than that, of the fierce hostility to anything which infringed the exclusive crown rights of Yahweh over his people which motivated Judas of Galilee in 6 CE and later on the Zealots.

All this is true despite the fact that Judaism was already substantially 'Hellenized'. 'Hellenism', in fact, was simply the international culture of the time – as Latin was in the Middle Ages. Consequently it was impossible to avoid 'Hellenization' in matters of language and

---

22. 'What made a Jew a heretic was not a slackness in observing the precepts, or even alienation from tradition, but the act of denying the election of the Jews . . .' (Urbach, 'Self-Isolation', pp. 292–3). W. D. Davies sums up the position regarding the rabbis thus: 'Pharisaism so cherished the view that there was an unseverable connection between Israel and Yahweh and the land that this view has been referred to as a "dogma" of the Pharisees' – *The Gospel and the Land*, University of California 1974, p. 55. See also Sanders, *Paul and Palestinian Judaism* index 'Election'.

23. See my *Romans*, p. 603.

24. The text is drawn from the Palestinian Recension as given in Schürer, 2.460–1.

25. Several scholars think the possibility is strong that Jesus as a craftsman worked on the rebuilding of Sepphoris; see discussion in Hengel, *'Hellenization'* p. 74 n. 90.

organization. 'Hellenism' was not an issue in 'neutral' matters, where the distinctives of the faith were not threatened. So too a significant proportion of the ruling elite were more open to 'hellenistic' culture – including not least the later Hasmoneans, and certainly the Herodians – Herod the Great being a friend first of Mark Anthony and then of Augustus, and Herod Agrippa a friend from boyhood of Claudius.[26] Nonetheless, the sense of Israel's distinctiveness and of the land as given them by God, setting them apart from other nations, remained a fundamental and constitutive element in Israel's self-understanding. Nor will readers need to be reminded that the same is still true today for many Jews.[27]

2.3 Covenant focussed in Torah

Absolutely crucial for any understanding of second Temple Judaism is an appreciation of *the centrality of the Torah in Israel's self-consciousness of being God's chosen people*.[28] This comes to clearest expression in Deuteronomy, which is the classic statement of Israel's covenant theology, and which evidently quite quickly succeeded in stamping its pattern on Jewish self-understanding.[29] It provides the classic statement of what Sanders has fittingly described as 'coven-antal nomism' – fittingly, since the phrase puts the emphasis on the two key words – *Torah* as given to Israel as part of God's *covenant* with Israel, *obedience to the law* of Moses as Israel's *response to God's choice of Israel* to be his people, 'nomism' as the way of living within the 'covenant', maintaining and manifesting status as the people of Yahweh.[30] The heart of the book (Deut. 5–28) is set out as a restatement of the covenant made at Horeb/Sinai (5.2–3). 29.1

---

26. See also above §1.3.

27. See e.g. the Foreword by D. Flusser to C. Thoma, *A Christian Theology of Judaism*, New York: Paulist 1980, pp. 9–10 – 'a Christian theology of Judaism that does not affirm the divinely willed tie between Israel and the Land appears to me impracticable in our day.'

28. 'It is essentially the Torah which holds Judaism together and gives it its identity' (Mussner, *Tractate*, p. 141). As with 'covenant' (above n. 18), Segal calls the Torah 'the root metaphor of Israelite society' (*Rebecca's Children*, p. 38). 'The centrality of the Torah of Moses to Judaism was the centrality of a national flag' (P. Alexander, 'Jewish Law in the Time of Jesus: Towards a Clarification of the Problem', *Law and Religion. Essays on the Place of the Law in Israel and Early Christianity*, ed. B. Lindars, Cambridge: James Clarke 1988, pp. 44–58, here p. 56.

29. See e.g. E. W. Nicholson, *God and his People: Covenant and Theology in the Old Testament*, Oxford: Clarendon 1986.

30. See Sanders, *Paul and Palestinian Judaism*, pp. 75, 180. I have found Sanders categorization here to be very helpful and illuminating in my earlier work in this area; see my *Jesus, Paul and the Law*, index 'covenantal nomism'.

sums up the whole of that block of teaching thus: 'These are the words of the covenant which the Lord commanded Moses to make with the people of Israel in the land of Moab, besides the covenant which he had made with them at Horeb.' And throughout the book the emphasis of covenantal nomism is sustained and reinforced in numerous restatements of the promise (and warning): 'This do and live' (4.1, 10, 40; 5.29–33; 6.1–2, 18, 24; 7.12–13; etc.) – a phrase which itself is one of the most concise summaries of covenantal nomism.

In view of the often repeated observation that the Hebrew *torah* is a much broader category than Greek *nomos*, and that the LXX rendering of the former by the latter distorted Jewish thought and gave unjustified foundation to the perception of Jewish 'legalism',[31] it is important to realize that the equation *Torah* = law is firmly rooted in Deuteronomy itself. In Deuteronomy *torah* denotes the collection of ordinances/commandments/statutes which spell out Israel's covenantal obligations – 'all this law' (4.8), 'all the words of this law' (32.46); and the basis of the equation, *Torah* = Pentateuch, is already firmly established (30.10 – 'this book of the law'). This does not support the further unjustified association of *nomos* with legalism – another outworking of the traditional denigration of 'late Judaism'. But it does mean that Paul's subsequent use of *nomos* to sum up Israel's obligations as set out by Moses cannot be dismissed as a Hellenistic Jew's Septuagintal distortion of his heritage, and that Paul's theological argument was interacting with a very important strand of Jewish thought and life.[32]

The Ezra reforms placed the Torah firmly at the centre of Israel's life once again. And as with other fundamental features of second Temple Judaism, the pattern of covenantal nomism was massively reinforced by the Maccabean crisis. In that crisis it was precisely Israel's identity as the covenant people, the people of the law, which was at stake (I Macc. 1.57; 2.27, 50; II Macc. 1.2–4; 2.21–22; 5.15; 13.14). And the response to that crisis was expressed in terms of 'zeal for the law' as the watchword of national resistance (I Macc. 2.26–27, 50, 58; II Macc. 4.2; 7.2, 9, 11, 37; 8.21; 13.14).[33] From these

---

31. See S. Schechter, *Aspects of Rabbinic Theology* 1909; New York: Schocken 1961, p. 117; Herford, *Judaism*, pp. 30–2; C. H. Dodd, 'The Law', *The Bible and the Greeks, Light of Jewish Religious History*, London: Lutterworth 1961, ch. 5.

32. See particularly S. Westerholm, 'Torah, Nomos and Law: A Question of "Meaning"', *Studies in Religion* 15 (1986), pp. 327–36; also A. F. Segal, 'Torah and *nomos* in Recent Scholarly Discussion', *Studies in Religion* 13 (1984), pp. 19–28, reprinted in *Other Judaisms*, pp. 131–45; and the earlier protest to the same effect by Urbach, *Sages*, pp. 288–90.

33. See further below §7.2.

passages it becomes clear that in the piety crystallized and cherished among the Maccabees and their successors, zeal for the law, devotion to the covenant and loyalty to the nation had become inextricably interwoven.

So too in the period following the Maccabean crisis, the tie-in between election, covenant and law remains a fundamental and persistent theme of Jewish self-understanding. Ben Sira, for example, echoes Deuteronomy's assumption both of Yahweh's universal sovereignty and of his special covenant choice of Israel (Deut. 32.8–9; Sir. 17.11–17). And ben Sira is the first clearly to identify universal divine wisdom with 'the book of the covenant of the Most High God, the law which Moses commanded us as an inheritance for the congregations of Jacob' (24.23). Elsewhere he speaks naturally of the law and the covenant in a single breath – 'the law of the covenant' (39.8; see also 28.7; 42.2; 44.19–20; 45.5). Jubilees is another classic expression of covenantal nomism, with its repeated emphases on the covenants made by Yahweh, the statutory obligations which follow from them, and his special choice of Israel from among the nations (e.g. 1.4–5; 2.21; 6.4–16; 15; 22.15–16; 23.19 – 'the law and the covenant'). Similarly with the Qumran community, membership of the covenant was understood precisely in terms of observing God's precepts and holding fast to his commandments (e.g. CD 1.15–18, 20; 3.10–16; 1QS 1.7–8; 5.1–3). No different is Pseudo-Philo, for whom the link between covenant and law, or, which is the same thing, (Israel's) election and commandments, is equally axiomatic (9.7–8; 23.10; 30.2; 35.2–3). So when *Pss.Sol.* 10.4 speaks of 'the law of the eternal covenant', or when we read, later on, in *Mek.Exod.* 20.6, 'By covenant is meant nothing other than the Torah', we can be sure we are in touch with one of the most basic strands of Jewish self-understanding.

Despite the variety of Judaism(s) represented in the above literature, then, and with surprisingly few exceptions, we can speak of *a common pattern of 'covenantal nomism' as characteristic of the Judaism of Paul's day.*[34] That is to say, it was part of the basic framework of

---

34. For the importance of the covenant within 'intertestamental' Judaism see particularly A. Jaubert, *La notion d'alliance dans le Judaïsme*, Editions du Seuil 1963. The dominance of the pattern of 'covenantal nomism' has been established by Sanders, *Paul and Palestinian Judaism*, though his work has to be supplemented by D. Garlington, *'The Obedience of Faith': A Pauline Phrase in Historical Context*, WUNT 2.38; Tübingen: Mohr Siebeck, 1991, who has demonstrated the presence of the pattern throughout the whole of 'the Apocrypha', and J. J. Collins, *Between Athens and Jerusalem: Jewish Identity in the Hellenistic Diaspora*, New York: Crossroad 1983, who notes, however, that the pattern is not quite so consistent through all the diaspora literature. 'Intertestamental'

reference, taken for granted by many or most Jews, that *God had made a special covenant with Israel to be his own, and as integral to that covenant had given Israel the law to provide Israel with the means of living within that covenant.*[35]

Several corollaries followed from this basic axiom of covenantal nomism; and since the issue of the law is one of the most crucial, and certainly has been the most controversial in attempts to understand the how and the why of the partings of the ways, it is necessary to give further attention to this third pillar. Two of these corollaries fill out the outline of the characteristic Jewish self-understanding of the period in which we are interested and deserve fuller note, as of particular relevance to our overarching question.

(*a*) The first is that the law so understood became a basic expression of Israel's *distinctiveness* as the people specially chosen by the one God to be his people. In sociological terms the law functioned as an 'identity marker' and 'boundary', reinforcing Israel's assumption of distinctiveness and distinguishing Israel from the surrounding nations.[36] This sense of separateness was deeply rooted in Israel's national-consciousness (Lev. 20.24–26; Ezek. 44.9; Joel 3.17; *Pss. Sol.* 17.28): it had been brought to pointed and practical expression in the enforced divorces of the Ezra reforms (Ezra 10.11; Neh. 13.3), was reinforced by the example of the heroes and heroines of the period, such as Daniel, Judith and Tobit,[37] and comes to powerful expression particularly in *Jub.* 22.16 –

> Separate yourself from the Gentiles,
>   and do not eat with them,
>   and do not perform deeds like theirs.

---

literature may not be the only witness to the Judaism(s) of Paul's day, but it is certainly a primary witness, and in any description of first century Judaism the consistency of that witness should not be discounted by contrasting it with pre-exilic or rabbinic literature. 'There is a consensus of covenantal theology underlying all of first century Judaism' (A. F. Segal, 'Covenant in Rabbinic Writings', *Other Judaisms*, pp. 147–65, here p. 153).

35. Cf. Fackenheim *Judaism*, p. 47, who offers as the traditional answer to the question, *Who* or *what* is a Jew?: 'A Jew is one obligated to the covenant that God made with Israel, a process that . . . reached its climax . . . with the revelation of the Torah at Mount Sinai.'

36. J. Neusner, *Judaism: The Evidence of the Mishnah*, University of Chicago, 1981, pp. 72–75; W. A. Meeks, *The First Urban Christians: The Social World of the Apostle Paul*, Yale University, 1983, p. 97; J. D. G. Dunn, 'Works of Law and the Curse of the Law (Galatians 3.10–14)', *NTS* 31 (1985), pp. 523–42, here pp. 524–7, reprinted in *Jesus, Paul and the Law*, ch. 8, here pp. 216–9. 'One of the characteristic themes of Jewish thought throughout the ages is this sense of contrast between the "us" and the "them"' (Cohen, *Maccabees to Mishnah*, p. 35).

37. See further below §2.3(3).

> And do not become associates of theirs.
> Because their deeds are defiled,
>   and all of their ways are contaminated,
>   and despicable, and abominable.

The letter of Aristeas expresses the same conviction in terms which reinforce the sociological insight.

> In his wisdom the legislator . . . surrounded us with unbroken palisades and iron walls to prevent our mixing with any of the other peoples in any matter . . . So, to prevent our being perverted by contact with others or by mixing with bad influences, he hedged us in on all sides with strict observances connected with meat and drink and touch and hearing and sight, after the manner of the Law (*Ep. Arist.* 139, 142).

Similarly Philo, *Mos.* 1.278 – a people 'which shall dwell alone, not reckoned among other nations . . . because in virtue of the distinction of their peculiar customs they do not mix with others to depart from the ways of their fathers'. And a funerary inscription from Italy praises a woman 'who lived a gracious life inside Judaism' – Judaism understood as 'a sort of fenced off area in which Jewish lives are led'.[38] This characteristic of Jewish self-understanding and social practice did not go unnoticed by others and formed part of the anti-Jewish polemic of Roman intellectuals, most emphatically expressed by Tacitus in the *Histories*, particularly 5.5.2.

Consistent with this is the characterization of the Gentile as *anomos* and their works as *anomia*: by definition they were 'without the law, outside the law', that is, outside the area (Israel) which was coterminous with the law, marked out by the law; so already in the Psalms (28.3; 37.28; 55.3; 73.3; 92.7; 104.35; 125.3), in I Maccabees (Gentiles and apostates – 3.5–6; 7.5; 9.23, 58, 69; 11.25; 14.14), and in the self-evident equation, Gentile = 'sinner' (as in I Macc. 2.44, 48; Tobit 13.6 [LXX 8]; *Jub.* 23.23–4; *Pss. Sol.* 1.1; 2.1–2; 17.22–5; Matt. 5.47/Luke 6.33; Gal. 2.15). Not surprisingly this desire to live *within* the law, and marked off from the lawless and sinner, became a dominant concern in the factionalism, which, as we shall see, was a feature of Judaism in the period from the Maccabeans to the emergence of rabbinic Judaism.[39]

---

38. Y. Amir, 'The Term *Ioudaismos*: A Study in Jewish-Hellenistic Self-Identification', *Immanuel*, 14 (1982), 35–6, 39–40.

39. See further below, §6.2.

(*b*) A second, natural and more or less inevitable converse of this sense of distinctiveness was the sense of *privilege*, privilege precisely in being the nation specially chosen by the one God and favoured by gift of covenant and law. This comes out particularly clearly in writings which could not simply ignore and dismiss Gentiles as sinners, but which had to attempt some sort of apologetic for the claims of Israel in the face of a much more powerful Gentile world. Thus both Philo and Josephus speak with understandable if exaggerated pride of the widespread desire among Greek and barbarian to adopt Jewish customs and laws:

> Philo, *Mos.* 2.17–25 – they attract and win the attention of all . . . the sancity of our legislation has been a source of wonder not only to Jews and to all others also;

> Josephus, *Ap.* 2.277–86 – The masses have long since shown a keen desire to adopt our religious observances . . . Were we not ourselves aware of the excellence of our laws, assuredly we should have been impelled to pride ourselves upon them by the multitude of their admirers.

Expressive of the same pride in the law of Moses is what seems to have been a fairly sustained attempt in Jewish apologetic to present Moses as 'the first wise man', who was teacher of Orpheus and from whose writings Plato and Pythagoras learned much of their wisdom.[40]

Pride in the law as the mark of God's special favour to Israel is also well illustrated in the identification of divine Wisdom with the Torah, the assertion that the universally desirable Wisdom, immanent within creation but hidden from human eyes, was embodied precisely in the law and nowhere else so completely or so clearly – as already in Sir. 24.23 cited above.[41] The same claim is expressed more forcefully in Bar. 3.36–4.4 –

> . . . (He) gave her to Jacob his servant
> and to Israel whom he loved
> She is the book of the commandments of God,
> and the law which endures for ever.

---

40. Eupolemus, *frag.* 1; Artapanus, *frag.* 3; Aristobulus, *frag.* 3–4; from Eusebius, *Praeparatio Evangelica* 9.26.1, 9.27.3–6 and 13.12.1–4. Texts in Charlesworth, *Old Testament Pseudepigrapha*, Vol. 2. See also J. G. Gager, *Moses in Greco-Roman Paganism*, SBLMS 16, Nashville: Abingdon 1972, ch. 1.

41. See above p. 25.

> All who hold her fast will live,
>> but those who forsake her will die.
> Turn, O Jacob, and take her;
>> walk towards the shining of her light.
> Do not give your glory to another,
>> or your advantages to an alien people.
> Blessed are we, O Israel,
>> for what is pleasing to God is known to us.

For those confronted by the crushing power of Rome within Palestine this sense of privilege was difficult to maintain. The Psalms of Solomon found a solution in pressing the older distinction (e.g. II Macc. 6.12–16) between discipline and punishment (particularly *Pss. Sol.* 3, 10 and 13) – thus 13.6–11:

> The destruction of the sinner is terrible
>> but nothing shall harm the righteous, of all these things,
> For the discipline of the righteous (for things done) in ignorance
>> is not the same as the destruction of the sinners
> For the Lord will spare his devout,
>> and he will wipe away their mistakes with discipline.
> For the life of the righteous (goes on) for ever,
>> but sinners shall be taken away to destruction . . .

Less easy to satisfy was *IV Ezra*, who in common with his fellow Jews saw the law given to Israel as a mark of divine favour (3.19; 9.31), but who could not understand how God could spare the sinful nations and yet allow his law-keeping people to be so harshly treated (3.28–36; 4.23–4; 5.23–30; 6.55–9).[42]

In short, *characteristic of early Judaism was the sense of Israel's distinctiveness and privilege as the people chosen by God and marked out from the other nations by this covenant relation and by the Torah practice of those loyal to this covenant (and thus to God).* It is not necessary to document such conviction from every strand of Judaism; it is enough to say that a broad spread within early Judaism shared these convictions, as integral to their self-understanding and as fundamental to their perception of their social world.

A sociological perspective also helps us to see how *conviction of privileged election and covenantal nomism almost inevitably came*

---

42. See now B. Longenecker, *Eschatology and the Covenant: A Comparison of 4 Ezra and Romans 1–11*, JSNT Supp. 57, Sheffield Academic Press 1991.

to expression in focal points of distinctiveness – particularly laws, especially ritual practices, which reinforced the sense of distinctive identity and marked Israel off most clearly from other nations, test cases of covenant loyalty. Three of them in particular stand out in Jewish looking out 'from inside' and Graeco-Roman looking in 'from outside' – circumcision, sabbath and food laws.

(1) The covenantal requirement of *circumcision* was clearly laid down beyond any doubt or peradventure already in Gen. 17.9–14:

> ... This is my covenant, which you shall keep, between me and you and your descendents after you: Every male among you shall be circumcised. You shall be circumcised in the flesh of your fore-skins, and it shall be a sign of the covenant between me and you ... So shall my covenant be in your flesh an everlasting covenant. Any uncircumcised male who is not circumcised in the flesh of his foreskin shall be cut off from his people; he has broken my covenant.

Here again the importance of circumcision as marking out identity and defining boundary was massively reinforced by the Maccabean crisis. Hellenistic antipathy to such bodily mutilation caused many Jews to abandon this key covenant marker. In the words of I Macca-bees, 'They built a gymnasium in Jerusalem, according to Gentile custom, and removed the marks of circumcision, and abandoned the holy covenant' (I Macc. 1.14–15). In the consequent revolt and suppression circumcision was clearly for many the make or break issue. Thus on the one side, in accordance with the Syrian decree, women who had their children circumcised were put to death with their (circumcised) infants hung from their necks (I Macc. 1.60–61; II Macc. 6.10); enforced abandonment of circumcision was evidently recognized to be the best way to break down the barrier which pro-tected and maintained Israel's distinctiveness. Equally, on the other, the Maccabean rebels made a particular point of forcibly circumcising 'all the uncircumcised boys that they found within the borders of Israel' (I Macc. 2.46); for them circumcision obviously had the same function as the *sine qua non* of Israel's self-definition. For the same reason, when, subsequently, the Hasmonean kingdom was able to extend its borders during the period when Syrian power was in decay, they made a particular point of forcibly circumcising the inhabitants of the conquered territories of Galilee and Idumea (Josephus, *Ant.* 13.257–8, 318); evidently it was impossible to conceive of the inhabi-tants of these territories belonging to Israel unless they had been circumcised.

That circumcision had this distinctive function for Jews was well recognized in the wider Graeco-Roman world and quite often commented on.[43] This is all the more remarkable since it was also well enough known that other peoples practised circumcision, including Samaritans, Arabs and Egyptians.[44] Clearly in the case of the Jews the rite had been given a particular prominence and significance, at the insistence of Jews themselves, as *essential to the definition and maintenance of their national and religious (covenant) distinctiveness.* As Tacitus was to put it in his own abrupt manner: 'They adopted circumcision to distinguish themselves from other peoples by this difference' (*Hist.* 5.5.2).[45]

(2) The *Sabbath* was also maintained and recognized as a distinctively Jewish institution. In Jewish self-understanding, of course, it was part of the decalogue and rooted in creation itself (Gen. 2.2–3; Ex. 20.8–11). Already in Ex. 31.16–17 and Deut. 5.15 its status as a key expression of covenantal responsibility is emphasized; in Isa. 56.6 keeping the sabbath is bound up with holding fast to the covenant, an essential mark of acceptability for the would-be proselyte; and Josephus notes that already before the Maccabees 'violating the sabbath' was one of the chief hallmarks of covenant disloyalty (*Ant.* 11.346). Again the Maccabean crisis reinforced its boundary defining status (I Macc. 1.43), and the increasing importance of the sabbath within Palestine at our period is clearly indicated by *Jub.* 2.17–33, 50.6–13, CD 10.14–11.18 and Mark 2.23–3.5.[46]

Within the diaspora the importance of the sabbath, as *a badge of ethnic identity and devotion to ancestral custom,* was also widely recognized by Gentile as well as Jew. Diaspora Jews had special dispensation to congregate on the sabbath, even when similar gatherings in clubs or societies were banned.[47] Such a regular day of rest

---

43. See particularly Petronius, *Satyricon* 102.14; *Fragmenta* 37; Tacitus, *Hist.* 5.5.2; Juvenal, *Sat.* 14.99 – texts in *GLAJJ*, §§194, 195, 281, 301.

44. Herodotus, *Hist.* 2.104.2–3; Strabo, *Geog.* 16.4.9; 17.1.51; Celsus in Origen, *c. Celsum* 5.41 – texts in *GLAJJ*, §1, 118, 123, 375; in Jewish sources cf. Jer. 9.25–6; Philo, *Spec. Leg.* 1.2.

45. See further L. H. Schiffmann, 'At the Crossroads: Tannaitic Perspectives on the Jewish-Christian Schism', *JCSD*, 2.115–56, here pp. 125–7; also *Who was a Jew?*, Hoboken: Ktav 1985, pp. 23–5; J. Nolland, 'Uncircumcised Proselytes?', *JSJ* 12 (1981), pp. 173–94; J. J. Collins, 'A Symbol of Otherness: Circumcision and Salvation in the First Century', *'To See Ourselves as Others See Us'. Christians, Jews, 'Others' in Late Antiquity,* ed. J. Neusner and E. S. Frerichs, Chico: Scholars, 1985, pp. 163–86; Schürer, 3.169; Dunn, *Romans,* pp. 119–120.

46. See further below §6.1(a).

47. Philo, *Legat.* 155–8, and Josephus, *Ant.* 14.241–6, 258, 263–4; both take care to document the right of sabbath observance granted to Jewish diaspora communities.

was unusual at the time and exercised a considerable attraction for many Gentiles. Josephus is even able to make the claim in the passage already cited: 'The masses have long since shown a keen desire to adopt our religious observances; and there is not one city, Greek or barbarian, not a single nation, to which our custom of abstaining from work on the sabbath day has not spread . . .' (*Ap.* 2.282). However exaggerated Josephus' claim, the fact that he could make such a claim at all indicates how widely known was this distinctively Jewish custom.[48]

(3) The third most distinctive boundary-defining feature of second Temple Judaism was the Jewish *food laws*. Their importance is clear in the Torah (Lev. 11.1–23; Deut. 14.3–21). But once again it was the Maccabean crisis which made these laws in particular a test-case of Jewishness and of Jewish loyalty to the covenant. 'Many in Israel stood firm and were resolved in their hearts not to eat unclean food. They chose to die rather than to be defiled by food or to profane the holy covenant; and they did die' (I Macc. 1.62–3). Here again *the fact that these laws marked out Jews as different made it inevitable that they should receive particular prominence in expressing and defining Israel's covenant status*.[49] It should occasion no surprise, therefore, that in the popular stories of Jewish heroes and heroines, which no doubt were well-loved by Jewish children and others of our period, it was precisely the refusal to weaken on this key issue, that is, by eating 'the food of Gentiles', which enabled Daniel, Tobit, Judith, Esther and Joseph to maintain their Jewish identity and express their covenant loyalty (Dan. 1.3–16; 10.3; Tobit 1.10–12; Judith 12.2, 19; Add. Esth. 14.17; *Jos. Asen.* 7.1; 8.5; *III Macc.* 3.4).

Jewish scruples on these matters were also well-known in the ancient world, with Jewish refusal to eat pork quite often a matter of interested, puzzled or amused comment. Philo, for example, reports the episode where he was leading a delegation to the Emperor Caligula, in which Caligula interrupted Philo's pleading with the abrupt and irrelevant question, 'Why do you refuse to eat pork?' (Philo, *Legat.* 361). And Plutarch devoted one of his 'table talks' to a discussion of why Jews abstain from pork (Plutarch, *Quaest. Conviv.* 4.5).[50] Here again, then, it is evident that these dietary rules

---

48. See further my *Romans*, pp. 805–6.

49. 'Avoiding pork (among other unclean animals) as well as practising circumcision . . . emerged at this point as symbolic boundary-marking actions far in excess of their original meanings within biblical lore . . . emblems of Jewish identity par excellence . . .' (Segal, *Rebecca's Children*, pp. 34–5).

50. See further and for other examples my *Romans*, p. 800.

constituted one of the test cases for Jewish identity, *one of the clearest boundary markers which distinguished Jew from Gentile and which were recognized as such.*

We have spent so much time on this subject since the role and issue of Torah in the definition of the people of God and the practice of the covenant was to become such a major issue in the beginnings of Christianity and subsequently in the self-definition of rabbinic Judaism. *The degree to which Torah was bound up with Jewish self-understanding and identity can hardly be over-emphasized for our period.* And in focussing particularly on circumcision, sabbath and food laws, that is neither to deny the importance of the rest of the law and of what was involved in covenantal nomism,[51] nor to suggest that at the root of Jewish self-understanding was a too great emphasis on ritual (the sabbath was not a 'ritual' anyway).[52] Rather it is to note that *in the circumstances which confronted Israel, particularly from the Maccabean crisis onwards, the importance of the law for Israel's self-understanding as the covenant people of God was bound to come to focus in those elements of the law which brought their sense of distinctiveness and separateness to most explicit and visible expression and which thus functioned for good or ill as test cases of loyalty to the covenant people and their God.* As we shall see, it was precisely because circumcision, sabbath and food laws defined Jewish identity and marked out its boundary so clearly that they inevitably became the chief flash-points in the agonizing reappraisal which Jesus and faith in him as the Messiah brought to many Jews.

2.4 Land focussed in Temple

The description of the Judaism of the pre-70 period as 'second Temple Judaism' is not a matter of mere convenience; it also indicates clearly *the role of the Temple at the centre of Israel's national and religious life at that time.* This can be readily documented.

(a) The Temple was not least *a political centre.* Judaea was technically a temple state or temple land. That is to say, the Jerusalem Temple provided the rationale for Judaea's existence as a separate entity within the Hellenistic and Roman empires. According to the

---

51. See above n. 49.

52. A. F. Segal, however, slips into this trap, by identifying 'the special laws' of the Jews with the ceremonial law, despite the fact that Philo's treatment of *The Special Laws* is basically an exposition of the Ten Commandments (*Paul the Convert. The Apostolate and Apostasy of Saul the Pharisee*, New Haven: Yale University 1990).

same rationale, the territory attached to the Temple was the amount of land needed to provide the resources (wood, animals for sacrifice, etc.) for the temple cult. Here becomes evident a further reason why it was necessary to circumcise the inhabitants of Galilee and the other territories annexed to Judaea by the Hasmoneans. By thus 'judaizing' them, making them 'Judaeans', the new territories could be seen as an extension of Judaea.[53]

Recognition of the Temple's political significance also helps explain the political power of the High Priests and high-priestly families within the extended Judaea.[54] It was awareness of this power which had prompted the merging of royal authority with that of High Priest in the case of Jonathan (brother and successor to Judas Maccabaeus) in 153 or 152 BCE; and the Hasmoneans took care to keep the two united so far as possible thereafter. No doubt Herod (the Great) would have continued the practice after his conquest of Jerusalem in 37 BCE, had he not been disqualified by reason of race (he was an Idumean).[55] Moreover, since Israel was a religious state, its religious law was also its state and civil law. Consequently also its chief court, the Sanhedrin, was the chief instrument of a wide range of legislative and executive power, much wider under Roman rule.[56] It is significant therefore that throughout the hundred years before the Temple's destruction (in 70 CE) the High Priests and the high priestly party (the Sadducees) seem to have been able to maintain a tight control of the Sanhedrin.[57]

(*b*) The Temple was also *an economic centre*. It needs to be recalled that the economic rationale for the location of Jerusalem was exceedingly weak. The city did not sit on any trade route, or river crossing, nor was it a port. The only reason for its continued existence, the only reason why people came to it was the Temple, directly or indirectly. The Temple was undoubtedly Jerusalem's main source of revenue. In material terms we need think only of the constant flow of daily sacrifices and offerings, and the half-shekel temple tax, due every year from every male Jew of twenty years and over, for the collection and transmission of which from all over the diaspora the Romans made special provision.[58] The pilgrim traffic for the three main pilgrim feasts (see below) must have been immense; at Passover

---

53. See also B. Reicke, *The New Testament Era*, 1964; ET Philadelphia: Fortress 1968; London: SCM Press 1969, pp. 68–9.

54. Jeremias, *Jerusalem*, pp. 193–4 notes that this power was concentrated in the hands of four key families.

55. On Herod's ancestry see Schürer, 1.234.

56. Schürer, 2.377.

57. See in much more detail Schürer, 2.199–236.

58. See Schürer, 2.271–2; *GLAJJ*, 1.198–9.

it is reckoned that the normal population of Jerusalem was swollen several times over.[59] Every devout Jew was obligated to spend one-tenth of the produce of his land in Jerusalem (the so-called 'second tithe').[60] The trade and business which this generated and supported must have been enormous.

In addition, the trades probably regarded the Temple as the centre of their operations too. If what we know of the integration between market-place and principal sanctuary in the typical cities of the eastern Mediterranean was reflected in any degree in Jerusalem, and given the enormous level space provided by Herod's immense Temple platform, it becomes quite possible to envisage the large outermost of the Temple courts functioning as a major economic centre where deals were struck and business transacted. The Temple itself certainly seems to have functioned as a financial centre; as one of the most secure places available it could serve very effectively as a bank. We know from *IV Macc.* 4.3 that it held private fortunes, and it is quite possible that it was able to make loans. So it is also possible that the Temple platform provided the facilities necessary for an actual trading centre or market place. In the light of the meagre evidence actually available, the point is speculative, but at least it warns us against assuming too quickly that the tables which Jesus overturned in the Temple area were solely to do with Temple business as such.[61]

It should also be recalled that during the period of Jesus' activity the Temple was being rebuilt. The vastness of Herod's reconstruction is still evident today. The amount of high quality materials involved (cedar wood, alabaster, marble and gold) would be significant in themselves; but the further influx of labour and expenditure of money would swell the economic activity still more, and again underlines the centrality of the Temple to the whole Judaean economy.

(c) Finally, of course, the Temple was most significant of all as *a religious centre*. Here the supreme importance of the intertwined motifs of Jerusalem, Zion and Temple as focus of elect people and promised land achieves profound lyrical not to say mythological expression. It was the city of God, the place where Yahweh had put his name, where the one God's presence was manifested on earth – a religious centre and theological symbol of tremendous emotive power

---

59. Jeremias, *Jerusalem*, p. 84.
60. For details see Schürer, 2.264–5 in n. 23.
61. Cf. Jeremias, *Jerusalem*, p. 49; and see further below §3.4.

(see e.g. I Kings 8.48; 9.3; Ps. 76.1–2; 87.1–3; Isa. 49.14–16; Ezek. 43.6–7; Sir. 36.18–19).[62]

The whole literature and liturgy of the Jewish people is full of the centrality of Zion, past and future. Who can not be moved, for example, by the beauty and depth of feeling expressed in Ps. 137.1ff.?

> By the waters of Babylon,
>> there we sat down and wept,
>> when we remembered Zion.
> On the willows there we hung up our lyres.
> For there our captors required of us songs,
>> and our tormentors, mirth, saying,
>> 'Sing us one of the songs of Zion!'
> How shall we sing the Lord's song in a foreign land?
> If I forget you, O Jerusalem,
>> let my right hand wither!
> Let my tongue cleave to the roof of my mouth,
>> if I do not remember you,
>> if I do not set Jerusalem above my highest joy!

The idealization of Jerusalem is well expressed in a sequence of texts stretching over the centuries: Isa. 60.14 –

> The sons of those who oppressed you shall come bending low to
>> you;
> and all who despised you shall bow at your feet;
> they shall call you the City of the Lord,
>> the Zion of the Holy One of Israel;

Jub. 8.19 – 'Mount Zion in the midst of the navel of the earth'; *Sib. Or.* 5.248–50 – 'the divine and heavenly race of the blessed Jews, who live around the city of God in the middle of the earth'.[63]

Here again it was the cult which gave Jerusalem and its Temple this supreme significance. For example, Philo in describing his fellow countrymen's devotion to the law and the ancestral customs, continues: 'Still more abounding and peculiar is the zeal of them all for

---

62. See further E. Lohse, *TDNT*, 7.307–19; J. D. Levenson, *Sinai and Zion*, San Francisco: Harper & Row 1985; B. C. Ollenburger, *Zion the City of the Great King*, *JSOTSupp*. 41, Sheffield: JSOT 1987. For the power of the idea of Zion and Zionism in the present century, see e.g. M. Buber, *On Zion. The History of an Idea*, 1952; New York: Schocken 1973.

63. See further Lohse, *TDNT*, 7.324–5; Davies, *Land*, pp. 7–8.

the temple' (*Legat.* 210–2). 'One Temple for the one God', says Josephus (*Ap.* 2.193). The importance of the pilgrim feasts – Passover, Weeks = Pentecost, and Booths (autumn) – has already been mentioned; clear echoes of their importance are also evident in Luke 2.41ff., John 7.1–10 and Acts 2.5. Above all, we should not forget that the whole system of sacrifice, atonement and forgiveness, so fundamental to the Judaism of the period,[64] was focussed entirely on the Temple. As Neusner notes, 'The Torah made (the) Temple the pivot and focus ... The life of Israel flowed from the altar; what made Israel Israel was the center, the altar.'[65] Nor should we underestimate the power which this gave those who controlled the sanctuary, cult and sacrificial system, since it meant that they controlled also access to God – an awesome and fearful power.

Was the Temple quite so central for *all* Jews? Three possible qualifications suggest themselves. (1) The Essenes at Qumran seem to have abandoned the Temple and to have established their own community as an alternative. However, their critique was not of the Temple as such, but only of the Temple as defiled by a false priesthood. They constituted themselves as the place where true worship of God could be maintained only as a temporary measure, until the reconstitution and rededication of the Temple proper.[66]

(2) We also hear of other actual Jewish temples – most notably at the earlier Jewish colony at Elephantine on the Nile, and, more important, currently at Leontopolis in Egypt, built in the second century BCE and not closed by the Romans till 74 CE (Josephus, *War* 7.420–36; *Ant.* 13.62–73).[67] Since the split in the Jewish priesthood which resulted in the Leontopolis temple is probably the same schism which resulted in the establishment of the community at Qumran, it is a fair guess that both actions were motivated by a very similar critique of the Jerusalem Temple and priesthood by two Zadokite groups.[68] However, the silence of the various Hellenistic Jewish writings, presumably composed not far away in Alexandria, probably implies that the great bulk of Jews in Egypt saw the Leontopolis

---

64. See further above §1.4d and below §3.3.

65. Neusner, *Judaism* p. 74.

66. See G. Vermes, *The Dead Sea Scrolls: Qumran in Perspective*, London: Collins 1977, pp. 181–2; also *The Dead Sea Scrolls in English*, London: Penguin ³1987, pp. 50–51.

67. See also *GLAJJ*, 1.405–6. On the significance of the Samaritan temple on Mt Gerizim, see below §4.6a.

68. C. T. R. Hayward, 'The Jewish Temple at Leontopolis: A Reconsideration', *JJS* 33 (1982), pp. 429–43.

temple as no real challenge to the Jerusalem Temple, or as such an insignificant challenge as to be not worth even mentioning.[69]

(3) Finally we may simply note the establishment of the synagogue as a centre for Jewish prayer and the reading of the law, particularly in the diaspora, where they are described precisely as 'prayer-houses'. This growth of the synagogue was almost certainly due in part at least to the desire among the diaspora Jews to compensate for their inability to offer their worship at the Temple itself, with morning and evening prayer offered at the hour of sacrifice, and offered probably with the people standing with their faces towards the Temple in Jerusalem.[70] But such practice can hardly be construed as an opposition to the Temple, rather as an inadequate substitute for what the great majority would still have regarded as the real thing. We also read of 'synagogues' within Palestine, most notably in Jerusalem itself (Acts 6.9),[71] but it is quite likely that within a pre-70 CE Palestinian setting *synagogē* would be more accurately translated 'meeting-house', thus reducing any possible implication that it functioned as a kind of alternative to the Temple.[72]

In short, it would still be a fair assessment to claim that the Jerusalem Temple stood at the heart of the various Judaisms of the second Temple period, as embodying the common conviction of Jews of the time that God had chosen Israel and given them the land centred on Mount Zion, the dwelling place on earth of the name and glory of the one God.

2.5 Conclusion

These then can be fairly described as the four pillars on which the Judaism(s) of Jesus' time was/(were) built, *the axiomatic convictions round which the more diverse interpretations and practices of the different groups within Judaism revolved.* The parting of the ways

---

69. The significance of the other temples is thus overstated by Kraft and Nickelsburg, *EJMI*, p. 19. Contrast Cohen, *Maccabees to Mishnah* – 'As the focal point of the religion, the temple was the central communal institution not just for the Jews of the land of Israel but also for those of the diaspora' (p. 106).

70. See Schürer, 2.449, and further pp. 423–54; Cohen, *Maccabees to Mishnah*, pp. 64–9.

71. 'The beginnings of the synagogue of Theodotus, which is probably connected to the synagogue mentioned in Acts 6.9, go back to Herodian times' (Hengel, '*Hellenization*', p. 13).

72. For a judicious assessment of the current debate about the origin of the synagogue see Cohen, *Maccabees to Mishnah*, pp. 111–5; also H. C. Kee, 'The Transformation of the Synagogue after 70 CE: its Import for Early Christianity', *NTS* 36 (1990), pp. 1–24.

came about because the new movement which stemmed from Jesus found it increasingly necessary to question and redefine each of these four axioms in greater or less degree – at any rate, to a degree unacceptable to mainstream Judaism.

When did the ways begin to separate? When did the seams begin to pull apart? When did these pillars begin to be undermined? Did the process begin with Jesus? Or only afterwards? Or did his ministry make the outcome inevitable? And did it happen all at once? Or did the undermining happen in a more staggered way? These are all questions which we must take up in the following pages.

How to begin? The most obvious procedure is to examine earliest Christian attitudes to each of the four pillars in turn. That procedure runs the risk of making artificial distinctions for the sake of analysis. We will attempt to stay alive to that danger, but some separation out of particular elements in much more complex pictures is always necessary, otherwise analysis would be impossible (this is as true of contemporary historical and political commentary as of our current task).

Where to begin? Even a cursory examination of the earliest history of the infant Christian movement (Mark 11.15–18 pars.; 14.58 par.; Acts 6–7) suggests that it was the status and continuing importance of the Temple and the Temple cult which made it the first of the four pillars to be called in question. But if so, how and why? It is that issue to which we first turn.

3

Jesus and the Temple

We begin our inquiry into the partings of the ways proper by focussing first on the Temple in Jerusalem – the last of the four pillars of second Temple Judaism examined in ch. 2. And we begin with Jesus – where else could a study of the emergence of Christianity from its Jewish matrix start? What was Jesus' own attitude to the Temple? Given that the Jerusalem Temple did lose its significance for Christians sooner or later, was it Jesus himself who began to undermine that pillar for his followers? If so, did he do so deliberately, for what reasons, and with what objectives in mind? If not, how may subsequent Christianity justify its disregarding or pulling down of this pillar with reference to Jesus' own attitude and ministry? And what does all this say about the relation of Jesus, and of the Christianity which followed, to Judaism, or at least to a Temple-centred Judaism? Such are the questions which drive this first stage of our inquiry forward.

3.1 Jesus' positive attitude to the Temple

There is a significant portion of evidence which shows that Jesus had a very positive attitude to the Temple. This includes, not least, the Gospel traditions of Jesus attending the Temple (Luke 2.41–51; John 5.1; 7.10). In Mark 14.49 Jesus reminds those sent out to arrest him that he had been in the Temple day after day teaching. The Q tradition of Matt. 23.37–9/Luke 13.34–5 ('O Jerusalem, Jerusalem . . . How often would I have gathered your children together as a hen gathers her brood under her wings . . .') suggests more frequent visits to Jerusalem, and so presumably also to the Temple, than the Synoptics mention. And to that extent the tradition of the Fourth Gospel, which focusses the bulk of its account of Jesus' ministry in Jerusalem and round the Temple, is reinforced. We might also simply note that the saying of Matt. 5.23–4 –

> If you are offering your gift at the altar, and there remember that
> your brother has something against you, leave your gift there before

the altar and go; first be reconciled to your brother, and then come
and offer your gift –

seems to indicate a presupposition on Jesus' part of continued use of
the Temple cult.[1] Matthew also records Jesus' readiness, albeit after
some protest, to pay the Temple tax (Matt. 17.24–27). Finally it is
worth recalling how Luke goes out of his way both to begin his
Gospel in the Temple and to end it there (Luke 1.5–23; 24.52).

Jesus is also presented as a good, devout Jew in other relevant
ways. There is the tradition of him attending the synagogue 'as his
custom was' (Luke 4.16).[2] There is also a strong implication in Mark
1.44 and Luke 17.14 of Jesus' readiness to work within the current
religious and social system (he sends the cleansed lepers to show themselves to the priest and to 'offer for your cleansing what Moses commanded').[3] Striking also is the degree to which the prayer which he
taught his disciples as their prayer was so closely modelled on Jewish
prayers of the time – particularly the Kaddish, which the strong echoes
show to have been probably already current in parallel form at this
time, and which was prayed by the pray-er on behalf of the people:[4]

Kaddish	*Lord's Prayer*
Exalted and hallowed be his great Name	Hallowed by your Name;
in the world which he created according to his will	
May he establish his kingdom in your lifetime.	Your kingdom come.
and in the lifetime of the whole household of Israel,	
speedily and at a near time.	

---

1. Cf. D. J. Antwi, 'Did Jesus Consider His Death to be an Atoning Sacrifice?', *Interpretation* 45 (1991), pp. 17–28, here pp. 20–1.

2. See also Mark 1.21–7 par., 1.39 pars.; 3.1 pars.; 6.2–6 pars.; Matt. 9.35; Luke 4.15;
13.10.

3. 'For a testimony/as proof to them' is the least contentious translation of the concluding phrase in Mark 1.44 (so e.g. V. Taylor, *The Gospel According to St Mark*, London:
Macmillan 1952, p. 190; R. Pesch, *Markusevangelium*, Band I, Herder; Freiburg: Herder
[2]1977, p.146; J. Gnilka, *Markus*, EKK 2; Benziger: Zürich 1979, 1.91), though some
maintain that the phrase should be taken in the sense, 'as evidence against them' (so F.
Hahn, *The Worship of the Early Church*, Philadelphia: Fortress 1973, p. 24; R. Guelich,
Mark 1–8, WBC 34A; Dallas: Word 1989, pp. 76–7).

4. J. Jeremias, *New Testament Theology. The Proclamation of Jesus*, ET London: SCM
Press/New York: Scribners 1971, pp. 198–9; text as in J. Petuchowski and M. Brocke (ed.),
The Lord's Prayer and Jewish Liturgy, 1974, ET London: Burns & Oates 1978, p. 37.

At all these points Jesus is represented as a good, pious Jew. Certainly there is nothing here to imply a development out of or breach with the Judaism of his day.

Yet, at the same time, there are a number of areas where question marks do begin to arise.

3.2 The issue of purity

The issue and importance of purity was at the heart of second Temple Judaism. This is evident in the very structure of the Temple itself.

The symbolism thus represented is clear – that is, of an innermost

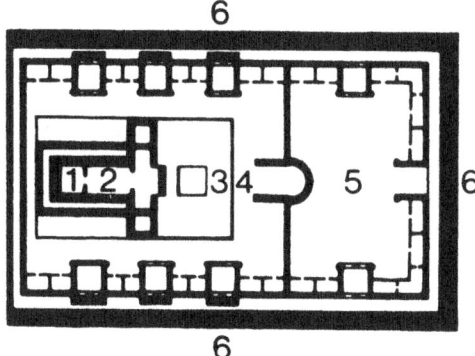

1. Holy of Holies
2. Holy Place
3. Court of Priests, including the altar of burnt offering
4. Court of Israel
5. Court of Women
6. Court of Gentiles

(a simplified outline of the Herodian temple)

sanctuary protected by what in effect was a sequence of concentric circles to ensure maximum protection from defilement. The Temple mount and Jerusalem itself constituted further circles, and the land of Israel a still further circle.[5]

The attitude was most fully set out subsequently in the tractate *m. Kelim* 1.6–9:

> There are ten degrees of holiness. The land of Israel is holier than any other land ... The walled cities (of the land of Israel) are still more holy, in that they must send forth the lepers from their midst ... Within the wall (of Jerusalem) is still more holy, for there (only) they may eat the Lesser Holy Things and the Second Tithe. The Temple Mount is still more holy, for no man or woman that has a flux, no menstruant, and no woman after childbirth may enter

---

5. Jeremias, *Jerusalem*, p. 79; Davies, *Land* pp. 58ff. – '... Jewish sanctity is only fully possible in the land' (p. 60).

therein. The Rampart is still more holy, for no Gentiles and none that have contracted uncleanness from a corpse may enter therein. The Court of the Women is still more holy, for none that had immersed himself the selfsame day (because of uncleanness) may enter therein ... The Court of the Israelites is still more holy, for none whose atonement is yet incomplete may enter therein ... The Court of the Priests is still more holy, for Israelites may not enter therein save only when they must perform the laying on of hands, slaughtering and waving. Between the Porch and the Altar is still more holy, for none that has a blemish or whose hair is unloosed may enter there. The Sanctuary is still more holy, for none may enter therein with hands and feet unwashed. The Holy of Holies is still more holy, for none may enter therein save only the High Priest at the time of the (Temple-)service.

Worth noting is the range of items which counted for impurity in different degrees in the above list – Gentile territory, leprosy, bleeding, corpse defilement, physical blemish and unloosed hair, unwashed hands and feet. Another much quoted example is *m. Hagiga* 2.7.[6] It is also worth recalling that the sixth division of the Mishnah is devoted to the subject of Purity, 12 tractates out of 63, nearly one quarter of the length of the whole.[7]

The texts just cited, of course, represent developed rabbinic views. But, as already indicated, the attitude is clearly implicit in the very construction of the sanctuary, and it was already spelt out in principle in the Torah, particularly the P legislation embodied in Leviticus, with the same purity logic explained by Josephus in *Ap.* 2.102–9. Note, for example, the concern for the purity of sacrifices expressed in Lev. 7.19–21 and the institution of an annual purification of priesthood and altar and holy place in the Day of Atonement ritual (Lev. 16.11, 15–16, 18–19). And not least the summary of the other various purity rules in Lev. 15.31 – 'Thus you shall keep the people of Israel separate from their uncleanness, lest they die in their uncleanness by defiling my tabernacle that is in their midst.' Or again Num. 35.34 – 'You shall not defile the land in which you live, in the midst of which I dwell; for I the Lord dwell in the midst of the people of Israel.'[8]

All this was particularly important for second Temple Judaism.

---

6. Cited, e.g., in my *Jesus, Paul and the Law*, p. 141.

7. See further Neusner, *Judaism*, in his summary treatment of his much more detailed studies – here pp. 63–9, 77–8, 101–10, etc.

8. For a list of biblical impurities see E. P. Sanders, *Jewish Law from Jesus to the Mishnah*, London: SCM Press/Philadelphia: TPI 1990, pp. 137–9, 147–8, 151.

Ezra 9–10 is all about cleansing the reconstituted Israel and restored land from the abominations and uncleanness of the surrounding nations (Ezra 9.1–4, 11, 14). The P revision of the Torah presumably gave the Torah and the cult their definitive form and stamped its priestly character on the whole, to become specially constitutive of second Temple Judaism. The nadir of the Maccabean crisis was reached in the sacrifice of a pig (most typical of the unclean animals) on the great altar of the Temple, the 'desolating sacrilege' of I Macc. 1.54 (cf. 1.47), the 'desolating transgression/abomination' of Dan. 8.13, 9.27, 11.13 and 12.11 (the note of horror still rings through the repeated descriptions); just as the high point of the Maccabean revolt was the cleansing of the sanctuary from its defilement and the rededication of the Temple (I Macc. 4.36–59), an event whose importance is still commemorated in the Feast of Dedication (*Hanukkah*). The horrified reaction of the inhabitants of Judaea to Pilate's bringing of the Roman standards into Jerusalem at the beginning of his term as governor of Judaea (bearing the abomination of the Emperor's image), and the similar reaction to Caligula's attempt to have a statue with his own effigy set up in the Temple in 39–40 CE, tell the same story (Josephus, *War* 2.169–74, 192–8; *Ant.* 18.55–9, 261–78; Philo. *Legat.* 207–53; Tacitus, *Hist.* 5.9.2).

At the time of Jesus the deep concern on the part of many Jews to maintain the purity laws is illustrated by such passages as Judith 12.7 (bathing each night), *Jub.* 3.8–14 (the laws of purification after childbirth dating from creation), *Pss. Sol.* 8.12, 22 (accusations about defiling the cult with 'all kinds of uncleanness'), in the Dead Sea Scrolls, 1QS 3.5 (the scorner is unclean), CD 5.6–7 (like *Pss. Sol.* 8.12) and 12.9–20 (various purity regulations), and Josephus, *Ant.* 3.261–2 (seven days seclusion for menstruant and corpse-impure). The discovery of many immersion pools from the pre-70 period in Jerusalem and elsewhere provides clear corroborative testimony.[9] A similar concern within the diaspora is also indicated by such passages as Philo, *Spec. Leg.* 3.205–6 (regarding corpse impurity) and *Sib. Or.* 3.591–2 ('always sanctifying their flesh').[10]

Such evidence indicates that *purity was a matter of wide concern within the Judaism of Jesus' time.* But it can also be documented as *a major concern of three of the main groups in particular.*

---

9. Sanders, *Jewish Law*, pp. 31, 38, 214–27.

10. See the discussion in Sanders, *Jewish Law*, pp. 258–71. Paul's use of purity language metaphorically (see below §5.4) indicates his awareness of the need both to affirm purity concerns and thus to counter what he now saw to be the unacceptable or unnecessary outworking of these concerns elsewhere in the Judaism of his day.

(*a*) *Priests.* The special importance of priestly purity was a consequence of the priests' crucial role in the sanctuary (see especially Lev. 21–22). This is the obvious background to the parable of the Good Samaritan (Luke 10.30–37). The clear implication is that it was fear of the defiling effects of a dead or possibly dead body which prevented the priest from coming to the injured man's aid: such defilement would have prevented him from fulfilling his functions at the Temple (Lev. 21.1–3). Although not mentioned on the surface of the story, the implication would be clear to any Jew.[11] Jeremias also notes the evidence of concern on the part of priests to maintain purity of descent, which although later documented, was presumably of long standing. According to *m. Kiddushin* 3.12 'only the daughter of a priest or Levite qualified to officiate, and the daughter of a pure-bred Israelite, were fit for legal marriage with a priest'. And in practice, 'it was customary for a priest to marry the daughter of a priest'.[12]

(*b*) *Pharisees.* The received wisdom is that the Pharisees at the time of Jesus were a purity sect.[13] Their concern was to keep the purity laws, which governed access to the Temple and participation in the cult, outside the Temple – to extend the holiness of the Temple throughout the land of Israel. The biblical warrant would have been obvious: 'You shall be a kingdom of priests and a holy nation' (Ex. 19.5–6). Taken literally, that would have meant, in order to be a holy people, those who were not themselves priests had to live as priests; which in turn would have meant, in particular, observing the purity laws by which the holiness of the Temple was preserved even outside the Temple. Neusner in particular sees this concern for purity focussed especially on the meal table: even secular food, that is, ordinary, everyday meals, should be eaten in a state of purity, as if one was a priest serving in the Temple.[14] Sanders objects to this as an exaggerated and over-blown picture,[15] but nevertheless demonstrates a strong active concern on the part of Pharisees to maintain purity at a level which must have marked them out if not as a purity sect as such, at

---

11. Sanders, *Jewish Law*, pp. 41–2. The same rationale might apply in the case of the Levite (Sanders). Or the criticism might be more severe in the case of the Levite: he would not even run the risk of incurring an impurity which could be easily removed. Hence the ordering of the events: the more excusable action (of the priest) is narrated first, followed in climactic sequence by the less excusable action of the Levite.

12. Jeremias, *Jerusalem*, pp. 217–18.

13. See e.g. Schürer, 2.396–400; Segal, *Rebecca's Children*, pp. 124–8; others in Sanders, *Jewish Law*, p. 152.

14. Neusner, e.g. *Rabbinic Traditions*, 3.288; also *From Politics to Piety*, Englewood Cliffs: Prentice Hall 1973, p. 83; also *Judaism*, p. 70.

15. 'There is absolutely *no* evidence that the Pharisees really tried to live like priests ... gross overstatements ... completely misleading' (Sanders, *Jewish Law*, pp. 248–9).

least in the degree of their concern.[16] A degree of punctiliousness certainly seems to be at least implied in some of the traditions examined below and in the traditions used by Matthew in Matt. 23.24–26.[17] That is not to say that such concerns were peculiar to the Pharisees; nor to deny that Pharisees were more liberal than others in many of their rulings;[18] but it is to affirm that purity was a concern of the Pharisees and was probably a reason for their very name, 'separatists'.[19]

(c) *Essenes*. Whatever may be the appropriate conclusion regarding the Pharisees, it is clear enough that the Essenes regarded themselves as a priestly community (see particularly CD 3.12–4.12; 4QFlor. 1.1–7). The anomaly was that they rejected the current priesthood in Jerusalem: the Temple had been defiled by 'the Wicked Priest' (1QpHab 8.8–9), and the current priesthood was illegitimate.[20] So in effect they set themselves up as an alternative Temple community.[21] With them concern for purity was even more dominant. This is clearly evident, for example, in the importance they placed on purificatory washings and in the rules to preserve the purity of the community meal.[22] 'The purity of the many' is a phrase which occurs quite frequently in reference to procedures for admitting new members and in the administration of discipline: a one year's probation was required before the novice could 'touch the purity of the Many' (1 QS 6.16–17); similarly, discipline regularly involved exclusion from the 'purity of the Many' (1 QS 6.24–5; 7.2–3, 15–6, 19).[23] Moreover, despite

---

16. Sanders, *Jewish Law*, ch. 3; summary of results, pp. 245–52. Much of Sanders' critique is directed against the idea that the Pharisees sought to debar others on grounds of impurity. This may be fair comment on the basis of the rabbinic evidence he reviews; but the indications that a concern for their *own* righteousness resulted in several 'sects' classifying those who differed from them or their opponents as 'sinners' at the time of Jesus must also be considered; see below ch. 6.

17. See again below §6.2.

18. See below n. 23; of course, a relatively 'liberal' concern to avoid impurity is still a concern to avoid impurity.

19. See further Cohen, *Maccabees to Mishnah*, pp. 119, 129–32, 154–9, 162; Saldarini, *Pharisees*, pp. 215, 220–5, 233–4, 290–1; and below p. 140 n. 32.

20. Vermes, *Dead Sea Scrolls*, pp. 30–33.

21. See further B. Gärtner, *The Temple and the Community in Qumran and the New Testament*, SNTSMS 1; Cambridge University, 1965, chs 2–3; G. Klinzing, *Die Umdeutung des Kultus in der Qumrangemeinde und im NT*, Göttingen: Vandenhoeck & Ruprecht 1971, II. Teil.

22. See further below §6.3.

23. See Vermes, *Qumran*, pp. 95–6; M. Newton, *The Concept of Purity at Qumran and in the Letters of Paul*, SNTSMS 53; Cambridge University 1985, pp. 10–26. The unpublished 4QMMT shows that purity disputes attested in rabbinic sources (here especially *m. Yad.* 4.6–7) were already current, with 4QMMT siding with the stricter view of the Sadducees on several points; see L. H. Schiffman, 'The Temple Scroll and the Systems

their divorce from the current Temple cult, the Temple remained of supreme importance for them, as the Temple Scroll indicates. And here again a primary accent is on purity: 'The city which I will sanctify, causing my name and (my) sanctuary to abide (in it) shall be holy and pure of all iniquity with which they can become impure. Whatever is in it shall be pure. Whatever enters it shall be pure . . .' (11QT 47).

In short, concern for purity was characteristic of (what we would today call) practising Jews and particularly of the most devout at the time of Jesus. And in each case it was a concern stimulated by and given its point by the sanctity of the Temple. Nor should such concerns be played down as of minor significance (a tendency on the part of Sanders).[24] Even though most impurity could be removed without much difficulty, *the level of concern to maintain purity and avoid impurity shows how important the whole issue was.* Moreover, it is precisely in a sectarian context that differences over such 'minor' matters become the stuff of polemic and denunciation – as *Pss. Sol.* 8.12, 22, 1 QS 3.5 and 4QMMT (referred to above) clearly indicate.[25]

In view of all this, several episodes in the ministry of Jesus immediately become more luminous. We need refer only to the Markan account.

Mark 1.40–45 – given the importance of skin disease in the purity legislation (Lev. 13–14), the significance of Jesus touching the leper (1.41) would not be lost on anyone familiar with the Torah.

Mark 1.23, 26–27, 3.11, etc. – Jesus casts out 'unclean spirits', but is accused himself of having 'an unclean spirit' (3.30).

Mark 2.25–26 – Jesus cites as precedent the disregard shown by David and his followers for the sanctity of the tabernacle and the bread of the presence.

Mark 5.1–17 is all about purity – unclean spirit(s), living in tombs (subject to corpse impurity, the greatest of all impurities), unclean spirits sent into pigs (unclean animals), and all happening in Gentile territory (outside the holy land).

Mark 5.21–43/24–34 – the woman with the haemorrhage. Even

---

of Jewish Law of the Second Temple Period', *Temple Scroll Studies*, ed. G. J. Brooke, Sheffield Academic Press 1989, pp. 239–55, here pp. 245–51.

24. Cf. Sanders, *Jewish Law*, p. 235 – 'minor gestures towards extra purity'. He immediately qualifies the point, but still fails to appreciate the importance which a factional dispute can give to (what an outsider might well see as) a minor matter.

25. See again Segal, *Rebecca's Children*, p. 34, cited above, ch. 2, n. 49; and again below ch. 6, including p. 145 n. 49.

without the clear echo of Lev. 15.25 in Mark 5.25, the significance would be clear to any Jew. Since menstrual bleeding rendered a woman unclean, and since the period of uncleanness stretched seven days beyond the day when the bleeding stopped, this woman would have been in a state of uncleanness most if not all of the time (Lev. 15). She would never have been able to take part in the major religious ceremonies, visiting the Temple or participating in the pilgrim festivals. Her social life would have been very restricted: Pharisees in particular, but by no means only they, would not have permitted her in their company for fear of defilement. Within the context of Judaism's purity laws her condition was about as crippling socially and religiously as one could imagine. And in the story she *touches* Jesus! And Jesus makes no objection! certainly not on grounds that her touch rendered him impure. Moreover, Jesus immediately goes on into the synagogue ruler's house in a condition which many devout Jews of the time would have regarded as a state of impurity which would have rendered others impure!

Mark 7 focusses on the issue of purity quite explicitly: not only is there Mark 7.15, 19, but Mark immediately goes on to tell the story of Jesus' dealings with a Gentile woman (outside the purity of the holy land) (Mark 7.24–30). Given the obvious importance of the whole theme for Mark, it is worth reflecting on the basic issue in its significance as a record of Jesus' own concerns. Sanders protests that 7.2, 5 are unlikely to be historical – part of his larger argument that 'there was no substantial conflict between Jesus and the Pharisees'.[26] It cannot be assumed, he would maintain, that concern for the purity of hands had developed so far before 70 CE; rather, Mark 7.1f. reflects later disputes when Christians and the successors to the Pharisees were at loggerheads and when the rulings which were to build up into Mishnah tractate Yadaim were being developed. But Mark 7.2 is clearly *pre*-Markan tradition: Mark (or his source) has to explain it for his Gentile readers (7.3–4); and since Mark can hardly be dated much (if at all) after 70, the implication is clear that the conflict presupposed in 7.1f. between the disciples of Jesus and Pharisees must have occurred *before* 70 (*pre*-Markan can hardly mean other than pre-70). This undercuts Sanders' attempt to drive a wedge between the development of the halakoth on this matter among the pre-70 Pharisees and the development thereafter. Already before 70

---

26. Sanders, *Jesus*, pp. 178, 199, 209, 264–5. In *Jewish Law*, pp. 31, 39–40, 90–1, 228–31 he observes that Pharisees practised hand-washing at their own sabbath and festival meals, but again notes that there is no evidence in rabbinic literature that Pharisees washed their hands before eating ordinary meals.

such concerns on the part of Pharisees are attested.[27] Whether this enables us to speak of the Pharisees as 'a purity sect' may be a moot point; but it certainly bears comparison with the developed halakoth of Qumran on such questions; and since the concerns of pre-70 Pharisees can hardly have differed greatly from those of many Pharisees contemporary with Jesus, we need not doubt that purity was indeed an issue of some significance between Jesus and at least some Pharisees. In which case, the key factor is indeed the disregard for such purity traditions on the part of Jesus' disciples, and, presumably, on the part of Jesus himself. So too in Jesus' reply there is at least a marked devaluation and relativization of purity concerns (7.15). To this subject we must return. Here all that need be noted is that in the Markan form of the saying, what Jesus said could be understood as legitimating the complete abandonment or abrogation of the laws of clean and unclean foods (7.19).[28]

A consistent picture begins to emerge, therefore – of a Jesus who did not share the concerns or degree of concern regarding purity of many (most?) of the Pharisees, and who indeed sat loose to, disregarded or discounted some at least of the outworkings of the purity legislation as it governed social contact (people with skin diseases, corpse defilement, discharge of blood). To what extent such actions would have been an aggravation to those who took such purity concerns more seriously or observed them more rigorously than Jesus, we cannot say. It would depend on their relative importance and on the degree of provocation (deliberate or otherwise) in the incidents themselves. And we have no way of gauging that accurately. What we can say, however, is that Mark's ordering of such a sequence evidences a clear memory of actions likely to be provocative on purity matters as a feature of Jesus' ministry, as well as his involvement in a particular dispute with Pharisees regarding the necessity of handwashing. Since purity was so much at the heart of Jewish religion, and since that concern focussed so much on the Temple, *someone who was so cavalier regarding purity, and popular despite that, could very well have been perceived as something of a threat to the whole religious system which centred on the Temple.*[29]

27. Note again the significance of 4QMMT in this connection (above n. 23).

28. See further my 'Jesus and Ritual Purity. A study of the tradition history of Mark 7.15', *A cause de l'evangile* J. Dupont FS, Lectio Divina 123; Editions du Cerf 1985, pp. 251–76; also 'Pharisees, Sinners and Jesus', *The Social World of Formative Christianity and Judaism*, H. C. Kee FS, ed. J. Neusner et al., Philadelphia: Fortress 1988, pp. 264–89; both reprinted in *Jesus, Paul and the Law*, chs 2 and 3.

29. J. Riches, *Jesus and the Transformation of Judaism*, London: Darton, Longman & Todd 1980, ch. 6, and M. J. Borg, *Conflict, Holiness and Politics in the Teachings of Jesus*, New York: Edwin Mellen 1984, both focus their discussion of Jesus the controversialist

3.3 The issue of forgiveness

The issue and the point can be easily overstated here too. N. Perrin, for example, characterized one of the distinctive features of Jesus' ministry as his offer of forgiveness to those who were debarred from it by an unfeeling Judaism: 'The central feature of the message of Jesus is ... the challenge of the forgiveness of sins.' 'Palestinian Judaism was confronted by a crisis when Jesus proclaimed the eschatological forgiveness of sins, and "tax collectors and other Jews who had made themselves as Gentiles" responded in glad acceptance.'[30] Against this parody Sanders has justifiably protested: 'Is it a serious proposal that tax collectors and the wicked longed for forgiveness, but could not find it within ordinary Judaism?'[31]

The protest is just, for the simple fact is that Judaism was a religion of forgiveness. The whole cult was geared to the restoration and maintenance of a positive relation between God and his people. The sacrificial system, particularly the sin-offering and Day of Atonement, were designed precisely to provide forgiveness. In Lev. 4–5, the legislation governing sin-offerings and guilt-offerings, the phrase occurs repeatedly at the end of the instructions: 'so the priest shall make atonement for him for his sins, and he shall be forgiven' (4.26, 31, 35; 5.10, 16, 18). Note not least the range of sins against God and neighbour covered by such provision (Lev. 6.1–7). Judaism, in short, was and is a religion of repentance and atonement.

Of course, forgiveness is a divine prerogative, and the Psalmist can speak very directly of God's forgiveness – as in Psalms 32 and 51 – and in some contrast to the cult (51.16–17). But no Jew would have understood that as countenancing an abandonment of the cult (so the Psalmist continues, 51.18–19). There is similar ambiguity in Jer. 31.31–4, climaxing as it does in the promise of divine forgiveness (31.34). In its structure the passage certainly invites or at least allows a contrast between outward ritual (the covenant of Sinai) and the new covenant (a different kind of covenant – immediate, non-cultic? – 31.33–4). But the contrast in fact is the familiar one between a genuine obedience and dedication from the heart (circumcision of the

---

round the theme of purity. The insight is well founded, though the overall balance of their claims is open to dispute and I would demur on various points of exegesis. On K. Berger, 'Jesus als Pharisäer und frühe Christen als Pharisäer', *NovT*30 (1988), pp. 231–62, see my *Jesus, Paul and the Law*, p. 87.

30. N. Perrin, *Rediscovering the Teaching of Jesus*, London: SCM Press 1967, pp. 107, 97.

31. Sanders, *Jesus*, p. 202; see pp. 200–4.

heart) and a *merely* outward, formalistic obedience (cf. particularly Jer. 9.25–6; 1QpHab 11.13). Here again a devout Jew would not have seen this as countenancing any disregard for cult or sacrificial system; as with the prophetic critique of the cult generally, it was a case of both-and, not either-or. It was, after all, God's law which was to be written in the heart, not a different law; the promise would then be understood as describing the whole-hearted embracing of the whole law, including the law of the cult.[32]

Was there then an issue over forgiveness in the ministry of Jesus? And if so, what was it?

The key passage is Mark 2.1–12 – especially 2.5–7, 10. Here again the point can be obscured or missed. At first the issue seems to be christological – 'Who can forgive sins but God alone?'; '. . . that you might know that the Son of Man has authority on earth to forgive sins . . .' (2.7, 10). But that in fact is a dubious interpretation. What Jesus actually says is, 'Your sins are forgiven' – something the priest could say in the Temple to everyone who had brought a sin-offering.[33] In Mark's telling of the story the christological emphasis is highlighted in the formulation of 2.7 and 10. But it is also noticeable that the phrase 'the Son of Man' evokes no comment: as the episode was recalled, it was evidently not seen as a claim to exalted or divine status by the crowd; indeed, in Matthew's version the force of the phrase in Aramaic idiom (as = 'man')[34] may be brought out in the final words about the crowd who 'were afraid, and glorified God, who had given such authority to *men*' (Matt. 9.8). Moreover, John the Baptist presumably pronounced sins forgiven (such at least seems to be the implication of Mark 1.4/Luke 3.3) without apparently provoking any accusation of breaching divine prerogative. And in the fragmentary Prayer of Nabonidus from Qumran, Nabonidus says

---

32. This is borne out even in the case of the Qumran covenanters, who regarded themselves as the fulfilment of the new covenant hope (CD 6.17–20; 19.32–35; 20.8–12), since they clearly understood that new covenant in terms of an intensification of the law given on Sinai; see Y. K. Yu, *The New Covenant: the Promise and its Fulfilment*, PhD Diss., Durham University 1989, chs 3–4.

33. As Sanders, *Jewish Law*, p. 61 notes, others have recognized that the issue was the propriety of going beyond 'delegated or prophetic 'authority' to speak in God's name the divine forgiveness of the man's sin' – V. Taylor, *The Gospel According to St Mark*, London: Macmillan 1952, p. 196, citing J. V. Bartlet, *St Mark*, Century Bible; Edinburgh 1922, p. 125.

34. That the Hebrew/Aramaic idiom 'son of man' means simply 'man' (as in Ps. 8.4) is well known. That this is the usage lying behind Mark 2.10 is also widely maintained – see e.g. those cited in Taylor, *Mark*, p. 197; also C. Colpe, *TDNT*, 8.430–1; M. Casey, *Son of Man. The Interpretation and Influence of Daniel 7*, London: SPCK 1979, pp. 159–61, 228–9; B. Lindars, *Jesus Son of Man*, London: SPCK 1983, pp. 44–7.

'an exorcist pardoned my sins', where human *mediation* of divine forgiveness is clearly implied (4QprNab 4).

Yet in the Synoptic accounts, Jesus' pronouncement caused offence. Why so? What is the issue in Mark 2.1–12? Or to be more precise, given the christological concern evident in Mark's telling of the story what is the underlying issue? In these circumstances, what was it that would have caused offence? Not that a forgiveness was being offered which might otherwise have been denied the man; he could, after all, have taken his offering to the Temple and/or benefited from the Day of Atonement like other Jews. Nor that Jesus was claiming a special status for himself by saying these words (which any priest could say). The answer seems to be rather that he pronounced the man's sins forgiven *outside the cult and without any reference* (even by implication) *to the cult*. It was not so much that he usurped the role of God in announcing sins forgiven. It was rather that he usurped the role of God *which God had assigned to priest and cult*.[35] God could forgive sins no doubt when and as he chose. But man could only promise and pronounce the forgiveness of sins when he operated within the terms and structures provided by God – the Temple, priesthood and sacrifice. In that sense, as usurping a prerogative of God in disregard for the terms laid down by God, what Jesus said and did could be counted a kind of blasphemy.[36]

We can also add that such pronouncing of sins forgiven was something of a feature of Jesus' ministry (Mark 3.28; Luke 7.47–9), and he may have taught his disciples to do likewise (John 20.23, but post-Easter; cf. Matt. 16.19 and 18.18, but do 'binding and loosing' include pronouncing sins forgiven?).[37] This is also a subject to which we must return.[38]

Here again we can see something of an implied challenge to a Temple centred religion, where forgiveness and therefore pronounce-

---

35. Cf. Antwi, pp. 26–7, who, however, overstates his case.

36. Cf. Sanders, *Jewish Law*, pp. 61–3, who suggests rather that it was the presumption of pronouncing sins forgiven in the absence of confession and restitution which would have been provocative. Presumably it was a similar boldness of claim by the Baptist which led to speculation about his possible messianic significance (cf. Luke 3.15; John 1.19–20). The significance of the Nabonidus forgiveness is lost, since only the beginning of the first column of writing has been preserved.

37. See discussion on 'binding and loosing' (probably teaching authority) e.g. in G. Bornkamm, 'The Authority to "Bind" and "Loose" in the Church in Matthew's Gospel', ET in G. Stanton (ed.), *The Interpretation of Matthew*, London: SPCK/ Philadelphia: Fortress 1983, pp. 85–97; J. Gnilka, *Das Matthäusevangelium*, Vol. 2, Freiburg: Herder 1988, pp. 66–7; R. H. Hiers, '"Binding" and "Loosing": the Matthean Authorizations', *JBL* 104 (1985), pp. 233–50 (exorcistic activity).

38. See further below §3.7.

ment of acceptability to and by God lay primarily and cultically in the hands of the priests. *He who took upon himself the priestly task of pronouncing absolution, without the authorization of the Temple authorities and without reference to the cult, might well be seen as putting a question mark against the importance and even the necessity of the cult, and, more threateningly, as undermining the authority of those whose power rested upon that system.*

3.4 The 'cleansing of the Temple'

There is little question in scholarly circles that underlying the tradition in Mark 11.15–17 pars. is a historical incident. But what?

(*a*) One suggestion is that it was a *revolutionary act* – as argued, for example, by Brandon.[39] The suggestion is not so far-fetched as might at first seem to be the case. For the Temple was a natural strong point, which any group of revolutionaries would endeavour to seize as a primary target, crucial to the success of their rebellion. This was already true at the time of the Maccabean revolt (I Macc. 4.36–41, 60–61), and was even more so following Herod's construction of the huge Temple platform, the first objective of the revolt in 66 CE (Josephus, *War* 2.320, 328–30, 422–4, 535–7). It may therefore be significant that Mark 15.7 speaks of a recent 'insurrection' in which Barabbas had been involved. Brandon also draws attention to three striking pieces of information preserved only by Luke: the presence of Simon a 'Zealot' among the disciples of Jesus (Luke 6.15);[40] the otherwise very puzzling instruction of Jesus to his disciples that they should purchase a sword (Luke 22.36); and the fact that Jesus was denounced to Pilate on a charge of subversion (Luke 23.2). Such evidence does at least raise the question as to whether there has been a Christian 'cover-up' at this point.

The explanation is unlikely however. With the fortress Antonia overlooking the Temple mount (by Herod's design), any significant military or military-like action in the Temple courts would have been met by an immediate response from the Roman garrison stationed therein, who were particularly alert for possible trouble at the crowded Passover season anyway (the point is vividly illustrated by

---

39. S. G. F. Brandon, *Jesus and the Zealots*, Manchester: Manchester University 1967; also *The Trial of Jesus*, 1968; London: Paladin 1971.

40. Mark and Matthew leave the Aramaic untranslated, Simon 'the Cananaion' (Mark 3.18; Matt. 10.4) – conceivably out of embarrassment at the later significance of the word 'Zealot' (see also e.g. Hengel, *Zealots*. pp. 69–70).

the episode in Acts 21.30–35).[41] It is almost impossible to conceive that the leading participant of such a military action was then left free for the next four days, teaching openly in the same Temple court. In other words, the issue is not simply one of a political whitewash obscuring the historical details of the event; the fact is that the whole tradition of Jesus' last week in Jerusalem would have to have been radically altered in order to accommodate Brandon's thesis.[42]

(*b*) Most have found the view more convincing that Jesus engaged in *a symbolic action*, like the prophets of old. But symbolizing what? Ferdinand Hahn argues that what Jesus did constituted a very radical criticism of the Temple. To hinder or prevent the provision of pure animals for sacrifice was tantamount to calling for *an end to the whole sacrificial system*.[43] The difficulty in this case is that the significance is not immediately obvious in the text and has to be inferred from the action; otherwise there is no hint that this is what Jesus intended. Nor does it square with the implication drawn in Mark 11.17 (the Temple is still intended to function as such for the Gentiles); or indeed with the subsequent history of the earliest Christian communities.[44]

(*c*) Sanders has strongly argued that the symbolism of Jesus' action must indicate *the destruction of the Temple*.[45] This certainly fits with other closely related evidence: particularly Mark 13.2 and 14.58, to which we must return; also the fact that Mark sets the 'cleansing of the Temple' between the two halves of the story of the cursing of the fig-tree, with the obvious implication that the fig-tree represents for the Markan Jesus the barrenness and condemnation of the Temple (Mark 11.12–14, 20–21); and not least the echo in Mark 11.17 of Jeremiah's own prediction of the imminent destruction of the Temple ('den of robbers' – Jer. 7.11). In Mark at least, all these can certainly be related to the action of Jesus as a way of interpreting it. But the symbolism is hardly self-evident from the action itself (overturning tables); whereas in the prophetic tradition the symbolism of the prophetic action is usually fairly clear-cut in its reference (e.g. I Kings 11.29ff.; 22.11; Isa. 20.1ff.; Hos. 1, 3).

(*d*) Perhaps, then, a more likely interpretation is one closer to that enshrined in the traditional title for the episode – *the cleansing of the*

41. See further Schürer, 1.366. In the initial events of the revolt in 66 it was sheer force of numbers which enabled the insurgents to hold the Temple platform against the Romans and their supporters.

42. See further particularly E. Bammel and C. F. D. Moule, *Jesus and the Politics of His Day*, Cambridge University 1984.

43. Hahn, *Worship*, pp. 27–30.

44. See further below §4.1.

45. Sanders, *Jesus*, pp. 61–71.

Temple – that is, an action expressing the conviction that the Temple had to be sanctified and made ready for its eschatological function. That an eschatological purification for Zion would be necessary is clearly implied in such passages as Isa. 4.4, Mal. 3.1–4, *Jub.* 4.26 and 11QT 29.8–10.[46] How much of a criticism of the present cult was indicated by such passages is not clear. Some such criticism may be implied in Mark 11.17, in the clear contrast between the explicit quotation from Isaiah and the allusion to Jer. 7.11, added to what looks like an echo (Mark 11.16) of the last sentence of Zechariah ('And there shall no longer be a trader in the house of the Lord of hosts on that day' – Zech. 14.21).[47] But more important may be the conviction that Jerusalem had to be purified in order to display the glory of God, in order to attract the Gentiles – as in *Pss.Sol.* 17.30:

> And he (the royal Messiah) shall purify Jerusalem, making it holy as of old; So that nations shall come from the ends of the earth to see his glory . . .

Not least of significance is the fact that it is to just this expectation that Mark 11.17 refers – Isa. 56.7 – that is, the strongly attested hope in second Temple Judaism that in the last days the Gentiles would come in large numbers to Jerusalem as eschatological proselytes.[48] That Jesus himself shared this hope is fairly clearly implied in Matt. 8.11–12/Luke 13.28–9 and Mark 12.9.

The implication would then be clear: that the action was eschatological in significance – *a symbolical representation of the 'cleansing' of the Temple which would be necessary if it was to serve its intended eschatological function,* and possibly even a symbolical attempt to bring about these conditions. That such a purification of the Temple involved also its destruction may very well be the proper implication of the evidence cited above (c);[49] though the symbolical action itself probably speaks more of protest and purification than of destruction

---

46. We have already noted (§2.4) that in Jewish thought Jerusalem, Zion and Temple were interlocking themes.

47. Note the possibility alluded to above (§2.4b) that the main Temple court served as a general market-place. For recent restatements of the view that Jesus' criticism was directed against specific abuses see R. Bauckham, 'Jesus' Demonstration in the Temple', *Law and Religion. Essays on the Place of the Law in Israel and Early Christianity*, ed. B. Lindars, Cambridge: James Clarke 1988, pp. 72–89; C. A. Evans, 'Jesus' Action in the Temple: Cleansing or Portent of Destruction?', *CBQ* 51 (1989), pp. 237–70.

48. Ps. 22.27; Isa. 2.2–3; 56.6–8; Zeph. 3.9–10; Zech. 14.16; Tobit 13.11; *Pss.Sol.* 17.33; *Sib. Or.* 3.702–18, 772–6; *T.Ben.* 9.2; see also Sanders, *Jesus*, pp. 213–8.

49. See also §3.5 below; cf.now B. Witherington, *The Christology of Jesus*, Minneapolis: Fortress 1990, pp. 107–16.

as such. One problem with this solution is that both Matthew and Luke omit the 'for all nations' of Mark 11.17 (and Isa. 56.7), and the echo of Zech. 14.21 is nowhere explicit. Nevertheless, all the evangelists are agreed in interpreting the episode as some sort of symbolical purification of the Temple cult; and all three Synoptics do refer to Isa. 56.7. So, despite everything, it probably remains the best solution.[50]

In which case it is important for our present inquiry to note how fully Jesus' action fits into prophetic tradition – both in terms of his use of symbolic action, and in terms of protest against abuse of the Temple system, such as we find in Isaiah, Amos and Micah. *However radical the criticism involved in Jesus' action, it is a prophetic critique with which we have to do.*

3.5 Jesus' word about the Temple

Here the key evidence is Mark 14.58 – the testimony given against Jesus at the hearing after his arrest, that he had said, 'I will destroy this temple made with hands, and after three days I will rebuild another made without hands'. In Mark, to be sure, it is presented as a false testimony; though Matthew softens the point by weakening the form of the saying ('I am able to destroy . . .') and by making it less clear that it was false testimony (Matt. 26.60–61). But Mark and Matthew do not hesitate to show that the accusation of Jesus' having so spoken was widely known in Jerusalem (Mark 15.29/Matt. 27.39–40); and, more important, all three Synoptic evangelists do not hesitate to report Jesus' prediction of the destruction of the Temple (Mark 13.2 pars.). Still more important, John 2.19 reports his equivalent to the accusation *on the lips of Jesus himself* – 'Destroy this temple, and in three days I will raise it up.' We should also note that the accusation against Stephen in Acts 6.14 echoes the same charge: 'We have heard him (Stephen) say that this Jesus of Nazareth will destroy this place . . .'; and that the Gospel of Thomas attributes to Jesus a not dissimilar saying – 'Jesus said: I shall destroy [this] house, and no one will be able to [re]build it' (*Gospel of Thomas* 71).

What are we to make of all this? Surely that Jesus must have said something at least about the destruction of the Temple, or of its passing away. This word of Jesus is recalled in the Synoptics as a prediction of the destruction of the Temple, which was to find fulfilment in the events of 70 CE; but beyond that it is treated as a false

---

50. See also Borg, *Conflict*, pp. 171–7.

testimony, falsely attributed to Jesus. John recalls the fuller saying (destruction and rebuilding) as a saying of Jesus himself, but interprets it differently (of Jesus' own body – John 2.21). As for Acts 6.14, the accusation against Stephen, it might at first seem that Luke was trying to pattern the first martyr's death on that of Jesus (cf. Luke 23.34 with Acts 7.60). But then we have to ask why Luke has no parallel to Mark 14.58 in his first volume; to *omit* the accusation against Jesus seems an odd way to bring out the parallel. The more likely answer is that Luke wanted to give the impression that the role of the Temple was not called into question until the time of Stephen and the Hellenists; and that he was encouraged or enabled so to do by drawing on the remembered fact that Stephen had taken up and used the tradition of Jesus' words regarding the Temple.[51]

Given then that Jesus almost certainly did say something on the subject, what could he have meant? If only the first half of the saying goes back to Jesus (as a variant of 13.2),[52] then he could have looked for a new age *without* the Temple (cf. Rev. 21.22). Alternatively, if the fuller form goes back to Jesus,[53] then probably he was echoing the apocalyptic hope of a new Temple in the new age. The most frequently cited expression of this is *I Enoch* 90.28–9 –

> Then I stood still, looking at that ancient house being transformed: All the pillars and all the columns were pulled out; and the ornaments of that house were packed and taken out together with them and abandoned in a certain place in the South of the land. I went on seeing until the Lord of the sheep brought about a new house, greater and loftier than the first one, and set it up in the first location which had been covered up – all its pillars were new, the columns new; and the ornaments new as well as greater than those of the first, (that is) the old (house) which was gone.

It was, however, a natural interpretation of the great temple vision of Ezek. 40–48, which we know exercised considerable influence on

---

51. See further below §4.3.

52. J. R. Donahue, *Are You the Christ? The Trial Narrative in the Gospel of Mark*, SBL Diss 10; Missoula: SBL, 1973, pp. 103–13; D. Lührmann, 'Markus 14.55–64: Christologie and Zerstörung des Tempels im Markusevangelium', *NTS* 27 (1980–81), pp. 457–74; Borg, *Conflict*, pp. 177–98; J. Schlosser, 'La parole de Jésus sur la fin du Temple', *NTS* 3 (1990), pp. 398–414.

53. E.g. Taylor, *Mark*, pp. 566–7; R. J. McKelvey, *The New Temple. The Church in the New Testament*, Oxford University 1969, pp. 67–72; G. Theissen, 'Die Tempelweissagung Jesu', *TZ* 32 (1976), pp. 144–58; Sanders, *Jesus*, pp. 71–6. In contrast to both positions, L. Gaston, *No Stone on Another*, NovTSupp 23; Leiden: Brill 1970, ch. 3 (Conclusion, pp. 242–3) argues that only the *second* half of the saying goes back to Jesus.

Qumran expectation (5Q15; 11QT). *Jub.* 1.17 and 27–8 pointed in the same direction – 'I shall build my sanctuary in their midst . . . Write for Moses from the first creation until my sanctuary is built in their midst forever and ever' (cf. Ps. 102.15–16; Tobit 14.5). And it is also a feature of (subsequent) Jewish apocalyptic expectation (as attested in *IV Ezra* 9.38–10.27; *II Bar.* 32.3–4; *T. Ben.* 9.2; *Sib.Or.* 5.423f.).[54] Most interesting of all is 4QFlor. 1.10ff., where the promise to David of a son who would build the Temple (II Sam. 7.12–14), is interpreted of the royal Messiah in the last days. We shall see in a moment how well such an expectation fits with the accusation of Mark 14.58.

All this is to say that *Jesus' expectation regarding the future of the Temple*, whatever its precise form and significance, *seems to set Jesus firmly within the expectation of Jewish apocalypticism so far as we know it for the time of Jesus* – critical of the present Temple, or at least recognizing the need for it to be sanctified afresh, and not necessarily mainline Jewish (if we can so speak for the period prior to 70), but certainly Jewish through and through.[55]

Can we say more? If Jesus intended any talk of a new Temple to refer to a new eschatological community,[56] that would imply a greater sense of divorce from the present Temple. This concept, a new eschatological (Temple) community, certainly seems to have emerged quickly in earliest Christian thought, though initially at least with less critique of or divorce from the current Temple than in the case of Qumran.[57] But quite what Jesus himself envisaged in any talk of a (re)new(ed) Temple remains tantalizingly obscure anyway.

3.6 Who or what killed Jesus?

A popular belief of long standing within Christian circles is that Jesus' chief opponents were the Pharisees and that it is they who brought about his death – a belief, which, of course, is given some credence by Mark 3.6 in particular. But the belief is problematic nonetheless and cannot be sustained, at least in its customary form – for two main reasons.

For one thing the view has been tied to an exaggerated assessment

---

54. See also Sanders, *Jesus*, ch. 2.

55. Borg's conclusion is similar, *Conflict*, p. 198.

56. See particularly D. Juel, *Messiah and Temple. The Trial of Jesus in the Gospel of Mark*, SBLDS 31; Missoula: Scholars 1977, but dealing with the issue at the level of Mark; Gaston, *No Stone*, pp. 229–43 argues that the image of the Temple as the (new) community goes back to Jesus himself.

57. See below §4.1e.

of the opposition between Jesus and the Pharisees – that Pharisees were legalists, narrow-minded, joyless busybodies, who hated Jesus because he brought forgiveness and acceptance to outcasts. Sanders in particular has rightly protested against this parody;[58] indeed, he and others are prepared to argue quite the contrary view, that Jesus and the Pharisees differed on no matter of consequence.[59] The issue will have to be discussed later; for the moment we should simply note that the traditional view that the Pharisees brought about Jesus' death is now under severe and justified challenge.

More important is the fact that Pharisees hardly feature at all in the passion narratives of the Gospels. In Mark no mention is made of Pharisees after 12.13 (early in passion week). In Matthew Pharisees appear only at 27.62 subsequent to the polemic of ch. 23. In Luke no mention is made of Pharisees after 19.39 (the entry into Jerusalem). And in John the only mention made of Pharisees after ch. 12 is 18.3. Contrast the use of *archiereis* (high priests) – 16 times in Mark 14–15; 19 times in Matt. 26–28; 13 times in Luke 19–24; and 14 times in John 18–19. Quite clearly, so far as the passion narratives themselves are concerned, on the Jewish side the chief actors in bringing about the death of Jesus were the high priests; Pharisees may not have had much, if indeed any part in it! The point for us is that if high priests rather then Pharisees were most responsible on the Jewish side for Jesus' death, *that clearly implies that the crucial issue was the Temple and not the law.*

Can we say more? Here again there are two problems. First, the Gospels all make some attempt to shift the blame for Jesus' death away from the Romans and on to the Jews. Note particularly Mark 15.6–15 pars. (cf. John 18.38). But there is no doubt that Jesus was crucified, and crucifixion is undisputably a *Roman* penalty.

Second, in the view of Sanders, though he is by no means alone, the trial scene before the Sanhedrin is historically incredible.[60] For one thing the charge of blasphemy (Mark 14.64 par.) is questionable: Mark 14.62 may very well reflect post-Easter christology;[61] and John

---

58. Sanders, *Jesus*, index 'Pharisees'.

59. Sanders, *Jesus*, e.g. p. 291 – 'I find no substantial conflict between Jesus and the Pharisees'. Others go further and speak of Jesus as a Pharisee – e.g. H. Falk, *Jesus the Pharisee*, New York: Paulist 1985; Maccoby, *Mythmaker*, pp. 29–44. Sanders criticizes one phrase of my critique of him (*Jewish Law*, p. 344 n. 1) but ignores the substantive issue raised in my 'Pharisees, Sinners and Jesus' (*Jesus, Paul and the Law*, ch. 3); see further below ch. 6 and n. 19.

60. Sanders, *Jesus*, pp. 297–8.

61. N. Perrin, 'Mark 14.62: The End Product of a Christian Pesher Tradition?' *NTS* 12 (1965–66), pp. 150–5.

18.19 and 24 make no mention of it. For another, how would the tradition of the exchanges between Jesus and the High Priest have become known to his disciples? And for another, a formal meeting of the court on the first night of Passover (Matthew and Mark) is incredible; Luke places the hearing on the morning; and John makes no report of a trial before the Sanhedrin at all; while Matthew and Luke report two trials – one at night and the other in the morning.

However, Sanders may be too sceptical here. In fact the sequence of questioning in Mark 14.57–61 is historically very plausible. Any talk, false witness or no, of rebuilding the Temple would almost certainly, or at least very easily, be heard as a claim regarding the fulfilment of the prophecy of Nathan – II Sam. 7.12–14: God's promise to David that his son 'shall build a house for my name, and I will establish the throne of his kingdom for ever. I will be his father, and he shall be my son . . .'. Note the combination of elements – son of David (royal Messiah), would build the Temple, and be counted by God as his son (son of God). We have already observed that II Sam. 7.12–14 featured in the Dead Sea Scrolls expectation regarding the royal Messiah (4QFlor. = 4Q174 1.10ff.); and in this expectation another feature of II Sam. 7.12–14 was evidently taken up as well – the Son of David would also be God's son.[62] In the light of this, the High Priest's question becomes a most natural one – 'Are you (accused of saying you would rebuild the Temple, therefore) the (royal) Messiah, the son of the Blessed?'[63] According to our accounts this exchange is the core of the case against Jesus, and it is not difficult to imagine how that could have become known to Jesus' followers (through sympathetic participants of the hearing then or later), just as it may well have become the subject of public rumour at the time (Mark 15.29 par).

All in all, then, it becomes very probable that there was a hearing before the leading members (high-priestly faction) of the Sanhedrin, *in which Jesus' challenge to the Temple*, however it may have been perceived, *was the central issue*. If the high-priestly faction had already decided that Jesus was too much of a trouble-maker who had to be silenced, then a natural procedure would have been to make

---

62. This is implied in the way 4Q174 seems to be linking Ps. 2 as a messianic psalm with II Sam. 7, even thought the text itself breaks off before Ps. 2.7 is reached. But the description of royal Messiah as God's son is present elsewhere in the Dead Sea Scrolls (1QSa 2.11f.; 4QpsDan Aᵃ; cf. *T.Levi* 4.2; IV Ezra 7.28f.; see those cited in my *Christology*, p. 273 n. 19). Consequently Sanders is wrong when he claims that royal Messiah and son of God are not combined outside the Christian movement (*Jesus*, p. 298).

63. See particularly O. Betz, *What do we Know about Jesus?*, 1965, ET London: SCM Press 1968, pp. 83–93.

the link provided by II Sam. 7.14, between Jesus' words regarding the Temple and the (royal) Messiah, son of God, and to transpose this into political terms (Royal Messiah/King of Jews) as the basis of a denunciation of Jesus to the Romans. This fits completely into the recollection of a trial before Pilate and the crucifixion of Jesus as constituting such a threat – 'the King of the Jews' (Mark 15.26).

Such a reconstruction does not solve all the problems relating to the Gospel accounts.[64] But no more is necessary at this point for our inquiry. The basic outline has a high degree of credibility and fits the records which we have, while allowing quite adequately for further elaboration and tendentious presentation on the part of the Evangelists.

In short, *the most probable historical reconstruction of the death of Jesus is that on the Jewish side the principal movers were the high-priestly faction.* In which case once again we see that *the primary issue would have been the Temple and Jesus' perceived challenge to it* – a challenge understood in theological terms, or, probably more likely, in political terms – that is, as a challenge to the priestly and principal power base within the Judaism of the time. We might simply note in passing that such a conclusion would have strong backing from several contemporary Jewish scholars of the period.[65]

3.7 Did Jesus see his death as a sacrifice, to end all sacrifices?

That Jesus' death did mark the end of the Jewish sacrificial system is clearly a view which finds strong expression subsequently – for example, and particularly in Hebrews.[66] But in fact it is very hard to discern when it first emerged in earliest Christian thinking – an issue to which we will have to revert more than once. Here the question is how Jesus would have seen his own death. Obviously if we must give a Yes answer to our question, then the corollary at once follows that Jesus anticipated and intended(?) a radical break with the Temple and the continuing sacrificial practices of Judaism.

We need not go in any detail into the prior question of whether Jesus anticipated his death. Although an affirmative answer has been disputed in the past, it is rendered highly probable by an important

---

64. For an excellent summary see D. R. Catchpole, 'Trial of Jesus', *IDBS*, pp. 917–19. For a confident assessment of the trial narratives' substantial reliability see A. Strobel, *Die Stunde der Wahrheit*, WUNT 21; Tübingen: Mohr-Siebeck 1980.

65. S. Zeitlin, *Who Crucified Jesus?*, New York: Bloch [5]1964; E. Rivkin, *What Crucified Jesus?*, Nashville: Abingdon 1984; London: SCM Press 1986; Maccoby, *Mythmaker*.

66. See further below §5.6.

range of evidence, which it is probably sufficient simply to note. (1) The saying about sharing his baptism and drinking his cup (Mark 10.38/Matt. 20.22–3/Luke 12.50), not to mention the 'passion predictions' of Mark 8.31, 9.31 and 10.33, 45. (2) The tradition about the fate of prophets (Mark 12.12 pars.; Matt. 23.29–36/Luke 20.47–51; Luke 13.33; Matt. 23.37/Luke 13.34). (3) The deeply rooted Jewish tradition of the suffering righteous (Pss. 22, 34, 69; Wisd.Sol. 3.1–10; 5.1–5), of which Isa. 53 and the vision of Dan. 7 are important expressions.[67] (4) The words of institution at the Last Supper (Mark 14.22–24 pars). (5) The precedent of John the Baptist and the hostility Jesus had already engendered – for example, the charges of sorcery and breach of sabbath which later on were certainly counted as worthy of death (*m.Sanh.* 7.4). It is not necessary to demonstrate the historicity of all this material, were such a demonstration technically possible, for the conclusion to be soundly based that *Jesus must have anticipated his death, or at least reckoned on death as a likely outcome of his mission*, some time before he died.[68]

The question for us here is rather, given the likelihood that Jesus did anticipate his death, how would he have understood it, or how did he in fact understand it? Not, assuredly as a disaster to be avoided at all costs; otherwise he would not have left the comparative security of Galilee, where his popularity was strongest, and gone to Jerusalem, putting himself thereby within the clutches of his chief opponents. Rather he must have viewed his likely rejection ultimately as something positive, intended by God as part of his good purpose for Israel.[69] But what would it mean for the Temple cult? That is our question. Here the evidence is unclear and its interpretation inevitably somewhat speculative.

(1) A rejection and death understood in terms of *the suffering righteous*, as in Wisdom of Solomon 3 and 5, would almost certainly carry no implication of undermining the cult.

(2) Likewise, *a martyr death*, as in II Macc. 7.37–8, or even possibly

67. See further E. Schweizer, *Erniedrigung und Erhöhung bei Jesus und seinen Nachfolgern*, Zürich: Zwingli ²1962; L. Ruppert, *Jesus als der leidende Gerechte?*, SBS 59; Stuttgart: KBW 1972; G. W. E. Nickelsburg, *Resurrection, Immortality, and Eternal Life in Intertestamental Judaism*, Harvard Theological Studies 26; Cambridge: Harvard University 1972.

68. See further e.g. Jeremias, *Proclamation*, pp. 277–99; H. Schürmann, 'Wie hat Jesus seinen Tod bestanden und verstanden?', *Orientierung an Jesus. Für Josef Schmid*, ed. P. Hoffmann, Freiburg: Herder 1973, pp. 325–63; V. Howard, 'Did Jesus speak about his own death?', *CBQ* 39 (1977), pp. 515–27; H. F. Bayer, *Jesus' Predictions of Vindication and Resurrection*, WUNT 2.20; Tübingen: Mohr-Siebeck 1986.

69. E. Schweizer, *Lordship and Discipleship*, London: SCM Press 1960, p. 36.

in the sacrificial terms used in *IV Macc.* 17.22, again need have no implication of undercutting or doing away with the sacrificial cult. Even if the martyr theology of *IV Maccabees* reflects some sense in Alexandria of the need to compensate in some degree for diaspora Judaism's inability to take regular part in the Temple sacrifices, the whole thrust of these Maccabean texts, as of the Maccabean revolt itself, was to defend and support Israel's relationship with God as expressed precisely in the Temple cult.

(3) *A suffering of the end-time tribulation*, later called 'the Messianic woes', may be expressed particularly in Luke 12.49–50 –

> I came to cast fire upon the earth;
>   and would that it were already kindled!
> I have a baptism to be baptized with;
>   and how I am constrained until it is accomplished!

The implication of this text is probably that Jesus was remembered as taking up and transforming the prediction of John the Baptist regarding the Coming One: Matt. 3.11/Luke 3.16 –

> I baptize you with water;
> He will baptize you with the Holy Spirit and with fire.

The significance lies in the fact that the Baptist's words are best understood as his own attempt to put into his own metaphor the expectation of a time of tribulation in the last days – an already well established apocalyptic motif, as in Zech. 14.12–15, Dan. 7.19–22 and 12.1, and especially Isa. 30.27–8, which so closely parallels the Baptist's own imagery. The point then is that Jesus would have seen his death as *somehow vicarious*, a suffering of the labour pains of the end-time as a necessary part of the process by which the new age would be born, the kingdom of God come.[70] However, just what that would mean for the Temple and the cult is not at all clear.

(4) *A covenant sacrifice* to introduce the new covenant, is clearly expressed in the Lukan and Pauline version of the 'words of institution' at the last supper – 'This cup is the new covenant in my blood' (Luke 22.20/I Cor. 11.25) – as indicated by the parallel of Ex. 24.5–8. How much more we can say, however, is not clear. Precisely at the

---

70. See further my 'The Birth of a Metaphor – Baptized in Spirit', *ExpT*89 (1977–78), p. 134–8. The passion predictions, including Mark 10.45, fall somewhere within the range covered by (1) to (3).

point which most interests us in this study, the question of what it was that Jesus originally said remains tantalizingly unclear. In the word over the bread, Matthew and Mark have no interpretative addition, nothing except, 'This is my body'; only Luke's and Paul's version add 'given/broken for you'. While in the word over the cup, the position is reversed: only Matthew and Mark have 'which is poured out for many (for the forgiveness of sins' – Matt.).[71] The point for us is that the covenant sacrifice was a different kind of sacrifice from the daily and annual sin-offerings. And it remains uncertain as to whether Jesus saw his death in terms of the latter. So, once again, *it is not at all clear that Jesus would have thought of his death as a sacrifice which rendered unnecessary the sacrificial cult.*

The issue here is very difficult for modern scholarship because it is tied to the question of what it was that Jesus expected to happen. What would the coming of the kingdom mean for the Temple? What would the destruction and reconstitution of the Temple mean for the sacrificial cult? Was the implication of a renewed or purified Temple, and of the eschatological pilgrimage of the Gentiles, that the name and presence of God would still be understood as located or focussed in the Temple? And would that still depend on the continuation of a cult and of cultic sacrifice? How was the presence of God to be mediated in the new age? Unfortunately we can only ask the questions, but cannot give the answers.

3.8 Conclusions

It is clear that the issue of the function and continuing role of the Temple was of some importance for Jesus and for the outcome of his mission in death. But what precisely was that importance?

(*a*) His actions and words could be said to contain an implicit critique of the cult in regard to purity issues. But was this necessarily any more severe in its ramifications than the critique of Temple and priesthood made by the *Psalms of Solomon* or the Qumran covenanters? Or the earlier prophetic critique as the prophets pressed for a proper balance and priority in Israelite spirituality?

(*b*) His actions and words contained an implicit critique of the cult in regard to the pronouncement of sins forgiven. But John the Baptist is also remembered as speaking of a forgiveness experiencable outside

---

71. For discussion of the earliest form of the 'words of institution' see e.g. my *Unity and Diversity in the New Testament*, London: SCM Press/Philadelphia: Westminster 1977; London: SCM Press/Philadelphia: TPI [2]1990, pp. 165–7 and those cited there in n. 23.

the cult (Mark 1.4/Luke 3.3)[72] – in connection with a ritual act, to be sure, but still without reference to the Temple cult. And presumably the Qumran covenanters experienced the grace (of forgiveness and acceptance) in which they evidently rejoiced in the saying of their hymns (1QH), even though they never went near the Temple. So, once again, Jesus is still within the parameters of the debate and practice of second Temple Judaism at this point too.

(*c*) The 'cleansing of the Temple' and the word about the Temple could simply be some sort of critique of the present functioning of the Temple and expressive of the desire for it to be purified or reconstituted for its eschatological function as the focal point for the new age, for the eschatological pilgrimage of the Gentiles and the eschatological worship of God. What all this says regarding the cult and its function in that future is once again unclear.

(*d*) The reason why Jesus was put to death is not much clearer. It could simply have been the result of a fierce (unnecessarily fierce) priestly reaction to what was perceived (rightly or wrongly) as a threat to their prerogatives and power. It does not follow that Jesus had actually rejected the Temple as such.

(*e*) Jesus' own understanding of his likely death is also unclear, particularly in its potential implications for the continuation of the cult and of the sacrificial system.

(*f*) Finally we may simply anticipate by noting that the practice of Jesus' followers in the earliest Jerusalem congregation seems to imply continuing loyalty to and focus on the Temple.[73] In which case it is hardly likely that Jesus had come out clearly and unequivocally against the Temple.

In short, *Jesus appears on this subject to stand well within the diversity of second Temple Judaism.* Nor should we forget that the Pharisees or their successors were able to reconstitute normative Judaism even after the destruction of the Temple – a Judaism which has continued for eighteen or nineteen centuries while *still* there is no Temple or sacrificial cult. Jesus stands certainly *within* that diversity. Of course there are elements in his ministry and teaching (§§3.2–7) which could be appealed to, in support of such a break away from

---

72. Note however, that Matthew omits the reference to the forgiveness of sins in connection with John's baptism (Matt. 3.2, 11) and that he inserts the same phrase ('for the forgiveness of sins') into his account of the words of institution at the last supper (Matt. 26.28), presumably with the implication that forgiveness of sins *did* depend on Jesus' sacrificial death.

73. See below §4.1.

the Temple in the future. But *nothing which required or compelled a development out of or breach with a Judaism focussed on the Temple of Jerusalem.*

4

A Temple 'made with hands'

In these chapters we are examining the way in which the Temple was viewed in the beginnings of Christianity – not least in its function as focus of the holy land of covenant promise, the place which God had appointed as the primary expression of his presence on earth. This pillar of Judaism (§2.4) was soon undermined and before long had become considerably less significant for most Christians. That is not in dispute. But why, and how soon? Can we gain a clear enough impression of the beginnings of Christianity to answer the question? We have seen how ambiguous is the evidence in regard to Jesus. So ambiguous that we cannot give a clear answer to the question: Did Jesus envisage or intend a worship no longer centred on the Temple and on the sacrificial cult in Jerusalem? But what about the first Christians, the earliest grouping of his disciples following the events remembered in the Christian calendar as Good Friday, Easter and Pentecost? How did they see themselves in relation to the Temple and the cult, particularly in the wake of these same events?

These are the questions we attempt to answer in this chapter. First by reference to the very earliest post-Easter community, and then by reference to the Hellenists, and the sequence of events they set in train.

4.1 The first Christians' attitude to the Temple

We need not argue the case that there was in Jerusalem from the early or at latest mid-30s a body of Jews who believed Jesus to be Messiah and to have been raised from the dead.[1] What then was their attitude to the Temple? Was it the same as that of Jesus, or different? Or is the evidence just as ambiguous? The answer seems to be that *they remained very much focussed on the Temple*. This at least is the impression which comes through consistently and strongly from the evidence, such as it is.

---

1. For considerations in favour of the essential historicity of the Pentecost tradition see e.g. my *Jesus*, ch. 6.

(*a*) Luke portrays a consistent picture from the end of his Gospel and throughout the first five chapters of Acts: that the first members of the sect of the Nazarenes never stirred from Jerusalem and remained focussed on the Temple (Luke 24.53; Acts 2.46; 3.1; 5.42). Why? The most obvious answer, though never expressed by Luke, is that they saw the Temple as the focal point of the eschatological climax of God's purpose for Israel (cf. Acts 1.6, 21–22; 3.21), and, not least, as the place to which Jesus would return (cf. Mal. 3.1; Acts 3.20; Rom. 11.26). We have already seen how strong was the strand of Jewish 'restoration theology', both in terms of an eschatological pilgrimage of Gentiles to Mount Zion, and in terms of a renewed Temple; also that Jesus himself seems to have shared it at least to some extent (Matt. 8.11–12, etc.); and that the 'cleansing of the Temple' and Jesus' word about the Temple are best understood in the context.[2] Naturally, in those circumstances, there would be no sense of a need or compulsion to take the gospel out *from* Jerusalem *to* Gentiles, since the expectation would have been of the Gentiles coming *in*.[3]

(*b*) The first believers in Jesus Messiah seem also to have attended the Temple and to have participated in the Temple cult. This is a disputed claim, but the evidence, such as it is, points firmly towards that conclusion. (1) The clear implication of Acts 3.1, and perhaps also 5.21, is that the first followers of Jesus observed the traditional hours of prayer. The point is that the hour of prayer was also the hour of sacrifice: Ps. 141.2 and Luke 1.10 indicate that the offering of incense was seen as occasion for prayer, and the offering of incense was itself part of the morning and evening sacrificial ritual.[4] (2) The fact that the instruction of Matt. 5.23–4 was retained within what was probably a catechetical manual, or simply a collection of Jesus' teaching for the continued guidance of his disciples' conduct (Matt. 5–7), likewise indicates a continued use of the provision for offering and sacrifice in the cult on the part of those who preserved that

---

2. See above §§3.4, 3.5.

3. It is difficult to see 'the great commission' as given out in its present form at the time indicated (Matt. 28.18–20). Or was it ignored so completely as Luke implies? Certainly the evidence of the rest of the NT indicates that the baptismal formula in the three-fold name is a later elaboration (all the Christian baptisms referred to in the NT were 'in the name of Jesus'). So the words of the commission reflect a later perception of the missionary task, and it becomes impossible to say what its original impulse was; see e.g. the discussion in B. J. Hubbard, *The Matthean Redaction of a Primitive Apostolic Commissioning: An Exegesis of Matthew 28.16–20*, SBLDS 19; Missoula: SBL 1974; also below n. 61. What weight Matt. 28.18–20 has against the testimony of Acts 1–5, if any, is therefore incapable of computation. See further below §7.1.

4. Schürer, 2.302–7.

teaching.[5] (3) According to the later account of Acts 21.24, the Jerusalem believers expected Paul to demonstrate his loyalty to the Temple by observing the prescribed purificatory rituals. Presumably they shared in some degree at least the attitude expressed in Acts 21.28 – the Temple a 'holy place' still to be kept free from impurity. And according to Acts 21.26 Paul did indeed take part in the purification rites, completed by 'the sacrifice offered for each one of them'. (4) The very fact that the first believers remained in Jerusalem presumably carries with it the same implication: since the Temple was the primary reason for Jerusalem's continued existence and status, the only reason why they would stay in Jerusalem was to be near the Temple and to participate in its services and benefits.[6] The logic of any significant degree of criticism of the Temple was already clear in the case of Jesus (death)[7] and the Qumran Essenes (departure from Jerusalem). Conversely, a decision to stay in Jerusalem could hardly be other than an affirmation of *continued identification* with Jerusalem and the Temple cult.

(c) There is a striking absence in the early speeches and sermons of Acts of the theology of the cross so prominent later. The historical fact of Jesus having been killed is mentioned, of course; but it is not interpreted soteriologically, or in terms of sacrifice (Acts 2.23, 36; 3.13–15; 4.10; 5.27–8; see also 7.52; 10.39; 13.27–8). Insofar as anything is made of the reference, it is to highlight the responsibility of those who put Jesus to death and God's consequent vindication. There are some possible allusions to Jesus as the Servant of Yahweh (3.13, 26; 4.27, 30); but they function to emphasize the theme of vindication following suffering, not of vicarious suffering as such. Similarly the allusions to Deut. 21.22–3 in Acts 5.30 and 10.39 indicate more the shame and disgrace of crucifixion, and are quite undeveloped in comparison with the more elaborate theology of Paul in Gal. 3.13.[8]

How much of this motif in the Acts speeches is a reflection of

---

5. Contrast L. Goppelt, *Theology of the New Testament. Vol. 1. The Ministry of Jesus in its Theological Significance*, 1975; ET Grand Rapids: Eerdmans 1981: Matt. 5.23 'did not presuppose that Jesus' disciples continued to offer gifts in the temple; it had a purely metaphorical quality' (p. 96). That however is a quite arbitrary judgment and runs counter to the other evidence cited by Goppelt on the same page.

6. 'The notion that the temple should serve some function other than sacrifice would seem to be extremely remote from the thinking of a first-century Jew' (Sanders, *Jesus*, p. 64).

7. See above §3.6.

8. See E. Kränkl, *Jesus der Knecht Gottes*, Regensburg 1972, p. 102–29; and below §7.2.

Luke's theology is very hard to tell. In this respect the weakness of the Lukan parallel to Mark 10.45 should be noted (Luke 22.27 – 'I am among you as one who serves' – nothing of Mark's talk of Jesus' giving his life 'as a ransom for many'). It is also a striking fact that the more clearly sacrificial language of the last supper in Luke 22.19–20 and Acts 20.28 is caught up in some of the most difficult textual questions in Luke–Acts[9] – which suggests at least that the original text called forth some reworking for some reason (an inadequate theology of the cross?). Whatever the true facts of the matter, the absence of a clear theology of Jesus' death as sacrifice at this very earliest stage (according to Luke's account) is notable and strengthens the impression that Jesus' death at that time may not yet have been seen as a (vicarious) sacrifice which removed the need for any further cultic sacrifice.[10]

(*d*) Here we might mention also the significance of the fact that the earliest Jerusalem community differed from the community at Qumran. The *parallels* were noted early on[11] – a consciously eschatological sect, a vivid experience of the Spirit, a community of goods, in particular. But on this point the *differences* are even more marked. (1) For one thing, the Qumran covenanters had abandoned Jerusalem and the Temple in Jerusalem; whereas, as already noted, the sect of the Nazarenes seem to have stayed firmly fixed in Jerusalem. (2) For another, Qumran was a priestly community, evincing a clear sense of functioning as an alternative to the corrupted cult of Jerusalem.[12] Whereas there is no indication of such a self-understanding and practice among the first Christians; no hint of the priests who joined them (Acts 6.7) functioning as priests within the house churches or groups; no hint of the twelve having priestly functions with regard to the rest

---

9. On the former see B. M. Metzger, *A Textual Commentary on the Greek New Testament*, London/New York: United Bible Societies 1975, pp. 173–7; on the latter see J. H. Ropes, *The Beginnings of Christianity. Part I. The Acts of the Apostles*, ed. F. J. Foakes-Jackson and K. Lake, *Vol. 3. The Text of Acts*, London: Macmillan 1928, pp. 197–9.

10. The early formula quoted in I Cor. 5.3–5 ('that Christ died for our sins') can not be counted as firm evidence for the views of the first Palestinian believers, since it was probably formulated in Greek, with semitic influence coming through the LXX. So H. Conzelmann argues strongly; see e.g. his *I Corinthians* 1969; ET Hermeneia; Philadelphia: Fortress 1975, pp. 252–4. See also below §4.5h.

11. See particularly the essays by O. Cullmann, 'The Significance of the Qumran Texts for Research into the Beginnings of Christianity', pp. 18–32, and S. E. Johnson, 'The Dead Sea Manual of Discipline and the Jerusalem Church of Acts', pp. 129–42, in K. Stendahl (ed.), *The Scrolls and the New Testament*, London: SCM Press 1958. See also (*e*) below.

12. See above ch. 3, p. 42 and below ch. 6, pp. 147–8.

of the believers as 'laity'.[13] There is nothing in all this to imply a divorce between the earliest Jerusalem church and the Temple. (3) We might perhaps add that the closest contemporary model of the form of teacher-taught relationship which characterized Jesus' disciples was probably provided by the Pharisees.[14] Just as the closest model for the form of communal meeting of the first believers was presumably the synagogue. At any rate, the subsequent pattern of leadership in the Jerusalem church was almost certainly modelled on the pattern of the community synagogue/'house of meeting': the ruler of the synagogue – James, the brother of Jesus (Acts 12.17; 15.13; Gal. 2.9); surrounded by the elders of the community (Acts 11.30; 15.2, 4, 6, 22–3; 16.4; 21.18).[15] The point is that neither Pharisees nor synagogues were at odds with the Temple, so that what would appear as the Nazarene equivalents would imply no kind of breach with the Temple.

(e) All this remains true even though the earliest church in Jerusalem may already have regarded itself as in effect the eschatological temple of God, the eschatological assembly of God's people ('the church of God')[16] – at this point at least sharing an eschatological self-consciousness with the Qumran community.[17] Such a conclusion is suggested by Paul's reference in Gal. 2.9 to James, Cephas and John as 'pillars'. The word is most frequently used in the LXX in reference to the supports of the tabernacle and pillars of the temple. Particularly notable are the twin pillars set up in front of Solomon's temple (I Kings 7.15–22; II Chron. 3.15–17), named Jachin and Boaz, which evidently had a covenant significance (II Kings 23.3; II Chron. 34.31) about which we know nothing.[18] It is likely then that the reference here is to the three as 'pillars in the temple' (as in Rev. 3.12); of what or where else would they be 'pillars'?

---

13. If Matthew reflects anything of this earliest period (as he presumably does in such passages as Matt. 10.5–6 and 15.24), we should not make too much of Matt. 16.19 at this point, since Matthew also makes a point of formulating 'the community rule' of Matt. 18 in the broadest terms as referring to 'the disciples'/'brothers'/'the church'.

14. Though see particularly M. Hengel, *The Charismatic Leader and his Followers*, 1968; ET Edinburgh: T. & T. Clark 1981.

15. Note that the elders would be elders of the community, and elders in relation to the synagogue precisely because the synagogue was the meeting place for the community. There is no need then to look to the superior (*mebaqqer*) and council of the Qumran community as the model for James and his circle of elders.

16. 'I persecuted the church of God' (I Cor. 15.9; Gal. 1.13; cf. Phil. 3.6) has something of a formulaic ring, probably reflecting a well established self-understanding of the earliest Jerusalem (or Judaean) church(es).

17. See again above ch. 3 p. 50.

18. See *IDB*, 2.780–1.

C. K. Barrett is probably correct in the further suggestion that the reference was eschatological:[19] this would tie in with the speculation regarding the destruction and reconstitution of the Temple already noted, in which Jesus was remembered as being caught up;[20] and it would certainly accord with the self-understanding shared by such as Paul, Hebrews and I Peter later on.[21] That is to say, James, Cephas and John were probably regarded by the Jerusalem church as pillars of the eschatological temple of God's people, that is, as the main support on which their own community was built. But even that self-perception does not seem to have made any difference to their adherence to Jerusalem and its cult. It is precisely at this point that contrast with the Qumran sect comes once again to the fore: whereas Qumran's self-perception of themselves as a priestly community led them to distance themselves from the Temple,[22] the first Christians did not stir from Jerusalem or set themselves up in opposition to the Temple.

We must conclude therefore that *the continuing function of the Jerusalem Temple was not an issue for the first Christians.*

4.2 What about the Hellenists?

The Hellenists are important for our inquiry precisely because they confront us with the issue of the Temple's significance. We first meet them, rather abruptly, in Acts 6.1 – 'Now in these days when the disciples were increasing in number, the Hellenists murmured against the Hebrews because their widows were neglected in the daily distribution.' That Luke delays in mentioning them till this point need not mean that they only appeared on the scene, within the group of believers in Jesus Messiah in Jerusalem, some time after the events related in Acts 1–5. The implication is that the problem outlined in Acts 6.1 had been boiling up for some time previous, presumably as a result of 'the disciples increasing in number'; but Luke has already reported that the audience for the first sermon on the day of Pentecost

---

19. C. K. Barrett, 'Paul and the "Pillar" Apostles', in *Studia Paulina in Honorem J. de Zwaan*, Haarlem: Bohn 1953, pp. 1–19.

20. See above §3.5. It is quite probable that Mark at least interpreted the prediction of which Jesus was accused in Mark 14.58 of a new community; see again Juel, *Messiah and Temple*. See also below §4.5b.

21. See below ch. 5.

22. Cullmann p. 21 and Johnson pp. 133–4 (Stendahl, *Scrolls*) noted the parallel between 1QS 8.1–4 (twelve men and three priests among the leadership of the community) and the twelve including (?) three 'pillars' of the earliest Christian community. But once again it is more significant here that James, Peter and John were *not* priests.

consisted in peoples 'from every nation under heaven' (2.5), and he goes on to date the initial increase in number of the first church to that same day (2.41). So the progression implied between chapters 1–5 and chapter 6 may be as much if not more editorial than historically sequential. And the following analysis makes no presuppositions regarding historical development, but simply follows Luke's own progression.

The word translated 'Hellenists' means basically 'Greek speakers'.[23] But we have already noted that Greek was the international language of the day, and that most residents of the main cities in Palestine would have been able to use and understand Greek in some measure.[24] So the other group in Acts 6.1, the 'Hebrews', could probably also speak some Greek; this was certainly the case with Paul who calls himself a 'Hebrew' in the only two other occurrences of the word in the NT (II Cor. 11.22; Phil. 3.5). Which suggests that the Hellenists were so called primarily because they could speak *only* Greek. Whereas native Jews living in Jerusalem could at least 'get by' in Greek, even though their main language was Aramaic, the Hellenists were distinguished by the fact that Greek was their only language of communication.[25]

This in turn suggests that in the case of the Hellenists we are dealing more or less exclusively with Jews from the diaspora, since that fact alone would explain their distinctively 'Hellenistic' character. Here we should bear in mind that the majority of Jews at this time lived in the diaspora, particularly in Mesopotamia, Egypt, Syria, Asia Minor and Rome itself;[26] for all but the first of whom Greek must have been the primary if not exclusive language of communication. It would be wholly natural that a fair number of them should wish to return to Jerusalem and to settle there, because they were Jews first and foremost, and 'Hellenists' only secondly. This suggestion, likely in itself, is substantiated in some measure by Acts 6.9, which speaks of a (or possibly more than one) synagogue in Jerusalem of the Freedmen, and of the Cyrenians, Alexandrians,[27] and those of Cilicia and Asia.

---

23. LSJ and BAGD, *hellēnistēs*.

24. See above §1.3(b).

25. See particularly C. F. D. Moule, 'Once More, Who Were the Hellenists?' *ExpT* 70 (1958–59), pp. 100–2; M. Hengel, *Between Jesus and Paul*, 1975; ET London: SCM Press 1983, pp. 4–11; R. Pesch, ' "Hellenisten" und "Hebräer". Zu Apg 9.29 und 6.1', *BZ* 23 (1979), pp. 87–92.

26. See again Schürer, 3.3–5 and ch. 2 n. 5 above.

27. Most likely a single synagogue is in view, identified by the fact that it was used mainly by returnees from three of the main areas of Jewish dispersion – Rome (see nn. 26 and 28), Alexandrians (Philo, *Flacc.* 43 – not less than a million Jews in Alexandria and Egypt) and Cyrenians (I Macc. 15.23; Mark 15.21; Acts 11.20).

The 'freedmen' were probably the Jews enslaved by Pompey when he captured Jerusalem in 63 BCE and/or their offspring.[28]

At this point the evidence can lead in different directions. On the one hand, the word 'Hellenist' would probably in and of itself carry a pejorative note for any devout Jew who recalled with pride the Maccabean defence and reaffirmation of the distinctiveness of Israel's election and covenant responsibilities.[29] The very fact that the Hellenists could speak or function effectively only in Greek is sufficient to indicate how much they must have been influenced by Hellenistic culture (language as the expression and vehicle of culture). It is likely then that the name itself betokens some suspicion, particularly when set over against 'Hebrews' (cf. again Phil. 3.5), as to the covenant loyalty of such 'Hellenizing' or 'Hellenized' Jews.[30] Did such a Jew keep the law? Did such a Jew maintain adequately the boundaries which marked off Jew from Gentile (food laws, sabbath, etc.)? And in particular, could such a Jew do enough to maintain the centrality of the Temple, in tithing, in sacrifices, in observing the pilgrim feasts?

On the other hand, we know that many, if not most diaspora Jews did remain devout. We have already noted that the temple tax invovled a major transfer of resources from the diaspora to Judaea, for which the Romans made unusual provision. And we know from Philo and Josephus that pilgrimage from the diaspora was popular (Philo, *Spec. Leg.* 1.69; Josephus, *War* 2.14). More to the point in this case, many if not most of the Hellenists of Acts 6.1 were precisely those who had returned to Jerusalem to settle there; despite the fact that as freemen they would be Roman citizens,[31] even so they had chosen to return to Jerusalem. That must indicate a level of devotion to the Temple of which we still have visible testimony in the many graves located in the vicinity of the Temple. Yet, at the same time, their ability to function only in Greek must have left them at a disadvantage so far as full participation in the Temple cult was concerned; and the reference to the synagogue in Acts 6.9 presumably indicates that that was the primary focus of their gatherings (where Greek would be used as the common language) for prayer and Torah reading(?).[32]

---

28. Schürer, 3.133.

29. So M. Simon, *St Stephen and the Hellenists in the Primitive Church*, London: Longmans 1958, pp. 12–13. On the importance of the Maccabean crisis in forging the character of 'Judaism' see above ch. 2.

30. It is precisely the antithesis between 'Hellenism' (II Macc. 4.13) and 'Judaism' (II Macc. 2.21; 8.1; etc.) which marks out II Maccabees.

31. Schürer, 3.132–3.

32. Cf. Hengel, *Between*, pp. 14, 25–9.

All this is in effect simply to set the scene for the Stephen affair. We do not need to go in here to the questions of what precisely was the issue indicated in Acts 6.1, of whether all the seven chosen were Hellenists (6.3–6), and what their status was vis-à-vis 'the apostles', the rest of the Hellenists and the rest of the Christian community. The one point which should be noted, however, is that the 'Hebrews' and 'Hellenists' of whom Luke speaks (6.1) all belonged to the community of the Jesus 'sect'. The implication of some tension between them (an almost unavoidable implication when just these two words are set in contrast) is therefore an implication that *on the side of the (Christian) Hebrews there was likely to be some of the same suspicion outlined above regarding the (Christian) Hellenists' faithfulness to the covenant distinctives, including the Temple.*[33]

4.3 A community divided over the Temple

However, the events leading up to the trial of Stephen swing the readers' attention away from the Christian community to the larger Hellenist community (6.8ff.). Although Luke uses 'Hellenist' only of the Christian Greek-speakers, it is sufficiently clear that they were part of a more substantial Greek-speaking community 'who belonged to the synagogue(s) of the freedmen, etc.' (6.9). Evidently some of this larger Hellenist group had come to believe in Jesus as Messiah and been baptized in his name. We may envisage not a little disquiet within this larger Hellenist community at so many of their members, including perhaps some of their finest younger members, becoming members also of the 'sect' of the Nazarene. And Stephen seems to have been very active in promoting his new loyalty, at least according to Luke's account (6.8, 10).

What caused the trouble within this larger Hellenist community was evidently that Stephen, in preaching his new faith, spoke out against the Temple. According to Luke the complaint brought against Stephen was that he 'spoke blasphemous words against Moses and God' (6.11). Or in the fuller terms of the charge on which he was indicted, 'This man never ceases to speak words against this holy place and the law; for we have heard him say that this Jesus of Nazareth will destroy this place, and will change the customs which Moses delivered to us' (6.14). The echo of the charge against Jesus is striking (Mark 14.58 par.). We have already observed that Jesus must have said something about the destruction of the

---

33. See also my *Unity*, pp. 268–75.

Temple.[34] Also that the echo here is clearly not intended merely to highlight a parallel between Stephen and Jesus, since Luke has no equivalent to Mark 14.58 in the trial of Jesus. The more likely explanation of the echo is that it occurred in Stephen's preaching and that it was picked out by his accusers for the same reason that the equivalent charge had been brought against Jesus. In other words, *Stephen seems to have seized upon that emphasis in Jesus' teaching with regard to the Temple which was the substance of the case against Jesus* (Mark 14.58), and this caused sufficient hostility within the larger Hellenist community as to result in Stephen's arrest and summary trial.[35] The other elements in the accusations of 6.11 and 14 are consistent with *an issue focussing more or less exclusively on the Temple*, since the law of Moses and 'customs' which grew upon its basis were so largely concerned with the regulation of the Temple cult.[36]

All this points to something of a split within the larger Hellenist community itself, or at least a deepening crisis over the views held by some within the larger Hellenist groupings in Jerusalem. If Greek-speaking Jews had returned from the diaspora to Jerusalem, one of the principal reasons for them doing so, as we have already indicated, would be to locate themselves near Mount Zion, where God had put his name. For such Hellenists Stephen's line of argument or preaching would be highly provocative, offending, as it must inevitably have done, against one of their central beliefs and motivations. To diminish the significance of the Temple was to undercut their whole reason for being in Jerusalem in the first place.[37]

It may not be too fanciful to see here a hint of what we today might call a generation split. Those who had returned to Jerusalem would probably be older, perhaps having spent their accumulated savings in order to return to the centre of the holy land of promise. Stephen, on the other hand, may well have belonged to a younger element; perhaps somewhat resentful at being brought by their elders to what they might well regard as a cultural backwater (in Hellenist terms at least); perhaps also in Stephen's case somewhat headstrong and outspoken

---

34. See above §3.5. The fact that Luke also reports it as a false accusation (cf. Mark 14.58) suggests that the tradition of such hostility to the Temple was a source of some embarrassment to the Evangelists.

35. See e.g. Simon, *Stephen*, pp. 95–6; G. Lüdemann, *Early Christianity according to the Traditions in Acts*, London: SCM Press/Philadelphia: Fortress 1989, pp. 81–5.

36. It is assumed far too readily that Stephen 'criticized the law' as such and was so accused (see e.g. Lüdemann in n. 35). But see also below §§4.5e, 7.2 and further my *Jesus, Paul and the Law*, particularly pp. 91–3.

37. Cf. P. F. Esler, *Community and Gospel in Luke–Acts. The Social and Political Motivations of Lucan Theology*, SNTSMS 57; Cambridge University 1987, pp. 139–48.

on behalf of his new commitment, with the enthusiasm of the new and young convert. That is all, of course highly speculative; but it is consistent with and makes good sense of the evidence which we possess, such as it is.

The most significant feature of the episode, however, is that *it was the Temple, not a claim regarding the messiahship of Jesus as such which led to the hostility against Stephen*. Evidently to claim that Jesus was Messiah was not regarded as a matter requiring strong counter measures; the Hebrew believers were left largely unmolested, according to Acts 1–5. So too the evidence of Greek cultural influence was not something too serious in itself; Hellenism was too widespread throughout Palestine for 'Hellenists' as such to arouse much comment. But the combination of the two, Hellenists who believed in Jesus, was something different and proved in the event to be an explosive mixture. And when the new teaching was directed against the Temple, the warning lights started to flash. The larger community of Hellenists had invested too much in the Temple to allow any kind of radical criticism of the cult to go unchallenged; and the larger circle of the inhabitants of Jerusalem, including the high priests, depended on the Temple too much in economic and political as well as religious terms to sit idly by in such circumstances. Even the larger community of those baptized in the name of Jesus can hardly have been very pleased, if the fact that they are identified precisely as 'Hebrews' is anything to go by.

This brings us to the evidence of Acts 7.

4.4 Stephen's defence

Can Acts 7 be used as evidence for Stephen's views or for the views of those of the Hellenist group who believed in Messiah Jesus? The point is much disputed. (1) There is no question that the speech has at least been worked over by Luke; the marks of his style are clear and not in doubt.[38] On the other hand, the content of the speech is quite distinctive. It has no real parallel elsewhere in Acts.[39] More important,

38. See J. Kilgallen, *The Stephen Speech*, (AnBib 67; Rome: Biblical Institute, 1976); E. Richard, *Acts 6.1–8.4. The Author's Method of Composition*, SBLDS 41; Missoula: Scholars 1978.

39. It is noticeable that many of the generalizations made about the speeches in Acts depend on a comparison limited to those containing overt missionary proclamation; i.e., omitting reference to the speeches of Acts 7 and 17. See e.g. U. Wilckens, *Die Missionsreden der Apostelgeschichte*, WMANT; Neukirchen: Neukirchener, ²1963; E. Schweizer, 'Concerning the Speeches in Acts', *Studies in Luke–Acts*, ed. L. E. Keck and J. L. Martyn, Nashville: Abingdon/London: SPCK 1966, pp. 208–16.

Luke's attitude to the Temple elsewhere in Luke-Acts is very positive: as noted earlier, the Gospel begins and ends in the Temple (Luke 1.8ff.; 24.52); so does his account of the first believers in Acts 1–5 (2.46; 5.42); and later on he almost bends over backwards to show Paul in a conciliatory mood towards the Temple (21.26; 22.17; 24.12, 18; 25.8).[40] So the sharp critique of the Temple in the speech attributed to Stephen, as we shall see, is less likely to be simply Luke's creation or expressive of his own more conciliatory attitude, and is best explained as an emphasis which Luke has drawn from his source.[41]

(2) It is sometimes said that the speech of ch. 7 does not fit well with its context, as being for the most part irrelevant as an answer to the charge levelled against Stephen (6.14).[42] But this is a serious misreading of the speech, as we shall also see.

(3) In fact the character and content of chs 6–8 are all of a piece and strongly support the suggestion that Luke has drawn the material from some Hellenistic source, oral or written. In the case of the speech itself, all we need suppose is that it represents Hellenist teaching, perhaps a Hellenist tract, used by them to explain the views which had caused their expulsion from Jerusalem (8.4; 11.19). In which case, if Stephen was a leading Hellenist, the speech could be regarded as a fair representation of his own views. The historiography of the time would require no more, and the question of whether Stephen had actually spoken these words on the occasion narrated would simply not arise for the typical reader of Acts. It would be quite sufficient that the speech expressed what Stephen would or could have said, whether in the event he was able to do so or not.[43] For our present purposes we need assume no more than that.

The speech itself contains two main themes: (*i*) the rejection of the Temple as the focal point of God's presence and purpose; (*ii*) the

---

40. See further particularly M. Bachmann, *Jerusalem und der Tempel. Die geographisch-theologischen Elemente in der lukanischen Sicht des jüdischen Kultzentrums*, Stuttgart: Kohlhammer 1980, with bibliography; J. B. Chance, *Jerusalem, the Temple, and the New Age in Luke-Acts*, Macon, Georgia: Mercer 1988.

41. See e.g. G. Lüdemann, *Acts*, p. 88; R. Pesch, *Die Apostelgeschichte*, EKK V; Zürich: Benziger/Neukrichen: Neukirchener 1986, Vol. 1, pp. 244–7.

42. Particularly M. Dibelius, *Studies in the Acts of the Apostles*, ET London: SCM Press 1956, pp. 167–9; E. Haenchen, *The Acts of the Apostles*, 1965; ET Oxford: Blackwell 1971, p. 286.

43. This seems to be the most sensible way to evaluate the evidence discussed in such treatments of the theme as H. J. Cadbury, *The Making of Luke-Acts*, 1927; London: SPCK 1958, pp. 184–90; Dibelius, *Studies*, pp. 138–85. See again n. 35.

rejection of Jesus as the climax of the repeated rejection of God's messengers.[44] Here we need deal only with the first.

At first glance the speech appears to be a straight recital of Israel's history – hence the misunderstanding already alluded to (2). But that is far from being the case. The following points should be noted. (*a*) The bulk of the speech deals with the period of Israel's history prior to the building of the Temple. And a consistent emphasis in the first half, as becomes more apparent when the speech is read as a whole, is that *the presence of God in Israel's history had not been restricted to one land or building*. Thus in the case of Abraham: God revealed himself to Abraham outside the promised land, 'when he was in Mesopotamia, before he lived in Haran' (v. 2); although promised the land for his posterity, in the event God 'gave him no inheritance in it, not even a foot's length' (v. 5), and told him that 'his posterity would be aliens in a land belonging to others' (v. 6). So too Joseph: 'God was with him' – in Egypt (v. 9). So too Jacob: Jacob's burial was in Shechem, in Samaria (v. 16), *not* in Hebron (despite Gen. 49.29–32; 50.13)[45] – that is, outside Judaea. And so also and not least Moses: he spent all his life outside the promised land (vv. 29, 36); God's angel appeared to him far from the land of promise (vv. 30ff.), the 'holy ground' on which he met God being outside Palestine, having no temple or altar. These points are not given much if any emphasis, of course, but for the speech to have picked on just these elements in the much fuller account of God's dealings with the patriarchs is hardly likely to have been an accident. On the contrary, the history of Israel's retelling its own story is itself a history of reassessment, of nuance and redaction.[46]

(*b*) In the second half of the speech the emphasis switches more to the subject of Israel's worship. The first point of emphasis is that the wilderness period had a nearly ideal form of worship: they had Moses, who had received the revelation of Mount Sinai; they had the *ekklesia*, the word used in the LXX for the assembly of Israel, but taken over by the Christians to become 'church'; they had the angel of God's presence; they had the 'living oracles'; all this was theirs before they

---

44. I gladly acknowledge my indebtedness here to the treatment by Simon, *Stephen*.

45. For the possibility of Samaritan influence on the Stephen tradition see e.g. C. H. H. Scobie, 'The Origins and Development of Samaritan Christianity', *NTS* 19 (1972–73), pp. 390–414, particularly pp. 391–8; J. Coggins, 'The Samaritans and Acts', *NTS* (1982), pp. 423–34; disputed e.g. by R. Pummer, 'The Samaritan Pentateuch and the New Testament', *NTS* 22 (1975–76), pp. 441–3; E. Richard, 'Acts 7. An Investigation of the Samaritan Evidence', *CBQ* 39 (1977), pp. 190–208.

46. In so doing, of course, Stephen/Luke follow a well trodden path, with such prominent predecessors as the books of Chronicles.

reached the promised land (v. 38). In sharpest contrast, from that point on, Israel's history had been one of frighteningly swift decline: they had rejected that pure worship of the wilderness period for tangible idolatry (vv. 40–41); and then in a remarkable jump, the speech proceeds immediately to draw a direct line of apostasy, from the tangible idolatry of the golden calf in the wilderness (v. 41), to the worship of the planetary powers, the 'host of heaven' (v. 42), which any Jew would know had been the reason for the Exile (vv. 42–3 – Amos 5.25–27). Not to be missed is the implication that *the whole sweep of Israel's time within the promised land itself was embraced within these two periods of blatant apostasy.*

(*c*) In the next few verses the point begins to become clear, the point being one of sharp contrast between the earlier, better days when Israel's focus and medium of worship was the tent of the wilderness period, and the days of the Temple, itself expressive of that decline. 'The tent of witness in the wilderness', made by Moses in accordance with God's direction, 'according to the pattern that he had seen' (Ex. 25.9, 40), had been brought in to the promised land, and remained the focus and medium of Israel's worship right up to and throughout the reign of David, 'who found favour in the sight of God', Israel's golden age (vv. 44–46). But David had *not* been permitted to build a temple; it was Solomon who did so (vv. 46–47).

'Yet the Most High does not dwell in houses made with hands' (v. 48). This last would be the most shocking feature of the Hellenist exposition. The adjective chosen, *cheiropoiēton*, 'made with hands', would be a horrifying word to use in this context. Why so? Because that was the word used by Hellenistic Jews to condemn idolatry, just this word summing up the typically dismissive Jewish polemic that Gentile gods were human artifacts, 'made with hands'. The idol was by definition *to cheiropoiēton*, 'the thing made by human hands';[47] an implication which any Greek speaking Jew, and Luke too, could not mistake, since the word had already been used with this disparaging overtone in v. 41 (cf. also 17.24). For just that word to be used *of the Temple* would certainly have sent shock waves through any Jewish audience or readership – the Temple itself a breach of that most fundamental axiom of Israelite/Jewish religion, that God's presence cannot be encapsulated or represented in any physical or man-made entity! – *the Temple itself an idol!* A proper parallel would be if an Englishman claimed that the Queen was illegitimate.

But the speech is not yet finished. In vv. 49–50 there follows

---

47. See LXX of Lev. 26.1, 30; Isa. 2.18; 10.11; 16.12; 19.1; 21.9; 31.7; 46.6; Dan. 5.4, 23; 6.27; Judith 8.18; Wisd.Sol. 14.8.

immediately a quotation from Isa. 66.1–2, one of the strongest critiques of a false evaluation of the Temple in the whole of Jewish scripture:

> Heaven is my throne, and earth my footstool.
> What house will you build for me, says the Lord,
>   or what is the place of my rest?
> Did not my hand make all these things?

Although the text, taken within the sweep of the prophetic critique of the cult, would have caused little problem for devout Jews and only stimulated them to proper use of the cult, coming as it does immediately after the description of the Temple as an idol, it takes on a much more negative tone and would add insult to injury. The Temple was so central for Jewish worship and Jewish identity, and the speech's attack, at first so subtle, but latterly so blatant and so blunt . . .[48] Anyone who put forward these views, and in Jerusalem (rather than from the safety of, say, Qumran or Leontopolis),[49] must have enraged a Jewish audience beyond bearing.

The rest of the story is well known and need not be repeated here.

4.5 The significance of the Stephen affair

If then we may assume that Stephen was indicted on a charge of speaking against the Temple (Acts 6.11, 14), and if the speech of Acts 7 can be taken as sufficiently representative of his views, both of which certainly seem to make best sense of the evidence, we can draw a number of conclusions from the Stephen episode which are directly relevant to our inquiry.

(a) Above all for us, *Stephen marks the beginning of a radical critique of the Temple on the part of the infant Christian movement.* Even if we have to qualify that conclusion and talk more generally of the Hellenists (rather than of Stephen in particular), or even if we can talk only of a tradition to that effect (without drawing such clear-cut historical conclusions), the point is the same in effect. Second- or third-generation Christianity looked back to Stephen and the Hellenists as *the beginning of the breach* between Christianity and the predominant Temple-centred Judaism of the mid-first century.

---

48. W. Schmithals, *Paul and James*, 1963; ET London: SCM Press 1965, p. 21 fails to appreciate the sharpness of the attack. See also S. G. Wilson, *The Gentiles and the Gentile Mission in Luke-Acts*, SNTSMS 23; Cambridge University 1973, pp. 148–50.

49. See above p. 34.

(*b*) Since the Hellenist Christians would have been unable to join in the prayers which were said in the Temple, they probably no longer attended the Temple (whether as a result of their baptism in the name of Jesus or before, we cannot now tell). The focus of their liturgical life was probably exclusively in the house churches, functioning as the Christian Hellenist equivalent or supplement to the synagogue of the freedmen (6.9), where Greek alone was used.[50] This would be in contrast to the Hebrews who, as we have seen (§4.1), seem to have functioned liturgically in the Temple as well as in the house churches. This presumably means also that *the sacrificial system* (for which the Temple existed) *had ceased to be used or to be meaningful for the Christian Hellenists* – once again in some contrast with the Hebrews. The life-style might not be all that different, but for Jews living in Jerusalem the transition in attitude and perspective regarding the means by which human beings related to God would have been profound, even if only beginning to be worked out (see below (*h*)).

(*c*) Stephen seems to have seen significance in a particular strand of Jesus' teaching, regarding the Temple, which had apparently been largely ignored by the other Jerusalem disciples. Up to this point the first followers of Jesus evidently had emphasized those elements in Jesus' teaching which brought out the *continuity* of that teaching with their Jewish heritage, and thus had lived, as members of the sect of the Nazarene, in faithful observance of Temple cult and law. But Stephen highlighted an element of potential *dis*-continuity and had developed it in a controversial way. Not least of the importance of Stephen's contribution, then, is that without him, such elements of Jesus' teaching might have been submerged and lost sight of, with Jesus remembered simply as a teacher and reformer *within* Judaism. Equally important for Christian self-understanding and apologetic is the fact that the impulse for such a radical critique can be traced back to a tradition of Jesus' teaching.

(*d*) In Stephen we see the beginning of the interaction between the Jesus-tradition and the traditions of diaspora Judaism, the beginning of the process of translating and thus interpreting the gospel into hellenistic terms. In this case the most striking feature is the use of the distinctively Hellenistic Jewish word, *cheiropoiētos*. Here we should simply note that in Mark's version of the accusation against Jesus (Mark 14.58), which is precisely the accusation then brought against Stephen, the same word is used – Jesus remembered as saying, 'I will destroy this temple *which is made with hands* and after three days

---

50. See above at nn. 25, 27.

I will build another *not made with hands*'. What is perhaps significant is that Matthew's version omits precisely these two words, *cheiropoiē-ton* and *acheiropoiēton* (Matt. 26.61). Since Matthew often seems to omit Markan phrases which he knows to be Markan elaborations of the common tradition,[51] it is likely that the same is true in this case. That is to say, we may already see in Mark's version of the charge concerning the Temple, evidence of the influence of the Hellenist re-expression of what Jesus had originally said into Greek.[52] The transposition of Jesus' teaching on the Temple into Greek language and Hellenistic categories helped to make the Temple an issue between Christian and Jew, as probably also in some measure between Christian (Hebrews) and Christian (Hellenists).

(*e*) We should not over-emphasize the extent of Stephen's critique of the Judaism of his time. The speech of Acts 7, Hellenistic tract or whatever, does not attack the law, apart, that is, from the law as it would have been seen to be integrated with the Temple.[53] The speech in fact gives considerable prominence to Moses and holds him in high regard: his was 'the time of the promise' (v. 17); he was 'beautiful before God' (v. 20); he was 'instructed in all the wisdom of the Egyptians, and he was mighty in his words and deeds' (v. 22);[54] he knew that 'God was giving them (his brothers) deliverance by his hand' (v. 25); and so on. Likewise the law is spoken of in the most positive of terms: it consists of 'living oracles' (v. 38); it was 'delivered by angels' (v. 53) – here a positive description (cf. vv. 30, 35, 38);[55] the problem identified in the speech's climax is not the law, but Israel's failure to keep it (v. 53). In short, the criticism contained in the speech is confined to the Temple, and the Temple as distinct from the tent of the wilderness, for which the legislation of the Pentateuch was actually designed. It is this fact which gives credibility to the view that Stephen was more a reformer than an apostate, that is, one who idealized the wilderness period of Israel's history and who wanted to get back to the discipline and relative purity of that period, back to

---

51. E.g. Mark 3.7–12, 20–21, 23a, 30.

52. That *cheiropoiēton* and *acheiropoiēton* are such interpretative additions is a matter of wide consensus; see e.g. Taylor, *Mark*, p. 566; R. Pesch, *Das Markusevangelium*, Band II, Frieburg: Herder 1977, p. 434.

53. The point is surprisingly often ignored; see above n. 36. But see S. G. Wilson, *Luke and the Law*, SNTSMS 50, Cambridge University 1983, pp. 61–3; Esler pp. 122–5.

54. The portrayal of Moses at this point is very comparable to the eulogizing of Moses which is a feature of much Hellenistic Jewish writing of history at this period; see above ch. 2, n. 40.

55. As in Deut. 33.2 LXX; *Jub* 1.29ff., Philo, *Som.* 1.143; Josephus, *Ant.* 15.136; Heb. 2.2. Gal. 3.19 is the exception.

first principles.[56] Of similar importance is the link made in the speech with the earlier prophetic critique of misplaced trust in the Temple. As a 'troubler of Israel' (I Kings 18.17) Stephen stood in a distinguished line. In other words, *for all the radicalness of his critique of the Temple, Stephen speaks still as a Jew eager to live within the terms actually laid down in the scriptures of his people.*[57]

(f) In so doing, however, he took a step towards a wider mission. It is indeed possible to argue that he did so consciously. Perhaps there is in the speech an implication that the new movement should be like Abraham – always on the move (vv. 2–4); like the *church* in the wilderness (v. 38); the mobile tent travelling with them as they journeyed, a superior sign of God's presence than a Temple 'made with hands'.[58] That may well be to read too much into the speech. But a criticism of the Temple in the terms used by the speech would soon have had the corollary effect of cutting the rope which, if we are right, had tied the first Christians so firmly to Jerusalem.[59] And such views as are attributed to Stephen in Acts 6–7 would certainly provide the possibility for a very crucial transition in the thought of the first Christians – from belief that God would convert Gentiles by bringing them *in* to worship in the Temple (the more traditional Jewish view),[60] to a recognition that God may actually want them to go *out* to the Gentiles.[61]

(g) Stephen's martyrdom led to the first major persecution of the infant church (Acts 8.1–4; 11.19). The combination of 'heterodox' belief about Jesus as Messiah, and radical criticism of the Temple, was evidently too much. It was this persecution, of course, which forced the new movement to look outward, whether willingly or no, whether by (fresh) conviction or no. It led directly to the mission outside Israel, to Samaria, to Antioch and then the Gentiles, as we shall see. But it also involved Paul in the persecution, as one of the devout diaspora Jews who tried to stamp out this disturbing set of beliefs from his fellow Hellenists, which led in turn to his conversion, with incalculable consequences for Christianity.

---

56. So particularly Simon, *Stephen*, pp. 46–7.

57. See also below ch. 8, pp. 212–13.

58. So particularly W. Manson, *The Epistle to the Hebrews*, London: Hodder & Stoughton 1951, ch. 2; L. D. Hurst, *The Epistle to the Hebrews. Its Background and Thought*, SNTSMS 65; Cambridge University 1990, ch. 4.

59. See above §4.1.

60. See above p. 77.

61. This would be the most natural setting for the decisive elaboration of the conviction contained in the great commission, that Jesus' apostles were being called by the risen Christ to 'Go and make disciples of all nations' (Matt. 28.19; cf. I Cor. 15.7); see above n. 3.

(*h*) In view of all the above, it becomes increasingly likely that it was with Stephen and the Hellenists that a theology of Jesus' death as a sacrifice which ends all sacrifice first emerged – one of the points of difference or of developing understanding of Jesus' death which marked this broadening out of the spectrum of infant Christianity. (1) Such a hypothesis would fit with the degree of divorce or estrangement from the Temple and its sacrificial system already noted (*b*). (2) We saw no clear indication of such a view already in the earliest Jerusalem church (the 'Hebrews'); whereas the Hellenists do seem to have developed Jesus' teaching in related areas in at least some measure ((*c*) and (*d*) above). (3) The only direct quotation from Isa. 53 in Acts appears on the lips of Philip, one of the Hellenists (Acts 8.32–33 = Isa. 53.7–8), and following the LXX. (4) As to the early tradition of I Cor. 15.3, 'that Christ died for our sins', Paul clearly indicates he learned this when he was first instructed in his new faith following his conversion. And that would presumably have been at the hands of the Hellenists whom he had been in the process of trying to persecute (those scattered abroad in the persecution following Stephen's execution – Acts 8.1–4; 9.1–2).[62] Moreover, the other early tradition of I Cor. 11.24, as we already noted, seems to be something of a development of the still earlier formula, a development evidently designed precisely to bring out the sacrificial and vicarious significance of Jesus' death.[63] (5) Finally, if there is anything in the suggestion of a link between Stephen and Hebrews (above (*f*)), then it is presumably significant that Hebrews is the most emphatic of all NT writings on the once-for-allness of Jesus' death, as a sacrifice ending all sacrifice.[64]

All in all, then, the contribution of Stephen and the Hellenists to the developing self-understanding and expression of Christian thought may have been much greater than even Luke's account indicates, and particularly in forcing the Nazarenes, or at least Hellenists among them, to reassess their attitude to the Temple. So far as the Temple is concerned, this major pillar of second Temple Judaism, *the Stephen episode marks the beginning of a clear parting of the ways*, between Christian and Jew, as also probably to some extent between 'Hebrew' Christian and 'Hellenist' Christian – at all events *the first*

---

62. It is generally agreed that it was the (Christian) Hellenists who were the primary, if not the almost exclusive focus of the persecution (by fellow Hellenists). See also above n. 10. Cf. M. D. Hooker, *Continuity and Discontinuity. Early Christianity in its Jewish Setting*, London: Epworth 1986: 'It is probable that the idea that Christ was the replacement of Jewish sacrifices was worked out as the result of being cut off from these sacrifices, rather than vice versa' (p. 14).

63. See above ch. 3, pp. 72–3.

64. See also below §5.6.

*rending of a major seam in a Judaism still best designated 'second
Temple Judaism'.*

4.6 The sequel

It is presumably significant, not least for our study, that *the issue of
the Temple and the Temple cult is the almost hidden counterpoint in
the succeeding narratives in Acts* – hidden, as not appearing on the
surface of the narratives, but not at all difficult for those well versed
in Jewish tradition and history to discern.

(*a*) *Philip's mission to Samaria (Acts 8.5–25).* Every Jew would
know well that a major, perhaps the major issue dividing Jew and
Samaritan, was the question of the Temple. The Samaritans had built
a temple on Mount Gerizim in the fourth century BCE with the
permission of their Persian overlords, on the basis of Gen. 22.2 and
Deut. 12.5 understood as a reference to Mount Gerizim, and as a
protest against the Jerusalem Temple's claim to be the one true sanctuary of Yahweh.[65] The dispute, its ongoing and fundamental character,
despite the fact that the Gerizim temple had been destroyed by John
Hyrcanus in about 128 BCE, is clearly reflected in John 4.20: the
'woman of Samaria' observes, 'Our fathers worshipped on this moun-
tain; and you say that in Jerusalem is the place where men ought to
worship'.[66]

The point, then, is that the free and unhindered acceptance of
Samaritans by the sect of the Nazarene would have been seen as a
sign of disregard for, even of disloyalty to the Jerusalem Temple and
the claims made for it by all the (other) main strands of second
Temple Judaism. Luke, it is true, does make a point of maintaining a
heilsgeschichtlich continuity between Jerusalem and the Samaritan
expansion, by showing how the Spirit was not given until Peter and
John came down from Jerusalem and laid hands on the new converts
(8.14–24). But in the narrative this continuity is established and maintained without any reference or allusion to the Temple whatsoever –
a fact whose significance is perhaps underlined by the concluding note
that Peter and John (the leading Hebrews as well as leading members

---

65. 'It was this contention (Schechem/Gerizim as the divinely ordained centre of Israel's
cultic life), not simply the existence of a Samaritan temple, which drove the permanent
wedge between the Samaritans and the Jews' (J. D. Purvis, 'The Samaritans and Judaism',
EJMI, pp. 81–98, here p. 89). The 'hatred' between the Samaritans and the Jews of that
period is illustrated by Josephus in *Ant.* 20.118–24; noted also by Tacitus, *Ann.* 12.54.

66. See further e.g. Schürer, 2.16–20. As Schürer and Purvis, pp. 90–5 note, part of
the current debate is as to whether the Samaritans should be regarded as a sect or group
within the diversity of Judaism.

of the sect as such) returned to Jerusalem preaching the gospel to many Samaritan villages (8.25).

(b) *Philip's conversion of the Ethiopian eunuch (Acts 8.26–40).* There is a particular irony in Luke's opening description of the Ethiopian eunuch and of the reason for his visit to Jerusalem, which no Jew would have missed. He 'had come to Jerusalem to worship' (8.27); but Deut. 23.1 makes it quite clear that a eunuch was prohibited from entering 'the assembly of the Lord'. The Ethiopian eunuch, therefore, is deliberately presented as one keen to share in the worship in Jerusalem, that is, in the Temple cult, but as debarred from doing so. Particularly significant in this connection is the fact that it is not his race or status which is the focus of Luke's narrative; rather it is his condition which is emphasized. After the initial identification ('an Ethiopian, a eunuch, a court official . . .' –8.27), he is referred to, and repeatedly so, simply as 'the eunuch' (8.34, 36, 38, 39).[67] The counterpoint is thus picked out clearly and would not have been missed by a Jewish auditor.[68]

The point then is that here we have another who was cut off from the worship of the Lord God by the laws regulating the Temple and the cult. It was precisely such a one, immediately following the breakthrough with the Samaritans, to whom Philip ministered. A clear implication is that the gospel was being extended beyond the limits allowed for in the Temple cult, and that in this way the breach with the Temple and its traditions was being widened still further. It is true, of course, that Isa. 56.3–5 looked for a day when eunuchs *would* be accepted within the Temple (so also Wisd.Sol. 3.14); and Luke no doubt saw Philip's mission as the fulfilment of this hope. The point, however, is that the breakthrough came as both Philip *and* the eunuch were moving out, *away from* Jerusalem and its Temple.[69]

(c) *The conversion of Paul (Acts 9.1–30).* Is it also significant in the same connection that Paul is represented as setting out to Damascus as the representative of and with the authority of the High Priest (9.1–2), despite the fact that Paul describes himself as a Pharisee and

---

67. The Greek word *eunouchos* can have the secondary sense of 'chamberlain'. But since his status is given by the title 'court official' (*dunastēs*), the term 'eunuch' must refer to his physical condition (BAGD, *eunouchos* 1). It would be taken for granted at that time that male attendants of a middle Eastern queen would include those who had been castrated. Three of Herod the Great's personal attendants had been eunuchs (Josephus, *War* 1.488; *Ant.* 16.230).

68. The hostility within Judaism towards eunuchs in the period of our concern is illustrated by Philo, *Spec.Leg.* 1.324–5 and Josephus, *Ant.* 4.290–1.

69. I am indebted to my pupil, F. S. Spencer, *The Portrait of Philip in Acts*, JSNTS 67, Sheffield: JSOT, 1992, pp. 185–7 for these observations.

is so described later in Acts (Acts 25.5; Phil. 3.5)? Perhaps we should conclude that it was precisely as agent of the cult and of the power represented by the cult that Paul was both persecutor and converted. There may also be some deliberate irony in the second account of Paul's conversion, in that Paul receives the confirmatory vision of his mission to the Gentiles precisely in the Temple (22.17–21). And the message is abrupt – to get out of Jerusalem: 'Depart; for I will send you far away to the Gentiles' (22.21). We may, of course, be reading in too much to Luke's account at these points. On the other hand, by setting the record of Paul's conversion immediately after ch. 8, Luke may have intended just such overtones to be picked up.

(d) *Peter's mission in the coastal plain (Acts 9.32–11.18)*. This is the last of the group of stories which provides a bridge back to the Hellenists, in Antioch (11.19ff.). The connecting thread in these records of Peter's mission is probably purity. That is certainly true in the case of Cornelius (10.10–16 and 11.5–10 – 'I have never eaten anything that is impure or unclean' . . . 'What God has cleansed you must not call impure'); an explicit note picked up in 10.28 ('God has shown me that I should not call any person impure or unclean'), and implied in the talk of the Spirit, baptism and cleansing (10.44–48; 15.9 – 'God cleansed their hearts by faith'). But the thread also probably ties in the episodes at the end of ch. 9 to the main theme of the Cornelius incident by describing Peter's host as 'Simon the tanner' (9.43; 10.6, 32).[70] Implicit here is a multiple breakthrough of various purity regulations or limits whose rationale in the last analysis was to preserve the sanctity of the cult. Above all is the striking lesson learned, that a Gentile, one who as such was debarred from entering closely to the presence of God in the Jerusalem Temple, was to be recognized as 'acceptable to him' (10.35), the distinction between Jew and Gentile epitomized by the cult no longer to be counted a factor (10.45–47; 11.12, 15–18; 15.8–9).

Here we might also observe the likely significance, in part at least, of Luke's omission of Mark's whole record of Jesus' teaching on purity (Mark 7.1–23), which for Mark clearly indicated the abrogation of the whole range of purity legislation (Mark 7.15, 19). The omission is closely parallel to Luke's omission of the charge against Jesus about the Temple in Mark 14.58.[71] The significance presumably

---

70. Tanning was an unpleasant and despised trade, regarded as a defect and ground for divorce, or to be kept at a distance, like corpses and graves (*m. Ketuboth* 7.10; *Baba Bathra* 2.9). Is it also significant that Luke only begins to speak of the Nazarenes as 'saints' in 9.13, 32, 41? – the analogy of cultic set-apartness being first evoked for those at some remove from Jerusalem and the cult.

71. See above pp. 66, 84–5.

lies in the fact that both have to do with the Temple cult, and its protecting purity laws. Luke evidently did not want to trace the breach between the new movement and the Temple at these crucial points back to Jesus. Since, unlike Mark, he had a second volume in view, he could leave the account of the breach with the Temple cult till these later points in his narrative. It was not until first the Stephen affair and then the conversion of Cornelius at the hands of Peter himself that the breach between Christianity and the Temple cult began to open up.

(e) *The Hellenists in Antioch (Acts 11.19–26)*. Perhaps it is not accidental therefore that when the narrative returns to the Hellenists and goes on to describe the breakthrough at Antioch, Luke also notes that it was precisely there, and following the introduction of Paul into the circle of leadership in the Antioch church, that the name 'Christians' first emerged. The implication, for those who have heard and followed the counterpoint of the sequence of stories from Stephen onwards, probably is that a new identifying description was proving necessary precisely because here was a group of Jews welcoming Gentiles – as Jews had done before,[72] but now in measured disregard for the Temple and its cult, and for the various ritual safeguards which the law provided to protect it. No longer were they simply 'Jews', (*Ioudaioi*) with their focus on the Temple state of Judaea (*Ioudaia*),[73] but Jews (and Greeks) whose most clear hallmark, and one which distanced them from the other Temple-centred Jews, was their faith in Jesus as the 'Christ' – hence the nickname by which they came to be known – 'Christ-ians'.[74]

4.7 Conclusions

Whether every observation in §4.6 can be sustained or not, the overall picture is certainly clear enough; that the Stephen affair and the Hellenist outreach from Jerusalem marked a development from and a growing breach with Temple-centred Judaism. The movement stemming from Jesus was beginning, on this point at least, to become something different from second Temple Judaism in one of the latter's most fundamental features.

How much of this significance was clear at the time is something we can no longer fully ascertain. Was Stephen's attack on the Temple

---

72. See e.g. Cohen, *Maccabees to Mishnah*, pp. 49–58.
73. See further below §8.2.
74. See also W. A. Meeks and R. L. Wilken, *Jews and Christians in Antioch in the First Four Centuries of the Common Era*, Missoula: Scholars 1978, p. 18.

in fact a recall to early ideals? And was it the pressure of the resulting persecution which pushed the logic of his attack into outright antithesis? To what extent was the momentum of Philip's boundary-breaching mission sustained (Acts 21.7)? How fundamental a transformation was the Cornelius episode for Peter (cf. Acts 10.28 with Gal. 2.12)? Did the name 'Christians' amount to recognition of a new sub-group within Judaism (like Pharisees, or Essenes, or Herodians), or of a group somewhere on the margin, partly in and partly out (like the Samaritans), or of a distinctively new entity recognizably different from 'Judaism'? Can we, at the remove of nineteen and a half centuries, distinguish between a broadening out of Judaism and the beginning of a splintering away from Judaism?

However we answer these questions, we need to recall two things. First, that the more we see a split opening up between 'Judaism' and 'Christianity' at this point, the more we must recognize that it was *also* a split within the new movement, between (the majority of?) Jewish Christians and others. And second, the Judaism which emerged from the first century was *also* able to reconstitute itself without the resource of the Temple and its cult. But our investigation of earliest Christian attitudes to the Temple is incomplete and we should return to that before attempting to draw any larger conclusions.

5

A Temple 'made without hands'

Thus far we have seen that Jesus' attitude to the Temple (in word and action) lay well within the diversity of attitudes to the Temple then current in second Temple Judaism. So also with the earliest Jerusalem community of his followers; if anything they were more closely identified with the Temple cult than Jesus himself had been. But with Stephen and the Hellenists we saw a marked change and development – the Temple itself put in radical question, and the widening circle of Hellenist-inspired mission breaking through barriers intended to protect the Temple and in effect leaving it still further behind. We left Luke's record of this development at the point where Paul had emerged as a leading figure in the church at Antioch, and it is with Paul that we enter upon the clearest treatment of the subject to date. As we shall see, Paul in effect seems to pick up from the Hellenists and to take the same line of re-interpretation a step further.

5.1 Categories transposed – (1) Paul and the Temple

When we look at Acts, the picture given is of Paul attempting to demonstrate at least some continuing loyalty to the Temple (Acts 21.26–30; 22.17; 24.18; 25.8; 26.21).[1] But in Paul's own letters nothing of the same concern emerges. And the implication is clearly that the Temple no longer functioned for him as the focus of God's presence and as providing the means whereby a positive relation with him can be maintained. Thus he transposes the category of the Temple from a geographical place to persons and their immediate relationship with God through the Spirit: 'Do you not know that you are God's temple . . . ?'; 'Do you not know that your body is a temple of the Holy Spirit?'; 'We are the temple of the living God . . .'

---

1. The emphasis is usually regarded as the result, in part at least, of Luke's attempt to show the earliest churches more unified and in stronger continuity with the Israel of old than was in effect the case. See e.g. my *Unity*, pp. 352–8; Wilson, *Luke and the Law*, pp. 64–8. See also below §8.4.

(I Cor. 3.16–17; 6.19; II Cor. 6.16).[2] The whole imagery is extended in Eph. 2.19–22, where the more static image of a building is merged into that of a living organism, the one new human being, the community or household of God.[3]

More striking still is the way in which the focus of divine presence (in 'structural' terms) was located for Paul not so much in the Temple as a sacred building, but in *the body of Christ* – particularly in Rom. 12.4–8 and I Cor. 12, but also Eph. 4. To the bulk of his first readers the significance of this body imagery would be clear. In so saying I make no reference to the speculation as to whether it was derived from a gnostic primal man myth (individuals understood as pieces of an original heavenly man); despite its popularity in the early and middle decades of this century, that view has now been almost totally abandoned.[4] In fact we need look no further than the quite common comparison in Greek thought between the *polis* (city) and the human body (still retained in our talk of 'the body politic'); the fable regarding Menenius Agrippa in Livy, *Hist.* 2.32 is the best known example (so also Epictetus 2.10.4–5).[5] The point, then, which Paul's first readers would readily have appreciated, is that the Christian communities of the diaspora could be said to have a corporate identity, as distinct in their own way as that of any city or corporation.

What was it that gave them their distinct corporate identity? Not ethnic identity as Jews; there were too many Gentiles involved for that; though whether they appeared to others as formally distinct from the synagogue communities is a question to which we will have to return.[6] Not any obvious loyalty to or focus on a particular Temple (in Jerusalem or wherever); the Pauline churches were in large measure at least the product of the Hellenist split with the Temple. What gave their corporate identity its distinctiveness, at least from their own point of view, was Christ – the fact that they were 'the

---

2. For detailed discussion of these texts see B. Gärtner, *The Temple and the Community in Qumran and the New Testament*, SNTSMS 1; Cambridge University 1965, pp. 49–66; McKelvey, *New Temple*, pp. 92–124.

3. If 'the barrier formed by the dividing wall' of Eph. 2.14 includes a reference to the partition which excluded Gentiles from the Temple (see e.g. discussion in McKelvey, *New Temple*, pp. 109–10; M. Barth, *Ephesians*, AB 34; New York: Doubleday 1974, pp. 283–91), then we may say that the breaking through was also a breaking out and away from the Temple cult in Jerusalem (cf. above §§4.5 and 6); see further below §5.4.

4. See above §1.3(c). The view is still found, e.g. in W. G. Kümmel, *The Theology of the New Testament*, Nashville: Abingdon 1973/London: SCM Press 1974, p. 210.

5. See also H. Lietzmann, *I & II Korinther*, HNT 9; Tübingen: Mohr-Siebeck 1949, on I Cor. 12.12; E. Schweizer, *TDNT*, 7.1038–9, 1041.

6. See below ch. 12.

body *of Christ*'; it was their commitment to Christ and focus on Christ which marked them out as *his* body.

Three other points are worth noting with regard to the church as the body of Christ.

(*a*) For Paul 'the body of Christ' was not yet a universal concept in I Corinthians and Romans (though, probably subsequently, in Ephesians). In I Cor. 12.27 Paul was able to say to the Corinthian believers: 'you are the body of Christ . . .'; that is, 'you (in Corinth) are the body of Christ (in Corinth)'. This ties in with the fact that Christians did not have any church buildings until the third century. The first churches were all, properly speaking, house churches (Rom. 16.5; I Cor. 16.19; Col. 4.15; Philemon 2; cf. Acts 12.12). The implication of Rom. 16.23 (Gaius, 'host to the whole church') is that Gaius was exceptional: he had a house big enough to take the whole church in Corinth.[7] Otherwise the 'church in Corinth' presumably had to meet in smaller groups, in the smaller houses of various of its members.[8] This means that *Paul saw the small group of Christians meeting in a member's home as the body of Christ come together as church* (I Cor. 11.18).[9] To be noted, then, is the fact that it was this coming and worshipping together, rather than the place where they met, which made them Christ's body. At that time there were private houses with cult rooms, as at Pompeii.[10] But not in the Pauline churches.

(*b*) Paul makes much of the metaphor of the body when he describes ministry within the Christian community; indeed, it is precisely in order to speak of ministry that he draws in the body imagery (Rom. 12; I Cor. 12). For Paul the point is clear: as members of the body of Christ, *each* has a function (Rom. 12.6), *each* has a ministry (I Cor. 12.5), *each* has a charism (I Cor. 12.5, 7; Rom. 12.4ff.). The body of Christ for Paul is essentially a 'charismatic community'.[11] In all this imagery there is no suggestion of, or even room for, a concept of ministry which focusses it all on a few or which confines it all, in either theory or effect, to the one or two. There is no conception of

---

7. See my *Romans*, pp. 910–1. There is more or less universal agreement that Romans was written from Corinth.

8. It is worth bearing in mind that a typical well-to-do home of the time could accommodate 30–40, or at best about 50. See e.g. J. Murphy-O'Connor, *St Paul's Corinth: Texts and Archaeology*, Wilmington: Glazier 1983, pp. 153–9. Other bibliography in my *Romans*, p. 911.

9. R. Banks, *Paul's Idea of Community*, Exeter: Paternoster 1980, particularly ch. 3.

10. I refer to the so-called 'house of mysteries', illustrated e.g. in T. H. Feder, *Great Treasures of Pompeii and Herculaneum*, New York: Abbeville 1978, pp. 110–17.

11. See further my *Jesus and the Spirit*, London: SCM Press Philadelphia: Westminster 1975, ch. 9.

some as ministers or charismatics, and the rest as (merely) ministered to. The strength of Paul's insistence on this point is often lost sight of; but he certainly intended his readers to be in no doubt about it. Particularly worthy of note is the cartoon or caricature effect of I Cor. 12.17–19: a whole body reduced (in ministry) to one member! Ridiculous! In such a case there is no body (no Christ! – 12.12), but only a grotesque parody.

(*c*) Of course, Paul recognized that Christian groups (like all groups) have a ritual boundary (baptism in the name of Jesus – I Cor. 1.13) and a ritual focus (the Lord's Supper – I Cor. 10.16–17). And in the case of the Lord's Supper he both ties it into the body of Christ language and imagery, and likens it to the sacrificial meals of the Jerusalem cult and of pagan temples (I Cor. 10.18–21). But the point of comparison all the way is the corporateness and the sharing (the thematic words are *koinōnia/koinōnos* = 'participation/partner or sharing/sharer', and *metechein* = 'to share or participate in');[12] not the idea of sacrifice or of a cult meal, nor, it must be said, any implication of a meal requiring priestly administration. Hence too the ambiguity of what *sōma Christou* ('body of Christ') refers to in I Cor. 10–11: the bread (10.16; 11.24, 27), or the company of Christians (10.17; 11.29?).[13] The oneness of the Christian group was constituted by the act of *sharing* the one loaf in the context of a shared meal (10.16; 11.23 – only the cup was 'after supper').[14]

In short, in the communities of the Pauline mission *the structural focus of the 'temple of God' and the embodiment of divine presence was quite markedly different from that of Temple-centred Judaism.*

5.2 Categories transposed – (2) Paul and sacrifice

A similar point emerges from Paul's treatment of the category of sacrifice.

(*a*) Whatever we may or may not be able to say about the earlier 'sect' of the Nazarenes in Jerusalem and about the Hellenists,[15] with Paul the position is clear: Christ's death was a *sacrifice*; and (the implication is unavoidable) as a result, no more sacrifice is necessary.

---

12. *Koinōnia/koinōnos* – I Cor. 10.16, 16, 18, 20; *metechein* – I Cor. 10.17, 21, 30.

13. See e.g. discussion in C. K. Barrett, *I Corinthians*, London: Black 1968, pp. 273–5; G. D. Fee, *I Corinthians*, NICNT; Grand Rapids: Eerdmans 1987, pp. 563–4.

14. The implication of I Cor. 11.23 is clearly that the bread was broken during the meal, and probably, in accord with Jewish practice, at the beginning of the meal. That is to say, at this stage the whole meal probably came in between the two 'elements' of bread and wine, as most commentators recognize.

15. See above §§4.1, 4.5h.

Thus in Rom. 3.25, Jesus' death is described as a *hilastērion*, where the word can hardly be other than an allusion to the cover of the ark of the covenant (the 'mercy seat'), on which the blood of the sacrifices was sprinkled on the Day of Atonement, making atonement for the people, in accordance with the provisions of Lev. 16.[16] In which case it is impossible to escape the conclusion that Jesus' death was being seen in sacrificial terms. It is true that the same word is also used in *IV Macc.* 17.22 in reference to the death of the Maccabean martyrs, and evidently without being seen to call the cult in question. But in Paul's case the implication is clear: the benefit of Christ's sacrificial death is to be received by faith – that is, without further recourse to the cult;[17] and Jesus' *hilastērion* is effective for *former* sins as well (3.26), which may even imply that Paul thought the whole sacrificial system in the Jerusalem Temple was merely a 'holding operation', pending God's provision of the one, decisive atonement for sins – Christ.

Similarly with Rom. 8.3 – God sent his Son 'in the very likeness of sinful flesh and concerning sin and condemned sin in the flesh'. That Paul refers here to the death of Jesus is not disputed. And the phrase translated here literally, 'concerning sin' (*peri hamartias*), is almost certainly used in conscious echo of and allusion to the same phrase in the LXX, where it translates the phrase 'for a sin offering' (*lᵉFhatta'th*; so, for example, Lev. 5.6–7,11).[18] So, again, a sacrificial allusion is clear. And for us the point once again is the extent of the effectiveness of Jesus' sacrificial death: Christ sent to 'condemn sin in the flesh' – that is, to provide the decisive answer to the problem and power of sin in human life ('sinful flesh'). The implication is the same as with Rom. 3.25: such a comprehensive counter to the problem of 'sinful flesh' renders unnecessary any further sacrifice for sin.

The same deduction follows from II Cor. 5.21 –

For our sake he made him to be sin who knew no sin,
so that in him we might become the righteousness of God.

For anyone familiar with Jewish sacrificial ritual the sacrificial allusion was unmistakable: Christ likened to the pure animal slaughtered

---

16. The word is almost exclusive to the LXX where it is used 21 times in Exodus, Leviticus and Numbers for the lid of the ark, the 'place of expiation' (see particularly Ex. 25 and Lev. 16). That it probably also has the extended sense of 'means of atonement' does not affect the point here. See for fuller details my *Romans*, pp. 170–2.

17. If the 'through faith' of Rom. 3.25 has been added by Paul to an earlier formula, as seems quite likely (and as many commentators think; see discussion in my *Romans*, pp. 163–4), then Paul wanted to make it a point of particular emphasis.

18. Further references and bibliography in my *Romans*, p. 422.

in sacrifice to meet the problem of the impure person.[19] And again it has to be noted that Jesus' death was not seen thus simply as a means of meeting the problem of a single individual or of a single sin, but as a means of achieving God's righteousness for those 'in Christ' – that is, presumably, once and for all.

Other references could be cited. But hopefully the point is already clear enough, and has been sufficiently well demonstrated by means of the above texts. The point rests on the fact that for Paul, Jesus' death (and resurrection) was not just one event in a sequence of other events, let alone other similar events (martyr deaths). It was *the* event which introduced a whole new state of affairs – a new age, even a new creation (II Cor. 5.17). As Adam and his sin introduced and established the character of the age of sin and death, so Christ and his obedience introduced and established the character of the new age of Spirit and life (Rom. 5.12–21; I Cor. 15.21–22, 45–49). For Paul there was a unique once-for-allness about Jesus' death and resurrection, which means that that one event has set the scene for all time to come. It needs no repetition; that would destroy its epochal character. 'The death he died he died to sin, once for all' (Rom. 6.10). The one sacrifice is the ground for his sustaining and continuing intercession which ensures God's final acquittal of those for whom he intercedes (Rom. 8.34).

The point needs no further elaboration. *With such a theology, there is no need any longer for a sacrificial cult.*

(*b*) In some ways still more striking is Paul's use of sacrificial terminology in Rom. 12.1 – 'present your bodies as a sacrifice, living, holy, acceptable to God, which is your spiritual worship'. *Sōma* ('body') here stands for the person (compare, for example, 6.13, 16, 19 with 12.1); hence the quite proper translation – 'present your (very) selves'. But it is the person seen precisely in his or her corporeality, in her or his relationships within this world; it is because they are bodies that they can experience the world and relate to others. What is in view is the physical embodiment of the individual's consecration in the concrete realities of daily life. It is as *sōma*, part of the world and within the world that the believer offers worship.[20] Also to be noted is Paul's use of the word *latreia*, 'worship', since eight out of the nine occurrences in the LXX refer to Jewish cultic worship.[21] The implication is therefore that *Paul saw this commitment of daily life*

---

19. See further my 'Paul's Understanding of the Death of Jesus as Sacrifice', *Sacrifice and Redemption*, ed. S. W. Sykes, Cambridge University 1991, pp. 35–56.

20. See further my *Romans*, pp. 709–712.

21. H. Strathmann, *TDNT*, 4.61.

as the Christians' equivalent to the priestly service of the Jerusalem cult. His exhortation is to the effect that *each* believer is to be engaged in the priestly act of sacrifice; but that it is to be carried out on the altar of everyday relationships.

It is noticeable that this is the first thing Paul says following his attempt, in effect, to redefine the people of God in chapters 9–11 of Romans.[22] The implication is that Paul was thereby attempting to redefine the cultic markers of the covenant people, which were no longer to be understood in terms of or focussed in the sacrificial cult at Jerusalem. *The Christian is also priest and also engaged in priestly ministry;* the language and what it stands for is important and not to be set aside. But the priestly ministry Paul has in view is the priestly ministry of a disciplined social life in the world. The cult has been secularized: or, alternatively, the market-place has been spiritualized. At all events, *the boundary between cult and world has been removed.* The space where the priestly worship of God is carried out is no longer to be conceived as a tightly controlled sacred space, but as the world itself.

Here even the fundamental rationale of having such a sacred space, where only those specially priested can enter, is put in question. With this discussion and conclusion we are already into a third category – priesthood.

5.3 Categories transposed – (3) Paul and priesthood

Historically the categories of sacrifice and priest go hand in hand. Any study of Paul's concept of sacrifice thus inevitably leads into and is already bound up with his concept of priesthood. Here we should note particularly Rom. 15.16, where Paul reminds his readers

> of the grace given me from God, so that I might be a minister (*leitourgon*) of Christ Jesus for the Gentiles, serving the gospel of God as a priest (*hierourgounta*), in order that the offering (*prosphora*) of the Gentiles might be acceptable (*euprosdektos*), sanctified (*hēgiasmenē*) by the Holy Spirit.

The language of priesthood and cult is unmistakable. By *leitourgos* Paul almost certainly had in mind its specific cultic sense ('priest'), as in Neh. 10.39, Isa. 61.6, Sir. 7.30, Heb. 7.30 and I Clem. 41.2. The cultic language of the following clauses puts this effectively beyond dispute: *hierourgein* – 'to perform the work of a priest' (so consistently

---

22. See further my *Romans*, pp. 705–706.

in Philo and Josephus); *prosphora* – either, the 'act of presenting an offering', or the 'offering' itself (as here): *euprosdektos* and *hagiazein* are also both very apposite in reference to sacrifice.[23]

There can be no question, therefore, that Paul here described his ministry in priestly terms. That however should not be taken to indicate that he thought of himself as a priest in a special way distinct from the ministries of other believers. There is no suggestion of that anywhere else in Paul. The whole imagery of priesthood has clearly been transposed entirely out of the cult and applied in its transformed sense to Paul's ministry of preaching the gospel to Gentiles. Why it should be assumed that Paul uses the word 'priest' in any kind of literal sense, when all the other priestly imagery in the verse is obviously being used in a symbolical sense (his ministry to the Gentiles = the eschatological equivalent to the priestly ministry of the old age) must remain a puzzle. Nor can we assume that he intended to imply that the priestly language was peculiarly appropriate to, or to be reserved for apostolic ministry (apostles as priests in a sense not true of all believers).[24] For he also describes Epaphroditus as a *leitourgos* in Phil. 2.25, where the ministry is that of tending to Paul's needs while in prison;[25] and, as we have already seen, Paul has already encouraged *all* his readers to engage in the priestly action of offering their own bodies (themselves) in sacrifice (Rom. 12.1). The point then is that *all ministry and service on behalf of the gospel can be considered as priestly ministry*, the new covenant equivalent of the ministries of grace (charisms) reserved in the old covenant for those specially anointed. By applying such cultic language to such non-cultic ministry on behalf of the gospel, Paul confirms that the cultic barrier between sacred and secular has been broken down and left behind.

It is difficult for us now to appreciate how *very odd* these earliest Christian home churches must have seemed in the cities of the Roman Empire. They had no cult centre or temple, no priests, no sacrifices. At all these points they would have been *unlike* the typical cults of the time. The nearest parallel would be the *collegia* – formally recognized associations for shared purpose or interest – most typically burial societies. Synagogues could be given formal recognition under such

---

23. For full details see my *Romans*, pp. 859–861.

24. So e.g. A. Vanhoye, *Old Testament Priests and the New Priest According to the New Testament*, Petersham, Mass.: St Bede's 1986, p. 269.

25. Of course, Paul also describes Epaphroditus in the same verse as 'apostle'; but as 'your apostle', that is as 'emissary' of the Philippian church to Paul; as also in II Cor. 8.23–'emissaries of the churches'.

legislation.[26] But typical of meetings of the *collegia* would be formal religious acts of a priest, including a ritual libation. Or trade guilds would meet on premises of the god or goddess who acted as their patron(ess). And in the synagogues, a priest would still be honoured as priest; and orientation of the synagogue towards the cult centre (the Temple) at Jerusalem would still be fundamental. But in meetings of the Christian home churches there were *none* of the usual cultic trappings. For many of the first Christians' contemporaries, a *religion* without a cult centre, without priests, without sacrifices, must have seemed a plain contradiction in terms, an absurdity – so far from the normal pattern of religious groups was this new movement. Here again the eschatological consciousness of the first Christians included the sense of having broken down the division between cult and world, between sacred and non-sacred space, between priest and people, or between specially sacred individuals and not so sacred people.

5.4 Categories transposed – (4) Paul and purity

The same point becomes evident in the matter of purity.

(*a*) In Paul the concept of purity has been spiritualized. Particularly notable here is Rom. 14.14 – 'I know and am persuaded in the Lord Jesus that nothing is unclean (*koinon*) in itself . . .' In ordinary Greek *koinos* meant 'common, ordinary'. It gained its characteristic Jewish sense, as here, by being used to translate the Hebrew, *tamē* or *ḥol*, both in the sense, 'profane, unclean'. This translation was not yet established in the LXX, but it had become a matter of primary concern from the Maccabean crisis onwards, as I Macc. 1.47, 62 and the evidence reviewed above (§3.2) indicates, as also confirmed by Mark 7.2 and Acts 10.14. The point here is Paul's complete renunciation of such a view as a matter of principle.[27] Similarly, I Cor. 10.25–26 – 'Eat whatever is sold in the meat market without raising any question on the ground of conscience. For "the earth is the Lord's, and everything in it".'

In the same context Paul uses another important purity word in the Jewish vocabulary: 'everything is clean (*kathara*)' (Rom. 14.20). In this context, *katharos* is clearly the opposite of *koinos* (v. 14), and so has primarily the issue of clean and unclean foods in view. In the

---

26. See e.g. discussion in E. M. Smallwood, *The Jews under Roman Rule*, Leiden: Brill 1976, pp. 134–6.

27. However much he might adapt his own principle out of pastoral concern (14.14b). For discussion of the relation of Rom. 14.14 to Mark 7.15 see my 'Jesus and Ritual Purity', *Jesus, Paul and the Law*, ch. 2; also *Romans*, pp. 819–20.

OT *katharos* is regularly used in this connection, and, like *koinos*, *katharos/akathartos* ('clean/unclean') came to denote an issue of great moment in the 'intertestamental' period.[28] Here again we might simply note the emphatic protest of Peter on the roof top in Joppa, as representative of traditional Jewish wisdom on this topic: 'I have never eaten anything common (*koinon*) or unclean (*akatharton*)'. The point again here is Paul's equally forthright, but quite contrary assertion: so far as food is concerned, '*everything* is clean'!

The same implication follows from his other uses of cleansing/ cleaning imagery. I Cor. 6.11 – 'you were washed (*apelousasthe*)', where the reference is clearly to the list of moral defilements given just before ('... thieves, greedy, drunkards, revilers, robbers'). The washing in view then is a washing of heart and conscience (cf. Mark 7.21–22; Acts 15.9; Heb. 9.14). Similarly with other *katharos/ katharizein* references in the Pauline corpus (I Tim. 1.5; 3.9; II Tim. 1.3; 2.22 – 'clean heart', 'clean conscience'; so probably also II Cor. 7.1 and Eph. 5.26).[29] In all these cases the language has long left behind the cultic sphere of ritual purity and stands for a spiritual cleansing and moral purifying *without reference to the cult*.

(*b*) We can also illustrate the same point with reference to the circles of purity round the Temple and the Holy Place.[30]

We have already seen that the boundary distinguishing priest and people had been breached: all engaged in the service of the gospel were engaged in priestly ministry; there was no longer any sacred space limited to a few, the specially sanctified; all have direct access to the presence of God in Christ by virtue of each equally being 'in Christ' (§5.3). The boundary between the court of the priests and the court of Israel had been broken through: each could bring the sacrifice now required by God and offer it on the altar of everyday vocation (§5.2).

In the same way, an even more major boundary had also been broken through – that surrounding the court of Israel, which marked Israel off from the Gentile world, the ritual expression of Israel's election and special set-apartness for God. This may be explicit in Ephesians' talk of 'breaking down the barrier formed by the dividing wall' (Eph. 2.14).[31] But it can be seen at once already in the way Paul

---

28. See e.g. Gen. 7.2–3, 8; 8.20; Lev. 4.12; 6.11; 7.19; Ezra 6.20; Mal. 1.11; Judith 12.9; I Macc. 1.48; *Pss.Sol.* 8.12, 22; *Ep.Arist.* 166; *T. Levi* 15.1; 16.4–5; Philo, *Spec.Leg.* 4.106; *Virt.* 147; Josephus, *Ap.* 1.307.

29. See further my *Baptism in the Holy Spirit*, London: SCM Press/Philadelphia: Westminster 1970, pp. 120–3, 162–5.

30. See above § 3.2.

31. See above n. 3.

uses the language of 'set-apartness' – *hagios* ('holy'), *hagiazein* ('to render holy, consecrate'). In the OT *hagiazein* is used particularly of sacrifices (Ex. 29.33, 36–37; 30.29. etc.), of priests (Ex. 19.22; 29.1, 21, 44; etc.) and of temple (I Kings 9.37; II Chron. 2.4; 7.16, 20; etc.); and not least of the people of Israel itself (Ex. 19.14; Lev. 11.44; 20.8; 22.32; etc.) – that is, 'holy' as 'sanctified', set apart and marked off from the surrounding nations. But in Rom. 15.16[32] Paul uses the word *hagiazein* of the sacrifice (*prosphora*) which probably consists of the Gentiles.[33] That is to say, the very ones who by definition were *un*-sanctified, unable on pain of death to cross the boundary excluding them from the inner courts of the Temple,[34] outside the boundary of national purity, are themselves conceived by Paul as the sacrifice. The barrier has gone. So with Paul's use of *hagiazein* for Christians generally, Gentile as well as Jew (I Cor. 1.2; 6.11). In the eschatological transformation effected by Christ and the gospel such cultically determined distinctions had now been left behind.

So also, not least, with Paul's use of *hagios* for Christians generally. 'The saints' is a frequent title in Jewish literature for the nation of Israel as a whole in its set-apartness for God and separation from all other people (Pss. 16.3; 34.9; 74.3; 83.3; Isa. 4.3; etc).[35] But Paul uses it of *all* his converts, *all* the members of the churches to which he wrote – without reference to whether they be Jew, proselyte, or Gentile (e.g. Rom. 1.7; I Cor. 1.2; II Cor. 1.1; Phil. 1.1). Once again, the cultic boundary round the nation had been broken through. Worth noting, once again, is the astonishing character of these first congregations consisting of Gentiles and Jews without distinction, who offered no sacrifice, called no man priest, practised no circumcision, and yet saw themselves as 'saints'.

(c) We should also note that the same is in effect true of the boundary which marked off the court of Israel from the court of women.[36] Paul certainly seems to have conformed to at least some of the norms of a patriarchally ordered society (I Cor. 11.2–16; 14.34–36). But some of that may have been determined by the particular situation in Corinth (notorious for its licentiousness),[37] or may have referred

---

32. Cited above, §5.3.

33. See discussion in my *Romans*, p. 860;

34. Schürer, 2.284–5; though sacrifices could be presented by Gentiles and accepted, rather as an act of courtesy and political good will (Schürer, 2.309–313).

35. See further my *Romans*, pp. 19–20.

36. See above §3.2.

37. See e.g. B. W. Witherington, *Women in the Earliest Churches*, SNTSMS 59; Cambridge University 1988, pp. 79–82.

particularly to married women.[38] And such teaching has also to be married with other statements of principle, particularly Gal. 3.28 – 'There is neither Jew nor Greek, there is neither slave nor free, there is neither male nor female; for you are all one in Christ Jesus.' That is to say, as the boundary of race and the boundary of social status no longer count or function 'in Christ', neither does the boundary between male and female. What this meant in practice is presumably indicated by the role which women actually filled in the Pauline mission and churches.

The best documentation of this role is given in Rom. 16, where the prominence of women among those listed is very striking.[39] Even more striking is the prominence of the roles they filled. Phoebe (16.1) is the first to be designated 'deacon' in all the NT. She is also called *prostatis*, which any Greek reader would have taken in its usual sense of 'patron', a role by no means unfamiliar for women in Roman society.[40] Prisca (16.3–5) was evidently the leading partner of the couple (Prisca and husband Aquila; also Acts 18.18, 26 and II Tim. 4.19), and as such was probably prominent in the leadership of the church which met in their home; as presumably was also Nympha, host(ess) of the church referred to in Col. 4.15. Junia (16.7) is certainly a female name, as the record of names of the period certainly shows.[41] She, together with Andronicus, probably her husband, were evidently leading members among the apostles from before the time of Paul's conversion ('outstanding among the apostles, who also were in Christ before me'). That is, she and Andronicus must have belonged to the circle of apostles mentioned by Paul in I Cor. 15.7.[42] Finally Paul greets Mary, Tryphaena and Tryphosa, and Persis (16.6, 12), all of whom he describes as 'hard workers'. Where this word is used elsewhere in similar contexts (I Cor. 16.16; I Thess. 5.12) it is usually taken as a description of leadership (hence Paul's call in these passages

---

38. See E. E. Ellis, *Pauline Theology. Ministry and Society*, Grand Rapids: Eerdmans/ Exeter: Paternoster 1989, pp. 67–71.

39. For detailed exposition of what follows see my *Romans*.

40. The assumption that the word could not have this, its regular meaning, here, which dictated such translations as RSV's 'helper', tells us more about the assumptions of the translators than about the text itself.

41. 'Junia' as a name occurs over 250 times; whereas the masculine form, 'Junias', is unattested. Translators' assumption that the masculine must be meant is an even more astonishing expression of what can only be described as uninformed prejudice.

42. Had Paul intended the 'weaker' sense of *apostolos*, 'emissary of some church', he would almost certainly have indicated this by some qualifying phrase, as in his only two uses of *apostolos* in this sense (II Cor. 8.23; Phil. 2.25). In contrast, 'the apostles' must designate the well-known circle, of which I Cor. 15.7 also speaks.

for his readers to respect such people). What is significant here is that in Rom. 16, these four women are the *only* ones so described. Overall the implication seems to be clear that *women were prominent in the leadership of the earliest churches in Rome*; indeed, if anything, *more* active in leadership than the men whom Paul knew and greeted.

In short, as with the boundary between Jew and Gentile, as with the boundary between priest and people, so with the boundary between male and female ministry. Culturally determined taboos which debarred women from service in the cult were no longer operative now that the cult itself was no longer a factor in the understanding and practice of ministry.

5.5 Categories transposed – (5) Jerusalem

Finally we need to recall that Jerusalem, Mount Zion, and the Temple were all interlocked in Jewish self-consciousness,[43] and ask about Paul's attitude to Jerusalem itself. The question of Paul's earlier attitude to Jerusalem is one to which we will have to return.[44] At this point we need deal only with his mature attitude, as expressed in his major letters. Here the factor of primary importance is undoubtedly *the collection*.

The collection was a matter of major concern for Paul. This is clear from the prominence he gives to the subject in his main letters (Rom. 15.25–32; I Cor. 16.1–4; II Cor. 8–9; cf. Gal. 2.10). Also from the overpowering desire on Paul's part to deliver it personally to 'the saints' in Jerusalem: it evidently marked for him the close of his missionary endeavours in the eastern Mediterranean area (Rom. 15.15–21, 23);[45] but before he could feel free to fulfil his burning ambition to go to Rome and begin the western phase of his mission to the Gentiles, he had to deliver the collection (Rom. 15.22–29).

What was its significance? From the perspective of the Jerusalem believers the collection could be understood as the equivalent of the Temple tax, which flowed annually from the diaspora and provided a major source of funds for the Temple in Jerusalem;[46] or, if anything more likely, as fulfilment of the Jewish expectation of Gentile homage to Jerusalem in the last days (Isa. 45.14; 60.5–17; 61.6; Micah 4.13;

---

43. See above §2.4.
44. See below §7.4.
45. See my *Romans*, particularly on 15.19 and 23 (pp. 864, 871).
46. So K. Holl, 'Der Kirchenbegriff des Paulus in seinem Verhältnis zu dem der Urgemeinde', *Gesammelte Aufsätze zur Kirchengeschichte*, Band II, Darmstadt: WB 1964, pp. 44–67. See also above §2.4.

Tobit 13.11; 1QM 12.13–15).[47] But it is most improbable that *Paul* saw the collection in these terms: that would have been too much a reaffirmation of the sense of Jewish prerogative which he had been at such pains to undermine earlier in the same letter (2.17ff.; 9.6ff.). Nor need we indulge in such speculation, since Paul lays down the rationale for the collection so clearly in Rom. 15.27: Gentiles have come to share in Israel's *spiritual* blessings; for such Gentiles to share their *material* blessings with the saints in Jerusalem was a quite proper act of gratitude and brotherly concern (cf. Rom. 12.8 and I Cor. 12.25–26 with Acts 24.17). No doubt also he would hope thereby to consolidate the Gentile mission in the eyes of the Jerusalem leadership (since it fulfilled the agreement of Gal. 2.10), and so maintain the unity of the Christian churches in their common *heilsgeschichtlich* continuity with the heritage of Abraham's promise, the covenant and the (Jewish) scriptures.[48]

However, it was a risky strategy in view of the possible misunderstanding which the collection permitted. And if, in the event, the collection was not accepted, as Paul had feared might be the case (Rom. 15.31),[49] that presumably must mean either that it did not prove acceptable on Paul's terms, or that it was judged to be politically inexpedient for the Jerusalem Christians to accept such alms (Acts 24.17)[50] from one already widely regarded within Jerusalem as an apostate (Acts 21.21, 28). Either way, the tragedy of the collection would be that it not only failed to bind Jewish and Gentile mission together, but also reinforced the division already opening up between Jew and Christian. Here again, as with Stephen and the Hellenists, the parting of the ways over Jerusalem and Temple was to leave the Jerusalem Christians caught uncomfortably in the middle.

Two other passages should be at least mentioned. The first is the allegory of Gal. 4.21–31, where Paul draws on the strand of Jewish apocalyptic thought which speaks of a heavenly Jerusalem.[51] In Paul's

---

47. See particularly R. D. Aus, 'Paul's Travel Plans to Spain and the "Full Number of the Gentiles" of Rom. 11.25', *NovT* 21 (1979), pp. 232–62.

48. Though the relation between Gal. 2.10 and the collection may have been a good deal more complicated; see N. Taylor, *Paul, Antioch and Jerusalem. A Study in Relationships and Authority in Earliest Christianity*, JSNTS 66, Sheffield Academic, 1992, p. 198.

49. See e.g. my *Unity*, pp. 256–7.

50. It should be recalled that this happened within ten years of the Jewish revolt (66 CE), and that the beginning of the revolt was marked by the decision to suspend the daily sacrifice for the emperor and 'to accept no gift or sacrifice from a foreigner. This action laid the foundation of the war with the Romans' (Josephus, *War*, 2.409).

51. This theme comes to clearest expression in *II Bar.* 4.2–6, *IV Ezra* 7.26, 10.44–59, 13.36, and *II Enoch* 55.2. But it is an obvious outworking of Ex. 25.9, 40; and Paul does not introduce the theme as though it was a new idea. See also below, §5.6(*c*).

reworking of the theme it is clear that the present equivalent ('the now Jerusalem') is an inadequate copy of the ideal Jerusalem of God's purpose, which is better identified with the line of promise through Sarah and Isaac. In other words, the new, or heavenly Jerusalem for Paul did not denote any geographical location, but rather stood in contrast to the city nestling in the Judaean highlands. Rather, it denoted a divine ideal or purpose, which the Jerusalem of traditional Judaism was not fulfilling, but which was already finding fulfilment in the groups of Jews and Gentiles who reckoned their relationship with God not in terms of law and physical descent, but in terms of promise fulfilled and Spirit received (Gal. 3.1–14; 4.28–31). In short, the heavenly Jerusalem for Paul was already a reality of experienced promise, in union with others who rejoiced in the same experience, something which, in Paul's view at least, was known in free measure in the home churches of the diaspora more than in the temple of Jerusalem.

The other passage is again from Paul's most mature work – Rom. 11.26. The ground of Paul's confidence that 'all Israel will be saved' was the hope expressed in Isa. 59.20–21: 'The Deliverer will come from Zion, he will banish ungodliness from Jacob . . .' What is interesting for us, however, is that where the Hebrew of Isa. 59.20 reads, '. . . will come *to* Zion', and where the Greek reads '*for the sake of* Zion', Paul reads '*from* Zion'. The implication once again is of Paul's readiness to reaffirm the eschatological significance of Jerusalem without reinforcing the old Jewish assumption that Zion would literally be the focus of the eschatological climax (cf. again Gal. 4.25–26). On the contrary, the Temple is where 'the man of lawlessness' would take his seat, 'proclaiming himself to be God' (II Thess. 2.3–4; Paul's *only* explicit reference to the Jerusalem Temple). It may even be that he thought the 'mystery of lawlessness' (2.7ff.) was already operative in the Jerusalem Temple, since elsewhere he clearly regards 'lawlessness' as an appropriate description of the perversion of covenantal grace as currently perceived and practised within the rest of Judaism (Rom. 2: Jew as guilty as Gentile – 3.9, 19–20; Gal. 3.10–11). Be that as it may, the Gal. 4.25–26 passage is already proof that for Paul the central category of Jerusalem itself had been transformed from an expression of nationalistic self-confidence to one of more universal, or spiritual significance, and as such was able to serve as an expression of hope (both realized and unrealized) for Gentile as Gentile as well as Jew.

In sum, so far as Paul was concerned, *the whole conception of sacred space, cultic sacrifice, priestly ministry and the question of who may enter and engage in their eschatological equivalents had been wholly transformed*. The imagery was still of value in a transposed sense; but no longer the actuality as such.

5.6 The Epistle to the Hebrews

When talking about the relationship between Christianity and second Temple Judaism's sacrificial cult, there is one writing above all else in the NT which demands attention – the letter to the Hebrews.

(*a*) First, some preliminary remarks. It is difficult to locate Hebrews within the time and area covered by the NT writings. But certainly we can call it an expression of Hellenistic Jewish Christianity. Indeed, it is the nearest parallel we have in the NT to the views of Stephen and/or the Hellenists.[52] It is dominated by concerns of primary interest to Jews. In particular it deals almost exclusively with the question of the traditional cult – priesthood, tabernacle, sacrifice: do they continue in Christianity in some sense, or have they been superceded? what is their new covenant equivalent? This in effect is the main thrust of the central section of the letter – 4.14–10.25. In striking echo also of Stephen, the letter does not really take issue over the law.

At the same time, however, Hebrews shows awareness in at least some measure of Greek philosophical thought. In particular of the Platonic world view of two worlds, above and below: above is the world of ideals or ideas, which is the real world; below is this world, the world of shadows and copies. The heavens are now where Christ is (4.14; 7.26; 8.1); he is the means of access to the heavenly, that is, the real presence of God (9.23–24). In contrast, the earthly sanctuary is described as 'a copy (*hypodeigma*) and shadow (*skia*) of the heavenly sanctuary' (8.5), where both words seem clearly to reflect the fundamental Platonic schema.[53]

---

52. See above §4.5(*f*).

53. See e.g. S. Schulz, *TDNT*, 7.396 (*skia*); set in conjunction with *skia*, *hypodeigma* seems to be used by Hebrews as the earthly 'copy' or 'imitation' of Plato's heavenly original or archetype (*paradeigma*), for which see LSJ. We do not need to argue that Hebrews was influenced directly by Plato, or by Philo in particular (see especially C. Spicq, *Hebreux*, EB; Paris: Gabalda; Vol. I 1952, pp. 25–91); it is enough to recognize that he shares with Philo something at least of the same Alexandrian-Platonic background. See e.g. J. Moffatt, *Hebrews*, ICC; Edinburgh: T. & T. Clark 1924, pp. 105–7; H. Braun, *An die Hebräer*, HNT 14; Tübingen: Mohr-Siebeck 1984, pp. 232–3; H. W. Attridge, *Hebrews*, Hermeneia; Philadelphia: Fortress 1989, p. 219. But even if we were to label the thought of Hebrews exclusively 'apocalyptic' the significance of its line of argument as developed in the text (§5.6b) would be the same.

From this we can build up a picture of the community (or communities) to which Hebrews was written. It was familiar with Platonic philosophy, or at least sufficiently familiar to appreciate an important element in the letter's argument. It was very much concerned with priesthood and sacrifice within the Jewish tradition. But it was not caught up in any dispute about the whether-or-not of law observance. All of which strongly suggests a *Jewish*-Christian community. It is difficult to imagine a *Gentile*-Christian community who were so entranced with questions relating to the Jewish cult, but where questions regarding the Torah were of little moment. More likely we have to envisage a fairly homogeneous Christian-Jewish community somewhere in the diaspora, untouched by the sort of questions Paul raised; but hankering after the ritual and tangibility of the Temple cult, such as the primitive Jerusalem church had enjoyed. In other words, quite likely a group of Christians who had migrated from Jerusalem or Judaea, during or as a result of the Jewish revolt (66–70) and of the Roman suppression of it.

There is a strongly held view that the letter must have been written before 70 CE, since otherwise it would surely have mentioned the destruction of the Temple.[54] But that does not necessarily follow. Other post-70 Christian writings which had good reason to mention the destruction of the Temple fail to do so: I Clement and the Letter to Diognetus both speak as though the sacrificial cult in Jerusalem was still in operation (I Clem. 41.2–3; Diognetus 3.5). As indeed does Josephus (*Ap.* 2.193–8). In fact, most Jews of the time would probably assume or hope that the Temple would soon be rebuilt again (as it had after the exile in Babylon); such a hope is probably implicit in the choice of 'Ezra' and 'Baruch' as pseudonyms in the two main Jewish apocalyptic writings of the period between the Jewish revolts (*IV Ezra* and *II Baruch*).[55] And it is notable that the rabbis continued to give rulings relating to the Temple cult after 70, presumably on the same assumption.[56] Indeed, this may provide the main reason why Hebrews speaks all the while in terms of the tabernacle or tent of the wilderness, and never of the Temple: *it was the very principle of a special cult and special priesthood and continuing sacrifice which the author wished to contest*, thus undercutting the theological rationale

---

54. E.g. J. A. T. Robinson, *Redating the New Testament*, London: SCM Press/Philadelphia: Westminster 1976, pp. 200–15; B. Lindars, *The Theology of Hebrews*, Cambridge University 1991, pp. 19–21.

55. See further below §12.1(c).

56. 'The sages made every effort to keep alive as many Temple ceremonies as possible' (G. Alon, *The Jews in their Land in the Talmudic Age*, Jerusalem: Magnes, 2 vols, 1980, 1984, p. 115; see further pp. 114–18, 253–65).

on which any renewed or rebuilt Temple might be reconstituted. Which also means that at this point Hebrews goes beyond Stephen's critique of the Temple.

(*b*) Let us now look more closely at the argument itself. It is widely agreed that Hebrews was written to warn against the danger of a relapse into traditional Judaism.[57] The problem confronting the author can probably be most simply summed up in terms of a 'guilty conscience' – as is clearly enough implied by the several references on this theme as the argument builds up to its climax (9.9, 14; 10.2, 22; also 13.18).[58] Presumably the problem was that Christian Jews, accustomed to the powerful impact of the sacrificial ritual of the Jerusalem cult, were finding the bare pronouncement of forgiveness in the Christian gatherings, somewhere in the diaspora (no cult centre, no priest, no sacrifice), symbolically and liturgically empty and unsatisfying. Hence what appears to have been the yearning on the part of many of the letter's readers for the old familiar tangibilities and rituals.

Whatever the precise details of context and chronology, the writer meets the challenge by developing a unique extended argument to the effect that Christ has wholly superseded and transcended the older Jewish cult. The new covenant (Jer. 31.31–34 – Heb. 8.8–12 – one of the longest OT quotations in the NT) is not to be conceived simply in terms of entering into Israel's blessings, as Paul had understood it; but rather in terms of wholly leaving behind this central feature of the parent religion, the cult. He attempts to demonstrate this by a fascinating combination of the Platonic world view and Jewish eschatology. As the one saw the cosmos divided vertically between heavenly reality and earthly shadow, so the other saw history divided into the two epochs of old age/present age and age to come/new age.

The genius of Hebrews' schema is the author's success in combining these two disparate views of reality. He identifies the *old age* of Jewish eschatology with the Platonic view of *this world* of shadow and copy. Whereas the *new age* of Jewish eschatology is identified with Plato's *real, heavenly world*. Christ's death marks the point at which the transition from old covenant to new took place, but also the transition from shadow to real, from earth to heaven. Christ broke through both barriers at one and the same time. Traditional Judaism with its cultic ritual, earthly temple, repeated sacrifice and Aaronic priesthood belongs to the old age, that is, to the age of shadow, provisional and

---

57. See e.g. F. F. Bruce, *Hebrews*, NLC; Edinburgh: Marshall, Morgan & Scott, 1964, p. xxiii–xxx; Attridge, pp. 21–3.

58. So particularly Lindars, *Hebrews*.

imperfect. With Christ's death and exaltation the old age, the old covenant is past, the age expressed in the Jewish cult; the new age, that is the reality for which it only prepared, has come. The tabernacle/tent was only a shadow of the heavenly temple, of heaven, God's dwelling place (8.5 – Ex. 25.40); the Aaronic priesthood was only a shadow and preparation for the priesthood of Christ, a unique and unrepeatable priesthood, the order of Melchizedek (7.3); the priestly sacrifices of the old covenant were only a foreshadowing of Christ's death. Where only the High Priest could enter into the Holy of Holies in the old age of Judaism (on the Day of Atonement), now Christ *the* High Priest has entered the heavenly Temple with the blood of his own sacrifice, and opened the way into the very presence of God for *all* believers (9.11–14). Hence the thematic repetition of the call to 'draw near to God' (4.16; 7.25; 10.22; 11.6; 12.22).

The whole sweep of the argument from chapters 5–10 needs to be read if its full force is to be appreciated, but the keynote is struck in such verses as 9.9–12, 23–24 and 10.1.

> 9.9–12 – According to this arrangement [an outer tent which symbolizes the present age], gifts and sacrifices are offered which cannot perfect the conscience of the believer . . . but when Christ appeared as a high priest of the good things that have come, then through the greater and more perfect tent (not made with hands, that is, not of this creation) he entered once for all into the Holy Place, taking not the blood of goats and calves but his own blood, thus securing an eternal redemption.

> 9.23–24 – It was necessary for the copies of the heavenly things to be purified with these rites [of the old covenant], but the heavenly things themselves with better sacrifices than these. For Christ has entered not into a sanctuary made with hands,[59] a copy of the true one, but into heaven itself, now to appear in the presence of God on our behalf.

> 10.1 – For since the law has but a shadow of the good things to come instead of the true form of these realities, it can never, by the same sacrifices which are continually offered year by year, make perfect those who draw near.

In short, the *reality* of access to God, of a conscience cleansed from sin, of Christ's continuing priestly role, *has made the Jewish cult*

---

59. Note the reappearance (twice) of the key term in Stephen's critique of the Temple (Acts 7.48); see above §4.4.

wholly redundant. 'Christ (has) offered for all time a single sacrifice for sins'; 'where there is foregiveness of these, there is no longer any offering for sin' (10.12, 18). Who remains satisfied with the shadow when the substance is present? The message surely was clear enough: there is no further need of tabernacle or Temple, no need of sacrifice or priesthood; to go back to that (as some of his readers seem to have wanted) was to go back to the shadow, the inferior copy. In particular, for the author of Hebrews, there is now only one who can properly be called 'priest' – Jesus himself. His priesthood is a unique kind: he qualified for it by virtue of his resurrection ('indestructible life' – 7.16);[60] no ordinary human being can match that type ('the order of Melchizedek' – 7.3). Moreover, by virtue of this one real priest's effective ministry, all believers can now enter directly into the very presence of God, without mediation of human priest. Consequently those who yearn for a priesthood of the old kind, like the order of Aaron, an order of priesthood *within* the people of God, are in danger of falling back into the era of preparation and imperfection from which the advent of Christ had delivered them, and of losing the immediacy of communion with God which it was Christ's whole purpose to bring about. Where only priests could enter the sacred space and the place where God had put his name, now *all believers* can enter the very presence of God by direct mediation of Christ; *a distinct priesthood is no longer necessary.*[61]

(*c*) Not surprisingly, the writer to the Hebrews also makes use of the theme of *the heavenly Jerusalem* (cf. his use of the theme of 'rest' in Heb. 3 and 4). But, somewhat surprisingly, he leaves it until he has completed the main argument of the letter (in Heb. 10) and only then introduces it in explicit terms:

11.10, 15 – Abraham looked forward to the city which has founda-tions, whose builder and maker is God ... They (the patriarchs) desire a better country, that is, a heavenly one. Therefore God is not ashamed to be called their God, for he has prepared for them a city.

---

60. See e.g. R. McL. Wilson, *Hebrews*, NCB; Basingstoke: Marshall Morgan & Scott/ Grand Rapids: Eerdmans 1987, p. 125–6; Attridge, p. 203.

61. At this point in the original lectures in Rome I continued with the paragraphs which now form the extended note at the end of this chapter. But the digression somewhat disrupts the flow of argument and analysis (it certainly did in Rome: I had to abandon the rest of the lecture to engage in vigorous discussion); so it seems wiser in the published version to leave the more contentious corollaries till later.

12.22–23 – But you have come to Mount Zion and to the city of the living God, the heavenly Jerusalem, and to innumerable angels in festal gathering, and to the assembly of the first born who are enrolled in heaven, and to the judge who is God of all, and to the spirits of just men made perfect . . .

13.10–14 – We have an altar from which those who serve the tabernacle have no right to eat.[62] For the bodies of those animals whose blood is brought into the sanctuary by the high priest as a sacrifice for sin are burned outside the camp. So Jesus also suffered outside the gate in order to sanctify the people through his own blood. Therefore let us go forth to him outside the camp, and bear the abuse he endured. For here we have no lasting city, but we seek the city which is to come.

Why Hebrews should have left the theme of the heavenly city to the end like this and then drawn on it so consistently in all three chapters is not at all clear.[63] More clear is the fact that it is a variant on the theme which dominated the main body of the argument. As in Gal. 4.25–26, the heavenly city is another way of speaking (1) of the reality of God's purpose for his people for which the earthly city and its cult is an inadequate substitute, and (2) of the future goal of God's purpose in relation to which the present Jerusalem is an inadequate prefiguration. Moreover, the point being made by the author is also the same: this heavenly reality, this future hope is *already present* for those who follow in Jesus' train. Already they are enrolled in the citizenship of that heavenly city. What is poignantly true too, however, as clearly expressed in the final passage quoted above, is the fact that this orientation of theirs towards this heavenly city has as its reverse side *an already deep sense of alienation from the present Jerusalem*. Discipleship of Jesus means going 'outside the camp'; looking for the heavenly city to come means also looking away from the earthly Jerusalem.[64]

Here again, then, we see a use of the motif of the new Jerusalem not as a reinforcement of loyalty to the old, nor as an affirmation of

---

62. A eucharistic reference is unlikely to be present here; see Bruce, *Hebrews*, p. 401–2; Braun, *Hebräer*, pp. 463–4; Wilson, p. 243.

63. For detailed exegesis of these passages see particularly Braun, *Hebräer*, ad loc.; Attridge, *Hebrews*, ad loc.

64. Note the double play on 'going out' in 13.13: it is the converse side of the 'entering in' (to the heavenly rest – 3.18–4.11; to the heavenly sanctuary – 6.19–20; 9.12, 24–25), and is parallel to the 'going out' of Abraham (11.8; so linking in to the first announcement of the heavenly Jersualem theme – 11.9–10).

the power of the symbol which strengthens devotion to the symbol; far less any continuing sense that God's purpose will climax in the geographical Jerusalem and vindicate the historic people of Israel in the eyes of the nations. In Hebrews the motif of the new/heavenly Jerusalem reinforces instead the symbol of the people of God in the wilderness, a wandering people, a pilgrim people, still looking for the promised 'rest', without any 'fixed abode' on earth (Heb. 3–4). And by its antithetical juxtaposition of earthly Jerusalem with heavenly Jerusalem, of an outmoded cult with an effective reality 'outside the camp', Hebrews provides a powerful warning to any religious institution too well rooted in this age. The heavenly Jerusalem in Hebrews is not to be identified with any particular city or geographical location, but is characterized precisely by contrast to such – that to which one looks away while in the midst of earthly living, that to which one comes by going forth 'outside the camp'.

In short, it is difficult to avoid talking of a parting of the ways in the case of Hebrews. In Hebrews, more than in any other NT passage at which we have so far looked, we find a clear sense of a decisive breach with what had gone before. Together with other NT writings, Hebrews wishes, of course, to insist on the continuity between the old and the new – the 'rest' still outstanding (Heb. 3–4), the promise of the new covenant fulfilled (8.8–12), the same race being run (11.1– 12.2), and so on. But the corollary note of complete rejection of the old is sounded in a way which goes well beyond those struck by Stephen and by Paul. Certainly the great body of Jews who continued to value and cherish the cult, even when they could no longer practise it, must have felt deeply alienated by such a writing. And the writer's own sense of rejection and departure is climactically clear in 13.13. *For Hebrews and a Judaism still focussed on the Temple and its cult the ways had parted.*

5.7 I Peter and the Revelation of John

The conclusions to which Paul and Hebrews came as regards priesthood were not idiosyncratic or exceptional within earliest Christianity. On the contrary, they seem to have been the common self-understanding of Christians and of the diaspora congregations as they spread round the north-eastern quadrant of the Mediterranean. This is the clear implication to be drawn from I Peter and Revelation in particular:

I Peter 2.5 – '. . . like living stones be yourselves built into a spiritual house, to be a holy priesthood (*hierateuma*), to offer spiritual sacrifices acceptable to God through Jesus Christ';

I Peter 2.9 – 'You are a chosen race, a royal priesthood (*hierateuma*), a holy nation . . .'

Rev. 1.5–6 – 'To him who loves us and has freed us from our sins by his blood and made us a kingdom, priests (*hiereis*) to his God and Father . . .'

Rev. 5.10 – 'You have made them a kingdom and priests (*hiereis*) to our God, and they shall reign on earth.'

The point is that these descriptions refer to *all* Christians. In the thought of these writers, all Christians are priests, either in a corporate sense (I Peter 2.5, 9 – *hierateuma*),[65] or individually (Rev. 1.6; 5.10 – *hiereis*), not simply a sub-group within the ranks of Christian believers. This fits with the evidence of the NT as a whole. In all the references to Christian worship and Christian community within the NT *there is simply no allusion to any order of priesthood within the Christian congregations*. There are many ministries referred to – but never that of an individual Christian exercising a priesthood which was not shared by other Christians. And this cannot be accidental, particularly when priesthood was such a common factor in other cults of the time. The silence on this point can hardly be other than deliberate. It must mean simply that there *was no* such ministry or order in the churches of the first two generations.[66]

And the reason for this is sufficiently clear too – viz. the sense of eschatological fulfilment which was one of the main features of the infant Christian movement. What had required the mediation of priest previously was now open to all through the direct mediation of Christ. The immediacy of direct knowledge of God for which the prophets had longed (as in Isa. 54.13; Jer. 31.31–34; Joel 2.28–29) was now being experienced in the last days (John 6.43–51; II Cor. 3.2–18; Acts 2.17–18). The old ideal of a 'kingdom of priests' (Ex. 19.6; cf. Isa. 61.6) was being realized in the movement inaugurated by the eschatological events of Christ's death and resurrection, and by the outpouring of the Spirit at Pentecost. The Christian faith as it comes to expression in these passages *saw its distinction from traditional*

---

65. Vanhoye, *Old Testament Priests*, p. 261–2.

66. Vanhoye again maintains that the 'elders' of I Peter 5.1 must have had an implicitly priestly role but recognizes that some special pleading is involved (*Old Testament Priests*, pp. 264–7).

Judaism precisely in that *the delimitation of sacred space reserved for special priesthood, and requiring specially priestly acts which only some can perform, is no longer appropriate in the age of Christ.* It was this strong eschatological consciousness of immediacy of relation with God through Christ and his Spirit which made inevitable the parting of the ways on this key feature of second Temple Judaism.

We should simply add that in Revelation the theme of the new Jerusalem is again taken up in characteristically apocalyptic fashion (3.12; 21.1–3; 21.10–11, 22–27). A striking feature of the seer's handling of the theme is his interweaving of the correlate theme of the temple.[67] Already in heaven he can see a temple which lies open to the apocalyptist's gaze and from which issue the angels of judgment and the voice of God (11.19; 14.15, 17; 15.5–8; 16.1, 17). His vision is of the elders 'serving God day and night within his temple' (7.15). The faithful believer who conquers is promised a central structural role as a pillar in this temple of God (3.12). And yet 21.22 makes it clear that this is all *imagery*: where else could God be said to dwell but in a 'temple'? where else would God be worshipped but in a 'temple'? This is simply human imagery, an aid to human conceptuality. The reality for the seer is that heaven is where God is; and *where God is in reality needs no temple to mediate his presence.* So in the heavenly city to come there is no temple, 'for its temple is the Lord God the Almighty and the Lamb' (21.22). The means is not allowed to obscure the end; the instrument is not allowed to become the thing itself.

5.8 John's Gospel

Not least of importance for this part of our inquiry is the degree to which the Fourth Evangelist emphasizes that *the movement for which he speaks has parted company with mainstream Judaism precisely at the point of the cult.*

(*a*) Jesus is depicted as overshadowing and superceding *the Temple*. Jesus' word about the rebuilding of the Temple (2.19), which had been so important at an earlier stage of the Christian movement (Mark 14.58; Acts 6.14),[68] is now interpreted unequivocally as a reference to his resurrection: 'he spoke of the temple of his body' (2.21). As with Paul, 'the body of Christ' has become the social focus of the people of the Messiah in the new age which he introduced. Even sharper is Jesus' reply to the woman at the well in Samaria

---

67. See further McKelvey, *New Temple*, pp. 155–76.
68. See above §§3.5 and 4.3.

(4.21–24), when she asks him to resolve the old dispute between Judaean and Samaritan as to where was the proper place for the sanctuary to have been built (Mount Zion or Mount Gerizim) –

> Woman, believe me, the hour is coming when neither on this mountain [Gerizim] nor in Jerusalem will you worship the Father . . . But the hour is coming, and now is, when the true worshippers will worship the Father in spirit and truth, for such the Father seeks to worship him. God is spirit, and those who worship him must worship in spirit and truth

Here again the claim is plain: *the worship made possible by Jesus has left behind and rendered redundant all the old disputes and concerns over holy places, sacred spaces, sanctified traditions.* Such concern now hinders or prevents the real worship for which God looks. That worship does not depend on a particular sanctuary, central or otherwise. For the Fourth Evangelist the position is clear: Christ has taken the place of the Temple; the concept of a particular sacred space to be guarded and defended against rivals and defiling encroachment is no longer appropriate in the eschatological 'now' inaugurated by Christ's coming.

(b) Jesus is depicted as superceding the great *pilgrim festivals.* Particularly the Passover: *Jesus* is the Passover lamb (1.29); the bread at Passover (6.4) symbolizes himself (6.51); his death occurs at the time of slaughtering the Passover lambs (19.14);[69] of him is fulfilled the scripture concerning the slaughter of the Passover lamb (19.33) – 'Not a bone of him shall be broken' (19.36 = Ex. 12.46). In a similar way he fulfils the symbolism of the Feast of Tabernacles, which included a ceremony of pouring water down the altar, particularly on the seventh day of the feast, and which on the first night included the ritual of lighting four golden candlesticks in the court of women. Hence 7.37–38 –

> On the last days of the feast, the great day, Jesus stood up and proclaimed,
>> 'If any one thirst, let him come to me;
>> and let him drink, who believes in me'.
> As the scripture has said,
>> 'From his belly shall flow
>> rivers of living water'.

---

69. Hence the well-known conflict between John's Gospel and the Synoptics as to the chronology of the last supper and Jesus' crucifixion.

Hence also 8.12, which carries forward the theme of ch. 7 – 'I am the light of the world'. *Where the reality and truth is in Jesus, there is no need for such feasts in their traditional cultic form to be celebrated any longer.*

(c) Finally, Jesus is depicted as fulfilling and thus superceding *the purity regulations* of Judaism, as, less explicitly, the law (1.17; 4.10; 5.39–40; 6.31–35). The description of the water jars in 2.6, as standing there 'for the Jewish rites of purification (*kata ton katharismon tōn Ioudaiōn)*' is no doubt deliberate. And the consequent symbolic significance of the following 'sign', of turning just this water into wine, would hardly be lost on any Jewish reader: the 'good wine' (2.10) of Jesus has replaced the water of Judaism and is far better. Similarly in the only other reference to 'purification' (*katharismos*) in John's Gospel, the evangelist speaks of a dispute about purification between the disciples of the Baptist and a Jew (3.25), where once again the sequel makes it clear that the dispute is at the level of the old age, 'from the earth', whereas Christ and his teaching is 'from above', 'from heaven' (3.27, 31–34). Cleanness (*katharos*), the cleanness which matters, comes now through the ministry of Jesus himself (13.10–11) and through the word which he speaks (15.3; the only other references to the theme of cleanness in the Fourth Gospel). So, we might simply note, in the only use of the related verb in the Johannine corpus, *katharizein* ('to make clean'), cleansing is said to come from the blood of Jesus experienced through a sharing in his walk 'in the light', and requiring from the sinner only that 'we confess our sins' (I John 1.7, 9). Once again the implication is clear: *such purity concerns, and the cult which they exist to safeguard, are outmoded*; there is a purity and cleansing which comes through Jesus and which makes the old Jerusalem cult irrelevant.

In all these ways, and in his own way, John echoes the common view of the NT writers: that in Jesus the Messiah the old Temple and cult has been rendered redundant; to worship 'in Spirit and truth' is no longer to be determined by such concerns.[70]

5.9 Conclusions

The teaching of the NT documents is therefore uniform on this issue. As far as these writers were concerned, and those for whom they spoke, one of the major characteristics and underpinnings of second Temple Judaism had been left behind as *passe*, no longer appropriate

---

70. See also my *Jesus*, pp. 353–5.

for the eschatological people of God, including, not least, the idea of a sacred space requiring the mediation of a special priestly order offering sacrifices on behalf of the rest. That which the sacred space represented and sought to protect – the presence of God among his people – was now something focussed in Christ in such a way as to render the idea and continuation of such a protected sacred space unnecessary. There was no need for the Temple. The presence of God could be known by individual and body of believers in a direct and unmediated way. Grace could and should be mediated and experienced through any and every member of the body of believers. While there was every need for a multiplicity of ministry, and for leadership, there was clearly felt no need for a special order of priesthood. The cleansing and forgiveness of God could be known directly through the mediation of Christ, the only priest. There was no need for bloody sacrifice or altar; Christ himself is the once for all and final sacrifice. In the new Jerusalem there is no temple, 'for its temple is the Lord God Almighty and the Lamb' (Rev. 21.22).

This then was the first of the four pillars of second Temple Judaism which was undermined by the earliest Christians. *On this point at least there was a pulling apart and a parting of the ways at a very early stage.* Yet, even so, its significance should not be exaggerated. For, on the one hand, *the same process could be described as more of a broadening of the spectrum of second Temple Judaism.* For some of the critique of the Temple is better seen as a call for reform within Judaism, a call to return to more primitive ideals. Not only so, but the earliest Christian movement apparently included those who held firm to the Temple as well as those who abandoned it. In that respect, the parting of the ways has also to be seen historically as something of *a schism within earliest Christianity*; though, at the same time, we should not forget that it is only the voice of the latter (those who regarded the Temple as no longer relevant) which has been preserved in our canonical texts. And on the other hand, once again, we should not forget that the Judaism which emerged as Christianity's chief competitor after 70 CE, that is, rabbinic Judaism, has itself been able to survive and thrive without having any continuing temple or cult. In that sense, circumstances dictated that the second pillar of Judaism was going to be undermined in one way or another anyway. Even here, on this one point, the 'parting of the ways' is something far more complex than is usually recognized.

Extended Note:[71]

In the light of all this, and particularly of what certainly seems to me, the clarity of the argument of Hebrews, may I pause at this point to confess to some bewilderment at the way the argument of Hebrews can be so lightly ignored or set aside by those Christian traditions which wish to continue to justify a special order of priesthood within the people of God, a special order whose priestly ministry is distinct in kind from the priesthood of all the faithful. I recognize, of course, that an argument from *tradition* as over against scripture can carry great, and indeed decisive weight. What I find puzzling is the attempt to use *Hebrews* of all texts to expound the doctrine of a continuing special order of priesthood within the people of God. To use Heb. 5.1 to justify or explain Christian priesthood, as the Second Vatican Council does, while ignoring the clear thrust and argument of the letter as a whole,[72] seems to me to constitute a form of eisegesis and special pleading which cannot really be justified from tradition. I have no quarrel in principle with tradition taking up and developing a possible but less probable interpretation of some text; but can it be justified in making doctrinal use of an interpretation which runs counter to the main point of the text itself?

Similarly with the argument that the function of Christian priests is to represent the one true priesthood of Christ, which reads more like a *post hoc* rationalization than a defensible exegesis of Hebrews. For by clear implication it interposes once again one who is an indispensable mediator of grace between the believer and God, despite the fact that the concern of Hebrews was precisely to convince its readers that such mediation was no longer necessary. Vanhoye in his often excellent study of the high priesthood of Christ in Hebrews properly argues that 'in 10.14 the participation of all believers in the priesthood of Christ is therefore affirmed'.[73] But otherwise he seems to miss the whole sense of eschatological transformation, which pervades the central argument of the letter, of a new which renders the old redundant, of a real which leaves the copy far back in the shadow. So in particular when he goes on to suggest that the 'leaders' of 13.7 and 17 are representatives of Christ's priestly ministry and instruments of his priestly authority, that is, priests in a way that other members of the community are not,[74] the argument would most probably have

---

71. See above n. 61.
72. *Lumen Gentium*, §28.
73. Vanhoye, *Old Testament Priests*, p. 220.
74. Vanhoye, *Old Testament Priests*, pp. 229–232, 234–235. 'Leader' in itself, of course, has no priestly overtone; and nothing can be made of the talk of altar and sacrifice

been quite unacceptable to the author himself. In which case, it is no longer simply a matter of tradition interpreting scripture, but of tradition riding roughshod over scripture.

---

in 13.10 and 15 in view of the spriritualization clearly in view in 13.15–16 (on 13.16 see Vanhoye, p. 224).

6

Jesus, Covenant and Torah

Thus far we have seen how the importance of the Jerusalem Temple and its cult was undermined for the first Christians as they moved more and more out of Jerusalem, and how Jerusalem itself, while still a potent theological symbol, became an expression of universal rather than of national significance. What of the other pillars of Judaism indicated in chapter 2?

As was already evident in ch. 2, and will become still clearer as we proceed, it is impossible to study the interrelation between emerging Christianity and the next two 'pillars' separately – election and Torah. The Jewish understanding of election was wholly bound up with their understanding of Torah. The Torah was a fundamental expression of covenant status. Indeed in a quite proper sense the Torah itself was the covenant.[1] That is precisely why the phrase 'covenantal nomism' (despite its ugliness) is such a good summary of second Temple Judaism's self-definition – the Torah given by God to enable the chosen people of God to live within the covenant.

How did Jesus and his disciples react to this understanding of covenant grace, of law and election? Did this too become a bone of contention between Christian and Jew, between Christian Jew and Christian Gentile? As before, we must start with Jesus and ask how he related to the Torah, and whether the axiom of Israel's election was in any way a problem or issue for him.

6.1 Did Jesus set himself against the law?

What was Jesus attitude to the law? This is how the issue is often posed – as though the Torah was a free-standing entity whose relation to Jesus could be discussed in isolation, 'Jesus and the Law'. So, for example, W. Gutbrod:[2]

---

1. Cf. again *Mekilta* on Ex. 20.6, 'By covenant is meant nothing other than the Torah', cited above p.25.
2. *nomos*, TDNT, 4.1060–1 – a section headed 'Jesus' Negation of the Law'; followed by a longer section on 'Jesus' Affirmation of the Law'. See also e.g. W. Pannenberg, *Jesus: God and Man*, London: SCM Press/Philadelphia: Westminster 1968, p. 255; J. Moltmann,

> The essential and basic negation of the Law in Jesus consists in
> the fact that he deposes it from its position of mediation. What
> determines man's relation to God is no longer the Law and man's
> relation to it.

The issue is also regularly but somewhat misleadingly posed in terms
of a distinction between written and oral law. By 'oral law' is meant
the Halakah – legal interpretations of the (written) Torah.[3] The best
examples of such interpretation are those preserved in rabbinic tradition. The Mishnah was the initial codification of these traditions,
(completed about 200 CE), but the practice long predates the
Mishnah, which refers back explicitly to Pharisaic teachers of the
pre-70 period, particularly Hillel and Shammai and the schools
(houses) which carried on their characteristic emphases.[4]

It should be noted at once that the concern expressed in these oral
rulings is wholly admirable. It sprang from the recognition that the
Torah derived from and referred primarily to a different age and to
different situations (then more nomadic, now more urban; then with
a view to an independent state, now no longer a sovereign nation).
So there was a need to interpret the Torah for changed and changing
circumstances, a need to expound and elaborate the simpler rules and
principles to take account of the complexity of daily life. In recognizing and responding to this obvious need the Pharisees showed themselves to be more progressive and practical than the Sadducees, who
thought the written Torah alone was sufficient (Josephus, *Ant.*
13.297).[5] The natural consequence was the development of a sequence
of more specific rulings, that is, the 'oral law'. 'Halakah', it should
be recalled, is derived from the Hebrew word meaning 'to walk'
(*halak*). As a collective name for these rulings (*halakoth*), therefore,
Halakah denotes simply guidance on how one should walk, the
response to specific requests for direction on how life should be lived
in obedience to the law, how the devout Israelite should fulfil the

The Crucified God, London: SCM Press/New York: Harper & Row 1974, p.32; Goppelt,
Theology, vol. 1, pp. 101–5; and those cited by R. Banks, *Jesus and the Law in the Synoptic
Tradition*, SNTSMS 28; Cambridge University 1975, pp. 3–5. For typical Christian
characterization of the law in negative terms see C. Klein, *Anti-Judaism in Christian
Theology*, 1975; ET London: SPCK/Philadelphia: Fortress 1978, pp. 39–66. See also the
criticisms of W. Pannenberg and J. Moltmann in J. T. Pawlikowski, *Christ in the Light of
the Christian–Jewish Dialogue*, New York: Paulist 1982, pp. 37–47.

   3. See e.g. Schürer, 2.339–46.

   4. See H. Danby, *The Mishnah*, Oxford University 1933, index, 'Hillel, School of',
'Hillel the Elder', 'Shammai, School of', and 'Shammai the Elder'.

   5. Schürer, 2.407–411.

often repeated call to 'walk in the law/statutes/ordinances/ways of God.'[6] The Mishnah then can be properly regarded as, in the main, a collection of case law – the rulings (and controversies) preserved from earlier generations as the ever enlarging basis for future rulings. This also means that the Pharisees in particular would not have regarded the 'oral law' as something distinct from the written law, since the 'oral law' was simply the exposition and application of the (written) law, the Torah itself.[7]

The issue can then be posed: What was Jesus' attitude to the law written and/or oral? A classic treatment of the theme is that of J. Jeremias, who sees Jesus' criticism as directed particularly against the *oral* law, the Halakah, and Jesus as very critical of the Pharisaic elaboration of the law.[8] For Jeremias the critique is clearest at three points. A restatement of his exposition might run as follows.

(a) *Sabbath halakah* – Mark 2.23–3.5. We know from *Jub.* 2.17–33, 50.8–12 and CD 10–11 how far the Sabbath halakah had already developed by the time of Jesus. For example, *Jub.* 2.29–30 already warned against preparing food on the Sabbath or drawing water on the Sabbath. *Jub.* 50 elaborates the work that is forbidden on the Sabbath in terms of going on a journey, ploughing a field, kindling a fire, riding an animal, etc. CD 10–11 is even more rigorous, and includes the firm instruction: 'No man shall assist a beast to give birth on the Sabbath day. And if it should fall into a cistern or pit, he shall not lift it out on the Sabbath.' Both documents predate Jesus' mission by a hundred years or so; and both show therefore that there was a well developed Sabbath halakah many years before Jesus. The level of Halakah reflected in Mark 2.23–3.5 is well within the range of Halakah already developed (and no doubt being practised at Qumran at that very time). There is no problem therefore with the argument that the Pharisaic Halakah reflected in Mark 2–3 is highly plausible for the time and circumstances.[9] The point then is that Jesus is presented as rejecting such Halakah: it prevented him from fulfilling the command to love his neighbour.

(b) *Corban* – Mark 7.9–13. The passage seems to indicate that it

---

6. See e.g. Ex. 16.4; Lev. 18.3–4; Deut. 28.9; Josh. 22.5; Jer. 44.23; Ezek. 5.6–7; Dan. 9.10; Micah 4.2.

7. Schürer, 2.389–391.

8. Jeremias, *Theology*, pp. 208–211; similarly Goppelt, *Theology*, §9.

9. Against Sanders, *Jesus*, pp. 265–6, who overreacts against such as Jeremias at this point and weakens his case by resorting to ridicule – 'Pharisees did not organize themselves into groups to spend their Sabbaths in Galilean cornfields in the hope of catching someone transgressing (Mark 2.23f)'.

was possible for a son to avoid all obligations to his parents by fictitiously dedicating to the Temple all the support he owed them – apparently even if he acted out of spite or anger.[10] This presumably would be based on Num. 30.2 –

> When a man vows a vow to the Lord, or swears an oath to bind himself by a pledge, he shall not break his word; he shall do according to all that proceeds out of his mouth.

Num. 30.3ff. gives precedent for circumstances where the command of v. 2 could be disregarded. And *m.Nedarim* (Vows) shows similar concern to alleviate the strict principle enunciated in Num. 30.2. But from Mark 7.9–13 it would appear that at this time the ruling in force was that a vow made in the circumstances indicated could *not* be retracted.[11] Here again Jesus is shown as rejecting the halakah: the elaborated exposition of this law was running directly counter to the obvious and prior obligation of the law regarding a child's responsibility to its parents.

(c) *Purity law* – Mark 7.1–8. We have already dealt with this passage under §3.2. It depicts Jesus as rejecting halakoth regarding the purity of hands which appears also to have been then current; and doing so on the grounds that it gave outward purity an importance to be accorded only to inward purity (Mark 7.15ff.).[12]

In each case it is very easy to argue along with Jeremias: that Jesus rejected the Pharisaic Halakah 'in a radical way';[13] and that for Jesus such rigorous elaboration of the law too often offended against the higher obligation to love one's neighbour as oneself.

If the issue regarding Jesus and the 'oral law' may be said to be fairly clear cut (at least on the evidence as we have it), there is much more dispute regarding Jesus' attitude to the *written* Torah, to the law as such.

On the one hand, Jesus is shown without contrivance to have been willing to observe the law. He is recalled as wearing the tassels required by law (Num. 15.38–39; Deut. 22.12) on the four corners of his outer garment (Mark 6.56 par.; Matt. 9.20/Luke 8.44; Matt.

---

10. Jeremias, *Theology*, p. 210.
11. Sanders, *Jewish Law*, p. 56–7 is dubious (though less confident on the point) that such a ruling was current among Pharisees of the time, but notes a similar ruling in Philo (*Hypothetica* 7.5).
12. See also below §6.3.
13. Jeremias, *Theology*, p. 208; likewise Goppelt, *Theology*, vol. 1, p. 90.

14.36). He tells the cleansed leper to 'Go, show yourself to the priest, and offer for your cleansing what Moses commanded' (Mark 1.44 pars.;[14] Luke 17.14). To the rich young man's request, 'What must I do to inherit eternal life?', Jesus replies by directing his attention to the second table of the ten commandments (Mark 10.19). And it is obvious from not a few passages that Jesus drew much at least of the authority for his own teaching from the Jewish scriptures and that he drew freely on them in his controversies (e.g. Mark 7.10; 10.6–7; 12.26, 29–31). Not least we should note Matt. 5.17–20 –

> Think not that I have come to abolish the law and the prophets; I have come not to abolish them but to fulfil them. For truly, I say to you, till heaven and earth pass away, not an iota, not a dot, will pass from the law until all is accomplished. Whoever then relaxes one of the least of these commandments and teaches men so, shall be called least in the kingdom of heaven; but he who does them and teaches them shall be called great in the kingdom of heaven.

Whether or not Jesus actually said these words,[15] the point to be noted here is simply the fact that Matthew could present Jesus as teaching in this vein, as an acceptable portrayal of Jesus. By 'fulfil' we may take the Matthean Jesus to mean 'complete'; that is, in terms of Matthew's overall depiction of Jesus, 'reveal the true meaning of the law and demonstrate it in action'.[16]

On the other hand, at certain points Jesus does seem, at least on the surface, to set aside the most relevant law. (1) Matt. 5.38ff. – 'You have heard that it was said, "An eye for an eye and a tooth for a tooth". But I say to you, . . .'. Here it is not a later ruling on a law but the law itself, the *lex talionis* (Ex. 21.24; Lev. 24.20; Deut. 19.21) which Jesus sets aside. (2) Mark 10.2–9 – Jesus' teaching on divorce, where he is remembered as repealing the Mosaic permission for divorce (Deut. 24.1). (3) Mark 7.14–23 – where he seems to cut at the whole basis of the laws on clean and unclean foods, particularly his words in 7.15, 'There is nothing outside a man which by going into him can defile him.' Mark himself understood the text in such radical terms: 'Thus he declared all foods clean' (7.19).

The question is, Do these last three examples really undercut the

---

14. See above p. 50 and n. 3.

15. For discussion see e.g. Banks, *Law*, pp. 204–26; W. D. Davies and D. C. Allison, *Matthew*, ICC; Edinburgh: T. & T. Clark; Vol. 1 1988, pp. 482–503. See also below §8.5.

16. See review and discussion in R. A. Guelich, *The Sermon on the Mount. A Foundation for Understanding*, Waco: Word 1982, pp. 139–41.

law, or do they fall within the range of the then current, and currently acceptable, debate about the law and its interpretation? Matthew clearly understood the antitheses of ch. 5 in the light of 5.17–20, and intended them to be so understood, by placing just these four verses at the head of the teaching on the law which was to follow. That is to say, he clearly understood the antitheses ('You have heard it said . . .; but I say to you . . .') as a radical, in the sense of deeper, interpretation, *not* as an abrogation of the related laws. And that applies no doubt to his record of Jesus' teaching on the *lex talionis* as well. Likewise Matthew's version or redaction of the Mark 10 (divorce) and Mark 7 (true cleanliness) passages indicates that he understood Jesus' teaching as a *relativizing*, not as an abrogating of the laws in question. Where scriptural rules are in conflict, one has to be given a higher priority than the other, but without necessarily implying that any are to be wholly dispensed with. So, Gen. 2.24 (the paradisial order of marriage) shows that Deut. 24.1 should be interpreted very tightly (unchastity the only allowable cause of divorce) (Matt. 19.3–9). And in Matthew's rendering of Mark 7.15–19, the sharpness of Jesus' antithesis between outward cleanness and inward cleanness disappears, and the words become an example of 'both-and' teaching: inner purity as more important than outward, but as not thereby necessarily rendering all ritual purity unnecessary (Matt. 15.17).[17]

If, therefore, Matthew's is a legitimate way of taking such teaching of Jesus, it then becomes very plausible to argue that Jesus' teaching was within the range of the then acceptable debate regarding the interpretation and application of the law. So much so that Sanders and others can argue that Jesus did not dispute the law's authority[18] and that there was no real point of dispute between Jesus and the Pharisees.[19]

---

17. See also B. Lindars, 'All Foods Clean: Thoughts on Jesus and the Law', *Law and Religion. Essays on the Place of the Law in Israel and Early Christianity*, ed. B. Lindars, Cambridge: James Clarke 1988, pp. 61–71; and further above §3.2 and below §8.5.

18. See e.g. Thoma, pp. 115–16, also cited by Mussner, *Tractate*, p. 120; J. Koenig, *Jews and Christians in Dialogue. New Testament Foundations*, Philadelphia: Westminster 1979, p. 26.

19. Sanders, *Jesus*, p. 291 – 'I find no substantial conflict between Jesus and the Pharisees'. In private correspondence Sanders adds: 'In discussing the synoptic passages on the law, I have argued that it is hard to find any substantial disputes with *anyone*; that is, no dispute that goes beyond the normal range of disagreement. I do not think that Jesus was especially close to the Pharisees. They, like others, upheld the sabbath law and the food laws. Jesus seems to have transgressed neither, in the view of anyone, as far as we can tell from any and all evidence from the first century. Other people may have turned down his appeal to scriptural analogy as justifying e.g. plucking grain, but the synoptic passage does not even say this: the dispute ends with his defence. The Houses disagreed with one another over more-or-less equal issues. Neither seems to have regarded the other as *transgressing*,

6.2 'Friend of sinners'

To pose the issue as we did at the beginning of §6.1, however, is misleading. It invites the inference that the whole issue was simply a question of law-keeping in the sense of moral choice and ethical conduct, or, more profoundly, of knowing and doing God's will. On this point the discussion through most of the century has continued to be determined to a remarkable extent by the older Liberal Protestant emphasis on Jesus as the ideal moral teacher.

The issue, however, has to be seen much more in terms of coven- antal nomism – *law-keeping as an expression of covenant status, of covenant membership* – law-keeping as what the covenant members needed to do in order to affirm and maintain their status within the covenant people of God.[20] The issue as it came to the fore at the time of Jesus, as we shall see, was not merely about points of law, or of ethical decision, but about how Jews should live as being the people of God, about what walking (halakah) according to God's statutes actually involved. The result was, as we shall also see, considerable factional dispute – and, more important, an effective *dis*-covenanting by each faction of those who disagreed with its halakah.

The point can be seen most clearly by analysing the jibe levelled against Jesus: that he was 'a friend of tax collectors and *sinners*' (Matt. 11.19/Luke 7.39). The jibe implies clearly that this 'friendship with sinners' was something customary on the part of Jesus, and that it caused offence to other Jews, including at least some Pharisees (Mark 2.15–16 and Luke 15.1–2). But who were these 'sinners'? Sanders criticizes Jeremias with some justification for identifying the 'sinners' in a too straightforward manner with 'the people of the land' ('*amme ha-arets*').[21] But in focussing his discussion of 'The Sinners' too exclusively on this issue, he understates the full force of the term 'sinner' and seems to forget how condemningly judgmental it was for one Jew to describe another as 'sinner'. For 'sinner' meant not just the morally or ethically wicked, 'deliberate and unrepentant transgressors of the law'[22] (as e.g. Pss. 1.1, 5; 37.32–36; Sir. 41.5–

---

just as having a weak argument in favour of their own practice.' This response does not seem to me to take enough account of the significance of the use of the term 'sinners' in the reported criticisms of Jesus; hence the main thrust of §6.2.

20. It is this recognition of the *covenant* function of the law which the present stage of the debate owes to Sanders, *Paul and Palestinian Judaism* (see above §§ 1.4d; 2.3).

21. Sanders, *Jesus*, pp. 176ff.: 'I know of no passage in Jewish literature which indicates that any group which can reasonably be connected with the Pharisees considered the common people as beyond the pale' (p. 180).

22. Sanders, *Jesus*, p. 385 n. 14 cites Jeremias approvingly here.

8). It was also, as Sanders recognizes, a term of *exclusion* – 'those beyond the pale and outside the common religion by virtue of their implicit or explicit rejection of the commandments of the God of Israel'.[23] And, more to the point, at the time of Jesus it was a very *factional* term – denoting those outside the boundary as defined by the group who used it, where 'wickedness', by definition, was *conduct outside the boundary*, conduct deemed unacceptable *to God* by those who counted themselves as inside.[24]

The most obvious example is where 'sinner' is used more or less as a synonym for '*Gentile*'.[25] Thus *Jub.* 23.23–24:

> He will rouse up against them the sinners of the nations
>   who have no mercy or grace for them . . .
> And they will cause turmoil in Israel and sin against Jacob;
>   . . .
> In those days, they will cry out and call and pray
>   to be saved from the hand of the sinners, the gentiles . . .

Or the *Psalms of Solomon*, written after the conquest of Jerusalem by the Roman legions of Pompey – so *Pss. Sol.* 2.1–2:

> Arrogantly the sinner broke down the strong walls with a
>   battering ram and you did not interfere.
> Gentile foreigners went up to your place of sacrifice;
>   they arrogantly trampled (it) with their sandals.

As we shall see, Paul reflects this typical usage when he points out to Peter that 'We are Jews by birth and not Gentile sinners' (Gal. 2.15).[26] In such passages the unifying concept is not that Gentiles by definition were murderers and robbers. Rather it is that *their conduct lay outside*

---

23. Sanders, *Jesus*, p. 210. Schiffman also understates this significance of 'sinner' as an abusive epithet when he claims: 'Even the most virulent never accuse the members of other groups of having left the Jewish community. Sinners they were, but Jews all the same' ('Crossroads', *JCSD*, p. 116; *Who was a Jew?*, pp. 3–4 and passim).

24. Sanders drew attention to this same feature in his *Paul and Palestinian Judaism*, index 'The Wicked'; e.g. on *Jubilees*, pp. 364–75. Unfortunately, he failed to integrate this evidence into his treatment of 'sinners' in *Jesus*.

25. The following paragraphs are an abbreviated version of part of my 'Pharisees, Sinners and Jesus', *The Social World of Formative Judaism and Christianity*, H. C. Kee FS, ed. J. Neusner et al., Philadelphia: Fortress 1988, pp. 264–89 reprinted in my *Jesus, Paul and the Law*, pp. 61–88.

26. See also Ps. 9.17; Tobit 13.8(6); *Pss.Sol.* 1.1; Luke 6.33 ('sinners')/Matt. 5.47 ('Gentiles'); Mark 14.41. pars.

the boundary of the law. They were literally 'law-less'. They did not have the law, therefore did not belong to the people of the law, and therefore did not keep the law.

The point which must be noted here, however, is that boundaries could also be drawn *within* the people of Israel, with 'sinners' used to describe those of whom a particular faction disapproved. So in I Maccabees: 'sinners and lawless men' (1.34; 2.44,48) evidently include those whom the writer regarded as apostates, that is, as *apostate Jews*. And in the period following the initial Maccabean revolt factionalism seems to have become very intense, with 'sinner' or equivalent regularly used to rebuke and denounce opposition groups and parties. Thus, for example, *Jubilees* and *I Enoch* show that the calendar became a crucial bone of contention. In each case the attitude is clear: to observe a festival or ordinance whose date has been wrongly computed is *non*-observance, failure to observe the covenant, 'walking in the feasts of the Gentiles' (*Jub.* 6.32–35; 23.16, 26). Likewise in *I Enoch* 'the righteous', 'who walk in the ways of righteousness' mark themselves off clearly from those who 'sin like the sinners' in wrongly reckoning the months and feasts and years (*I Enoch* 82. 4–7) – that is, *Jews condemning other Jews as 'sinners', as putting themselves in the status of Gentiles.*

Particularly notable in such factionalist polemic is the sharp antithesis between 'righteous' and 'sinner'. The writers, of course, regard themselves as (or speak for) 'the righteous', that is, as those (the only ones) who live in accordance with the law and thus maintain their covenant status. They castigate and denounce the 'sinners', that is, as living in effect outside the covenant. In each case it is the voice of Jewish factionalism (the righteous) condemning other Jews as 'sinners'. So in *I Enoch* 1–5, the 'righteous/chosen' rebuke the 'sinners/impious' (1.1, 7–9; 5.6–7) – 'You have not persevered, nor observed the law of the Lord' (5.4). Once again, *'sinners' denote Jews who practised their Judaism differently from the 'righteous'.* Similarly in the Dead Sea Scrolls. The covenanters had developed their own particular interpretation of the Torah – in reference to the Teacher of Righteousness, their sense of being the new covenant, their disowning of the Temple cult in Jerusalem, and their intensification of the law as practised at Qumran. Those who had not gone along with them, the political and religious opponents with who they had parted company in the second century BCE, are denounced roundly: they are the men of Belial, 'those who seek smooth things', 'deceivers'; they have departed from the paths of righteousness, transgressed the covenant, and so on (e.g. CD 1.13–21; 1QS 2.4–5; 1QH 2.8–19; 4.6–8; 1QpHab 2.1–4; 5.3–8; 4QpNah 2.7–10). According to the usual interpretation of these passages, these opponents included the Pharisees in particular.[27]

Characteristic also are the Psalms of Solomon, composed about a hundred years before Jesus' mission. They were written by those who considered themselves the 'righteous/devout' (e.g. 3.3–7; 4.1, 8; 9.3; 10.6; 13.6–12; 15.6–7). Their opponents were 'sinners' – that is, not just Gentiles or blantantly wicked individuals, but including their factional opponents within Judaea, probably the Hasmonean Sadducees who had usurped the priesthood and defiled the sanctuary (1.8; 2.3; 4.8; 7.2; 8.12–13; 17.5–8, 23). In other words, once again *'the righteous' are Jews who were condemning other Jews as 'sinners'.* Finally we might note *Test. Mos.* 7 – a forthright attack on 'godless men, who represent themselves as being righteous'; 'with hand and mind' they 'touch unclean things', even though they themselves say, 'Do not touch me lest you pollute me' (7.3, 9–10) – an attack quite probably once again on Pharisees, and clearly reflecting deeply felt disputes over issues of ritual purity.

This range of literature just reviewed includes most of the main writings which have come down to us from Jewish groups in Palestine in the 150–200 years before Jesus. They also stretch across that period. And, most strikingly, they all bear the stamp of factional dispute. Indeed, this period in Judaism seems to have been riven with factional dispute.[28] We do not have evidence from any other period of ancient Judaism where the picture is so clear. *Evidently within the Judaism of Jesus' day there were various groups who regarded themselves as alone loyal to the covenant and the law, and who regarded and denounced their fellow Jews as being disloyal.* And key and characteristic terms in the several polemics were 'righteous' and 'sinner'.

The significance of all this becomes clearer thanks to the insights of sociology and social anthropology – particularly with regard to *the role of conflict in group self-definition.*[29] In order to form and maintain their identity, groups have to differentiate themselves from other groups. The closer other groups are to them, and the more alike to

---

27. See e.g. those referred to in Saldarini, *Pharisees*, p. 279 n. 6.

28. 'The heyday of Jewish sectarianism was from the middle of the second century BCE to the destruction of the temple in 70 CE' (Cohen, *Maccabees to Mishnah*, p. 143); see also Saldarini, *Pharisees*, pp. 65, 210–1; J. A. Overman, *Matthew's Gospel and Formative Judaism. The Social World of Matthean Community*, Minneapolis: Fortress 1990, ch. 1.

29. In the article just mentioned (n. 25) I was drawing particularly on L. A. Coser, *The Foundations of Social Conflict*, London: Routledge 1956.

them, the more important it is to define the boundary between them. This has two corollaries. (1) In this process, conflict can play an important part, in binding a group together in the face of a common enemy, and in strengthening its sense of distinctiveness and of its rightness in that distinctiveness. *Where the groups are close or very similar, the conflict is likely to be more intense*: it is the brother who threatens identity most (the well-known phenomenon of 'sibling rivalry'); it is the party most like your own which threatens to draw away your support and to undermine your reason for existence as a separate entity.

(2) In this process it will be *the points of distinctiveness*, the matters on which they disagree, which inevitably will become the chief differentiation and boundary markers between the rival groups. This will mean that features of their respective profiles, which otherwise may not have been very important in relation to other features in that profile, assume a much larger importance, precisely because they are the points of differentiation, the boundary markers. We have already seen this in relation to second Temple Judaism as a whole, in terms of self-differentiation of Jew over against Gentile, by reference to circumcision, Sabbath and food laws in particular.[30] When it comes to differentiation *within* Judaism, *the boundary markers were bound to be precisely those points of disagreement over halakah*, over covenantal nomism: how to live as a devout and faithful Jew. Hence the exaggerated emphasis on calendar, on legitimate priesthood, and on ritual purity, which are a feature of the evidence just reviewed.

The point is that such conflict is not simply a matter of 'sweetly reasonable' schoolroom disagreement. It is not like the House debates, where the differing opinions could be retained within rabbinic tradition as examples of quite acceptable diversity of opinion. Such an assessment does not take adequate account of the depth of feeling evident in such writings. The language could be so fierce because the distinguishing issue was seen quite simply as a matter of life and death: personal and group identity was at stake; salvation was at stake; the meaning and character of God's covenant with Israel was at stake. And these different interpretations, which might seem minor to the onlooker but as expressing fundamental differences by the factions themselves, had to be defended at all costs by those who represented the groups. All this is implicit in the word 'sinner' as a term of inter-factional polemic. At the time of Jesus, to call a fellow Jew a 'sinner' was both to *condemn* that person as effectively outside the covenant and to defend one's own identity and boundaries,

---

30. See above §2.3.

the group's interpretation of what walking within the covenant meant.

Where do *Pharisees* fit into all this? We cannot attribute any of the second Temple Jewish literature just reviewed to the Pharisees with any confidence (perhaps the *Psalms of Solomon*).[31] Nevertheless, we can be confident that they shared much of that party-spirit and factional outlook. The following evidence should be considered. (1) It is generally agreed that 'Pharisees' probably meant originally, 'separated ones'. They were marked out, even from other Jews, by their determination to keep themselves 'set apart' for God.[32] This chimes in with what was said above regarding the Pharisaic ideal as a purity group,[33] and indicates what must be regarded as basically a factional attitude: in order to preserve their own ideal and identity they were bound to be critical of others who seemed to them to threaten that ideal and identity. We shall see later how this probably worked out in relation to table-fellowship.[34] (2) We saw above that Pharisees are among the most likely groups to have been the targets for the barbs of the Dead Sea Scrolls and the Testament of Moses. If so we need have little doubt that some at least of their number would have responded by drawing the lines of distinction between themselves and their attackers with equal vigour. (3) We know from Josephus and Acts that Pharisees were marked by *akribeia*, that is, by concern to keep the law with scrupulous accuracy and exactness (Josephus, *War* 1.108–109; 2.162; *Life* 191; *Ant.* 20.200–1; Acts 22.3; 26.5).[35] It should cause no surprise, then, if they regarded those who did not share that *akribeia* as insufficiently faithful to the law, as lawless or 'sinners'. (4) We know from Paul that there was at least one Pharisee who was prepared to go beyond verbal criticism of his fellow Jews to

---

31. See e.g. G. W. E. Nickelsburg, *Jewish Literature between the Bible and the Mishnah*, Philadelphia: Fortress/London: SCM Press 1981, p. 212; R. B. Wright in Charlesworth, *Old Testament Pseudepigrapha*, Vol. 2, pp. 641–2.

32. Schürer, 2.396–7: Since all Israel was obligated to a separation from uncleanness, 'the Pharisees must have obtained their name from a separation in which the main body of the people did not participate, in other words, from having set themselves apart, by virtue of their stricter understanding of the concept of purity, not only from the uncleanness of the Gentiles ... but also from that uncleanness which, in their opinion, adhered to a great part of the people itself. It is in this sense that they were called the "separated" or "self-separating".' See also Saldarini, *Pharisees*, pp. 215, 220–1.

33. See above §3.2(*b*).

34. See below §6.3.

35. See particularly A. I. Baumgarten, 'The Name of the Pharisees', *JBL* 102 (1983), pp. 413–417.

outright physical force, in order to defend the integrity of Israel's covenant status.[36]

Against this background, the Gospels' attribution to Pharisees of the jibe 'sinners' in relation to Jesus' halakah and conduct makes perfect sense – particularly when set over against 'righteous', as in Mark 2.16. As with so many of these other factions, the claim to righteousness would undoubtedly have been fundamental to their identity. They believed that they were being faithful to their covenant obligations and therefore were 'righteous'. Since some at least of that claim was bound up with their own distinctive halakah, the claim to being righteous was a way of affirming and defending that halakah. And inevitably such a claim would carry with it the corollary that those who ignored that halakah, disputed it, or interpreted and practised the law differently and in a way which called in question their own interpretation, were *not* righteous; that is, they were 'sinners'. Consequently, the severity of their condemnation of other Jews (whoever they were) and of Jesus for consorting with such should not be played down. The depth of this factional hostility towards Jesus should not be ignored. The importance of what was at stake for both Pharisee and Jesus regarding the true understanding of God's will should not be ignored. This is the dimension of 'sinners' which Sanders has left out of account and which undercuts what would otherwise be an impressive critique of Jeremias.[37]

6.3 Jesus and the halakah of Pharisees and Qumran – the issue of table-fellowship

In the light of all this the question of Jesus and the law can be, and indeed must be wholly recast. It was not simply a question of 'law and gospel', or to be transposed into these terms as quickly as possible. It was not simply a question of how one might or should reach ethical decisions – an ethic of rules or an ethic of love – however much such

---

36. See further below §7.2. The continued failure to use Paul as a source for our knowledge of pre-70 Pharisaism, albeit a 'hostile witness', is regrettable, not least since he is the *only* Pharisee from the pre-70 period and writing in the pre-70 period from whom we have *any* testimony whatsoever. Segal, *Paul*, hopefully marks a step in the right direction.

37. This is true also of Sanders' most recent work, *Jewish Law*, particularly pp. 236–42 on 'Exclusivism', where the issue is still focussed on the Pharisees' attitude to the ordinary people and on whether they 'controlled Judaism as a religion' (with Jeremias still the target). What Sanders fails to note, however, is that clear boundaries and vigorous defence of them is necessary precisely when a group does *not* control society and must mark itself off from the dominant or majority groups (see Saldarini, *Pharisees*, p. 8, n. 11). And again, no account is taken of the factional use of 'sinner' in Mark 2.16.

questions may follow from what Jesus said and did. It was much more a matter of *challenging a factional attitude to and expression of the law*, an attitude which was undermining the basic principle expressed in God's choice of Israel.

We can see something of this in the *Sabbath* disputes already examined. According to Mark 2.23–3.5 what Jesus evidently resisted and criticized was an attitude which made a fellow Jew's well-being subservient to an elaborated Sabbath halakah, in such a way as to call the principle of the Sabbath itself in question. In all three Synoptic accounts, the criticism here is directed against Pharisees. But just as interesting is the Q material which Matthew includes in the account of the healing of the man with the withered hand (Matt. 12.9–14) and which Luke includes in his variant account of a man being healed of the dropsy on the Sabbath (Luke 14.1–6): 'Which of you, if he has one sheep and it falls into a pit on the Sabbath, will not lay hold of it and lift it out?' (Matt. 12.11/Luke 14.5; cf. Luke 13.15). Since, as we saw above, CD specifically *dis*-allows any member of the sect to lift a beast, which had fallen into a cistern or pit, out again on the Sabbath (CD 11), the implication of Jesus' saying is clear: he was appealing to the fact that Pharisees disagreed on this very point of halakah with the Essenes, appealing to the logic of their own more liberal halakah.[38] The argument, then, is not only a good example of rabbinic argument – *a minore ad maius (qal wahomer)*; it is also to be seen as an attempt to turn factional dispute to good account. In effect Jesus says, 'If you Pharisees can see the need to disagree with the Essenes on this point, if you see that the life of an animal is more important than this point of halakah, then you should also recognize that the same principle applies in the case of meeting *human* need on the Sabbath.'

However, the distinctive point for which Jesus contended in dispute with Pharisee and Essene comes out most clearly in the question of *table-fellowship*. It is on this issue that the jibe about Jesus and sinners almost always comes to focus: 'Why does he eat with tax collectors and sinners?' (Mark 2.16); 'the son of man came eating and drinking, and they say, "Behold, a glutton and a drunkard, a friend of tax collectors and sinners!"' (Matt. 11.19); 'This man receives sinners and eats with them' (Luke 15.2); 'He has gone in to be the guest of a man who is a sinner' (Luke 19.7). *It is on this point that Pharisees*

---

38. This is consistent with Matthew's redaction of Mark elsewhere (see below §8.5*a*), where he sets Jesus' teaching into the context of rabbinic debate. But the fact that Luke also has this particular tradition indicates that in this case Matthew's material cannot be attributed solely to his own editorial reworking.

were remembered as having been most regularly critical of Jesus, and at this point therefore, we may deduce from the above survey of second Temple Jewish factionalism, that *they perceived their own identity and boundaries to be most under threat from the criticism implicit in Jesus' own practice of table-fellowship.*[39]

Here we need to remind ourselves of how important was the principle and practice of hospitality in the ancient world, and particularly of the religious and social significance of the meal table in the Ancient Near East. In Jewish thought Abraham and Job were extolled as the models of hospitality, where it was precisely the shared food which was the expression of that hospitality (Gen. 18; Job 31.31–32).[40] Jeremias has expressed this significance of the meal table well:[41]

> . . . to invite a man to a meal was an honour. It was an offer of peace, trust, brotherhood and forgiveness; in short, sharing a table meant sharing life.
>
> . . . In Judaism in particular, table-fellowship means fellowship before God, for the eating of a piece of broken bread by everyone who shares in the meal brings out the fact that they all share in the blessing which the master of the house had spoken over the unbroken bread.

We also should recall that table-fellowship was of great importance for Jesus himself. (1) Much of his teaching took place in the context of the meal table; it was quite literally 'table-talk' (Mark 2.15–17 pars.; 14.3–9 par.; Luke 7.36–50; 10.39–40; 11.37–41; 14.1–24; 19.5–7). Indeed, Jesus' enjoyment of the meal table was proverbial – 'a glutton and a drunkard' (Matt. 11.19/Luke 7.34). (2) The meal was also a feature of his teaching – especially the wedding banquet with its clear eschatological overtones (Mark 2.19 pars.; Matt. 22.1–14; 25.10; Luke 14.16–24; 22.30). Particularly significant is the indication that he wanted his practice of table-fellowship to be determined by and thus to foreshadow the eschatological banquet in character (Luke 14.13, 21 – those whom the master calls to be brought into the eschatological banquet are those whom Jesus encouraged his Pharisaic host to invite to his own table).

It was the message which Jesus thus both taught and lived out

---

39. Cf. particularly Saldarini, *Pharisees*, pp. 133, 136, 168–9.

40. Abraham – Philo, *Abr.* 107–114; Josephus, *Ant.* 1.196; I Clement 10.7; probably Heb. 13.2; Job – *Test.Job* 10.1–3; 25.5; 53.3. See further those cited in my *Romans*, p. 744.

41. Jeremias, *Theology*, p. 115. He cites appositely II Kings 25.27–30 (par. Jer. 52.31–34) and Josephus, *Ant.* 19.321.

which made his table-fellowship a focus of controversy. His eating with tax-collector and sinner was evidently a primary cause of offence. 'Tax-collectors', we can readily understand, would have been regarded as apostates – collaborators with and instruments of the occupying power. 'Sinners' we can now see to have been a factional term. The point of criticism against Jesus, then, as it is recalled in the Synoptic Gospels, was that this eating with such people was perceived by many Pharisees to constitute a *challenge to their own self-understanding as faithful covenant members* ('the righteous'), and so also as *a threat to their own identity and the boundary marking out that identity*.

In the last two decades Jacob Neusner has provided a remarkable confirmation of the Synoptic picture from the side of rabbinic tradition, particularly by his documentation of the considerable importance which the pre-70 rabbinic traditions placed on table-fellowship. His study of the rabbinic traditions specifically attributed to the period before 70, to the debate between the Houses of Hillel and Shammai, produced a very striking conclusion.[42]

> Of the 341 individual Houses' legal pericopae, no fewer than 229, approximately 67 percent of the whole, directly or indirectly concern table-fellowship ... The Houses' laws of ritual cleanness apply in the main to the ritual cleanness of food, and of people, dishes, and implements involved in its preparation. Pharisaic laws regarding Sabbath and festivals, moreover, involve in large measure the preparation and preservation of food.

Neusner also points out that this concern, part, as he would see it, of Pharisaic concern to extend the holiness and purity of the Temple throughout the land, was expressed not in special or ritual meals, but in all meals, the daily meal table.[43] The relevance of all this to our subject is clear.

Sanders has now heavily criticized Neusner at this point, for offering a substantial misreading of the rabbinic material. His own study of the rabbinic traditions leads him to the conclusion that Neusner is one hundred percent in error on these points.[44] There is no possibility within the scope of these pages to examine again all the evidence in dispute between Neusner and Sanders. Suffice it to say, it is very doubtful whether Neusner can be dismissed so completely.

---

42. Neusner, *Politics*, p. 86.
43. Neusner, *Politics*, pp. 87–8. See also above §3.2(*b*).
44. Sanders, *Jewish Law*, pp. 166–236.

(1) Neusner's findings, even if overstated, tie in so well to the rest of the evidence: Pharisees as 'separated ones', 'scrupulous' in their observance of the Torah;[45] the factionalism of pre-70 Judaism, coming to sharpest expression in points of differentiation and disagreement; the meal table as a focus of so much religious and social significance, and so a likely point at which boundary markers would be set out and maintained;[46] in a moment we will also see how important the whole issue was for one of the Pharisees' major rivals, the Essenes.[47]

(2) Sanders' own analysis has to be qualified. For one thing, he recognizes the high level of concern over corpse impurity and midras impurity among the Pharisees, but argues that they were making only 'minor gestures towards extra purity'.[48] Such a categorization ('minor gestures'), however, ignores the fact that in factional dispute such 'minor' matters can become major flash-points.[49] For another, Sanders himself accepts the difficulty of distinguishing Pharisees from *haberim* ('associates').[50] But in the latter case the importance of guarding the meal table from impurity is not open to much dispute.[51] So the force of Sanders' own argument is much blunted. Finally, caution is necessary at this point in particular when the rabbinic traditions are used as evidence for pre-70 Pharisaism. For these traditions were codified at a time when the rabbis were indeed the established and controlling power within the normative Judaism they themselves were well on the way to establishing. These traditions may therefore not reflect the full force of the factional rivalry of the pre-70 period when the Pharisees had to fight for and defend their definition and practice of Judaism against others within the Judaism of that time.[52]

(3) Once again it must be insisted that the Synoptic traditions are part of, or at least include some of our most important evidence for pre-70 Judaism, including the Pharisees. It can not all be dismissed to a post-70 date, and on this point not least (criticism of Jesus for

---

45. See above pp. 140–1.

46. Cf. again particularly Saldarini, *Pharisees*, particularly pp. 212–16. Jews today would be among the first to observe that it is precisely at the meal table that the current different forms of Judaism come to clearest expression. The rules one follows at the meal table show what kind of religious Jew one is.

47. See below pp. 146–8.

48. Sanders, *Jewish Law*, pp. 232–5.

49. Contrast Kraft and Nickelsburg: 'In such instances, differences in interpretation and disputes about law are raised to the level of absolute truth and falsehood and have as their consequences salvation and damnation' (*EJMI* p. 18). See also above §2.3 and pp. 55–6.

50. Sanders, *Jewish Law*, pp. 154–5, 250.

51. See e.g. Schürer, 2.398–400; also Sanders in preceding note. See also the careful discussion in Saldarini, *Pharisees*, pp. 216–220.

52. See again Saldarini, *Pharisees*, p. 8, n. 11.

eating with 'sinners') it certainly goes back to the pre-70 period,[53] and therefore interlocks in a most impressive way with the rest of the evidence.

Thus, even if Neusner has overstated his point, a point of considerable significance nevertheless still emerges. Table-fellowship would most probably be one of the elements of Pharisaic halakoth which functioned as an identity marker and boundary, marking them out and marking them off as 'separated' from others. Moreover, for others to live or teach in such a way as to call such Pharisaic halakah in question, or even to dispute it, would most likely be perceived by the Pharisees, or at least by the *haberim* within the Pharisees, as a threat to or even attack on their own identity – something to be fiercely resisted and met with counter attack. Evidently Jesus appeared to many Pharisees as just such a threat – one who challenged the boundary-marking rituals of hand-washing by which Pharisaic *haberim* preserved their separateness from the uncleanness of other Jews – one who challenged their sense of what righteousness was and what righteousness required by eating with 'sinners'. He was threatening their identity, challenging their boundaries. And in their eyes *that would be tantamount to challenging the covenant, breaking the covenant, even abandoning the covenant.* To call in question their own well-defined understanding and practice of covenantal nomism was to threaten not just the law, but the covenant of which the law was a fundamental expression, was therefore in effect *to put in question one if not two of Israel's foundational pillars.*[54]

The issue of table-fellowship would have been even more serious for *the Qumran covenanters.* We knew already from the description by Josephus of how important the daily meal was for them: after purification they would repair to the refectory as to some sacred shrine; the meal began and ended with prayer and was eaten in reverential silence; the garments they wore for the meals were like 'holy vest-

---

53. Sanders accepts that such criticisms were made of Jesus (*Jesus*, p. 179); but since he has missed the factional context and significance of the criticism of Jesus, he has also failed to recognize its full significance on this point of dispute with Neusner.

54. It is worth noting in passing that Jesus would probably have been regarded by many of the Pharisees as himself a sinner (the fact that he is not remembered as being so called in the Synoptic tradition is presumably a mark of the respect which they nevertheless had for him as a teacher – cf. Mark 12.32–33; Luke 7.36; 11.37; 13.31; 14.1). The question as to whether Jesus was a 'sinner' is therefore not to be answered by Christians by a sweeping and dismissive denial. What is meant by 'sinner' in such a charge is precisely what has to be analysed before it can be discussed – an important example, therefore, of the need for contextualized exegesis and for the historical research which makes such exegesis possible.

ments' (Josephus, *War* 2.129–133). Likewise it was only after a careful and rigorous novitiate that the would-be covenanter was permitted to touch 'the common food' (*War* 2.138–139). This picture has now received first-hand confirmation from the Dead Sea Scrolls. 1QS 6 confirms the religious significance of the common meal, each meal requiring as its initial act the blessing of the bread and wine by the priest (6.2, 4–5). And after describing the hierarchical character of their seating in the assemblies (6.8–9),[55] it goes on to describe the requirements and stages for the novitiate in language which closely parallels that of Josephus (6.16–17, 20–21). Particularly interesting for us is the comparison between 1QS 6 and 1QSa 2 – the latter a description of the eschatological meal in which the Messiah of Israel would participate. The point being that the two meals are described in very similar terms. That is to say, clearly, the daily meal of the Qumran community was seen as a foretaste of the eschatological banquet in the presence of the (royal) Messiah. The parallel with Jesus at this point is striking.[56]

Even more striking, however, is the concern shown by the community to protect the sanctity of the community as expressed in the common meal table. Not only did novices have to go through a lengthy period of preparation before they could participate; but even those expelled from the community or under discipline by the community were expected to continue to observe the rigorous oaths they had taken before being admitted to the common meal (Josephus, *War* 2.143). More to the point, the list of those excluded from the assembly and from the common meal was clearly drawn and quite often referred to:

> No man smitten with any human uncleanness shall enter the assembly of God . . . No man smitten in his flesh, or *paralysed in his feet or hands* or *lame or blind* or deaf or dumb or smitten in his flesh with a *visible blemish* . . . for the angels of holiness are (with) their (congregation) . . . let him not enter among (the congregation), for he is smitten (1QSa 2.3–10 Vermes).

The list and its concerns are echoed in 1QM 7.4–6, 4Q D[b] and 11QT 45.12–14, and is obviously based on Lev. 21.17–24, describing those debarred from the priesthood:

55. This matches Philo's description of the Essenes in *Prob.* 81; cf. Josephus, *War* 2.150.
56. See above p. 144.

Say to Aaron, None of your descendents throughout their generations who has a *blemish* may approach to offer the bread of God.
For no one who has a *blemish* shall draw near, a man *blind, or
lame* . . . or a man who has an *injured foot* or an *injured hand* . . .
(Lev. 21.17–21).

Here is a clear expression of the Qumran sect's sense of being a
priestly community: the regulations regarding who is debarred from
the *priesthood* were taken to apply to their *own* community. The
parallel with the Pharisees or the *haberim* in particular, is notable
again: of both groups we can say, with varying degrees of confidence,
that they sought to maintain in their daily meals a level of purity
which in principle was required only for the Temple and its service.
In the case of the Essenes, particularly the closed community at
Qumran, it is clear that the purity norms and boundaries were intensi-
fied and more rigorously policed.

What is particularly striking for us in this case is the way Jesus'
words in Luke 14.13 and 21 seem to echo these very same Qumran
regulations.

He said also to the man who had invited him, 'When you give a
dinner or a banquet, do not invite your friends or your brothers or
your kinsmen or rich neighbours, lest they also invite you in return,
and you be repaid. But when you give a feast, invite the poor, the
maimed, the *lame*, the *blind*, and you will be blessed, because they
cannot repay you' . . . '. . . Then the householder in anger (at the
refusal of his original guests to attend his banquet) said to his
servant, "Go out quickly to the streets and lanes of the city, and
bring in the poor and *maimed* and *blind* and *lame*"' (Luke 14.12–
14, 21).

The parallel is both positive and antithetical. Positive, because both
Jesus and Qumran evidently regarded their table-fellowship as of
eschatological significance (Luke 14.13 with 14.21; parallel to 1QS
6 with 1QSa 2). But much more striking is the echo of the list of
those excluded from the Qumran table-fellowship – the maimed or
crippled,[57] the lame, the blind. *The very ones whom Qumran went
out of its way to exclude from its table-fellowship and so from the*

---

57. The word translated 'maimed' (RSV), *anapeiros*, would probably be better translated 'disabled', 'seriously disabled', and is an appropriate Greek equivalent to the words
used in Lev. 21.17–21 and in the Dead Sea Scrolls to indicate physical 'blemish' or 'crippled'
or paralysis.

eschatological banquet, are the very ones Jesus says firmly are to be in-cluded. Those to whom he speaks and of whom he speaks in Luke 14 are urged to make particular point of including in their table-fellowship just those whom Qumran excluded. It is very difficult to imagine that Jesus was unaware of this parallel: the repetition of the list of those excluded from the Qumran table-fellowship indicates that it was a point of emphasis for the Qumran covenanters, and that it would probably be quite widely known.[58] Almost certainly, therefore, Jesus said what he is remembered as saying in Luke 14.13 and 21 precisely as a protest against and challenge to the Qumran practice of table-fellowship and vision of the messianic banquet.

It thus becomes clear what it was that Jesus was doing in eating so deliberately with those called 'sinners' by Pharisees and in calling others to welcome to their table the disabled, the lame and the blind. *He was challenging the boundaries which were being drawn by these two major factions within second Temple Judaism.* He was protesting against an understanding and practice of God's covenant grace which excluded other Jews by drawing such boundaries and by drawing them too tightly. He was protesting against what he must have perceived as an attempt to corner for themselves the covenant grace of God, to monopolize the covenant righteousness of the Lord God. Alternatively expressed, he was attempting to restore the wholeness of Israel.[59]

And thus the earlier issue becomes clearer too. It was not the law or law as a principle which Jesus called in question. *It was the law understood in a factional or sectarian way* – interpreted in narrowing terms so that those who could not accept, or who would not conform, or who challenged that interpretation, were *ipso facto* categorized as 'sinners', even though they were Jews themselves and willing or indeed eager to live within the covenant as they understood it.

6.4 Jesus and Gentiles

What are the consequences of this conclusion for our perception of how Jesus understood the covenant people? In challenging such factional or sectarian attempts, in effect, to 'hijack' or take over the covenant and its righteousness, did he in fact call in question the very

---

58. We have already seen how accurate was Josephus' knowledge of the rules governing the Qumran sect.

59. Cf. P. von der Osten-Sacken, *Christian–Jewish Dialogue. Theological Foundations*, Philadelphia: Fortress 1986, pp. 50–3.

idea of a covenant people as such? How does his attitude to *Gentiles* tie in to his attitude to the Jewish factions of the time? So far we have looked only at Jesus in relation to what we designated as the third pillar of second Temple Judaism (Torah); what about his attitude to the second – Israel as God's elect people, and as such distinct from the Gentiles? If he challenged the boundaries being drawn *within* Judaism, did he also challenge the boundary around Judaism?

The evidence here is again rather striking.[60] (*a*) Matthew records Jesus as expressly restricting his disciples' mission, or their share in his mission: 'Go nowhere among the Gentiles, and enter no town of the Samaritans, but go rather to the lost sheep of the house of Israel' (Matt. 10.5–6). The passage is very notable since Matthew himself evidently believed in a mission to all nations (Matt. 28.19); it must therefore belong to earlier tradition, and was probably a memory of Jesus' teaching preserved by a strong Jewish Christian tradition within earliest Palestinian Christianity. The same deduction follows from the material found only in Matt. 10.23 and 15.24: 'Truly, I say to you, you will not have gone through all the towns of Israel, before the Son of Man comes' (10.23); Jesus 'answered, "I was sent only to the lost sheep of the house of Israel"' (15.24). We may note also John 4.22: 'salvation is from the Jews'. Since John was so anxious to show the extent to which Christianity superceded Judaism,[61] it is again probably a case of his here drawing from an old and deeply rooted tradition of Jesus' ministry. Jesus' choice of twelve to be his closest group of disciples, with its obvious symbolism (12 = the twelve tribes) tells the same story; as indeed the picture of the final judgment in terms of the twelve judging the tribes of Israel (Matt. 19.28/Luke 22.30).[62]

The only real exception from within Jesus' mission is Mark 13.10 – 'the gospel must first be preached to all nations'. But that is almost certainly an interpretative addition by Mark (or his source), with a view to the expanding Gentile mission: (1) the vocabulary is wholly and distinctively Markan; (2) it interrupts the flow of argument from vv. 9–13; and (3) it runs so very sharply counter to the evidence just being reviewed.[63] The weight of evidence remains clear: that Jesus,

---

60. For fuller discussion cf. particularly J. Jeremias, *Jesus' Promise to the Nations*, 1956; ET London: SCM Press 1958; F. Hahn, *Mission in the New Testament*, 1963; ET London: SCM Press 1965, pp. 26–41.

61. See above §5.8.

62. See further Sanders, *Jesus*, Part One, 'The Restoration of Israel'. Cf. the third thesis of P. Lapide (with U. Luz), *Jesus in Two Perspectives. A Jewish–Christian Dialog*, 1979; ET Minneapolis: Augsburg 1985: 'Jesus never repudiated his people' (pp. 85–110).

63. See particularly Taylor, *Mark*, p. 507.

during his mission, did not encourage his disciples to think of any missionary outreach beyond Israel.

In addition, we might simply note Jesus' attitude to what we have earlier characterized as the three principal boundary markers distinguishing Israel from the nations. There is no indication whatsoever that Jesus ever questioned circumcision, though it could be argued that his undifferentiated call for repentance, like that of the Baptist, effectively relativized its significance. As for the sabbath, it is not unimportant to realize that the two principal disputes over the sabbath (Mark 2.23–3.5) do not question *whether* the sabbath should be observed, only *how* it should be observed,[64] even though, as we shall see in a moment, the principle uttered was capable of more far-reaching application. Precisely the same is true in regard to the food laws, as the different ways of taking Jesus' saying about true cleanliness again remind us (Mark 7.15, 19; Matt. 15.17).

(*b*) At the same time, however, Jesus is not remembered as one who was hostile to Gentiles. The response he is recalled as making to the two Gentiles who pleaded for his help, the centurion and the Syrophoenician woman, is sufficient proof to the contrary (Matt. 8.5–13/Luke 7.1–10; Mark 7.24–30 par.).[65] And we have already seen that Jesus very likely shared the Jewish hope of the eschatological pilgrimage of the Gentiles to Jerusalem[66] – a deduction drawn from the 'cleansing of the Temple', and borne out by Matt. 8.11–12/Luke 13.28–29 ('many will come from east and west and sit at table with Abraham, Isaac and Jacob in the kingdom of heaven, while the sons of the kingdom will be thrown into outer darkness'), as also by Mark 12.9 pars (the vineyard of Israel taken from the rebellious tenants and given to others). The more threatening note of these last two passages also seems to fit within the Jewish tradition of prophetic warning against Jewish presumption over Gentiles: as in Amos 9.7 ('Did I not bring up Israel from the land of Egypt, and the Philistines from Caphtor and the Syrians from Kir?' – in other words, 'what makes you so special?'); and John the Baptist's preaching ('Do not think to say among yourselves, "We have Abraham as our father"; for I say to you that God is able from these stones to raise up children

---

64. See my 'Mark 2.1–3.6', in *Jesus, Paul and the Law*, pp. 21–2.

65. According to Mark 7.27 Jesus, by implication, refers to Gentiles as 'dogs', presumably a traditional term of abuse (cf. Phil. 3.2); but it is notable that the Greek uses the word *kunarion*, 'little dog' (house-dog or lap-dog), rather than *kyōn*, a dog of the street. And if he referred to Gentiles as 'sinners' (Luke 6.34; cf. Matt. 5.47) he would simply be reflecting characteristic Jewish usage of the time (see above n. 26).

66. See above §3.4.

to Abraham' – Matt. 3.9/Luke 3.8). At this point Jesus seems to stand well within the tradition of self-critical Judaism.

What we can say, however, is that Jesus' attitude to Gentiles showed much of the same character as his attitude to Jewish factionalism.[67] (1) Even if he did not go out looking for Gentiles or encourage preaching the good news of the kingdom to Gentiles, nevertheless he responded positively to Gentiles who approached him with faith. The emphasis on the faith of the centurion and of the Syrophoenician woman is obviously highlighted in the Evangelists' retelling of the stories. But there is no reason to doubt that the basis for their doing so was the memory that Jesus did act with such positive good will (in the end) to Gentiles who called on him for help, and did so, impressed by their faith. In which case we can say fairly confidently that Jesus regarded faith expressed by whomsoever as more important than the ethnically understood and ritually expressed boundaries surrounding and protecting the elect people.

(2) The parable of the Good Samaritan (Luke 10.30–37) is obviously aimed in large part at the racial prejudices within Judaism which regarded the Samaritans as racial half-breeds and religious apostates.[68] Here we again see Jesus showing the same disregard for the boundaries by which the righteous sought to protect themselves. Where he seems mostly to have concerned himself with challenging the boundaries drawn *within* Israel, here we see one case at least where he challenged the boundary *round* Israel. The point should not be overemphasized, since the Samaritans were more like a sect of Judaism than another religion.[69] But in view of the significance which Acts clearly attributed to the breakthrough to the Samaritans in Acts 8,[70] the parable of the Good Samaritan can be seen as a first challenge to an attitude probably shared by all Jews that Samaritans were 'beyond the pale'.

(3) We may even be able to go a little further. For there are hints that Jesus did look to a more universal experience of God's grace. Mark 2.27–28 may contain an original *bar ʾnasa* saying, where the phrase originally had the force of the Aramaic idiom = 'man':[71] 'the Sabbath was made for man . . . therefore (the son of) man is lord also of the Sabbath.' That is to say, in the eschatological condition of a restored paradise (man as crown and lord of creation), the Sabbath

---

67. See above §6.3.
68. See above §4.6a.
69. See Purvis, *EJMI*, pp. 90–5.
70. See again above §4.6a.
71. See below §9.4.

would function as a day of rest and recreation for humankind as a whole. If so, there would be implicit an important challenge to the more typical Jewish use of the creation stories as a way of heightening Israel's own significance; as classically in Dan. 7 – the man-like figure (representing the saints of the Most High) fulfils the creation order of Adam's dominance over the beasts, by being given dominion over the beast-like figures (representing the nations hostile to Israel). Again, in Mark 7.15 it is still possible that Jesus enunciated a principle which he knew and intended could apply to the distinction between clean people (Jew) and unclean people (Gentile) – as Mark began to recognize and to point out (Mark 7.19).[72] And if we may assume that the parable of the sheep and the goats goes back to Jesus (Matt. 25.31–46), it would appear that he even envisaged a brotherhood in openness to God's grace which extended across national boundaries.

All these, however, are undeveloped hints. For the most part we again see Jesus functioning within the boundaries of second Temple Judaism, sharply critical of its current widely prevailing factionalism, challenging the boundaries being drawn by various groups within the people of God, exercising a prophetic critique against Israel's presumption and tendency to spiritual arrogance, looking for an eschatological pilgrimage of the Gentiles, for a renewed Judaism, an eschatological Israel – but still all within characteristic Jewish terms. *There is no parting of the ways evident here, on either Torah or covenant*, even though we can say with hindsight that the principles or fundamental insights which informed his mission were bound to raise far-reaching questions as soon as the issue of whether and how the gospel of Jesus should be preached also to Gentiles came to the fore.

---

72. See above §6.1.

7

Paul and 'covenantal nomism'

7.1 The first Christians and the law

If Jesus was an uncomfortable figure within second Temple Judaism, calling in question its internal boundaries and various attempts at self-definition in terms of the Torah, the same seems to have been less so for his first followers in the aftermath of Good Friday and Easter. They seem to have sat at least a little more comfortably within the spectrum of the prevailing Judaism(s) of Judaea in the middle decades of the first century.

It is important to remind ourselves that these first 'Christians' (at this stage, of course, the term itself is anachronistic) were *all Jews – and loyal Jews*. They did not see themselves as a new religion. To be sure they believed that the crucified Jesus was both Messiah and risen from the dead; but while that made them something of an oddity within the spectrum of second Temple Judaism, it left them still well within the parameters of what it meant to be a Jew at that time – as we shall see.[1] As far as our present theme is concerned, Israel's election and the law, the following evidence should be considered.

(*a*) The first believers evidently regarded themselves as *the climax of Judaism*, as the renewed or eschatological Judaism for which the prophets had looked. Thus the twelve were seen as the focal point of the reconstituted Israel, representative of the regathered twelve tribes. Such at least seems to be the implication of the final Q saying as remembered by the first Christians – Matt. 19.28/Luke 22.28–30 (the twelve to share in the judgment of the twelve tribes of Israel); the desire to replace the traitor Judas attests a need felt to re-establish the inner circle of twelve for the same obvious reasons (Acts 1.21–22); and already, in the early formula of I Cor. 15.5, 'the twelve' is an established term for the founding group of witnesses. Similarly the fact that the last supper was remembered as a meal symbolizing the

---

1. See below §10.2.

new covenant attests a sense of eschatological fulfilment of prophetic hope.[2]

(*b*) Our records indicate that the first group of believers in Jerusalem *continued to observe the Torah*, apparently without question. Particularly significant here is Peter's own testimony as given in Acts 10.14 and 11.8, that he had never eaten anything common or unclean; as also the reaction of 'the brothers in Judaea' – 'Why did you go to men who were uncircumcised and eat with them?' (Acts 11.3). Clearly implicit in both cases is a still well established covenantal nomistic mindset – a still unquestioned assumption of the rightness or necessity of operating fully within the boundaries marked out by the Torah. Such testimony as to the earliest community's continuing faithfulness on the matter of food laws and table-fellowship provides one of the strongest reasons for questioning whether Jesus was so clearly as radical on the subject of food laws as Mark 7.15 and 19 indicate.[3]

(*c*) As we have already seen, the first Nazarenes seem to have remained *firmly attached to the Temple*.[4]

(*d*) They also seem to have made very little, if any, attempt to stir from Jerusalem. There is *no evidence on their part of any sense of mission to the Gentiles*. (1) The implication of a sequence of passages in Acts 1–5 is that they were thinking only in terms of Israel:[5] 1.6 – 'Will you at this time restore the kingdom to Israel?'; 1.21–22 – the completion of the twelve; 2.5 – 'Jews, devout men from every nation under heaven'; 2.39 – 'the promise is to you and to your children and to all that are afar off', where the last group probably refers to those symbolized in the Pentecost crowd (2.5), Jews and proselytes (2.11) of the diaspora, whose restoration to Mount Zion was a constant theme in covenant and prophetic promise;[6] 3.25 – 'you are the sons of the prophets and of the covenant which God gave to your fathers . . .'; 5.31 – 'God exalted him . . . to give repentance to Israel and forgiveness of sins'. (2) Similarly the fact that the very restrictive, Israel-centred sayings of Jesus (Matt. 10.5–6, 23; 15.24) were preserved through this period suggests that these sayings continued to express the priorities of those who preserved them. If they did think

2. See above pp. 72–3.

3. See e.g. Sanders, *Jesus*, p. 266; other bibliography in my 'Jesus and Ritual Purity' in *Jesus, Paul and the Law*, p. 55 n. 17. See also above pp. 57–8, 134, 151, 153.

4. See above §4.1.

5. I assume here only that such a sequence of references in Acts 1–5 reflects a characteristic feature of the earliest Jerusalem community.

6. E.g. Deut. 30.1–5; Isa. 27.12–13; Zech. 9.11–17. Note the use of the 'far off' theme in Isa. 46.12–13; Jer. 2.5; 31.10; Ezek. 11.15; Zech. 6.15; 10.9. Commentators on Acts, however, usually see 2.39 as including a reference to the Gentiles.

of the Gentiles (cf. Acts 2.39?; 3.25), it would presumably have been, once again, in terms of Gentiles coming *in to* Jerusalem (the eschatological pilgrimage of the nations),[7] rather than of mission *out to* Gentiles (so also the implication of the words attributed to James in Act 15.16–17).[8] (3) And, as already noted,[9] it is almost certain that the 'great commission' of Matt. 28.19–20 reflects an understanding of mission which only came to such clear and full expression at a later stage – whatever may have been the historical root of the saying itself. The total disregard of it by the first Jerusalem disciples (they baptized only 'in the name of Jesus'; they did *not* go out and make disciples of other nations) is very hard to explain otherwise. Similarly with Acts 1.8, which Luke sets at that point to provide a 'table of contents' for his second volume. In short, the idea of a mission *to* the Gentiles cannot be attributed to the earliest Jerusalem community of the Nazarenes with any conviction.

(*e*) Equally striking is the account of *Pharisaic sympathy towards the new group*: 5.33–39 – Gamaliel, a leading Pharisaic teacher, defends it with some sympathy; 15.5 – the new 'sect' was of such a character as to attract several Pharisees, who evidently did not cease to be Pharisees when they came to believe in Jesus Messiah. We might note the confirmation at this point from Paul – that the Jerusalem church attracted strictly law-observant individuals, whom he calls 'false brothers' (Gal. 2.4) And later on, Acts 21.20 speaks of thousands among the Jews who had believed and who were 'all zealous for the law'. This relative warmth on the part of Pharisees towards the followers of Jesus is one of the most marked differences between the Synoptic records of Jesus' ministry and the Acts picture of the earliest Jerusalem church. Evidently the new sect was not perceived, initially at least, to be so much a threat as Jesus had been. The best explanation for this disparity is that *the first Nazarenes' attitude to and practice of the Torah remained within the more traditional guidelines recognized by the Pharisees*, which in turn must mean that the first believers maintained a relatively strict level of observance of Torah and halakah.

In short, the new movement of Jesus' followers saw itself as part of second Temple Judaism and remained very much within that matrix.

---

7. For the eschatological pilgrimage of the nations see above §3.4(*d*).
8. See further below §8.4.
9. See above p. 77 and n. 3.

7.2 From persecutor to apostle

When then did the second and third main pillars of second Temple Judaism come under question from the first Christians? The fourth pillar (the Temple) had been put into radical question by Stephen and the Hellenists.[10] Was it so also with regard to election, covenant and Torah? It is often maintained that the answer is Yes, at least so far as the Torah was concerned: radical critique of the Torah began with the Hellenists; so what Paul converted to was just such a radical view of the law.[11] But this is a highly questionable assertion, at least so far as our evidence is concerned.

None of the evidence most likely to be traced or to be linked directly back to the Hellenists indicates a questioning of the Torah independently of a questioning of the Temple. (1) In the whole of the material closely associated with the Hellenists, only Acts 6.13 raises the issue of the law ('he speaks against this holy place and the law'). And this is presented as a false accusation against Stephen. The main thrust of the accusation against Stephen comes in the charge that Jesus would destroy this place (the Temple) and change the customs Moses delivered (Acts 6.14); but since so much of the law deals with regulation of the Temple cult anyway, what was perceived as an attack on the Temple as such could be so described. And the speech of ch. 7 reads like a defence of Stephen's high regard for the law (7.38, 53), with his criticism directed solely against the Temple.[12] (2) So too with the immediate sequel to the Stephen affair: the overtones have all to do with Temple rather than law;[13] in Acts the wider question of law and circumcision is only raised during the mission of *Peter* (not a Hellenist). (3) If John 4 and Hebrews reflect anything of a pre-Pauline Hellenistic background,[14] the implication is the same – Temple, but *not* law put in question. So the 'Hellenistic evidence' seems to deny the claim that the Hellenists advocated abandonment of the law beyond what was involved in attendance at the Temple and participation in the Temple cult.

But does this settle the matter? There is also the evidence of Paul, the self-confessed persecutor of the church (that is, primarily or exclusively the Hellenists). Phil. 3.5–6 – 'in terms of the law, a Pharisee;

---

10. See above §4.3–6.

11. See e.g. Hengel, *Between Jesus and Paul*, pp. 23–4; S. Kim, *The Origin of Paul's Gospel*, WUNT 2.4; Tübingen: Mohr-Siebeck 1981, pp. 44–8; stated in an extreme way by Schmithals, *Paul and James*, pp. 25–6. See also above §4.3.

12. See above §4.5e.

13. See above §4.6.

14. See above pp. 93, 115.

in terms of zeal, a persecutor of the church; in terms of righteousness which is in the law, blameless'. Is it not the most obvious exegesis to take all three clauses as referring to the law, and thus to deduce that Paul persecuted the church because he saw it as abandoning the law? Gal. 3.13 – 'Christ redeemed us from the curse of the law, by becoming accursed for us; as it is written, "Cursed is everyone who hangs on a tree" (Deut. 21.23).' Again the implication is readily drawn that Jesus' crucifixion was seen as his being accursed by God. Certainly it is the case that Deut. 21.23 had already been referred to crucifixion at the time of Jesus (4QpNah 1.7–8; 11QT 64.6–13). And the probability must be high that the text had been used in earliest Jewish polemic against earliest Christian proclamation of a crucified Messiah[15] – indeed, probably by Paul himself. So it is certainly plausible to argue that Gal. 3.13 marks a reversal in Paul's own earlier logic. Hence the common line of argument in current scholarship: Paul had thought Jesus accursed by the law; then he encountered Jesus on the Damascus road and recognized that God had vindicated Jesus; from which the corollary followed that if *God* had vindicated him whom the *law* cursed, then the law must be wrong, and God has thereby indicated that the law is no longer to be regarded as a determiner of God's will. Not untypical is Kim's reasoning: Paul was confronted with the alternative – either the law or the crucified Christ; Paul's belief that Christ was 'the end of the law' (Rom. 10.4) must go back to the Damascus road encounter.[16]

In my view, however, such reasoning too is fatally flawed, particularly in that it ignores once again the social function of the law as defining and marking off Israel from other nations. What comes to the surface when the evidence is examined more closely is *not the issue of the law as such*, particularly not the issue of gospel versus law as traditionally posed in Reformation exegesis. The following clues have been missed.

(*a*) '*Zeal*'. The reason why Paul persecuted the church was out of 'zeal' (Phil. 3.6 – 'in terms of zeal, a persecutor of the church'). Presumably this affirmation of his earlier zeal ties in with his description of his 'former life in Judaism' as 'exceedingly zealous for the traditions of his fathers' in Gal. 1.13–14. Any Jew reading these words would have recognized the implicit allusion in such talk of

---

15. See e.g. G. J. Brooke, 'The Temple Scroll and the New Testament', *Temple Scroll Studies*, ed. G. J. Brooke, Sheffield Academic 1989, pp. 181–99, here pp. 181–2 with bibliography in n. 3.

16. Kim, *Origin*, pp. 3–4. See also those cited in my *Jesus, Paul and the Law*, pp. 102–3, nn. 11–12.

'zeal'. For 'zeal' was an important word in the history of Jewish self-identification, particularly in the senses echoed here – zeal for God, zeal for the law. In Jewish circles the classic examples of this zeal were well known and highly regarded: *Simeon and Levi*, whose zeal for God consisted in the defence not only of the honour of their sister, but also of the integrity of Israel against the stranger and Gentile (Judith 9.2–4; *Jub.* 30.5–20; referring to the episode in Gen. 34);[17] *Phinehas* likewise was remembered as one whose zeal caused him to destroy the one who transgressed the boundary round Israel and thus to make atonement for the people (Num. 25.6–13; Sir. 45.23–24; I Macc. 2.54; *IV Macc.* 18.12);[18] *Elijah's* zeal for the law was expressed particularly in his opposition to the syncretism patronized by Ahab and Jezebel (I Kings 18; Sir. 48.2; I Macc. 2.58); and 'zeal for the law' was a much repeated theme in the history of the *Maccabean revolt* against the Syrian attempts to destroy Israel's ethnic and religious identity (I Macc. 2.19–27, 50, 58; II Macc. 4.2; Josephus, *Ant.* 12.271).[19] Clearly it is this same zeal which Paul attests for his fellow Jews in Rom. 10.2–3 – 'they have a zeal for God . . . and seek to establish righteousness as theirs alone . . .' – as is confirmed by the echo these words contain of Matthias's rallying cry in I Macc. 2.27 ('Let everyone who is zealous for the law and establishes the covenant come out with me!').[20]

The point is clear enough. In every case the *zeal referred to was a dedicated defence of Israel's distinctiveness.* Anything or anyone that seemed to adulterate the purity of Israel's belonging to God or to obscure Israel's distinctiveness as the covenant people of God was to

---

17. Note (1) the importance of circumcision as a boundary marker is already clear in Gen. 34.14 ('to give our sister to one who is uncircumcised . . . would be a disgrace to us'); (2) the link between zeal and maintaining ethnic purity in Judith 9.4 ('beloved sons who were zealous for you and abhorred the pollution of their blood'); (3) the elaboration of the Gen. 34.14 point in *Jubilees*: any mixed marriage brings uncleanness on Israel (*Jub.* 30.13ff.); this zeal is the basis of Levi's priesthood (30.18). We should note in passing the dramatic irony (or treachery) in the story of Simeon and Levi: they used circumcision, the rite of *inclusion*, as a means to incapacitate and destroy the Shechemites, and so to defend the boundary marked by circumcision.

18. On the basis of this act Phinehas was given a 'covenant of perpetual priesthood' (Num. 25.12–13; Sir. 45.24; I Macc. 2.54). He was regarded as a great hero and role-model by the Zealots (Hengel, *Zealots*, pp. 149–77, see the whole section – pp. 146–228; Schürer, 2.598–606).

19. Note also *m. Sanh.* 9.6 – 'If a man stole a sacred vessel or cursed by Kosem or made an Aramean woman his paramour, the zealots may fall upon him. If a priest served [at the altar] in a state of uncleanness his brethren the priests did not bring him to the court, but the young men among the priests took him outside the Temple court and split open his brains with clubs.'

20. See in fuller detail my *Romans*, p. 588.

be resisted and removed. And in every case the zeal was expressed *by taking up the sword* and by resort to open force: in the destruction of the Shechemites (*Jub.* 30.18 – 'zeal to execute righteousness and judgment and vengeance on all those who rose up against Israel'); in the killing of the Israelite who brought the Midianite woman to his bed; in the slaughter of the prophets of Baal (I Kings 18.40); in the act which began the Maccabean rebellion – the killing of an apostasizing Jew who had betrayed the covenant ('Thus he burned with zeal for the law, as Phinehas did . . .' – I Macc. 2.23–26).

This is clearly the zeal which Paul has in mind in recalling his own career as a violent persecutor (Gal. 1.13–14; Phil. 3.5–6) – *zeal for the law expressed in defence of Israel's covenant distinctiveness by the sword.*[21] He could call himself a 'zealot' precisely because (in the words of Rom. 10.2–3) he had sought to establish righteousness as the peculiar prerogative of Israel – Israel's and not anyone else's.[22] He was 'in advance' of his contemporaries in zeal for the traditions of his fathers because he was like other Pharisees and those documented in §6.2: he wanted to draw a tighter, stricter line round the 'righteous', to mark them off even more clearly from the Gentile 'sinner'. Hence the violence of his reaction to the Hellenist believers: it had to do with their opening the door to Gentiles, not with the law as a measure of moral or self-achievement; his persecution was born of zeal for the law as a boundary marking off righteousness with God as a special privilege to be promoted and defended. Evidently he saw the Hellenists as a threat to his own identity as a covenant member and as a threat to the covenant itself. Like Simeon, Levi and Phinehas, he sought to be counted righteous by virtue of such zeal (Ps. 106.30–31; *Jub.* 30.17).[23]

(*b*) *Conversion.*[24] It is a striking fact that Paul never refers to his encounter with the risen Christ on the Damascus road as a 'conver-

---

21. Cf. T. L. Donaldson, 'Zealot and Convert: The Origin of Paul's Christ-Torah Antithesis', *CBQ* 51 (1989), pp. 655–82. We should not underestimate the violence indicated by both the evocation of the tradition of Phinehas-like 'zeal' and the description of his 'persecution' as an attempt to 'destroy' (*porthein*; BAGD – 'pillage, make havoc of, destroy, annihilate') the church (Gal. 1.13; so Acts 9.21).

22. For this exegesis on Rom. 10.2–3 see again my *Romans*, pp. 586–9.

23. The fact that Gen. 15.6 is drawn in in these passages to describe the righteousness of such zeal will no doubt have been part of the reason why Paul gave Gen 15.6 such prominence in his own exposition of righteousness in Gal. 3 and Rom. 4.

24. In what follows I draw on and develop the case argued in my ' "A Light to the Gentiles": the Significance of the Damascus Road Christophany for Paul', *The Glory of Christ in the New Testament. Studies in Christology in Memory of G. B. Caird*, ed. L. D. Hurst and N. T. Wright, Oxford: Clarendon 1987, pp. 251–66; reprinted in *Jesus, Paul and the Law*, ch. 4.

sion', but *always and only as a commissioning.*[25] Thus in probably his earliest reference, in Gal. 1.15–16: 'when it pleased (God) . . . to reveal his Son in me in order that I might preach him among the Gentiles . . .' So also with I Cor. 9.1–2 ('Am I not an apostle? Have I not seen Jesus our Lord? If to others I am not an apostle, at least I am to you; for you are the seal of my apostleship in the Lord'); and 15.8 ('Last of all . . . he appeared also to me. For I am the least of the apostles, unfit to be called an apostle, because I persecuted the church of God').

More important for us here, Paul understood the appearance as a commissioning for apostleship *to the Gentiles.* For him being an apostle always meant, so far as we can tell, 'apostle to the Gentiles' (Rom. 11.13); hence the 'in order that' of Gal. 1.16 (just cited). It is most unlikely that Paul ever thought of himself as an apostle (in some general, unspecific sense) and then later on concluded that his apostleship was to the Gentiles. That would be quite at odds with his concept of apostleship, as a particular commissioning (cf. especially I Cor. 9.1–2; Gal. 2.8; II Cor. 10.13–16). So far as Paul was concerned what he received in his encounter with the risen Christ was grace and apostleship to win faith among the Gentiles (Rom. 1.5; 15.15–16). This ties in to a remarkable degree with the emphases in Acts. In all three accounts of Paul's 'conversion' nothing at all is said about the law; it has all to do with his *commissioning* to the *Gentiles* (Acts 9.15; 22.15; 26.17–18). Clearly, in Paul's own recollection of his entry into the new movement, and in the recollection preserved by Luke, *the major factor was his conviction of a calling to take the gospel to the Gentiles.*

This finding also ties in with the conclusions drawn above with regard to 'zeal' (*a*). When looking back before his Damascus road encounter, Paul recalled his zeal to keep Gentiles *out,* to defend the boundaries of the covenant people, by force of persecution, as had Phinehas and others before him. But in the Damascus experience a *reversal* occurred: he now recognized that through this risen Jesus God's purpose of grace had been extended to include the Gentiles, and that he was being called to be a minister of that grace to the Gentiles. Understandably, Paul was converted to the convictions he had previously attacked so vigorously.[26]

---

25. The observation is not new, of course. See e.g. Stendahl, *Paul Among Jews and Gentiles*, pp. 7–12; others in my *Jesus, Paul and the Law*, p. 101, n. 1.

26. I am very open to the possibility that Paul's understanding of his calling developed over the years following his conversion (see §§7.3ff.), not least in terms of 'post-conversion autobiographical reconstruction' (see particularly Segal, *Paul*, ch. 4; Taylor, *Paul, Antioch and Jerusalem*). Nevertheless, the correlation between the evidence marshalled under (*a*)

(c) *Gal. 3.13.* In the light of these findings, Gal. 3.13 also begins to make clearer sense. Verse 13 does not stand alone, but continues with a purpose clause: Jesus' being cursed on the cross had the objective of extending the blessing of Abraham *to the Gentiles* 'in Christ' (3.14). The curse being removed was, by implication, a curse which prevented Gentiles being accepted into the covenant people, which rendered them ineligible for participation in the covenant promise to Abraham. What precisely Paul meant by that 'curse' is unclear, but the two other most relevant facts in Gal. 3.10–14 provide some clues. (1) Gal. 3.10 – the curse lies on those who are *ex ergōn nomou*, 'from the works of the law', on those who are *en nomō*, 'within the law' (v. 11). As we shall see,[27] these phrases indicate a typical covenantal nomistic attitude on the part of his fellow Jews; they imply an understanding of the law and a practice of the law as marking out those within the people of God from those outside the law (*anomoi*). (2) Also significant is the double reference to Deuteronomy: Deut. 27.26 – 'Cursed be everyone who does not abide by all things written in the book of the law to do them' (Gal. 3.10); Deut. 21.23 – 'Cursed be everyone who hangs on a tree' (Gal. 3.13). F. F. Bruce draws out the significance of these texts well.[28]

> The curse of Deut. 27.26 was pronounced at the end of a covenant-renewal ceremony and had special reference therefore to the covenant breaker;
> The penalty of being hanged on a tree until one dies is prescribed in the Temple Scroll for an Israelite who . . . has been guilty of breaking the covenant-bond. To be exposed 'in the sun' was judged in OT times to be a fitting punishment for Israelites who were guilty of covenant violation.

The implication of the application of Deut. 21.23 to Jesus' crucifixion therefore was that *Jesus was being regarded by many Jews as a coven-*

---

and (*b*) above points strongly to the conclusion that a major, if not the major feature in Paul's conversion was the transformation of a theology of exclusiveness to one of inclusiveness. Thus, it will not be insignificant that as in Gal. 1.13–16, so in I Cor. 15.9, Paul sets in sharp contrast his previous career as a persecutor with his new calling as an apostle of Jesus Christ to Gentiles (like the Corinthians). Segal also notes that 'one result of postdecision dissonance is a strong desire to proselytize' (p. 127).

27. See below §7.6.

28. F. F. Bruce, *Galatians*, NIGTC; Exeter: Paternoster 1982, p. 164; 'The Curse of Law', *Paul and Paulinism*, C. K. Barrett FS; ed. M. D. Hooker and S. G. Wilson, London: SPCK 1982, pp. 27–36, here p. 31.

ant breaker, as one who had been put out of the covenant people.[29] Once again it was the law in its boundary function which was in view – marking out the limits of what and who count as acceptable within the covenant. Consequently we may surmise that the revelation of the Damascus road for Paul was more likely to involve the following conclusion and corollaries: God has affirmed one whom the law had cursed, that is, counted guilty of breaking the covenant, that is, excluded from the covenant and its benefits, which is tantamount to being reckoned a Gentile.[30] If God is 'for' one such, then he is 'for' Gentiles; to be 'in Christ' is to be in one who was reckoned outside the covenant, but nevertheless acceptable to God. Thus Paul can proclaim that in Christ the good news of God's saving vindication, the blessing of Abraham, the gift of the Spirit, is after all for those *outside* the covenant, that is, for Gentiles.

If all this is on the right lines, then we have to part company with Kim and others who think the primary point of Paul's theology to emerge from the Damascus experience was his doctrine of justification by faith understood in classic Lutheran terms – as antithetical to any notion of earning God's acceptance, and therefore as antithetical to (the) law in principle. If we are right, the turning point for Paul was *not* a reassessment of the law in these terms, but specifically in terms of the law's significance *for Gentiles*, as limiting God's grace to those *en nomō*, 'within the law', and as excluding those *anomoi*, 'outside the law, not having the law.' To draw this conclusion is not to deny the importance of the classic Lutheran restatement of the doctrine of

---

29. Whether they so concluded in the case of other Jews crucified by the Romans we cannot say. It is hard to believe that this would have been the case, given the numbers of Jews crucified by the occupying forces before and after this period. All we can say is that there is evidence that Deut. 21.23 was applied to the crucified *Jesus*. Of course there may have been a particular factor in the case of Jesus which meant that Deut. 21.23 was referred to his death and not to that of other Jews who suffered the same fate. Our findings in ch. 6 would suggest that such a factor was the degree to which Jesus sided with 'sinners' against the 'righteous' who were trying to define and defend the boundaries of covenant righteousness more tightly within Israel. In which case there would be a direct link between Jesus' ministry to 'sinners', and the opposition to it on the one hand, and, on the other, Paul's persecution of Jesus' followers, and subsequent commissioning to open the good news of God's righteousness to Gentile sinners. That is to say, the opening towards the Gentiles by the Hellenists probably reactivated the criticism of Jesus' association with sinners in a fiercer form.

30. If in Jewish factionalism a Jew observing the law inadequately (in terms of dates of feasts, or unacceptable priesthood) could be regarded as equivalent to or worse than a Gentile (*Jub.* 6.32–35; *Ps.Sol.* 8.13), it would be natural and probably inevitable for a Jew who was a 'friend of sinners' and 'hung on a tree' to be identified with Gentile sinners outside the covenant.

justification or the fact that it is bound up with and emerges directly from Paul's teaching on the subject. It is simply to affirm that *the primary thrust and cutting edge of the doctrine of justification* as it emerges in Paul's writings is as an expression of his Damascus-road-given insight that *God's covenant grace is also for the Gentiles as Gentiles, that the eschatological fulfilment of the promise through Abraham does not require Gentiles to merge their ethnic identity into that of the Jewish people.*[31]

How much of all this was hindsight? How soon did Paul begin his missionary work among the Gentiles? The point is disputed, particularly with regard to the implications of Gal. 1.17 (did he embark on missionary work right away in Arabia?). Fortunately we do not need to gain a clear answer. It is enough for us that Paul identified himself as from the beginning sympathetic to and active with Hellenistic Christians who were already beginning to open the gospel to Gentiles. And the fact is that from about the middle 30s (or even earlier?) Gentiles were being accepted by Jewish Nazarenes in (presumably) increasing numbers.

7.3 The issue of circumcision

To speak of Gentiles entering the new Jewish sect in increasing numbers at once raises the next question – circumcision; for the clear implication of our texts is that these Gentiles were accepted by the Nazarenes without first requiring them to be circumcised. And this, despite the fact already noted,[32] that circumcision was such an important identity and boundary marker for more or less all Jews. With any number of uncircumcised Gentile converts to a Jewish sect, given the importance of circumcision for Jewish self-identity, one would have expected that the issue of circumcision would have been inescapable for the new movement more or less from the start. And yet it appears that the issue of whether such Gentile converts should be circumcised did not emerge till about the year 50 (Gal. 2.1–6; Acts 15.1–5).[33] Why the delay? Why

---

31. This is not a new insight. It was expressed early in the century by W. Wrede, *Paul*, ET London: Philip Green, 1907, pp. 122ff.; but most influentially in recent decades by Stendahl, 'The Apostle Paul and the Introspective Conscience of the West', *HTR* 56 (1963), pp. 199–215; reprinted in *Paul Among Jews and Gentiles*.

32. See above pp. 38–9.

33. The persecution in which Paul was involved was occasioned by Stephen's or the Hellenists' views about the Temple and at least began as intersectarian Jewish strife, of a piece with that which was documented in ch. 6. How far Paul's view that the Hellenists threatened the boundaries between Jew and Gentile (§7.2) was shared by others involved in that persecution we cannot tell (Rom. 10.2 could reflect the later situation ten years before the Jewish revolt). And whether there was much concern to pursue the Hellenists

did the circumcision of these Gentile converts not become an issue earlier? Several factors may point to the answer.

(*a*) The precedent of Cornelius (Acts 10–11). Luke certainly highlights the significance of the Cornelius episode with the benefit of hindsight: he has inserted it (Acts 9.32–11.18) together with the account of Paul's conversion (Acts 9.1–31) into the otherwise unbroken sequence of Hellenist history (Acts 6.1–8.40; 11.19–30) so that in his narrative at least it clearly precedes the breakthrough at Antioch. Moreover, the threefold reference to it (Acts 10.1–48; 11.1–18; 15.7–9) gives it a prominence in Luke's narrative which only the threefold account of the conversion of Paul outweighs (Acts 9.1–30; 22.3–21; 26.2–23). Even so, however, in the event, the Cornelius episode must have provided an important precedent: a Gentile had been accepted into the new community of the Nazarene's disciples (baptized in the name of Jesus Christ), without having first been circumcised, and by Peter himself.

At the same time, however, we should note two important qualifying factors. (1) Cornelius is represented as a very pious person – one 'who feared God' and who had judaized, that is, adopted a Jewish way of life to a considerable degree (Acts 10.2).[34] So he was already very close to Judaism. (2) In his case, Luke emphasizes, there were clear and indisputable manifestations of the Spirit (Acts 10.44–47; 11.15–18). Where such grace was being so clearly manifested, the first Jewish Christians found themselves with no other alternative but to recognize that God had short-circuited the hitherto normal means of entry into the people of God (as also in Acts 11.23 and Gal. 2.7–9) – the cleansing (or circumcision) of the heart rendering the circumcision of the flesh of doubtful necessity (cf. Acts 15.7). Perhaps then those of the first believers in Messiah Jesus who saw no reason for otherwise changing their practice of the Torah could regard Cornelius and such cases simply as *exceptions* – posing no real threat to the normal pattern of entry into the covenant people.

(*b*) A high proportion of the earliest converts, perhaps all of them

---

beyond Judaea apart from that reported of Paul (Acts 9.2) is open to some question: Paul's description of himself at that period as displaying an excess of zeal (Gal. 1.14) implies that he was exceptional in the singlemindedness of his pursuit of the Nazarene sect (Phil. 3.6); on the other hand, Gal. 4.29, II Cor. 11.24 and I Thess. 2.14 certainly seem to indicate some ongoing persecution, though whether the issue was the openness to Gentiles remains unclear. Even Gal. 5.11 implies that circumcision became an issue as a result of Paul's own missionary work. See also below p. 289 n. 42.

34. On 'God-fearers' and 'judaizing' see the next paragraph. Cornelius' practice of almsgiving is given particular prominence (Acts 10.2, 4); and almsgiving was regarded as an especially important act of piety within Judaism (see below §7.4c).

in the early days, would have been proselytes and God-fearers. This claim does not depend on 'God-fearer' being an already recognized category, which is a matter of some dispute.[35] The point is that there can be no disputing the fact that many Gentiles were attracted to Judaism and attached themselves to the local synagogues in varying degrees of adherence. Josephus and Philo indicate the considerable attractiveness of Jewish customs for non-Jews, including the sabbath and the food laws (Josephus, *Ap.* 2.123, 209–210, 280, 282; Philo, *Mos.* 2.17–20). *Ioudaizein*, 'to live like a Jew', was already a well established term to indicate the adoption of Jewish practices.[36] And when we look at the main areas of Jewish settlement in the Roman Empire, the story is the same. The testimony of Philo, just mentioned, refers to Alexandria, the second largest city of the Roman empire. Archaeological and inscriptional evidence from Asia Minor shows how highly Jewish communities could be regarded within cities where they had settled.[37] A string of Roman sources confirms that Judaism exerted considerable attraction for many in Rome itself.[38] Most striking for us at this point is Josephus's report that in Syria, of which Antioch was the capital, many Gentiles had 'judaized' and become 'mixed up' with the Jews during the first century (*War* 2.462–3; 7.45).[39]

The deduction which may be drawn from all this is that the Hellenist Nazarenes, when they first came to Antioch, found many Gentiles, both proselytes and god-fearers, who had attached themselves to the synagogues in Antioch; and that this is where the first substantial body of Gentile converts to the new movement of Jesus the Christ came from.[40] If so, very important factors would be (1) the degree to

---

35. See particularly A. T. Kraabel, 'The Disappearance of the God-fearers', *Numen* 28 (1981), pp. 113–26. But see also e.g. J. Reynolds and R. Tannenbaum, *Jews and Godfearers at Aphrodisias*, Cambridge Philological Society Supp. 12, 1987, pp. 48–66; Schürer, 3.160–71; S. McKnight, *A Light Among the Gentiles. Jewish Missionary Activity in the Second Temple Period*, Minneapolis: Fortress 1991, pp. 110–14.

36. So, e.g., in the LXX of Esther 8.17; Theodotus in Eusebius, *Praep. Evang.* 9.22.5; Plutarch, *Life of Cicero* 7.6; Josephus, *War* 2.454. They are cited in my *Jesus, Paul and the Law*, p. 149.

37. See particularly the forthcoming study by P. Trebilco, *Studies on Jewish Communities in Asia Minor*, SNTSMS; Cambridge University 1991.

38. E.g. Plutarch, *Life of Cicero*, 7.6; Juvenal 14.96–106; Cassius Dio 67.14.1–3; Suetonius, *Domitian* 12.2.

39. See further S. J. D. Cohen, 'Crossing the Boundary and Becoming a Jew', *HTR* 82 (1989), pp. 13–33; McKnight, *A Light Among the Gentiles*, ch. 5 (McKnight's important and convincing thesis is that second Temple Judaism was largely unconcerned with missionary activity and that it was not a missionary religion).

40. It may be relevant to recall here that the Hellenist source on which Luke was able to draw makes a point of noting that one of the seven chosen in Acts 7.5 was 'Nicolaus, a proselyte of Antioch'.

which these Gentiles had already 'judaized', and (2) the degree to which they had already proved acceptable to the Jewish synagogues in Antioch. Such adherents and sympathizers would presumably appear less threatening to most of the Jerusalem believers: after all, the boundaries were not being pushed back very far, and baptism (into the name of Jesus) could well be regarded as a further step into Israel.[41] The more traditional Jerusalem believers might also have been content for the time being to allow such Gentiles to remain in an anomalous status, as presumably the synagogues did with regard to their God-fearers – God-fearing attachment to the synagogue/Nazarene community being seen as a step towards full proselyte commitment, judaizing practice as a step towards the complete commitment of circumcision.[42]

But if all this provides some explanation of why it took so long for the issue of circumcision to emerge in the infant Christian communities, the next question is obvious: *why then did the issue of circumcision arise when it did?* We may guess at three reasons at least. (1) Cornelius was proving less an exception and more the rule. The numbers of uncircumcised Gentile converts were increasing too rapidly. What could be regarded as a regrettable but acceptable anomaly when only a relative few were involved became much more of a threat when numbers increased. The boundary markers were no longer being simply obscured; they were being abandoned.

(2) We should not forget the success of the Nazarenes' outreach to their fellow Jews ('the Jewish mission' – Gal. 2.7–8). As already noted,[43] this increased number of Jewish members seems to have included a significant number of Jews who saw their new belief in Jesus as completely consistent with their more traditional beliefs and Pharisaic halakoth. Certainly the difference in attitude between the Judaean brothers in Acts 11.18 (full acceptance of the Cornelius precedent) and Acts 15.1–5 (Christian Pharisees insisting on circumcision) points in this direction; as also Paul's reference to the 'false brothers' in Jerusalem making the same demand, after having 'slipped in to spy out our freedom' (Gal. 2.4).

(3) We should also bear in mind the deteriorating political situation in Judaea during this period, not least the crisis caused by Emperor

---

41. If proselyte baptism was in process of being introduced at this time (for discussion see those cited in my *Jesus, Paul and the Law*, p. 168 n. 70; McKnight, *A Light Among the Gentiles*, pp. 82–5), baptism 'in the name of Jesus' would belong to the same grey area.

42. Cf. again Juvenal 14.96–106 – the son of the God-fearing father takes the natural next step by accepting circumcision.

43. See above §7.1.

Caligula's attempt to have a statue of himself set up in the Jerusalem Temple (40 CE), a threat every bit as serious as that which occasioned the Maccabean revolt.[44] The death of King Agrippa (44) was probably a blow to more moderate hopes (given Agrippa's friendship with Emperor Claudius, and therefore potential for securing favourable treatment for his people). The succeeding Roman procurators were weak and heavy handed. Cuspius Fadus (44–46?) demanded that the vestments of the High Priest be returned to the Romans for safe-keeping and had to act against the threatened rebellion of Theudas (Josephus, *Ant.* 20.6, 97–99). His successor, Tiberius Iulius Alexander, himself a Jewish apostate, (46?–48) crucified James and Simon, sons of Judas the Galilean, presumably because like their father they were thought to be fomenting unrest against Roman rule which would see as a threat to Israel's loyalty to God alone (*Ant.* 20.102). Under his successor the situation continued to deteriorate (48–52) with a near riot in Jerusalem resulting in thousands dead (according to Josephus) and increasing banditry (Zealots) in Samaria and elsewhere (*War* 2.223–38; *Ant.* 20.105–24).[45]

Under these circumstances, and given the characteristic Jewish sense of covenant prerogative and religious distinctiveness in relation to other nations, it would occasion little surprise if the more relaxed attitude in Jerusalem indicated in Acts 11.18 began to change. Since religious identity and national identity were so inextricably intertwined in Jewish self-understanding,[46] any factors perceived as a threat to national identity would make it necessary for both national and religious boundaries to be defended with vigour. Conversely, religious innovations would all the more easily be seen as a threat to national identity. The pressure would build up for boundaries to be more carefully monitored and more fully observed – as is usually the case when a group feels under threat. And since circumcision was such a primary marker, *the* sign of God's everlasting covenant with Abraham and his seed (Gen. 17.9–14),[47] it would immediately come to prominence as an issue as soon as any group of Jewish believers took it upon themselves to draw the lines of definition and identity more tightly in communities of the diaspora as well as in Judaea.[48]

---

44. Philo. *Legat.* 184–338; Josephus, *War* 2.184–203; *Ant.* 18.261–309 – note the space given to it. Tacitus was also aware of it (*Hist.* 5.9).

45. Fuller details in Schürer, 1.455ff.

46. See further below §8.2.

47. See again above pp. 38–9.

48. This national-religious importance of circumcision is again highlighted by the decision of Emperor Hadrian to ban circumcision as part of his response to the Bar Kokhba revolt (Schürer, 1.538–9).

It must have been somewhat in this way that the issue of circumcision arose for the new movement in the late 40s – the second great dispute to rend earliest Christianity (the first having been the views of Stephen and the Hellenists regarding the Temple). Whatever the pre-history, this was the issue which evidently dominated what history has called the council of Jerusalem (Gal. 2.1–10; Acts 15.1–29).[49]

7.4 The council at Jerusalem

When the issue of circumcision did come to the surface and provoke vigorous disagreement within the new movement (Gal. 2.1–10) there were three parties involved.

(a) *Paul and Titus.* Paul chose his language in Gal. 1–2 very carefully. He wanted to make it quite clear that at the time he wrote Galatians he did not regard himself as in any degree dependent on or subordinate to the leaders of the Jerusalem church. We should note particularly Paul's repeated insistence on the independence of his apostleship (1.1, 12, 16–17); the distancing description of the Jerusalem leaders in 2.2 and 6 – *hoi dokountes*, 'those who are held in repute';[50] and the striking parenthesis in 2.6 – 'what they once were makes no difference to me, God shows no partiality'. But, *at the same time*, his language also indicates that at the time of the Jerusalem meeting he *had* regarded the Jerusalem apostles highly and probably acknowledged their authority; as a missionary of Antioch (cf. Acts 13.3), itself a daughter church of Jerusalem (Acts 11.19–24), he would presumably have seen it as quite proper at that time that he should come to Jerusalem to have the matter under dispute resolved. This attitude is probably implicit in the verbs used in Gal. 1.16 (*prosanatithesthai* = 'consult for authoritative ruling or interpretation' of the revelation received; although he did not go to Jerusalem for such a consultation, his language is a tacit acceptance that the Jerusalem leadership would have been the proper authorities to consult for such a ruling); and 1.18 (*historeō* = 'get to know Peter', which would no doubt include the traditions about Jesus for which Peter would be a primary authority). But the point is clear in Gal. 2: 2.2 – the judgment made by the Jerusalem leadership would make all the difference to

---

49. The discussion here does not depend on the identification of the Gal. 2.1–10 consultation with that of Acts 15; what is primarily in view here is the agreement on circumcision reached at Jerusalem between Paul and the Jerusalem leadership (Gal. 2.1–10).

50. See particularly H. D. Betz, *Galations*, Hermeneia; Philadelphia: Fortress 1979, pp. 86–7, 92, 94.

the effectiveness of Paul's work ('I laid before them . . . the gospel . . . lest somehow I should be running or had run in vain'); 2.3 – they did not *compel* Titus to be circumcised, the implication being that they could have insisted had they so chosen; 2.6 – they 'added nothing' to Paul's message, but once again with the implication that they could have done so if they had so decided; 2.9–10 – it was they who recognized Paul's mission, they who gave Paul the right hand of fellowship, they who called on Paul to remember the poor. Quite clearly, Paul had fought his corner with great vigour and courage, and it was his argument which had won the day. But equally evident is the fact that it was for the pillar apostles to accept or reject that argument. The awkwardness of Paul's position was that *in order to stress the fact that the pillar apostles accepted his understanding of the gospel and of his vocation he had also to acknowledge their authority to grant that acceptance.*[51]

(*b*) The 'false brothers'. This, of course, is Paul's description of them (Gal. 2.4). But presumably they were also Christians, believers in Jesus as Messiah crucified and raised, and baptized in his name. Evidently they were much more conservative on the matter of maintaining Israel's distinctive identity and boundaries than the Jerusalem leaders, and certainly than Paul. Here we must note again that they evidently saw their new loyalty (to Messiah Jesus) as an extension of their traditional faith, the new movement of the Nazarenes as wholly *within* the Judaism of the second Temple period. They did not see the new movement as in any way separate or distinct from the Judaism of their ancestral faith. There was no clash of loyalties involved, no sense that they had to make a choice between this further belief and Judaism. On the contrary, their logic was clear: to be a member of the new movement one had to be a Jew or to become a Jew, that is, to enter into the covenant in the normal way, as with all proselytes.

(*c*) '*Those of repute*', *the* '*pillar*' *apostles* (2.2, 6, 9). This group evidently stood in the middle, between the competing and antithetical advocacies of Paul and the 'false brothers'. What is particularly interesting is the implication of 2.3 that the 'pillars' were sympathetic to the 'false brothers'.[52] They would have welcomed Paul's conforming to the traditional practices by agreeing to the circumcision of Titus. Apart from anything else, *by his refusal to conform, Paul was blurring their own identity as Jews and members of the covenant people* whose

---

51. For a fuller exposition on which the above paragraph is based see my 'The Relationship between Paul and Jerusalem according to Galatians 1 and 2', *NTS* 28 (1982), pp. 461–78, reprinted in *Jesus, Paul and the Law*, ch. 5.

52. See again the insightful exposition by Lightfoot cited above p. 4.

status as such (in their own eyes at least) was enhanced rather than threatened by their belief in Jesus as Israel's Messiah.

In the event, however, it was Paul's advocacy which won the day: the manifestations of divine grace were so clear in Paul's missionary work, as they had been in Peter's, that they could not withhold agreement (2.7–9; cf. Acts 11.23 and 15.7–12). Despite the explicit instruction of the Torah on the point (Gen. 17.9–14), God's will now to the contrary had been made clear in a way which none of them could deny. *And so the momentous decision was made: circumcision was not to be regarded as necessary for Gentile membership of the Nazarenes.* An increasingly serious anomaly which could be ignored so long as nothing was said about it in public had been brought into the public forum and made an issue; and the issue had been resolved in Paul's favour.

The one thing the 'pillar' apostles did ask was that the mission to the Gentiles should remember the importance of almsgiving, something Paul agreed to readily enough (Gal. 2.10). This codicil to the Jerusalem agreement should not be seen merely as a casual afterthought born of a charitable disposition, or merely as an act of charity. Almsgiving was understood within second Temple Judaism as a central and crucial expression of covenant 'righteousness' (Ps. 112.9, cited in II Cor. 9.9; Dan. 4.27; Sir. 29.12; 40.24; Tobit 4.10; 12.9; 14.10–11; Matt. 5.20/6.2–4).[53] It had been precisely almsgiving which had marked out Cornelius as an acceptably judaizing Gentile (Acts 10.2, 4). In a real sense almsgiving was the next best thing to circumcision; so having conceded the latter, it would be important, perhaps essential to the Jerusalem apostles that Paul should affirm the former, as an expression of their common integrity as Jews, both theirs and Paul's. We should not miss the fact that *the mind-set thus indicated was still that of traditional covenantal nomism*: what was in view was the typical righteous act by which one attested and maintained one's status within the covenant.

And so was resolved the issue of circumcision for the sect of Messiah Jesus – temporarily for some, unacceptably for others, as would all too soon become apparent. That decision would seem to cut the nerve or at least undermine the principle of covenantal nomism as

---

53. K. Berger, 'Almosen für Israel: zum historischen Kontext der paulinischen Kollekte', *NTS* 23 (1976–77), pp. 180–204. In the LXX *eleēmosunē*, 'kind deed, alms, charitable giving', is frequently used to translate the Hebrew, *sedeq/s'daqah*, 'righteousness' (G. Schrenk, *dikaiosunē*, *TDNT*, 2.196). For subsequent rabbinic traditions see Strack-Billerbeck 4.536–58; e.g. the Midrash on Deut. 15.9 elaborates: 'Be careful not to refuse charity, for every one who refuses charity is put in the same category with idolaters, and he breaks off from him the yoke of heaven, as it is said, "wicked", that is, "without yoke".'

understood and practised within the Judaism of the day. So Paul may have thought. At the very least *a decisive precedent* had now been set and agreed to for other disputes in this area. However, the further agreement regarding almsgiving, precisely because it was also counted as a benchmark of covenantal righteousness, may well have muddied the issue. What Paul understood by it at the time is not clear.[54] But it probably left some at least of those in the middle ground (particularly James) under the impression that *an exception had been permitted rather than a principle conceded*. The almost inevitable result was the incident at Antioch.[55]

7.5 The issue of food laws – the incident at Antioch

Circumcision had to do only with the issue of how a Gentile might *enter* the covenant people. As an entry requirement it was a one-off act. To that extent it was easier to make an exception in the case of circumcision, as other Jews may occasionally have been prepared to do (Josephus, *Ant.* 20.40–42). However, there was *also* the question of how one lived *within* the covenant; how did one express one's continuing obligation to God *under* the covenant? As observed before, for the devout Jew, obedience to the law was not a way of entering the covenant, not a way of winning a place in God's favour. Obedience to the Torah was what God demanded of those already *within* the covenant, already part of his chosen people. The law told the covenant member how to live as a covenant member. 'Covenantal nomism' is what the devout Jew did to express his Jewishness, that which distinguished him from the other nations.[56] Since what was involved was the praxis of every day life, *to that extent the ongoing issue of covenantal nomism was even more serious than the one-off issue of circumcision.*

We have also noted that within the scope of covenantal nomism the food laws held a very central place.[57] Here we need to remind ourselves of the overlapping and interacting series of concerns bound up with observance of these laws: the laws on unclean foods themselves (Lev. 11; Deut. 14); the law of ritual slaughter requiring the blood to be properly drained (Lev. 3.17; 7.26–27; 17.10–14; Deut. 12.16, 23–24; 15.23); the fear of being contaminated by idolatry,

---

54. See further above §5.5 (pp. 112–13).

55. In what follows I draw on and develop my 'The Incident at Antioch (Gal. 2.11–18)', *JSNT* 18 (1983), pp. 3–57; reprinted in *Jesus, Paul and the Law*, ch. 6.

56. See above §2.3.

57. See above §2.3 (pp. 41–2) and §6.3.

that is, by meat which had been offered to idols (*IV Macc.* 5.2; cf. I Cor. 8–10); and ritual purity, a concern for all Jews, but particularly for Pharisees and Essenes at the time.[58] Religious Jews would have observed all these rules and rulings with varying degrees of strictness; as also, probably, judaizing God-fearers, since just these rules provided definition for that distinctively Jewish way of life which proved so attractive to many Gentiles and which the word 'judaize' covers.[59]

At Antioch we read that Jewish and Gentile believers ate together (Gal. 2.12). That probably means that the basis of their table-fellowship was at least a modest observance of the food laws. Complete abandonment of the law *in toto* in this area would have created a stir among the local Jews long before this, such was the importance of the food laws in Jewish self-identity.[60] And most of the initial converts to the new group had probably been God-fearers or proselytes, drawn from that large group of Gentile judaizers of whom Josephus speaks (*War* 7.45); that is, they had been accustomed to observe the food laws in at least some measure prior to their joining the Nazarenes. On this basis Peter and the other Jewish believers, identified as 'the rest of the Jews' (rather than as Hellenists – 2.13), would have been quite happy to share in table fellowship with uncircumcised Gentile believers.[61]

But then, Paul tells us, 'certain men came from James', and 'when they came, he (Peter) drew back and separated himself, fearing those of the circumcision. And the rest of the Jews joined with him in playing the hypocrite, so that even Barnabas was carried away with their insincerity' (Gal. 2.12–13). It is obvious from this that the men from James were hostile to the table-fellowship of Jew with Gentile as being practised at Antioch; and that their hostility resulted in Peter and all the other Jewish believers withdrawing from that fellowship. Why should they be so hostile? We need not go into the full detail of

---

58. See above §3.2; also §§6.2–3.

59. On the meaning of *ioudaizein*, 'judaize', see my *Jesus, Paul and the Law*, pp. 149–50.

60. See again as n. 57. E. P. Sanders, 'Jewish Association with Gentiles and Galatians 2.11–14', *The Conversation Continues. Studies in Paul and John. In Honor of J. L. Martyn*, ed. R. T. Fortna and B. R. Gaventa, Nashville: Abingdon 1990, pp. 170–88, agrees with the basic position here argued, though he questions whether ritual purity was a factor.

61. Esler criticizes my earlier study of this episode by disputing that there could be any table-fellowship between Jews and Gentiles in this period (*Community*, pp. 76–86); but he greatly oversimplifies the evidence (see my response in *Jesus, Paul and the Law*, pp. 179–81). As Segal, *Paul*, pp. 231–3 points out: 'there is no law in rabbinic literature that prevents a Jew from eating with a gentile'. The question was rather on what terms such table-fellowship might be possible – as the Antioch incident itself confirms. See again Cohen, 'Crossing the Boundary'.

a fascinating text, and must allow for the fact that it was penned from Paul's own point of view; nevertheless the answer is sufficiently clearly hinted at in Paul's response, which probably echoes in critical rejoinder some of the attitudes with which we are now familiar.

(1) Particularly noticeable is the use of *hamartōloi*, 'sinners', in 2.15 – 'We (Peter and Paul) are Jews by nature and not Gentile sinners'. As we have already seen,[62] *hamartōloi* was perhaps the word above all others which Jews used to indicate those outside the covenant, both Gentiles who were law-less by definition, and other Jews who, in the eyes of the 'righteous', did not observe the law properly. In this phrase Paul almost certainly was echoing the attitude of the men from James, and the attitude which had proved decisive for Peter and the others: that the law, here particularly the food laws, should mark a boundary separating Jew from Gentile, the people of the covenant from those outside the covenant; and that these laws had to be observed if Jewish identity as the covenant people was to be preserved, and observed the more strictly the more that identity was under threat from Hellenistic syncretism or Roman oppression. *What shocked the men from James was that Peter and the other 'Jews by nature' were eating so freely with 'Gentile sinners',* as if God intended no distinction between those within and those outside the covenant people.

(2) If in 2.15 Paul was echoing the shock of the men from James, the same is probably true in 2.14 – 'you (Peter) a Jew live like a Gentile and not like a Jew'! Notice again the language of clear differentiation – 'Jew' and 'Gentile'. Despite the protests of some, 'to live like a Gentile' need not mean a complete abandonment of the law.[63] Once again we are probably confronted with factional language: 'living like a Gentile' was the accusation which one sect within Judaism would throw at another which denied or disputed its halakoth (as in *Jub.* 6.32–35 and *Pss. Sol.* 8.13).[64] *From the perspective of the men from James, the modest level of law-observance in the table-fellowship at Antioch was tantamount to abandoning the law altogether;* the Jewish believers at Antioch were already too far down

---

62. See above §6.2.

63. Betz, *Galatians* – 'total emancipation from Judaism' (p. 112); T. Holtz, 'Der antiochenische Zwischenfall (Gal. 2.11–14)', *NTS* 32 (1986), pp. 344–61, here pp. 351–2. P. C. Böttger, 'Paulus und Petrus in Antiochien. Zum Verständnis von Galater 2.11–21', *NTS* 37 (1991), pp. 77–100, also misses the factional and polemical character of the language (p. 80). That the language echoes the rebuke of 'those from James' to Peter is sufficient to explain the present tense used by Paul.

64. Sanders, 'Jewish Association', pp. 186–7, likewise recognizes that the language is 'exaggerated'.

the slippery slope to complete apostasy. To maintain table fellowship at a level governed, say, by the conventions later regularized in the 'Noahide laws' (Gen. 9.3–4),[65] was quite inadequate for a child of Abraham, a member of the covenant people governed by the law of the covenant as distinct from the other nations.

(3) There may be a further echo of the attitudes Paul attacks in Paul's report that Peter and the other Jews 'separated themselves' from the rest of the believers in Antioch (2.12).[66] For, again as noted above, 'Pharisee' probably meant originally 'one who separated himself' from others, in order to maintain a more strict level of purity, of dedication to God.[67] In the light of the other clearer echoes of Pharisaic attitudes among the men from James (cf. Acts 15.5), not to mention the use of the word 'sinner', Paul probably implies that Peter and the other Jewish believers, by withdrawing from the table-fellowship of Antioch, were acting like Pharisees, at least in the sense that by their action and attitude they were criticizing and condemning other Jews for failure in commitment and devotion to the covenant.

Whatever the finer nuances of this passage (Gal. 2.11–15), the result of the hostility of the men from James is not disputed. Peter gave a lead in separating himself from the common table-fellowship of the Antioch community, the rest of the Jewish believers followed suit, and even Barnabas (there is a hint of considerable misgiving on his part) was swept along in the unanimity of Jewish action. Paul speaks of the action as 'insincere/hypocritical', as 'not straight as regards the truth of the gospel' (2.13–14). But that is *Paul's* view of the matter. How would Peter have put it? (1) He would certainly have seen the logic of covenantal nomism – that a Jew should continue to live in accordance with the law. (2) He would no doubt have felt the pressure of mounting nationalism and zeal; this is obviously alluded to when Paul says he 'feared those of the circumcision' (2.12), that is, those who continued to define themselves by means of circumcision, whether belonging to the Nazarenes or not (cf. Gal. 2.7–8). (3) He would have been concerned for the continuing viability of his mission to the circumcised; to be identified as a 'sinner', and not least by those of his own 'sect', would have made him unacceptable to many Jews. (4) Moreover, to ask the Gentile believers to go a fair way in law-keeping was nothing unusual, but on the contrary, quite normal; as

---

65. For full discussion see D. Novak, *The Image of the Non-Jew in Judaism. An Historical and Constructive Study of the Noahide Laws*, Lewiston/Queenston/Lampeter: Edwin Mellen 1983, particularly ch. 1.

66. A similar, though contrasting, word-play may have been intended at Gal. 1.15.

67. See above §6.2, p. 140 and n. 32.

we have already seen, probably most if not all of the first Gentile converts had been proselytes or God-fearers and so, like Cornelius, had practised the Jewish way of life to a considerable degree; with the main stumbling block for such adherents (circumcision) no longer an issue, why should such Gentiles not be asked to take sympathetic account of the scruples of their Jewish brothers and make it possible for the latter to retain the regard of their devout kinsmen? All in all, we might justifiably think, Peter's policy was really rather sensible: he was concerned for the genuine and deeply felt beliefs of his fellow Jews, and he was not putting too heavy an additional demand on the Gentiles – only a difference in degree of law observance, nothing that conflicted with the principle of the gospel itself.

Paul, however, saw things differently. Indeed, it was perhaps this very episode which brought the issue into focus for him. For him the issue now became whether believing in Jesus was simply an extension of being a Jew, or whether believing in Jesus was something distinct from or at least not dependent on being a Jew – whether the logic of covenantal nomism as normally understood applied to uncircumcised Gentiles as well – whether the blessing of God originally offered to and through Abraham continued to be tied to membership of the Jewish people as such. For almost all his fellow Jews the answer was obvious: 'Yes! They followed the logic of covenant: God had made his covenant with the Jewish people; the law was part of that bargain (covenant); membership of the covenant people could not be separated from keeping the law which defined and governed that people.

Paul, however, followed a different logic – the logic of faith. Entry into the people of God was by faith, and circumcision was no longer necessary; that was common ground (Gal. 2.16). But at that point Peter and the others stopped short: they seem to have confined this principle to the question of circumcision, to the question of Gentile *entry* into the covenant people, and to see 'works of the law' (food laws in particular) as the necessary corollary to faith; 'works of the law' could be seen and required as the outworking of this faith.[68] But Paul pressed the logic of faith. If *entry* into the covenant is by faith, the same principle should apply to life *within* the covenant; membership of the covenant people should *not* be tied to or be made to depend on particular rulings regarding food and table-fellowship; *it*

---

68. Gal. 2.16 can be translated, 'We are Jews by nature ... knowing that no one is justified by works of the law, except through faith in Jesus Christ ...'. Although the exegesis is a matter of some dispute (see my *Jesus, Paul and the Law*, pp. 206–14, particularly points 3 and 9), the Antioch incident indicates that this was in fact the attitude and understanding of Peter and the other Jewish believers. On 'works of the law' see below §7.6.

should depend solely on faith (2.16). He goes on to recall how he used to see things as Peter and the men from James did: if eating with uncircumcised Gentiles constitutes someone a sinner, then Christ himself falls victim to the same logic (2.17–18); but that was all behind him, *now* he lived by faith in the Son of God (2.19–20). And so, he goes on to urge the Galatians, having *begun* with the Spirit, through faith, continue as you began (3.1ff).

Paul thus in effect accused Peter of thinking in too narrowly nation-alistic terms. Faith in Christ *is* the climax of *Jewish* faith, but it is no longer to be perceived as a specifically *Jewish* faith; *faith should not be made to depend in any degree on the believer living as a Jew (judaizing)*.

The *consequences* of the Antioch incident were far-reaching. In this instance Paul was probably unsuccessful in his appeal to and rebuke of Peter.[69] The traditional view is that Peter recognized the force of Paul's arguments and gave way; table-fellowship was resumed as before. But the critical point is that Paul does not say so. If he had been successful, it is most probable that he would have indicated this clearly to his Galatian readers – as he had done with regard to the Jerusalem agreement (Gal. 2.1–10); the matter was of such impor-tance to the Galatians, he could hardly have refrained from indicating that his policy had been given the influential backing of Peter and the others, had that in fact been the case. Instead the rebuke of Peter in Gal. 2.14ff. tails off into a restatement of Paul's own position – the implication being that he had to restate it because the argument had not been accepted the first time. Moreover, the more weighty we recognize to have been the reasons why Peter withdrew from the common table in the first place, the less likely is it that he would have agreed with Paul that the principle of justification by faith was in danger. To observe the law as a regulator of conduct was *not* to undermine the principle of justification by faith (James 2 in effect argues for just this point of view). All that the Gentiles were being asked to do was to make it easier for Jewish believers to remain in good standing with their fellow Jews in Judaea.

The further consequences take us too far from our present concerns, but we should just note that they probably involved *a significant break between Paul and others, and a new stage in the still young Christian mission*. (1) It probably meant a break with Antioch: pre-viously Paul had worked as a missionary of Antioch; from now on the picture is much more of an independent missionary, making the

---

69. That Paul was defeated in the confrontation at Antioch is a view which commands a wide consensus in modern scholarship.

centre of his operations first in Corinth and then in Ephesus (Acts 18.11; 19.10). (2) It probably meant a break with Barnabas: previously they had been close colleagues; now they went their separate ways (cf. Acts 15.36–41). (3) It probably meant a break with Jerusalem: as we have seen, whereas at the time of the Jerusalem council he had been willing to acknowledge the authority of the Jerusalem leadership, by the time he wrote Galatians he wanted to stress his independence of Jerusalem;[70] almost certainly it was the Antioch incident which soured the relationship and which proved the crucial turning point in Paul's attitude to Jerusalem.

The point of particular importance for us, however, is the likelihood that the Antioch episode and its outcome resulted in *a clarification and crystallization for Paul himself of what the principle of justification by faith involves.* Now, if not before, he realized that the experience of faith and the promise of the Spirit freely shared by Gentile as well as Jew, without the law, 'outside the law', must affect Israel's traditional understanding and practice of covenantal nomism – not simply of circumcision as a rite of entry for Gentiles into the covenant people, but also of the law as defining the people of God in ethnic distinctiveness. In other words, *the Antioch incident was probably a decisive factor in the undermining of the third great pillar of second Temple Judaism, the Torah.*

Have we then reached the parting of the ways on this second matter so central to Jewish self-understanding? As the Stephen incident proved decisive for Christianity in undermining the centrality of the Temple, did the Antioch incident settle the matter of the law for Christianity? Does it mean that Paul from that time on, or earlier, abandoned the law, as some would maintain? And what about the election of Israel, the second pillar of Judaism, on this analysis; since covenantal nomism is so much an expression of covenant and election, did Paul draw what many would think the obvious corollary, that Israel had forfeited its election by its failure to acknowledge Jesus as Messiah?

In no case is the answer a simple Yes or No. Apart from anything else, the parting of the ways, if we can already so speak, was at this point also as much a parting of the ways *within* the new movement as *between* Christianity and Judaism, or better, as within Judaism. If our analysis is correct, Paul moved on from Antioch a relatively isolated figure. Within the NT itself the epistle of James in particular seems much closer to the attitude to the law with which Paul broke

---

70. See above §7.4(a).

at Antioch.[71] In order to gain a clearer picture we will have to extend the discussion beyond Paul. So too the question of Paul's understanding of Israel's election will take us into the next chapter.

Here, however, we should at least take up the issue of how deep and serious was Paul's disillusion with the law as determining conduct for the people of God. Did he indeed wish to abandon the law completely? Is the logic of his position inevitably antinomian, however much he might have protested to the contrary? What was left of this third pillar of Judaism for Paul after Antioch?

7.6 Paul's mature view of the law

Did Paul abandon the law completely? Did he no longer consider it a positive factor in God's saving purpose? A thorough study of the question would require a full-scale monograph. But there is at least one point which arises out of the present study, which can make an important contribution to the wider debate,[72] and which deserves more attention than it has so far received. It focusses on the phrase *'works of the law'* – the phrase by which, in fact, Paul sums up his objection to Peter in the Antioch incident: that 'no man is justified by works of the law' (Gal. 2.16). To what was it that Paul was objecting?

Unfortunately exegesis of Paul's teaching here has become caught up in and obscured by the Reformation's characteristic polemic against merit, against the idea that anyone could earn salvation, make himself or herself acceptable to God by good works.[73] The mistake was to assume too readily that this was what Paul too was attacking. To be fair, such an interpretation can be built quite quickly on Rom. 4.4–5 – 'Now to him who works the reward is not reckoned as a favour but as a debt; but to him who does not work but believes on him who justifies the ungodly, his faith is "reckoned for righteousness".'[74] But that passage is probably intended simply to contrast a human contract with the divine-human relationship, in order to show that in the latter *logizesthai* ('to be reckoned') has the meaning, 'reckoned as an act of grace'. It does *not* say that the Jewish understanding of Israel's covenant relationship was conceived in terms of

71. Note how James 2.18–24 seems to take up the line of argument used by Paul in Rom. 3.28–4.22 and to refute it point by point.

72. For the wider debate see those cited in my *Jesus, Paul and the Law*, p. 8, nn. 2–6.

73. See above §1.4d.

74. See particularly S. Westerholm, *Israel's Law and the Church's Faith. Paul and his Recent Interpreters*, Grand Rapids: Eerdmans 1988, particularly pp. 109–21. I respond to Westerholm in *Jesus, Paul and the Law*, pp. 237–41.

a human contract.[75] We have already seen that it was not so: Judaism typically was (and is) a religion which emphasizes repentance and atonement provided by God, a very different model from that of the human contract. Besides which, it is surely incredible that Paul should be thought to say that God does not want his human creatures to do good works (contrast Rom. 2.10; 12.21; 13.3). There was always something odd, not to say suspect, about the assumption that Paul's polemic against 'works of the law' was a polemic against 'good works'.

How then should we understand 'works of the law'? As ever in exegesis, the phrase needs to be set primarily within the context both of its times and of its usage by Paul himself.

(*a*) The phrase itself is best taken in the sense, 'service of the law' or 'nomistic service'.[76] That is, it does not denote actions already accomplished, so much as obligations laid down by the law, the religious system determined by the law. In fact, 'works of the law' is the Pauline expression of what we have been calling 'covenantal nomism' – the obedience to the law laid upon the member of the covenant by virtue of his membership.

(*b*) The nearest parallel to Paul's phrase comes in fact in the Qumran writings – 'deeds of the law' (*ma'seh torah*).[77] In 4QFlor. 1.1–7 'deeds of the law' are what marked out the Qumran community in its distinctiveness from outsiders and enemies. In 1QS 5.20–24 and 6.18, 'deeds in reference to the Torah' are what the community member has to be tested on every year. And the so far unpublished 4Q *Miqsat Ma'aseh Ha-Torah* (4QMMT) consists in a sequence of sectarian halakic regulations.[78] In other words, 'deeds of the law' denote the interpretations of the Torah which marked out the Qumran community as distinctive, the obligations which members took upon themselves as members and by which they maintained their membership. The implication is that the 'deeds of the law' over which the covenanters had to show greatest sensitivity, on which they had to demonstrate their loyalty most clearly, were precisely those points of halakoth which were most in dispute between them and the other sects of second Temple Judaism.

(*c*) When first used by Paul, in Gal. 2.16, the phrase clearly looks

---

75. See further my *Romans*, pp. 203–204.

76. E. Lohmeyer, 'Gesetzeswerke', *Probleme paulinischer Theologie*, Stuttgart n.d., pp. 33–74; J. B. Tyson, ' "Works of Law" in Galatians', *JBL* 92 (1973), pp. 423–31.

77. L. Gaston is thus quite wrong (though he is hardly alone) when he attempts to make sense of the phrase on the assumption that it 'is not found in any Jewish texts' (*Paul and the Torah*, Vancouver: University of British Columbia 1987, e.g. pp. 25 and 69).

78. See above p. 55 n. 23.

back to the immediately preceding issue – that of the *food laws* at Antioch. Probably also included is the other great issue of Gal. 2 – *circumcision*. In other words, the sense of the phrase as used by Paul comes close to what we have just seen in the Dead Sea Scrolls. 'Works of the law' had in view particularly (but not exclusively) those acts of covenantal nomism which served as tests of covenantal loyalty – in the Antioch incident, the food laws (this was the view of the men from James which prevailed with Peter and the other Jewish believers) – and in the Jerusalem council, circumcision (this was the view of the 'false brothers'). In view of what we saw earlier about the importance of just these two obligations of the Torah for Jewish self-identity (particularly I Macc. 1.60–63),[79] it is hardly surprising that the issue of covenant loyalty should come to focus in just these two 'works of the law'.

(*d*) The same is true of Paul's use of the same phrase in Romans. It occurs for the first time in 3.20, where it seems clearly to function as a summary of the attitude indicted by Paul in the preceding section, particularly the Jewish presumption in view in 2.1ff., and especially 2.17ff. This is confirmed by 3.27–28, where it is linked with the 'boasting' attacked in 2.17 and 23. To be noted is the fact that 'boasting' here is not the boasting of self-achieved merit, as once again in typical Reformation exegesis;[80] but boasting in status as a 'Jew' (2.17), boasting in the privileged position given to Jews by their possession of the law (2.17–20). 'Works of the law' here denotes the attitude of covenantal nomism as typically understood in second Temple Judaism in general, and as focused in the principal identity confirming/boundary defining acts (like circumcision and food laws), since they excluded the Gentile by definition. Hence Paul's line of argument in Rom. 3.27–30: to say 'a man is justified by works of the law' is tantamount to saying 'God is the God of Jews only' (3.28–29).

Thus it begins to become clear that Paul was *not* against the law as such – far less against 'good works'! What he aimed his arguments against was *the law understood and practised in such a way as to limit the grace of God, to prevent Gentiles as Gentiles enjoying it in full measure.* Paul regarded the issue very seriously for that reason. So to understand the law was also to understand Jewish identity in too formal, outward, physical and ethnic terms (Rom. 2.28–29). It prevented a 'doing' of the law which was not dependent on 'having

---

79. See above §2.3; see also p. 145 n. 49.
80. See e.g. Bultmann, *Theology*, 1.242; Käsemann, *Romans*, ad loc.

the law', on being 'within the law' (2.12ff.). Such an attitude stood
under the condemnation of the law as much as the grosser Gentile sins
(3.9–20). By implication such pride in the law was also an example of
sin's abuse of the law (7.7ff.), a different kind of failure to keep the
law, but equally falling under the law's curse (Gal. 3.10–12).[81]

In contrast, *Paul did expect the law to be fulfilled by believers.*
That is, the law understood in terms of faith, 'the obedience of faith'
(Rom. 1.5), faith as confirming the law (3.31), 'faith working through
love' (Gal. 5.6), where faith for Paul was the basis and means by
which the human relates to the divine, rather than by works of the
law. Hence too the emphasis of Rom. 8.4: the purpose of God in
sending his Son was 'in order that the just requirement of the law
might be fulfilled in us, who walk not according to the flesh but
according to the Spirit', where 'walking according to the Spirit' is
obviously posed in contrast also to the typical OT talk of 'walking
in the law/statutes/ ordinances of God', which in Paul's eyes had
become an expression of covenantal nomism. Hence too the emphasis
of 13.8–10 – the law fulfilled in the command to 'love your neighbour', a command which in Jesus' exposition of it did not presuppose
maintenance of boundaries dividing the people of God from the rest,
but precisely the abolition of such boundaries (Luke 10.30–37).[82]

So, we may say, in attacking the covenantal nomism of the Judaism
of his day Paul was attacking neither the law, nor the covenant (as
we shall see), but *a covenantal nomism which insisted on treating the
law as a boundary round Israel, marking off Jew from Gentile, with
only those inside as heirs of God's promise to Abraham.* In short, it
was the law abused to which Paul objected, not the law itself. To be
sure, this latter distinction is not a simple one; Paul's position is easily
misunderstood, then (Rom. 3.8;6.1) as now. But at least the reason
for the misunderstanding should now be fairly plain. Paul was making
*a distinction between different ways of understanding what the law
required, different ways of doing the law.* One he argued, is a false
understanding ('works of the law'), to be distinguished quite sharply
from fulfilling the law by faith through love, or by 'walking in accord-

---

81. See further my 'Works of the Law and the Curse of the Law (Gal. 3.10–14)', *NTS*
31 (1985), pp. 523–42, reprinted and elaborated in *Jesus, Paul and the Law*, ch. 8.

82. That Paul was aware of and influenced by Jesus' teaching on this theme is highly
probable; see my *Romans*, p. 779; also 'Paul's Knowledge of the Jesus Tradition. The
Evidence of Romans', *Christus Bezeugen. Festschrift für W. Trilling*, ed. K. Kertelge et al.,
Leipzig: St Benno 1989, pp. 193–207. A similar deduction is made by A. J. M. Wedderburn,
'Paul and Jesus: Similarity and Continuity', *NTS* 34 (1988), pp. 161–82, revised in *Paul
and Jesus. Collected Essays*, ed. A. J. M. Wedderburn, JSNT Supp. 37; Sheffield Academic
1989, pp. 117–43.

ance with the Spirit'. The problem was that most of his fellow Jews did not or could not see that distinction. For them, naturally, doing the law *included* doing the works of the law to which Paul objected – particularly the boundary defining deeds of the law that marked out Israel as God's own. Paul, in other words, was beginning to make *a distinction within Jewish identity which his fellow Jews simply could not see*. For them it was a total package, as passages like Gen. 17.9–14 and Lev. 18.5 indicated. So Paul was inevitably a 'loser' so far as the bulk of his fellow Jews were concerned.[83] What he stood for was simply incomprehensible to them, for the simple reason that works of the law were integral to the covenant for them, integral to their own identity as Jews.[84] It is not surprising then that Paul should be regarded with such suspicion in Jerusalem itself (Acts 21.20–21): *he was seen as undermining the foundation of Judaism itself.* Nor that he should be remembered in the Jewish Christianity of the second and third centuries as the enemy of Peter and in virulently hostile terms.[85] For those who could not understand their religious identity except as Jews, as the people of the law, Paul appeared inevitably as an apostate.

What Paul had done, however, was to extend Jesus' attack on the *internal* boundaries being drawn within Judaism to the *external* boundaries drawn round Judaism. Jesus had objected to the Pharisaic (and others') belief that non-sectarians were 'sinners', excluded by God from covenant grace because outside the boundaries of their particular faction. In just the same way, Paul objected to the typically Jewish idea that the Gentiles were 'sinners' by definition, excluded by God from covenant grace because outside the boundary determined by the law, a boundary to be defended most resolutely at the points of historic significance and particular sensitivity (above all, circumcision and food laws). To that extent, therefore, we can indeed say that *it was Paul who effectively undermined this third pillar of second Temple Judaism.* Not, we should repeat, the law itself, but the law understood as the means of protecting and guaranteeing Israel's

---

83. Note also W. A. Meeks, 'Breaking Away: Three New Testament Pictures of Christianity's Separation from the Jewish Communities', *'To See Ourselves as Others See us'. Christians, Jews, 'Others' in Late Antiquity*, ed. J. Neusner and E. S. Frerichs, Chico: Scholars 1985, pp. 93–115: *'Theologically* it is correct to say that the scriptures and traditions of Judaism are a central and ineffaceable part of the Pauline Christians' identity. *Socially*, however, the Pauline groups were never a sect of Judaism' (p. 106).

84. In a very similar way the suggestion that Christians need or should not be baptized would be incomprehensible and shocking to *most* Christians today.

85. *Epistula Petri* 2.3; *Clem. Hom.* 17.18–19; Irenaeus, *adv. Haer.* 1.26.2; Origen, *cont. Cels.* 5.65; Eusebius, *HE* 6.38; Epiphanius, *Pan* 28.5.3; 30.16.8–9.

covenant prerogatives. Insofar as Judaism regarded the law thus understood as integral to its identity, and continued to do so in a rabbinic Judaism which organized itself round the Torah, Paul's stand at Antioch and thereafter *made a parting of the ways inevitable, and already probably a factor for the churches of his foundation.* But did this also mean that Paul or Christianity in general had broken with *Judaism* and in effect denied Israel's election? Had Paul, in taking the stand he did, opened the door to Christian antipathy to Judaism as such, to anti-Judaism? To these questions we must now turn.

8

The Israel of God

8.1 The issue of 'anti-Judaism' in the New Testament writings

If our findings in chapter 7 are correct, it was Paul who above all others undercut the self-understanding of Judaism as expressed particularly in the Torah. It was he who decisively undermined the third pillar of Judaism in its characteristic function within second Temple Judaism. What does this say with regard to his attitude to Judaism as such? Since Torah was so much bound up with Jewish identity as the covenant people of God, what was his attitude as a Christian to Israel as the people of God, to the fundamental Jewish axiom of election and covenant? It is quite possible to argue, as some have, that Paul was totally alienated from his ancestral faith, from Judaism.[1] As evidence we will have to consider several passages in his writings. Principally I Thess. 2.14–15, where Paul attacks 'the Jews' as persecutors of Jesus and the churches. Also the sharp dismissal of Jewish claims on the inheritance of Abraham in Galatians, particularly Gal. 3.19–22 and 4.30. And not least the apparent illogicality of Paul's argument in Romans: particularly 3.1, where the more obvious response to the question, 'Then what advantage has the Jew?', seems to be None![2] and the incoherence of chs 9–11, where it would appear that 'the word of God' *has* 'failed' (9.6), with Israel assigned to the role of 'vessels of wrath' previously filled by Esau and Pharaoh.[3] Do such passages not betray Paul's complete alienation from his heritage – election now nothing but an empty cypher, the Jews abandoned by God?

---

1. So, in varying degrees, H. Räisänen, *Paul and the Law*, WUNT 29; Tübingen: Mohr-Siebeck 1983, and F. Watson, *Paul, Judaism and the Gentiles*, SNTSMS 56; Cambridge University 1986.

2. C. H. Dodd, *Romans*, London: Hodder and Stoughton 1932: 'The logical answer on the basis of Paul's argument is, "None whatever!"' (p. 43).

3. See e.g. Watson, *Paul*, pp. 168–70; H. Räisänen, 'Römer 9–11: Analyse eines geistigen Ringens', *ANRW*, II.25.4 (1987), pp. 2893, 2910–12. Others in my *Romans*, pp. 539–40. On II Cor. 3 see below p. 195 n. 34 and p. 327.

This critique of Paul is part of a wider reassessment of the attitude towards the Jews within the New Testament, itself part of the continuing revulsion among Christians and students of the period against the Holocaust. A feature of this reassessment has been the increasing awareness, and increasingly uncomfortable awareness of the extent to which subsequent anti-semitism is rooted in the NT itself; though most today prefer to speak of anti-Judaism, since 'anti-semitism' is a more explicitly modern phenomenon, more appropriate to describe the powerful blending of ideas of race and of nationalism which reached their nadir in Nazism.[4] Whatever the term used, however, the question cannot be escaped and has been posed with increasing sharpness in recent years: Is the NT itself anti-semitic, or at least anti-Jewish?[5] In effect, this is simply another way of posing our question: Did the first Christians abandon and deny Israel's election, the second foundational pillar of second Temple Judaism?

The charge of anti-Judaism has been levelled in recent days most emphatically against Luke-Acts, particularly Luke's second volume. At the beginning of the century Adolf Harnack had called Acts 'the first stage of developing early Christian anti-semitism'.[6] But J. T. Sanders (the brother of E. P.) has no hesitation in describing Acts as 'antisemitic' without qualification.[7] And Norman Beck describes Acts as the most anti-Jewish document in the NT.[8] Particularly important here is the frequent and consistently negative portrayal of 'the Jews': they dog Paul's footsteps and cause nothing but trouble – 'a picture of increasing Jewish hostility and opposition to the gospel'; with the climax coming in 'the Pauline passion narrative' (21.11, 30, 36; 22.22, 30; 23.12; 25.24; 26.2, 21). In the end the opposition is simply 'the Jews' – 'Jewish opposition to Christianity is now universal and endemic'.[9] The final note of Acts (28.26–28) refers the dismissive Isa. 6.9–10 to all Jews, and shows that for Luke salvation is for the

---

4. See e.g. S. Sandmel, *AntiSemitism in the New Testament*, Philadelphia: Fortress 1978, pp. xix–xx.

5. Much of the material which follows is drawn from the fuller treatment of my paper 'The Parting of the Ways and the Question of Anti-semitism in the New Testament Writings of the Period', in Jews and Christians: *The Parting of the Ways 70–135 CE*, The Durham–Tübingen Research Symposium on Earliest Christianity and Judaism (1989), ed. J. D. G. Dunn, Tübingen: Mohr-Siebeck 1992, pp. 177–211.

6. Cited by J. T. Sanders (n. 7 below).

7. J. T. Sanders, *The Jews in Luke-Acts*, London: SCM Press/Philadelphia: Fortress 1987, pp. xvi–xvii.

8. N. A. Beck, *Mature Christianity. The Recognition and Repudiation of the Anti-Jewish Polemic of the New Testament*, London/Toronto: Associated University Presses 1985, p. 270.

9. Sanders, *Jews*, pp. 77, 80.

Gentiles and was never intended for the Jews. In the words of Ernst Haenchen, 'Luke has written the Jews off'.[10]

So far as Matthew is concerned, we need only refer to the sustained polemic against the Pharisees in Matt. 23 and Matt. 27.25 – 'All the people answered, "His blood be on us and on our children!"' The former has been the principal basis for the denigration of the Pharisees which has given the word 'Pharisee' such negative connotations in English usage.[11] And the latter has provided one of the most virulent roots of (or excuses for) the anti-semitism which has marred Christian history, providing as it has a scriptural warrant for countless denunciations of Jews of later centuries as 'Christ killers'.[12] Some would see here evidence of a *Gentile* Christian author arguing against the Judaism of the day.[13] And though most agree that Matthew was a *Jewish* Christian, the view is strongly maintained that so far as he was concerned the final breach between church and synagogue had *already* happened. Matthew sees himself and his community as *extra muros*, outside the walls of Judaism: 'Matthew's community has recently parted company with Judaism after a period of prolonged hostility.'[14]

In the case of John's Gospel it is easy to argue that the sense of looking in from outside is even stronger. Even more than in Acts, 'the Jews' are presented as hostile to Jesus and to all that he stands for.[15] To be especially noted is John 8.44 and the depth of hostility expressed there – 'Jesus said to them (the Jews) . . . "You are of your father the devil, and your will is to do your father's desires"' – another tap-root of anti-semitism, giving ground for later identification of Jews with all that is evil.[16] Hence the widely held view that John is 'either the most anti-Semitic or at least the most overtly anti-Semitic of the Gospels'.[17] So far as our inquiry is concerned, equally significant is the repeated use of *aposynagōgos*, 'excommunicated, expelled from

---

10. E. Haenchen, 'The Book of Acts as Source Material for the History of Early Christianity', *Studies in Luke-Acts*, ed. L. E. Keck and J. L. Martyn, Philadelphia: Fortress/London: SPCK 1966, pp. 258–78, here p. 278; regularly quoted by Sanders, *Jews*, here pp. 80–83, 297–9.

11. Thus *The Concise Oxford Dictionary of Current English* gives as the second meaning of 'Pharisee', 'self-righteous person, formalist, hypocrite'.

12. Sandmel, *AntiSemitism*, p. 155, gives examples from his childhood.

13. E.g. D. R. A. Hare, 'The Rejection of the Jews in the Synoptics and Acts', in A. T. Davies (ed.), *AntiSemitism and the Foundations of Christianity*, New York: Paulist 1979, p. 38.

14. G. N. Stanton, 'The Gospel of Matthew and Judaism', *BJRL* 66 (1984), pp. 264–84, here p. 273.

15. For references see below §8.6.

16. Ruether, *Faith and Fratricide*, p. 116.

17. Sandmel, *AntiSemitism*, p. 101.

the synagogue' (John 9.22; 12.42; 16.2), where the implication is clear: the breach between church and synagogue is already past; Christianity now defines itself in opposition to Judaism.

As noted in the first chapter,[18] the whole issue has become more serious in recent years, for two main reasons. (1) In the initial post-war discussion of anti-semitism in Christianity and the NT it was argued plausibly that anti-Jewish trends in the NT were peripheral and accidental and were not grounded in the NT itself.[19] But the contribution of Rosemary Ruether has sharpened the issue immeasurably by arguing that anti-Jewish attitudes are endemic to Christianity, an inevitable corollary to the church's proclamation of Jesus as Messiah: 'Is it possible to say "Jesus is Messiah" without, implicitly or explicitly, saying at the same time "and the Jews be damned"?'[20] Thus the question stands in all its naked horror: Is anti-semitism or anti-Judaism integral to Christianity and to the NT? (2) The same period has seen a welcome re-emphasis on the *Jewishness* of Jesus.[21] But one consequence of this has been to re-open and deepen the gulf between Jesus and what followed (from the Hellenists and Paul onwards). The irony is, that the more Jewish Jesus is seen to be, the more divorced from the Judaism and Jewishness even of Jesus, seem to be Paul and the others cited above. The old gap between the simple moralizing message of Jesus and the hellenizing gospel of redemption in Paul, which was such a feature of the late nineteenth-century Liberal Protestant reconstruction of Christian beginnings, has been re-opened, deepened and widened in a way that no Christian can find other than unnerving.

Our question is clear, then, and can be posed in different ways: Is there evidence of an anti-Judaism in the NT writings which indicates that all thought of Israel as the people of God had been abandoned? Had the pillar of Jewish election been so undermined already for the first Christians that Christianity henceforth can be defined only in antithesis to Judaism? Do such sentiments as those recorded above indicate that the parting of the ways between Christianity and Judaism had already happened within the time span of the NT, so that

---

18. See above §1.4(e).

19. J. Isaac, *L'Antisémitisme a-t-il des racines chrétiennes?*, Paris: Fasquelle 1960, p. 21, cited by Davies, *AntiSemitism* p. xiv; G. Baum in Introduction to Ruether, *Faith and Fratricide*, p. 3, referring to his earlier study, *The Jews and the Gospel*, New York: Newman 1961. See also J. G. Gager, 'Judaism as Seen by Outsiders', *EJMI*, pp. 99–116, here pp. 99–101.

20. Ruether, *Faith and Fratricide* p. 246.

21. E.g. G. Vermes, *Jesus the Jew*, London: Collins 1973; and the 'third quest of the historical Jesus' referred to above in §1.5.

the Christianity of the NT was already well launched on the trajectory of anti-semitism?

8.2 Who is a Jew?

There is a problem underlying all this which has not been given sufficient attention – the problem that *the key categories were not yet fixed*. I refer not simply to the fact that 'Christianity' as a clearly definable entity was only in process of emerging throughout our period. Still more important here is the fact that the other key terms, 'Jew' and 'Judaism' were also in some state of flux. 'Who is a Jew?' is a question *still* unresolved in the modern state of Israel. Does 'Jew' denote *ethnic* or *religious* identity? And if the latter, that simply shifts the problem to the definition of 'Judaism'. 'What is Judaism?' is a central question for scholars of the second Temple period and beginnings of Christianity. As we have already seen, there are Jewish scholars who prefer to speak now of the Judaisms (plural) of our period.[22] Can we then use 'anti-Judaism' for the factional polemic so characteristic of Jesus' time? Are the *Psalms of Solomon* 'anti-Jewish' because they attack another form of Judaism? – in fact a form of Judaism (probably Sadducean control of the Temple) which might well be said to have a greater claim than the Psalmist(s) to the title of 'normative Judaism'. Are the Qumran scrolls 'anti-Jewish' because they attack another form of Judaism? – including, probably, the Pharisees, who were to become the founders of normative Judaism.[23]

The point underlying all this is crucial to our discussion: *'Judaism' was a term or concept whose reference was in some dispute, whose range of application was shifting, whose identity was in process of developing.* That being the case, what meaning can we give to a term like 'anti-Judaism'? When it is a case of one group of Jews criticizing another, is that 'anti-Jewish'? Does polemic by some Jews against other Jews signify that the former have become internally disoriented or alienated from 'Judaism'? Where 'Jew' is a form of religious identity, can those caught up within the debate about that identity, or claimants to that identity be classified as 'anti-Jewish'? Even this brief analysis should make it clear that the question of anti-semitism or anti-Judaism in the NT, and its implications for Christian understanding of Israel's election, need a good deal more careful analysis than has usually been offered.

As a first step, three features of significance relating to these basic

---

22. See above ch. 2 (p. 24), n. 1.
23. See above §6.2.

terms should be noted. (*a*) As already indicated, *Ioudaios*, 'Jew', embraces both ethnic and religious identity. In its basic and most traditional sense it was the name used by foreigners for a person belonging to Judaea. But in the Hellenistic period Judaea functioned politically as a temple state, so that *Ioudaios* soon came to include a religious as well as geographical and ethnic reference. Following the expansion of Judaea's political authority under the Hasmoneans, and the increasing experience of diaspora, it could thus be used characteristically of those who ethnically derived from Judaea or the expanded temple state, and whose religious world of meaning focussed on the Temple in Jerusalem.

In the second Temple period, therefore, 'the Jews' would normally denote *a group identified by ethnic origin and religious practice*, and *as such* distinct from others around. The precise reference of the group would depend on who the others were from whom the group was being distinguished – the Jews distinct from the Samaritans, or the Jews as opposed to the Syrian overlords of the Maccabean period, or the Jews as a distinct entity within a diaspora city; the customs of the Jews, which distinguished them from those with different customs, and so on. This covers the great preponderance of usage in the documents of the time, not least Philo and Josephus. For example, Philo speaks regularly of 'the nation of the Jews' or of Moses as 'the lawgiver of the Jews'. But in *In Flaccum* and *de Legatione ad Gaium* he can often speak of 'the Jews' when it is quite clear that he means the Jews of a particular region or city. Josephus likewise in *The Jewish War* speaks typically of 'the Jews' in opposition to such as Antiochus, Pompey, Herod and Pilate, and in the build-up to the revolt against Rome; but he can also speak with equal meaningfulness of 'the Jews' of specific cities such as Alexandria or Damascus, or switch from a specific reference to Jews in general (as in *War* 2.532) without confusion.

The consequences for our discussion are obvious: in analysing the significance of any occurrence of the phrase 'the Jews', *we must always ask whether this was not the most natural way to describe a group who stemmed ethnically from Judaea and whose religious identity focussed in Jerusalem*, and how else they might be distinguished from other groups and actors in the story.

(*b*) There is another factor of considerable importance for us: the fact that *religion and specific religious assertions were so fundamental to Jewish identity*. For these religious assertions were a matter of some dispute, so that the description of some as 'Jews' was a way of *making a religious claim to that epithet over against others*, including other claimants to the same epithet. John Ashton has noted two cases in Josephus.[24] In *Ant.* 11.173 Josephus observes that 'the Jews' was 'the name by which they (the returnees from Babylon) have been called from the time when they went up from Babylon'. This reflects a claim that 'the Jews' properly speaking were *not* those who had remained in Judaea (a *geographical* designation), but those who had remained faithful in Babylon and returned to the land of covenant promise at the earliest opportunity to become the basis of the renewed and revitalized people in the post-exilic period (a *religious* designation). From the same period comes Josephus' account of the Samaritans who were prepared to identify themselves as 'Jews' when it seemed propitious to do so, but whom Josephus regarded as 'apostates from the Jewish nation' (*Ant.* 11.340–341). Hence too Josephus' attitude to Herod the Great, designated a 'half-Jew' because he was Idumean (*Ant.* 14.403), and his unwillingness to use the term 'Jew' of the apostate Tiberius Alexander (cf. *Ant.* 20.100). On the other hand, there are indications that the term 'Jew' could be used irrespective of nationality, that is in a 'purely' religious way.[25]

It is important at this point to recall also the emergence of the term *Ioudaismos*, 'Judaism', during the Maccabean period, as a way of designating the religion of the Jews in its self-conscious distinctiveness and fierce loyalty to the law and the traditional customs (initially in II Macc. 2.21; 8.1; 14.38). 'Judaism' from the first understood itself as distinct and different from, and defined by opposition to the Hellenizing policies and influences of the Syrians and the apostate Jews who sided with the Syrians. We see the same sense of distinctiveness and fierce loyalty present in Paul's use of the word in Gal. 1.13–14, in his description of his way of life as a Pharisee: his former life 'in Judaism' marked by his zeal for the traditions of his fathers, that is, his 'zeal' to protect and maintain Israel's covenant prerogatives, as demonstrated not least by his persecution of the church.[26]

Here again the question will have to be asked: to what extent the 'anti-Jewishness' of any NT writing is of a piece with the factional disputes of the last two centuries of the second Temple period in which the claim was regularly made by different groups to be in effect more truly 'Jewish' than others?

(c) The other factor of relevance which should be noted here is that *Ioudaios* was not the only name by which a Jew might identify

---

24. J. Ashton, 'The Identity and Function of the *Ioudaioi* in the Fourth Gospel', *NovT* 27 (1985), pp. 40–75, here pp. 52–52, 73.

25. See W. Gutbrod, *TDNT*, 3.370–1; R. S. Kraemer, 'On the Meaning of the Term "Jew" in Greco-Roman Inscriptions', *HTR* 82 (1989), pp. 35–53.

26. See above §7.2.

himself. Indeed, *Ioudaios* was not the most natural self-designation for many Jews. K. G. Kuhn notes that in the post-biblical ('intertestamental') period, *Israel* was the people's preferred name for itself (cf. e.g. Sir. 17.17; *Jub.* 33.20; *Pss. Sol.* 14.5), whereas *Ioudaios* was the name by which they were known to others.[27] In other words, *'Jew' was a designation by which Jews were distinguished from other ethnic and religious groups.* But 'Israel/Israelite' denoted a *self*-understanding in terms of election and covenant promise. 'Jew', we might say, always had something of an outsider's perspective;[28] whereas 'Israel(ite)' was much more an *intra muros*, intra-Jewish designation. Most striking here is the usage of the Damascus Document (CD), where 'Israel' is clearly the preferred self-designation (e.g. 3.19 – 'a sure house of Israel'), and the sect sees itself as those who 'have gone out from the land of Judah' and who will 'no more consort with the house of Judah' (4.2–3, 11).

It would be possible, then, for an early Jewish believer in Jesus Messiah to cede the use of the name 'Jew' to others within the broad spectrum of late second Temple Judaism, while clinging to the title 'Israel(ite)' – as did the Qumran covenanters. In other words, *Ioudaios* would not necessarily be regarded as catching the essence of Jewish identity, but rather could be seen as lending itself to too much superficial (external) an identification; whereas *Israel* was much the more worthy of retention, as reaching to the true heart of Jewish identity. In analysing our texts, therefore, we will need to be sensitive to the comparative use of these two terms.

In the light of these three observations we can make a clearer assessment of the four main NT authors to whom anti-Judaism has been attributed. In each case we can do no more than scratch the surface of much more extensive debates, but at least we may hope to do enough to indicate how these texts bear upon our own inquiry.[29]

8.3 Paul and Israel

Each of the above observations has immediate application in the case of Paul.

---

27. K. G. Kuhn, *TDNT* 3.359–65.

28. Hence the regularity of its use by Philo, in *Flacc.* and *Legat.*, and by Josephus.

29. The fact that other NT writings from the post-Pauline period are so *lacking* in anti-Jewish content should be given more notice in the current round of debate; see my 'The Deutero-Pauline Literature', *Faith and Polemic: Studies in Anti-Semitism and Early Christianity*, ed. C. A. Evans and D. A. Hagner, Minneapolis: Fortress 1991.

(*a*) I Thess. 2.14–16 –

You became imitators, brothers, of the churches of God which are in Judaea in Christ Jesus; because you suffered the same things from your own countrymen as they also did from the Jews, who killed both the Lord Jesus and the prophets, and drove us out, and are displeasing to God and opposed to all men by hindering us from speaking to the Gentiles in order that they might be saved – so as always to fill up the measure of their sins. But God's wrath has come upon them at last!

Here we need simply note that the reference to 'the Jews' is quite specific – the Jews in Judaea who killed Jesus and the prophets, and who persecuted the churches of God in Judaea. Paul evidently had in mind those Jews whom he would have known well. It should not be counted a problem that Paul, himself a Jew, should so refer to fellow Jews. No more than if a Scot should refer to his fellow countrymen, involved in a sequence of incidents where other nationalities were involved, as 'the Scots'. It is a historical fact that there was a strong body of Jews who were hostile to the Gentile mission of the Nazarene sect, and that there was a number of them (Paul had been one himself) who actively persecuted the members of the sect for that reason.[30] And the most straightforward way to refer to them was to describe them as 'the Jews who . . .', without thereby being understood to include all Jews in the indictment or to deny that many Jews were themselves members of the sect being persecuted.[31] The sharp comment that Paul goes on to make at the end of v. 16 ('God's wrath has come upon them at last') is consistent with the belief more fully articulated in Rom. 1 and 9–11: most Jews by their attitude to the covenant, their presumption regarding the law, and their unwillingness to recognize that their God accepted people through faith, were now putting themselves under the wrath of God (cf. Rom. 1–3); a grievous state of affairs, but one which was itself part of God's mysterious plan to save all Israel (Rom. 9.22–24; 11.11–12, 28–32).[32]

---

30. See above pp. 119–22, 305 n. 33.

31. Cf. F. Gilliard, 'The Problem of the Antisemitic Comma between I Thessalonians 2.14 and 15', *NTS* 35 (1989), pp. 481–502.

32. See further particularly I. Broer, ' "Antisemitismus" und Judenpolemik im Neuen Testament. Eine Beitrag zum besseren Verständnis von I Thess. 2.14–16', *Biblische Notizen* 29 (1983), pp. 59–91. There are helpful reviews of the discussion of these verses in R. Jewett, *The Thessalonian Correspondence. Pauline Rhetoric and Millenarian Piety*, Philadelphia: Fortress 1986, pp. 37–41; and C. A. Wanamaker, *1 and 2 Thessalonians*, NIGTC; Grand Rapids: Eerdmans 1990, pp. 114–19. Against the argument of B. A. Pearson, '1 Thessalonians 2.13–16: A Deutero-Pauline Interpolation', *HTR* 64 (1971),

(b) Rom. 2.28-29-

For the true Jew is not the one visibly marked as such, nor circumcision that which is performed visibly in the flesh, but one who is so in a hidden way, and circumcision is of the heart, in Spirit and not in letter. His praise comes not from men but from God.

Here it is quite clear that Paul too was wrestling with the question, 'Who is a Jew?' and was concerned to contest the definition of 'Jew', or at least the assumption that the 'Jew' is to be defined in ethnic ('in the flesh') and outward (circumcision, 'in the flesh') terms. It cannot be unimportant for our inquiry that Paul should thus think it necessary or desirable to contest the definition of 'Jew' and, moreover, to press for a definition which emphasizes the hiddenness of the real person and the danger of obscuring that reality by focussing on what is more immediately apparent to the onlooker. Equally striking is the fact that he should end with a word-play, which only worked in the Hebrew and would therefore have been lost on his Greek readership,[33] but which deliberately reached back into the patriarchal narratives (Gen. 29.35; 49.8) to define the essence of a *Ioudaios* in terms of recognition given by God rather than of the distinguishable features of the ethnic Jew or ritual Judaism. He who so argues had hardly abandoned either concept ('Jew' or 'Judaism') or disowned that for which they stood. On the contrary, he thereby indicates his desire to remain faithful to the reality which scripture indicates should lie at the heart of these concepts. The 'Jew' who recognizes the true character of his heritage *is* advantaged (Rom. 3.1).

(c) Again in Romans, we should note the way in which Paul switches emphasis from *Ioudaios* early in the letter to *Israel(ite)* in chs 9-11. In chs 2-3 *Ioudaios* is used (1.16; 2.9, 10, 17, 28, 29; 3.1, 9, 29), evidently because the thought is principally of Jews in distinction from Greeks (1.16; 2.9, 20; 3.9; 29); and what Paul is resisting is the idea that 'Jewishness' is to be defined in terms of this distinction (2.17-20, 28). In chs 9-11, however, *Israel(ite)* dominates (9.4, 6, 27, 31; 10.19, 21; 11.1, 2, 7, 25, 26), where Paul speaks much more as an insider (9.1-3; 11.1). Both designations and their proper reference were evidently still in dispute (2.28-29 – see above; 9.6 – 'Not all those descended from Israel are "Israel"'); but whereas

---

pp. 79-94, that the passage presupposes a 'final break' between Judaism and Christianity (and therefore a post-70 date for the interpolation), see also J. W. Simpson, 'The Problems Posed by I Thessalonians 2.15-16 and a Solution', *HBT* 12 (1990), pp. 42-72.

33. Judah/*hodah* = praise; הודה/יהודה

Paul addresses his imaginery Jewish interlocutor as *Ioudaios* in 2.17, in 11.1 he identifies *himself* as an *Israelite*.

Thus it begins to become clear what Paul was trying to do in both Galatians and Romans. In his eyes, Israel had become, as it were, Judaism. It had shifted the focus of the covenant in which God chose Jacob by grace and made him Israel, and had focussed the covenant in a law understood as limiting that grace and preventing the Jacobs of his day from participating in it. In the terms used in Galatians, the Judaism which he criticized had confused the age of immaturity and childhood with the age of maturity and full sonship, failing to recognize the eschatological maturity which had come through Christ and the gift of the Spirit (Gal. 3–4). He writes as though he was hostile to his own people and their ancestral faith, a faith which he had once confessed and practised so fervently himself. *But it was the form which his ancestral faith currently took against which he was protesting.* And he was able to insist without dissimulation that his own understanding and proclamation of that faith was *truer to what it had started as and was intended to be.* In a real sense, we may say that Paul stood for the reformation of Judaism rather than its abandonment, although the result was not unlike that of the sixteenth-century Reformation. The point of Gal. 4.30, then, the scriptural quotation from Gen. 21.10–12 – 'Cast out the slave and her son; for the son of the slave shall not inherit with the son of the free woman' – is not that Israel, or Jews in general had been cast off irrevocably by God; but rather that so long as his fellow Jews remained more devoted to the earthly Jerusalem and the covenant of Sinai, and failed to appreciate that the Jerusalem above is a larger reality and that the fulfilment of the promise to Abraham is richer than can be contained within Judaism as then understood and practised, they effectively limited themselves to the role of the other son of Abraham, still in the stage of the promise to Abraham unfulfilled.[34]

So too with Rom. 9–11. It is important not to fall into the mistake of thinking that chs 9–11 are about 'the church and Israel', as though already in Paul's mind these were distinct entities.[35] Not at all! The

---

34. See further my commentary on *Galatians*, London: Black 1992, *ad loc*. For Paul's attitude to the church in Jerusalem see above §5.5. On the difficulty of who Paul means by 'the Israel of God' in Gal. 6.16 see particularly the discussion in P. Richardson, *Israel in the Apostolic Church*, SNTSMS 10; Cambridge University 1969, pp. 74–84; Betz. *Galatians* pp. 322–3; Bruce, *Galatians* pp. 273–5. The contrast between old covenant and new in II Cor. 3 is in effect the same; although it has been sharpened by a context of polemic and self-defence (2.17–3.6), Moses still provides the type of the one who turns to the Lord (3.7–18, particularly v. 16).

35. See e.g. those referred to in my *Romans*, p. 520.

discussion of those chapters is exclusively about *Israel* (9.6). Israel is the factor of continuity; the chief question is whether God's purpose has been sustained and will be fulfilled in Israel (11.26). Gentiles are only heirs of the promise and covenant as having been grafted into the olive tree of Israel – *not* into a different tree, but into the *same* tree (11.17–24).[36] The Israel of God's purpose consists of Jew first, but also Gentile (9.24 and 10.12 – the only two references to 'Jew' in chs 9–11; and note the climax to the whole argument in 15.7–12). The point of 9.6 is *not* to disown Israel, but to point out that Israel is defined and determined by promise and election, *not* by physical descent, and *not* by works of the law (9.7–11).[37] Those who are Israelites, but who fail to recognize the covenant character of their status as Israelites, have to that extent sold their own birthright for a bowl of bread and pottage (Gen. 25.29–34). Whereas those who recognize the totally gracious character of God's call and respond in faith are Israel, whether descended from Jacob or not.

There is therefore no contradiction on this point between Rom. 9 and Rom. 11, as some have argued.[38] What was at stake was the *essence* of Judaism, the true character of *Israel*. Paul may have been disowning the *Judaism* in which he had been brought up (Gal. 1.13–14), but he did so self-consciously as an *Israelite* – that is, as one who sought to maintain and promote the true character of Israel's election against the majority of his fellow Israelites who were currently interpreting it in a more narrowly particularistic or ethnic sense. To put the point in terms drawn from Eph. 2: in Christ the two men, Jew and Greek, have been recreated in the Israelite of God's purpose (cf. Eph. 2.15), wherein Gentiles are united with Christ, become members of the commonwealth of Israel, participate in the covenants of promise, and rejoice in hope and in the knowledge of God, brought near by the blood of Christ (2.12–13), 'no longer strangers and sojourners' (2.19). The axiom of Israel's election is thus not denied or abandoned; instead it is reaffirmed and re-expressed, in terms which are no longer restricted by but rather which transcend the old Jew/Gentile division (2.14–19), anticipation of a truly universal church (1.22–23).[39]

In short, *Paul would by no means have regarded himself as outside*

---

36. So e.g. Richardson, *Israel*, p. 130 – 'The Church has no existence apart from Israel and has no separate identity.'

37. On 'works of the law' see above §7.6.

38. See above n. 3.

39. A. T. Lincoln, 'The Church and Israel in Ephesians 2', *CBQ* 49 (1987), pp. 605–24 understates the significance of the passage: Paul still uses the language of an elect people (2.19) but now in an inclusive rather than exclusive way.

Israel looking in. Outside Judaism, perhaps; but Judaism as defined by his Pharisaic contemporaries, Judaism as distinct from Israel; Paul an Israelite still.

8.4 The testimony of Acts – a people rejected?

The use of *Ioudaios* as an ethnic/religious identification also helps explain most of the usage in Acts. As well as the more negative references to 'the Jews', Luke regularly uses what we might call 'neutral' references, denoting simply the ethnic/religious identity of those so referred to: for example, 'the synagogue(s) of the Jews' (13.5; 14.1; 17.1, 10), like the fragmentary inscription found at Corinth ('the synagogue of the Hebrews'); or 'the customs of the Jews' (26.3), as in Josephus' regular phrase (e.g. *Ant.* 15.268). There are also a number of *positive* references, particularly to Jews who believe and respond positively to Paul's message (13.43; 14.1; 21.20; 28.24). In addition we may recall an element of 're-judaizing' of Paul: he accepts the apostolic decree, circumcises Timothy, makes a vow at Cenchreae, takes part in temple purificatory ritual, and appeals to 'the promises made by God to our fathers, to which our twelve tribes hope to attain . . .' (16.3–4; 18.18; 21.26; 26.6–7). Nor should we forget Paul's own and repeated self-affirmation, 'I am a Jew' (21.39; 22.3).[40] Moreover, according to Luke, James responds to Paul's success in converting Gentiles by citing Amos 9.11–12: the rebuilding of the dwelling of David has in view (also) the salvation of the Gentiles (Acts 15.14–18).[41]

As for the more 'negative' references to 'the Jews', they hardly fall outside the scope of normal usage. Most consist of quite natural references, where 'the Jews' denote simply the bulk of the Jews in a place already indicated by the context, or 'the Jews' actually involved in the incident being narrated ('the Jews' of Antioch – 13.45, 50; 'the Jews of Iconium' – 14.4; and so on; 'the Jews' bringing the indictment against Paul – 24.9 and 26.2). Linked into this may also be the *religious* factor noted above (§8.2b). That is to say, where an attitude was being expressed by the bulk of the Jews in any place or region, and where that attitude consisted of a strong affirmation of what had usually been recognized as characteristically and distinctively Jewish,

---

40. See further E. Franklin, *Christ the Lord. A Study in the Purpose and Theology of Luke-Acts*, London: SPCK 1975, pp. 108–15; R. L. Brawley, *Luke-Acts and the Jews*, SBLMS 33; Atlanta: Scholars 1987, particularly ch. 5.

41. J. Jervell, *Luke and the People of God. A New Look at Luke-Acts*, Minneapolis: Augsburg 1972, pp. 51–3; G. Lohfink, *Die Sammlung Israels. Eine Untersuchung zur lukanischen Ekklesiologie*, München: Kösel 1975, pp. 58–60.

those who maintained that attitude with some force could and would lay special claim to the designation 'Jews'. Hence the characteristically 'Jewish' nature of the opposition to Paul (particularly 21.20ff. – including Jewish Christians).

In the light of such considerations, the question needs to be asked whether in all this Luke is any more tendentious and motivated by anti-Jewish malice than, say, Suetonius in his much quoted report that Claudius 'expelled (the) Jews from Rome because of their constant disturbances at the instigation of Chrestus' (*Claudius* 25.4), or Paul in his own description of his hardships – 'At the hands of Jews five times have I received forty (lashes) less one' (II Cor. 11.24)?

The charge of 'anti-semitism' against Luke, as brought by Sanders, depends most of all on the weight given to the final paragraph of Acts – 28.17–30.[42] For him it is the climax of Luke's anti-semitism: it was because 'the Jews' objected that Paul has come to Rome; the final quotation, from Isa. 6.9–10, 'must refer not only to Jews in Rome, but to all Jews'; and the final word, the Lukan interpretation of the passage (28.28), shows that for Luke salvation is for the Gentiles and was never intended for the Jews, the cycle of rejection and further mission ends with rejection. 'Luke has written the Jews off.'[43]

But here at least Sanders has surely overstated his case. (1) Luke does not go out of his way to blacken the character of 'the Jews': Paul is still speaking positively of the ancestral customs (v. 17), of 'my nation' (v. 19), of 'the hope of Israel' (v. 20); the part played by 'the Jews' is hardly a point of emphasis or indeed of exaggeration (v. 19); and the Jews of Rome are depicted as remarkably open, with nothing having been said against Paul or his message by other Jews from elsewhere (vv. 21–22).[44]

(2) Paul succeeds in 'convincing' some, which was what he was trying to do (vv. 23–4), and which could mean a full acceptance of Paul's message (if 17.4 and 19.26 are anything to go by). Or, if we give weight to the imperfect tense (cf. 13.43; 18.4), the implication

---

42. The crucial nature of this final passage for the present debate is also indicated by the volume edited by J. B. Tyson, *Luke-Acts and the Jewish People*, London: SCM Press 1988. See particularly the essay by Tyson, 'The Problem of Jewish Rejection in Acts' (pp. 124–37), especially pp. 124–7 and nn. 3–5.

43. Sanders, *Jews*, p. 80–3, 297–9. In v. 25 'Paul turns viciously on his auditors' (p. 80)! For those who agree with Sanders see Tyson, *Luke-Acts*, p. 159 n. 5.

44. The Roman Jews' description of the movement represented by Paul as a *hairesis*, 'sect', has, of course, no note of rejection in it; as already noted, Josephus uses the same word to describe the 'sects' within Judaism (see above p. 24); and Luke is well aware of this usage (Acts 5.17; 15.5; 26.5; so also 24.5, 14).

would presumably be that many of the Roman Jews were on the verge of accepting the message – at any rate, hardly a negative portrayal.[45]

(3) The portrayal of the Jews (of Rome) as divided between those persuaded by and those unbelieving in Paul's message is a regular feature of Acts (13.43–5; 14.1–2; 17.4–5, 10–14; 18.4–8); what is noticeable here, though, is that Luke depicts them as continuing to be divided as they departed, *after* Paul's final statement (v. 25); the implication being that whatever the force of that final statement it does *not* refer to the Jews *en masse*.[46]

(4) This raises the further possibility that this final turning of Paul to the Gentiles is no more final than the earlier turnings (13.46–8; 18.6; 22.21; 26.17–18), no more final indeed than the words of Isa. 6.9–10 were for Isaiah's mission to his people.[47] Certainly the implication of 28.30–31, that Paul continued to preach openly to 'all who came to him', must be that the 'all' included Jews as well as Gentiles – at the very least those Jews already (being) 'persuaded' by Paul. And Luke has made no attempt to exclude that most natural inference.[48]

In short, Sanders has oversimplified the evidence of Acts on 'the Jews' by reading it resolutely through and in conformity with one sequence of references, a sequence which at the very least may be better explained by reference to other factors and considerations. There is clearly something wrong when, for example, despite Paul's repeated self-identification, 'I am a Jew' (21.39; 22.3), Sanders can still conclude that for Luke 'all Jews are equally, in principle at least, perverse'.[49]

To sum up, Sanders must be judged to have greatly overstated his case. He has been selective in his choice of evidence and tendentious in his evaluation of it. He has not given enough weight to the positive elements in Luke's presentation of Jews and Judaism. Even the most negative of Luke's statements regarding the Jews may be best explained by a combination of historical fact, rhetorical effect, stylistic variation, and awareness of current tensions between the different groups claiming the heritage of second Temple Judaism. Luke certainly does intend to demonstrate how Christianity took on an

---

45. So also particularly R. C. Tannehill, 'Rejection by Jews and Turning to Gentiles: the Pattern of Paul's Mission in Acts', in Tyson, *Luke-Acts*, pp. 83–101, here p. 97.

46. Cf. Particularly Jervell, *Luke*, pp. 49 and n. 21, and 63.

47. Note that Luke follows the LXX almost verbatim, that is, without tendentious modification.

48. So also Brawley p. 75–7; 'Acts 28 does not write off the Jews, but explains their unbelief' (p. 75).

49. Sanders, *Jews*, p. 317.

increasingly Gentile face, and 'the Jews' of various cities and regions are often foil to that purpose; like others he remained puzzled by the fact that the bulk of Jews continued to reject their Messiah. But the continuity between (second Temple) Judaism and Christianity is a much more living reality for Luke than Sanders allows, and Luke portrays a Gentile Christianity in the person of its great apostle as much more positive about its Jewish heritage and as more effective among and open to Jews to the last, than Sanders allows. In short, Luke's 'anti-semitism' is much more in Sanders' reading of the text than in the text itself. The continuity in terms of substance and fulfilment between the elect Israel and the church of the new age is much more pronounced for Luke than the discontinuity.

8.5 The Evidence of Matthew – church and synagogue in dispute

Matthew was probably writing for a Jewish Christian community in Palestine or Syria in the 80s, when the lines of confrontation between Christianity and rabbinic Judaism were becoming more sharply drawn, and when the successors of the Pharisees were trying to define Judaism in their own terms.[50] An hypothesis along these lines certainly seems to be required to explain the violence of the attack on the Pharisees in Matt. 23. But again the question arises: does this demonstrate a degree of disengagement with Judaism on the part of Matthew and/or his community, or indeed of anti-Judaism properly so called? Are Matthew and his community outside the walls of Judaism, or did they still regard themselves as inside?[51] Outside the walls as being defined by the Pharisees/rabbis, presumably; hostile to *that* understanding of Judaism, no doubt. But is that the same thing? Here too it is not possible to give the issue comprehensive consideration, but at least the following evidence should be considered.

(*a*) Matthew was evidently concerned to demonstrate his (and his community's) *loyalty to the law*. To the Pharisees/rabbis with whom he was in conflict he says in effect, We are as loyal to the law as you (5.18–19; 23.3, 23), indeed *more* loyal (5.20; 23.1–36). Particularly significant here is his use of two words distinctive to his vocabulary. He is the only Evangelist to speak of *anomia* 'lawlessness' (7.23;

---

50. So most commentators; see e.g. W. G. Kümmel, *Introduction to the New Testament*, 1973; ET Nashville: Abingdon/London: SCM Press 1975, pp. 119–20; Davies & Allison, *Matthew*, pp. 127–38. On post-70 rabbinic Judaism see further below, §§11.5–7 and 12.1–2.

51. See above §8.1 (p. 187).

13.41; 23.28; 24.12); clearly it was *his own* word. In warning against lawlessness, as he does in these passages, he was clearly proclaiming his own, and the gospel's loyalty to the law. Almost as distinctive to Matthew is his use of *dikaiosunē*, 'righteousness' (seven times in Matthew; elsewhere in the Gospels only in Luke 1.75 and John 16.8 and 10). Note again 5.20 – 'Unless your righteousness exceeds that of the scribes and Pharisees, you will never enter the kingdom of heaven'.

Here we may also mention Matthew's redaction of the divorce pericope. In Mark 10.1–9 the debate is about divorce as such; and 10.11 ('Whoever divorces his wife and marries another, commits adultery against her') amounts to a critique or an annulment of the Mosaic ruling understood as permitting divorce (10.4; Deut. 24.1–4). Matthew, however, subtly alters the subject of the debate, so that it is no longer about divorce as such, but about divorce 'for any cause' (Matt. 19.3). In other words, it is presented as a debate about the *interpretation* of Deut. 24.1, 3, rather than about its validity as law. In fact, Matthew sets Jesus' teaching at this point within the then current debate between the schools of Hillel and Shammai, at a point where the Hillelite position (divorce for any cause) seems to have been dominant. Jesus' response is similarly modified: whereas Mark 10.11 envisages no divorce at all, Matt. 19.9 regards divorce as permissable in cases of adultery (which was equivalent to the more rigorous Shammaite view). So also in Matt. 5.32. Thus a case which in Mark's version could be read as an abrogation of the law has been transformed into a question about current rabbinic debate on the interpretation of the law, in which Jesus is shown to favour the more rigorous position.[52]

It is evident from his insertions (Matt. 12.5–6 and 11–12) into the two sabbath day controversy stories (Matt. 12.1–8/Mark 2.23–28; Matt. 12.9–14/Mark 3.1–6) that Matthew has achieved the same effect with regard to the sabbath.[53] So too, the clear implication of Matthew's insertion into Mark 13.18 ('Pray that it may not happen in winter') to read, 'Pray that your flight may not be in winter or on a sabbath' (Matt. 24.20), is that the Matthean community continued to observe the sabbath. In Matthew's perspective Jesus had not called for any abandonment of the basic law regarding the seventh day.[54]

---

52. See further D. R. Catchpole, 'The Synoptic Divorce Material as a Traditio-historical Problem', *BJRL* 57 (1974), pp. 92–127; J. A. Fitzmyer, 'The Matthean Divorce Texts and some new Palestinian Evidence', *TS* 37 (1976), pp. 197–226.

53. E. Levine, 'The Sabbath Controversy according to Matthew', *NTS* 22 (1975–76), pp. 480–483.

54. Cf. P. Sigal, *The Halakah of Jesus of Nazareth according to the Gospel of Matthew*, Lanham/London: University Press of America 1986, here ch. 5.

To similar effect Matthew was able to present Jesus' teaching about the law in such a way as *to make it clear that Jesus set himself only against the oral tradition and did not intend to abrogate the law itself.* So 5.17–20 is set at the head of the section of antitheses in the Sermon on the Mount, thus undoubtedly indicating how Matthew wanted the antitheses interpreted: what Jesus was doing was giving a deeper *interpretation* of the law and setting *that* against the oral tradition which the rabbis accepted as the authoritative interpretation of the law. Note also how effective is Matthew's redaction of Mark 7. According to Mark 7.15, Jesus had said 'Nothing from outside can defile a man'; and Mark draws out the obvious implication: 'Thus he declared all foods clean' (Mark 7.19). But Matthew completely departs from Mark's version at just these two crucial points. He *omits* the two key phrases of Mark; he is unwilling to have Jesus affirm that the law on unclean foods no longer applies. And he *adds* material (15.12–14, 20b), thus directing the force of Jesus' teaching back to the issue of hand washing, which was already presumably becoming a matter of increasing importance in rabbinic oral tradition (resulting in the Mishnah tractate *Yadaim*, 'Hands').[55]

The alternative way to interpret the law is presented by Matthew in terms of *love*. In a manner only partly paralleled in the other Gospels, Matthew draws on Jesus' teaching to underscore his conviction that the commandment of love is the heart and essence of the law, in contrast to the more typical rabbinic scrupulosity (5.43–48; 7.12; 22.34–40). Not least, he evidently saw Jesus' own ministry as displaying this interpretation, as showing how the law should be obeyed, interpreted by love (12.1–8, 9–14; 18.12–35). Note particularly the repeated appeal to Hos. 6.6, in 9.13 and 12.7, in both cases directing the prophetic critique of a superficial law observance against the Pharisees – Jesus as the climax of the prophetic interpretation of the law. This presumably is the clue to Matthew's understanding of 5.17 ('I have not come to abolish the law and the prophets but to fulfil them'): it was through his ministry of love that Jesus 'fulfilled' the law, that is, brought it to complete expression, fully realized it. And thus Jesus in his ministry and teaching becomes a model for Christians in their own understanding of and obedience to the law, in the face of the exclusive rabbinic claim to it, a righteousness superior to that of the rabbi and his pupils (5.20).

(*b*) One possible indication of Gentile authorship, or at least of a Jewish Christian looking at Judaism 'from outside', and who can therefore be categorized in terms of 'anti-Judaism', is the appearance

---

55. See also above §3.2.

of the phrase '*their* synagogue(s)' (4.23; 9.35; 10.17; 12.9; 13.54) in five of Matthew's nine references to 'synagogues', four of them unique to Matthew. Here, however, is another case where the evidence can be easily misinterpreted and unbalanced conclusions drawn. For 'their' can be a quite natural adjective to describe something belonging to others, without necessarily implying a great distance between 'theirs' and 'ours'. In other words, 'their synagogues' may simply mean the synagogues of the people to whom Jesus was at that time ministering, as in Mark 1.23 and 1.39 (= Matt. 4.23). And even where a more negative note enters (as in 10.17 and 23.34), 'their synagogue' may denote simply *their* synagogue and not *ours*, rather than their (the Jews') *synagogues*.[56]

This possibility is given support by several factors. (1) Matthew also speaks simply of 'the synagogue' (6.2, 5; 23.6), and does so precisely where he is comparing and contrasting the spirituality and behaviour of 'the hypocrites' with the spirituality and conduct he seeks to encourage within his own community;[57] note also 23.7–8 – the hypocrites 'love to be called rabbis by others, but you are not to be called rabbi'. This suggests not a set of completely antithetical values, but *a set of shared practices*, where antagonism is so fierce precisely because they are so close ('sibling rivalry'). (2) Matthew also speaks of 'their scribes' (7.29); but in 8.19 and 23.34 scribes are portrayed in a positive light, and the view has been long popular which sees in 13.52 Matthew's own description of himself and of the task he set himself in compiling his Gospel, or at least a reference to scribes in his own community.[58] This is a clear reminder that any hostility to scribes in Matthew's Gospel is *not a hostility to scribes as such, nor, therefore to Judaism as such*. On the contrary, it reflects rather the conflict of two groups who share the same heritage (particularly the Torah – 5.17–20; 23.2–3) and style of teaching ('binding and loosing' – 16.19 and 18.18; the rabbinic-style treatment of 19.3–9); and *that* is why their mutual hostility is so fierce.[59] (3) It is also

---

56. G. D. Kilpatrick, *The Origins of the Gospel According to St Matthew*, Oxford: Clarendon 1946, pp. 110–11; R. Hummel, *Die Auseinandersetzung zwischen Kirche und Judentum in Matthäusevangelium*, München: Kaiser 1966, pp. 28–33; S. Brown, 'The Matthean Community and the Gentile Mission', *NovT* 22 (1980), pp. 193–221, here p. 216.

57. Cf. B. Przybylski, 'The Setting of Matthean Anti-Judaism', in P. Richardson, (ed.), *Anti-Judaism in Early Christianity. Vol. I. Paul and the Gospels*, Waterloo, Ontario: Wilfrid Laurier University 1986, pp. 181–200. here pp. 193–5.

58. Cf. e.g. Przybylski, pp. 190–1.

59. Similarly the warning of Matt. 8.11–12 parallels the intra-covenantal warning of Amos 9.7–8 and John the Baptist (Matt. 3.9); see above §6.4b (so also Mussner, *Tractate*, p. 159). See further also above pp. 138–40, and S. Freyne, 'Vilifying the Other and Defining

important to recall that Matthew alone of the Evangelists uses *ekklē-sia*, 'church' (16.18; 18.17), and that behind it lies the familiar OT concept of the *qahal Israel*, 'the congregation of Israel'. In other words, we see a claim that the Matthean community represents the eschatological people of God (cf. also Matt. 19.28). This is certainly *a claim from within the heritage of second Temple Judaism, not from 'outside'*. And though that claim would no doubt have been contested by 'their scribes' (and Pharisees), and though his claim invites an antithesis between 'church' and 'synagogue', the implication for the self-definition of Matthew's own community is clear enough.

(c) This brings us finally to the infamous Matt. 27.25, where we started. But even here Matthew's 'anti-Judaism' needs much more careful statement than it usually receives. (1) Matthew's use of *laos*, 'people'. The negative force of 27.25 ('all the people') is unsurpassed in Matthew. However, it is paralleled at least in some measure by 13.15 and 15.8, both of them in quotations from Isaiah (13.15 = Isa. 6.10; 15.8 = Isa. 29.13). In other words, the other negative references to 'the people' in Matthew belong, once again, to the category of prophetic polemic and warning. They also have to be set alongside the more positive references: 1.21 – Jesus 'will save his people from their sins'; 4.23 – Jesus 'was healing every disease and every malady within the people'; and 26.5 – the chief priests decided to arrest Jesus 'not during the feast, lest there be a tumult among the people'. In many ways the most striking of all is 27.64: the chief priests and (NB) the Pharisees ask Pilate to secure Jesus' tomb lest his disciples steal the body and 'tell the people, "He has risen from the dead"', and the last fraud will be worse than the first'. Here there is a clear distinction between leaders (including Pharisees) and people.[60] And, more notable still, 'the chief priests and the Pharisees' fear lest the gospel of Jesus' resurrection will find favour with 'the people'. That is to say, even after 27.25, 'the people' may still be won to the gospel, and are an object of competition between the Pharisees and the bearers of the resurrection message.

(2) Related to this is the one use of 'Jews' which seems to parallel

the Self: Matthew's and John's Anti-Jewish Polemic in Focus', '*To See Ourselves as Others See Us'. Christians, Jews, 'Others' in Late Antiquity*, ed. J. Neusner and E. S. Frerichs, Chico: Scholars 1985, pp. 119–23, 132–4; cf. Meeks, 'Breaking Away', pp. 108–14.

60. Similarly Matt. 21.43 is intended by Matthew as a warning primarily for the leaders of the people, as 21.45 makes clear. So also Matt. 23. See further S. van Tilborg, *The Jewish Leaders in Matthew*, Leiden: Brill 1972, particularly pp. 142–65; D. Garland. *The Intention of Matthew 23*, SuppNovT 52; Leiden: Brill 1979; R. T. France, *Matthew – Evangelist and Teacher*, Exeter: Paternoster, 1989, ch. 6.

John's more extensive negative usage: Matt. 28.15 – 'this story [the deception that Jesus' disciples stole Jesus' body from the tomb while the guards slept] has been spread among Jews to this day' – in Stanton's view 'a thoroughly Johannine' formulation which 'seems to indicate that the Matthean community saw itself as a separate and quite distinct entity over against Judaism'.[61] But even that is an over-statement. *Ioudaios* here is anarthrous: the story has been spread among Jews in general (not 'the Jews'). The reference, in other words, is purely descriptive, and hardly different, for example, from the typical usage of Josephus described earlier (§8.2). One who was him-self a Jew and who still hoped to counter that story among his own people would hardly have spoken otherwise.

(3) It should not be assumed that the self-indictment of 27.25, 'His blood be on us and on our children', was so sweeping and comprehensive as has often been inferred (all Jews then and there-after). The most closely related of Matthew's other references to 'children' imply a more limited scope (2.18; 3.9; 15.26; 23.37). And no Jewish reader could fail to recall the much tougher and more far-reaching terms laid down in one of the central statements of the covenant – 'visiting the iniquity of the fathers upon the children and the children's children, to the third and fourth generation' (Ex. 20.5; 34.7; Num. 14.18; Deut. 5.9). In other words, *even Matt. 27.25 can be ranked as an intracovenant statement*, milder in its force than the classical warnings of the covenant contract, and so also holding out (by implication) the classical covenant hope of restoration for those who experienced the curses of the covenant but who returned to the Lord their God, they and their children (Deut. 30.1ff.).[62]

In the debate as to whether Matthew is writing *intra muros* or *extra muros*, therefore, the evidence on the whole seems to favour *the former*. No doubt Matthew's opponents and the opponents of Matthew's community (the Pharisees and 'their scribes') regarded them as 'outsiders', meaning outside the walls of (early rabbinic) Judaism. But Matthew still speaks as an 'insider' and is attempting to portray a Jesus who would be attractive to others who also considered themselves 'insiders'. In other words, once again we seem to find ourselves confronted with the situation where the narrowing channels

---

61. G. N. Stanton, 'The Origin and Purpose of Matthew's Gospel. Matthean Scholar-ship from 1945 to 1980', *ANRW*, II.25.3 (1985), p. 1914.

62. T. B. Cargal, ' "His Blood be Upon Us and Upon our Children": A Matthean Double Entendre?' *NTS* 37 (1991), p. 101–12, suggests the possibility that Matthew intended a play on the only other reference to 'blood' in the Gospel (26.28), implying the hope of forgiveness for 'the people', echoing Deut. 21.8 (pp. 110–2).

of rabbinic Judaism and Christianity respectively were still in competition for the head waters flowing from the broader channels of second temple Judaism.[63] In which case, once again, *the charge of anti-semitism or anti-Judaism against Matthew has either to be dismissed or to be so redefined within its historical context as to lose most of its potential as justification for the anti-semitism of later centuries.* And, once again, it is more a matter of continuity than discontinuity, of Israel's special place in the purposes of God reaffirmed as well as redefined.

8.6 The polemic of John – 'sons of the devil'?

John's Gospel highlights afresh the importance of the earlier question, 'Who is a 'Jew'?, since a most crucial issue for the interpretation of John is the question, Who are 'the Jews'? The issue is inescapable for us, since it is the fierce hostility against 'the Jews' in John which leads directly to the charge of anti-semitism or anti-Judaism, particularly the 'diabolizing' of 'the Jews' implicit in John 8.44, as noted in §8.1. If a consistent reference for 'the Jews' is sought, the most inviting one is that John uses the phrase to refer to 'the Jewish authorities';[64] in which case it would become appropriate to speak of John's Christianity disowning or already disowned by the official representatives of Judaism (9.22; 12.42). However, there is also a whole string of references where 'the Jews' clearly denote the common people, the crowd;[65] not to mention neutral references (such as 2.6, 13; 3.1, 22; 4.9b; 5.1; etc.), and the two very striking 'positive' references in 4.9 and 22 (Jesus himself is 'a Jew', who affirms that 'Salvation is from the Jews'). Unfortunately, too much of the discussion has been vitiated by the abstraction of references from the dramatic context of the Gospel itself. In particular, the whole discussion of these issues has almost entirely ignored a major Johannine theme, central to the drama of the Gospel, which C. H. Dodd illuminated, which provides a plot context for the bulk of the references to 'the Jews', and without which the significance of these references cannot be understood.[66] I refer to

---

63. Overman, *Matthew's Gospel and Formative Judaism*, reaches the same conclusion (see particularly pp. 141–61).

64. So 5.10, 15, 16, 18; 7.1, 13; 8.48, 52, 57(?); 9.18, 22; 10.31, 33; 11.8(?); not to mention 18.12, 14, 31, 36, 38; 19.7, 12, 14, 31, 38; 20.19. See particularly U. C. von Wahlde, 'The Johannine "Jews". A Critical Survey', *NTS* 28 (1982), pp. 33–60.

65. 6.41, 52; 7.11(?); 7.15; 7.35(?); 8.22, 31; 10.19, 24(?); 11.19, 31, 33, 36, 45, 54; 12.9, 11; 13.33(?); 18.20; 19.20–21.

66. C. H. Dodd, *The Interpretation of the Fourth Gospel*, Cambridge University 1960, particularly pp. 352–353.

the theme of *krisis*, 'separation, judgment' (3.19; 5.22, 24, 27, 29, 30; 7.24; 8.16; 12.31) and *schisma*, 'division' (7.43; 9.16; 10.19).

The point is, as Dodd noted, that 'the Book of Signs' (chs 3–12) has been constructed in order to bring out the divisive effect of Christ (1.11–13), the escalating process of separation (*krisis*) and division (*schisma*) which was the inevitable effect of the light shining (3.19–21). Throughout the Book of Signs there is a sifting going on. Some are attracted and follow, like the disciples and the Samaritans. Others are repelled ('the Jews' = the authorities). But in the middle are the ambivalent crowd (also 'the Jews') who cannot make up their mind. They also 'follow' him (6.2) but remain confused throughout the bread of life discourse, and in the end 'many of his disciples drew back and no longer went about with him' (6.66). Throughout ch. 7 'the Jews'/'the crowd'[67] debate back and forth the significance of Jesus, with many believing (7.31) or reaching a positive though inadequate verdict (7.40), but with others sceptical (7.35), and the end result 'a division among the people' (7.43). In ch. 8 the process of sifting continues, the process occasioned by the shining of 'the light of the world' (8.12), with continued debate among 'the Jews', some believing (8.31) and others rejecting (8.48); and in ch. 9 the episode of the blind man receiving his sight becomes a further illustration and occasion for further division (9.16). In ch. 10 the process is maintained, with further 'division among the Jews' (10.19–21), with some rejecting (10.31–9)[68] and other (many) believing (10.41–2). In ch. 11 the references to 'the Jews' are unusually positive (11.19, 31, 33, 36, 45), with the note of division clearly enunciated in 11.45–6: 'many of the Jews ... believed in him; but some of them went to the Pharisees ...' Ch. 12 forms an effective climax, with 'the crowd' again prominent (12.9, 12, 17, 18, 29, 34), and once again a division between those Jews who believe (12.11) and bear witness to him (12.17–19) and those who refuse (12.37–40), and with the *krisis* process occasioned by the light continuing to the end (12.31–43).

All this seems to indicate something of a *contest* between the Johannine gospel and 'the Jews' = the Jewish authorities, for the loyalty of 'the Jews' = the people, with the gospel itself as the sifting, divisive factor. Even in the passion narrative, where the hostile references are most intense, John preserves the memory that Jewish responsibility for Jesus' execution was largely confined to the high priestly party, as distinct from the Pharisees (the main representatives

---

67. 'The Jews' – 7.11, 15, 35; 'the crowd' – 7.12, 20, 31–32, 40, 43.
68. The fact that 'the Jews' here and in 8.48–59 are part of the sifting/division motif raises the question as to whether these references also should not be referred to the crowd.

of the Jewish authorities of his own day).[69] And at the crucifixion the absence of any taunting by the crowd/people (such as we find in Matthew and Mark) actually softens and narrows the polemic against the Jews.[70] In short, however hostile John may be to the Jewish leadership of his day, *we cannot yet conclude that he has disowned or has been disowned by the Jewish people.*

The complexity of John's treatment of 'the Jews' is best explained by the historical situation confronting the Fourth Evangelist. There is a large scale consensus that John was writing at around the end of the first century, during the period when the rabbinic council at Yavneh, under the leadership first of Yohanan ben Zakkai and then Gamaliel II, began the lengthy process of rebuilding the nation round the Torah and of defining Judaism more carefully in face of other claimants to the heritage of second Temple Judaism, including Christianity. In these circumstances it is very likely that John's use of 'the Jews' (= the Jewish authorities) refers to a local Jewish leadership who identified with the objectives of the Yavnean rabbis, or possibly even to the Yavnean rabbis themselves.[71] But it is also likely that John's usage reflects the claim beginning to be made at that time by the Yavnean authorities to be the only legitimate heirs to pre-70 Judaism, to be, in fact 'the Jews'. At the same time, however, there were other (ethnic) Jews who must have been 'caught in the middle', the heirs of the much more diverse forms of late second Temple Judaism caught between the competing claims of Yavnean rabbis and others (already designated by Yavneh as *Minim*, 'heretics'), including the believers in Jesus Messiah.[72] These will be 'the Jews' = the ambivalent crowd, uncertain which competing claim to accept. As Lou Martyn in particular has perceived, ch. 9 seems clearly to reflect the sort of pressures and uncertainties and hard decisions which must have confronted many ethnic Jews of that time.[73]

If there is anything in this we can also say that *John's usage indicates not so much a clear distancing of the Johannine congregation from*

---

69. After ch. 12 Pharisees are mentioned only at 18.3; contrast the prominence given to the high priests (particularly 18.3, 35; 19.6, 15, 21). And see above §3.6.

70. See further R. Leistner, *Anti-Judaismus im Johannes-Evangelium? Darstellung des Problem in der neueren Auslegungsgeschichte und Untersuchung der Leidensgeschichte*, Bern/Frankfurt: Lang 1974; D. Granskou, 'Anti-Judaism in the Passion Accounts of the Fourth Gospel', *Anti-Judaism* Vol. 1, ed. Richardson, pp. 201–16, here pp. 214–15.

71. See further below §11.5.

72. See again below §11.5 and further §§12.1–2; and cf. above §8.5 on Matthew.

73. J. L. Martyn, *History and Theology in the Fourth Gospel*, Nashville: Abingdon, 1968 [2]1979, ch. 2; see again below §11.5.

'the Jews,' as an acknowledgment of a dispute over the pre-70 Jewish heritage. This was a dispute in which the believers in Messiah Jesus were in part involved and in part distant: in part involved as 'the Jews' = the crowd indicates; in part distant, as indicated by the sharp antithesis between Jesus and 'the Jews' = the religious authorities. Furthermore, since the process of *krisis* in John in the end results in the crowd eventually siding against Jesus (12.37–40), we could say that John was aware that Christian Jews were losing the battle, that 'the Jews' = the crowd would side with 'the Jews' = the authorities (the dominant usage in chs 18–19) – that is, that the Yavnean authorities would succeed in imposing their definition of Judaism on the more diverse patterns (Judaisms) of the second Temple period. To that extent John would in effect be ceding the claim to the title 'Jew' to the rabbis, and with it something of the claim to the heritage of post-exilic Judaism. But only something of that claim, if our earlier observations on the distinction between *Israel(ites)* and *Ioudaios* (§8.2c) are sound. In other words, John may have been willing to yield the self-understanding of Judaism which largely comes to expression in the distinction of 'Jew' from 'Gentile', while continuing to claim that the 'true Israelite' recognizes Jesus to be 'king of Israel' (1.47, 49). Moreover, John's handling of the passion narrative, noted above, suggests a polemic more carefully directed against the Jewish authorities, with some hope still entertained regarding the crowd, not to mention those symbolized by Nicodemus (19.39).[74]

We have still to draw out the significance of John's christology at this point (§§11.5–6), but enough has been said for the moment to show that *while the parting of the ways between Christianity and the Judaism of the Yavnean rabbis seems already an accomplished fact, John, in his own perspective at least, was still fighting a factional battle within Judaism rather than launching his arrows from*

---

74. Cf. Freyne, 'Vilifying the Other', who speaks of 'the community's resolve to locate (its) self-identity within, not outside Judaism. Johannine Christianity is convinced that salvation "is of the Jews" (4.22)' (p. 128). Contrast W. A. Meeks, '"Am I a Jew?" Johannine Christianity and Judaism', *Christianity, Judaism and Other Greco-Roman Cults. Studies for Morton Smith*, ed. J. Neusner, Leiden: Brill 1975, Vol. 1, pp. 163–86: 'the Johannine community is separate from "the Jews" and no longer expects "Jews" to convert' (p. 182); also 'Breaking Away' pp. 98–9. On the ambivalent role and significance of Nicodemus, see e.g. M. de Jonge, 'Nicodemus and Jesus', *Jesus: Stranger from Heaven and Son of God*, Missoula: Scholars 1977, pp. 29–47; R. E. Brown, *The Community of the Beloved Disciple*, London: Chapman 1979, p. 72, n. 128; D. Rensberger, *Johannine Faith and Liberating Community*, Philadelphia: Westminster 1988, chs 2–3. One of the most intriguing references on this theme is 12.42: 'many of the leaders/rulers believed in him, but because of the Pharisees they were not confessing him lest they be expelled from the synagogue.'

without, still a Jew who believed that Jesus was Messiah, Son of God (20.31), rather than an apostate from his people, far less an anti-semite.

This suggests in turn that the dualism of John's polemic is a matter more of *rhetoric* than of calculated *prejudice*. It is true that *kosmos* in John represents the 'world' of humanity in its otherness from God and in its hostility to his Son,[75] so that the implicit identification of 'the Jews' with 'the world' in ch. 8 intensifies the anti-Jewish polemic. But this is all part of John's rhetorical schema devised to focus attention on Jesus. So, for example, he alone is 'from above' (3.31; 8.23), they are 'from below', 'of this world' (8.23). But so also is Pilate's authority (19.11). And so also are Nicodemus, the secret believer (3.3, 7, 13), and John the Baptist, the model witness (3.31). By intensifying the focus on *Jesus* in this way, *any* or *all* other claimants to final or definitive revelation from God, not just 'the Jews', are set in the shadow. And since this christological claim is contested at this point chiefly by 'the Jews' (the Yavnean[?] authorities), it is they who bear the brunt of John's dualistic polemic. But it is not an ontological dualism, far less a dualism dividing Jews from others (*all* are 'from below', 'of the flesh' – 1.13; 3.6; 8.15), rather a *rhetorical* dualism which intensifies the alternative in order to provoke a decision (3.19–21; etc. again).[76]

More important, the dualism is a central part of John's salvation schema.[77] *The dualism is deepened precisely in order to emphasize the scope of God's saving purpose through his Son.* 'The Word became flesh' (1.14), his flesh is given for the life of the world (6.51), and it is precisely by eating this flesh that life is received (6.53–6). God loves the world and gave his Son for it; the number of positive references to 'the world' in this vein is striking (1.29; 3.16–17; 4.42; 6.33, 51; 8.12; 9.5; 12.19), and the theme is particularly prominent in the conclusion to the Book of Signs (12.46–7). Although 'his own' reject him (1.11), he also loves 'his own' (13.1). And the fact that Jesus dies for 'the people', as a necessity recognized by the High Priest, is given emphasis by being repeated (11.50; 18.14). Here again we

---

75. Particularly 1.10c; 3.17b; 8.23; 12.31; 14.17, 30; 15.18–19; 16.8, 11, 33; 17.6, 9, 14, 16, 25; 18.36.

76. See particularly J. H. Charlesworth, 'A Critical Comparison of the Dualism in 1QS 3.13–4.26 and the "Dualism" Contained in the Gospel of John', *John and Qumran*, ed. J. H. Charlesworth, London: Chapman 1972, pp. 76–106.

77. Cf. E. Grässer, 'Die antijüdische Polemik im Johannesevangelium', *NTS* 11 (1964–65), pp. 74–90, here pp. 85, 88–90.

can hardly speak of anti-semitism or even anti-Jewish polemic.[78] What lies behind these themes, as behind the whole treatment of 'the Jews', was evidently *a contest for the minds and hearts of the Jewish people*, a contest which 'the Jews' = the Jewish (Yavnean?) authorities seem to have been winning, but a contest which the Fourth Evangelist had not yet given up as lost.[79]

It is the rhetoric of factional polemic which also probably explains even the (to us) horrifying dismissiveness of John 8.44 – 'You are of your father the devil' (§8.1). For in the blunter language of those days, the description of the opposition (within Judaism) as 'the sons of Belial' (as in *Jub.* 15.33 and 4QFlor. 1.8)[80] was a particularly pointed and forthright way of asserting their error. But we should also recall that within Christian documentation, *Jesus* rebuked Peter as 'Satan' (Matt. 16.23/Mark 8.33), and *Paul* denounced the 'apostles of Christ' as 'servants of Satan' (II Cor. 11.13–15). Even with John 8.44, therefore, we are still in the realm of intra-Jewish polemic. Even here, once we set it within the rhetorical conventions of factional dispute of the time, we cannot fairly speak of an anti-semitism, or of John disowning Israel's election as the people of God.

All this suggests that there is a grave danger of misreading John's treatment of 'the Jews'. The danger is (1) of failing to appreciate the complexity of that treatment even when abstracted from the rest of the Gospel, (2) of failing to give enough attention to the historical context within which John was writing and enough weight to the pressures under which he was writing, and (3) of failing to integrate that treatment into the Gospel as a whole, to appreciate the overall positive purpose of his portrayal, and to take account of the rhetoric he used to achieve that purpose. The problem of definition indicated at the beginning (§8.2) cannot be escaped even in John. *The Fourth Evangelist was still operating within a context of intra-Jewish factional dispute*, although the boundaries and definitions were themselves part

---

78. The point can be applied even to the fierce language of ch. 8 cited at the beginning. Cf. *T.Dan.* 5.6: 'your prince is Satan' – 'not an antisemitic but inner-Jewish invective' (as Thoma, *Christian Theology*, p. 157 notes).

79. Cf. C. K. Barrett, *The Gospel of John and Judaism*, London: SPCK 1975, pp. 65–9: 'the fact is that there was a continuing relation between Christianity and Judaism which involved both attraction and repulsion' (p. 69).

80. Cf. e.g. the fierceness of the language in 1QS 2.4–10: 'And the Levites shall curse all the men of the lot of Satan, saying: "Be cursed because of all your guilty wickedness! May he deliver you up for torture at the hands of the vengeful avengers! May he visit you with destruction by the hand of all the wreakers of revenge! Be cursed without mercy because of the darkness of your deeds! Be damned in the shadowy place of everlasting fire! ..."' (Vermes).

of that dispute. It is clear beyond doubt that once the Fourth Gospel was removed from that context, and the constraints of that context, it was all too easily read as an anti-Jewish polemic and became a tool of anti-semitism. But it is highly questionable whether the Fourth Evangelist himself can fairly be indicted for either anti-Judaism or anti-semitism, and highly questionable whether John would have agreed that he had undermined the pillar of Israel's election.

8.7 Conclusions

(a) The main effect of the present study has been to reinforce the impression that Paul and the other authors examined above were writing *within a period when the character of what we have to call 'Judaism' (or Judaisms) was under dispute and its boundaries in process of being redrawn*. All four certainly reflect the fact that the bulk of the Jewish people had (so far) rejected the message of Jesus the Christ. All four reflect the puzzlement, hurt, and, yes, anger which that rejection provoked. But *they still wrote as those for whom the issue was not closed*. In the period following 70 CE the Christian case may have been regarded as lost so far as the rabbinic successors of the Pharisees, the Jewish authorities at Yavneh and their supporters were concerned. But they were by no means the only Jews. And they did not succeed in establishing their authority over the other Jews as quickly as is often assumed.[81] For Luke, Matthew and John, the match was not over; all was still to play for. Judaism was not yet solely rabbinic Judaism. Christian Judaism was not yet simply Christianity. Others may have been building the walls in a tighter circle round the Torah. But Matthew, John and even Luke, as well as Paul, still saw themselves as within the older walls of the Judaism of Jesus' time.

(b) Most, if not all of the so-called 'anti-Jewish' polemic in these four authors has the character and the intensity of sibling rivalry – able to be so hurtful, because the weak points were so well known; having to be so dismissive, in order to establish their own identity in distinction from the other. But there is at least something also of prophetic critique in the polemic. For example, Matthew's rebuke of 'an evil and adulterous generation' (12.39; 16.4) has strong echoes of Ezek. 23 and Hos. 3.1, not to mention James 4.4. And the fact that Stephen's denunciation in Acts 7.51–3 deliberately draws on OT language is well known (Ex. 33.3, 5; Lev. 26.41; Num. 27.14; Isa.

---

81. See further below §12.1.

63.10; Jer. 6.10; 9.26). There is a robustness in all this which Enlightenment liberalism finds profoundly disturbing. In the more sensitive, sophisticated and mild-mannered present, not only an Inquisition's treatment of 'heretics', or a Calvin's burning of Servetus disturbs and offends. But also the bluntness of a prophet's denunciation of unfaithfulness, or Jesus' rebuke of Peter as 'Satan', or Paul's similar denunciation of other 'apostles of Christ'. We should beware of reading such language with pedantic literalism, not least because we hear only one side of the several disputes involved. We should certainly be slow to let our own sensitivities dictate a verdict of anti-Judaism or anti-semitism on those whose world of discourse was so very different from our own.[82]

(*c*) What then about the second and third 'pillars' of Judaism with which we have been most concerned in these last three chapters? Can we be more precise? So far as the *Torah* was concerned, we can see that the split which seemed inevitable so far as Paul and his Pharisaic contemporaries were concerned did not appear so clear-cut for those writing after 70. Paul had not abandoned the law either, as we saw; but his claim to fulfilment of the law was probably posed in terms too sharply removed from that of the rabbis and too challenging to the rabbis. Matthew, however, was prepared to mount his claim in terms the rabbis would have understood and appreciated much more ('doing and teaching the law', 'lawlessness' and 'righteousness'). Even in Acts the care taken to show Paul as law-observant is striking, though in John the issue of the law has evidently been swallowed up in the central issue of christology (John 5, 9). However, *none of these first-century Christian writers would have accepted the proposition that they had denied or abandoned the law.*

So far as *election* was concerned, it looks as though *there was a certain readiness on the part of all four to concede 'Judaism' to 'the Jews', but* not *the axiom and heritage of election.* Israel was still the Lord's olive-tree (Paul), still the Lord's vineyard (Matthew). Jerusalem was still the hinge of salvation-history (Luke). Salvation was still 'from the Jews' (John). Thus we might say that there was a readiness to yield 'the gifts and the call of God', insofar as they were being understood in terms of a Judaism over against and exclusive of the

---

82. Contrast D. Flusser in Thoma, *Christian Theology*: 'Do not tell me that such statements and ideas are merely inner-Jewish disputes or prophetic scoldings' (p. 17); with L. T. Johnson, 'The New Testament's Anti-Jewish Slander and the Conventions of Ancient Polemic', *JBL* 108 (1989), pp. 419–41: 'by the measure of contemporary Jewish polemic, the NT's slander against fellow Jews is remarkably mild' (p. 441). But it is also Flusser who notes that 'all the motifs of Jesus' famous invective against the Pharisees in Matt. 23 are also found in rabbinical literature' (cited by Koenig, *Jews and Christians*, p. 24).

Gentile world. And *to the extent that Judaism could only and did define itself in these terms a split was inevitable*; the difficulty (or is it impossibility?) of disentangling ethnic and religious Judaism, still today, continues to confuse (might we say 'bedevil') the whole question. But the real issue was, and still is, *which of the two chief strands emerging from second Temple Judaism was being truer to the original and most characteristic impulse of God's call and gifts*, and whether *both* can be so regarded.

(*d*) At least so far as 'the partings of the ways' are concerned, we have to say that there was nothing like a clean break over the issues and in the period covered by the writers reviewed above. There were varying degrees of disengagement, and the extent of disengagement was by no means a matter of agreement by those on either side of the disputes. A break which was clearer to Paul's Jewish (including Jewish Christian) opponents was not so to Paul. A break which was already final to the 'Pharisees' of Matthew's Gospel was not so to Matthew. A break which was sharper to 'the Jews' of John (and Acts?) was not so to Luke and John. It might even have been the case that while *some* strands of Christianity would have proved unacceptable to continuing Judaism on these issues (the Pauline churches; but was Acts attempting to remedy that?), *others* continued to be tolerated by many (most?) Jews (Matthew and John in particular), at least for a time. But if so, it may simply mean that *the issues of Torah and election need not have proved sufficient in themselves to cause the final split between Christianity and rabbinic Judaism*.

However, we have still to take up the issue posed by Ruether: whether it was Christian belief in and claims for *Jesus* which made anti-semitism unavoidable and the 'parting of the ways' which that presupposes inevitable. And so we turn to the final issue, the pillar of Jewish monotheism and the question of christology.

9

Jesus and the One God

So far we have seen how emerging Christianity found it necessary to question three of the four pillars of second Temple Judaism: the Temple, beginning with Stephen and the Hellenists; and the Torah as the mark of election, understood in terms of ethnic identity, by Paul. In retrospect the first need not have been too serious a breach: the rabbis after 70 were able to reconstitute Judaism round the Torah without having the Temple as a physical focus. The second was more serious. Whatever his intentions, Paul's treatment of the Torah made a breach with a Judaism centred on the Torah almost inevitable; though Matthew was able to contest the issue on the basis of the teaching of Jesus; and the issue may have been less decisive for other strains of Judaism. Even in the case of Israel's election the matter was not straightforward. There always had been a degree of ambiguity in Jewish identity, with proselytes, resident aliens and God-fearers clouding any definition in simple ethnic terms. And with the majority of Jews living in the diaspora, for most of them the land was bound to be more of a theological ideal than a practical reality. Nevertheless, the degree of identity between 'Judaism' (the religion) and 'Jew' (ethnic identity) probably meant that *a form of Judaism which ceased to equate Israel with the Jews* per se *was bound to part company with a Judaism which maintained the identity of race and religion more closely.*

What about the one remaining pillar of second Temple Judaism (§2) – monotheism? Was that too undermined or realigned? If so, when and how, and to what extent? We follow the same pattern of inquiry as before, starting once again with Jesus' own teaching and attitude. That means starting with the extremely difficult question of Jesus' self-consciousness,[1] where a proper evaluation of the evidence

---

1. I have defended the proposition that 'statements of historical personalities can so embody their feelings and a consciousness (or conviction) as to their own significance, even if only at a particular point in their lives, that we today can know something of their feelings and sense something of that consciousness through these same statements' in my *Christology*, pp. 25–6.

would run far beyond the scope of this chapter, so that here not least we shall have to be content with a summary treatment at many points requiring fuller discussion. We shall also have to bear in mind that the issue 'bites' most deeply at the level of popular Christian faith (Was not Jesus God?) and move forward with sensitive circumspection.

9.1 Jesus the devout worshipper

How did Jesus see himself in relation to God? The question could be framed far more profoundly, but this simple formulation suffices to pose the issue clearly enough. And the obvious place to start is with the question of *how Jesus functioned in the Jewish worship of his time*. Before we begin to explore more problematic areas we should at least be clear as to whether Jesus did in fact worship, confess, and pray to the one God. Unfortunately, or perhaps significantly, we have little to go on within the Gospel traditions. But what we have at this point does build together into a consistent picture of *Jesus as a faithful Jew*.

(a) *The proclamation of God's kingly rule.* This was evidently the chief feature of Jesus' preaching (see e.g. Mark 1.15; Luke 6.20/Matt. 5.3; Matt. 10.7/Luke 10.9; 13.11, 19, 24, 31, 33, 44, 45, 47).[2] We may note here simply that it was the kingdom of *God* which he preached, *God's* kingly rule.[3] He teaches his disciples to pray for God's kingdom, not his own, and to pray first for the sanctification of the divine name, which, as a good Jew, he does not utter (Matt. 6.9/Luke 11.2).[4] There is no implication in all this that Jesus saw himself in any sense as a rival to God, or looked for anyone else to be such. An advocate before God, yes (as in Matt. 10.32); an agent of God, likewise (as in Luke 22.29). And there are, of course, other elements within the Jesus-tradition, for example, the Son of Man passages,[5] to which we must return. But on this point we can recognize the force of the claim made by the old Liberal Protestants: Jesus proclaimed God and not himself.[6]

---

2. The most recent comprehensive study of the theme in English is G. R. Beasley Murray, *Jesus and the Kingdom of God*, Grand Rapids: Eerdmans/Exeter: Paternoster 1986.

3. Riches, *Jesus*, ch. 5, argues that Jesus reworked the conventional associations of the notion of the kingdom and so radicalized and transformed first-century Judaism (p. 87); but his case depends on these 'associations' and thus is covered by what follows (§§9.2ff.). The same is true of his treatment of Jesus' theism (ch. 7).

4. Osten-Sacken, *Christian-Jewish Dialogue*, p. 49 (cf. p. 123).

5. See below §9.4.

6. Cf. Harnack, *What is Christianity?*, p. 108: 'The Gospel, as Jesus proclaimed it, has to do with the Father only and not with the Son.'

(b) *Jesus' prayer life.*[7] As a Jewish child Jesus would have been taught to pray daily; he is recalled describing the Temple as 'a house of prayer' (Mark 11.17); and it was evidently his regular practice on the Sabbath to attend the synagogue (Luke 4.16), known at least in the diaspora as a 'prayer house'.[8] In addition, three times Mark recalls Jesus at prayer (1.35; 6.46; 14.32–9); and Luke has a much fuller picture of the praying Jesus (3.21; 5.16; 6.12; 9.18, 28–9; 11.1; 22.41–2; 23.34, 46).[9] In no sense could these be described as merely mouthing traditional forms or going through the motions, as his recorded teaching on prayer also confirms (e.g.Matt.7.7–11/Luke 11.9–13). Rather we must speak of such prayer as expressing a clear sense of dependency on God.

(c) *The Temple and sacrifice.* This is a topic with which we have already dealt.[10] Unfortunately we have no testimony either way as to whether Jesus ever offered up a sin-offering or guilt-offering on his own behalf. It would presumably have been regarded as extremely odd if he had never done so (cf.Luke 2.22–24). But the issue is complicated by our uncertainty regarding the number or frequency of his visits to Jerusalem, and by the fact that sacrifice was required for 'unwitting' sins and for ritual impurities (Lev. 4–5). In the absence of viable evidence it is probably wiser not to speculate further.

(d) *The importance of the Shema'.* (1) Jesus' answer to the question, 'Which commandment is the first of all?' is particularly striking. In Mark he begins by quoting the *Shema'*: 'The first is, "Hear, O Israel: The Lord our God, the Lord is one; and you shall love the Lord your God with all your heart, and with all your soul, and with all your mind, and with all your strength"' (Mark 12.29–30; citing Deut. 6.4). That is to say, Jesus affirmed the foundational Jewish confession of the unity of God.[11] (2) In the same connection we might note that the temptation narratives (Matt. 4.1–10/Luke 4.1–12), particularly Matthew's, take the form of a midrash on Deut. 6–8[12] – the same passage, so fundamental in Israel's self-understanding of its obligation to acknowledge Yahweh as God alone. Note particularly Matt. 4.10, the climax of the Matthean account, where Jesus is portrayed as citing

---

7. For the importance of prayer within Jewish worship at this period, see e.g. Cohen, *Maccabees to Mishnah*, pp. 62–73.

8. See LSJ and BAGD, *proseuche.*

9. See further below §9.3.

10. See above §3.1.

11. See above §2.1.

12. See particularly B. Gerhardsson, *The Testing of God's Son (Matt. 4.1–11 and par.),* Con B; Lund: Gleerup 1966.

Deut. 6.13 – 'You shall worship the Lord your God and him only shall you serve'. (3) Equally striking in this connection is Jesus' reply to the question of the rich young man: 'Good teacher, what must I do to inherit internal life?' Jesus answers, 'Why do you call me good? No one is good but God alone' (Mark 10.17–18).[13]

(e) *His call for faith.* Jesus' talk of faith/believing comes predominantly (nearly two-thirds of the references) in relation to miracles.[14] The implication is that the faith looked for was faith in God, or faith in God's power working through Jesus. There is no indication that Jesus called for faith in *himself as such*, and certainly not for faith in the later Christian sense of belief in him as risen, commitment to him as exalted Lord. Besides, any such talk of faith in him at the earlier stage would not have been understood as trust in God somehow *transferred* to Jesus. It would presumably have been understood more along the lines of the Qumran covenanter who had 'faith in the Teacher of Righteousness', with no sense whatsoever that this was in any way or degree inconsistent with their basic monotheistic faith.[15]

Here, then, we have the basis of the modern Jewish willingness to reclaim Jesus as one of their own – a great prophet, a controversial rabbi, perhaps, but *at heart a devout Jew whose basic springs and expressions of piety were Jewish through and through.* But is there not further evidence that Jesus saw himself in some sense as God? Or at least as so much the spokesman for and representative of God that he must have appeared as a threat or rival to the one God? The evidence on this point is complex and would require a much more detailed examination than we can give here. It must suffice to sketch out the main areas of discussion and to highlight the most relevant features.

9.2 Jesus as Messiah

For the question of Jesus' potential significance within a Jewish milieu, the most obvious starting point is the messiahship of Jesus, Jesus as

---

13. Matthew's redaction sticks close to Mark's wording, but subtly alters it to remove the potential problem posed by Mark: 'Teacher, what good deed must I do, to have eternal life?'; to which Jesus replies, 'Why do you ask me about what is good? One there is who is good' (Matt. 19.16–17). The fact that Matthew felt it necessary thus to modify Mark's text confirms both that Mark's is the older tradition and that the memory of Jesus so speaking was not problematic prior to Matthew.

14. Details in my *Jesus*, pp. 74–6.

15. 1QpHab 8.2–3 interprets Hab. 2.4 thus: 'Interpreted, this concerns all those who observe the Law in the House of Judah, whom God will deliver from the House of Judgment because of their suffering and because of their faith in the Teacher of Righteousness.'

'Messiah'. This is the title which became so quickly established in earliest Christianity in its Greek form ('Christ') that already within the earliest writings of the NT (the Pauline letters) it functions in effect as a proper name – Jesus Christ. There is also a long-rooted tradition in Christianity which speaks of Jesus' 'messianic consciousness', particularly prominent in older Lives of Jesus. And often with the implication that this was the historical equivalent of his divinity, or, in terms closer to those used by Baur referred to at the beginning of these lectures, that Jesus' messianic self-consciousness was the historical form of his divinity.[16] At all events, the association of Jesus' Messiahship with his divinity is still firmly established in popular Christianity. What, then, are the facts so far as we can uncover them?

(a) There is certainly evidence that the identification of Jesus as messiah, that is as the royal Messiah, son of David, was a topic of speculation at the time of Jesus. Among the chief points which would call for consideration in a more extensive treatment are the following.[17]

(1) There was popular expectation of such a figure, based on such passages as II Sam. 7.14, Isa. 11.1–2 and Ezek. 34.23–4. Such expectation is attested for groups nearer the time of Jesus, as we can see, for example, in *Pss. Sol.* 17.23ff. and 4QFlor 1.10–13 (citing II Sam. 7.14). Though the royal Messiah was not the only figure of Jewish expectation (see e.g. 1QS 9.11), he was probably the one who featured most in popular hope and expectation.

(2) There had been other claimants to the crown, particularly in the period of anarchy following the death of Herod the Great (Josephus, *War* 2.57–65).[18] According to both Luke and John, the Baptist's mission raised the question as to whether *he* might be 'the Messiah' (Luke 3.15; John 1.19–20). And subsequently the rebel leader Simon bar Kokhba was hailed as Messiah by many Jews including the famous rabbi Akiba.[19] We may fairly deduce, then, that one who aroused the sort of enthusiasm that Jesus evidently did would

---

16. See above §1.1.

17. See further my 'Messianic Ideas and their Influence upon the Jesus of History', *The Messiah. The First Princeton Symposium on Judaism and Christian Origins*, ed. J. H. Charlesworth et al., New York: Doubleday 1991. Cf. e.g. M. de Jonge, *Christology in Context. The Earliest Christian Response to Jesus*, Philadelphia: Westminster 1988, pp. 209–11.

18. See further R. A. Horsley and J. S. Hanson, *Bandits, Prophets and Messiahs. Popular Movements at the Time of Jesus*, Minneapolis: Seabury 1985, ch. 3, here pp. 111–17.

19. See Schürer, 1.544.

most likely also arouse speculation as to whether he was the hoped for Messiah.

(3) According to John 6.15 the episode of the 'feeding of the five thousand' climaxed in an attempt by the crowd to make Jesus king by force. Whatever the historical basis of the miracle story, any event which recalled the manna miracle in the wilderness, or the prophetic hope of a fruitful desert in the age to come, or of the shepherd king providing for his flock (Ezek. 34.23; *Pss. Sol.* 17.45), was likely to arouse such messianic hopes.

(4) Not least of relevance is the account of Peter's confession – 'You are the Messiah' (Mark 8.27ff.). The historical value of the account is disputed, but is nonetheless well grounded.[20] The specification of the place where it happened (in the territory of Caesarea Philippi) is one indication, since no other episode (including no resurrection appearance to the twelve) is located so far north. Moreover, given the impact of Jesus' mission and the interest he aroused, it would have been most odd if his own disciples had not, sooner or later, asked themselves whether Jesus was the hoped for Son of David. And certainly it must be judged highly unlikely that a story was allowed to gain acceptance in Christian circles of Jesus calling Peter 'Satan' (Mark 8.33), had it not been rooted in the memory of an actual incident.

(5) Above all there is the record of Jesus' trial and condemnation (Mark 14.55–65; 15.1ff.). We have already noted the strong likelihood that the accusation against Jesus recalled in Mark 14.58 the memory of Jesus having said something about the destruction and rebuilding of the Temple.[21] The point here is that such a prophetic utterance would fit in well with a messianic interpretation of II Sam: 7.14, such as we know to have been entertained at Qumran: any claim to (re)build the Temple could all too readily be read as a claim to royal messiahship, and divine sonship (II Sam. 7.12–14). As already pointed out, therefore, the High Priest's question was entirely plausible and indeed wholly to be expected: 'Are you the Messiah, the son of the Blessed?' (Mark 14.61).[22] Even stronger is the evidence that the charge before Pilate was that of being a royal pretender – and that Jesus was executed as such: the title over the cross, 'King of the Jews', was not a Christian title, and so, almost certainly historical. Jesus was crucified as a messianic pretender![23]

---

20. Cf. e.g. Taylor, *Mark*, p. 374; F. Hahn, *The Titles of Jesus in Christology*, 1963; ET London: Lutterworth 1969, pp. 223–5.

21. See above §3.5.

22. See above (1) and earlier p. 69; and further below §9.3b.

23. This is one of the most firmly anchored 'historical facts'; see e.g. A. E. Harvey, *Jesus and the Constraints of History*, London: Duckworth 1982, pp. 11–35.

In short, so far as it is a question as to whether the messiahship of Jesus was an issue during his life or not, the answer is clearly in the *affirmative*. Can we therefore continue to speak quite happily of Jesus' 'messianic consciousness'? How did he respond when this issue was raised?

(*b*) The rather surprising feature of our records is that *Jesus did not respond positively to the role of Messiah*. He apparently did not warm to the idea of being the royal son of David. This becomes clear from the same three episodes reviewed above.[24]

(1) In the feeding of the five thousand we should note the way in which a surprising feature of Mark's account dovetails into that of John.[25] According to Mark 6.45 Jesus '*compelled*' his disciples to embark on the lake when it was already evening, *before* dismissing the crowd. The odd choice of language and order of events is left unexplained in Mark but becomes clear in the light of John 6.15. The picture indeed becomes fully coherent if we simply infer that Jesus' *disciples* were also caught up in the messianic fervour of the crowd. The only way to handle the dangerous situation was to detach the disciples from the crowd and to despatch them on to the lake, even though the evening wind was likely to be against them. Only then was Jesus able to dismiss the crowd – and then, probably significant, go off into the hills to pray. If this reconstruction is at all accurate, then the point is that Jesus reacted *against* the popular role being offered to him. Presumably he saw it as a false understanding of his mission. The fact that he went off to pray may also imply that he saw the role of popular ruler, or military leader, as dangerously attractive; hence the need to pray in the face of such temptation (cf. Mark 14.36). The account of Jesus' temptation in the wilderness (Matt. 4.8–10/Luke 4.5–8) may be based, in part at least, on such an episode. The point for us, however, is that *Jesus rejected the role of royal Messiah thus thrust at him.*

(2) A similar conclusion comes from a closer look at the account of Peter's confession. In the earliest account (Mark) Jesus replies to the confession by forbidding his disciples to speak to anyone about him (Mark 8.30). This is not a refusal of the confession and the role it implied. But neither is it a word of welcome (though Matthew understandably develops the tradition in that direction – Matt.

---

24. I am drawing here on my 'The Messianic Secret in Mark', *Tyndale Bulletin* 21 (1970), pp. 92–117, here pp. 110–12.

25. See particularly C. H. Dodd, *Historical Tradition in the Fourth Gospel*, Cambridge University 1963, pp. 212–16.

16.17–19). Mark 8.30 is neither a rebuke, nor a word of congratu-
lation. Given the sustained emphasis in Mark on the disciples' dull-
ness, the implication is that Peter's understanding of Jesus as Messiah
was inadequate and misleading – not much different, in fact, from
that of the Galilean crowd in the feeding episode. That would be why
a command to silence was appropriate: such a view was not to be
encouraged. Instead, according to all three Synoptic evangelists, Jesus
began at once to describe what his mission really involved – suffering,
rejection and death (Mark 8.31 pars.). The implication is, once again,
that 'messiah' as popularly understood (as also by the disciples) was
not a suitable vehicle for Jesus' self-understanding.

(3) In the accounts of Jesus' trial the important question for us here
is once again, How did he reply to the question of the High Priest,
'Are you the Messiah?' (Mark 14.61). In Mark 14.62 the longer
reading, though weakly attested, may well be correct – 'You have said
that I am'. The texts of Matthew and Luke are more readily derived
from it than from the shorter reading ('I am') than vice versa.[26] And
it is more probable that in the course of textual transmission, the
equivocal longer text was abbreviated to the strong affirmation ('I
am'), than that the strong affirmation was watered down by lengthen-
ing it ('You have said that I am'). In which case, the reply of Jesus to
the High Priest is closely similar to his reply to Pilate's equivalent
question – 'Are you the king of the Jews?' – namely, 'You say so'
(Mark 15.2 = Matt. 27.11 = Luke 23.3). In both cases, in all three
Synoptic Gospels (with the sole exception of Mark's shorter reading),
the answers are tantamount to saying, 'The words are yours, not
mine'; 'That's your way of putting it.' Once again, then, there is
indication on the part of Jesus of *an unwillingness to accept what
those who put the question would understand by the term* (Messiah/
King).

We may conclude, therefore, that although the question of whether
Jesus was Messiah was almost certainly aired during his life, *the
idea of messiahship was* not *one which Jesus warmly welcomed or
embraced.* In consequence, any talk of Jesus' *messianic* consciousness
becomes more than a little complex, if not altogether dubious.

(c) More to the point: even if Jesus had warmly embraced the
idea of messiahship and we could speak readily of his messianic
self-consciousness, it would still say nothing of immediate relevance
to our topic.

---

26. Mark 14.61 – τὸ εἶπας   ὅτι ἐγώ εἰμι.
    Matt. 26.64 – τὸ εἶπας. Luke 22.70 – ὑμες λέγετε ὅτι ἐγώ εἰμι.

(1) The expectation of a messianic king fitted fully within the religious framework of Judaism. In the texts cited above, the royal Messiah was not understood as a supernatural figure, although such an identification was made subsequently in what are probably later texts (*I Enoch* 45–62; *IV Ezra* 7.28; 12.32; 13.32–40).[27] But for a Jew to identify someone as Messiah was in no way to dilute or put in question his faith in God as one. Still in the middle of the second century Trypho the Jew asserts, 'We all expect the Christ to be born as a human being from a human being' (Justin, *Dial.* 49).[28]

(2) The same point can be made in reference to the other figures also mentioned above. The royal pretenders in the aftermath of Herod the Great's death were just that – somewhat pathetic royal pretenders. The speculation regarding John the Baptist did not disturb any faith in God as one, even if it included the thought that the Baptist might be Elijah returned from heaven (as in Matt. 11.14; John 1.21). And rabbi Akiba presumably saw his recognition of bar Kokhba as Messiah as wholly consistent with his saying the *Shema'*.

(3) In the event, Jesus was denounced by the High Priestly party not so much for blasphemy (whatever the language used), but rather as a political threat to their power and power base (the Temple).[29] It was as such that he was crucified – not because he dared to say he was God's son, but on the political charge of being 'King of the Jews'.

In short, even if Jesus had claimed to be Messiah, that would have been a claim wholly within the categories and expectations of second Temple Judaism. In fact, however, he seems to have resisted the title and role as inappropriate or inadequate to his mission, at least as understood at the time.[30] Either way, talk of Jesus' 'messianic consciousness' raises more problems than answers and does not contribute much to our inquiry.

---

27. See further below §9.4 particularly p. 229.

28. See further Schürer, 2.518–23.

29. See further above §3.6. That Jesus was charged with 'blasphemy' is attested in Mark 14.64/Matt. 26.65. But if so, it was not because he claimed to be Messiah (see (2) above; also J. Marcus, 'Mark 14.61: "Are You the Messiah-Son-of-God?", *NovT* 31 [1989], pp. 125–41, here pp. 127–30). The technical charge of 'blasphemy' (the word could be used more loosely) would be appropriate only where the prerogatives or authority of God were being improperly usurped. See further below n. 35 and §9.7. On Mark 2.7/Luke 5.21 see above pp. 60–1. On John 10.33, 36, see below §11.6.

30. The first Christians were able to establish their claim for Jesus as Messiah only by reinterpreting what messiahship involved. This they could do only in the light of the known facts of Jesus' death and their firm conviction of his resurrection and by drawing in scriptural texts which hitherto had not been referred to the Messiah. See e.g. U. Luz in his agreement with Lapide's first thesis: 'Jesus did not declare himself to his people as Messiah', Lapide and Luz, *Jesus*, pp. 27–56, 129–37.

9.3 Jesus as God's son

When Christians think of Jesus as divine the title which most naturally comes to mind is 'the Son of God'. Did Jesus see himself as such?

(*a*) Somewhat surprisingly, in scholarly circles there is a widespread agreement that *Jesus probably did indeed see himself as God's son, or understood himself in relation to God as son.* In terms of historical critical analysis the point is most securely based on the tradition of Jesus' prayer to God using the Aramaic form of address, 'Abba' ('Father'). I have argued the case in detail elsewhere,[31] and so need not repeat myself unnecessarily. I remain convinced that the key evidence, which is not usually given sufficient weight,[32] is Rom. 8.15f. and Gal. 4.6–7. (1) The evidence is clear that the early *Greek* speaking churches cherished the *Aramaic* prayer form – why? (2) The evidence is also clear that it was seen as an expression of sonship: 'When we cry "Abba! Father!" it is the Spirit himself bearing witness with our spirit that we are children of God . . .' (Rom. 8.15f.). (3) And the implication is almost as clear that this prayer was understood as proof positive and adequate that the pray-er shared in Jesus' sonship: those who so pray demonstrate that they are 'joint heirs with Christ' (Rom. 8.17). Taken together with the Synoptic Gospels' testimony that Jesus' characteristic prayer address was 'Father', that is, probably 'Abba' (Mark 14.36), and that Jesus taught his own disciples so to address God (Luke 11.2), the conclusion seems inescapable: that *'Abba' was cherished by the first Christians precisely because it was remembered as Jesus' own characteristic prayer language,* a mark of his circle of discipleship (Luke 11.1–2); *and so remembered and cherished precisely because it was understood by the first Christians as expressive of Jesus' own sense of sonship,* a sonship in which they could now participate through the Spirit of God's Son (Gal. 4.6).

There is more evidence, and more contentious evidence, particularly from John's Gospel (see §9.6), but we need not go further into it here. The point is already secure: that Jesus saw himself in relation to God as son to father, as God's son.

(*b*) But here again we must ask ourselves the significance of such a self-consciousness or lived out claim. And here we have a problem. The problem for us is that the title 'Son of God' is something very specific for Christian tradition; for Christians and the whole European tradition, 'the Son of God' has one sole referent – Jesus Christ. Moreover, for us Christians who live post-Nicaea it is hard to avoid the

---

31. See my *Jesus*, ch. 2, and *Christology*, pp. 22–33.
32. As e.g. by Osten-Sacken, *Christian-Jewish Dialogue*, pp. 46–7.

full force of the title in Christian tradition: since the council of Nicaea, Son of God has been *the* key title for Christ; and since Nicaea 'Son of God' has all the overtones of the full blown Trinitarian formula – 'Son of God' means second person of the Trinity, 'true God from true God, begotten not made', etc. In other words, our problem is the difficulty of hearing 'son of God' other than from this side of Nicaea.

It often comes, therefore, as something of a shock to realize that it was *not* the same *pre*-Nicaea – not, at any rate, at the time of Jesus. At the time of Jesus, in Jewish thinking of the early first century, 'son of God' was not a specific title or description.[33] (1) In the Jewish scriptures it could be used collectively of Israel (Ex. 4.22; Jer. 31.9; Hos. 11.1), or in the plural in reference to angels, the heavenly council (e.g. Gen. 6.2, 4; Job 1.6–12), or in the singular of the king (II Sam. 7.14; Ps. 2.7; 89.26–7). (2) At a period much closer to Jesus it was used of the Davidic Messiah at Qumran: the collection of texts put together in 4QFlor 1.10 to end uses II Sam. 7.14 in this way, probably linking it with Ps. 2.7 (but the text breaks off too soon for us to be sure); and 1QSa 2.11f. speaks of a time when God will have begotten the Messiah among them.[34] Hence, presumably, the full question put by the High Priest to Jesus in Mark 14.61 – 'Are you the Messiah, the son of the Blessed?'[35] (3) More striking still is the fact that the righteous man could also be called God's son (e.g. Sir. 4.10; Wisd. 2.13, 16, 18; *Pss. Sol.* 13.8). And also charismatic rabbis, like Honi 'the circle drawer' (first century BCE), who prayed to God like a son of the house, and Hanina ben Dosa (from the generation after Jesus), whom a heavenly voice addresses as 'My son' (*m. Taan* 3.8; *b. Taan* 24b).[36]

We need not belabour the point, since it is clear enough. *At the time of Jesus 'son of God' was a way of characterizing someone who was thought to be commissioned by God or highly favoured by God.* It was not necessarily a title of divinity; not only angels were sons of God. The idea of Jesus as 'God's son' need only imply such a commissioning by God of one specially favoured by God. *As used of*

---

33. For a fuller, though still summary treatment, see my *Christology*, pp. 14–16.

34. See further J. A. Fitzmyer, 'The Contribution of Qumran Aramaic to the Study of the New Testament', *NTS* 20 (1973–74), pp. 382–407, reprinted with Addendum in *A Wandering Aramean: Collected Aramaic Essays*, Chico: Scholars 1979, pp. 85–113.

35. See above §§3.6 and 9.2a. Any charge of blasphemy at the trial (Mark 14.64; above n. 29) would thus not be occasioned by the implication that Jesus by claiming to be Messiah was also claiming to be son (nor does Mark imply that it was); so rightly Juel, *Messiah and Temple*, pp. 77–82, 107–14, against Marcus, 'Mark 14.61'. The charge in John 10.33, 36 is occasioned by the notably 'higher' Son of God christology of the Fourth Gospel (see again below §11.6).

36. See particularly Vermes, *Jesus the Jew*, pp. 69–78, 206–7.

Jesus, initially at least, 'son of God' did not necessarily imply any overtones of divinity. And in terms of Jesus' own self-consciousness, all we can talk about with full confidence is of his sense of intimate sonship to God as Father, whose nearest parallels would place him among the righteous of the Wisdom literature or identify him as a charismatic rabbi like Honi or Hanina.

9.4 Jesus as son of man/Son of Man

If we are looking for 'titles of majesty' which could signify Jesus' own consciousness of divinity the next most obvious one is 'Son of Man'. Here, however, as anyone familiar with the study of the Gospels will be well aware, opinions range over a wide spectrum: from those who think that Jesus called himself the Son of Man by identifying himself with the heavenly figure, 'one like a son of man', of Daniel's vision in Dan. 7.9–14; to those who deny that he used the phrase at all.[37] The point is that if the former are correct, Jesus may have identified himself with one who could easily come to be understood as a rival to 'the Ancient of Days',[38] not least because he sat on the other throne indicated in Dan. 7.9.[39] How then does this phrase or title contribute to our inquiry?

(a) It is certainly *hard to doubt that Jesus used the phrase ('the son of man') to speak of himself.* The evidence could hardly be clearer. The phrase itself occurs eighty-six times in the NT – sixty-nine in the Synoptics, thirteen in John, with only four other occurrences (Acts 7.56; Heb. 2.6; Rev. 1.13; 14.14), of which the last three are quotations from the OT and only in Acts 7.56 is it a title. This is a striking fact: that the phrase belongs almost exclusively to the Gospels. Even *more* striking is the fact that in all four Gospels it appears in effect *only* on the lips of Jesus. He is never addressed as 'Son of Man' in the narratives, or subsequently in the churches' worship, or confessed as 'Son of Man'. The contrast with other titles (Messiah, Son of God, Lord) at this point is remarkable.

These facts must mean that 'Son of Man' did not appear in early Christian theology as an independent feature.[40] It was always, from

---

37. See e.g. the bibliography in my *Unity*[2], pp. 431–2.

38. It was the identification of the Messiah as the Son of Man in *IV Ezra* and *I Enoch* which gave the concept of 'Messiah' a transcendence it lacked before (see above §9.2c).

39. The question of who the other throne was for was fruitful of considerable controversy towards the end of the first century (see further below §11.6b).

40. On the possibility that a 'Son of Man' christology lies behind some other NT texts see my *Christology*, pp. 90–1.

the first, part of their tradition of *Jesus'* teaching, and must have originated there. Had it originated independently of the Jesus-tradition and then been introduced to the Jesus-tradition, we would surely have more evidence of that usage independently of the Jesus-tradition. When the evidence is so clear-cut (of a characteristic *Jesus'* usage, and an *un*-characteristic post-Easter usage), it is verging on the perverse to argue that Jesus did not himself use the phrase or to deny that its use in Christian tradition began with Jesus.

This is not to say that *all* Son of Man sayings go back to Jesus. We have evidence of tradition being interpreted and reworked, and there are passages where the most plausible explanation is that the phrase has been introduced by the evangelist or his source (e.g. Matt. 16.28; see also Matt. 26.2/Mark 14.1; Mark 13.26 appears to have been expanded by the addition of Matt. 24.30a). But in that case it is all the more significant that this reworking has been confined *within* the Jesus-tradition, and maintains the pattern where the phrase is *confined to Jesus' own words*. This must be because that pattern was so firmly stamped on the tradition from the first, and was from the first so massively consistent that the evangelists naturally copied it in their own editorial work. Which is to say, *the phrase must have been a very firm and clear characteristic of Jesus' own speech*.

(*b*) But once again, we have to ask, So what? What is the significance of this usage? The fact is that 'son of man' is an Aramaic phrase or idiom. *Ho huios tou anthrōpou* is barbarous Greek, for the simple reason that it is a literal translation of the Aramaic, *bar ʿᵉnasa*, 'the son of man'. The point is that the Semitic idiom uses 'son of' where we would use an adjective; so 'son of wisdom', a wise man; 'son of war', a war-like man. So, 'son of man' means simply 'man', or 'man-like, a human being'. Thus in Ps. 8.4 we see a good example of Hebrew poetry where the two lines say the same thing in different words:

What is   man   that you are mindful of him,
and the son of man   that you care for him?

In Hebrew and Aramaic idiom 'man' and 'son of man' are two ways of saying the same thing. Thus in Ezekiel, the regular address to Ezekiel as 'Son of Man!' (Ezek. 2.1, 3, 8; 3.1, 3, 4, etc.), could be translated colloquially as, 'Hey, man!'

There is good evidence that Jesus spoke of himself in this sense. That is the best explanation of a number of sayings in the Synoptic tradition. For example, (1) in Mark 2.28 Jesus says:

> The Sabbath came about on account of man
>   and not man on account of the Sabbath;
> So that the son of man is lord also of the Sabbath.

Here, as in Ps. 8.4, 'the son of man' seems to be parallel to and equivalent of 'man'. (2) Similarly in the earlier reference in Mark – Mark 2.10 ('in order that you might know that the son of man has authority to forgive sins on earth'). A reference to Jesus himself must be at least present. But, as noted before,[41] the point for us here is that the hearers are not shown as taking any offence at the phrase, as though Jesus was heard to identify himself with some heavenly figure. In contrast, Matthew ends by noting that the crowds glorified God 'who had given such authority to *men*' (Matt. 9.8). (3) In the parallel verses Matt. 12.31/Mark 3.28/Luke 12.10, it looks very much as though a common Aramaic saying has been taken different ways, with the phrase *bar ᵉnasa* taken as a general reference by Mark ('sons of men' 'men' in Matthew), but taken as a title for Jesus ('the Son of Man') in Luke (Q).[42] (4) There are also a number of parallel passages between the Synoptics where the personal reference of the Aramaic idiom is still clearer, since one version reads 'the son of man', and the other reads 'I'. The implication is most natural that one rendering of the Aramaic saying into Greek recognized the self-reference in the Aramaic idiom, while another took it as a title (Luke 6.22/Matt. 5.11; Luke 12.8/Matt. 10.32; Matt. 16.13/Mark 8.27). This small but not uncharacteristic sample of the evidence indicates strongly that Jesus used the phrase in a somewhat ambiguous way, an ambiguity preserved in the tradition and resolved in different ways in our present texts. The best conclusion, then, is that *Jesus used the phrase, not as a title, but primarily in a more idiomatic sense, which could be translated, 'I, a man', or more idiomatically in the older-fashioned polite English, 'one'.*[43]

(c) The key question, however, is whether Jesus (also) spoke of himself in terms of the vision of Dan. 7. The point is hotly disputed. Some think that the phrase itself would have carried clear reference

---

41. See above pp. 60–1.

42. For more detail see my *Jesus*, pp. 49–52.

43. So particularly Vermes, *Jesus*, pp. 188–91; M. Casey, *Son of Man. The Interpretation and Influence of Daniel 7*, London: SPCK 1979, ch. 9; also 'General, Generic and Indefinite: The use of the Term "Son of Man" in Aramaic Sources and in the Teaching of Jesus', *JSNT* 29 (1987), pp. 21–56; B. Lindars, *Jesus Son of Man. A Fresh Examination of the Son of Man Sayings in the Gospels*, London: SPCK 1983, chs 2–5; D. R. A. Hare, *The Son of Man Tradition*, Minneapolis: Fortress 1990, ch. 8.

to Dan. 7.13 – as though anyone who said *bar ᵉnasa* would at once be linked to Daniel's vision. This is unlikely, since, as we have seen, the phrase was a familiar semitic idiom and would not carry with it any clear reference to any single earlier use of it in particular.[44]

There are, however, some Synoptic passages where a reference to Daniel's vision is indisputable – the reference indicated *not* by use of *bar ᵉnasa*, but by the fuller reference to 'coming in clouds'. So particularly Mark 13.26/Matt. 24.30 and Mark 14.62. A strong strand of scholarship would see these as post-Easter references: either Jesus spoke of someone *else* as 'the Son of Man';[45] or else the whole element reflects the attempt of the first Christians to make sense of what had happened to Jesus by drawing on texts like Ps. 110.1 and Dan. 7.13 and giving them a new and pointed significance by referring them to Jesus.[46] At the other end of the spectrum of scholarship there are those, myself included, who dispute whether there was a Son of Man expectation in Jewish theology: the man-like figure of Daniel's vision is best understood as symbolizing Israel, 'the saints of the Most High' (as the beasts of the preceding part of the vision symbolize the nations hostile to Israel);[47] and the Jewish writings which interpret the man-like figure as an individual, the Messiah (*I Enoch* 37–71 and *IV Ezra*) were probably written after the period of Jesus' ministry.[48] Which would, of course, explain why no formal identification is made between Jesus and 'the Son of Man' anywhere in the NT; there was no such recognized figure to identify him with!

But even if we accept that Jesus himself did refer to Daniel's vision and see in it a picture of his own ministry, as is quite possible, we still have to ask what would have been the significance of such allusions to Daniel's vision on the lips of Jesus. Jeremias suggests that Jesus used

---

44. This is true despite the regular presence of the definite article ('the son of man'), despite my revered teacher, C. F. D. Moule, *The Origin of Christology*, Cambridge University 1977, pp. 11–20, since it is not clear whether we should translate simply 'the son of man' (without any emphasis on the article), or '*the* son of man', or 'that son of man', where the reference would be to an already identified and well known 'son of man' (in Daniel?). Contrast both *I Enoch* and *IV Ezra* where 'that Son of Man' always refers back to the initial reference to and identification of the Dan. 7 figure (*I Enoch* 46.1; *IV Ezra* 13.3).

45. E.g. Hahn, *Titles*, pp. 28–34; R. H. Fuller, *The Foundations of New Testament Christology*, London: Lutterworth 1965, p. 119–25.

46. E.g. E. Käsemann, 'The Beginnings of Christian Theology', *New Testament Questions of Today*, ET London: SCM Press 1969, pp. 82–107, here pp. 101, 107; Perrin, *Rediscovering*, pp. 164–85.

47. Not to be forgotten is the fact that in Dan. 8.17 Daniel himself is addressed as 'son of man'!

48. See particularly Schürer 3.259; also Dunn, *Christology*, pp. 67–82.

the vision only to give expression to his own hopes of vindication following his rejection and death – he would *become* Son of Man[49] – a not implausible suggestion, at least insofar as the man-like figure of the vision clearly represents 'the saints of the Most High' in their vindication after suffering (Dan. 7.14 = 7.22, 27). But even if we go further and maintain that Jesus saw himself as already the Son of Man – his role as Son of Man running unbroken through to its climax in the living out of Daniel's vision – the significance remains unclear. For in sayings like Luke 12.8 ('Everyone who acknowledges me before men, the Son of Man also will acknowledge before the angels of God'), or Mark 14.62 ('You will see the Son of Man seated at the right hand of Power, and coming with the clouds of heaven'), the Son of Man is not presented as any kind of alternative to God – rather as God's agent in judgment. There was nothing un-Jewish about that; on the contrary, as we shall see, various heroes of the past featured in first-century Jewish speculation as playing a role in the final judgment, as God's scribe, and so forth.[50] Only in Matt. 25.31ff. (the parable of the sheep and the goats) is the Son of Man spoken of as a king in his own right, and many would be doubtful about the authenticity of the Son of Man reference at this point for that very reason – so unusual is it in the Jesus-tradition. Even so, it would then be on a par with Matt. 19.28 – Jesus as the Son of Man, as chief judge along with the twelve – God having presumably bestowed the role of judge on each (cf. the parallel in Luke 22.29–30).

In short, *even if Jesus did draw on Dan. 7.13 to express his hope and conviction regarding his future vindication in particular, that would not be un-Jewish in character, and would be quite consistent with a strongly held monotheism.*

9.5 Jesus' authority

For those who are suspicious about a discussion too much dependent on 'titles', the issue can be focussed much more clearly in terms of Jesus' *authority*. Whatever title Jesus did or did not use or lay claim to, did he not speak and act in a way which showed him to be *the*

---

49. Jeremias, *Theology*, pp. 274–6.

50. See below §10.2. In the LXX the text of Dan 7.13 reads, 'Behold on the clouds of heaven there came one like a son of man, and came *like* the Ancient of days . . .'; instead of the Hebrew,' . . . and came *to* the Ancient of days . . .'. But the significance of the distinctive Greek is not evident, it is not drawn out in any Jewish or Christian text making use of Dan 7, and anyway the text would not have been familiar to Jesus, or indeed probably to those who made the earliest and most creative use of the Jesus-tradition at this point.

representative or spokesman for God, and so to have understood himself?

There can be little doubt that Jesus was remembered for the authority with which he spoke. The fact that he was able to call various individuals literally to follow him is evidence enough. Moreover, a note of amazement among the crowds at the authority of his words and actions is struck on several occasions in the Synoptic traditions (particularly Mark 1.27 par.; 6.2 par.). And the Jerusalem authorities are recalled as asking him 'By what authority' he acted, following his action in the Temple (Mark 11.28). The surprise was occasioned, presumably in part at least, by Jesus' lack of formal training as a teacher. Yet we must recall that there were others who were remembered for the authority with which they taught. Not least, the Teacher of Righteousness at Qumran, who obviously stamped his teaching and interpretation of the scriptures on the sect who formed round him (e.g. 1QpHab 6.14–7.5; CD 1.12–13; 6.7–11).[51] Both Jesus and the Teacher of Righteousness could be seen as a threat to the organized and traditional methods of teaching and channels of tradition. But that would not make them subversive of divine authority, any more than the earlier prophets in their critique of the religious authorities of their day.

The same is probably true of Jesus' pronouncing sins forgiven in Mark 2.5, as we saw earlier.[52] To pronounce sins forgiven was already the prerogative of the priest in the cult. Only God could dispense with the authorized channels. But in the event, what was put in question by Jesus' pronouncement was not God's authority so much as the cult's. And if he authorized his disciples in turn (cf. Matt. 18.18 with John 20.23), that is presumably to be understood as a re-channelling of authority *from* God, not as any usurpation of God's authority.

The same is probably true of passages where Jesus seems to link himself with the figure of divine Wisdom. In Luke 7.35 he calls himself a child of Wisdom. In Matt. 11.25–27/Luke 10.21–22 the claim to speak with a uniqueness of authority and knowledge is framed in characteristic Wisdom language. And in Luke 11.49–51 the implication is that Jesus spoke as the emissary of Wisdom. Whatever the origin of these passages, the point is that in the earliest form in which we have them, Jesus is shown as speaking within the tradition of a teacher of divine wisdom, as indeed a spokesman for divine Wisdom.

---

51. See Vermes, *Dead Sea Scrolls*, p. 40.
52. See above §3.3.

Only with Matthew's editing and elaboration of these passages (Matt. 11.19, 28–30; 23.34–37) does the transition come from Jesus the *emissary* of Wisdom to Jesus *identified with* the figure of Wisdom herself.[53]

The same is true not least of Jesus' actions, including his healings and exorcisms. We should not fall into the trap of thinking that such miracles *prove* anything. Matt. 12.27 ('by whom do your sons cast out demons?') reminds us that there were plenty of other Jewish exorcists at the time of Jesus. And Jesus refused to produce a sign as 'proof' (Mark 8.11–12 pars.). The history of Christianity shows beyond dispute that a 'miracle' is only a miracle to faith; where faith is lacking, there is no 'miracle'.

There is more to be said here, but at first glance it does not seem to take us any further than the approach through titles. For all that Jesus spoke and acted with authority, *he still stood within the traditions of Jewish religiosity and inspiration*.

9.6 Jesus in the Fourth Gospel

The only clear exception to the testimony thus far adduced is the Jesus of the Fourth Gospel. There Jesus speaks with an unclouded consciousness of a divine existence with God from before his time on earth. We need think only of such discourses and dialogues as John 5.19ff. and 8.12ff. for the point to be clear. *The Jesus of the Fourth Gospel would have put a severe strain on Jewish monotheism* and probably could not have been retained within Judaism – as indeed events proved, but we shall come back to that.[54] Here the question which cannot be ducked is whether the Jesus of the Fourth Gospel was intended as a *historical* portrayal, whether Jesus of Nazareth actually spoke in the terms used by the Fourth Gospel. Were the christological claims of John's Gospel already in place from the beginning of Christianity? It is hardly likely. The following considerations which, once again require fuller discussion to do them real justice, should be noted.

(*a*) The points at which the Fourth Gospel makes its highest and most unequivocal claims regarding Jesus are all points where the Fourth Gospel goes *beyond* the Synoptics' portrayal of Jesus. (1) Jesus as the Son. In the Synoptics Jesus rarely speaks of God as Father.[55]

---

53. See also below §11.3 and further my *Christology*, pp. 197–202.
54. See below §11.5–7.
55. For discussion of Matt. 11.27, Mark 12.6, 13.32 and Luke 22.29–30 see my *Jesus*, pp. 26–37.

But in John this language is all pervasive.[56] So, for example, the talk of Jesus as the Son sent by the Father, that is from heaven (about forty times in John), is something we never find in the Synoptic accounts. (2) Jesus as the Son of Man. Wholly distinctive of the Fourth Gospel is talk of the descending/ascending Son of Man, and the Son of Man as 'lifted up' (John 3.13–14; 6.62; 8.28; 12.34). (3) Not least, there is the whole new category of sayings of Jesus – the 'I ams' ('I am the bread of life', 'I am the light of the world', etc.), including 8.58: 'Before Abraham was, I am'. There is *nothing* like them in the Synoptics.[57] If they were historical, their omission by the Synoptic Evangelists is absolutely astonishing and inexplicable.

(b) The way Jesus speaks in the Fourth Gospel is consistently Johannine, and consistently distinct from the way he speaks in the Synoptics. In John, Jesus speaks in the *same* way, whether in Galilee or in Jerusalem, whether to Galilean peasants or to Jerusalem intelligentsia, whether to opponents or to disciples. He uses the same language as John the Baptist, the same language as I John. Where in the Synoptics his characteristic style is the wisdom saying, the pungent epigram, in the Fourth Gospel he uses long, often convoluted discourses. In the Synoptics he speaks rarely of himself, and much of God's kingdom; in the Fourth Gospel the position is completely the reverse.[58] With such differences the most obvious explanation is that this is the style of the *Fourth Evangelist, not* of Jesus. The style and content of Jesus' teaching in the Synoptics is too consistent to allow any other conclusion than that it closely reflects the teaching of Jesus. Whereas the teaching of the Fourth Gospel can hardly be explained as other than the much developed theological reflection of the fourth evangelist.[59]

(c) Particularly striking is the contrast between the different portrayals of Jesus' teaching on and practice of prayer. In the Synoptics Jesus is portrayed as a man who needed to pray, sometimes all night, and in the garden of Gethsemane with great distress (Mark 14.33; 'with loud cries and tears' – Heb. 5.7); and as one who warned against

---

56.

	Mark	Q	Luke	Matthew	John
'Father'	3	4	4	31	100
'the Father'	1	1	2	1	73

57. Including Mark 6.50 and the longer text of 14.62.

58.

	Matthew	Mark	Luke	John
'Kingdom'	47	18	37	5
'I'	17	9	10	118

59. For a fuller, though popular treatment see my *The Evidence for Jesus*, London: SCM Press/Philadelphia: Westminster 1985, pp. 30–45.

praying for show (Matt. 6.5).[60] But in the Fourth Gospel Jesus is portrayed rather as one who is so far above events that no real prayer is necessary; and the parody of prayer in John 11.41–42 ('I have said this on account of the crowd standing by . . .') simply underlines how far removed is the Johannine Jesus from the Synoptic Jesus, and thus also, at these points at least, from the historical Jesus.

(d) Finally we might simply note that if Jesus had so spoken as in the Fourth Gospel, it is astonishing that there is no greater mark of it elsewhere in the NT, not just in the Synoptics, but also in the other NT writings. For, so far as our present inquiry is concerned, the simple fact is that the Jesus of the Fourth Gospel is barely containable within second Temple Judaism as we know it. And those who followed this Jesus and affirmed of him what the Fourth Evangelist affirms could not have remained undisturbed within the synagogues of Palestine as long as they evidently did. We have already seen that the movement towards a final parting of the ways was a fairly drawn-out process running through the first century. But *had Jesus spoken in the terms ascribed to him in the Fourth Gospel the crisis must have come much sooner.* Whereas, as we shall see, christology did not become a critical factor in the parting of the ways till much later.[61]

In short, the only obvious conclusion to be drawn from the above is that the Fourth Gospel's portrayal of Christ is evidence for a later stage of christology and of the resulting tensions between 'the Jews' and the believers in Messiah Jesus, *not* for the first stage.

9.7 The eschatological plus

So far, then, we have found little enough in the ministry and teaching of Jesus itself which could explain how it was that Jesus came to be accorded the divine significance which soon became a feature of Christian claims. We cannot, of course, exclude the possibility that these claims all stem from later events, including the resurrection – a subject to which we will return (§§10.1–2). Yet it would be surprising if there was complete discontinuity between Jesus' pre-Easter self-understanding and such post-Easter assertions. Is there perhaps more to be said? – some indications from the earliest Gospel traditions of why it was that Jesus became the figure round which divine significance gathered, rather than, say, John the Baptist. Not a full blown christological claim which must have broken out of the categories

---

60. See also above §9.1(*b*).
61. See again below §§11.5–7.

and language of second Temple Judaism straight away. That we would already have noted. And if that is what we have been looking for, the quest has been unsuccessful. But elements which must have been uncomfortable from the first, even within the variegated forms of first-century Judaism – so uncomfortable as to force a choice for or against this Jesus and for or against those who followed him. Here there may indeed be something more to be said. Once again, however, we can only indicate the scope of the data rather than give it the thorough examination it requires.

(*a*) Jesus evidently was seen as a prophet, and indeed saw himself in prophetic terms (e.g. Mark 6.4, 15; 8.28).[62] But the category was inadequate (as the opinions reported in Mark 6.15 and 8.28 indicate). Here was someone, or something, greater than Jonah the prophet (Matt. 12.41/Luke 11.30). Probably we have to say, therefore, that it was not simply as a prophet that Jesus called for attention, but as one who is better described as the '*eschatological prophet*'. One of the end-time figures of Jewish expectation was the prophet envisaged in Isa. 61.1–2. Jesus evidently saw this prophecy as programmatic for his own mission: this is the testimony not only of Luke 4.18f., but is also clearly implicit in the Q material preserved in Matt. 5.3–4 and 11.5.[63]

Jesus is also recalled as having spoken of himself as sent by God, as a prophetic emissary (Matt. 10.40/Luke 10.16), but perhaps with a sense of transcending the category of prophet (cf. Mark 12.1–9 – his prophetic predecessors as 'servants'; himself as 'son').[64] C. H. Dodd made the interesting suggestion that just as Jesus' words 'I say to you' may take us beyond the prophetic consciousness expressed in the typical prophetic formulation, 'Thus says the Lord', so Jesus' words, 'I came' (Mark 2.17 pars.; Matt. 11.19; Luke 12.49), might likewise take us beyond the more typically prophetic formulation, 'I was sent'.[65]

Something more than a prophet was here.

---

62. See also my *Jesus*, pp. 82–4.

63. For fuller discussion see my *Jesus*, pp. 53–62. We should note the influence of this passage also in Qumran expectation as indicated at least by 11QMelch.

64. This is the nearest the Synoptic tradition gets to the full blown 'Son sent by the Father' christology of the Fourth Gospel (above §9.6a), and presumably shows us one of the roots of that full growth.

65. C. H. Dodd, 'Jesus as Teacher and Prophet', *Mysterium Christi*, ed. G. K. A. Bell and A. Deissmann, London: Longmans 1930, pp. 53–66: 'We may perhaps trace here the same transition from the prophetic to the more-than-prophetic which is marked by the difference between "Thus saith the Lord", and "I say unto you"' (p. 63).

(*b*) Similarly we should note that our traditions portray Jesus not simply as an exorcist, but as *one who made striking claims regarding his exorcisms.*

(1) He saw them as *the defeat of Satan*, as the casting out of Satan himself (Mark 3.23; Luke 10.18), as the plundering of his goods (Mark 3.27). The significance of this is that, though exorcisms as such were not regarded as a mark of the new age, the binding of the powers of evil *was* looked forward to at the end of the age.[66] We may deduce, therefore, that Jesus saw his exorcisms as a demonstration that the end of the age was already present, that the final reign of God was already in operation. He is recalled, indeed, as making precisely that claim: that his exorcisms were evidence that the kingly rule which God would exercise in the new age was already in effective operation (Matt. 12.28/Luke 11.20). The claim that the expected blessings of the new age, healings and restoration to wholeness, were evident in his ministry (Matt. 11.5/Luke 7.22; Matt. 13.17/Luke 10.24), is simply the positive side of the same conviction.

(2) He also understood his exorcisms as *empowered by the Spirit.* Particularly worthy of note is the antithesis in Matt. 12.27–28 – '. . . by whom do your sons cast them out? . . . But since it is by the Spirit of God that I cast out demons, then has come upon you the kingdom of God' (where 'Spirit' and 'kingdom of God' are in the places of emphasis in the sentence). Hence the rather frightening conclusion Jesus drew regarding the sin of blaspheming against the Holy Spirit (Mark 3.29): the effect of his ministry of exorcism was so obviously beneficial, that to deny it was the worst kind of perversity; so to confuse deliberately the power of God for good and the power of Satan for evil, was to turn one's back on God and so also on his forgiveness.

(3) Also implicit is a further difference between Jesus' exorcisms and other exorcisms. Typical of exorcisms at that time was the use of physical aids: in Tobit, burning the heart and liver of a fish (Tobit 8.2–3); in the case of the Jewish exorcist, Eleazar, exorcising before Vespasian, the smell of a root in a ring (Josephus, *Ant.* 8.46–47); in the magical papyri, amulets. Also typical was the invocation of some authority or power source, regularly using the formula, 'I adjure you by . . .' (as in Acts 19.13). But Jesus evidently used no such aids, and, more important, used no such formula. Rather we find the straight command – 'I command you' (Mark 9.25) – with the implication, once again, that Jesus acted *in consciousness of his own authority, in*

---

66. See Isa. 24.21–2; *I Enoch* 10.4ff.; 11ff.; 1QS 4.18–19; *Test. Levi* 18.12; *Test. Jud.* 25.3; so also Rev. 20.1–3.

the immediacy and directness of an authority and power from God.[67]

Here too we may justly conclude, there was something more than just an exorcist present – and in his own self-estimation at that.

(*c*) So too, if we return to the subject of Jesus' authority, we may say that Jesus taught not simply as a teacher, like one of the contemporary Pharisees of whom we know, but *with a self-conscious authority.*

(1) The word 'Amen', meaning 'certainly' in both Hebrew and Aramaic, was clearly characteristic of Jesus' teaching style (used thirteen times in Mark, and eighteen times in the non-Markan tradition of Jesus' teaching). As Jeremias points out, in Jewish usage 'amen' affirmed, endorsed and appropriated the words of *someone else* (cf. I Cor. 14.26). But in the Jesus-tradition it is used *without exception* to introduce and endorse Jesus' own words.[68]

(2) Equally striking is the emphatic 'I' in the formula, 'But I say to you'. We should note particularly the antitheses which use this formula in Matt. 5.21–48 and which embody a claim to authority which seems to rival that of Moses.[69] Where the prophet typically said, 'Thus says the Lord', Jesus said, 'But I say . . .'.[70] Presumably implicit is the claim to be fulfilling the hope of a 'prophet like Moses' (Deut. 18.15, 18).

(3) Not only so, but we should also note the significance Jesus is remembered as putting upon his own words. In the final parable of the Sermon on the Mount Jesus portrays his hearers' whole lives as dependent on whether or not they build their lives on the foundation of his teaching (Matt. 7.24–27). And in speaking of the final judgment Jesus speaks with similar gravity. 'Whoever is ashamed of me and of my words . . . of him will the son of man be ashamed when he comes in the glory of his father . . .'. (Mark 8.38 par.). 'Everyone who acknowledges me before men, I also will acknowledge before my

---

67. See further J. D. G. Dunn and G. H. Twelftree, 'Demon-Possession and Exorcism in the New Testament', *Churchman* 94 (1980), pp. 210–25; G. H. Twelftree, *Christ Triumphant. Exorcism Then and Now*, London: Hodder and Stoughton 1985, ch. 3.

68. J. Jeremias, *The Prayers of Jesus*, London: SCM Press 1967, p. 112.

69. Even if some of the antitheses were put into that form by Matthew, he most probably worked from a model provided by the Jesus-tradition itself. So e.g. R. Bultmann, *The History of the Synoptic Tradition*, ET Oxford: Blackwell 1963, pp. 134–6. Cf. particularly E. Käsemann, 'The Problem of the Historical Jesus', *Essays on New Testament Themes*, ET London: SCM Press 1960, pp. 15–47, here pp. 37ff.

70. E. P. Sanders in an unpublished paper ('The Question of Uniqueness in the Teaching of Jesus', delivered at the Historical Jesus seminar at the Milan SNTS Conference, 1990) denies that there is anything 'unique' about the formula, 'But I say', by comparing the formula in 4QMMT, 'and concerning [this] we say'. But the distinctiveness of the first person singular formulation of Jesus remains.

Father who is in heaven' (Matt. 10.32 par.). How his hearers would fare in the final judgment was dependent on their reaction to him and his teaching.

It is in this context that a charge of blasphemy (Mark 14.64) begins to make sense. For the claim to play a decisive role in the final judgment could be regarded as usurping divine authority, if it was an unauthorized claim. Contrariwise, in making such a claim Jesus would have been claiming an authority which had only been accorded to other exceptional heroes of the faith like Enoch,[71] though an authority nevertheless accorded by God (cf. again Luke 22.29–30), and to that extent *not* liable to the charge of blasphemy.

In all this we can say that Jesus taught with *a degree of self-consciousness of being God's spokesman, able to act and speak in God's stead, which is only partially paralleled within the Jewish tradition.* He claimed an immediacy of apprehension of God's will which outstrips and surpasses anything else we know of for the period.[72]

(d) Finally we should note again *Jesus' call to discipleship.* We have time to mention here only a few features. (1) The exclusiveness of the claim: 'He who loves father or mother more than me is not worthy of me; and he who loves son or daughter more than me is not worthy of me' (Matt. 10.37/Luke 14.26). (2) Jesus chose twelve. He did not choose another eleven, who, together with him, would make up the symbolical representatives of the twelve tribes of the new age. *Evidently he held himself in self-conscious distinctiveness from the representatives of eschatological Israel.* (3) His use of 'Abba' in prayer to God may be said to imply a similar sense of distinctiveness. For although he evidently taught his disciples to pray in the same way (Luke 11.2), it was precisely *his disciples* whom he so taught. The implication being, presumably, that their saying 'Abba' was an expression of their discipleship, as somehow dependent on his 'Abba'. This is certainly implied also in Rom. 8.15–16 and Gal. 4.6 – that to say 'Abba' was to share *his* sonship.[73] Perhaps then it is significant that while we have Jesus on a number of occasions saying 'my Father' and 'your Father', we have no instance of him joining with his disciples to say 'our Father'.[74]

---

71. See below §10.2.

72. Sanders, *Jesus*, p. 271, accepts that 'Jesus claimed to be spokesman for God', without wishing to put so much weight on the point.

73. See also above p. 170.

74. The point is treated more fully in my *Jesus*, pp. 24–6.

To sum up. When we review the Jesus-tradition, we find an impressive build up of evidence, all of which would be hard to deny to the historical Jesus on sound criteria of critical scholarship, which carries with it *clear implication that Jesus acted and taught with a consider-able degree of self-conscious authority as the eschatological spokes-man for God.*

At the same time, we should take note of the ordinariness of it all. In the age of Jesus there were plenty of parallels of people who laid claim to or whose office embodied the claim to divine authority: individuals who spoke in ecstasy in the person of the god who was thought to possess them;[75] and kings whose very title expressed the claim to be manifestations of the deity ('Epiphanes'). But there was nothing quite like this son of an artisan, who, in sober and wholly rational speech, claimed to speak for God as his representative at the end of the age; nothing quite like the unassuming arrogance of his egotism – 'But *I* say to you . . .'[76]

9.8 Conclusion

We have had to cover a great deal of ground at a considerable pace. The picture which emerged from most of the discussion was of a Jesus who used, or resisted, categories which were familiar to his Jewish audience, and which could be claimed for or applied to a first-century Jew without putting in question the daily saying of the *Shema'*. Even when we looked at his authority our initial finding had similar effect.

In the final section, however, it became necessary to complement the findings of the earlier part of the chapter by drawing attention to a number of resonances within the Jesus-tradition, all of which indi-cated a 'something more', an 'eschatological plus'. The point, how-ever, is that it was (and is) all implicit. We today can certainly hear these resonances. We can readily see how such words must have sounded to the first Christians, how evocative and expressive of the explicit claims they found it necessary to formulate on their own account. In other words, we can see the roots of future christology quite clearly – including the high and developed christology of the Fourth Gospel.

But at the level of Jesus, that was all in the future. *There was nothing yet which called in question the traditional understanding of God and of his revealing his will through chosen emissaries.* 'Messiah'

---

75. The word 'enthusiasm' in its original usage denoted someone who was thought to be inspired, possessed by a god (see LSJ, *enthousiazō*).

76. Cf. the conclusions of Riches, *Jesus*, ch. 8, particularly pp. 187–9.

was yet to receive and establish its peculiarly Christian interpretation. 'Son of God' was yet to be focussed on Jesus in an exclusive way. 'Son of man' was yet to become a clear title. The claim to authority implicit in his teaching was like new wine fermenting within old wineskins; but the old wineskins had by no means yet burst; the fermenting process had some way to go. In all this, despite Mussner, there was nothing 'un-Jewish' in what Jesus said or did.[77] The reason why Jesus was done to death in the end of the day was more due to political than to religious considerations – less because he claimed an unacceptable authority for himself and his teaching, more because he was in danger of undermining the authority of the Temple and the status quo. Only in the Fourth Gospel do we find claims on the lips of Jesus which could be understood as subversive of the unity of God. Otherwise the most we find is a claim to exercise an authority bestowed in a direct and immediate way by God alone.

For all that Christians can and did make much of what Jesus did and said in the light of Good Friday and Easter, therefore, *Jesus himself still stood well within the boundaries of second Temple Judaism at the point of Jewish monotheism.* For all the ferment he caused, this Jesus could have been absorbed and retained within a Judaism which did not become Christianity.

---

77. Mussner, *Tractate*, pp. 215–20.

One God, One Lord

10.1 The significance of the resurrection for Jesus

The conclusion of chapter 9 was in effect that the significance of the ministry (including the death)[1] of Jesus could have been contained within the complex of Israel's history of great heroes – particularly its prophets, but also those who in retrospect were seen best to represent or embody Israel's destiny.[2] This is true even if the effort to contain him would have meant the stretching of some of these categories: Jesus as prophet, when prophecy was thought to have ceased long since; Jesus as eschatological prophet, as revealer of God's purpose (kingdom) and will, with an authority which rivalled that of Moses; and so on. The very fact that many Jews today are prepared to make room for Jesus within their tradition, as one of the greatest prophets and rabbis is sufficient proof of this.[3]

It is equally clear that what *began* to make the decisive difference was *the resurrection of Jesus* – the belief that God had not abandoned Jesus to death, but had raised him from the dead. There is no need here to discuss the 'what' of the resurrection. Suffice it to say that the first Christian preachers made this claim *the basis or hinge of their proclamation*. The point is easily documented. The evangelistic sermons in Acts consistently give the resurrection of Jesus the place of primary importance – typically in the form, 'Jesus was delivered to death; but God raised him up. Of this we are witnesses' (Acts 2.24–32; 3.15, 22–26; 10.40–41; 13.30–37; 17.31). The complaint made against the first disciples was that they were 'proclaiming in Jesus the resurrection from the dead' (4.2). In Athens those who heard Paul thought he was proclaiming two new divinities, evidently because he spoke so much about Jesus and Anastasis ('resurrection'); that is to

---

1. See also above pp. 71–2.
2. I put it thus to include the categories of Messiah and Son of Man at all the stages of their development, both prior to and within Christianity.
3. See e.g. D. A. Hagner, *The Jewish Reclamation of Jesus: An Analysis and Critique of the Modern Jewish Study of Jesus*, Grand Rapids: Zondervan 1984.

say, they thought that 'Resurrection' was the female consort of Jesus (17.18).

So too in the pre-Pauline confessional and kerygmatic formulae it is the resurrection of Jesus which receives most prominence. In Romans, for example, we need only cite 1.3–4, 4.24–25 and 8.34, passages which most commentators recognize to contain pre-Pauline statements.[4] Rom. 10.9 is widely recognized as one of the earliest baptismal confessions: 'If you confess with your lips that Jesus is Lord and believe in your heart that God raised him from the dead, you will be saved' – belief in the resurrection of Jesus as the decisive factor in salvation. To take but one other example, I Cor. 15.1–8 contains Paul's own testimony regarding the fundamental statement of the gospel which he himself had received when first converted, and which he had preached to the Corinthians as the basis of salvation – where, once again, it is the witness to the resurrection of Jesus which is given most prominence. So much so that Paul could go on to indicate that for him it was the resurrection of Jesus which made the decisive difference between the viability and relevance of his message or other-wise: 'If Christ has not been raised, your faith is futile and you are still in your sins' (I Cor. 15.17).

In fact, *it is impossible realistically to envisage a form of Christianity which did not have this conviction at its heart and basis.* The main point for us, however, is the *significance* of the resurrection for christology. What was it that God did in raising Jesus from the dead?

Here we must void two side-tracks or mistakes: the one of *under-estimating* the significance of the resurrection; the other of reading in to it *too much too soon.* (1) The first mistake is seen in the interpretation of the resurrection formulae as evidence solely of something having happened to the *disciples.* Thus Rudolf Bultmann wanted to speak of no more in historical terms than 'the rise of Easter faith'.[5] And Willi Marxsen has maintained that the message of the resurrection reduces to the recognition or conviction that the cause of Jesus could not die.[6] Of course, it is technically possible to see Easter faith as a projection or expression of some other more basic conviction about Jesus. But the fact remains that its irreducible formal expression

---

4. See e.g. W. Kramer, *Christ, Lord, Son of God,* 1963; ET London: SCM Press 1966, pp. 29–26, 108–11.

5. R. Bultmann, 'New Testament and Mythology', in H. W. Bartsch (ed.), *Kerygma and Myth,* ET London: SPCK 1957, p. 42 – 'If the event of Easter Day is in any sense an historical event additional to the event of the cross, it is nothing else than the rise of faith in the risen Lord . . . the historical event of the rise of Easter faith . . .'

6. W. Marxsen, *The Resurrection of Jesus of Nazareth,* ET London: SCM Press/Philadelphia: Fortress 1970, pp. 125–6: 'Easter meant that the cause of Jesus continues.'

is of something having happened to Jesus, not just to the disciples. God raised *Jesus*; he did not simply bring comfort to the disciples. If 'the resurrection of Jesus' does not mean that something happened to Jesus himself, then the character of Christian faith becomes so radically different from what it has been understood to be from the beginning that it has actually become something else – not simply a difference in degree, but a difference in kind.

(2) The other danger is of assuming that the full significance of the resurrection of Jesus, which we now see so clearly with the benefit of hindsight, was already so clear from the first. Like every other piece of earliest Christian tradition or data we have to set earliest Christian belief in Jesus' resurrection within its historical context. As with the material reviewed in §9 (particularly Messiah, Son of God, Son of Man), the earliest expressions were probably different, less well formed. There is no doubt that christology, properly speaking, was in process of coming into existence and developing at this time; apart from anything else, there were things believed about a man (Jesus) at the end of the first century which had not been said of any other man within Jewish tradition before Christ. So it is not a question of *whether* these developments happened. The question is simply *how quickly* did these developments take place? We who see how these developments worked out in the subsequent credal forms should discipline ourselves by attempting to enter within the limited horizons of these first Christians who could have had no idea how the classic creeds would come to expression.[7]

The point for us, then, is not to call that development in question, but simply to note that in its *earliest* expressions the christology which grew out of the resurrection (or resurrection faith, if you prefer), *continued to remain within Jewish categories and without offering, or being seen to offer, any threat to the traditional Jewish belief in God*. The point becomes clear when we take note that contemporary Jewish thought was even then making considerable use of the concept of the exaltation or vindication of heroes of the faith.

10.2 Exaltation to divine functions

To those who are accustomed to thinking of Christian belief in Jesus' resurrection as something unique, the number and range of possible parallels already current within second Temple Judaism is something of a surprise.

---

7. See also the Foreword to the second edition of my *Christology*, pp. xi–xxxix.

(*a*) The category of *resurrection* itself is certainly not un-Jewish. On the contrary, belief in the resurrection was an already established feature of faith for many Jews – particularly Pharisees.[8] Such a belief could be traced back at least as far as Dan. 12.2. Jesus himself shared that belief, along with the Pharisees, over against the Sadducees, as the well-known story in the Gospels reminds us (Mark 12.18–28 pars.). And the report of Paul using the Pharisaic belief in the resurrection to split the council consisting of Pharisees and Sadducees has a strong ring of truth (Acts 23.6).

It is certainly surprising that a number of Jews should believe that the resurrection had happened for a single individual *before* the final resurrection (that is, the 'general' resurrection, prior to the final judgment). But it would appear that *the first Christians actually believed that Jesus' resurrection was (literally) the beginning of the general resurrection*. Thus the early credal formula in Rom. 1.4 speaks of Jesus' exaltation *not* as from *his* resurrection *from* the dead, but 'as from the resurrection of the dead'. And the image of Christ's resurrection as the 'first-fruits' of the general resurrection has the same implication, since in the harvest, from which the metaphor is drawn, the first-fruits was literally the first sheaf to be reaped – that is, the beginning of the harvest itself (Rom. 8.23). Likewise the most obvious explanation of the ancient tradition preserved in Matt. 27.52–53 (the saints raised from their tombs at Jesus' crucifixion, but only appeared 'to many' after his resurrection) is that Jesus' resurrection was early on thought of as the 'trigger' for a more general resurrection. If anything, *that* is the surprising feature of earliest Christian belief – not so much the use of the category of 'resurrection' itself.

It may even be that a 'one-off' resurrection of an individual was something believable at the time of Jesus. Such could be the testimony of Mark 6.14 pars. and Luke 9.8. In the former, the popular belief is reported that Jesus was 'John the baptizer raised from the dead'. And in the latter, the similar belief or speculation is reported that Jesus was 'one of the ancient prophets risen (from the dead)'. Whether these reports are historical, or reflect some influence of Christian belief in Jesus as raised need not concern us here. The fact is that such beliefs or speculations could be credited to the Jewish populace without any sense of impropriety – because belief in the resurrection was something characteristically Jewish. Certainly it cannot be irrelevant to our inquiry that a Jew like Pinchas Lapide can conclude

---

8. Schürer, 2.391–2, 498, 501, 539–44.

that Jesus was indeed raised from the dead and affirm it precisely as a Jew.[9]

(*b*) *Ascension* to heaven is also attested of Jesus, whether as a category coincident with or subsequent to his resurrection (Luke 24.50; Acts 1.9; 3.13; Rom. 10.6; Eph. 4.8–10; etc.). Here again Jewish writers were quite familiar with such a thought. Enoch and Elijah had been translated to heaven (Gen. 5.24; II Kings 2.11). The righteous martyrs of Wisd. 5 fully expected to be numbered with the sons of God/angels (Wisd. 5.5, 15–16). Towards the end of the first century CE Jewish writings could speak of Ezra and Baruch as having been taken up to heaven (*IV Ezra* 14.9; *II Bar.* 13.3; etc.) without any sense of their having thereby crossed a decisive boundary between the human and the divine.

(*c*) *Apotheosis* is also a relevant category, since several texts clearly imply that the resurrection-exaltation of Jesus made him something more than he had previously been: by means of the resurrection 'God made Jesus both Lord and Christ' (Acts 2.36); the words of Ps. 2.7 are referred to the resurrection of Jesus in both Acts and Hebrews – 'You are my Son, today I have begotten you' (Acts 13.33; Heb. 5.5); Jesus was 'appointed Son of God in power as from the resurrection of the dead' (Rom. 1.4).[10] But this category too has its context within a Judaism which could embrace speculation about Enoch being transformed on his translation to heaven (*Jub.* 4.22–23; *I Enoch* 12–16; *II Enoch* 22.8). In a famous text, *I Enoch* 71.14, Enoch is even identified as the heavenly Son of Man.[11] In Sir. 45.2 we read that God made Moses 'equal in glory to the holy ones (angels)'.[12] And Josephus reports speculation as to whether Moses had been taken or had returned to 'the deity' (*Ant.* 3.96–7; 4.326; cf. Philo, *Sac.* 8–10; *Mos.* 2.290).[13] Likewise in the (probably Christian) Ascension of Isaiah, Isaiah is transformed into heavenly form when taken up to heaven (particularly 9.30). Nor should we forget that Jesus himself is recalled

---

9. P. Lapide, *The Resurrection of Jesus*, ET London: SPCK 1984. To that extent therefore one would have to qualify Osten-Sacken's judgment that 'Christian . . . confession of faith in Jesus' resurrection and . . . the development of what this confession of faith means . . . is the parting of the ways for the Jewish and Christian understandings of the man from Nazareth' (*Christian–Jewish Dialogue*, p. 58).

10. The word translated 'appointed' is often taken in a weaker sense (e.g. NEB, NIV – 'declared to be'). But see my *Romans*, p. 13 and those cited there.

11. See further below §11.6b.

12. L. W. Hurtado, *One God, One Lord. Early Christian Devotion and Ancient Jewish Monotheism*, Philadelphia: Fortress/London: SCM Press 1988, p. 56.

13. See also J. D. Tabor, ' "Returning to the Divinity": Josephus's Portrayal of the Disappearance of Enoch, Elijah, and Moses', *JBL* 108 (1989), pp. 225–38.

as speaking of the resurrected as 'like the angels in heaven' (Mark 12.25).

(*d*) The exalted Jesus is spoken of as *sharing in divine functions*, particularly that of judge: 'God will judge the world in righteousness by a man whom he has appointed...' (Acts 17.31; similarly Rom. 2.16); 'We must all appear before the judgment seat of Christ' (II Cor. 5.10). But here again the most striking parallel feature of the then current Enoch speculation is precisely the role attributed to Enoch in the final judgment (references as in (*c*)). Enoch is linked with Elijah in this role in *I Enoch* 90.31 and the *Apocalypse of Elijah* 24.11–15. In 11 QMelchizedek, Melchizedek is depicted as a heavenly being – apparently the angelic leader ('elohim') of the holy ones who execute judgment on Belial and his host (lines 13–14). In the *Testament of Abraham* 11 and 13 Adam and Abel are shown in similarly exalted roles. Perhaps above all we need to recall that in our own texts first the twelve are said to be given share in the final judgment (Matt. 19.28/Luke 22.30 – sitting on twelve thrones judging the twelve tribes of Israel), and then the saints as a whole – 'Do you not know that the saints will judge the world? ... Do you not know that we are to judge angels?' (I Cor. 6.2–3).

(*e*) The most striking function of the exalted Christ might seem to be his *power to bestow the Holy Spirit on others*: 'Being therefore exalted at the right hand of God, and having received from the Father the promise of the Holy Spirit, he has poured out this which you see and hear' (Acts 2.33).[14] Yet John the Baptist had evidently expected the Coming One to bestow the Spirit (Mark 1.8 pars.). Who he thought the Coming One to be is one of the unsolved mysteries of the period; John himself may not have had any clear idea. But at least we can say it is very unlikely that he thought the Coming One was divine, otherwise his talk of not being worthy to loosen the thongs of his sandals would have been ridiculous (Mark 1.7 pars.). And Simon Magus was rebuked for seeking to buy the power to bestow the Spirit, not for any overboldness in attributing such power to Peter (Acts 8.17–20).

The point is surely clear. Within second Temple Judaism there was nothing un-Jewish in thinking that a great man had been signally honoured by God by being taken to heaven, whether without death or after death. There was nothing un-Jewish in claiming that such a one had been given share in such definitively divine roles as the

---

14. M. M. B. Turner, 'The Spirit of Christ and Christology', *Christ the Lord. Studies in Christology presented to D. Guthrie*, ed. H. H. Rowdon, Leicester: IVP 1982, pp. 168–90 (particularly pp. 182–3).

exercise of final judgment over the world. Just as no point of constitutive substance in second Temple Judaism was called in question when a
Jew recognized another as Messiah or son of God, so *no fundamental
element in second Temple Judaism was shaken by the speculation,*
not uncharacteristic of the first century CE, *that God had exalted a
favoured servant of his to heaven and given him authority such as no
man on earth could think to enjoy.*

Of course Christian apologetic can make a great deal of the fact
that the first Christians used the primary category of *resurrection* to
describe what they believed had happened to Jesus, and not just
vindication by exaltation to heaven after death. And the fact that they
should thus believe that in Jesus' resurrection the general resurrection
had already begun remains astonishing, a fact from which much
greater significance can be drawn.[15] But the fact remains that the
categories used are thoroughly Jewish, and that *their use in reference
to Jesus was not enough in themselves to cause any fundamental
rupture within or with second Temple Judaism itself.* For all that we
see the beginnings of a christology which was to go on to claim much
more for this Jesus, nothing of what we have looked at so far in these
early claims or expressions of faith in Jesus would have shaken the
foundations of second Temple Judaism.

10.3 Jesus as Lord

Potentially more significant than any of the above was the claim that
by the resurrection-exaltation of Jesus, God had made him 'Lord',
kyrios. We have already cited Acts 2.36 – the resurrection as proof
that God had made Jesus 'both Lord and Christ'. Similarly in the
Christ-hymn of Phil. 2.6–11, God is extolled for highly exalting the
crucified Christ and giving him a name above every name, so that every
tongue should confess 'Jesus Christ is Lord' – where 'Lord' is presumably that 'name above every name' bestowed by God in his exaltation
of the crucified Christ. One of the most important 'proof texts' among
the earliest believers was Ps. 110.1 – 'The Lord said to my Lord: "Sit at
my right hand, till I make your enemies your footstool"' – where once
again it is the conjunction of the title 'Lord' with the thought of Jesus'
exaltation which is the point of significance.[16] The title was particularly

---

15. See e.g. my *The Evidence for Jesus*, pp. 71–4.

16. Ps. 110.1 is echoed or cited in several NT passages—Rom. 8.34; I Cor. 15.25; Eph.
1.20; Col. 3.1; Heb. 1.3, 13; 8.1; 10.12f.; 12.2; I Peter 3.22. The importance of Ps. 110.1
as a proof text in earliest Christianity is not affected one way or other by the issue of
whether Jesus himself had already used it in debate during his ministry (Mark 12.35–37

important for Paul: in the Pauline letters it is used about two hundred and thirty times for Jesus. For example, the confession of Jesus as Lord is the outward expression of the belief that God has raised him from the dead in the (probably) baptismal confession, Rom. 10.9. In I Cor. 12.3 it is likewise the confession 'Jesus is Lord' which provides proof of inspiration by the Spirit. And elsewhere Paul can sum up his preaching simply as a preaching of 'Jesus Christ as Lord' (II Cor. 4.5; Col. 2.6).

But what was the significance of this title in its application to Jesus? The title *kyrios* ('lord') was particularly important for the early History of Religions school, as being a key title in mystery cults. So the designation of Jesus as Lord meant that he could be described as *kyrios* of the Christ cult.[17] And it is true that the title was not uncommon in prominent cults of the time (cf. I Cor. 8.5), particularly the cults of Isis and Sarapis.[18] It was also probably in process of becoming increasingly significant as Emperor worship spread steadily from the Eastern empire,[19] with the confession 'Caesar is Lord' liable to become a test of political loyalty, as certainly was the case later on (*Martyrdom of Polycarp* 8.2). To be noted, however, is the fact that Paul (and here presumably Paul can serve as spokesman for Christianity as it spread more widely into the Graeco-Roman world) claims Jesus not simply as a *kyrios*, or even as the *kyrios* of a particular cult, but as *the kyrios*: 'For although there may be so-called gods in heaven or on earth – as indeed there are many "gods" and many "lords" – yet for us there is one God, the Father, . . . and one Lord, Jesus Christ' (I Cor. 8.5–6); in the Philippians hymn the vision is of *every* knee bowing, and *every* tongue confessing that 'Jesus Christ is Lord' (Phil. 2.11); 'For he must reign until he has put all his enemies under his feet' (I Cor. 15.25). Here at least we can say that Paul both recognized the category of 'Lord' in contemporary cults and religious movements, but also that he was not at all content for use of the title in reference to Jesus to be taken in the same way. *There is a claim here for an exclusiveness of significance for 'the Lord Jesus Christ' which is precisely parallel to the Jewish claim for the exclusiveness of its belief in the one God*, over against the competing syncretism of the wider Hellenistic world: 'for us there is one God, the Father, . . . and one Lord, Jesus Christ' (I Cor. 8.6).

---

pars.), quite apart from the fact that the significance of this particular Gospel tradition is far from clear itself.

17. So particularly Bousset, *Kyrios Christos*.

18. W. Foerster, *kyrios*, *TDNT*, 3.1050–2.

19. Foerster, *TDNT*, 3.1054–8.

The Christian use of *kyrios* for Jesus, therefore, probably reflects more of Jewish than of the wider Hellenistic influence – an expression of the awkward stubbornness of Jewish claims for the uniqueness of the revelation granted to them. But this simply brings us to an issue of still greater significance. For as soon as we shift the focus of our discussion back on to the Jewish significance of *kyrios* a point of primary importance for us emerges. The point is that *kyrios* had by this time become the accepted Greek rendering for the Hebrew 'Yahweh' in the diaspora. Paul attests this by his own use of *kyrios* for the tetragrammaton (YHWH) in OT quotations (about nineteen times). Some have noted that our evidence is confined to Christian manuscripts of the LXX, and that Jewish versions of the LXX leave a blank or write PIPI.[20] From which it may be concluded that *kyrios* was *not* used in diaspora synagogues for Yahweh. But the manuscript evidence is not actually to the point. For these manuscripts would have been *heard* rather than *read* by the great majority on any one occasion in any synagogue. And almost certainly when the Jewish scriptures were read in Greek the divine name was *not* rendered as 'PIPI'(!), but as *kyrios*. Just as the Hebrew YHWH was rendered *Adonai* in public reading of the Hebrew scriptures, so the divine name would assuredly have been rendered as *kyrios* in Greek speaking synagogues. Paul's practice in writing the divine name as *kyrios* in his letters was surely no surprise to those who came to the meetings of his churches from the synagogue.

The point of significance for us, however, is the well known fact that Paul applies several of such passages from the (Jewish) scriptures to *Jesus*. Where the *kyrios* of the text is clearly Yahweh, Paul does not hesitate to read it as speaking of *Jesus* as *kyrios*. Thus in Rom. 10.13 he quotes Joel 2.32 – 'Everyone who calls upon the name of the Lord will be saved'. But in the context it is clear beyond doubt that the 'Lord' here is Jesus (10.9–10). In I Cor. 2.16 he quotes Isa 40.13 – 'Who has known the mind of the Lord so as to instruct him?', and immediately adds, 'But we have the mind of Christ'. Most striking of all is the Philippian hymn already referred to, Phil. 2.10–11 – '. . . that at the name of Jesus every knee should bow, . . . and every tongue confess that Jesus Christ is Lord . . .'. The significance here lies in the clear echo of Isa. 45.23, and in the fact that the Isaiah

---

20. See H. Conzelmann, *An Outline of the Theology of the New Testament*, [2]1968; ET London: SCM Press 1969, pp. 83–4; G. Howard, 'The Tetragram and the New Testament', *JBL* 96 (1977), pp. 63–83. The Hebrew form of the divine name, YHWH (יהוה), transliterates most closely into the Greek, PIPI (*II I II I*).

passage is one of the strongest assertions of Jewish monotheism in the whole of the scriptures:

> . . . Turn to me and be saved,
>   all the ends of the earth!
> For I am God, and there is no other.
>   By myself I have sworn . . .
> 'To me every knee shall bow,
>   every tongue shall swear'.

That a Jew should use such a text of a man who had recently lived in Palestine is truly astonishing.[21]

Should we therefore conclude that in making such use of such scriptures Paul was *equating* or even *identifying* Jesus with God, with the one God of Jewish monotheism? Such a development would seem to go well beyond anything within the current diversity of first-century Judaism and constitute such a radical revision of the dogma of monotheism as to make a parting of the ways inevitable and in fact already irretrievable. However, the issue is not quite so straightforward.

Paul in fact calls Jesus 'Lord' as much as a means of distinguishing *Jesus from God as of identifying him with God*. We have already cited I Cor. 8.6 more than once: 'For us there is one God, the Father . . . and one Lord, Jesus Christ.' Evidently Paul could confess Jesus as Lord, while *at the same time* confessing that God is one; the two claims were not seen to be in any kind of competition. Paul could acknowledge the lordship of Christ, without apparently diminishing his commitment to Jewish monotheism. He could say 'Jesus is Lord' and confess the *Shema'* in one and the same breath.[22] Even the Philippian hymn with its echo of Isa. 45.23 ends with a significant phrase: '. . . and every tongue confess that Jesus Christ is Lord, *to the glory of God the Father*' (Phil. 2.11). The confession of Jesus as Lord is thus understood as a way of giving the honour to God for which Isaiah had looked. We should also note a phrase which recurs quite often in the Pauline corpus, 'the *God* and Father of our *Lord* Jesus Christ'.[23] Even Jesus as *Lord* has God as *his* God. Thus also it becomes significant to recall that Ps. 110.1, much used in early Christian apolo-

---

21. See also below §10.7 (*b*).

22. Note the importance of the *Shema* elsewhere in the Pauline corpus – Rom. 3.30; 16.27; Eph. 4.6; I Tim. 1.17; 2.5; 6.15–16; also James 2.19 and Jude 25. See also F. Hahn, 'The Confession of the One God in the New Testament', *HBT*2 (1980), pp. 69–84.

23. Rom. 15.6; II Cor. 1.3; 11.31; Eph. 1.3, 17; Col. 1.3; I Peter 1.3.

getic,[24] envisages Jesus being established as Lord by God the Lord. God is *Lord* also of the *Lord* Jesus (I Cor. 15.24–28).

To call Jesus 'Lord', therefore, was evidently not *understood in earliest Christianity as identifying him with God.* What Paul and the first Christians seem to have done was to claim that *the one God had shared his lordship with the exalted Christ.* Consequently Jesus could be hailed as Lord and receive the honour due to God alone, because God had so appointed Christ to this status and these roles; so that to call on him as Lord and to honour him as Lord was to honour the one God who had accorded him this position. Such talk of the Lordship of Jesus brings us to our next topic.

10.4 Jesus as Last Adam

One of the most striking features about the earliest Christian, particularly Pauline, understanding of the exalted Christ is that Christ was evidently thought of as a corporate being, as *one who was more than individual*.[25] Consider, for example, the frequent use of what we might call 'incorporative' phrases: Paul's regular use of the phrase 'in the Lord' (as in Rom. 16.2, 8, 11, 12, 13, 22), where 'Lord' is clearly Christ; and particularly of prepositional phrases with 'Christ' – 'in Christ' (about eighty times), 'into Christ' (e.g. Gal. 3.27), 'with Christ' (e.g. Rom. 6.8; 8.17; Gal. 2.19–20), 'through Christ' (about twenty times), and, not least, 'the body of Christ' (as in Rom. 12.4–5 and I Cor. 12.12–27).

Such a usage is equally astonishing for any thoughtful Jew. It is without any real parallel in the evidence reviewed under § 10.2. And it is also without real parallel in the mystery cults, despite the claims made by the History of Religions school that Christian belief here was based on the more widespread idea of the dying and rising God.[26] So far as we can tell, the thought in such cases was *not* of incorporation into Attis or Osiris, more of following the way to life which these legendary figures had already gone.[27] In contrast, the sense of

---

24. See above p. 247 and n. 16.

25. C. F. D. Moule, *The Phenomenon of the New Testament*, London: SCM Press 1967, ch. 2, and *Origin of Christology*, ch. 2, has made much of this.

26. Such claims continue to be dragged out from the dustbin, e.g. by G. A. Wells, *The Jesus of the Early Christians. A Study of Christian Origins*, London: Pemberton 1971, and Maccoby, *Mythmaker*, also *Paul and Hellenism*, London: SCM Press/Philadelphia: TPI 1991, ch. 3, despite the fact that they have long since been consigned there by careful scholarship; see particularly A. J. M. Wedderburn, *Baptism and Resurrection. Studies in Pauline Theology against its Graeco-Roman Background*, WUNT 44; Tübingen: Mohr-Siebeck 1987.

27. See also my *Romans*, pp. 308–11, especially 310.

Jesus as a corporate body, as more than an individual, and so soon within Christianity, is a powerful indication of just how quickly the earliest Christians found it necessary to reach for new ways of expressing their belief regarding Jesus.

As Paul uses such language, it seems to be an expression of *Adam christology*; that is, of attempts to express the importance of Christ by comparing him and his significance with that of Adam. Here we should note how one of the major concentrations of 'incorporative' phrases ('into/with/in Christ' – Rom. 6.3ff.) appears immediately after Paul's main exposition of Adam christology in Rom. 5.12–21. The implication is that such phraseology is a way of expressing the 'Adamic significance' of Christ. As Adam is the one man who can be said to represent the old age, the age of sin ruling over humanity to death (Rom. 5), so Christ can be said to be the one man who represents the new age, the age of life through death and beyond death. And as those under the power of sin and death can be 'summed up' in Adam, so those under the power of grace and life-through-death can be summed up 'in Christ' (Rom. 6.1–11). The same is true with the other most overt statement of Adam christology, I Cor. 15.21–22–

> For as by a man came death,
> by a man has come also the resurrection of the dead.
> For as in Adam all die,
> so also in Christ shall all be made alive.

Here again Adam is being understood as a representative figure: one can describe what is true of all, what is the fate of all 'in Adam' by describing what was true of Adam, what was the fate of Adam. So likewise, by analogy, Christ is being portrayed as a representative figure: what happened to him is what will happen to all 'in him'.

Alternatively expressed, 'in Christ' is a salvation-historical status. 'Into Christ' is transfer terminology – from Adam, into Christ. 'With Christ' and 'through Christ' describe the believer's participation in salvation-effective events – from death, through/with Christ to life. 'The body of Christ' reminds us that we experience this not as individuals but as a corporate entity. And as we shall see, there is also an experiential dimension to all this – the body of Christ as an expression of the shared experience of the Spirit (§10.6).

To be true to Paul, we should add that he would regard it as important that the distinctiveness of Christ be retained over against those whom he represents. Christ is more than 'the body of Christ';

the exalted Christ is not reducible to the body of Christ.[28] Paul was evidently concerned to make a point of this. As the last Adam, Christ represents a new race of humankind, as the first of this new race. So in I Cor. 15.20, he is the 'firstfruits' of the resurrection, followed by 'each in his own order' (15.23). In Col. 1.18 he is the 'firstborn from the dead, that in everything he might be pre-eminent'. In Rom. 8.29 he is 'the first-born among many brothers', the eldest of a new family of God. In particular, he was the first to be raised from the dead, and so the prototype of the resurrection. Hence the confidence of Paul that 'just as we have borne the image of the man of dust (Adam), we shall also bear the image of the man of heaven' (I Cor. 15.49); that is the 'spiritual body' of the resurrection will be patterned on *his* resurrection (15.44–45). The Lord Jesus Christ 'will change our lowly body to be like his body of glory' (Phil. 3.21). So the *uniqueness* of Jesus as the archetype is preserved.

The main point for us, however, is *the thoroughly Jewish character of such Adam christology*. 'Adam' in Hebrew, of course, means 'man', the 'man'/humanity that God made; that is, in Paul's schema, 'man'/humanity fallen under sin and death, 'man'/humanity fallen short of the glory God intended for him (Rom. 3.23; 7.7–12). Equivalently, Christ is 'man', come in the very likeness of sinful flesh (Rom. 8.3), obedient by free choice to the death which Adam died as punishment for his *dis*obedience (Rom. 5.19), but raised from the dead as the last Adam (I Cor. 15.45).[29] In other words, the purpose for which God made 'man', a purpose which failed in Adam, has been achieved in Christ. This theological claim can be set out as an exposition of Ps. 8.4–6, as Heb. 2.6–11 shows: God created man in order to make him the crown of creation, to put everything 'in subjection under his feet'; but it is only in Christ that this has actually happened.[30] In Paul, however, the theme is even more clearly expressed in terms of the *'glory'* or *'image'* of God. Thus in II Cor. 3.18ff., particularly 4.4, the implication is that the glory and image of God, lost or defaced in Adam, has been restored in the risen and glorified Christ who appeared to Paul on the Damascus road.[31] To become like Christ, therefore, was to become as God intended humanity to be. To be 'in Christ' etc. is the way of reversing or undoing, and indeed *more* than

---

28. A danger in J. A. T. Robinson, *The Body. A Study in Pauline Theology*, London: SCM Press 1952 – e.g. p. 58.

29. See further my *Christology*, pp. xviii, 107–8, 127; also *Romans*, p. 278.

30. See further below §11.1.

31. Contrast Kim, *Origin of Paul's Gospel*, pp. 193ff.

compensating for the damage done by Adam. Hence also the 'image' and 'glory' language in Rom. 8.29 and Phil. 3.21 already quoted.

What is most striking for us here, however, is the way in which *earliest Christian apologetic brought Ps. 8.6 in to supplement Ps. 110.1*. In Ps. 110.1 the talk of 'making your enemies your footstool' was often replaced or supplemented by Ps. 8.6's talk of 'putting all things under his feet'. This has happened in I Cor. 15.25–27: 'he must reign until he has put all his enemies under his feet (cf. Ps. 110.1) ... For God has put all things in subjection under him (Ps. 8.6).' Similarly in Eph. 1.20–22, I Peter 3.22 and again Phil. 3.21 ('the Lord Jesus Christ [who will] subject all things to himself').[32] The implication is plain: to be made '*Lord*' was to fulfil the design God had when he first made '*man*'; the Lordship of Christ was another way of describing his role as Last Adam; Christ as Lord triumphant over all his enemies fulfilled God's intention to put all things under Adam's feet. Hence the final emphasis of I Cor. 15.24–28 –

> Then comes the end, when he (Christ) delivers the kingdom to God the Father, after destroying every rule and every authority and power. For he must reign until he has put all his enemies under his feet (Ps. 110.1) ... When all things are subjected to him (Ps. 8.6), then the Son himself will also be subjected to him, who put all things under him (Ps. 8.6), that God may be all in all.

Adam christology is also probably the determinative clue to our understanding of Phil. 2.6–11. The claim is greatly disputed, but the following parallels from 'Adam theology' elsewhere need to be considered.[33]

2.6a – in the form of God (cf. Gen. 1.27);
2.6b – tempted to grasp equality with God (cf. Gen. 3.5);[34]
2.7 – enslavement to corruption and sin – humanity as it now is (cf. Gen. 2.19, 22–24; Ps. 8.5a; Wisd. 2.23; Rom. 8.3; Gal. 4.4; Heb. 2.7a, 9a);

---

32. Mark 12.36 = Matt. 22.44 is a similarly mixed quotation of Ps. 110.1 – 'The Lord said to my Lord, Sit at my right hand, till I put your enemies "under your feet" (Ps. 8.6).'

33. See fuller exposition in my *Christology*, second edition, p. xix and accompanying notes, in defence of the exposition in pp. 114–21.

34. Despite N. T. Wright, '*harpagmos* and the Meaning of Philippians 2.5–11', *JTS* 37 (1986), pp. 321–52, it remains the case that *harpagmos* would most naturally have been understood as 'act of robbery' (BAGD) or as equivalent to the gerund ('snatching, grasping'). There is no real evidence for the claim that the sense of 'retaining' inheres in the word; see now J. C. O'Neill, 'Hoover on *Harpagmos* Reviewed, with a Modest Proposal Concerning Philippians 2.6', *HTR* 81 (1988), pp. 445–9.

2.8 – submission to death (cf. Wisd. 2.24; Rom. 5.12–21; 7.7–11;
I Cor. 15.21–22);

2.9–11 – exalted and glorified (cf. Ps. 8.5b–6; I Cor. 15.27, 45;
Heb. 2.7b–8, 9b).

In other words, Phil. 2.6–11 seems to be framed primarily to draw
out the parallel between Adam and Christ: Christ confronted with
the same choice as Adam (2.6b); Christ embracing the lot of Adam
(2.8 – the obedience of Christ to death being the answer to the
outcome of Adam's disobedience); and Christ thus fulfilling the original destiny God had intended for Adam – dominion over all (other
created) things (2.9–11). If this is so, then even Phil. 2.6–11 has to
be seen as fulfilment not just of Ps. 110.1 (given the name and status
'Lord'), but also of Ps. 8.6 (all other created beings owning his authority over them). This insight simply serves to underline the significance of the final phrase – 'to the glory of God the Father'. *The last
Adam glorifies God by fulfilling the role God designed for humankind, by exercising Adam's authority over all other creatures as the
crown of creation.*

In this connection we should note also that some Jews of this period
were willing to conclude that since Adam was the image and likeness
of God, it was appropriate for worship to be offered to him – *Life of
Adam and Eve* 13–14:[35]

> When God blew into you the breath of life and your countenance
> and likeness were made in the image of God, Michael brought you
> and made (us) worship you in the sight of God, and the Lord God
> said, 'Behold Adam! I have made you in our image and likeness'.
> And Michael went out and called all the angels, saying, 'Worship
> the image of the Lord God, as the Lord God has instructed'. And
> Michael himself worshipped first, and called me and said, 'Worship
> the image of God, Yahweh'.

The speaker here is 'the devil' (Satan), who refuses to offer such
worship, coveting such worship himself; and it is for this reason that
he and other angels were expelled. To worship Adam, the image of
God, was thus considered to be an expression of obedience to the
Lord God; the refusal to offer such a worship a denial of God's
sovereign right. Here is a further indication that Adam christology

---

35. This can be seen as of a piece with subsequent rabbinic exposition of Adam's created
glory; see e.g. R. Scroggs, *The Last Adam. A Study in Pauline Anthropology*, Oxford:
Blackwell 1966.

goes a considerable way towards explaining much of the NT phenomena under examination, or at least how natural it was for at least some Jews to draw out the line Adam-image of God-worship without thinking to infringe their monotheism. It is also a reminder that the categorization of Paul's theology in Adam terms should not be thought of as a 'low' christology in contrast to Wisdom christology (§10.5). Rather the point is that the two run into each other, as the common use of 'image of God' language itself indicates.[36]

In short, then, one of the main categories of early christology which seems at first to go well beyond Jewish thought (Christ as a corporate individual, as more than individual) is in effect *an outworking and development of the more familiar Adam theology* drawn from Gen. 1–3 and from subsequent reflection on these chapters. And the use of Ps. 8.6 in particular as a christological text, in conjunction with Ps. 110.1, is a salutary reminder of just how much even the *kyrios* christology of Paul made use of essentially Jewish categories. The categories were certainly being stretched by such usage, but we cannot yet say that the new wine had already burst the old wineskins.

10.5 Jesus as divine Wisdom

We come now to what is probably the single most important category in the development of earliest christology – Wisdom christology. Here, as in other sections, I have to draw on material already published. Since the theme is so important to our present discussion a certain amount of repetition is unavoidable. But my object here is to document the central point for the present discussion: that *the usage is Jewish through and through*. Whether that usage also breaks through these Jewish categories in a way that transformed their significance within Judaism and threatened Jewish belief in the oneness of God is the crucial issue. At this point of the discussion we will confine ourselves to the most important Pauline texts.

The relevant range of material first comes to notice because it seems to lift early christology on to a wholly new plane – where *pre-existence and a role in creation are clearly attributed to Christ*. Such an attribution surely lifts the christology concerned well beyond any thought of a vindicated or glorified man; the lines of *deity* are being clearly sketched into this christology. A human figure might be considered capable of sharing in God's role as final judge without compromising

---

36. See further D. Steenburg, 'The Worship of Adam and Christ as the Image of God', *JSNT* 39 (1990), pp. 95–109.

God's oneness; Adam, and so too the last Adam, might be considered worthy of worship, as an act which glorifies the one God; but to attribute a role in creation itself to anyone other than God would seem to require a considerable revision of the classic Jewish understanding of the creator God as one. The most important texts in Paul are I Cor. 8.6 and Col. 1.15–20.

> I Cor. 8.6 – For us there is one God, the Father,
>   from whom are all things
>   and for whom we exist,
>   and one Lord, Jesus Christ,
>   through whom are all things
>   and through whom we exist.

> Col. 1.15–20 – He is the image of the invisible God,
>   the first-born of all creation;
>   for in him all things were created
>   all things were created through him and for him.
>   He is before all things,
>   and in him all things hold together.

It is possible that we should recognize pre-existence also attributed to Christ in Phil. 2.6–11. But that is not so clear as in the above cases. For if the Adam parallel is so dominant, as seems to be the case (§10.4), then it may simply be that the initial status spoken of is that of Adam – created, in 'the image of God', that is, in a primal mythic time before the history of human fallenness. Somewhat similarly with II Cor. 8.9 – 'though he was rich, yet for your sake he became poor, so that by his poverty you might become rich'. It is usually simply assumed that the intended contrast is between pre-existent richness and the poverty of the human condition. In fact, however, the contrast of both the verse and the whole section is one of *spiritual* wealth and poverty; and the saving act of Christ ('by his poverty') is always understood elsewhere in Paul as his *death*.[37] But whether or not pre-existence is attributed to Christ in these latter cases, it clearly is so in the case of I Cor. 8.6 and Col. 1.15ff. What is the significance of this?

The clue to exegesis of these passages is the recognition that they are using *Wisdom language* – that is, language is being used of Christ which at that time was typically used of divine Wisdom in Jewish

---

37. See further *Christology*, pp. 121–3. Rom. 8.3 and Gal. 4.4 are often cited here too, but they too are probably further expressions of the more pervasive Adam christology. See my *Christology*, pp. 38–45, 111–2; also *Romans*, p. 421.

circles. To I Cor. 8.6 and Col. 1.15ff. we may compare, for example, the following:[38]

Prov. 3.19 – The Lord by wisdom founded the earth;
        by understanding he established the heavens . . .

Wisd. 8.4–6 – For she (Wisdom) is an initiate in the knowledge
    of God, and an associate in his works.
        If riches are a desirable possession in life,
    what is richer than wisdom who effects all things?
        And if understanding is effective,
    who more than she is fashioner of what exists?

II Enoch 30.8 – On the sixth day I commanded my wisdom to
    create man.

Wisd. 7.26 – She (Wisdom) is an image of his goodness.

Prov. 8.22–30 – The lord created me at the beginning of
        his work,
    the first of his acts of old . . .
    Before the mountains had been shaped,
    before the hills, I was brought forth . . .
    When he established the heavens, I was there . . .
    When he marked out the foundation of the earth,
    Then I was beside him, like a master workman (or little child).

Sir. 24.9 – From eternity, in the beginning, he created me,
    and for eternity I shall not cease to exist.

To be noted is the fact that such Wisdom language was not simply that of diaspora Judaism, though it was particularly prominent in the Hellenistic Jewish literature which emerged from Alexandria (Wisdom of Solomon, Philo). But it is also present in the more domestic (Palestinian) traditions of Proverbs and ben Sira. Any Jew familiar with such passages would at once recognize what Paul was doing in I Cor. 8.6 and Col. 1.15ff. when they heard Paul's letters being read to them. Paul was describing Jesus in the language of divine Wisdom. That is to say, he was attributing to Christ the role of Wisdom. *He was in effect identifying Jesus with the figure of divine Wisdom.* That point is clear enough. The crucial issue, however, is what such language used of Jesus would have meant to such a hearer – or indeed

---

38. Fuller details in *Christology*, pp. 165–6. For a full discussion of the Wisdom tradition behind Col. 1.15–20 see J. -N. Aletti, *Colossiens 1.15–20. Genre et exégèse du texte. Fonction de la thématique sapientielle*, AB 91; Rome: Biblical Institute 1981.

to Paul himself. What was such language saying about Jesus? This crucial question can be answered *only if we are first clear what such language would have meant for the typical Jew of Paul's time quite apart from its application to Jesus.*

How then did Paul's Jewish contemporaries understand the figure of divine Wisdom?

(a) Not a few answer at once: Wisdom would have been understood as '*a divine being*', even 'an independent deity'. How else are we to understand such apparently straightforward language as Prov. 8.22–30 or II *Enoch* 30.8?[39] Certainly it is the case that within a polytheistic system, such language would have been so understood – Wisdom as simply another deity. But second Temple Judaism was by no means a polytheistic religion – quite the contrary, as we have seen.[40] And within such *different* religious systems the *same* language is bound to have different significance. As Larry Hurtado rightly notes, 'the actual significance of the language must be determined by the function of the language in the religious life of ancient Jews'.[41] In other words, *it must be judged highly unlikely that such widespread talk of the figure of divine Wisdom within second Temple Judaism was seen as any kind of threat to the oneness of God.* Whatever Wisdom was within Israel, she was not another god.

(b) Others prefer to see here a '*hypostatization*' of divine attributes – that is, something half-way between a person and a personification.[42] But the term 'hypostasis' is illegitimately used for this period, since it only gained its technical theological nuance in the third and fourth centuries CE, as a way of resolving a peculiarly Christian dilemma. That is to say, it is anachronistic for the period under discussion and its use here imports distinctions and categories which would have been meaningless for the first-century Jew.[43]

(c) The best answer to our question still seems to be to see here the

---

39. So e.g. those cited in *Christology*, p. 325 n. 20; also J. E. Fossum, *The Name of God and the Angel of the Lord*, WUNT 36; Tübingen: Mohr-Siebeck 1985, cited by Hurtado, *One God*, p. 47. I have been unable to verify the citation in Fossum, but his indiscriminate use of later sources undermines the value and reduces the relevance of his work for our inquiry; as again in his 'Colossians 1.15–18a in the Light of Jewish Mysticism and Gnosticism', *NTS* 35 (1989), pp. 183–201.

40. See above §2.1.

41. Hurtado, *One God*, p. 48.

42. See e.g. those cited in *Christology*, p. 325 n. 21.

43. 'The statement that hypostasis ever received "a sense midway between 'person' and "attribute", inclining to the former" is pure delusion, though it derived ultimately from Harnack' (G. L. Prestige, *God in Patristic Thought*, London: SPCK ²1952; paperback 1964, p. xxviii).

language of *personification* – the figure of divine Wisdom as a way
of speaking about *God* in his wisdom and in the wisdom of his action.

(1) Such vigorous metaphorical usage is wholly in line with the
vigour of Hebrew poetry and imagery. For example, Ps. 85.10–11
pictures 'righteousness' and 'peace' as kissing each other. Isa. 51.9
calls upon the arm of the Lord to 'awake, awake, put on strength'.[44]
In *Joseph and Asenath* 15.7–8 'Repentance' is depicted as 'the Most
High's daughter ... the guardian of all virgins ... a virgin, very
beautiful and pure and chaste and gentle'.[45] This is simply the language of personification, and Jewish readers familiar with such usage
would surely not interpret the similar language used of Wisdom any
differently. To be sure the metaphor is more sustained in a passage
like Sir. 24; but in essential character it is no different from these
briefer apostrophes. Sir. 24 itself, as we have noted before, identified
this figure of divine Wisdom explicitly with the Torah; and however
much Jews of the period valued the Torah, they were not in the
business of deifying it; to say divine Wisdom *is* the Torah is simply
to assert that the wisdom of God is contained in the Torah, visible
there as nowhere else.

(2) Jewish writers of this period also speak not just of Wisdom as
a being apparently independent of God, but also of the Word of God,
of the Spirit of God, of the Glory of God, of the Name of God (e.g.
Wisd. 18.15; Ps. 139.7; *I Enoch* 39.7, 9, 13; *m.Abot* 3.2).[46] Were all
of these 'hypostatizations'? Then we have to speak not just of a binity
or a trinity already in Jewish thought, but of a quinity! The traditional
Jewish rejection of the Christian understanding of God as Trinity
shows just how much credence would have been given such a suggestion at the time of Paul. The mistake in these cases has been to see
such language as a consequence of an increasing emphasis on the
transcendence of God. In consequence of which it became necessary
to envisage intermediaries between the now distant God and his
people.[47] In contrast, however, it makes much better sense to recognize that the function of such language was to express the *immanence*
of God – drawn in precisely as *a way of expressing God's nearness,
without infringing his transcendence.* Thus the Spirit of God is the
presence of God (Ps. 139.7). The Word of God is God's revelation of

---

44. Further examples in *Christology*, pp. 174–5.

45. Hurtado, *One God*, p. 47.

46. Further examples in *Christology*, pp. 129, 133–4, 217.

47. W. Bousset and H. Gressmann, *Die Religion des Judentums im späthellenistischer
Zeitalter*, HNT 21; Tübingen: Mohr-Siebeck 1966, speak of a 'whole host of intermediary
beings (who) forced their way in between God, who had become distant from the world,
and man' (p. 319; also cited by Hengel, *Judaism*, 1.155).

himself in rational utterance. The Glory of God is that of God which may be seen by human eye when God is present. And so on.[48] So with Wisdom. For example, in Wisd. 10ff., that which in earlier accounts was described as God's deliverance of his people, is attributed to the work of Wisdom. For *Wisdom was simply a way of speaking of God in his interaction with his creation and his people.* The Wisdom of God is God acting in his wisdom. Wisdom denoted God; its usage did not denote Wisdom rather than God. If we are to use later categories at all, then at most we can speak of a binity – God transcendent and God immanent.

(3) All this is confirmed by the constant stress in the same writers on the activity of God where it is quite clear that God himself is the acting agent and 'wisdom' just a way of expressing how he acts. For example, 'the Lord gives wisdom; from his mouth comes knowledge and understanding' (Prov. 2.6); 'All wisdom comes from the Lord and is with him for ever' (Sir. 1.1); 'Though we speak much we cannot reach the end, and the sum of our words is: "He is the all"' (Sir. 43.27); 'God is the guide even of wisdom and the corrector of the wise' (Wisd. 7.15); etc.[49] *Such is the language of a Jewish monotheism so confident of its major premise that it can speak vigorously of God's wisdom without any thought of attributing a separate divine status to this wisdom or of compromising that monotheism.*

In short, for the typical Jew of the period the figure of divine Wisdom was *a way of expressing God's self-revelation*, a way of speaking about his will and purpose as revealed in creation and pre-eminently in the Torah.

This then is the Wisdom imagery which the first Christians used in such passages as I Cor. 8.6 and Col. 1.15ff. If this is so, how would they have understood and intended its use in reference to Jesus? The same three alternatives are canvassed here too.

(*a*) *A divine being*, an 'independent deity'? So the language of Col. 1.15ff. could be understood; and indeed quite naturally so, if by that is meant what *we* today might regard as the natural meaning of the words. But did Paul mean such passages to be understood as saying that the man Jesus, Jesus Christ as such, had been with God at the beginning of creation?[50] For that is in fact the most natural meaning

---

48. See also e.g. Thoma, *Christian Theology*, pp. 124–5.

49. See further *Christology*, pp. 171–3.

50. Is there any justification at this stage for making a distinction between Jesus and Christ – so that statements are acceptable about the pre-existence of *Christ*, but not about the pre-existence of *Jesus*? There is no indication that Paul would have recognized or

of the words. But then indeed we would have two gods! – not a binity but a bitheism – *polytheism rather than monotheism*. Such insistence on the most 'natural meaning' also tends to be not a little selective in its reading of I Cor. 8.6 and Col. 1.15ff. For in I Cor. 8.6 we have already pointed out that in the first half of the verse Paul is equally insistent that 'for us there is (only) one God, the Father'. His monotheism is untouched by what he goes on to say about the 'one Lord, Jesus Christ'. And in Col. 1.15ff. the second clause is 'most naturally' understood as calling Christ the first created being ('first-born of all creation'). It is no secret or surprise that the verse provided a major plank for Arianism! Moreover, the second half of the Colossian hymn should not be neglected as much as is usually the case in these discussions. For it claims that Jesus was 'the first-born from the dead, in order that in everything he might be pre-eminent' (1.18); *his pre-eminence was the result of his resurrection*! And the very next sentence, 'For in him God in all his fulness was pleased to dwell', is 'most naturally' understood as some form of adoptionism![51]

The point is surely clear: that *this is the language of poetry and hymn, not of finished theological logic*. To interpret it in what *we* today might regard as its most straightforward sense is probably a sure recipe for *mis*-interpretation. *All* of it needs to be set firmly back into the context of the time and not read as though intended to be a theological contribution to the christological debates of subsequent centuries. And when we do set it back into the context of late second Temple Judaism that means *into the context of the Wisdom poetic imagery examined above*.

What then was the significance of this language as used of Jesus? Here *the decisive consideration must be that there is no evidence of such language used of Jesus causing any problem for the early Jewish Christians, or for Paul's fellow Jews*. At this stage the conflict was almost wholly over the *law*, not christology. Evidently such language used of Jesus was *not* seen as a threat to Jewish monotheism. Evidently Jesus Christ was *not* being presented or understood as a divine being distinct from or independent of God. No new ontological category was being formulated: the 'entity' was God in his self-revelation, not someone other than God.[52]

---

intended such a distinction. The 'one Lord' of I Cor. 8.6 is *Jesus Christ*, that is *Jesus* (I Cor. 12.3; Phil. 2.10–11); similarly in the case of Colossians (1.3; 3.17).

51. See further my *Christology*, pp. 192–3.

52. Cf. N. T. Wright, 'Poetry and Theology in Colossians 1.15–20', *NTS* 36 (1990), pp. 444–68, who argues that the passage has to be understood as an expression of 'christological monotheism', that is of a christology set 'within the framework of Jewish creational monotheism itself' (pp. 459–63).

(b) *An hypostatization*. But the term is still wholly anachronistic for our period. 'Hypostasis' was the term devised, with a new sense given to an old word, when the later fathers of the church were trying to fit a passage like Col. 1.15–20 into the emerging scheme of trinitarian theology. It does not emerge *from* Col. 1.15–20 but is an attempt to solve the problems for later theology caused by, among others, Col. 1.15–20.

(c) The great probability is that Jewish readers would have been no more perturbed by Wisdom language used of Jesus than they were by the vigorous poetic imagery used for 'righteousness', 'repentance', etc. They had used the same vivid metaphor of divine Wisdom to express the full significance for them of the Torah. They would understand that the first Christians were doing the same in the case of Jesus. Hellenistic Jews anxious to explain or commend their faith and way of life to sympathetic Gentiles would be saying in effect: If you wish to have access to the wisdom which lies behind the world, the creative rationale immanent within the cosmos, the wisdom by which God seeks to bring humankind to the highest good, you will find it in the law. So they would recognize that the first Christians were doing the same: If you want to see the fullest and clearest expression of God's wisdom, you will see it in Jesus Christ. This, in fact, is precisely what Paul says in his first reference on this whole theme – I Cor. 1.24, 30. To Corinthians who were seeking wisdom in words and in terms of knowledge of the divine, Paul says, 'You will find the true measure of divine Wisdom in the cross of Christ' (I Cor. 1.20–25).

To sum up. Here again we see how Jewish language and categories were being stretched by the first Christians. To refer the personification of divine Wisdom to the Torah was one thing. But to refer it to a man of living memory was a significant step beyond. However, the fact of decisive significance remains, that *it does not seem yet to have been perceived as a threat*. There is no indication for the time of Paul that such Wisdom christology had burst through the categories of Jewish Wisdom theology or was as yet perceived to be causing problems for Jewish monotheism.

10.6 Jesus and the Spirit

To round off our consideration of the significance of christology during the first generation of Christianity, in its relation to the 'pillar' of Jewish monotheism, we need to take brief account of two other areas. First the question of how the first Christians understood the relation between Jesus and the Spirit of God.

(*a*) One important feature is the way in which Paul and others began to speak of the Spirit as 'the Spirit of Jesus', 'the Spirit of Christ', 'the Spirit of God's Son' (Acts 16.7; Rom. 8.9; Gal. 4.6; Phil. 1.19; I Peter 1.11). I have attempted to reflect on the significance of this development elsewhere: that Jesus thus came to be seen as the definition of the Spirit – the Spirit as the power of God which had inspired Jesus' ministry; with the implication that the character of Jesus' life and ministry became the touchstone of the Spirit – only that power was to be recognized as the Spirit of God which manifests the character of Jesus.[53] But that dimension of the relationship between Jesus and the Spirit is not so much to the point here. The point of note here, rather, is that this way of speaking lay within the parameters of Jewish usage – where the Spirit of God could be linked with a particular example of one inspired – as in Luke 1.15–17, where it is predicted of the Baptist that 'he will be filled with the Holy Spirit . . . and he will go before him (God) in the spirit and power of Elijah'.

(*b*) But Paul goes further. He seems *to identify Christ with the Spirit*. Thus in Rom. 8.9–11 Paul can speak equivalently of 'the Spirit of God dwelling in you' and of 'Christ in you'. And particularly I Cor. 15.45 – 'The last Adam (Christ) became life-giving Spirit', where 'life-giving Spirit' would usually be taken as a description of the Spirit of God (as in John 6.63 and II Cor. 3.6).[54] At first this might seem simply a further example of what we examined in §10.5: the Spirit of God, like the Wisdom of God, understood as a way of expressing the immanent presence and activity of God (e.g. Ps. 33.6; 139.7; Isa. 63.9–14; Wisd. 9.1–2, 17).[55] There is, however, a difference. Divine Wisdom was identified with Christ from before his resurrection (from creation!). But the identification between Jesus and the Spirit was made *only from the point of Jesus' resurrection* (cf. Rom. 1.4); 'the last Adam (*became*) life-giving Spirit' (I Cor. 15.45). Moreover, when we look at it more closely, the identification seems to be in *the believer's experience* of God's saving power. Thus in Rom. 8.9–11 the parallel is precisely between 'Christ *in you*' and *having* the Spirit. And in I Cor. 15.45 the risen Christ became *'life-giving* Spirit', that is, the power of God experienced as life-giving. That is to say, Paul did not think of the believer as experiencing the Spirit and Christ

---

53. See further my *Jesus*, pp. 318–42.

54. See my 'I Corinthians 15.45 – Last Adam, Life-giving Spirit', *Christ and Spirit in the New Testament. Studies in Honour of C. F. D. Moule*, ed. B. Lindars and S. S. Smalley, Cambridge University 1973, pp. 127–41.

55. *Christology*, p. 317 n. 31.

separately, but of experiencing the Spirit as 'the Spirit of Christ', of Christ experienced in, through and *as* the Spirit. In terms of human experience the impact of the divine could not be so easily differentiated. At the same time, Christ's role as Lord in relation *to God* could be expressed without reference to the Spirit, as we have seen.[56]

(*c*) Still more, we can see a dynamic in the relation between Jesus and the Spirit which evidently made Paul cautious as to how he expressed that relationship. The point is clearest in Rom. 8.11, where Paul seems deliberately to go out of his way to avoid making the straightforward parallel: 'If God gave life to Jesus through the Spirit, so in the same way will he give life to your mortal bodies.' Instead the parallel is stated in a much more complex fashion, apparently to avoid making the simple statement that Jesus' resurrection was the result of the power of the Spirit: 'If the Spirit of him who raised Jesus dwells in you, he who raised Christ Jesus from the dead will give life to your mortal bodies also through his Spirit which dwells in you.' Only the resurrection of believers is attributed to the Spirit, not Christ's. Less clear is Rom. 6.4, where Paul also avoids making what would seem to be the most obvious connection – 'as Christ was raised by the *Spirit*, so we too might walk *in the Spirit*'. And in I Cor. 15.45 he likewise seems to avoid describing the resurrected Jesus as 'spiritual body', that is a body enlivened by the Spirit, even though the topic of the argument at that point is focussed exclusively on the nature of the resurrection body. The point would seem to be that *the Spirit is not to be thought of as related to Christ in just the way that the Spirit is related to the rest of resurrected humanity.*[57] At this pont the contrast with Paul's Wisdom christology is noticeable: evidently he could think of Christ as wholly identified with Wisdom, so that Christ absorbed the role of divine Wisdom without remainder; whereas in the case of the Spirit the identification was not so complete.

Evidently there is something of profound importance going on here which is not wholly clear on the surface or easy to articulate. Were it the case that Spirit of God, like Wisdom of God, was fully identified with Christ, then Christian thought would have been pushed toward a *bi*-nitarian (rather than *tri*-nitarian) formulation. Jesus would have been understood to have wholly 'taken over' the role of Spirit, Wisdom etc. as a way of expressing the immanence of God. In the Jewish 'binitarianism' of God transcendent and God immanent, Jesus

---

56. See above §§10.4–5.

57. Cf. above p. 252–3, where we noted that Paul's Adam christology seeks to maintain the distinctiveness of Christ.

would be seen as God immanent, God as Christ-Spirit.[58] But the fact that Jesus and the Spirit were seen to *overlap* in function, but *not wholly to coincide*, implies that already among the first Christian theologians there was *a recognition that the Spirit still had a role distinct from that of Christ*, even if Wisdom did not. In other words, already there was a recognition of that dynamic of relationship between Christ and God, Christ and the Spirit which pushed Christian thought inevitably, it would seem in retrospect, towards a *trinitarian* understanding rather than a *binitarian* understanding of God.[59]

In short, once again we seem to be moving well within traditional Jewish categories of God-talk. But once again the earliest Christian use of these categories was beginning to stretch them in ways which would become increasingly uncomfortable for traditional Jewish theology.

10.7 Jesus as God

In the light of all the above discussion, the one remaining question which we cannot avoid posing in explicit terms is whether Paul and other first generation Christians thought of Jesus as *God*. The *kyrios* formula which seemed at first to imply a straight transposition of the category Yahweh to the risen Christ, we saw to function equally within a sustained confession of God as one, the Lordship of Christ equally understandable as the Lordship of the last Adam. The identification of divine *Wisdom* with Christ, even when Wisdom was understood as the self-revelation of God him/herself, did not prove so immediately disturbing to Jews who had been equally willing to identify the same divine Wisdom with the Torah. And the identification of Jesus with the *Spirit* never approached a concept of incarnation, but moved between that of Jesus as inspired by the Spirit and the Spirit as the means by which the risen Christ could still work among and within his followers. But leaving all that aside, did Paul ever speak of Jesus as 'God' directly, or render him worship appropriate only to God?

(*a*) The most plausible example of Paul calling Jesus 'God' is

---

58. Cf. the more radical presentation of G. W. H. Lampe, *God as Spirit: the Bampton Lectures 1976*, Oxford University 1977; London: SCM Press 1983. I also imply, of course, that Christian Trinitarianism is not so far removed from Jewish monotheism as might at first appear, because the Jewish understanding of God was already implicitly binitarian in character. See further below §12.3.

59. See again my *Christology*, p. 266.

Rom. 9.5. On syntactical grounds a strong case can be made for reading the text as a doxology to Christ as God:[60]

> from whom (Israel) is the Christ according to the flesh, he who is over all, God blessed for ever.

The alternative punctuation however would make a break after '... flesh':

> ... the Christ according to the flesh. He who is over all, God, may he be blessed for ever.

And the weight of considerations seems to tip the balance in favour of the latter. (1) A doxology to Christ as God would be without clear parallel in Paul's letters and in first generation Christianity.[61] (2) The passage is thoroughly and characteristically Jewish: 'the Christ' is counted among Israel's privileges; and at the end of the list, Paul the Jew blesses God for these privileges in equally characteristic Jewish manner. In the mood of the passage it would be most unlikely that the reader of Paul's letter would have read the benediction as addressed to any other than God. (3) The benediction speaks of 'God over all'. That looks even more clearly a description of the one God, the God most high of Jewish monotheism (cf. I Cor. 15.28). The doxology at the end of the first paragraph of Rom. 9–11 thus looks to have been penned in the same mood as the doxology at the end of Rom. 9–11 – addressed to God alone. All this underlines the extent to which Paul was still functioning with the forms of characteristic Jewish worship and his thought still moving *within* characteristic Jewish monotheism, and was not yet thinking of Christ in a way which would be, or in the event was seen to be any kind of challenge to Jewish monotheism.[62]

(b) Did Paul nevertheless address worship, devotion or prayer to

---

60. See e.g. C. E. B. Cranfield, *Romans*, ICC; Edinburgh: T. & T. Clark; 2 vols. 1975, 1979, pp. 464–70.

61. While in Rome I was also able to check personally that Codex Vaticanus has a point (= semi-colon) after 'flesh'.

62. The use of 'God' in reference to Jesus may be clearer in the later, post-Pauline, Titus 2.13 – 'the appearing of the glory of our great God and Saviour, Jesus Christ'; though even there we should note that the talk is of '*the glory* of our God ...'; that is to say, the thought is still closer to Wisdom christology – Jesus Christ identified more in terms of the visible manifestation of God, God manifesting himself in and through Jesus Christ, rather than as God as such (see also *Christology*, p. 345 n. 87). On John 1.1, 18 and 20.28, see §11.6 below.

Jesus? Hurtado thinks the answer is Yes, and that 'the cultic veneration of Jesus in early Christian circles' was the decisive factor in the Christian modification of Jewish monotheism. It was religious devotion to Christ which distinguishes the Christian use of divine agency (the figure of divine Wisdom, etc.) from Jewish use of the same imagery elsewhere.

> This innovation was first manifested in the devotional life of early Christian groups, in which the risen Christ came to share in some of the devotional and cultic attention normally reserved for God: the early Christian mutation in Jewish monotheism was a religious devotion with a certain binitarian shape.[63]

That Hurtado is correct I have no doubt – in the longer term.[64] What I find questionable is *whether we can so speak at the earliest stage*, the first generation of Christian theology and worship.

Hurtado cites two main lines of evidence – (1) early Christian hymns, and (2) prayer to Christ.[65] (1) However, the earliest hymns of those cited (Phil. 2.6–11 and Col. 1.15–20) are hymns *about* Christ, not hymns *to* Christ. The earliest clear examples of worship of Christ do not appear until the hymns in the Revelation of John, one of the latest documents in the NT (e.g. Rev. 5.8–10).[66] (2) So far as prayer to Jesus is concerned, outside the Pauline letters Hurtado cites Acts 7.59–60: Stephen prays, 'Lord Jesus, receive my spirit'. In Paul he refers particularly to II Cor. 12.8 ('I besought the Lord three times about this') and I Cor. 16.22 ('Our Lord, come!'). In II Cor. 12.8, however, it may be significant that Paul uses the verb meaning 'beseech, exhort' (*parakaleō*), and not the regular word for prayer (*deomai*). And I Cor. 16.22 is more an invocation than a prayer. More typical is Paul's understanding of prayer as prayer ,to God *through* Christ (Rom. 1.8; 7.25; II Cor. 1.20; Col. 3.17).[67]

Hurtado also points to the benedictions at the beginning and end

---

63. Hurtado, *One God*, pp. 11–14, 124.

64. See further below §11.4.

65. Hurtado, *One God*, pp. 101–8. The other material reviewed by Hurtado (pp. 108–14) would lose most of its weight without these first two. See also R. T. France, 'The Worship of Jesus: A Neglected Factor in Christological Debate?', *Guthrie* Festschrift, pp. 17–36.

66. Hurtado also cites Eph. 5.19 – 'making melody to the Lord' (*One God*, pp. 102–3); but the significance of the reference is less than clear. See further below §11.4.

67. Cf. particularly C. F. D. Moule, 'The Influence of Circumstances on the Use of Christological Terms' (1959), *Essays in New Testament Interpretation*, Cambridge University 1982, pp. 165–83, here pp. 166–73.

of Paul's letters – 'grace and peace from God our Father and the Lord Jesus Christ';[68] likewise the closing benedictions, particularly II Cor. 13.14 ('The grace of the Lord Jesus Christ and the love of God and the fellowship of the Holy Spirit be with you all'), and I Thess. 3.11–13 ('Now may our God and Father himself, and our Lord Jesus, direct our way to you; and may the Lord make you increase and abound in love to one another . . .'). These are indeed remarkable and we should not allow our familiarity with them to dull the astonishing character of such language spoken of one who had so recently lived on earth. But we should also note that the balance and tension already referred to under §10.3 is maintained in such passages: Jesus understood as Lord, as God's 'right hand man', but without detracting from the glory of the one who is alone God and Father. Clearly the exalted Jesus was thought to be associated with the one God in his function as Lord. And this seems to go beyond the Jewish understanding of glorified heroes; but by how far is still unclear. In reflecting on such invocation of Jesus as I Cor. 16.22, we should recall, for example, Mark 15.35, where the Jewish crowd round the cross apparently found it quite conceivable that Jesus on the cross should be invoking Elijah. Nor is it clear what status was being attributed to Christ in these formulations. Was it like that discussed in §10.2 – the glorified heroes given a share in the divine function of judgment? Or like that in §10.4 – Jesus as the archetype of the new humanity, Lord over all things under God? Was he conceived as elder brother of the new family of God, as mediator between God and humankind, or more? How much does the language of veneration (Hurtado's word) go beyond the subsequent Christian veneration of Mary and the saints?[69]

Clearly then we can see a trend well established already in the earliest of the NT writings – *Christian devotion to the exalted Christ on the way to full-scale worship*. That is the strength of Hurtado's argument. What is not clear, however, is whether we can *already* speak of '*worship*' of the exalted Christ, or whether we are witnessing in such texts *a development only begun*. Clearly we are confronted within the NT with a spectrum of usage; the question is, where along that spectrum does this early reverence for Christ come? And once again *the crucial point has to be that nothing of what has been*

---

68. Hurtado, *One God*, pp. 105–6 – Rom. 1.7; I Cor. 1.3; II Cor. 1.2; Gal. 1.3–4; Phil. 1.2; Philemon 2.

69. We discussed with some Catholic students the significance of veneration offered to Mary within Catholic tradition during our time in Rome. 'I assume you venerate Mary, but do not worship her', I said. 'No', came the reply, 'we worship her, but do not adore her.' See also above p. 255.

covered above seems to have caused any question or concern among Paul's Jewish contemporaries. The silence on this score cannot be because we have no means of knowing what Jewish reaction to earliest Christian theology was at this stage; on the contrary, we can see well enough from the literature of first generation Christianity that Paul's understanding of the law was a sore bone of contention for those who valued their Jewish heritage highly. *Had Paul's christology been equally, or more contentious at this time for his fellow Jews, we would surely have heard of it from Paul's own letters.* The absence of such indicators points in the other direction: that *Paul's christology and the devotional language of the earliest Christian worship did not cause any offence to monotheistic Jews.* So far as both Paul and his fellow Jews were concerned, early Christian devotion to Jesus still lay within the bounds of the Jewish understanding of God in his dealings with his world and his people. At this stage the parting of the ways over christology still lies ahead of us.

Is Christianity Monotheist?
The first great
christological debate

Thus far we have examined the way in which the first Christians, Paul in particular, attempted to express the meaning they had found in Jesus by using categories drawn from or adapted from second Temple Judaism. The most significant of these, the categories of resurrection, exaltation and sharing in divine functions, of Lord, Adam, divine Wisdom and Spirit, all made crucially important contributions of language and conceptuality to this attempt to state the distinctiveness of Jesus the Christ. They constituted major aspects of the emerging christology which, taken together, soon began to transform the christology itself beyond what had been said previously within Judaism about divine agency or divine self-manifestation. But the categories were still characteristically Jewish, rather than distinctively Hellenistic. And this earliest Christian use of them, so far as we can tell, still stayed within the bounds of the Jewish monotheism of the period. At least we have no indication that during the first generation of Christianity such attempts to speak of Jesus' larger significance caused any problems whatsoever for Jewish belief in God as one. Even if, in the metaphor we have used several times already, the new wine was causing the old wineskins to be stretched, the point is that the wineskins were not yet burst; they were still holding.

However, the use of Jewish categories in early christology continued after Paul. And the wineskins did burst in due course. The ways did part over christology. But when? And in what circumstances? And why? And need it have been so? And did it actually involve the abandonment of Jewish monotheism by these Christian writers and theologians? We will have time only to pick out the main features from the NT writers who speak most directly to our theme.

11.1 The Epistle to the Hebrews

Hebrews contains an amazing mixture of christology, and not least in the first two chapters.

(a) *Wisdom christology.* 1.1–3 is a very striking expression of Wisdom christology, drawing on the Wisdom and Logos theology[1] of Alexandrian Judaism which we find so richly expressed in the Wisdom of Solomon and Philo in particular.[2]

Heb. 1.2 – the Son whom he made heir of all things. . .
Cf. Philo's treatise, *Who is the Heir of Divine Things.*

Heb. 1.2 – through whom he made the world.
Cf. above § 10.5 on I Cor. 8.6 and Col. 1.15

Heb. 1.3 – He is the radiance (*apaugasma*) of God's glory . . .
Wisd.Sol. 7.26 – She is the radiance (*apaugasma*) of eternal light,
                        a spotless mirror of the working of God . . .

Heb. 1.3 – . . . and the stamp (*charaktēr*) of his nature . . .
Philo, *Plant.* 18 – the stamp (*charaktēr*) is the eternal Word.

Heb. 1.3 – sustaining all things (*pherōn ta panta*) by the word
                        of his power.
Philo, *Plant.* 8f. speaks of the Word as the prop which sustains the
                        whole.

The writer's thought was clearly moving in the same circles as Paul's when the latter wrote I Cor. 8.6 and Col. 1.15ff., though with fuller dependence on the theology of Hellenistic Judaism.[3] And probably we have to come to the same conclusion in the case of Hebrews as in the case of Paul. Christ was being presented as the climax of God's revelation (Heb. 1.1–2). In Jewish Wisdom theology, divine Wisdom was a way of speaking of God's fullest and clearest self-revelation, the most that can be known of God, his will and purpose for his creation and his people.[4] Hebrews, like Paul, claimed that *divine Wisdom had come to fullest, definitive and final expression in Christ.*

---

1. Word (Logos) is the dominant category in Philo, with Wisdom (Sophia) little more than an occasional variant for the Logos when an allusion to a female figure was appropriate (cf. e.g. *Fuga*, 97, 108f.; *Som.* 2.242, 245; see further my *Christology*, p. 326, n. 34, p. 340, n. 24).

2. See more fully *Christology*, pp. 166, 207–8.

3. The point here does not depend on whether the author of Hebrews knew Philo's work directly; see above pp. 115 and n. 53.

4. See above §10.5 and *Christology*, pp. 168–76.

Something very similar is presumably true of the Psalm quotations in Heb. 1.8–9, 10–12. Note the ambiguity of verses 8–9 – 'Your throne, O God . . .', or 'God is your throne . . .'; there is a similar ambiguity in the Hebrew of Ps. 45.7 here cited. In verse 9 the writer continues, '. . . Therefore God, your God, has anointed you . . .' In other words, even if the one addressed is addressed as 'God', that is not to detract from the 'Godness' of God, who is still his God. The parallel to the balance of I Cor. 8.6 ('one God . . . one Lord . . .') is to be noted. So presumably also with Heb. 1.10–12, an application of Ps. 102.25–27 – 'You, Lord, in the beginning founded the earth . . .' In the Psalm, the words are manifestly addressed to God as Creator. But like the use of Wisdom language in reference to Christ in verses 1–3, it is presumably an attempt to express the conviction that *Christ embodied the creative power of the Creator God.*[5]

Such use of scripture and of these Wisdom motifs is indicative of the sense of these earliest Christians that the full divine significance of Christ could not be expressed without taking over such otherwise problematic material.

(b) *Adam christology.* The major objective of these opening verses of the letter is clearly to demonstrate Christ's superiority over the angels (1.4–8, 13–14). As part of that same objective (2.4), Hebrews also draws in the clearest expression of Adam christology in the whole of the NT. Heb. 2.6–9 is obviously intended as an exposition of Ps. 8.4–6 – God's design for humankind fulfilled only in the risen Christ.

> It has been testified somewhere [Ps. 8.4–6]:
> 'What is man that you remember him,
> or the son of man that you visit him?
> You made him for a little while lower than the angels,
> you crowned him with glory and honour,
> having put all things in subjection under his feet.'

But the writer at once goes on to note that this purpose had not been fulfilled:

But now we do not yet see all things in subjection to him.

The divine purpose to give the human creature dominion over the rest of creation has not yet achieved its end. What then?

---

5. For fuller treatment of these texts see particularly Braun, *Hebräer*, pp. 38–44, and Attridge, *Hebrews*, pp. 58–61.

> But we do see Jesus, who 'for a little while was made lower than the angels', 'crowned with glory and honour' because of the sufferings of death, so that by the grace of God he might taste death for everyone.

In other words, the goal and purpose which failed in man (Adam) had succeeded with Christ (last Adam). Of him alone was it true that he had been 'crowned with the glory and honour' which the Psalmist gave as the intention of God for humanity when he created male and female.

The final note of that exposition ('that he might taste death for everyone') leads directly to another important metaphor in Hebrews' christology – Christ as 'leader' or 'pioneer' (*archēgos* – 2.10; also 12.2).[6] Later on, the similar imagery of 'forerunner' is used (6.20; only here in the NT). The imagery is of Christ as leader or pioneer and forerunner, going ahead to open up the way for others to follow – going ahead, as will soon become clear, into the very presence of God, 'to lead many sons to glory'.

Even more striking is the use of 'Son' language. He who is described as 'son' in full-blown Wisdom christology in 1.2, is also described as 'son' in 1.5, where the use of Ps. 2.7 implies that his appointment as Son took place *at his resurrection* (so also 5.5). Moreover, the imagery of Jesus as pioneer is also tied in to talk of his 'being made perfect *through suffering*' (2.10). And this too is tied in to the Son christology in 5.7–9:

> In the days of his flesh, Jesus offered up prayers and supplications, with loud cries and tears, to him who was able to save him from death, and he was heard for his godly fear. Although he was a Son, he learned obedience through what he suffered; and being made perfect he became the source of eternal salvation to all who obey him.

The balance of the thought is striking: God's son, who yet learnt obedience through suffering and was *thus made perfect*.

It is of considerable importance in any attempt to assess Hebrews' christology, and to assess what a full blown Wisdom christology like that in 1.1–3 might have meant for the first Christians, to note that the same writer could speak of Christ in terms both of (*a*) *and* (*b*).

(*c*) *High Priest*. In many ways, however, the most striking of all is Hebrews' combination of both these paradoxical motifs in the

---

6. This may well be a primitive christology, since the metaphor is found elsewhere in the NT only in Acts 3.15 and 5.31.

christology of Christ as High Priest after the order of Melchizedek. Particularly noticeable are 7.3 (similar in christological weight to the Wisdom christology), and 7.16 (similar in emphasis to the thought of Jesus as Son through suffering and resurrection).

> 7.3 – He is without father or mother or genealogy, and has neither beginning of days nor end of life, but resembling the Son of God he continues a priest for ever.
> 7.16 – He has become a priest . . . by the power of an indestructible life.[7]

Here, just as with the Wisdom language of 1.2–3, it is clear that Hebrews is part of a wider Jewish theology; in this case the wider speculative use of the Melchizedek figure from Gen. 14.[8] Particularly notable here is the Melchizedek fragment from cave 11 at Qumran – 11QMelch 9–11:

> This is the time of the acceptable year of Melchize(d)ek . . . the holy ones of El to the rei(gn) of judgment, as it is written concerning him in the hymns of David who says: 'Elohim (stan)ds in the congre-(gation of God); among the Elohim he judges' [Ps. 82.1]. And concerning him he says: '(Above) them do you return on high; El shall judge the nations' [Ps. 7.8] . . .

Hardly insignificant for our present concerns is this Melchizedek's role in the final judgment, and his being called Elohim.[9]

It is also pertinent to recall,[10] that Hebrews, like Philo, has probably been influenced in some measure by Platonic idealism – particularly the world-view which saw the real world as above, of which this world is and contains only shadows and imperfect copies. The same world-view operates here too, with Melchizedek representing the ideal of heavenly priesthood, and Christ understood to embody this ideal become hard reality.[11] The claim is in effect the same as that made by Hebrews' Wisdom christology. Wisdom represents the ideal of divine

---

7. See above p. 119 and n. 60.

8. I am not claiming that Hebrews knew 11 QMelch.

9. Elohim, of course, is used in the OT both for angels or gods, and for God; see BDB.

10. See pp. 115 and n. 53. But, as there, the point is the same if we prefer to call it simply a Jewish apocalyptic perspective.

11. Note the ambivalence of 7.3 – Melchizedek resembles the Son of God. Who is the archetype – Melchizedek or the Son of God? In terms of Hebrews' Wisdom christology the answer would be the Son (1.2–3). But in terms of Hebrews' High Priest christology, Melchizedek represents the heavenly reality, over against the earthly shadow of the Aaronic priesthood; Christ is priest 'according to the order of Melchizedek, just like Melchizedek'.

self-revelation, superior to the imperfect revelation given through prophet (1.1–3), or angels (1.4–2.18), or Moses (3.1–4). Christ is that ideal become reality, his death and resurrection the breaking through the barrier from the old age to the new age of Jewish eschatology, from the shadow to the reality of Platonic philosophy, from earth to heaven.

The issue for us is this. Given the philosophical schema on which Hebrews was trading, at least in part, what was the reality which Wisdom and Melchizedek represented for the author? What was the deity that Christ thus expressed? Was the philosophical schema simply a borrowed robe, an *ad hominen* apologetic device to appeal to those who found it meaningful? Or did Hebrews' use of it take a step forward in Christian understanding of Christ? The degree to which Hebrews has been relatively tangential to the major christological developments of subsequent centuries suggests that the former may be closer to the truth.

For us, however, the point is that here we see a Christian comfortable with categories drawn from or meaningful to Greek philosophical thought, including talk of God's self-revelation, and to that extent just like his Alexandrian Jewish brothers. It would be fascinating to know what someone like Philo or the author of the Wisdom of Solomon would have made of Hebrews. Would either have found the author's use of such categories in relation to Christ surprising, or unacceptable? Would they have considered what Hebrews was doing as beyond the pale, beyond what might have been considered acceptable in Hellenistic Judaism? This is the area of comparison, it should be noted – Hebrews in comparison with Alexandrian Judaism, rather than with the more restrained categories we have dealt with elsewhere. Would Hebrews by itself have been any less acceptable to Alexandrian Jews than the middle Platonic philosophizing of Philo? If Philo remains within the spectrum of recognizable and acceptable first-century Judaism, would the same not be true for Hebrews also? It would be hard to answer anything other than Yes.

11.2 James and I Peter

James is the most characteristically Jewish and least distinctively Christian document in the NT. Here the only two overt features of christological significance for us are 2.1 and 5.6.

> 2.1 – My brothers, show no partiality as you hold the faith of our Lord Jesus Christ, the Lord of glory.

5.6 – You have condemned, you have killed the righteous man; he does not resist you.

The significance of James' language in 2.1 is not clear. 'The Lord of glory' is certainly an example of *kyrios* christology, but in view of the close connection already noted elsewhere between *kyrios* christology and Adam christology,[12] the glory could well be that of *Adam*: Jesus as the one who has been restored to the glory Adam lost and who has been given the fuller glory God had originally intended for humanity when he created Adam (cf. Rom. 3.23). In Paul, the phrase 'faith of our Lord Jesus Christ' would best be understood in the sense faith *in* Jesus Christ (as in Gal. 2.16). But given James' characteristic difference in emphasis from Paul (James 2.17–26), it would be no surprise that James intended the phrase to speak of Christ's faith, that is, Christ's faithfulness.[13] In which case Jesus would be presented here as a model for James' readers to follow. This ties in with the allusions to Jesus' teaching, which thus seems to have been regarded as a basic constituent of Christian wisdom or moral teaching[14] – Jesus being remembered as a teacher of halakah and wisdom. So too in 5.6, if there is indeed a reference to Christ here ('the righteous one'), as seems most probable, the reminiscence of Wisdom of Solomon's talk of 'the righteous' (Wisd. 2, 5) is striking – Jesus' death being understood in terms of the suffering of the righteous.

It is difficult to speak of James' christology. The references are too isolated, and the language too allusive for us to gain a real handle on the christology of the author. All that we can say is that the brief references we have are *wholly Jewish in language and thought*, and relatively undeveloped when compared with the christologies of other NT writers.

In I Peter the most striking text for our discussion is 1.20.[15] It would be possible to read it as an expression of Christian belief in the literal pre-existence of Jesus.[16] But a strikingly close parallel can be seen in

---

12. See above §10.4.

13. In 2.21–23 James interprets Abraham's faith as faithfulness, in contrast to Paul (Rom. 4), but in accordance with the normal Jewish understanding of the time (I Macc. 2.52; cf. Ps. 106.31 and *Jub.* 30.17–19).

14. Cf. particularly James 1.5, 17 with Matt. 7.7ff.; James 1.22f. with Matt. 7.24f.; James 4.12 with Matt. 7.1; and James 5.12 with Matt. 5.34–37. That all the echoes lie within the Sermon on the Mount is significant.

15. In a larger discussion of I Peter's christology, however, 3.18–22 should probably be given pride of place.

16. See e.g. J. N. D. Kelly, *Peter and Jude*, London: Black 1969, p. 76.

Test.Mos. 1.14, and the question has to be asked whether the two are so very different from each other in thought and theology.

> I Peter 1.20 – Jesus was destined before the foundation of the world but was made manifest at the end of the times for your sake.

> *Test.Mos.* 1.14 – Moses says, 'He designed and devised me, and he prepared me before the foundation of the world that I should be the mediator of his covenant'.

Evidently, in each case the author wanted to say that the work of Moses/Jesus was in no way accidental, but rather had been planned from the beginning. That is to say, the *Testament of Moses* and I Peter are examples of Jews of the first century using the language of pre-existence, or at least of predestination, to express *the claim that Moses/Jesus was the climax of the divine purpose prepared from the beginning of time.* In each case the language used is a way of expressing the sovereignty of God more than any idea that Moses or Jesus had themselves existed at the beginning of time.[17] Here too, in other words, the language and conceptuality is *well within the range of what we can find within Jewish theology of the time.*

11.3 The Gospel of Matthew

It is worth giving particular attention to Matthew, since his is the most Jewish of the Gospels, and since his christological claims mark important developments or phases or features in second generation Christianity.

(a) *Matthew's Wisdom christology.* We have already had occasion to note the wisdom language used by Jesus in his own teaching.[18] This emphasis, on Jesus as a teacher of wisdom is retained in the Q collection of the Jesustradition, where Jesus is remembered as the emissary or spokesman of divine Wisdom. But when we examine Matthew's use of the same material it becomes clear that he has strengthened that Wisdom christology, and that *for Matthew, Jesus is no longer simply the spokesman for Wisdom, but is to be identified with Wisdom herself.* The point has already been documented in detail elsewhere;[19] here we need only recall the chief evidence.

---

17. See also my *Christology*, pp. 236–7.

18. See above §9.5.

19. See particularly M. J. Suggs, *Wisdom, Christology and Law in Matthew's Gospel*, Cambridge: Harvard University 1970, chs 2–3; C. Deutsch, 'Wisdom in Matthew: Transformation of a Symbol', *NovT* 32 (1990), pp. 13–47; also my *Christology*, pp. 197–204.

(1) In Luke 7.35 Jesus is presented as Wisdom's *child* (so also the Baptist). In the Matthean parallel (Matt. 11.19) Jesus is identified as *Wisdom* –

Luke 7.35 – Yet Wisdom is justified by all her children;

Matt 11.19 – Yet Wisdom is justified by her deeds

– where it is clear that the 'deeds' are 'the deeds of the Christ' (11.2), a reference which is itself redactional (cf. Luke 7.18). (2) Matt. 11.28–30 seems to be Matthew's elaboration of 11.25–27. The first three verses (25–27) are parallel to Luke 10.21f., where Jesus speaks in language characteristic of the teacher of wisdom. But in verses 28–30 Jesus speaks more *as* Wisdom, echoing the language of ben Sira (Sir. 51.23–26): where Jesus ben Sira invites pupils to draw near and put their necks under the yoke of *Wisdom*, Jesus of Nazareth invites his followers to take *his own* yoke upon them. (3) In Luke 11.49, 'the *Wisdom* of God said, "I will send them prophets . . ." '. In Matthew's parallel (Matt. 23.34) it is *Jesus himself* who says, 'I send you prophets . . .'. Unless his readers were familiar with the Lukan form of the saying, of course, the fact of redaction would be lost on them. But the point remains that Matthew found it appropriate to make the modification and that the modification tells us something about his own christology. (4) Finally, in Matt. 23.37–39 (par. Luke 13.34f.), we have further use of Wisdom language and imagery by Jesus. Here the fact that Matthew thinks of Jesus as divine Wisdom only becomes apparent when Matthew's version of Jesus' words is read in the context of Matt.23.

In short, where in the Q material Jesus seems to speak consistently as the messenger of Wisdom, Matthew saw it as most natural to think of Jesus as speaking with the voice of *Wisdom herself*.

(b) Matthews' christology of divine presence. An important theme in Matthew is formed by the linkage between 1.23, 18.20 and 28.20. Although the motif is thus only briefly attested, the importance of the first and third of these references underlines the importance of the whole: at the beginning, the first of Matthew's formula quotations – so a thematic statement for what is to follow; and at the very end – a summary of the significance of what has gone before.

1.23 – Behold, a virgin shall conceive and bear a son, and his name shall be called Emmanuel [Isa. 7.14] (which means, God with us).

18.20 – Where two or three are gathered in my name, there am I in the midst of them.

28.20 – Lo, I am with you always, to the close of the age.

In 1.23 the significance of the quotation from Isa. 7.14 has usually
been located in its function as a proof text for the virginal conception
of Jesus. But in view of 18.20 and 28.20, it would probably be more
accurate to say that for Matthew the chief significance of the text lies
in the name 'Emmanuel' – the one thus conceived understood as *the
presence of 'God with us'*. As regards 18.20, most major commentators note the parallel with *m. Abot* 3.2, where the same thing is
said in effect of the Shekinah present with those who speak words of
Torah between them.[20] The Shekinah (glory) of God, we may recall,
is one of those phrases which serves to express God's immanence.[21]
We cannot assume, of course, that the rabbinic formulation of this
thought was as early as Jesus' time, though the parallel is sufficiently
close that Matt. 18.20 could be an argument for its early dating.[22] At
any rate Matthew's thought was probably not simply of Jesus himself
present with his disciples, but of Jesus present among them *as the
mode of divine presence*. 28.20 almost certainly has the same force,
since the promise follows the assertion of the risen Christ that 'All
authority in heaven and on earth has been given to me'. The one who
will be present with them to the close of the age is the viceroy of God,
God's representative and plenipotentiary, *God's effective presence on
earth*.[23]

The two emphases (*a*) and (*b*) amount to the same claim and reinforce
each other: Jesus-Wisdom as the self-revelation of God; Jesus-
Emmanuel as 'God with us'. That is, in Matthew's view, *Jesus was
nothing less than the supreme and final expression of God's presence*,
the embodiment of divine Wisdom, the definition of 'God with us'.
In a very important sense, Matthew's *christ*-ology is a subset of his
theo-ology. Even though Matthew resisted any weakening of traditional Jewish emphasis on the Torah,[24] it is clear that for Matthew
the clearest manifestation of God's self-revelation and saving-
revelation was *not*, or was no longer the Torah, but Christ. At the

---

20. *mAbot* 3.2 – 'If two sit together and words of the Law (are spoken) between them,
the divine presence (the Shekinah) rests between them.'

21. See above §10.5 pp. 261.

22. The saying is attributed to Rabbi Hananiah ben Teradion who was killed in 135 at
the time of the bar Kochba revolt (Danby, *Mishnah*, p. 450, n. 3).

23. Matthew's christology of divine presence has been studied in great detail by my
pupil, David Kupp, *Matthew's Emmanuel: Divine Presence and God's People in the First
Gospel*, SNTSMS 90; Cambridge University 1996. Cf. Davies and Allison, *Matthew*,
1.217.

24. See above §8.5(*a*).

same time, we should once again simply note that the terms of Matthew's christology are *thoroughly Jewish* and would have been so perceived by Matthew's Jewish readers when they made their own assessment of the significance of that christology.

11.4 The Revelation of John

The most striking feature of Revelation's christology is probably the opening vision which sets the scene for what follows – Rev. 1.12–16.

> [12]Then I turned to see the voice that was speaking to me, and on turning I saw seven golden lampstands, [13]and in the midst of the lampstands *one like a son of man, clothed with* a long robe and with a *golden girdle* round his breast; [14]*his head and his hair were white as white wool, white as snow; his eyes were like a flame of fire,* [15]his feet were *like burnished bronze,* refined as in a furnace, and *his voice* was *like the sound of many waters;* [16]in his right hand he held seven stars, from his mouth issued a sharp two-edged sword, and his face was like the sun shining in full strength.

What is particularly striking here is the clear echo and use of several OT passages – not just Dan. 7.9 and 13, but also Ezek. 1.24, 26, 8.2 and Dan. 10.5–6. The italics indicate the clearest parallels.

> Ezek. 1.24–27 – In his awe-inspiring vision of the chariot throne of God, Ezekiel heard the sound of the wings of the living creatures '*like the sound of many waters*'; 'and seated above the likeness of a throne was *a likeness as it were of a human form.* [27]And upward from what had the appearance of his loins I saw as it were *gleaming bronze,* like the appearance of a *fire* enclosed round about; and downward from what had the appearance of his loins I saw as it were the appearance of fire, and there was brightness round about him.'

> Ezek. 8.2 – Then I beheld, and lo, a form that had *the appearance of a man*: below what appeared to be his loins it was *fire,* and above his loins it was like the appearance of brightness, *like gleaming bronze.*

> Dan. 7.9, 13 – As I looked, thrones were placed and one that was ancient of days took his seat; his raiment was *white as snow,* and *the hair of his head like pure wool;* his throne was *fiery flames,* its wheels were burning fire . . . [13]I saw in the night visions, and behold,

with the clouds of heaven there came *one like a son of man*, and he came to the Ancient of Days and was presented before him.

Dan. 10.5–6 – I lifted up my eyes and looked, and behold, *a man clothed in* linen, whose loins were *girded with gold* of Uphaz. His body was like beryl, his face like the appearance of lightning, *his eyes like flaming torches*, his arms and legs like the gleam of *burnished bronze*, and the sound of *his words like the noise of a multitude*.

The significance of these parallels has been investigated particularly by Christopher Rowland.[25]

(1) Clearly we are in touch here with an apocalyptic tradition of *a glorious angelic figure* encountered by the apocalyptist in a vision. In addition to the texts already cited note also particularly 11QMelch (Melchizedek described as 'elohim'), *Apoc. Zeph.* 6.11–15,[26] *Apoc. Ab.* 10–11 (note the description of 11.1–4)[27] and *Joseph and Asenath* 14.9.[28] This tradition in turn was almost certainly drawing on the still older tradition of 'the angel of the Lord', who appeared, for example, to Hagar and Ishmael in Gen. 16.7–12, and to Moses in the burning bush, according to Ex. 3.2. Also significant here was Ex. 23.20f. –

Behold, I send an angel before you, to guard you on the way and to bring you to the place which I have prepared. Give heed to him and hearken to his voice, do not rebel against him, for he will not pardon your transgression; for my name is in him.

This identification of an angel in whom God had put his name was a major stimulus to the idea of a majestic angel, who might even be mistaken for God. Hence the name given to the glorious angel in the *Apocalypse of Abraham* – Yahoel – which was probably intended as

---

25. C. Rowland, 'The Vision of the Risen Christ in Rev. 1.13ff.: The Debt of an Early Christology to an Aspect of Jewish Angelology', *JTS* 31 (1980), pp. 1–11; also *The Open Heaven. A Study of Apocalyptic in Judaism and Early Christianity*, London: SPCK/New York: Crossroad 1982.

26. 'Then I arose and saw a great angel standing before me with *his face shining like the rays of the sun in its glory* ... And he was girded as if *a golden girdle were upon his breast. His feet were like bronze which is melted in a fire*' (6.11–13).

27. 'The appearance of his body was like sapphire, and the aspect of his face was like chrysolite, and *the hair of his head like snow*' (11.2).

28. 'Asenath raised her head and saw, and behold a man in every respect similar to Joseph, by the robe and the crown and the royal staff, except that *his face was like lightning*, and his eyes like sunshine, and the hairs of his head *like a flame of fire* of a burning torch, and hands and feet like iron *shining forth from a fire*, and sparks shot forth from his hands and feet.' Italics indicate what is obviously a common pool of imagery.

a combination of Yahweh and El; at any rate, the allusion of *Apoc. Ab.* 10.3 to Ex. 23.21 is clear.

(2) The same strand of material also puts us in touch with an early form of Jewish mysticism – *Merkabah* or *chariot mysticism*. The name derives from Ezekiel's vision of the chariot throne, including even the vision of God, so tentatively described in Ezek. 1.26. The ultimate objective of Merkabah mysticism was for the mystic to re-experience the vision of Ezekiel, to be granted the vision of God.[29] This is an important element in the context of second generation christology to which we must return (§ 11.6).

(3) The most striking feature of this whole tradition for us is *the degree of confusion between God and the glorious angel* which seems to have been involved. This was already implicit in talk of 'the angel of God'. For this 'angel of the Lord' was *a way of expressing the presence of God*. Thus in Gen. 16.13 Hagar asks, 'Have I really seen God and remained alive after seeing him?' In Gen. 21.17f. the angel speaks in the first person as God. In Gen. 31.11–13 the angel says, 'I am the God of Bethel'. And in Ex. 3.2–6 the one seen in the burning bush is identified both as the angel of the Lord and as the God of Abraham, Isaac and Jacob, who goes on to say 'I am who I am' (Ex. 3.14).

The same point is evident in the degree to which these visions and the descriptions used by the seer seem to overlap and merge. Particularly relevant here is the degree of closeness of the descriptions of the visions of Ezek. 8.2 and Dan. 10.5–6 to that of the vision of God in Ezek. 1.26. They seem to borrow from each other, to merge into each other. In the visions, distinctive details become lost in overpowering impressions of fire and of brightness. In similar vein Melchizedek can be described as Elohim, and Yahoel as the angel of the Lord in whom God has put his name.

All this is true of Revelation also. Not only does the vision of the son of man borrow descriptive language from these different visions.[30] But very striking is the fact that Rev. 1.13–14 is influenced *both* by Dan. 7.13, *and* by Dan. 7.9. That is to say, Jesus is described in terms used not only for the son of man, *but also for the Ancient of Days* ('his head and his hair were white as white wool, white as snow')! So too, not only God says 'I am the Alpha and the Omega' (1.8), but also the exalted Christ (22.13; cf. 1.17). And some of the descriptions of the exalted Christ's relation to the throne in the seer's vision seem

---

29. See e.g. G. G. Scholem, *Major Trends in Jewish Mysticism*, 1941; New York: Schocken, 1961, pp. 42–4.

30. Note also Rev. 10.1 – 'Then I saw another mighty angel coming down from heaven, wrapped in a cloud, and his face was like the sun, and his legs like pillars of fire.'

to imply that the Lamb was sitting on *God's* throne: 7.17 – the Lamb sits 'in the midst of the throne'; 22.1, 3 speak of 'the throne (singular) of God and of the Lamb'.

What is the significance of all this? Rowland sees what he calls a process of '*bifurcation*' taking place, a process already happening in the Jewish texts. By that he means a process whereby the divine human-like figure on the throne in Ezek. 1.26–28 seems to become separated from the throne and to function separately as 'the agent of the divine will' – 'a gradual splitting in the way the divine functions are described'. Ezek. 8.2–4 in particular reveals 'the separation of the form of God from the divine throne-chariot to act as quasi-angelic mediator'. And in reference to Dan. 10.5–9 Rowland speaks of 'the beginning of a hypostatic development'.[31] If all this were so, once again we would have grounds for speaking about *some kind of binitarian emphasis in Jewish thinking prior to or independent of the emergence of Christianity*.

At this point, however, I have to express some serious doubts. (1) 'The angel of the Lord' had provided an old and well established precedent for speaking of *God's immanent presence and activity* by the device of envisioning and talking about an angelic being. In effect 'the angel of the Lord' was simply the old way of speaking of God making himself visible to the human eye. Or should we say, 'the angel of the Lord' was early on understood simply as the extent to which God could make himself manifest to human perception.

(2) A question needs to be asked which Rowland fails to ask: how much of the similarity of the language of these visions is due to the fact that descriptions of glorious heavenly figures in visions could draw on only a limited pool of metaphors and images? Hence the prevalence of the impression of fire and brightness. That is to say, there could be a natural link at the *literary* or descriptive level between these accounts of such visions, simply because the imagery used by one prompted the use of the same imagery by another. But that need *not* imply any intention to suggest that the figures thus described in different visions were the same figure. On the contrary, where such glorious heavenly beings are identified they are specifically identified as different – Melchizedek, Eremiel (*Apoc. Zeph.* 6.15), Yahoel (*Apoc. Ab.* 10.3), Adam and Abel (*Test. Ab.* 11.9; 13.1–2).[32] Still less should

---

31. Rowland, *Open Heaven*, pp. 96–7, 100.

32. The implication of the full narrative of Dan. 10 presumably is that the one seen in 10.5–6 (and 10.16, 18) is one of the chief archangels, like Michael, leading the heavenly host against the angelic rulers of other nations (Persia, Greece; 10.13, 20) – probably

we deduce from mere similarity of description between the vision of Ezek. 1.26–28 and others that the figures so described were intended to be one and the same. Since man was made in the image of God, any attempt to envision God or one of his angels would almost inevitably envisage a human form. What is more striking in such comparison, if anything, is that the exceeding tentativeness of Ezekiel's description is *not* repeated ('the likeness as it were of a human form'). The angelic figures could be described more boldly, simply because they were *not* descriptions of God himself.

(3) With Hurtado, I question whether it is right to speak of a 'bifurcation' in God. Certainly it is true that *the vision of a glorious being on a throne in heaven was the source of what came to be regarded as one of the basic heresies within rabbinic Judaism*. Four rabbis from the early decades of the second century are remembered in rabbinic tradition as having 'entered the garden' (*t. Hag.* 2.3–4 pars.). As most agree, the tradition probably refers in a veiled way to a vision of the chariot throne of God.[33] One of them, Elisha ben Abuyah, is regarded in rabbinic tradition as an arch-heretic, because in his vision of heaven he mistook the glorious figure sitting on a great throne (Metatron) as a second divine power in heaven: 'There are indeed two powers in heaven', he exclaimed (*III Enoch* 16.3) – thus denying the unity of God. This is what came to be known as *'the two powers heresy'* (*b. Hag.* 15a; *III Enoch* 16).[34] But in the apocalyptic visions of angels cited above care seems to be taken to *avoid* any such possible conclusion. The angels spoken of are kept distinct from God – for example, *Apoc. Ab.* 16.3–4: 'God cannot be looked upon himself', that is, unlike angels. And a characteristic note in such visions is the firm refusal of the angelic figure to allow the seer to worship him. So *Apoc. Zeph.* 6.15 – 'He said to me, "Take heed. Do not worship me. I am not the Lord Almighty, but I am the great angel, Eremiel . . .".' And in *Apoc. Ab.* 17 'the angel knelt down with me (the apocalyptist) and worshipped' (17.2) and together they recite a hymn of adoration. In other words, the pre-Christian apocalyptic and mystical tradition seems to have *remained consciously within the constraints of Jewish monotheism*.

Gabriel, since earlier on he had been described as 'one having the appearance of a man' (8.15–17).

33. See particularly I. Gruenwald, *Apocalyptic and Merkabah Mysticism*, Leiden: Brill 1980, pp. 86–92; Rowland, *Open Heaven*, pp. 306–40.

34. R. T. Herford, *Christianity in Talmud and Midrash*, London: Williams & Norgate 1903, pp. 262–6; A. F. Segal, *Two Powers in Heaven: Early Rabbinic Reports about Christianity and Gnosticism*, Leiden: Brill 1977. See also Thoma, *Christian Theology*, pp. 121–3.

I am dubious therefore whether we can see in pre-Christian Jewish texts or in other first-century Jewish apocalyptic or mystical tradition any real precursor to the Christian revision of Jewish monotheism made necessary by Christian assessment of the significance of Jesus. In the case of Revelation, indeed, it is precisely at this point that we can probably detect the Christian seer taking a step beyond this earlier and contemporary Jewish apocalyptic vision tradition. For although he belongs thoroughly within that milieu, there is a point of significant difference. *In Revelation there seems to be clear and uninhibited worship of the Lamb.* In particular, the hymns of chapter 5, to the Lamb, are no different in character from the hymns in chapter 4, to God. And in such passages as 5.13 and 7.10 the Lamb is linked with God in a common ascription of adoration. This is all the more significant, since John the seer was fully aware of the danger of mistaking a glorious angel for God. In Rev. 19.10, indeed, he issues the same warning as his fellow apocalyptists: 'Then I fell down at his (the angel's) feet to worship him, but he said to me, "You must not do that! I am a fellow servant with you and your brethren who hold the testimony of Jesus. Worship God".' The fact, then, that *he both shared these inhibitions and abandoned them in the case of the exalted Jesus*, indicates a clear conviction on his part that the exalted Jesus was *not* to be understood simply in terms of a glorious angel: the glorious figure of Rev. 1.12–16, unlike the glorious angels of similar visions elsewhere, is worthy of worship.[35]

To sum up. Three points of central importance for us emerge from all this. (1) Revelation's christology is very much part of and in line with the visions which were already familiar within the tradition of Jewish apocalyptic. (2) The visions of Revelation, however, seem to be stretching that pattern and indeed beginning to break it; the constraints of monotheism previously observed were being challenged. (3) But at this point Revelation was not entirely alone, since round about the time that Revelation was written, or soon after, we have the emergence of 'the two powers heresy'.

The question which thus emerges is *whether what the seer of Rev-*

---

35. See also R. Bauckham, 'The Worship of Jesus in Apocalyptic Christianity', *NTS* 27 (1980–81), pp. 322–41. Cf. my critique of Hurtado above (§10.7(*b*)). The critique of Hurtado by P. A. Rainbow, 'Jewish Monotheism as the Matrix for New Testament Christology: A Review Article', *NovT* 33 (1991), pp. 78–91, however, underplays the importance of visionary experiences, which may not only be conditioned by and conform to older conceptualizations, but may very well contribute to their transmutation (cf. Paul's conversion-commissioning experience and the consequent development of distinctive Christian vocabulary and christology).

*elation did was a legitimate extension of a pattern already well estab-
lished, or a step beyond, breaking that pattern.* Revelation at this
point was clearly part of a larger Jewish apocalyptic and mystical
tradition engaged in *exploring the boundaries of how to speak of
God and how to envisage the transmission of divine revelation.* But
has Revelation broken through these boundaries or simply pushed
them out a little further? Did the concept of God need to be redefined
in the light of such visions? Or rather should the visions be rejected
in the light of the monotheistic axiom, and the seer of such visions
be regarded as having abandoned monotheism? We know what the
rabbinic reaction was to a similar challenge in the case of Elisha ben
Abuyah. But how would they have regarded the apocalypse of John?

The issue thus exposed comes to its sharpest expression in the case
of the Fourth Gospel.

11.5 The Fourth Gospel – christology and crisis

In what will perforce be a much compressed treatment, we start with
two points which are either fairly obvious or are widely agreed.[36]

(a) *Christology is manifestly central to the Fourth Gospel.* The
Evangelist makes this clear himself in giving as his objective in writing,
'that you may believe that Jesus is the Christ, the Son of God . . .'
(20.31). The same point is evident also in the 'Johannine distinctives'
– the features of the Fourth Gospel which mark it off most clearly
from the Synoptics: particularly, the Son sent from the Father from
heaven, conscious of his pre-existence, the descending and ascending
Son of Man, and the profound 'I am' sayings.[37] Moreover, *the points
at which the Evangelist betrays greatest sensitivity to real or potential
challenges have all to do with the Christian claims for Christ.* For
example, the repeated juxtaposition with the Baptist in chapters 1–
3, with the Baptist deliberately contrasted as inferior to Christ (1.6–
9, 15, 20; 3.28–31); the way in which the older battles over the law
and sabbath have become christological battles (especially chapters
5, 7 and 9); the dramatic unfolding of the *krisis* theme,[38] where it is
precisely the shining of Christ as the light (of the world) which forces
the separation of a choice for or against him (3.19–21); and the way

---

36. In what follows I draw on my 'Let John be John. A Gospel for its Time', *Das
Evangelium und die Evangelien*, hrsg. P. Stuhlmacher, WUNT 28; Tübingen: Mohr-
Siebeck 1983, pp. 309–39 = *The Gospel and the Gospels*, Grand Rapids: Eerdmans 1991,
pp. 293–322.
37. See more fully above §9.6.
38. See above §8.6.

in which the Fourth Gospel depicts the disciples' faith in Christ, going from initial confidence (1.41, 45, 49), through crisis (6.68–69) and clarification (14.5–11), to the climactic confession of Thomas, 'My Lord and my God' (20.28).

In short, the christological claim is very much at the heart of the Fourth Gospel, including not least the distinctively Johannine character and form of that claim.

(b) There is also wide agreement that the context of the Fourth Gospel is late first century CE and that *its writing reflects a crisis between the new sect and a dominant form of Judaism*, or at least a parting of the ways between the Johannine congregations and another form of late-first-century Judaism. We have already noted how often John speaks of 'the Jews' as hostile to Christianity.[39] There is a middle ground of Jews (the crowd) who have not yet decided; but strong opposition is already coming from 'the Jews', that is, from an authorized body who can be called 'the Jews' because they represent or at least claim to represent the authentic voice of 'Judaism' – religious authorities who determine matters of faith and polity for the people (1.19; 5.16; 9.18; 18.12; 19.31). The use of *aposynagōgos* ('expelled from the synagogue') in 9.22, 12,42 and 16,2 is similarly significant. Note particularly 9.22 – 'The Jews had already agreed that if anyone should confess him to be the Christ, he was to be put out of the synagogue.' This seems to presuppose a formal decision made by an authoritative Jewish body to excommunicate any Jews from the synagoguge who were making a Christian confession.[40]

The prominence and character of this tension between Jesus and 'the Jews' points to a primarily Jewish context for the Fourth Gospel in the period after 70.

(1) The sharpness of the breach between Jesus and 'the Jews' and the vehemence of the polemic in the middle section of the Gospel[41] is not matched anywhere else in the NT, not even by Matt. 23.

(2) The breach centred on the confession of Jesus as Messiah (9.22; 12.42). There is, however, *no* indication that such a confession

---

39. For what follows see again above §8.6.

40. See particularly Martyn, *History and Theology in the Fourth Gospel*, ch. 2, whose main thesis that the Evangelist presents a two-level drama (an *einmaliges* event during Jesus' earthly lifetime, and the situation facing his own community) has been widely accepted. See e.g. D. M. Smith, 'The Contribution of J. Louis Martyn to the Understanding of the Gospel of John', in *The Conversation Continues. Studies in Paul and John. In Honor of J. L. Martyn*, ed. R. T. Fortna and B. R. Gaventa, Nashville: Abingdon 1990, pp. 275–94.

41. See above §8.6 pp. 210–1.

became a make or break issue between Jewish Christians and leaders of Judaism prior to 70. The earlier disputes, as we have seen, were about the Temple and the Torah. But in Palestine, Jews were evidently able to believe that Jesus was Messiah and yet remain largely undisturbed before the Jewish revolt (cf. Acts 21.20–26).[42] Likewise in areas of Jewish mission: Josephus, for example, makes no mention of any faction being excluded from the synagogues of Syria during this period. Even in areas of the Gentile mission, those looking in from outside seem to have regarded the disputes as internal Jewish affairs: when the Jews of Corinth brought Paul before the Roman tribunal, Gallio's response was curt – 'Since it is a matter of questions about words and names and your own law, see to it yourselves' (Acts 18.15); the trouble in Rome caused by the preaching of Jesus as the Christ was regarded as a dispute internal to the Jewish community, resulting in (many? all?) Jews being expelled (Suetonius, *Claudius* 25.4; Acts 18.2).[43]

(3) In contrast, there is evidence from the Jewish side that the period between 70 and 100 saw the first proponents of rabbinic Judaism taking a deliberate step to mark themselves off from other claimants to the broad heritage of pre-70 Judaism. In particular, it would seem that the Twelfth Benediction (of the Eighteen Benedictions), the *birkat ha-minim*, was revised during this period to include a pronouncement against the *minim*, 'heretics', that is, those regarded as Jewish sectarians, whose views and practices were no longer acceptable to the rabbis (*b. Ber.* 28b).[44] That this emendation, to include a curse against the heretics, had the Christians specifically in view is not certain. It is true that one version, probably a further emendation, does specify the Nazarenes as such; and Justin confirms that there was a cursing directed against Christians in the synagogues of his period (*Dial.* 16, 47, 96). However, the probability is that the malediction was not so

---

42. The persecution referred to in I Thess. 2.14–16, Gal. 4.29 and 5.11 all seems to have been occasioned by Jewish hostility to the opening of the gospel to Gentiles, and thus to be, from the Jewish perspective, Torah-centred rather than Christ-centred (see further above chs 7–8). The devoutly Jewish believers in Jerusalem were evidently not affected; if anything, many of them may have supported such a policy of internal discipline. This is confirmed by Josephus' description of the death of James, brother of Jesus, in Jerusalem in 62 CE. James was arraigned by the Sadducean party on charges of 'having transgressed the law', and his execution caused offence to 'those of the inhabitants of the city who were considered the most fair-minded and who were strict in observance of the law' (*Ant.* 20.200–1). See also above p. 164 n. 33

43. See further below §12.2.

44. The effect of the revision would be to make it impossible for one of the *minim* to act as precentor in the synagogue in leading the prayers of the congregation, as he might be called upon to do by the *archisynagōgos*.

specific at first.[45] At the same time, it is equally probable that the *minim included* the Christians; since the boundary was beginning to be drawn more tightly round rabbinic Judaism to exclude some of the other Judaisms of the pre-70 period, (Jewish) Christianity would almost certainly be numbered among the other Judaisms thus targetted.[46]

In fact, the best explanation of John 9.22 is that it refers directly to something like the *birkat ha-minim*, if only a local equivalent. Either way, 9.22 would seem to provide sufficient confirmation that *by the time the Fourth Gospel was written, there was a form of official Judaism which no longer regarded it as acceptable for Jews to confess Jesus as Messiah, and which could enforce its ruling on the subject among the local synagogues.*

Why so? Why should the confession of Jesus as Messiah *now* provoke such a confrontation between Jesus and (the leaders of) 'the Jews'? Most likely the answer is two-fold. (1) The Christian claims for Jesus were being pressed or expressed with such force at this time that christology became an issue as never before, making it impossible for other Jews to remain agnostic about these claims; and (2) they were met by a rabbinic Judaism beginning to draw its own boundaries more tightly round 'Judaism'. *A Christianity which was continuing to push back the older boundaries was met by a Judaism trying to draw in the same boundaries more tightly.* The almost inevitable result was a split, a parting of the ways.

11.6 The Fourth Gospel – the divine revealer

What would it have been in Christian claims regarding Christ which would have provoked this result? We have a number of clues which together build up to a strong answer.

---

45. In the Palestinian recension the twelfth benediction reads: 'And for apostates let there be no hope; and may the insolent kingdom be quickly uprooted, in our days. And may the Nazarenes and the heretics perish quickly; and may they be erased from the Book of Life; and may they not be inscribed with the righteous. Blessed art thou, Lord, who humblest the insolent'. But the Nazarenes are included only in the Geniza version. See Schürer, 2.462–3; Schiffman, *JCSD*, pp. 149–52; *Who Was a Jew?*, pp. 53–61.

46. For a balanced assessment of the conflicting evidence and arguments see particularly W. Horbury, 'The Benediction of the *Minim* and Early Jewish–Christian Controversy', *JTS* 33 (1982), pp. 19–61. But see also important cautionary notes voiced e.g. by Thoma, *Christian Theology*, pp. 146–50; R. Kimelman, '*Birkat Ha-Minim* and the Lack of Evidence for an Anti-Christian Jewish Prayer in Late Antiquity', *JCSD*, pp. 226–44; Cohen, *Maccabees to Mishnah*, pp. 227–8; see also Overman, *Matthew's Gospel and Formative Judaism*, pp. 48–56, and further below §12.1.

(*a*) There were evidently two contentious points for Jewish ears which are clearly reflected in the Fourth Gospel. (1) *The question of Jesus' origin*: where had he come from? Was it from Bethlehem, or Galilee, or Samaria, or where (7.26–27, 41–42, 52; 8.48; 9.29; 19.9)? The reader of the Fourth Gospel, of course, would know the Evangelist's own answer – 'from his Father in heaven' (6.41; 7.27–29, 42, 52; 8.23; 9.29; 19.9). This emphasis on the heavenly origin and status of Jesus is also expressed in the idea of the Son of Man descending from and ascending to heaven (3.12–13; 6.61–62) – the most distinctive feature of the Son of Man motif in the Fourth Gospel. Most disturbing of all for 'the Jews' is the inference that in claiming to be Son of God, Jesus has made himself *'equal with God'* (5.18), has made himself *God* (10.33) – again a claim which the Fourth Evangelist clearly wanted to make on his own account (1.1, 18; 20.28).

(2) Bound up with all this is one of the most consistent emphases of the Fourth Gospel, on *Jesus as the bearer of divine revelation*. What he says has the stamp of heavenly authority, because as the Son of God he speaks what he has seen and heard with the Father; as the Son of Man, he speaks with the authority of one who has descended from heaven; as one who is from above, his message outweighs in kind and quality anything said by him who is from below.[47] This motif is the basis for Rudolf Bultmann's much quoted observation: 'Jesus as the revealer of God reveals nothing but that he is the revealer.'[48]

(*b*) When we set this against the context of post-70 Judaism we begin to recognize *an important area of overlap* – particularly with the strains of apocalyptic and mystical Judaism already touched on above (§11.4).

(1) It is important, first of all, to appreciate the extent to which both these strands were caught up with *the same concern regarding divine revelation*. Both apocalyptic and merkabah mysticism were characterized precisely by their claim to a direct knowledge of heavenly mysteries – either by means of a vision, or, more frequently, by means of an ascent to heaven. Such ascents to heaven are attributed not only to Enoch and to Abraham, but also to Adam, to Levi, to Baruch and to Isaiah[49] – most of these reports being either roughly

---

47. 1.17–18, 49–51; 3.10–13, 32; 7.16–18; 8.14, 28, 38; 12.49–50; 14.10; 15.15; 17.14.
48. Bultmann, *Theology*, Vol. 2, p. 66.
49. Enoch – *I Enoch* 14.8ff.; 39.3ff.; 70–71; *II Enoch* 3ff.
   Abraham – *Test. Ab.* 10ff.; *Apoc. Ab.* 15ff.; cf. also *IV Ezra* 3.14; *II Bar.* 4.4.
   Adam – *Life of Adam and Eve* 25–29.

contemporary with or pre-dating the period of our interest.[50] So too the account of Moses' ascent of Mount Sinai (Ex. 19.3; 24.18) evidently encouraged several circles within Judaism to view it as an ascent to heaven.[51] Similarly with the practice of *merkabah mysticism* – the aspiration, by means of meditation, particularly on the chariot vision of Ezekiel 1 (but also other visions, Isa. 6 and Dan. 7.9–10), to experience for oneself a mystical ascent to or revelation of the throne of God. Such practice seems to have become already well established in our period. It may be reflected already in *I Enoch* 14, is hinted at in Sir. 49.8, and is clearly attested in the so-called 'angelic liturgy' of Qumran (4QSl 40.24).[52] Not least of relevance here is the appearance in some of these visions of a glorious heavenly being, already referred to (§11.4), and the motif of the transformation into angel-like form of the one who ascends, notably Moses and Isaiah, and especially Enoch.[53] It is probably significant that it was just in this same period (post-70) that we find the *Dan. 7.13–14 vision* of 'one like a son of man' becoming a focus of speculation in both Jewish and Christian apocalyptic literature (*IV Ezra* 13; Rev. 1.13; and probably *I Enoch* 37–71); in the aftermath of the fall of Jerusalem it would be natural for Jewish apocalypticists to look to the manlike figure, who in Daniel's vision represented the saints of the Most High in their vindication after horrendous suffering, for inspiration in their own case.[54] The common concern in all these cases was *the revelation*

Levi – *Test. Levi* 2.5ff.

Baruch – *II Bar*, 76; *III Bar.*

Isaiah – *Asc. Isa.* 7ff.; cf. *Sir.* 48.24–25.

50. For fuller detail see A. F. Segal, 'Heavenly Ascent in Hellenistic Judaism, Early Christianity, and their Environment', *ANRW*, II.23.2, Berlin/New York: de Gruyter 1980, pp. 1352–68.

51. Philo, *Mos.* 1.158; *Qu.Exod.* 2.29, 40, 46; Josephus, *Ant.* 3.96; *II Bar.* 4.2–7; Ps-Philo 12.1; *Memar Marqah* 4.3, 7; 5.3; cf. *Ezekiel the Tragedian* in Eusebius, *Praep. Evang.* 9.29.5–6; *IV Ezra* 14.5; *II Bar.* 59. In Targum Neofiti Deut. 30.12–14 is elaborated thus: 'The law is not in the heavens, that one should say, Would that we had one like Moses the prophet who would go up to heaven and fetch it for us.' See particularly W. A. Meeks, *The Prophet-King: Moses Traditions and the Johannine Christology*, NovTSupp 14; Leiden: Brill 1967, pp. 110–11, 120–5, 147–9, 156–9, 206–9, 241–4.

52. J. Strugnell, 'The Angelic Liturgy at Qumran', *VT.S* 7 (1959), pp. 318–45. See further C. Rowland, 'The Visions of God in Apocalyptic Literature', *JSJ* 10 (1979), pp. 137–54.

53. See above §10.2.

54. Although *I Enoch* 37–71 is often dated prior to 70 CE, two factors weigh with me in pointing to a post-70 date: (1) in *I Enoch* 37–71 the interpretation of Daniel's vision is introduced as though it was entirely new and independent – just as in *IV Ezra* 13;(2) there is no indication of any influence between these passages, or between them and the Synoptic tradition of the Son of Man (prior to Matthew's Gospel at least – see my *Christology*, pp. 77–8); this includes the use of Dan. 7.13 in Revelation, which is more like what we

of divine mysteries which these visions and heavenly ascents provided.

(2) Secondly, we should note also that *both early Christianity and the Yavnean sages were not unaffected by such tendencies within Judaism*. Paul's account of a visionary ascent to the third heaven (II Cor. 12.2–4) may well support the view that Paul himself was familiar with the practice of merkabah mysticism.[55] And, as already noted (§11.4), the vision of John the seer (Rev. 1.13–16) has some striking points of contact with the earlier visions of Ezek. 1 and Dan. 7.9–14 and 10.5–6. As for the rabbis, there is strong evidence that Yohanan ben Zakkai, who played the leading role in initially re-establishing rabbinic Judaism at Yavneh after 70,[56] was himself greatly interested in the chariot chapter of Ezek. I and probably practised meditation on it (*t. Hag.* 2.1ff. pars.).[57] More striking is the indication that the 'two powers heresy' was dated back to much the same period – to the vision of the chariot throne of God (probably) by four rabbis, including the famous Akiba, which resulted in one of them, Elisha ben Abuyah, mistaking the glorious figure on the throne (Metatron in III *Enoch* 16) with a second power in heaven.[58] One of the starting points for this 'two powers' heresy seems to have been speculation on the plural 'thrones' in Dan. 7.9. For there is also a tradition that even Akiba was rebuked for his speculation as to the occupant of the second throne in Dan. 7.9 (*b.Hag.* 14a; *b.Sanh.* 38b). This evidence strengthens the hypothesis above that in the period between the Jewish revolts (70–132) the vision(s) of Dan. 7.9–14 were a focus of considerable reflection in the hope that they might provide a source of insight and inspiration in the crisis confronting Judaism during that period.

(3) We know, thirdly, that *there were already strong reactions against some of these tendencies in apocalyptic and merkabah speculation, in both Jewish and Christian circles*. Sir. 3.18–25 can be readily understood as an exhortation to refrain from speculations involving visionary experiences.[59] And *IV Ezra* 8.20–21 seems to be directed against claims to be able to see and describe God's throne.[60]

---

have in *I Enoch* 37–71 and *IV Ezra* 13 than in the Gospel tradition. Taken together these factors point to the post-70 period as a time in which apocalyptic thought generally was stimulated by, *inter alia*, Daniel's vision, resulting in several similar but not directly interdependent formulations. See also above ch. 9 (p. 230) n. 50.

55. J. W. Bowker, '"Merkabah" Visions and the Visions of Paul', *JSS* 16 (1971), pp. 157–73.

56. See further below §12.1.

57. See J. Neusner, *A Life of Yohanan ben Zakkai*, Leiden: Brill ²1970, pp. 134–40; Gruenwald, *Merkabah Mysticism*, pp. 75–86; Rowland, *Open Heaven*, pp. 282–305.

58. See above p. 285.

59. Gruenwald, *Merkabah Mysticism*, pp. 17–18.

60. Rowland, *Open Heaven*, pp. 54–5.

In specifically Christian circles we may recall the strong warnings against angel worship in Heb. 1–2 and possibly Col. 2.18,[61] and the early churches' hesitation over granting too much authority to the book of Revelation. Similarly the rabbinic polemic against angelology probably goes back to our period;[62] there are explicit cautionary notes concerning the chariot chapter in the Mishnah (*m. Hag.* 2.1; *m. Meg.* 4.10); and the apostasy of Elisha ben Abuyah is a notorious fact elsewhere in rabbinic tradition.[63] We should also note how frequently subsequent rabbinic polemic against the *minim* consists in a defence of monotheism, the unity of God.[64]

(c) Set against this context, the Fourth Gospel's christological claims become still clearer in their significance. There is time only to give three principal examples. In each case it is worth noting how the claim is made for Jesus explicitly over against Moses.

(1) The prologue ends with the highest claim for the revelatory significance of Jesus: 'No one has ever seen God; the only begotten God[65] ... has made him known' (1.18). The reader is probably intended to bear this blunt assertion in mind when he comes to the next climax of christological confession – the exchange with Nathanael (1.47–51).[66] The train of thought is at first puzzling, but it gains invaluable illumination from the background sketched above. In mystical thought 'Israel' is taken to mean 'he that sees', or 'he that sees God' (cf. Gen. 35.9; often in Philo).[67] Nathanael, then, is presented as 'a genuine Israelite', who has begun to believe in Jesus: he calls him 'rabbi', 'Son of God' and 'King of Israel' (1.49). But Jesus replies that he will see more than that – a vision just like that of the first Israel (Jacob – Gen. 28.12 – the ladder to heaven), where the

---

61. Col. 2.18 is usually taken as directed against the worship of angels, but may well refer to participation in the worship of God by angels (as in *Asc. Isa.* 7.13–9.33; *Test. Job* 48–50); so particularly F. O. Francis in *Conflict at Colossae*, ed. F. O. Francis and W. A. Meeks, Missoula: Scholars 1975, pp. 163–207. See discussion in P. T. O'Brien, *Colossians, Philemon*, WBC 44; Waco: Word 1982, pp. 142–5.

62. P. S. Alexander, 'The Targumim and Early Exegesis of "Sons of God" in Gen 6', *JJS* 23 (1972), pp. 60–71.

63. Rowland, *Open Heaven*, pp. 331–9.

64. See the texts collected by Herford, *Christianity in Talmud and Midrash*, pp. 291–307; also J. Jocz, *The Jewish People and Jesus Christ. A Study in the Controversy between Church and Synagogue*, London: SPCK 1954, pp. 185–90.

65. This is the most probable text; see e.g. Metzger, *Textual Commentary*, p. 198.

66. Cf. M. de Jonge, *Jesus: Stranger from Heaven and Son of God*, Missoula, Montana: Scholars 1977, p. 83 – '1.19–50 stands between 1.18 and 1.51, both dealing with the heavenly status of the One to whom all the designations in the intermediate section point in their own way'.

67. See references in vol. X of the Loeb edition of *Philo*, p. 334 note.

central feature will be the Son of Man serving as the ladder, that is, mediating between heaven and earth (1.51). For no one else has seen God – not Moses (1.17; cf. Ex. 33.20 and Deut. 4.12), and not even Israel ('he who sees God'). The true Israelite is thus encouraged to 'see' that *all God's self-revelation now comes to focus in and through Jesus* (1.18, 51); God can only be seen to the extent that one sees him in and through (the revelation of) Christ.[68]

(2) John 1 links with John 3 in that another sympathetic Jew (3.2) needs similar instruction. Though 'a teacher of Israel' (3.9), Nicodemus has no idea of how one can 'see the kingdom of God', how it is possible to 'enter the heavenly realm' (3.3, 5). Such knowledge cannot be attained by an ascent to heaven – '*no one* has ascended into heaven' (3.13). This sweeping assertion can hardly be other than a polemic against current beliefs in the possibility of such heavenly ascents, through contemplation on the divine chariot or otherwise.[69] Such knowledge of heavenly things is possible *only* for him who *descended* from heaven, the Son of Man (3.13). Mention of Moses in the following verse and the return to the same theme in 3.31–36 ('he who comes from above is above all') effectively distances this Son of Man from any competing claims about the heavenly commissions of Moses and John the Baptist (cf. 1.6, 17). Not even Moses ascended to heaven (despite current speculation to this effect),[70] and the Baptist remains rootedly 'of the earth'. True knowledge of heaven comes only from Christ, he who is from above and who bears witness to what he (alone) has seen there.

(3) In John 6 the narrative moves with fine dramatic sense from the enthusiastic recognition of Jesus as 'the prophet who has come into the world' (6.14), the prophet like Moses who could be asked to repeat the miracle of manna (6.31), to the point where many of his own disciples take offence (6.60–61, 66). In the context of the whole discourse, what causes the offence is the way in which these two categories (the prophet and Moses) are transcended and left behind. The prophet's insight into God's will could easily be transposed into talk of a heavenly ascent to 'listen in' on the heavenly council.[71] But

---

68. See also N. A. Dahl, 'The Johannine Church and History', *Current Issues in New Testament Interpretation*, ed. W. Klassen and G. F. Snyder, New York: Harper & Row 1962, pp. 124–42, here pp. 136–7.

69. See e.g. H. Odeberg, *The Fourth Gospel*, Uppsala 1929, pp. 72–98; Meeks, *Prophet-King*, pp. 295–301; F. J. Moloney, *The Johannine Son of Man*, Rome: Las 1976, ²1978, pp. 54–7.

70. See above §11.6b.

71. See further particularly J. A. Bühner, *Der Gesandte und sein Weg im 4. Evangelium*, Tübingen: Mohr-Siebeck 1977.

to speak of Jesus as 'him whom God sent' (6.29) is only adequate if by that phrase is meant 'sent from heaven', without implication of any previous ascent; Jesus' subsequent ascent is to 'where he was before', to his place of origin (6.62). Moses too is pushed to one side (6.32). The manna miracle does not exalt Moses, as 'the Jews' assumed;[72] that model of divine mediation (cf. Deut. 18.18) is inadequate to express the significance of Jesus. The direct communication from God promised by Isa. 54.13 ('All our sons will be taught by the Lord') is now a reality in Jesus (not the Torah); he is the yardstick by which all claims to knowledge from God must be tested, for only he has seen the Father (John 6.45–46).[73] Thus the experience which mediates eternal life is believing recognition that Jesus is himself from God, the living bread which came down from heaven, the life from God incarnate in Jesus (6.35–58).

In these ways John's Gospel attempts to articulate one of its chief claims: that *revelation from God, revelation of the heavenly mysteries is to be found in its fullest and clearest and final form in the fleshliness of Jesus, rather than in the Torah of Moses.*

(d) Here we can also begin to bring in the other main motif which proved so important in Christian writings prior to the Fourth Gospel – *Jesus as Wisdom.* It has long been recognized that the language of the Johannine prologue is considerably dependent on the Wisdom theology of second Temple Judaism.[74] For example:

John 1.1 – In the beginning was the Word,
                  and the Word was with God . . .
Wisd. 9.9 – With you is Wisdom, who knows your works and was
                  present when you made the world.

John 1.4 – The life was the light of men.
Aristobulus – All light comes from her (wisdom).[75]

---

72. Cf. particularly G. Vermes, '"He is the Bread": Targum Neofiti Exodus 16.15', *Post-Biblical Jewish Studies*, Leiden: Brill 1975, pp. 139–46.

73. See particularly, P. Borgen, *Bread from Heaven*, NTSupp. X; Leiden: Brill 1965, especially pp. 150–4.

74. See particularly R. Harris, *The Origin of the Prologue to St John's Gospel*, Cambridge University 1917, especially p. 43; R. Bultmann, 'Der religionsgeschichtliche Hintergrund des Prologs zum Johannes-Evangelium' (1923), *Exegetica. Aufsätze zur Erforschung des Neuen Testaments*, Tübingen: Mohr-Siebeck 1967; Dodd, *Interpretation*, pp. 274–5.

75. Eusebius, *Praep. Evang.* 13.12.10.

John 1.11 – He came to his own home, and his own people received
him not.

I Enoch 42 – Wisdom went forth to make her dwelling place among
the children of men, and found no dwelling place.

John 1.14 – The word became flesh and dwelt (literally, pitched his
tent) among us.

Sir. 24.8 – The one who created me assigned a place for my tent.
And he said, 'Make your dwelling (literally, set your
tent) in Jacob'.

Less familiar is the fact that Wisdom motifs extend well beyond the
prologue in the Fourth Gospel; in Jesus' teaching repeated use is made
of the language and imagery of divine Wisdom.[76] So, for example,
the closest parallels to the talk of Jesus descending from heaven are
to be found in Wisd. 9.16–17, Bar. 3.29 and *I Enoch* 42. The 'I ams'
are closely paralleled in the first person singular speech of Wisdom in
Prov. 8 and Sir. 24. Also in content – for example, Jesus-Wisdom as
light (Wisd. 7.26, 29; John 12.8), as food and drink (Sir. 24.19–22;
John 6.51–58), as shepherd (Philo, *Agr.* 51; *Mut.* 116; John 10.14).
Particularly significant is the recognition[77] that Wisdom is not just
another intermediary or agent angelic or human, but is precisely *a
way of speaking about God himself in his self-revelation.* Hence the
emphasis of John 12.45 and 14.9: 'He who sees me sees him who
sent me' (12.45); 'He who has seen me has seen the Father' (14.9).
Also of 12.41 (Isaiah 'saw his glory and spoke of him'): Christ is the
glory/Shekinah of God, the presence of God visible to Isaiah in his
vision in the Temple (Isa. 6).[78] Hence again the charge laid by 'the
Jews' against Jesus: he makes himself equal with God (5.18); he,
though a man, makes himself God (10.33).

Clearly, then, the Fourth Gospel has gone beyond anything which
we have so far read in Christian writing of the period to bring out
the full significance of Wisdom christology. The insistence on the
heavenly origin of Jesus is much more thoroughgoing and emphatic
than what we have in I Cor. 8.6 and Col. 1.15. The closeness of
continuity between the Father and the Son is much more than simply
an identity of will or function.

But John's christology has also gone well beyond anything that we
have seen being said in second Temple Judaism, and he has done so

76. See e.g. R. E. Brown *John 1-12*, AB 29; New York: Doubleday 1966, pp. cxxii-
cxxv; M. Scott, *Sophia and the Johannine Jesus*, JSNTS 71; Sheffield: JSBT 1992.

77. See above §10.5.

78. See Dahl, 'Johannine Church', pp. 131–4.

in a way that would have put him at odds with the rabbis of the post-70 period. For their part, they would no doubt have been willing and desirous of pursuing the identification of Wisdom with *the Torah* (Sir. 24.23, 25; Bar. 3.36–4.4); for them grace and truth came through *the law* (1.17); for them *the Torah* was the gift of God, the living water (4.10); for them the manna would speak of the heavenly nourishment provided by *Moses* (6.31–33); and so on. Following a similar logic to the Christians, the rabbis came in their turn to speak of *the Torah* as pre-existent.[79] The difference was that a pre-existent Torah could be maintained without threat to the unity of God; whereas in their eyes to speak in such terms with regard to the man Jesus must inevitably have meant the recognition of Jesus as a second divine power in heaven.

Which brings us to the inevitable question: Had, then, John taken a step too far? In going beyond what had been claimed for Christ in Christian circles, in going beyond what hitherto had been said of Wisdom in second Temple Judaism, and in putting his Jesus at such odds with the rabbinic authorities of his own day, had John gone too far?

11.7 A step too far?

When we put together all these pieces of the jigsaw of Johannine christology, what is the result?

(*a*) Johannine Christianity belongs within a broad stream of Judaism which, particularly in the aftermath of 70 CE, was exploring different ways of gaining access to heavenly knowledge, of discerning the secrets of God's purpose – heavenly journeys, visions of glorious angelic beings, mystical experiences, speculation regarding divine Wisdom, reflection on the visions of Dan. 7.9–14 and not least on the 'one like a son of man' in Dan. 7.13–14. Within this exploration, the claims of the Fourth Evangelist rang loud and clear; Jesus alone is the one able to reveal the secrets of heaven, to provide the vision of God; he *is* the Son of Man; he *is* Wisdom incarnate.

(*b*) One major strand of post-70 Judaism, focussed in the rabbis of Yavneh, was becoming increasingly nervous about this broader speculative Judaism and saw its task very much in terms of defining Judaism more carefully and of drawing the boundaries round Judaism more tightly. In their view the only safe way to handle such theological reflection and exploration was to focus it in the Torah: *the Torah*

---

79. See e.g. Strack-Billerbeck, 2.353–5; F. B. Craddock, *The Pre-existence of Christ in the New Testament*, Nashville: Abingdon 1968, pp. 46–53.

alone contained the necessary knowledge; *the Torah* alone is the embodiment of divine Wisdom. In consequence, this early rabbinic Judaism wished to warn off fellow Jews from all those other forms of Judaism which gave too much scope (in the view of the rabbis) to such explorations into the knowledge of God and his mysteries – including, though not only, early Christianity.

(*c*) Within this context the debate and conflict so characteristic of the central section of John's Gospel becomes still clearer: that is, the conflict between, on the one hand, 'the Jews' = the Jewish authorities claiming to be the only legitimate exponents of 'Judaism', and, on the other, those Jews represented by John, believers in Jesus Messiah, Son of God; a conflict for the allegiance of 'the Jews' = the people in the middle, swithering between the claims made for this Jesus and those of 'the Jew(ish authoritie)s'. That is to say, there were three parties in the debate.

(1) So far as the Jewish authorities were concerned, the claims made by the (Johannine) Christians had gone too far: *the Jesus of John's Gospel had made himself God.* That is to say, the believers in Jesus Christ for whom the Fourth Evangelist spoke, *had abandoned the fundamental confession that God is one.* They had named Jesus as a second power in heaven.[80] They had knocked away the final pillar of second Temple Judaism.

(2) So far as the Fourth Evangelist was concerned, and the Christian Jews for whom he spoke, however, this last was a false evaluation of their belief. In the view of the Fourth Evangelist, Jesus is *not* another divine power in heaven, a second divine being who therefore could be said to threaten the unity of God. Rather, *Jesus is the Wisdom-Logos of God, that is, the self-revelation of God himself.* To have seen him *is* to have seen the Father. In other words, *John saw himself still as a monotheist*; he understood what he was saying about Jesus Christ as *still within the bounds of Jewish monotheism.* This is why it would be wholly accurate at this point to sum up his christology thus: For John Jesus was the incarnation *not* of the Son of God, but of *God* – God's self-revelation become flesh and blood.

(3) It was clearly John's hope still to win 'the Jews' = the people in the middle to this faith in Jesus as the Christ, the Son of God, since in this belief was life (John 20.31). What John hoped for, the rabbis feared (e.g. John 7.45–52; 11.45–48; 12.10–11, 17–19). John no doubt recognized that his chances were slim: his dramatic presentation shows 'the Jews' of the middle ground in the end siding with

---

80. So also J. Ashton, *Understanding the Fourth Gospel*, Oxford: Clarendon 1991, p. 158.

'the Jews' = the authorities (12.37–40). But there were evidently still individuals like Nicodemus (7.50–51; 19.39–42) and the man born blind (ch. 9), even some of 'the authorities' themselves (12.42–43; 19.38), who needed to take their courage in both hands to make full and public confession of Jesus as the Christ, the Son of God. It was for them above all, or perhaps realistically, only them that the Fourth Evangelist wrote his Gospel.

(*d*) In short, for proponents of emerging rabbinic Judaism, those who claimed to be the only legitimate spokesmen for authentic Judaism, Christian claims for Jesus *had* taken a step too far. *From their perspective the parting of the ways had already happened.* And insofar as the bulk of the Jewish people (as represented by John) seemed already to be siding with these authorities, that may have meant, and in the event did mean, that the parting of the ways was already irreversible. But for John the Evangelist, the faith he proclaimed by means of his Gospel was still a form of second Temple Judaism, still part of that broader Judaism which was concerned to have clearer insight into the mysteries of God's purpose. Above all, *his proclamation of Jesus was still an expression of Jewish monotheism, still concerned with other Jews to explore ways of speaking of the one God and his revelation to Israel.* And, not least, he was still hoping to convince more and more of his fellow Jews by means of his proclamation that the Christian expression of traditional Jewish religion was the way of life for *all* Judaism.

The Parting of the Ways

We have now looked at each of the four pillars of second Temple Judaism and at the way in which each of them became an issue between the new Jewish sect (Christianity) and the rest of first-century Judaism. Or to be more precise, we have seen how within the diversity of first-century Judaism, the major strand which was to become Christianity pulled apart on a sequence of key issues from the major strand which was to become rabbinic Judaism. Or to change the metaphor, we have seen how within the various and often conflicting currents of the broad stream of late second Temple Judaism, two strong currents began to carve out divergent channels for themselves. The breach was not immediate or sudden. It began with Jesus, but without Easter and the broadening out of the gospel to the Gentiles the two currents might have been contained within the same banks.

Nor can we speak of a single breach, or, to resume our principal metaphor, of a single parting of the ways. For those who continued to stay focussed on the Temple, the Stephen episode and its sequel constituted a decisive enough schism; though the 'those' included many Jews who believed in Jesus as Messiah. And the writer to the Hebrews evidently felt himself and his community to be at some remove from the typical mind-set of Jewish cultic practice and worship. At the same time we should remind ourselves once again that rabbinic Judaism managed to survive and thrive despite the lack of a Temple and viable sacrificial cult. Nevertheless, here we can speak of *the first parting of the ways*. For the Judaism which focussed its identity most fully in the Torah, and which found itself unable to separate ethnic identity from religious identity, Paul and the Gentile mission involved an irreparable breach; though again, we do well to recall that many Christian Jews were involved on both sides, and that Paul in particular attempted to retain a full significance for the foundation axiom of Israel's election. Nevertheless, here we have to speak of *further partings of the ways*. And not least, for 'the Jews' who reaffirmed the unity of God in traditional terms and who turned their backs on all attempts to explore the boundaries of that axiom, the Christian affirmation of Jesus as the divine Word/Wisdom-become-flesh was the last straw; such no longer had right or place within the synagogue. Here we may speak of *a particularly crucial parting of the ways.*

To be sure, these views were not shared by the Christian writers themselves. All the NT writers in their own fashion protest that their understanding of the common Jewish heritage was true to that heritage and truer than that of other claimants. This is a claim which needs to be given renewed attention in promotion of a mutual spirit of continuing rapprochement between Judaism and Christianity. And to that we will return in the second half of this chapter. But in the event such claims from the Christian side were unavailing. And so the ways parted and have remained apart ever since.

One question remains to be clarified, however, before we turn to these concluding reflections. Was there a decisive point in time or period when the parting of the ways became irreversible? We have looked at the question almost exclusively in thematic terms. But was there a time in history before which the final parting might have been avoided and after which the situation was irretrievable? For many the most obvious candidate is the catastrophe of the defeat of the Jewish revolt and the destruction of Jerusalem in 70 CE.

12.1 The significance of the crisis of 70 CE

At the beginning of this century the dominant view was that 70 CE was the crucial date in the parting of the ways between Christianity and Judaism.[1] The reasoning for such a view is, after all, straightforward:[2] with the defeat of the first Jewish revolt and the destruction of Jerusalem in that year, the four 'sects' or factions within Judaism of which Josephus spoke were reduced to one – the Pharisees. The others perished with the unsuccessful revolt: the Essenes at Qumran when it was destroyed by the Roman legions in 68 CE; the Sadducees with the destruction of the Temple, since that meant also the destruction of their political and economic power base; the Zealots with the downfall of the last outpost of resistance at Masada in 73 or 74.[3] This left only Christianity to compete with the Pharisees for the heritage of

---

1. See e.g. those cited by Simon, *Verus Israel*, p.x. The view is also implicit in Robinson's *Redating the New Testament* prior to 70 CE.

2. Cf. e.g. S. Sandmel, *The First Century in Judaism and Christianity. Certainties and Uncertainties*, New York: Oxford University 1969, pp. 25–6, 58. The view is implicit in the assumption that Yavnean authorities were able to impose the *birkat ha-minim* on Jews generally; but see above §11.5 and below n. 6.

3. Cf. Schürer, 1.523ff.

pre-70 Judaism, and their ways were already set in opposing directions. The effective disappearance of the rest of the spectrum of second Temple Judaism in 70 CE left the two remaining heirs already separate and increasingly at odds.

This view, however, is too much of an oversimplification, if not, indeed, a distortion of the facts. It is true that out of the disaster of 70 CE emerged the two main heirs of second Temple Judaism, rabbinic Judaism, successors to the Pharisees, and a Christianity predominantly Gentile in composition. But if the analysis of Acts, Matthew and John in chapter 11 is at all accurate, it is *not* true to say that the parting of the ways had already happened in 70, or that there was anything like a single break. The situation can be surveyed quite briefly.

(a) *Rabbinic Judaism.* Following the destruction of Jerusalem, the Pharisees who had not taken part in the revolt were given permission by the Romans to establish an academy or rabbinical school at Yavneh (Jamnia), a Judaean city on the Mediterranean coast – first under Yohanan ben Zakkai, and then Gamaliel II, as already mentioned.[4] There they began to reformulate and define Judaism. We could say that they did so round the three remaining pillars (since the Temple had been destroyed). That would be misleading, however, since the Temple cult was *not* ignored or set aside. On the contrary, the rabbis continued to legislate with regard to the cult, presumably on the assumption that it would be restored, as it had been before, after the previous disaster in the era of Babylonian supremacy.[5] Nevertheless, the principal focus for the Yavnean scholars was the Torah. There they began the process of regularizing the transmission of the traditions by which they interpreted the Torah, of passing on and developing the halakah by which they believed Israel should live – a process which culminated in the Mishnah, published about 200 CE, which in turn became the basis for the Talmud. In so doing they succeeded in developing a form of Judaism which could maintain its identity without a geographical or cultic focus.

It is important to realize, however, that the Yavnean authorities were not in any position to impose their will on the rest of Judaism immediately. Far from it. Yavneh marked the beginning of a long, slow process whereby the rabbis extended their authority and gained widening recognition – initially, no doubt, in Palestine itself, but only

---

4. Above p. 209–10.

5. Cohen, *Maccabees to Mishnah*, p. 219, notes that 'more than half the Mishnah is devoted to one aspect or another of the temple and its cult'.

slowly through the diaspora. Indeed, it may not have been until the
fourth century that the rabbinic patriarch, now established in Galilee,
had established semi-formal control over the diaspora communities
within the Roman empire and gained official Roman approval to
send his *apostoloi* to collect contributions from them.[6] Whatever the
precise facts of the case, we can be sure that the Yavnean authorities
did not establish their authority over the rest of Judaism overnight.
And in the period following 70, the rabbinic sages were probably
in competition with other Jewish 'philosophies' and interpretations,
including Essenes and Sadducees, whose continuing existence and
influence Josephus may still imply by his present tense description of
them, as well as with Christians.[7] At all events, *it may not be possible
to speak simply of 'rabbinic Judaism' as the only acknowledged form
of Judaism throughout the Roman empire until well into the third
century.*

(b) *Jewish Christianity*. If Judaism did not become rabbinic Judaism
overnight, neither did Christianity become Gentile Christianity overnight. It is almost certain that the base of conservative Jewish Christianity, in Jerusalem, was effectively eliminated by the events of 66–70,
or at least decisively reduced in significance.[8] There exists, however, a
tradition of the Jerusalem church fleeing from Jerusalem, either before
the revolt, or at least before the Roman siege finally closed round
Jerusalem itself in 70 (Eusebius, *HE* 3.5.2–3).[9] The episode may be
referred to in two NT texts – Luke 21.20–21 and Rev. 12.14:

> Luke 21.20–21 – 'But when you see Jerusalem surrounded by
> armies, then know that its desolation has come near. Then let those
> who are in Judaea flee to the mountains, and let those who are
> inside the city depart . . .

6. This is now the consensus view of specialist studies. See particularly the major
treatments by Simon, *Verus Israel*, and Alon, *The Jews in their Land*; and more briefly in
e.g. S. T. Katz, 'Issues in the Separation of Judaism and Christianity after 70 CE: A
Reconsideration', *JBL* 103 (1984), pp. 43–76; Cohen, *Maccabees to Mishnah*, pp. 221–
4; Saldarini, *Pharisees*, pp. 196, 207–9; P. S. Alexander, ' "The Parting of the Ways" from
the Perspective of Rabbinic Judaism', *The Parting of the Ways: AD 70–135*, ed. J. D. G.
Dunn, Tübingen: Mohr-Siebeck 1992.

7. The Sadducees should not be identified completely with the high priestly party before
70; see further the brief review in Porton, *EJMI*, pp. 67–8.

8. Though Eusebius, *HE* 4.5 does contain the tradition of a continuing succession of
bishops 'all Hebrews by origin' over a church consisting of Hebrews, which persisted until
the expulsion of all Jews from Jerusalem by Hadrian after the bar Kokhba revolt.

9. For the essential historicity of the tradition, see now C. Koester, 'The Origin and
Significance of the Flight to Pella Tradition', *CBQ* 51 (1989), pp. 90–106.

Rev. 12.14 – The woman was given the two wings of the great eagle that she might fly from the serpent into the wilderness, to the place where she is to be nourished for a time, and times, and half a time.

According to the tradition preserved by Eusebius, the Jerusalem Christians fled to the city of Pella, in Transjordan. Significantly, it is to this region that the origin of the later Jewish Christian sect known as the Ebionites may be traced.[10]

Still more significant is the fact that such Jewish Christian sects could claim to stand in a more direct line of continuity with the original Nazarene community in Jerusalem than those churches which owed their origin and character to the Hellenists and Paul. Certainly it cannot be assumed that Christianity as understood and practised in Jerusalem disappeared altogether, or that the Jewish Christian sects which remained firmly loyal to the law, which regarded Paul as an apostate and held James of Jerusalem in highest respect, and which probably shied away from the high christology of the Johannine gospel,[11] began their existence *outside* the spectrum of first-century Christianity. Nor did these sects themselves disappear very quickly, lingering on into the fourth century at least. And as long as they continued in existence they blurred the otherwise sharpening distinction between Jew and Christian.[12]

Moreover, writings like Matthew and James probably retain some of the traditions on which such forms of Jewish Christianity continued to feed (e.g. Matt. 10.5–6; 15.24).[13] Despite the clear assumption in the Fathers that Jewish Christians were heretical sects from the beginning, we cannot assume that their representation of such groups was wholly objective and accurate, nor that a single pattern was stamped on Christianity right away, any more than in the case of rabbinic Judaism. When the parting of the ways between mainstream Christianity and Jewish Christianity took place is an even more

---

10. So particularly Epiphanius; see the discussion in A. F. J. Klijn and G. J. Reinink, *Patristic Evidence for Jewish–Christian Sects*, SuppNovT 36; Leiden: Brill 1973, pp. 19–43.

11. I have briefly documented the points of continuity in my *Unity* pp. 240–4. On the anti-Paulinism of the Jewish Christian communities see also G. Lüdemann, *Paulus, der Heidenapostel. Band II. Antipaulinismus im frühen Christentum*, Göttingen: Vandenhoeck & Ruprecht 1983, part II.

12. On the complexity of 'Jewish Christianity' see now J. E. Taylor, 'The Phenomenon of Early Jewish–Christianity: Reality or Scholarly Invention?', *VC* 44 (1990), pp. 313–34.

13. According to Epiphanius, the Ebionites used only Matthew's Gospel, in an incomplete, mutilated version (Irenaeus, *adv haer.* I.26.2: III.11.7; Epiphanius, *Pan*, 30.3.7).

obscure issue than that between Christianity and Judaism. _Like post-70 Judaism, post-70 Christianity was still a spectrum, and the two spectrums continued to overlap, precisely in the phenomenon of Jewish Christianity._

(c) _Others forms of Judaism._ We have already noted that other forms of Judaism survived the catastrophe of 70, observing that Josephus' description of the other 'sects' (as well as the Pharisees) in the present tense may indicate their continuing existence and influence in some form for some time. We have also referred to the lively expression and development of Jewish mysticism during the same period, influencing Yohanan ben Zakkai and perhaps Akiba among others.[14] And not least of significance is the fact that the years 70–132 can properly be regarded as the golden age of Jewish apocalyptic, since the two classic Jewish apocalypses, _IV Ezra_ and _II Baruch_, not to mention the apocalypse of John, were written during that period. Once again we have to insist that the spectrum of second Temple Judaism did not reduce to two sects (Pharisees and Nazarenes) overnight or all at once.

Moreover, as already noted,[15] the use of 'Ezra' and 'Baruch' as pseudonyms probably indicates a lively assumption that the Temple would be restored: Ezra was venerated as the one who had reconstituted the religion and worship of Israel following the exile; and Baruch was remembered as the scribe who had witnessed and preserved the record of Jeremiah's purchase of a field in Anathoth, token of his confidence that the judgment of the exile would be reversed (Jer. 32.12–15). Such an assumption would probably carry with it hope that some at least of the earlier breadth of second Temple Judaism would be maintained or restored (_II Bar._ 32.2–4;[16] cf. _Sib. Or._ 5.493–502). IV _Ezra_ in particular shows a different response to the crisis caused to ethnocentric covenantalism by the destruction of Jerusalem, in that it effectively abandons the second pillar of second Temple Judaism (election and covenant) and puts forward its own solution in terms of an individualistic works-righteousness model

---

14. See above §11.6b.

15. Above ch. 5, p. 116. The Epistle of Barnabas may have been written to counter an expectation that the Temple would be rebuilt; see M. B. Shukster and P. Richardson, 'Temple and _Bet Ha-midrash_ in the Epistle of Barnabas', _Anti-Judaism in Early Christianity. Vol._ 2. _Separation and Polemic_, ed. S. G. Wilson, Waterloo, Ontario: Wilfrid Laurier University 1986, pp. 17–31; R. S. MacLennan, _Early Christian Texts on Jews and Judaism_, Atlanta: Scholars 1990, ch. 1.

16. But see F. J. Murphy, 'The Temple in the Syriac _Apocalypse of Baruch, JBL_ 106 (1987), pp. 671–83.

(note the climax of *IV Ezra* 14.27–35).[17] *Mainstream Christianity and rabbinic Judaism were not the only attempts to claim and redefine the heritage of second Temple Judaism.*

(*d*) *Christianity remained Jewish Christianity*. As we move into the second century not only certain Christian sects can be described as 'Jewish-Christian', but Christianity as a whole can still properly be described as 'Jewish Christianity' in a justifiable sense.[18] The takeover of Jewish heritage included not just the Jewish scriptures (the 'Old Testament'), but also a degree of what may be called re-judaizing – the other side of the process of de-eschatologizing which marked the fading of the parousia hope. This is most apparent in the evolving ecclesiology of the late first century and early second century, as the pattern of synagogue ruler (overseer) and elders was extended through the churches founded by the Gentile mission,[19] and as the OT language of priestly sacrifice was taken over and steadily fleshed out in the idea of a priesthood set apart within the priesthood of the whole people.[20]

Even more striking is the fact that a whole sequence of non-rabbinic Jewish texts from before the second century were transcribed and preserved, not by the rabbis, but by Christians – including such important texts as the *Psalms of Solomon, Testament of Moses, Sybilline Oracles, IV Ezra* and *II Baruch*. In Alexandrian Christianity Philo could be regarded as in effect a Christian before Christ since his treatment of the Logos so prefigured Logos christology.[21] Clearly indicated here is a lively interaction between this broader stream of second Temple Judaism and mainstream Christianity – a greater degree of overlap and interaction than of rabbinic Judaism with either.

The same point emerges when we appreciate how much Jewish material was appropriated by the first Christians and incorporated into their own writing. For example, *IV Ezra* was expanded by the addition of two chapters at beginning and end, and forms part of

---

17. I am indebted here to the thesis of my pupil, Bruce Longenecker, *Eschatology and Covenant*. Simon, *Verus Israel*, pp. 35–6 also argues that 'for Jewish universalism the temple (had been) an obstacle and a hindrance'.

18. Cf. particularly J. Danielou, *The Theology of Jewish Christianity*, 1958; ET London: Darton, Longman & Todd 1964.

19. See my *Unity*, pp. 115–16.

20. See below §12.6.

21. Cf. e.g. the comment of J. N. D. Kelly, *Early Christian Doctrines*, London: Black[2] 1960, on the second-century Apologists: 'their thought was more Philonic than Johannine' (p. 96).

the Christian apocrypha as II Esdras. *The Testaments of the Twelve Patriarchs* are now generally recognized to be a Christian composition (or recension) using older Jewish material.[22] *The Ascension of Isaiah* combines the Jewish *Martyrdom of Isaiah* with two Christian works. Books Seven and Eight of the *Apostolic Constitutions* seem to have incorporated a sizable number of Jewish prayers.[23] Even if a strong case can be made for recognizing a major parting of the ways between mainstream Christianity and rabbinic Judaism from 70 CE on, such evidence as this indicates clearly that *the broader streams of second Temple Judaism continued to mingle and flow together for some time thereafter.*

(e) *Evidence of continuing contact between Jew and Christian.* On the one side, there is evidence within rabbinic writings of continuing contact between rabbis and *minim*, where the latter clearly refer to Jewish Christians. At least two strands of material deserve notice.

(1) Rulings have been preserved regarding 'the Gospels and the books of the heretics'.[24] Their status in relation to the canonical scriptures was evidently an issue for some rabbis. So we hear of debates as to whether such Christian documents 'defiled the hands', that is, whether they were inspired,[25] and whether they should be saved from burning, as being of canonical value.

> *t. Yad.* 2.13 – The Gospels (*gilyonim*) and the books of the heretics (*sifrei minim*) do not defile the hands. The book of ben Sira and all books which have been written from that time onward do not defile the hands.

---

22. See review of recent discussion by J. J. Collins in *EJMI* pp. 268–76.

23. Details in Charlesworth, *Old Testament Pseudepigrapha* 2.143ff., 671ff.; see also his 'Christian and Jewish Self-Definition in Light of the Christian Additions to the Apocryphal Writings', *JCSD*, pp. 27–55; and see further particularly R. A. Kraft, 'The Multiform Jewish Heritage of Early Christianity', *Christianity, Judaism and other Greco-Roman Cults. Studies for M. Smith*, ed. J. Neusner, Part 3. *Judaism before 70*, Leiden: Brill 1975, pp. 175–99.

24. See Herford, *Christianity in Talmud and Midrash*, pp. 146–61; Alon, *Jews*, pp. 290–307; Schiffman, *JCSD*, pp. 153–5; *Who Was a Jew?*, pp. 62–4; Katz, 'Separation', pp. 56–62; Alexander, 'The Parting of the Ways'. The significance of the traditions cited does not depend on being able to date them to a particular period. But, of course, the later the situations they reflect the more significant their testimony. Urbach argues that *gilyonim* are not the Gospels but 'the blank spaces of the book' (*JCSD*, pp. 290–1); similarly Herford, p. 155 n. 1; see discussion in Katz, pp. 58–9.

25. *t. Yad.* 2.14 – 'Rabbi Shim'on ben Menasya says: The Song of Songs renders the hands unclean, because it was composed under divine inspiration. Qohelet does not render the hands unclean because it is (merely) the wisdom of Solomon.'

t.Shab. 13(14).5 – The Gospels and the books of the heretics are not saved from a fire, but are burnt in their place, they and their sacred names. Rabbi Yose ha-Gelili says: On a weekday one cuts out the sacred names and hides them and burns the rest. Said Rabbi Tarfon: May I bury my sons! If they come into my hand, I would burn them along with their sacred names. For even if a pursuer were running after me, I would enter a house of idolatry rather than enter their houses. For the idolaters do not acknowledge him and then deny him, but *they* do acknowledge him and deny him ... Said Rabbi Ishmael: If in order to bring peace between a husband and his wife, the Omnipresent has commanded that a scroll (*sefer*) which has been written in holiness be erased by means of water, how much more should the books of the heretics which bring enmity between Israel and the Father who is in heaven be erased, they and their sacred names ...

The *Sifrei Minim* are probably not distinctive Christian compositions such as the NT Epistles, in contrast to the Gospels, but rather Christian Torah scrolls. Such scrolls written by Christians would be regarded as unfit for public worship, presumably because their origin put them under suspicion. Similarly the Gospels were not to be read as scripture in public worship. The implications of such a ruling would be far reaching. Apart from anything else, it would put Christian Torah scribes out of business and make it impossible for any synagogue obeying the ruling to make use of their services.

Moreover, to hear the Torah read from such a scroll would presumably not be a valid hearing of the law. Thus Rabbinic Jews would be discouraged from attending synagogues where there was Christian influence, still more so from frequenting distinctively Christian gatherings where the Christian Gospels might be read publicly as scripture. This ruling, then, seems to have been aimed primarily at a separation in worship between rabbinic and Christian Jews.[26]

The point for us is that such rulings clearly imply that there were Jews, those within the ambit of rabbinic authority, who read the Gospels and Christian Torah scrolls. Rulings of this nature had to be given because some non-Christian Jews may have regarded these writings as canonical, or at any rate questioned whether they might be so. At the very least they could be regarded as having the status of ben Sira. Such debates and rulings reflect the fluidity of the situation within Jewish Christian circles. The issues discussed presuppose *a*

---

26. I am indebted to Alexander, 'The Parting of the Ways' for these observations.

still unbroken spectrum stretching from Gentile Christianity through Jewish Christianity and other forms of Judaism to the rabbis.

(2) Rulings have also been preserved which were evidently intended to prevent or limit contact between those under the sway of rabbinic Judaism and *minim* = Jewish Christians.

> *t.Hull.* 2.20–21 – If meat is found in the hand of a non-Jew, it is permitted to derive benefit from it, but (if it is found) in the hand of a *min*, it is forbidden to derive benefit from it. That which comes from the house of a *min*, indeed it is the meat of sacrifices to the dead, for they said: The slaughtering of a *min* is idolatry; their bread is the bread of a Samaritan; their wine is the wine of libation; their fruits are untithed; their books are the books of diviners, and their children are mamzerim. We do not sell to them, nor do we buy from them. We do not take from them, nor do we give to them, and we do not teach their sons a craft. We are not healed by them, neither healing of property nor healing of life.

This seems to indicate that a key weapon used by the rabbis against Jewish Christians was ostracism. It was forbidden for rabbinic Jews to eat with Jewish Christians – the ruling achieved, significantly in view of our earlier discussion,[27] by applying the dietary rules more tightly. Once again the implication is clearly of the existence of such social contacts between rabbinic Jews and Jewish Christians, which thus made necessary such regulations and attempts at control.[28]

On the Christian side we need mention only the evidence of Ignatius, Barnabas and Justin.

(1) *Ignatius.* In *Magn.* 8–10 Ignatius warns his readers against 'living in accordance with Judaism (*kata Ioudaismon*)' (8.1) and against 'judaizing' (*ioudaizein*) (10.3). In *Smyrn.* 1.2 there is no sense of hostility towards 'Jews': '. . . saints and believers, whether among Jews, or among the heathen . . .'. Most interesting of all is *Philad.* 6.1–

> If anyone interpret Judaism to you do not listen to him; for it is better to hear Christianity from the circumcised than Judaism from the uncircumcised.

---

27. See above §§6.3 and 7.5.
28. See further Simon, *Verus Israel*, here particularly pp. 183–6; Schiffman, *Who Was a Jew?*, pp. 64–73.

Clearly implied here is some dialogue between Jews and Christians, in which Christianity and Judaism were topics of conversation or teaching between them. But also implied is the fact that some Gentile (uncircumcised) Christians(?) were attracted to Judaism and were ready to speak favourably of it and on behalf of it.[29]

(2) *Barnabas* may well have been written in response to a situation where Judaism continued to be so attractive to many Christians that there was a real danger of relapse into it (cf. Hebrews).[30] The key evidence here is 3.6 – 'lest we be shipwrecked as proselytes to their law'. Hence, probably, the bitterness and harshness of Barnabas's attitude to Judaism: Jews posed a real danger to his readers; there were real contacts and interchange between them. At the same time we need to recall that Barnabas himself shows contact with and influence from Jewish thought in his midrash-like interpretations of the Day of Atonement ritual and the Red Heifer (Barn. 7–8).

(3) With *Justin* the points of contact hardly require to be demonstrated. We need mention only his *Dialogue with Trypho*, which is not to be dismissed as wholly artificial, or Trypho the Jew as a straw man. But in addition Justin confirms contacts continuing more widely between the two communities; he speaks of Christians who have adopted Judaism and 'gone over' (*metabantas*) to the polity of the law' (*Dial.* 47.4); and he confirms the account of *t.Hull.* 2.20–24 (cited above) that Jewish authorities had had to prohibit Jews from conversing with Christians (*Dial.* 38, 112).[31]

In short, even if the ways had parted for most rabbinic Jews and most Christians, they still ran close together, with not a few contacts between them, and with Jewish Christians continuing to overlap both these otherwise separated ends of the spectrum. All of which is to confirm that *talk of a clearcut or final parting of the ways at 70* CE *is distinctly premature.*

---

29. See also C. K. Barrett, 'Jews and Judaizers in the Epistles of Ignatius' (1976), *Essays on John*, London: SPCK 1982, pp. 133–58.

30. See above §5.6.

31. See further Simon, *Verus Israel* chs 9–11; Meeks and Wilken, *Jews and Christians in Antioch*; J. N. Lightstone, *The Commerce of the Sacred. Mediation of the Divine among Jews in the Graeco-Roman Diaspora*, BJS 59; Chico: Scholars 1984, ch. 6; summary in Gager, *EJMI*, p. 104. It is generally accepted, not least in the light of archaeological evidence, that the fierceness of Melito's polemic reflects the situation of a small Christian community confronted with a large, well established and highly regarded Jewish community; see e.g. S. G. Wilson, 'Melito and Israel', *Anti-Judaism, Vol.* 2, ed. Wilson, pp. 81–102; MacLennan, *Early Christian Texts*, ch. 3.

12.2 When did the ways finally part?

The crisis of 70 CE did not settle the matter, then. There is other evidence, however, which strongly suggests that the following period, *the period between the two Jewish revolts (66–70 and 132–135) was decisive for the parting of the ways*. After the first revolt it could be said that all was still to play for. But after the second revolt the separation of the main bodies of Christianity and Judaism was clear-cut and final, whatever interaction there continued to be at the margins.

(a) *Rabbinic Judaism*. Although the rabbis took longer to establish themselves as the authorized voice of Judaism (§12.1a), the process did make a decisive beginning in the post-70 period. The revision of the *birkat ha-minim* during this period represents the other side of the process of reorganizing Judaism round the Torah and the rabbinic halakah. Whatever its earliest form,[32] it is remembered in rabbinic tradition (*b. Ber.* 28b) as stemming from the time of Rabban Gamaliel at Yavneh (probably the mid-80s), and certainly must be judged as marking a decisive step forward in the attempt to define rabbinic Judaism over against other forms of Judaism as heretics (*minim*).

This is not to say that only with the Yavnean rabbis and their successors do we find emerging a concept of orthodox or normative Judaism and of heresy. The Yavnean sages were simply carrying on in the same manner as the factions before 70 – regarding themselves as alone correct, alone faithful to the covenant, and others as 'sinners', effectively outside the covenant.[33] But after 70 there were crucial differences. For one thing, now they had a degree of authorization from Rome. They could now be regarded as the nearest thing to official representatives of Judaism and of the Jews, a status which became increasingly theirs and formally recognized over the years. In contrast, other possible claimants to be equally representative, even equally authoritative, fell by the wayside. The apocalyptic and mystical strands in Judaism were not sufficiently representative or sufficiently coherent as movements. And Christians, by virtue of their abandoning ethnicity as a primary feature of the covenant people, had effectively abandoned any claim to represent Jews as a whole.

In short, *with the emergence of rabbinic Judaism we have the beginnings of the first real or really effective form of orthodox or normative Judaism*. In these circumstances it became increasingly difficult for

---

32. See above §11.5.
33. See above §6.2.

Christian Jews to sustain any claim to be one of a number of legitimate forms of Judaism. From being heterodox, Christianity became heretical.

(b) *Jewish Christianity*. Although Jewish Christianity also continued for a long time in its various forms, and probably continued to serve as a dialogue partner for rabbinic Judaism, it seems nevertheless to have been unable to maintain the continuity of the spectrum between the diverging currents of mainstream Christianity and rabbinic Judaism. Having lost its base in Jerusalem, or been at least decisively diminished in significance, the Jewish-Christian wing of the Christian spectrum ceased to have that symbolical power as representing the focus of continuity between the older Judaisms and the newer movement of Jesus Messiah. The reason why the rest of Christianity should continue to respect and retain loyalty towards the Jewish Christian wing became crucially weakened, when the particular link of Jerusalem itself was first fractured and then finally broken in the 130s. Greatly significant here is the fact that the NT canon retains no document which is assuredly from that wing of the church. At best James contains clear echoes of an earlier, much more characteristically Jewish pattern and style. But Matthew, Hebrews and Revelation all display a Jewish Christianity already much more integrated into and facing towards the wider Graeco-Roman world.

The Jewish Christianity of which we read in the fathers is a group of heretical sects, already detached from mainstream Christianity.[34] And though they could claim a high degree of continuity with primitive Jerusalem Christianity,[35] the points at which the ways parted found them more on the traditional Jewish side than with Paul and John. Paul's view of the Torah was too much for them: he is remembered by them as an apostate. John's high christology was too strong for those who found it enough to continue regarding Jesus simply as a prophet. *The parting of the ways was more between mainstream Christianity and Jewish Christianity than simply between Christianity as a single whole and rabbinic Judaism.* Whether Jewish Christianity could or should have been retained within the spectrum of catholic Christianity is an important question which it may now be impossible to answer. Within two or three centuries it had ceased to be important anyway, once the Jewish Christian sects withered and died, presumably by absorption into rabbinic Judaism on the one side, and into catholic Christianity on the other, or just by the slow

---

34. See e.g. Klijn and Reinink, *Patristic Evidence for Jewish–Christian Sects*.
35. See above §12.1b.

death of failure to regenerate. But it is a question which we need to address now with renewed seriousness in the light of the current phenomena of messianic Jews (Jews who believe in Jesus as Messiah) in north America and Israel.

(c) Other signs that the parting of the ways between mainstream Christianity and rabbinic Judaism became effective in the early second century accumulate round that period.

(1) The growing absorption of Christian theologians of the second century with christological questions was bound to emphasize and broaden the gap which John's christology had opened up for 'the Jews'. The deity of Christ became more and more a matter of assumption (already regularly in Ignatius),[36] and the main debate more with Gnostic or docetic or monarchical alternatives than with the Jewish Christian option. At just the same time the rabbis were in process of defining heresy in terms of a failure to maintain the unity of God.[37]

(2) The writings retained by and regarded as expressive of mainstream Christianity became more controversial. For Barnabas and Justin the ways certainly had already parted, at least with the Judaism they knew, however close to each other they still ran.

(3) In a real sense the Christians took over the LXX; it became Christian scripture. In contrast, the synagogues continued to read the scriptures in Hebrew. It is very likely that the further translation of the Jewish scriptures into Greek by the Jew Aquila in 130 CE was intended as a replacement for the Christianized Septuagint. As a more literal translation, it would serve as a safer targum for Greek-speaking Jews. Indeed, it may be that Aquila should be seen as part of the rabbis' campaign to rabbinize their Greek-speaking co-religionists.[38]

(4) After the beginning of the second century the overlap which was provided when earlier Jewish documents were taken over by Christians effectively disappeared. The pattern provided by Christian use for example of the Jewish *Testaments* or *IV Ezra* ceased to operate. Either there were no more non-rabbinic Jewish writings after about 100 CE. Or, more likely, the diminishing contacts between Christians and other, broader currents of Judaism meant that the impulse to take over newer non-rabbinic Jewish writings diminished also.

(5) The emerging canons of Judaism and Christianity also point in

---

36. *Eph.* inscrp.; 1.1; 7.2; 15.3; 18.2; 19.3; *Trall.* 7.1; *Rom.* inscrp.; 3.3; 6.3; *Smyrn.* 1.1; 10.1; *Poly.* 8.3.

37. See the texts collected by Herford, *Christianity*, pp. 291–307; also Simon, *Verus Israel*, pp. 186–96; and above §2.1 p. 21.

38. See also M. Hengel, 'Die Septuaginta als christliche Schriftensammlung und die Entstehung ihres "Kanons"', *Parting of the Ways: AD 70–135*, ed. Dunn.

a similar direction. Rabbinic Judaism held to the narrowed down version, excluding elements already in the LXX;[39] Christianity held to the LXX, but was already beginning to give increasing and increasingly decisive weight as scripture to the 'memoirs of the apostles' (Justin) and the letters of Paul.

(6) Finally we may note that in Graeco-Roman writers the recognition that Christians are different from Jews only begins to become clear in the early second century. We have already observed that prior to 70 CE disputes occasioned by Christian preaching of Christ were regarded as intra-Jewish disputes (§11.5b). But thereafter too, Epictetus, writing about the turn of the century was probably thinking of Christians when he talks about those who do not simply 'act the part of a Jew' but 'have been baptized' and become 'a Jew in fact' (2.9.19–21).[40] And the charge of atheism brought against Flavius Clemens in 95 CE, 'a charge on which many others who drifted into Jewish ways were condemned' (Cassius Dio 67.14.1–2), has often been taken to indicate his conversion to Christianity.[41] In contrast, however, from the early second century on, a clear distinction is drawn, with Christianity increasingly recognized as a separate or independent religion. Tacitus, writing in the early second century, notes that the Neronian persecution of 64 CE was directed against those 'whom the crowd styled Christians' – although his fuller description of them parallels his earlier description of Jews and suggests that he himself thought of these 'Christians' as Jews.[42] But writing a little later, Suetonius speaks of punishment inflicted in the same period 'on the Christians', as 'a new and wicked superstition' (*Nero* 16.2). And in Pliny's correspondence with the emperor Trajan in about 112 CE it is clear that Christians are a definite, widespread and influential sect, where the issue was whether guilt could be determined by the very confession or denial of 'being a Christian' (*Epp.* 10.96–97). In other words, by

---

39. Note the ruling on ben Sira in *t. Yad.* 2.13, cited above (§12.1e).

40. At this period baptism was the distinctively Christian rite which alone was sufficient to mark the change of life in conversion to Christ, whereas even if proselyte baptism was already being practised within Judaism, circumcision still remained the most distinctively Jewish rite of transfer from status as Gentile to that of Jew.

41. But see *GLAJJ*, 2.380–3.

42. *Hist.* 5.4.1, 5.5.1 – 'The Jews regard as profane all that we hold sacred; on the other hand, they permit all that we abhor ... Toward every other people they feel only hate and enmity'. *Ann.* 15.44.2–4 – 'a class of men, loathed for their vices, whom the crowd styled Christians ... convicted ... for hatred of the human race'. As Simon, *Verus Israel*, notes: 'It is surely not coincidence that the popular imagination accused both Jews and Christians of exactly the same vices. It is quite probable that the Christians were the victims, in the first instance, of a kind of anti-Semitism' (pp. 118–19). He also points out that Christians seem often to have been buried in Jewish cemeteries (p. 124).

the time of Pliny the issue was clear: Christians are not Jews. By then the perception from outside reinforces the impression that *the parting of the ways had already become effective*, in Asia Minor and in the view from Rome at any rate.

(*d*) Perhaps we should make particular mention of two other factors which probably each played a decisive role in reinforcing the separatist trends between Christian and Jew. One was the changing policy of the Roman government to the *fiscus Iudaicus*.[43] This was the poll tax levied on Jews after the 66–70 revolt: every Jew, male or female, from the ages of three to sixty, was required to pay two drachmas a year. The original purpose was for the rebuilding of the temple of Jupiter Capitolinus in Rome, but it continued long after that project was completed. Initially it was levied only on Jews, that is, ethnic Jews, but apparently not on Gentile proselytes, let alone God-fearing Gentiles – the assumption being that *Iudaei* were an ethnic group, all of whom subscribed to the national cult. 'It is striking', as Martin Goodman has noted, 'that no gentile writer before the end of the first century AD seems to have been aware of the Jewish concept of proselytism', despite the numbers who had evidently been attracted by Jewish customs and had judaized.[44] Where such allegiance was noted, it would presumably either be ranked as equivalent to initiation to just another eastern cult, without affect on ethnic or cultural identity, or be regarded simply as anomalous.

Under Domitian, however, the *fiscus Iudaicus* was exacted *acerbissime*, 'with utmost rigour'. That is, according to Suetonius, people who had previously escaped from paying the tax were now compelled to do so. To whom did Suetonius refer? He explains himself – 'those who without publicly acknowledging that faith yet lived as Jews, as well as those who concealed their origin and did not pay the tribute levied upon the people' (*Domitian* 12.2), that is, judaizing Gentiles and non-religious Jews.[45] As Goodman notes, this more rigorous exaction of the tax would have been very unpopular with Jews who had renounced their faith, like Tiberius Julius Alexander, nephew of Philo the philosopher, who abandoned the religion of his fathers and took service with the Romans, to become, in fact, Roman Procurator of Judaea in the 40s.

---

43. See e.g. Schürer, 1.513, 528; 2.272–3.
44. M. Goodman, 'Diaspora Reactions to the Destruction of the Temple', *The Parting of the Ways ad 70–135*., ed. Dunn, For what follows see also his earlier 'Nerva, the *fiscus Judaicus* and Jewish identity', *JRS* 79 (1989), pp. 40–4.
45. Text and fuller details in *GLAJJ*, 2.128–30.

The strength of such reaction must have been a factor in Nerva's countermanding Domitian's unpopular action by reforming the *fiscus Iudaicus* in 96. Nerva's coins proclaim: *Fisci Iudaici calumnia sublata*, 'the malicious accusation with regard to the Jewish tax has been removed'. From this Goodman deduces that the reform of the tax would have allowed those who wished to deny their Jewishness (like Alexander) the right to do so. Since permission was also withdrawn for prosecution of non-Jews for 'adopting the Jewish way of life',[46] a corollary would be that people of non-Jewish origin could pay the tax and thus become 'Iudaei', 'Jews', in official reckoning at least. In other words, the tie-in between ethnic and religious identity was slackened: the weight in the term 'Iudaeus' shifted, so that it became more a *religious* than an *ethnic* identification.

More important for us, such a change in policy meant that *a clearer definition of apostasy could become possible*. Before 96 CE there was no recognized definition of apostasy agreed by all Jews. But now any ethnic Jew who refused to pay the tax thereby declared his apostasy for all to see. By failing to pay the tax he thereby denied that he was a Jew. Presumably there were few if any Gentile Christians who paid up; and many Jewish Christians no doubt also welcomed the opportunity to be free of the tax. At all events, there is something both sad and modern about the likely conclusion that government taxation policy played a significant part in the final parting of the ways.

(*e*) For others still living within Judaea the final breach may not have come till the second Jewish revolt (132–135).[47] The crucial factor here was the recognition of the leader of the revolt, bar Kokhba, as Messiah. The very name by which he was known, bar Kokhba, 'son of the star' was a clear allusion to the messianic text, Num. 24.17; the famous rabbi Akiba definitely announced him as such; and he was almost certainly widely regarded as Messiah among the people.[48] The significance of this is that in effect *for the first time within Judaism since Jesus there was a widely accepted alternative to the Christian claim that Jesus was Messiah*. For the Jewish Christians, still loyal to

---

46. Cassius Dio 68.1.2 notes that under Nerva's ruling, 'no persons were permitted to accuse anybody ... of adopting the Jewish mode of life' (*GLAJJ*, 2.384–5). See also Schürer, 3.122–3.

47. So e.g. Moore, *Judaism*, 1.90–1; Richardson, *Israel*, p. 203; Schiffman, *JCSD*, pp. 155–6; *Who Was a Jew?*, pp. 75–8; Katz, 'Separation' p. 76; Gager, *EJMI*, p. 104; Wilson, *Our Father Abraham*, pp. 81–3.

48. Schürer, 1.543–5.

the ideal of a Jewish state, the rise of bar Kokhba must have precipitated an agonizing choice. They had to choose between Jesus and bar Kokhba; and to choose Jesus was to deny the national leader and the rekindled sense of Jewish identity which he must have engendered. Some such dilemma must lie behind the report of Justin that in the Jewish war 'Bar Kokhba, the leader of the revolt of the Jews, gave orders that Christians alone should be led to cruel punishments, unless they would deny Jesus Christ and utter blasphemy' (*Apol.* 1.31.6). This inability of Jewish Christians to confess bar Kokhba and to identify with the sense of nationhood he embodied, and the resultant persecution from the Jewish side must have sealed the issue for many Jewish Christians, confirming once and for all that they could no longer be both Jews and Christians, but had to decide which of the now separated ways they should follow.[49] In turn, the failure of the revolt would have only added to the depth of the divide, increasing the sense of betrayal and bitterness on the one side, and the sense of vindication and superiority on the other, proto-typical of the troubled relationships which would characterize the encounter between Jew and Christian thereafter. That *the final issue should have been one of christology*, Who is the Messiah?, simply confirms that this in the end was the decisive make or break issue for most Jews-become-Christians, and for most Gentiles-become-Christians-but-not-Jews.

In short, if there is one period in which the seams uniting the two main segments of the heritage of second Temple Judaism finally pulled apart, that period is almost certainly the first thirty to thirty-five years of the second century. However many threads remained linking the sundered parts, however closely together they lay, and however much alike they were, *by the end of the second Jewish revolt, Christian and Jew were clearly distinct and separate.*

12.3 The significance of Christianity's Jewish origins and of the parting of the ways for Christianity

What then is the significance of Christianity's beginning within the matrix of second Temple Judaism and of the parting of the ways between Christianity and rabbinic Judaism? The answers (plural) to that question could be developed in many ways. But our inquiry has focussed the issue in four main subject areas – the four main pillars of second Temple Judaism. And in fact many of the most significant points emerge precisely in relation to these four pillars. So we shall

---

49. See also Alon, *Jews*, pp. 305–7.

confine ourselves to the areas and issues already marked out in the preceding discussion. Having traced the process of parting in reverse order from the initial description of the four pillars, we revert to the original order in an attempt to gather the threads of our conclusions together.[50]

(1) God is one

The fundamental question put to Christianity by rabbinic Judaism was simple: *Is God one? Is Christianity (still) monotheistic?* It remains the central issue between Christianity on the one hand and both Judaism and Islam on the other. At the end of chapter 11 we concluded that Christianity and rabbinic Judaism pulled apart finally over the issue of christology: in the view of rabbinic Judaism, Christianity was no longer monotheistic. But the point came through with equal insistence from the Fourth Evangelist that *the view of Christ presented in his Gospel remained wholly within monotheism*. This, it will be recalled, is the conclusion which follows from the recognition that *the chief expression of christology in the Fourth Gospel is that of Logos-Wisdom christology*. In the Fourth Gospel, Son of God christology is *not* distinct and different from Wisdom christology.[51] Nor did his Son of God language imply for John that the Son of God is a separate being alongside God; rather it is to be understood as an extension of the vigorous poetic Hebrew imagery used in talking of the personified figure of Wisdom.

The point can be underlined by noting the serious error in translating John 1.1 as, 'Before anything else existed, there was Christ with God'.[52] Not only is it simply an inadmissable translation, but it makes the mistake of identifying Christ as the Logos even before the incarnation. But in John's christology, Christ, properly speaking, is not the Logos so much as *the Logos incarnate*. Whereas to speak of *Christ* as 'in the beginning with God' is to imply that the Logos was a quite separate personality from God, a person in the sense that Jesus of Nazareth was a person, already distinct in that sense from God. But that points inevitably in the direction of tri-theism – the Logos-Son as a person, Jesus of Nazareth, and the Father as a person in the sense

---

50. Although I have reflected on these issues now for several years, I should stress that the following thoughts are still provisional, not least because they lead me quickly beyond my own specialisms.

51. Here again I should note the development in my own thinking marked by the second edition of *Christology* – pp. xxvi–xxviii.

52. *The Living Bible*, p. 993.

that Jesus is a person, and so on.[53] That *would* be an abandonment of monotheism. And, to be fair, that is more or less what the rabbis heard John's christology as saying. But if we are right in §11, it is not what *John* said or intended to be heard as saying.

The point of recognizing that Wisdom(-Logos) christology is the dominant category in John, however, is that *it shows how John's christology remained within the bounds of Jewish monotheism*. If Jesus was the incarnation of Logos-Wisdom, then Jesus was thereby understood as the self-expression of God, that of God which may be known by human creatures – *God* incarnate, rather than the *Son* of God incarnate, if the Son is understood as other than the Logos-Wisdom of God. As Paul's Wisdom christology could still be maintained alongside, and even in the same breath as the *Shema'* (§10.5), so with John's: *Jesus as God, in the sense that the Logos/Wisdom is God – that of God which may be manifested within the limits of human history and flesh*. And thus the Fourth Evangelist maintained its christology within a monotheistic frame-work. But not in the perspective of rabbinic Judaism. For the rabbis the thought of divine Wisdom incarnate in the Torah was acceptable within monotheism. But not a real 'in-carnation', not Wisdom become flesh in a man of living memory and in literal, not just allegorical, sense. Hence the parting of the ways.

The corollaries of all this for the Christian understanding of God, of Christ and of God as Trinity are of major importance. For a start, it is very important to realize that *this was the first great christological debate in which Christianity was involved*[54] – a debate not so much over christology as such, as over *theo*-logy, about the understanding of *God*, about *monotheism*. And even more important to realize that the belief which triumphed was the belief in God as one and in Jesus as the expression of the one God. Even though the rabbis thought Christianity had become polytheistic (two powers in heaven), the Christianity involved in that debate (Johannine Christianity) denied it. To put the point from the patristic side, the christological debates of the patristic period did not start with the issues of docetism or monarchianism. Nor did they begin with the issue of the relationship between Father and Son. The highway of second-century christological development was *the same Wisdom/Logos christology* – con-

---

53. One of the great merits of Lampe's *God as Spirit* is to highlight this problem of using 'person' as a category when its meaning has become so different from that intended in the Patristic usage.

54. Or the second, if the claim that Jesus was Messiah should be regarded as the first.

tinuing to emphasize the *continuity* between God and Jesus. The main debates of the second century started with the recognition of the deity of Christ, as attempts to spell out the implications of Logos christology, with docetism or modalism as the main alternatives – attempts in other words to spell out the implications of a christology operating *within* monotheism, of a monotheistic christology. It was *the givenness of Christian monotheism*, already disputed but firmly maintained, which dictated the framework of these debates and the alternatives open to those who took a Wisdom-Logos christology for granted.[55]

The givenness of the Christian monotheistic axiom is even more important to hang on to when assessing the subsequent and much more complex debates. This is true not least when we come to Nicaea, where 'Logos' in effect gave way to 'Son of God' as the key christological category, and where the key issue to be resolved became that of the *relation* between Father and Son. Indeed, it is evident that 'Son of God' became more important than 'Logos' primarily because it provided better *relational* imagery than the latter (whereas 'logos' better expressed the *continuity* between the unspoken and the spoken word). What is important here, however, is to appreciate that the issue of relationship could emerge safely, that is, without encouraging the idea of two divine beings, because the issue of continuity had been resolved long before, that the second person of the Nicene Trinity is the Son *only as the Logos*. Within the security of a Christian monotheism once disputed but now taken for granted, these further questions could be debated. From this perspective, Nicaea's Son of God Trinitarianism is essentially a refinement of the earlier established Logos monotheism.

The danger in assessing and reaffirming Nicene orthodoxy is that *it is all too easy to forget the earlier stage of the debate and development* (Logos-Wisdom christology as an expression of monotheism) and to *start* christological reflection from the classic Father, Son language of the Nicene creed. It is the danger of starting with the question of *relationships* between the persons of the Godhead, the danger of identifying Jesus as the Son of God *simpliciter*, or of thinking of the Son of God as a person in the same way that Jesus was a person. For the theological path which starts at that point leads assuredly into the trap of polytheism, of thinking of God as three persons (in the modern sense of 'person'), that is as three gods![56] Only by pushing back *behind*

---

55. See further Kelly, *Doctrines*, ch. 4 and 5.

56. Karl Rahner has given similar warnings; see particularly his *The Trinity*, London; Burns & Oates 1970, pp. 42–5; also *Foundations of Christian Faith*, London; Darton, Longman & Todd 1978, pp. 133–7; see also his 'Remarks on the Dogmatic Treatise, "De Trinitate",' *Theological Investigations*, Vol. 4, London: Darton, Longman & Todd 1974,

Nicaea, back to the presuppositions of the Nicene formulations, will such a danger be averted. And that means *back to John's christology* and the christology of the second century which followed on the path pointed out by John's Wisdom-Logos christology. In this understanding, *Jesus is the Son of God as the Logos, as the self-expression of God*. The continuity of the Logos-Wisdom-Son with the one God is more fundamental to John's christology than the subordination of the Son to the Father which the subsequent debate about the relationship between Father and Son brought to the fore.[57] In such discussions, Son of God christology begins as the refinement of a more basic monotheism reaffirmed, established and assumed.

In short, *monotheism is a non-negotiable starting point for Christian thought about Christ, and remains the axiomatic starting point within which any 'high' christology must continue to be expressed.* Christology 'from above', properly understood, is a subset within the doctrine of God.

The consequences of this conclusion for Jewish/Christian dialogue are equally profound. For it encourages the possibility of re-examining that final parting of the ways (over christology). *If Christianity is indeed genuinely monotheistic in its faith, then the question cannot be avoided: was it necessary after all for Jew and Christian to separate over christology?* If Jew (and Christian!) could be convinced of Christianity's monotheism, what scope might there be for a fresh re-examination of their mutual claims to the heritage of Israel's monotheism. Is it possible, for example, that a re-emphasis on the continuity of the claims made for Jesus with the preceding revelatory claims made by Jesus' predecessors (as in Heb. 1.1ff.), within the monotheistic given, might be sufficient once again to encourage Jews to see in Jesus an *essential complement* of the Torah? On the other side, can Christians be open enough to the universal within the *Christian*

---

pp. 77–102 (I owe these references to Mgr Jack Kennedy, Rector of the Venerable English College).

57. It is for this reason that I demur at C. K. Barrett's re-emphasis on John's 'subordinationist christology' – ' "The Father is Greater than I", John 14.28: Subordinationist Christology in the New Testament' (1974), *Essays on John*, pp. 19–36; similarly Osten-Sacken, *Christian-Jewish Dialogue*, pp. 130–1. That is to read John far too much against the later Nicene concern with relationships; whereas, or so it seems to me, John's concern was to stress the *continuity* between the Father and the Son – that is, a Logos-Wisdom emphasis more than a subordinationist emphasis; see particularly M. L. Appold, *The Oneness Motif in the Fourth Gospel*, WUNT 1; Tübingen: Mohr-Siebeck 1977. Barrett however does quite rightly emphasize the theocentricity of John's christology in the preceding essay – 'Christocentric or Theocentric? Observations on the Theological Method of the Fourth Gospel' (1976), *Essays*, pp. 1–18.

particular to step back from the most offensive (to Jewish sensibilities) and needlessly offensive claims regarding Christ (just as Jews earlier recognized the universality of Wisdom within the Torah)? Should the step of seeing Wisdom incarnate in Jesus rather than in Torah have been condemned as a step too far? Is a christological perception of God un-Jewish?[58] Can a Judaism (and Christianity) which was to accept as *de facto* legitimate a large mystical dimension not reappreciate the power of a christology rooted in the mysticism of John's Gospel?[59]

Or to take another tack: *the fact that both Jew and Christian await the coming of the Messiah*. Is the *incompleteness* of the fulfilment of messianic hope in the (first) coming of Christ and the *common* hope of Jew and Christian for the still future coming of the Messiah sufficient ground for a *mutual* reassessment of the christological claims which, for good or ill, resulted in the parting of the ways?[60] In writing my commentary on Romans I was deeply impressed by the way in which Paul expresses his hope for Israel in un-distinctively-Christian terms: the Christian Christ does not appear as Paul's exposition draws to its climax in Rom. 11; the hope is of a coming deliverer, in terms drawn directly from Isa. 59.20–21; and the final doxology focusses exclusively on God alone. It is almost as though Paul was falling over backwards to avoid language and claims which would be offputting to his Jewish kinsfolk. Is there here a lesson to be learned for Christian dialogue with Jew? – that that which unites us is sufficient ground for future reconciliation when the Messiah comes?

Whatever the realism or unrealism of such a vision, the fact remains that *Christianity is only Christianity when it is monotheistic*. Only so can Christians remain true to their roots, to their heritage within the religion of Israel. Only so can Christians continue to retain the Jewish scriptures within their canon. The *Shema'* is the common starting point of faith which Christians share with their Jewish brothers and sisters. Otherwise they have lost their connection with their Jewish heritage, and not only destroyed their chance of dialogue with

---

58. See Thoma, *Christian Theology*, pp. 124–36.

59. 'Jewish mysticism in its time absorbed many pagan elements and even found room for a kind of Trinitarianism which was perhaps cruder and more pagan than that of Roman Catholic Christianity' – Y. Kaufmann, *Christianity and Judaism. Two Covenants*, Jerusalem: Magnes 1988, p. 25. In pursuit of Kaufmann's thesis (see below n. 69) we could say that Christianity secured the defeat of idolatry by its Adam christology; that is, by focussing worship on and through Jesus as the only legitimate 'image' of God (see above §10.4).

60. The point, of course, is not new; see e.g. those reviewed by Pawlikowski, *Christ*, pp. 19, 26–7, 43.

Judaism, and any future *rapprochement* with Jews, but abandoned the christology of the apostles for a Jesus-ism or a Jesus-olatry which has effectively lost touch with that first faith and hope in 'the God and Father of our Lord Jesus Christ'. From the first, the importance of holding the uniqueness of God's revelation in Christ within the axiom of God as one has been an essential test of sound christology.

12.4 (2) The people of God

Another inescapable question which lies at the heart of Christian self-understanding as a result of its origins is: *Who are the people of God?* How stands now the axiom of Israel's election? So long as Christianity and Judaism were still part of an unbroken, continuous spectrum, it was not so much of a problem. It was possible to speak and think of a renewed or expanded Israel in continuity with the old, with the Christian claim as one of several competing claims within the first century.[61] But with the final parting of the ways the question becomes more pressing and unavoidable as such. Who are the people of God? All Jews? Or only those Jews who have become Christians = the remnant = eschatological Judaism? Or Gentiles as well? What about the great bulk of the Jewish people who have not believed in Jesus as Messiah and still show no signs of doing so?[62] And has Christianity taken over from Israel, the 'new Israel' superceding the old?

In the second century the problem was compounded with the steadily emerging sense of Christians as a third race[63] – Jews as well as Gentiles becoming 'them' to the Christian 'us', Christianity as alone the true Israel.[64] The other and tragic side of this emergence of a clear and distinctive Christian identity was the steady growth of anti-semitism. It is and remains a deeply disturbing fact that catholic Christianity found it necessary to define itself over *against* Judaism, all too often by vilifying the Jews – in early centuries most disturbingly in Chrysostom's *Homily Against the Jews*.[65] Here was a great irony: Christianity began by rejecting the ethnocentricity of Judaism and of Jewish Christianity; but in coming to think of itself as a separate

---

61. The issue is highlighted within the NT by such texts as Rom. 9.6, Gal. 6.16, James 1.1 and I Peter 1.1–2.

62. M. Barth has done much to bring the issue to the fore; see particularly his *The People of God*, JSNTSupp 5; Sheffield: JSOT 1983.

63. See particularly Simon, *Verus Israel*, pp. 107–11; Richardson. *Israel*.

64. Simon, *Verus Israel*, pp. 79–80; Richardson, *Israel*, pp. 9–14.

65. Text in Meeks and Wilken, *Jews and Christians in Antioch*, pp. 85ff.; see further Simon, *Verus Israel*, ch. 8.

'race', it opened the door to a different kind of racialism, where Christians defined themselves by *excluding* 'the Jews', making the very mistake against which Paul in particular protested so vehemently.

Can that process be reversed? The possibility is opened up if we are prepared to go back behind these centuries of anti-semitism and mutual suspicion. For our study has highlighted what was one of the most important features in the beginnings of Christianity – *the evangelistic necessity to challenge the religious and social boundaries* by which the people of God of that period defined themselves, their religion and their corporate identity. Jesus challenged the boundaries within the people of God – a central feature of his ministry. That has immediate and obvious implications for all sectarianism within Christianity, not simply between denominations, but between the factions within denominations – factions which so often speak and think in very similar terms to those whereby the 'righteous' within Israel distinguished themselves from 'sinners'. The claims to exclusive and solely normative insight into the will of God are as vigorously proclaimed today within Christianity, whether by Roman magisterium or Protestant fundamentalist sect. And *the rebuke of Jesus to such attitudes and claims is as valid and as important now as then.*

More to our present point, Paul, as we saw, pressed the logic of Jesus' good news for sinners by extending it to the 'sinners of the Gentiles'. The challenge today is in effect to recognize the same logic in reverse. That *as Jewish hope then could not be fulfilled without Gentile participation, so Christian hope now cannot be fulfilled without Jewish participation.* As the first Christians had to insist that the Jewish 'us' could not be completed without the Gentile 'them' (I have in mind, for example, the picture of Heb. 12.1–2), so present day Christians have to appreciate that the Christian 'us' cannot be complete without the Jewish 'them'. Here is the greatest challenge for the ecumenical movement.[66] The greatest schism within the people of God is not between Catholic and Protestant, or between Eastern and Western Christianity, but between Jew and Christian. Until Jew and Gentile can praise God together, the vision of a passage like Rom. 15.8–12 cannot be fulfilled.

Is such an ecumenical *rapprochement* between Jew and Christian conceivable? Probably not this side of the eschaton. But two factors may prove to be crucial. One is to appreciate and re-emphasize *the essentially Jewish character of Christian beginnings.* On the Christian

---

66. A challenge realized only in recent years; see above ch. 1, n. 69.

side that means recognizing the force of such treatments as Eph. 2.11–22, where the sense of the new people of God builds into that of the old – a hope fulfilled in terms not simply of 'one new man in place of the two', but a hope fulfilled also in terms of the commonwealth of Israel, the covenants of promise and the one God of Israel (2.12, 15, 19). Is it possible to return to a perspective like that of Paul, to rediscover and maintain afresh the tension of continuity/discontinuity with Israel, between the universal and particular of 'Israel'? The extremes to be avoided are clear – anti-semitism and narrow nationalism. But can we hold the two (the Israel of old and eschatological or enlarged Israel) together? Can we recover the sense of an inner-Israel critique as something very different from anti-semitism or anti-Judaism? Paul's answer may not have been sustainable within the flow of history. But the insights and arguments he put forward in Romans in particular still provide both challenge and means to mount a fresh reappraisal at this point. For example, the openness of Rom. 2.10–11 – 'Glory and honour and peace for everyone who does good, the Jew first and also the Greek. For God shows no partiality'. Or Rom. 4 – Abraham as the model of faith, prior to his taking on the distinctive and differentiating sign of circumcision. Or Rom. 9.6–12, where Paul reasserts the character of the divine call/election as without reference to physical descent or ethnic traditions. Or again Rom. 11, with its final climactic hope in characteristically Jewish and un-distinctively-Christian terms. In short, *does the period from before the parting of the ways provide us resources for present and future which will enable us to recover more of that earlier continuity and to rediscover that character of earliest Christian mission as a movement for renewal within the Judaism of the time?* The increasing numbers of Messianic Jews in Israel and north America add unnerving complications to the picture, particularly in giving a further twist to the sad history of exclusivist claims. But they also offer fresh bridging possibilities, since the Jew/Christian spectrum is more complete now than at any time since the early decades (when Jewish Christianity was a vital option).

Jewish/Christian dialogue in this area has tended to pose the issue in terms of one covenant or two;[67] and clearly I lean to the 'one covenant' side. But it is important to recall that these original terms, particularly the contrast of old covenant and new covenant, were not necessarily to be understood as alternatives. II Cor. 3 and Heb. 8

---

67. See particularly Pawlikowski, *Christ*; also *Jesus and the Theology of Israel*, Wilmington: Glazier 1989; see also e.g. P. Sigal, 'Aspects of Dual Covenant Theology: Salvation', *HBT* 5 (1983), pp. 1–48; Kaufmann, *Christianity and Judaism*.

certainly push in that direction. But the terms of Jer. 31.31–34 taken up in these passages implied a high degree of continuity (it was the *law* which was to be written upon their hearts). And those in view in the Damascus Document could take up the idea of a new covenant, as well as the Christians, without hereby moving themselves off the end of the spectrum of Judaism. In the end of the day, the difference between a renewed covenant and a new covenant is not so great.[68] In particular, we should recall our finding above (chs 7–8) that the law of the covenant was not abandoned, except in its ethnic particularity; for the Christianity of the NT, fulfilment of the law was still important. So, whether we see Christianity as fulfilling Israel's covenant task, a light to the nations, Judaism for the Gentiles,[69] or place weightier emphasis on the newness of the new covenant, it should not be forgotten that the common ground is the *covenant* given by God; nor that the faithfulness of God is as much 'on the line' with the one as the other. In both cases the particularism of historical contingency is in danger of obscuring the universalism of a belief in God as one, and creator of all.[70]

If such a policy of *rapprochement* was to have any hope of success, of course, it would depend in large part on both Jews and Christians showing the same willingness to go behind the centuries of antagonism and to build on their common foundations. The possibility of rapprochement depends on *each* being willing to recognize and acknowledge their *common* heritage from this earliest period (first century CE), the common roots of Judaism and Christianity both in second Temple Judaism. The problem has always been that each has tended to view that period of overlap from the perspective of what

---

68. It is important to avoid the mistake of thinking that Christianity emerged from and subsequent to Judaism, understood as rabbinic Judaism; rather *both* are descended from and redefinitions of the earlier Judaism, that is, second Temple Judaism. Hence the now quite frequent talk of Judaism and Christianity as 'siblings' is welcome; see e.g. Segal, *Rebecca's Children*; H. G. Perelmuter, *Siblings. Rabbinic Judaism and Early Christianity at Their Beginnings*, New York: Paulist 1989; W. Harrelson and R. M. Falk, *Jews and Christians. A Troubled Family*, Nashville: Abingdon 1990. Hence too the undesirability of speaking of Christianity as 'new Israel' (Koenig, *Jews and Christians in Dialogue*, p. 13), despite its attractiveness to second-century Christian writers; preferable is J. Neusner's characterization – 'you Christians, Israel with us (Jews)' (*Jews and Christians: The Myth of a Common Tradition*, London: SCM Press/Philadelphia: TPI 1991, p. 29; also pp. 2–5.

69. See particularly Kaufmann, *Christianity and Judaism*.

70. See particularly Mussner, *Tractate*, pp. 74–6: ' "Covenant" says that God will not forget his creation. The world knows this primarily through Israel' (p. 76). This, of course, becomes the basis of a covenant critique of renewed Jewish insistence on the land of Israel/Palestine as exclusively for Jews and other forms of extremist Zionism. For the justice of the *creator* God to become divorced from the justice of the *covenant* God would undermine the theological legitimacy of all covenant theology.

followed – through the grids of catholic Christianity and rabbinic Judaism respectively. Many scholars from the Christian side have begun to recognize this and to seek ways to compensate. It is less clear that a similar proportion of Jews have reached the same recognition.[71] There are still too many Jewish scholars who view the final phase of second Temple Judaism as though it was simply the beginnings of rabbinic Judaism, who read rabbinic Jewish traditions back into the earlier first century, who pay too little regard to non-rabbinic Jewish sources, including apocalyptic and 'sectarian' Jewish documents, and not least the Christian documents.[72] *A crucial step forward will be taken when Christian scholars recognize that the beginnings of Christianity cannot be understood without reference to Jewish documents and traditions from the late second Temple period; and when Jewish scholars recognize that the bulk of the NT writings are also Jewish documents and that many of them have a right to be counted as witnesses to the breadth and character of second Temple Judaism as much as their own later documents.* And if progress has already been made in terms of 'the Jewish reclamation of Jesus',[73] then that simply underlines the extent to which the storm centre shifts to *Paul* and to the question as to whether he is simply to be dismissed as an apostate or can be reclaimed in turn as a Pharisee whose interpretation of his Jewish heritage still lies within the breadth of legitimate inner-Jewish debate and mutual critique.[74]

The other crucial factor is to look forward rather than back – to recognize that *the character and 'shape' of the people of God in the future may be as different from what it is now as rabbinic Judaism and Christianity are different from second Temple Judaism.* If the Reformation can be regarded as a renewal movement within the mediaeval church which the mediaeval church was insufficiently flexible to contain within itself, so the emergence of Christianity may be regarded as a renewal movement within the people of God which resulted in an unnecessary and theologically undesirable schism within the people of God.[75] Equally, the hope of the great eschato-

---

71. Jacob Neusner has been the most notable exception.

72. See e.g. Maccoby, *Judaism*; and above §1.4c.

73. See again Hagner, *Jewish Reclamation of Jesus*.

74. A. F. Segal's *Paul the Convert* is a step in the right direction. But there is a noble tradition of Jewish scholarship which attempted to take Paul seriously, including particularly C. G. Montefiore, J. Klausner, H. -J. Schoeps, and S. Sandmel; see further W. Jacob, *Christianity Through Jewish Eyes. The Quest for Common Ground*, Hebrew Union College Press 1974; F. A. Rothschild (ed.), *Jewish Perspectives on Christianity*, New York: Crossroad 1990.

75. Though Neusner, *Jews and Christians*, questions such a perspective (here particularly pp. 20–2).

logical church can hardly be contained within a vision which is simply a projection forward of the present patterns of church structure, but must be open to a further renewal which results in 'one new man' instead of the two old ones. So too in the larger ecumenical vision which embraces Jew and Christian: the hope of a reunited people of God cannot be envisaged simply in terms of Judaism as presently understood and Christianity as presently understood coming together. One thing we can be sure of: *the eschatological people of God will be constituted differently from either the rabbinic Judaism or the catholic Christianity of today.*

In short, the crucial question to both Jew and Christian may be this: Can we let go our present sufficiently to recover our common past? And can we let go our separate past and present sufficiently to allow a common future to emerge from within the will of God in history?

12.5 (3) The law of God (scripture and tradition)

So far as the third pillar of second Temple Judaism is concerned, our study has focussed principally on the role of Torah as boundary, so that the comments just made (§12.4) have application here too. But there is another aspect of this third pillar and of its questioning by emerging Christianity which underlies all of the above discussion and which needs to be brought more to the surface. I refer to the character of *Torah as normative revelation* once given and recognized as of divine authority (= scripture), and to the tension which that assessment sets up between *the determinative revelation once given and its interpretation*, between, in other words, a normative revelation and claims to fresh revelation, between the law of God and evolving case law, or between scripture and tradition.[76]

(*a*) It is important to recognize that this tension *is* part of the *common* heritage from second Temple Judaism for both Jew and Christian. They shared a very similar problem: the tension between Torah (written = scripture) and tradition (oral); the tension, we may say, within first Temple Judaism between priest and prophet, and within second Temple Judaism between Sadducee and Pharisee.[77] So,

---

76. I am, of course, playing on the fact that in the NT 'the law' has a range of meaning, including the law (of Moses), the Pentateuch and scripture (the OT) generally (see e.g. BAGD, *nomos* 3–4); cf. also above §2.3 p. 33.

77. It will be recalled that according to Josephus (*Ant.* 13.297; 18.16) the Sadducees, in contrast to the Pharisees, regarded only the Torah as binding and rejected the developing body of tradition (see Schürer, 2.407–11).

in due course, in Christianity: the tension between the NT and tradition, where very soon the NT canon itself became a means of excluding false (particularly Gnostic) tradition, but was itself already caught in the tension between scripture (NT) and tradition (the rule of faith);[78] and the still current tension between canonical scripture and the magisterium within catholic Christianity, or between canonical scripture and each denomination's distinguishing tradition.

Not to be forgotten, however, is the fact that *the same tension was already there in the beginnings of Christianity itself*. For the only scriptures recognized by the first Christians were the same *Jewish* scriptures (what Christians call 'the OT'). The first expression of this tension in Christianity was between scripture (OT) and Jesus' halakah. And as there was a debate within second Temple Judaism about the relation of Torah and halakah, so too there was an equivalent debate within earliest Christianity – as illustrated by Matthew's and Mark's differing assessments of the consequences of Jesus' teaching for the continued validity of some key Torah commands.[79] Moreover, we should not forget that the hermeneutical principles and practices of the first Christian teachers, as represented not least by Paul, were wholly Jewish in character.[80] For the first Christians, the scriptures (OT) were as authoritative as for the first rabbis. The tension between a fuller canon (NT as well as OT) is in principle not so very different from the tension between the Torah and the Prophets and Writings or between the Torah and the Mishnah.

The point is that this tension is not an aberration within the people of God, but *constitutive of the human attempt to recognize and respond to divine revelation*. It is not a malaise to be healed, or a situation which can be wished away. So long as this world lasts, the revelation of God will always be expressed in the inadequacy and historical conditionedness of a human language which constantly requires interpretation and re-expression. Those who think they live by scripture alone, and that they can wholly dispense with tradition, simply confess their blindness to their own particular traditions which effectively govern their reading of scripture. To recognize this basic fact of our own historical conditionedness is both a bulwark against all fundamentalisms which make the written word into an idol, and a further cause for hope in Jewish/Christian relations. It is because

---

78. So particularly Tertullian; see Kelly, *Early Christian Doctrines*, p. 40.

79. See above §§6.1 and 8.5a.

80. For bibliography on 'The NT's use of the OT' see e.g. my *Unity*², pp. 434–5. That discussion should not be confined to explicit quotations is well demonstrated by R. B. Hays, *Echoes of Scripture in the Letters of Paul*, New Haven: Yale 1989.

both Jew and Christian believe in God, not simply as one who acted in the past but who still acts, in God as Spirit as well as God the Creator who called a people to himself, that we can cherish a hope for a further leading and revelation of God which will be recognized *on both sides* as completing what has already been revealed in Torah, prophet, sage and . . . As Christians want to add – and not least in Jesus and through Paul. So Jews want to add – and also through such great teachers as rabbi Akiba, rabbi Meir, etc.[81] The test of genuinely open dialogue will be whether Jew and Christian can recognize the other's 'and' without driving the debate to a mutually exclusive 'either-or'.

Perhaps only the coming of the Messiah will see the fulfilment of such a hope. In the meantime, to live in the tension between old revelation and fresh insight will require a good deal more openness to the insights which can come from others into one's own normative word, as well as an openness to wholly new insights given by the Spirit, than has hitherto been the case in any measure on either side.

(*b*) A sociological point is also worth some reflection. There is clearly a tendency for the liberating teaching of one generation to become the binding tradition of the next. The previous wave of renewal can so easily become the greatest obstacle to the next wave of renewal. So probably with the Pharisees. They themselves were a movement we might say to liberate the Torah and to respond creatively to the changed circumstances of their own time. But in turn too many of them came to regard the renewal movement begun by Jesus as a threat to be opposed; whereas, in the view of Jesus and the first Christians, the liberating tradition of the Pharisees had become merely 'the tradition of men' (Mark 7.8). Within the NT we may have to recognize something of the same in the case of the Pastorals, that is, as a second generation attempt to conserve and codify as tradition the teaching of Paul from the first generation, but perhaps running the same danger of transforming the teaching of Paul in the Spirit into the tradition of Paul the man.

In *Unity and Diversity in the New Testament* I was bold enough to suggest that one weakness of emerging catholic Christianity[82] was that unlike Jewish Christianity, unlike Hellenistic Christianity, unlike apocalyptic Christianity, early catholicism was not seen to have a

---

81. For sketches of the early rabbis see Perelmuter, *Siblings*.

82. I should remind readers that by 'catholic Christianity' I do not mean *Roman Catholicism*; see my *Unity*[2], pp. xxix–xxx and n. 40.

heretical extreme.[83] Another way to put the point is to ask whether catholic Christianity was sufficiently alive to the danger which the early Christians saw so clearly in rabbinic Judaism's emphasis on tradition. Here perhaps the parting of the ways broke part of this same crucial tension which is so fundamental to the character of the people of God – Christianity as most itself when living in the tension between scripture and tradition, between OT and the halakah and haggadah which bring home the continuing relevance of that scripture.

It is this recognition, then, that the tension between normative scripture and its interpretation for different situations cannot be easily resolved or escaped which gives further hope for Jewish Christian relations. The rabbis omitted much that might have been regarded as legitimate interpretation of scripture from second Temple Judaism – including, not least, the Christian documents. But within the Mishnah and the subsequent collections of traditions they have retained a marvellous range and diversity of insight. So too, Christianity refused the option, for example, of running all four Gospels into a single Gospel, as though there was one and only one legitimate form of the Gospel tradition. And the Pastorals, though imposing a conservative interpretation on the Pauline tradition neither decanonized Paul nor allowed Paul to decanonize them. In other words, both the scriptures themselves and the tradition which has been integral to rabbinic Judaism constantly push out against any attempt to define the identity and boundaries of either Christianity or Judaism too narrowly.

Is it so inconceivable, then, for Christians to recognize rabbinic halakah as at least in principle a legitimate interpretation of the Torah, however much that claim may have to be debated in its particulars? Is it so inconceivable for Jews to recognize the NT writings as at least in principle a legitimate interpretation or extension of the Jewish scriptures, however much that claim may have to be debated in its particulars? Is it so inconceivable for Jews and Christians to come together to discuss such issues openly, without abandoning their boundaries, but with the boundaries open rather than closed, endeavouring to be inclusive (as determined by the breadth of the scriptures) rather than exclusive (as determined by the particularity of our traditions)? Our common scriptures, and the diverse interpretations which both traditions can recognize as legitimate within their own confines, should provide all the stimulus and precedents we need.

----

83. *Unity* pp. 365–6 and again *Unity*[2], pp. xxix–xxx.

12.6 (4) Priesthood and ministry

The most interesting feature here is that the parting of the ways affected Christianity and rabbinic Judaism in a way which *reverses the pattern so far observed* – so much so that we should perhaps better speak of rabbinic Judaism parting from Christianity than of Christianity parting from rabbinic Judaism on this point. For rabbinic Judaism was able to survive the loss of a cult centre (the Temple), and so also the loss of the possibility and need for sacrifice and priesthood, by reorganizing itself round the Torah. *In rabbinic Judaism priest was replaced by teacher.* In contrast, and somewhat surprisingly, *it was Christianity which found it necessary to revert to OT categories of sacrifice and priesthood*, at first in a spiritual or allegorical way, as a means to expressing continuity with the ideal of OT spirituality, but then in an increasingly literal way. In view of the surprising character of this development, surprising in the light of the findings of chapter 5, and the contested nature of that development, it is perhaps worth briefly surveying its initial post-NT phase before further comment.

So far as the *Temple* was concerned, the position of the NT writers was in effect confirmed: the Temple was no longer relevant. Indeed, the point was made in fiercer tone, the destruction of the Temple being taken as a sign of God's having disowned Israel. So particularly Barnabas 16 – a forthright polemic against the Temple: 'the wretched men erred by putting their hope in the building and not in the God who made them . . . For they consecrated him in the Temple almost like the heathen. But learn how God speaks . . .'; and the writer goes on to cite several passages in support, including Isa. 66.1 (cf. Acts 7.49–50) and *I Enoch* 89.55–6, 66–7. He then proceeds to argue that we in whom God truly dwells are the habitation of God – '. . . a spiritual temple being built for the Lord' (Barn. 16.1–10).[84] In similar vein, Ignatius echoes earlier NT usage by speaking of individual believers as stones in the temple of God, or as themselves God's temples, or of Jesus as the temple of God (*Eph.* 9.1; 15.3; *Magn.* 7.2).

So there was really no change between the NT writers and those of the early second century with regard to the Temple. But since the Temple was no longer a living factor for Judaism anyway (any hope of the Temple being rebuilt was doomed to disappointment), the issue was that much more academic. With sacrifice and priesthood,

---

84. Note again the possibility that Barnabas was written in face of the expectation that the Temple would soon be rebuilt (see above n. 15).

however, the matter was different, and it is the significance of this difference on which the debate focusses. At first it seems that *only the metaphor or analogy* of sacrifice and priesthood was used; the question of when the language came to be more *literally* understood is the bone of contention.

On the issue of *sacrifice*, an early reference is Did. 14.2, where *thusia*, 'sacrifice', probably refers to the eucharist. But the significance is unclear since the language is drawn directly from Mal. 1.11, where the talk is of a pure sacrifice offered among the nations in contrast to the sacrifices offered on the altar in Jerusalem. I Clement also speaks of the episcopate offering sacrifices (*dōra*) (I Clem. 44.4). But again the significance is unclear. In 35.12 and 52.3–4 it is the sacrifice (*thusia*) of praise which is meant; and in 36.1 it is clear that he is drawing much more on the ideas of Hebrews than those of the Jerusalem cult – 'This is the way, beloved, in which we found our salvation, Jesus Christ, the High Priest of our offerings, the defender and helper of our weakness . . .' (36.1). The same range of imagery continues to be used in Ignatius. Referring to the eucharist he speaks of 'one flesh . . . one cup . . . one altar (*thusastērion*), as there is one bishop with the presbytery and deacons . . .' (*Philad.* 4). And Justin draws on the same Mal. 1.11 text in identifying the Gentiles there spoken of as 'us, who in every place offer sacrifices to him, that is, the bread of the eucharist, and also the cup of the eucharist . . .' (*Dial.* 41).

The question remains, however, whether these writers were taking over the language of sacrifice in the same sense, or in a *transferred* or *metaphorical* sense: whether the eucharist was understood as a sacrifice in a *literal* sense, or as the eschatological *equivalent* of Malachi's talk of a *pure* offering. The latter seems to be more likely. Ignatius, for example, used the language of sanctuary and purity in speaking of obedience to the bishop: 'He who is within the sanctuary (*thusastērion*) is pure (*katharos*), but he who is without the sanctuary is not pure; that is to say, whoever does anything apart from the bishop and the presbytery and the deacons is not pure in his conscience' (*Trall.* 7.2); so also *Eph.* 5.2 and *Philad.* 4. Note also *Rom.* 2.2, where he uses *thusastērion* in referring to his own martyrdom. Also Polycarp, who uses the same word of widows bringing to God tested gifts (4.3). And in the passage just quoted above from Justin's *Dialogue with Trypho*, Justin goes on immediately to spiritualize circumcision: circumcision is the 'type of the true circumcision, by which we are circumcised from deceit and iniquity . . .' (*Dial.* 41). And later on, still speaking of the pure offerings of Mal. 1.11, Justin identifies them with 'prayers and giving thanks' which 'are the only perfect and well pleasing sacrifice to God' (*Dial.* 117).

It is very unlikely, then, that these apostolic fathers were really restoring the language of sacrifice in any literal sense, or that the eucharist was being regarded as a sacrifice in a sense any different from the evangelistic ministry of a Paul, or the death of Ignatius, or the good works of a widow, or the praise and thanks of all Christians.

There is a similar issue with regard to the concept of *priesthood*. I Clem. 40–41 describes the obligation of religious service in typological language drawn from the OT and Jewish cult: not just sacrifices, but the High Priest, priests and Levites, *and* laity (*laïkos*). But how much this too was intended to be understood in a transferred or metaphorical sense, and how much was intended in a literal sense, remains in dispute. It must be metaphorical at least in the case of the Levites. J. B. Lightfoot was able to review all the (then) relevant talk of priests in the apostolic fathers and beyond and concludes that there is no clear idea there of a sacerdotal priesthood prior to Cyprian. Prior to that the dominant idea was that of Christians as a whole as a sacerdotal race, with the minister 'regarded as a priest, because he is the mouthpiece, the representative, of a priestly race'.[85] His understanding of the process leading up to Cyprian is that it was 'by the union of Gentile sentiment with the ordinances of the Old Dispensation (that) the doctrine of an exclusive priesthood found its way into the Church of Christ'.[86]

In modern times we would speak of a social pressure. At that period, priesthood and sacrifice were constitutive of a religion or cult; a religion or cult, indeed, was scarcely imaginable without priesthood and sacrifice. Rabbinic Judaism did not succumb to that pressure: the loss of its own Temple and the focus on Torah enabled it to resist the attraction of the social norm. In contrast, Christianity found itself unable to resist the pressure: the centrality of Christ was insufficient to withstand the pressure towards social conformity, whereby the typological use of OT cultic ideas and terms naturally tended to give way more and more to a literal transposition. Even so, as Schillebeeckx notes, as late as the fifth century, 'Augustine continues to refuse to call bishops and presbyters "priests" in the real sense, in the sense of being mediators between Christ and the community'.[87] In Schillebeeckx's view of the development, it was only when, during the decline of the Roman Empire, bishops assumed a power of

85. J. B. Lightfoot, 'The Christian Ministry', *Philippians*, London: Macmillan 1868, pp. 179–267, here p. 257.

86. Lightfoot, *Philippians*, p. 264.

87. E. Schillebeeckx, *The Church with a Human Face*, London: SCM Press/New York: Crossroad 1985, pp. 144–5.

jurisdiction like that of civil magistrates or prefects, that the concept of a different 'order' emerged, an order wielding 'secret power'. Prior to that the dominant idea was of a priesthood effective by virtue of being representative of the priesthood of the people. At this point, the work of the Catholic theologian confirms the earlier work of the Anglican scholar and bishop: particular 'priestly' ministry was initially understood in these early centuries as representative of the priestly ministry of the whole people of God gathered for worship.

I pursue the debate on these matters beyond the confines of my own area of speciality (the NT and Christian origins) not because I hope to be able to contribute anything to the discussion about ministry in the patristic period. It is simply to point out that the debate about Christian ministry as it develops from that period is not to be posed in terms of a straightforward contrast between NT teaching and developments immediately thereafter. The developments did not take place immediately thereafter, and the influence of the teaching of Paul and Hebrews extended much more fully into the patristic period than was often the case in other matters. But more important here is the positive and negative side of the matter as it affects Christian self-understanding and the relationship between Christianity and Judaism.

On the one hand the degree to which the early Fathers took over the language of priesthood and sacrifice from the OT helps further to underline *the degree of continuity between Christianity and its Jewish heritage*. Indeed, it strengthens the case to be made that the developments in Christianity and in Judaism are *complementary* rather than contradictory: the one re-employing the priestly and cultic heritage of second Temple Judaism; the other giving greater emphasis to the spoken and written heritage. Here too may be ground for fruitful inter-reflection between Jew and Christian.

On the other hand, the subsequent re-emergence of an order of priesthood *distinct and separate from the priesthood of the whole people* still seems to be something of a *retrograde* step back from the fulfilment claimed by the first Christians for their understanding and practice of worship and community. Apart from anything else, the teaching ministry, so central to rabbinic Judaism, so fundamental for the character and continuation of Judaism, and indeed so important in the earliest churches, was too quickly absorbed within and to too large an extent obscured behind a ministry conceived in primarily priestly terms. But most important of all, as is only now, belatedly, being realized, the focus of all ministry to such an exclusive extent on the ordained ministry within Christianity has resulted in *a crip-*

pling rather than a facilitating of the effective ministry of the whole people of God.[88] If ministry in name and fact is effectively confined to the ordained ministry ('the ministry'), then no wonder the body of Christ is less active than it should be, since the great majority of its members are underdeveloped, if not in effect paralysed! The re-assessment of Christianity's beginnings at this point too becomes an essential means of critiquing our present understanding and *mis*-understanding of Christianity. Our appreciation of Judaism as a different, but also valid appropriation of our common heritage may be a vital stimulus in that shaking of the foundations which will allow a new structure to arise more appropriate to the eschatological people of God.

12.7 A concluding reflection

For myself the lasting impression of this study must be *the enduring Jewish character of Christianity*. Christianity of course is not to be identified simply by reference to its beginnings. Nevertheless its birth and beginnings stamped an indelible character on Christianity – as its canon attests for all time with the Jewish scriptures numbered as part of its scriptures. All its leading figures in the most formative period of its existence were Jews who continued to understand themselves as Jews, still part of God's covenant purpose with and through Israel. And in Jesus above all we have the fulcrum figure on whom Christianity ever turns. The more divine significance we Christians recognize in Jesus, God's self-revelation in fullest form possible within humanity, the more we need also to recall that this incarnation took place precisely in a Jew – Jesus the Jew.

One thought in particular has returned to me again and again during my work in preparing these chapters: *Christianity began as a movement of renewal breaking through the boundaries first within and then round the Judaism of the first century.* At its historic heart Christianity is a protest against any and every attempt to claim that God is our God and not yours, God of our way of life and not yours, God of our 'civilization' and not yours; against any and every tendency to designate others as 'sinners', as beyond the pale of God's saving grace, or to insist that for sinners to receive forgiveness they must become righteous, that is 'righteous' as *we* count 'righteousness'.

---

88. This is only beginning to be recognized in the still largely lip service paid to the ministry of the whole people of God in the Vatican II statement on ministry (*Lumen Gentium*) and in the World Council of Churches' statement, *Baptism, Eucharist and Ministry*, Geneva: WCC 1982, 'Ministry' §§1–6.

Against any and every attempt to mark off some of God's people as more holy than others, as exclusive channels of divine grace over against others. At its heart it is a protest against every attempt to pigeon-hole and institutionalize the grace of God, to limit that grace in its expression to the safe confines that human minds can cope with and human capacities can organize. At its heart is an openness to the unexpectedness of divine grace, to the new thing which God may wish to do, even when it breaks through and leaves behind the familiar paths and forms. At its heart is the conviction that God revealed himself most fully not just in human word but in human person, not just in rational or even inspired propositions but in the human relationships which can never be confined within words and formulae alone.

And it is *this character of Christianity which is encapsulated and canonized within our NT writings*, and which gives them their distinctive character within the wider 'canon' of Jewish and Christian normative texts. Which also means that breathing through these writings is that same spiritual force which broke through barriers and boundaries once before and which can therefore do so again. The witness to the renewal of Judaism which was emerging Christianity gives us renewed hope of a yet further new thing which God will do once again for both Jew and Gentile, for his people Israel and for the world.

Appendix

Two Covenants or One?
The Interdependence of Jewish and Christian Identity[1]

I. INTRODUCTION

The subject I wish to address is that of the self-understanding of Judaism and Christianity in their relationships to each other in the early centuries of the common era (CE). My basic question is whether Judaism and Christianity can fully or adequately understand themselves unless they understand their mutual relationship; whether, despite long-established traditions of separation, their relationship to each other is actually an integral part of the identity of each. The larger thesis (in unrefined form) which I would like to explore is: that Christianity cannot understand itself except as an expression of Judaism; that Judaism is not true to itself unless it recognizes Christianity as a legitimate expression of its own heritage; and that, equally, Christianity is not true to itself unless it recognizes that Judaism is a legitimate expression of that same common heritage.[2] In a single paper, of course, I can deal only with a few aspects of the thesis.

Coming to the subject as a Christian, I do not apologize for having a strongly twentieth-century motivation in pursuing this thesis; nor

---

1. This essay first appeared in the Festschrift for Martin Hengel – *Geschichte-Tradition-Reflexion. III. Frühes Christentum*, ed. H. Lichtenberger, Tübingen: Mohr Siebeck 1996, pp. 97–122 = 'Zwei Bünde, oder Einer? Die wechselseitige Abhängigkeit der jüdischen und christlichen Identität', in P. Fiedler and G. Dautzenberg, (eds), *Studien zu einer neutestamentlichen Hermeneutik nach Auschwitz*, Stuttgarter biblische Aufsatzbände 27; Stuttgart: Kath. Bibelwerk 1999, pp.11 5–54. [Some additional material has been added to footnotes in square brackets.]

2. Cf. J. T. Pawlikowski, 'The Re-Judaization of Christianity: Its Impact on the Church and Its Implications for the Jewish People', in *People, Land and State of Israel: Jewish and Christian Perspectives, Immanuel* 22/23 (1994), pp. 60–74 – a plea for Jews to take more seriously the implications of Christian re-judaization for their own self-perception.

for focusing the analysis so narrowly on the beginning of the common
era. For one thing, the question of Jewish–Christian relationships
has, quite properly, assumed a central place in Christian theology and
ecumenical discussion in the second half of the twentieth century (the
post-Holocaust period). A prominent strand of this discussion has
revolved round the question whether that relationship should be
understood in terms of a single covenant (embracing both) or of two
distinct covenants:[3] does God have a single agreement with one
people, or distinct ways of dealing with two peoples, Jews and
Gentiles?[4] In effect I argue for a refinement of the former: the relationship between Jew and Christian is too symbiotic to be adequately
expressed in a theology of two covenants.

And for another, the period of common beginnings is so critical for
the self-perception of each that it deserves special attention. I need
not argue the case in terms of these decades having some kind of
formal canonical significance, though, of course, Christianity has traditionally regarded the 'apostolic age' with its chief literary product,
the New Testament, as somehow definitive, and rabbinic Judaism
looks back to the generations of the Tannaim with the chief literary
product, the Mishnah, in a not too dissimilar light. More to the point,
however, is the fact that in that period terms became established in
meaning and attitudes were fixed, terms and attitudes which still
dominate self-understanding and mutual perception today and which
do so in large part because of the way they were formulated in these
early days. In other words, whether formally stated or not, these
opening decades and centuries have had, for good or ill, a defining
influence on all subsequent discussion.

A third reason of particular importance in this instance is that the
essay is dedicated to Martin Hengel, some of whose concerns are
echoed in this paper, and whose breadth and detail of coverage of
period and documentation leaves most of the rest of us struggling
gratefully in his wake, immensely grateful and (if truth be told) rather
envious of his easy mastery of the sources. His contribution to a
refocusing of our modern perception of relations between Judaism
and the wider Hellenistic world through the Second Temple period,
and his magisterial deployment of historical criticism to provide often
decisive illumination of the NT writings has been unsurpassed in the

---

3. See the discussion surveyed in J. T. Pawlikowski, *What Are They Saying about
Christian–Jewish Relations?* New York: Paulist 1980, ch. 2; M. Braybrooke, *Time to Meet:
Towards a Deeper Relationship between Jews and Christians*, London: SCM/Philadelphia:
TPI 1990, ch. 6.

4. It is not possible within this paper to extend the discussion to consideration of
Judaism's and Christianity's relationship to other religions and ideologies.

second half of the twentieth century. It is an honour for Durham once again to honour its distinguished graduand and thus also to celebrate its ties with its partner university in Tübingen.[5]

I will begin by taking a brief look at the period of overlap during the early centuries CE, to remind ourselves of the character of Judaism's and Christianity's mutual relationship over the years in which they pulled steadily more and more apart. Then we will attempt to clarify the extent to which the very names used, particularly 'Judaism', may have contributed to the problem. And finally we will focus attention on the one who is usually given the chief credit or blame for making the parting of the ways inevitable – Paul, apostle and/or apostate![6]

2. THE MYTH OF CHRISTIAN BEGINNINGS[7]

There is a strong consensus that Judaism and Christianity effectively became separate religious systems in the early second century. The destruction of the Jerusalem Temple in 70 CE, the increasingly Gentile character of the Christian movement in the diaspora, the heightening claims made by Christians regarding Jesus at the turn of the first and second century, and the nationalist and messianic fervour of the bar Kokhba revolt begun in 132, all made it less and less possible for a Jew to remain both 'Jew' and 'Christian' in good standing in both synagogue and church.[8]

This was reinforced on the Christian side by a series of apologetic and polemical writings which all argued in effect that Christianity had superseded and replaced Israel in the divine purpose. Thus already in Hebrews, the talk of a 'new covenant' is understood to imply that the first covenant is 'obsolete' and will soon disappear (*gēraskon eggus aphanismou* – Heb. 8.13). Similarly according to Barn. 4.6–8, the people of Moses have forfeited the covenant; it is 'ours' and not 'theirs', or to be more precise, not 'both theirs and ours' (see also

---

5. For Martin's own moving personal account see his 'A Gentile in the Wilderness: My Encounter with Jews and Judaism', in *Overcoming Fear Between Jews and Christians*, ed. J. H. Charlesworth, American Interfaith Institute; New York: Crossroad 1992, pp. 67–83.

6. The echo of A. F. Segal's *Paul the Convert: The Apostolate and Apostasy of Saul the Pharisee*, New Haven: Yale University 1990, is intentional.

7. The echo of R. L. Wilken, *The Myth of Christian Beginnings*, London: SCM Press 1979, is also deliberate.

8. The growing crisis is already reflected in the Fourth Gospel, particularly chs 5 and 9, as has effectively been argued by J. L. Martyn, *History and Theology in the Fourth Gospel*, Nashville: Abingdon ²1979. See further my *The Partings of the Ways between Christianity and Judaism*, London: SCM/Philadelphia: TPI 1991.

Barn. 13–14).[9] According to Justin Martyr too the Christians have replaced Israel: 'The true spiritual Israel . . . are we who have been led to God through this crucified Christ' (*Dial.* 11.5); 'As, therefore, Christ is the Israel and the Jacob, even so we, who have been quarried out from the bowels of Christ, are the true Israelite race' (135.3, 6; see further 82.1, 117, 119–20, 123 and 125). And for Melito of Sardis 'the people (Israel) was a model (*tupos*)', but 'the church' is 'the reality (*hē alētheia*)', and now the people has been made void (*ekenōthē*) and the model abolished (*eluthē*); what was once precious (*timos*) (Jerusalem and its sacrificial cult) is now worthless (*atimos*) (*Peri Pascha* 39–45).[10] Thus within the first 150 years of Christian history was established the line of Christian self-definition in relation to Israel (that Christians have replaced Jews as the real people of God) and the fateful *adversus Judaeos* tradition,[11] a tradition of self-definition which has remained influential to the present day.[12] At

9. Barnabas is usually dated to the period 115–17 in Egypt; see e.g. the discussion cited by R. S. MacLennan, *Early Christian Texts on Jews and Judaism*, Atlanta: Scholars 1990, pp. 21–2.

10. Following the text and translation of S. G. Hall, *Melito of Sardis*, Oxford: Clarendon 1979.

11. See further A. L. Williams, *Adversus Judaeos*, Cambridge University 1935; R. Wilde, *The Treatment of the Jews in the Greek Christian Writers of the First Three Centuries*, Washington: Catholic University of America 1949; K. Hruby, *Juden und Judentum bei den Kirchenvätern*, Zurich: Theologischer Verlag 1971; J. N. Lightstone, *The Commerce of the Sacred: Mediation of the Divine among Jews in the Graeco-Roman Diaspora*, Chico, CA: Scholars 1984, ch. 6; J. G. Gager, *The Origins of Anti-Semitism: Attitudes Toward Judaism in Pagan and Christian Antiquity*, New York: Oxford University 1985; also 'Judaism as Seen by Outsiders', in *Early Judaism and its Modern Interpreters*, ed. R. A. Kraft and G. W. E. Nickelsburg, Atlanta: Scholars 1986, pp. 99–116 (with bibliography). On Tertullian see particularly D. P. Efroymson, 'The Patristic Connection', in *AntiSemitism and the Foundations of Christianity*, ed. A. T. Davies, New York: Paulist 1979, pp. 98–117; and MacLennan, ch. 4. On Origen see N. de Lange, *Origen and the Jews: Studies in Jewish–Christian Relations in Third-Century Palestine*, Cambridge University 1976. For the text of Chrysostom's *Homilia adversus Judaeos* 1 and 8 see W. A. Meeks and R. L. Wilken, *Jews and Christians in Antioch in the First Four Centuries of the Common Era*, Missoula: Scholars 1978, pp. 83–127. For Cyril of Alexandria see R. L. Wilken, *Judaism and the Early Christian Mind: A Study of Cyril of Alexandria's Exegesis and Theology*, New Haven: Yale University 1971. On the reasons why Christians called their scriptures 'the new testament' see now W. Kinzig, '*Kainē daithēkē*: The Title of the New Testament in the Second and Third Centuries', *JTS* 45 (1994), pp. 519–44. See also now J. Lieu, J. North and T. Rajak, *The Jews Among Pagans and Christians in the Roman Empire*, London: Routledge 1992; L. M. McDonald, 'Anti-Judaism in the Early Church Fathers', in *Anti-Semitism and Early Christianity: Issues of Polemic and Faith*, ed. C. A. Evans and D. A. Hagner, Minneapolis: Fortress 1993, pp. 215–52.

12. It lies behind the use of the term Spätjudentum (still current in NT scholarship through the latter decades of the twentieth century) to describe late Second Temple Judaism – that is, Judaism ended with the coming of Christianity! This indeed is explicitly stated by such scholars as W. Pannenberg, *Jesus: God and Man*, London: SCM/Philadelphia:

the same time, according to common perception, rabbinic Judaism became more withdrawn from the wider world and introverted, thus broadening the gulf with Christianity from its side.

It must be asked, however: How representative were such theological assertions from the Christian side? Did they reflect the reality of the time, or were they more in the nature of wishful thinking? And is it correct to speak of a Jewish withdrawal which restricted contacts between Christians and Jews? The impression is readily given by the preceding paragraph of a rampant, triumphant Christianity, explaining itself in relation to an enfeebled and despondent Judaism. But particularly since the important studies of James Parkes and Marcel Simon[13] this portrayal of early Jewish–Christian relations has become less and less tenable. The reality is that during the first three or four centuries of the common era Judaism was not on the retreat, withdrawn into itself. Quite the contrary. The boot was more often on the other foot – a still small and struggling Christianity trying to give itself the greater credibility by defining itself more sharply over against the stronger, more established Judaism.[14] One could almost make the rule: the fiercer the invective, the weaker the cause defended, the stronger the Judaism attacked.

The point is well illustrated by putting side by side two of the more significant discoveries of the last sixty years – the *Peri Pascha* of Melito of Sardis, with its vigorous polemic against Israel (72–99), and the archaeological uncovering of Sardis itself. An inescapable conclusion from the latter is that the Jewish community was large, well-established, well respected and thoroughly integrated into the civic life of the city.[15] In consequence, Melito's polemic cannot be understood as an expression of Christian success, but rather has to be seen as 'the product of a fledgling Christian church struggling for

---

Westminster 1968 p. 255; and L. Goppelt, *Theology of the New Testament*, vol. 1, Grand Rapids: Eerdmans 1982, pp. 101–5.

13. J. Parkes, *The Conflict of the Church and the Synagogue*, Jewish Publication Society 1934; reprinted New York: Macmillan; M. Simon, *Verus Israel: A Study of the Relations between Christians and Jews in the Roman Empire (AD 153–425)*, 1948, 1964; Oxford University 1989. The most recent survey of the extensive (and still growing) evidence is by L. H. Feldman, *Jew and Gentile in the Ancient World*, Princeton University 1993, ch. 10, particularly pp. 356–8, 368–82, 440–4.

14. On the strength of Judaism as a vigorous and thriving presence in the Empire up at least into the fifth century see also Wilken, *Judaism*, ch. 1; T. Rajak, 'The Jewish Community and Its Boundaries', in *The Jews* ed. Lieu *et al.*, pp. 9–29.

15. For a summary of the evidence see MacLennan, pp. 93–102, with particular reference to the contributions of A. T. Kraabel (his thesis advisor). MacLennan's chief thesis throughout is that the literary evidence of the period should not be interpreted without reference to the archaeological.

its existence ... overshadowed by the venerable Jewish community in the same area', written not so much to attack the Sardis synagogue as to defend the weaker church.[16] Given the strength of Jewish communities elsewhere in Asia Minor[17] and in Syria[18] throughout this period we should presumably make an equivalent allowance in the earlier case of Ignatius and the later case of Chrysostom.[19]

Nor can we say, and this is more to our immediate point, that dialogue between Christianity and Judaism was a thing of the past, as Harnack thought.[20] There were, in contrast, many who evidently resisted the suggestion of complete disjunction between the two, many who understood and tried to express in their practice of faith a much closer continuity between the two, many who did not see themselves forced to a choice between membership of one or other, many who evidently saw their identity in terms of both. It is this last point whose significance needs to be drawn out more fully than hitherto.

(a) Consider, first, the many warnings by *Christian* leaders against members of their congregations attending synagogues and observing Jewish feasts – indications, in other words, that, despite the hostile perspective of the writers, many Christians saw Christianity and Judaism as sharing common ground. Ignatius, for example, has to warn his Christian Jewish readers against living 'according to Judaism' and keeping the sabbath (*Magn.* 8–10). To the Philadelphians he says, 'If anyone interpret Judaism (*ioudaismon*) to you do not listen to him; for it is better to hear Christianity (*christianismon*) from a man having circumcision than Judaism from one having uncircumcision' (*Philad.*

---

16. MacLennan, pp. 115–16. See also S. G. Wilson, 'Melito and Israel', in *Anti-Judaism*, ed. Wilson, pp. 81–102, particularly pp. 95–102. (For a more cautious assessment, given the century or so gap between Melito and the relevant archaeological evidence, see my 'On the Relation of Text and Artifact: Some Cautionary Tales', in *Text and Artifact in the Religions of Mediterranean Antiquity*, P. Richardson FS, ed. S. G. Wilson and M. Desjardins, Waterloo, Ont.: Wilfred Laurier University 2000, pp. 192–206 (here pp. 194–5).)

17. P. Trebilco, *Jewish Communities in Asia Minor*, SNTSMS 69; Cambridge University 1991).

18. Meeks and Wilken.

19. See further Simon, *Verus Israel*, particularly chs 3, 5, 6 and 8: 'the most compelling reason for anti-Semitism was the religious vitality of Judaism' (p. 232).

20. A. von Harnack, *Die Altercatio Simonis Judaei et Theophili Christiani, nebst Untersuchungen über die anti-jüdische Polemik in der alten Kirche*, Berlin 1883, pp. 75 ff. Against Harnack, see Parkes, pp. 112–15; Simon, *Verus Israel*, pp. 137–41; Wilken, pp. 28–30, 35–8, 41–3, 50–3. Wilken also argues effectively that the preoccupation with scripture which is such a feature of patristic writing arose out of Jewish–Christian debate; see particularly pp. 13–21 and his conclusion: 'It is precisely because Cyril was so deeply rooted in the biblical tradition that his points of reference were almost wholly Jewish, and it was because he was so preoccupied with Judaism that the Bible was the chief source of his theology' (p. 227).

6.1). Clearly implied is an interest in Judaism on the part of Ignatius' readers and the conviction that Jews (presumably Christian Jews, like Paul) were most likely to have the best understanding of Christianity.[21] Justin in turn willingly acknowledges that there are Christians who observe Jewish customs, and though he regards them as 'weak-minded', he wishes to maintain association with them as 'kinsmen and brothers' (*Dial.* 47), and his very *Dialogue* itself almost certainly reflects continuing discussion and mutual respect between Jews and Christians.[22] Origen in his homilies frequently attacks Christians who observe the Jewish fasts and feasts and has to warn Christians listening to him on a Sunday against referring back to what they had learnt the day before in the synagogue (*Homilies on Leviticus* 5.8; *Selecta on Exodus* 12.46).[23] Aphrahat in his first homily (about 345) likewise warns his readers against observing sabbaths, new moons and festivals of the Jews, and the Council of Antioch (341) had to pass legislation (Canon 1) prohibiting Christians from dining at Passover with Jews.[24] And it is equally clear from Chrysostom's polemic that many members of his congregation observed the sabbath, joined in the Jewish feasts and fully respected the synagogue (*Hom. ad Jud.* 1, PG 48.844–5).[25] Such Christians were evidently commonly described as *nostri judaizantes*,[26] the 'our' indicating continuing willingness to 'own' such 'judaizers'.

Nearly two-and-a-half centuries after the parting of the ways, the continuing attraction of Judaism to many Christians in Asia Minor in particular is well indicated by the council of Laodicea (c. 363 CE), which prohibited Christians from practising their religion with Jews, in particular, 'celebrating festivals with them', 'keeping the sabbath', 'eating unleavened bread' during the Passover; Christians should

---

21. We need not go further into the complexities of the situation envisaged here by Ignatius; see e.g. W. R. Schoedel, *Ignatius of Antioch*, Hermeneia; Philadelphia: Fortress 1985, pp. 202–3; L. Gaston, 'Judaism of the Uncircumcised in Ignatius and Related Writers', in *Anti-Judaism in Early Christianity, vol. 2: Separation and Polemic*, ed. S. G. Wilson, Waterloo, Ont.: Wilfrid Laurier University 1986, pp. 36–8.

22. See further Gager, *Origins*, pp. 153–9; D. Trakatellis, 'Justin Martyr's Trypho', in *Christians Among Jews and Gentiles*, K. Stendahl FS, ed. G. W. E. Nickelsburg and G. W. MacRae, Philadelphia: Fortress 1986, pp. 287–97; H. Remus, 'Justin Martyr's Argument with Judaism', in *Anti-Judaism*, ed. Wilson, pp. 59–80, particularly pp. 71–80.

23. De Lange, pp. 36, 86; 'What he does not make clear is whether the offenders were Jews who had embraced Christianity or Christians who were attracted to the outward forms of Judaism' (p. 36).

24. Feldman, p. 376.

25. 'A widespread Christian infatuation with Judaism' (Meeks and Wilken, p. 31). Chrysostom's homilies 'show that the Judaizers' enthusiasm was not for any one rite in particular, but for the entire religious life of the Jews' (Simon, *Verus Israel*, p. 326).

26. Simon, *Verus Israel*, pp. 322, 328.

work on the sabbath and read the Gospels as well as the Jewish scriptures on Saturday (Canons 16, 29, 37, 38).[27] From about the same time the *Apostolic Constitutions* found it necessary to prohibit Christians (including bishops and clergy?) from entering Jewish synagogues, keeping feasts with the Jews, and following Jewish customs, though it still sanctioned observation of the Passover and keeping Saturday as well as Sunday as days of rest (2.61; 5.17; 6.27, 30; 7.23; 8.33, 47). And a few decades later, correspondence between Augustine and Jerome instances the converted Jew who circumcises his son, observes the sabbath, abstains from (unclean) foods and keeps the Passover (*Ep.* 67.4; 112.15).[28] Clearly, Christians who so acted understood there to be a much more vital and continuing relationship between the religion of the synagogue and that of the church than our written sources were willing to accept.[29]

(b) From the Jewish side we may simply recall some evidence regarding *minim*, who must at least have included Christians, which also implies continuing contact between Jews and Christians. The material has frequently been reviewed,[30] and we have time here to

---

27. Parkes, *Conflict*, pp. 175–6. See further Parkes, *Conflict*, pp. 174–7 and 381–2 for a summary of the canons of other councils prior to the Theodosian Code. 'The interest of the councils is only in Jewish Christian relationships, and they thereby reveal how close those relationships were' (p. 174). 'What we are faced with is an uninterrupted tradition of Judaizing, reaching down from the time when the epistles to the Galatians and the Colossians were written' (Simon, *Verus Israel*, p. 330).

28. Simon, *Verus Israel*, p. 325. Chrysostom likewise instances a Christian who has been circumcised, not as a convert to Judaism, but as a Christian (*Hom.* 2.2, PG 48.858B–860A; Meeks and Wilken, p. 32).

29. 'So far as the common people are concerned, it is indeed questionable whether any of these prohibitions (against contacts with Jews) succeeded in securing their objects. Their frequent repetition in the next century suggests their ineffectiveness' (Parkes, *Conflict*, p. 193; see further pp. 268–9, 320, 324). 'The active influence of Judaism upon Christianity in Antioch was perennial until Christian leaders succeeded at last in driving the Jews from the city in the seventh century' (Meeks and Wilken, p. 18). On the situation in Alexandria see e.g. B. A. Pearson, 'Christians and Jews in First-Century Alexandria', in *Christians Among Jews and Gentiles*, K. Stendahl FS, ed. G. W. E. Nickelsburg and G. W. MacRae, Philadelphia: Fortress 1986, pp. 206–16. For Spain see Feldman's references (pp. 373, 380, 398) to the Council of Elvira (about 300).

30. R. T. Herford, *Christianity in Talmud and Midrash*, London: Williams & Norgate 1903; Simon, *Verus Israel* ch. 7; G. Alon, *The Jews in Their Land in the Talmudic Age*, vol. 1, Jerusalem: Magnes 1980, pp. 290–307; L. H. Schiffman, 'At the Crossroads: Tannaitic Perspectives on the Jewish–Christian Schism', in *Jewish and Christian Self-Definition*, vol. 2; *Aspects of Judaism in the Graeco-Roman Period*, ed. E. P. Sanders, London: SCM 1981, pp. 115–56, here pp. 153–5; also *Who Was a Jew? Rabbinic and Halakhic Perspectives on the Jewish–Christian Schism*, Hoboken, NJ: Ktav 1985, pp. 51–73; J. Maier, *Jüdische Auseinandersetzung mit dem Christentum in der Antike*, Darmstadt: Wissenschaftliche Buchgesellschaft 1982; S. T. Katz, 'Issues in the Separation of Judaism and Christianity after 70 CE: A Reconsideration', *JBL* 103 (1984), pp. 43–76, here pp. 56–62; P. S. Alexander, ' "The Parting of the Ways" from the Perspective of Rabbinic Judaism',

mention only the most often cited texts.[31] First, the rabbinic rulings which have been preserved regarding 'the *gilyonim* and the *sifrei minim*', and their status in relation to the already recognized canonical scriptures – that is, whether they 'defiled the hands' (that is, were inspired), and whether they should be saved from burning (as being of canonical value) (*t. Yad.* 2.13; *t.Shab.* 13(14).5). The *gilyonim* are frequently taken to be the Christian Gospels, though the point is strongly disputed, and the *sifrei minim* probably at least included Christian writings or Christian Torah scrolls in particular.[32] At any rate the rulings attest a period during which many Jews probably read and prized documents written by Christians; that is, they were not conscious of a strong line of distinction between 'Judaism' and 'Christianity', and thought of Christian writings in the same category as writings like ben Sira, and perhaps also the Mishnah.

Second, just as Christian leaders attempted to limit Christian contact with the synagogue, so the rabbis seem to have made similar attempts to prevent or limit contact between those under their sway and *minim*, who again almost certainly must have included Jews who honoured Jesus as Messiah (*t. Hull.* 2.20–1). The parallel is still more interesting since the strictures are tighter in relation to a *min* than to a non-Jew – evidence of the same need to determine self-identity by marking themselves off most sharply from those closest to them.[33] The various allusions to Jews cursing Christ and those who believe in him in their synagogues (as early as Justin, *Dial.* 16.4; 47.4; 93.4; 95.4; 133.6) presumably confirms that there were many practising Jews of the time who believed in Jesus as Messiah.[34] Jerome certainly attests what he regards as 'a sect among the Jews', spread 'throughout all the synagogues of the East', called 'the Minaei' or 'Nazaraei', who, he notes, 'wish to be both Jews and Christians' (*Ep.* 112.13).[35] And

in *Jews and Christians: The Parting of the Ways* A D *70 to 135*, ed. J. D. G. Dunn, Tübingen: Mohr 1992, pp. 1–27.

31. For further examples of rulings re the *minim* in Herford, pp. 146–91 and Simon, *Verus Israel*, pp. 183–6 (more fully above pp. 305–10).

32. Alexander, ' "Parting" ', pp. 11–15.

33. 'According to the oldest rabbinic evidence, insofar as the evidence allows us to classify it chronologically at all, the *minim* appear to be mixed among the orthodox Jewish communities. They continue to attend the Synagogue services and take an active part in the worship' (Simon, *Verus Israel*, p. 198; see also pp. 406–9). Similarly Schiffman: 'the tannaim did not see the earliest Christians as constituting a separate religious community' ('Perspectives', p. 147; *Jew*, p. 51).

34. See further Schiffman, *Jew*, pp. 54–61; Alexander, ' "Parting" ', pp. 6–11.

35. De Lange, pp. 35–6. We should also recall the argument of A. Mamorstein, 'Judaism and Christianity in the Middle of the Third Century', *HUCA* 10 (1935), pp. 223–63, that those referred to in rabbinic literature as *posh'ei Yisrael*, 'Jewish sinners', were Jews who accepted Jesus as the Messiah but who continued to observe the *miswoth* (pp. 254ff.).

the previous allusions to Christian 'judaizers' presumably indicate that Christian Gentiles continued to find acceptance and welcome in many diaspora synagogues and thus further strengthen the impression that rabbinic Judaism took several centuries to impose itself on the synagogues of the diaspora.[36]

(c) As a final example of the substantial overlap between Judaism and Christianity in our period we may simply recall the extent to which Christianity in the event incorporated the wider heritage of pre-70 Judaism. I am referring here not to the theological assertion that Christianity was the new Israel, but to the fact that so much *Jewish* literature has come down to us only through *Christian* preservation. Not only the LXX, but also the pseudepigrapha, not to mention Philo and Josephus. There were evidently vigorous and (judging by the diverse translations in which these documents are preserved) widespread forms of Christianity which found such documents conducive to their own faith (albeit at times aided by appropriate editing). In addition we need to recall the thoroughly Jewish character of Christian documents like the *Didascalia* (where Jews are referred to as 'brothers' – vv. 14–15),[37] the degree to which writings like the *Testaments of the Twelve Patriarchs* and *Apostolic Constitutions* simply reworked or incorporated Jewish material,[38] and the extent to which the dispute over the date of Easter (the Quartodeciman controversy) hung in effect on the issue of whether the Christian celebration was a Christian version of the Passover (Eusebius, *EH* 5.23–5).

What needs to be remembered in all this is that the forms of orthodoxy with which we have been long familiar, both orthodox (that is, rabbinic) Judaism and orthodox (that is, catholic) Christianity, took

---

Similarly Simon: the *posh'e yisrael* designated Palestinian Christians who thought of themselves as Jews and who remained recognized members of the synagogue, albeit in rebellion against the law of Israel (*Verus Israel*, pp. 256–60).

36. Lightstone, p. 136.

37. Simon, *Verus Israel*, ch. 11, especially pp. 310–21; G. Strecker, 'On the Problem of Jewish Christianity', in W. Bauer, *Orthodoxy and Heresy in Earliest Christianity*, Philadelphia: Fortress 1971, pp. 241–85, here pp. 248–51. For the text see R. H. Connolly, *Didascalia Apostolorum*, Oxford: Clarendon 1929. On the *Didascalia*, Simon, *Verus Israel*, p. 315 observes: 'It is inconceivable that such a work could have been written except in a region with strong Jewish communities, where the whole population, men of all faiths, were impregnated with Jewish ways of thinking.'

38. For details see R. A. Kraft, 'The Multiform Jewish Heritage of Early Christianity', in *Christianity, Judaism and other Greco-Roman Cults: Studies for M. Smith*, ed. J. Neusner, part 3: *Judaism before 70*, Leiden: Brill 1975, pp. 175–99; J. H. Charlesworth, 'Christian and Jewish Self-Definition in Light of the Christian Additions to the Apocryphal Writings', in *Jewish and Christian Self-Definition*, vol. 2; *Aspects of Judaism in the Graeco-Roman Period*, ed. E. P. Sanders, London: SCM 1981, pp. 27–55.

many decades and indeed centuries to establish themselves in that position of dominance. In the meantime, that is, in the period of our concern, there is clear enough evidence of more diverse forms of both Judaism and Christianity. In particular, in the middle ground between them were evidently many who did not think of themselves as *either* Christian *or* Jew. I have in mind here not simply the Jewish-Christian sects as such, which seem to have adopted a more formal identity as recognizable 'sects', and which as such were condemned by the Christian Fathers.[39] I have in mind rather those (an unquantifiable number) who in a more inchoate way recognized the degree of interpenetration of things Jewish and things Christian and who instinctively found it most natural to live out their faith in the overlap. I have in mind those forms of Judaism which flourished in the diaspora and have left us several literary deposits, but which were never fully owned by the rabbis and yet provided nursery training and complementary syllabus for many godfearing catechumens and baptized. The Christian Judaism of the middle ground was evidently a lot more significant than either rabbinic or catholic tradition have cared to admit. As Parkes pointed out sixty years ago, 'there is every reason to believe that the common people were much more friendly with each other than the leaders approved of . . .'.[40] In this connection we should also note the warning of Meeks and Wilken against taking too literally the assertions that the Christian judaizers were to be found principally among women and the relatively uneducated; such claims 'are common coin in ancient attacks on religious deviance'.[41]

Of course, this middle-ground was regarded as heretical by both Christianity and Judaism. But perhaps that judgment owes more to sociological than to theological necessity. In other words, in a period when both groups, represented by the Christian fathers on the one side and by the rabbis on the other, were struggling to establish themselves, it was probably inevitable that they should mark themselves off more sharply from each other than either their heritage or

---

39. A. F. J. Klijn and G. J. Reinink, *Patristic Evidence for Jewish-Christian Sects*, NovT Supp 36; Leiden: Brill 1973.

40. Parkes, *Conflict*, p. 94. Simon reaches a similar conclusion: 'the anti-Jewish bias of official ecclesiastical circles was counterbalanced by equally well-marked pro-Jewish sentiments among the laity and among some of the clergy too . . . it is the existence of the pro-Jewish sentiments among the laity that is the real explanation of Christian anti-Semitism' (*Verus Israel*, p. 232).

41. Meeks and Wilken, p. 35. Also relevant is Gager's warning against a too simplistic distinction between 'Judaeo-Christians' (= judaizing Gentile Christians) and 'Jewish-Christians' (= Christian Jews who continue to observe Jewish halakhah): 'both groups show the same commitment to the position that observance of the Mosaic rituals is in no way incompatible with, may even be required by loyalty to Jesus' (*Origins*, p. 117).

theology required. The phenomenon of sibling rivalry is well documented. Perhaps in contrast, in the more relaxed context of today,
and when greater weight (or lip service) is being given to the theology
of the 'laity', some reassessment should be attempted. Whatever the
constraints and necessities of the period under review, in the light of
the full sweep of Christian history (including the present), not to say
the full sweep of the history of God's people, it may be necessary
(for the sake of historical and theological integrity) to give more
weight now to the voices silenced then and forgotten since. Such
an argument should not be interpreted on the Christian side as a
restatement of Walter Bauer's thesis (that 'heresy' in many cases pre-
ceded 'orthodoxy').[42] Rather it suggests that there may have been an
important dimension of both Judaism and Christianity, which was
marginalized and lost sight of in these early centuries by the emerging
orthodoxies on each side, and which needs to be recovered now if we
are to understand both Christianity and Judaism and their formative
periods aright.

3. WHAT'S IN A NAME?[43]

Central to the quest for self-definition is the name by which one
chooses to be known. Here we encounter a problem which has been
too little recognized as a factor in the separation of Judaism and
Christianity. I refer to the names themselves, 'Judaism' and 'Christianity'. For it has been too little appreciated that they contain overtones
which work against a proper recognition of their commonality.

The problem begins with the term 'Judaism'. It first appears in our
literary sources in 2 Maccabees' description of those who stayed
faithful to and fought for their distinctive ancestral traditions (2.21;
8.1; 14.38; similarly 4 Macc. 4.26). The only other occurrences from
before the end of the first century CE each speak of a life being lived
en tō Ioudaismō (Gal. 1.13–14; *CIJ* 537), where the implication is of
a lifestyle carefully marked out and defended from outside influences –
'Judaism' as a system of religion and way of life within which diaspora
Jews lived so as to maintain their distinctive identity.[44]

A point of considerable significance immediately emerges. In each
case the term 'Judaism' was being used in self-definition to indicate

---

42. Bauer, *Orthodoxy*.
43. The allusion this time is of course to Shakespeare's *Romeo and Juliet* Act 2 Scene 2.
44. On *CIJ* 537 see Y. Amir, 'The Term *Ioudaismos*: A Study in Jewish-Hellenistic
Self-Identification', *Immanuel* 14 (1982), pp. 34–41.

the character of belief and practice which distinguished the referent from the surrounding culture and ethos. In 2 Maccabees the term is obviously coined as a counter to 'Hellenism' (*Hellēnismos*) (2 Macc. 4.13). That is to say, for the author of 2 Maccabees, 'Judaism' is the summary term for that system embodying national and religious identity which was the rallying point for the violent rejection by the Maccabees of the Syrian attempt to assimilate them by the abolition of their distinctive practices (particularly circumcision and food laws – 1 Macc. 1.60–3; so also 4 Macc. 4.26). Paul uses the word with precisely the same overtone, characterizing his life 'in Judaism' as the life of a 'zealot' – that is, one who was totally committed to his people's religious traditions and who fiercely resisted anything which would dilute or defile Israel's set-apartness to God (Gal. 1.14; Phil. 3.6).[45] From the beginning, therefore, the term 'Judaism' expressed a strongly national and religious identity which was given its more definitive character by vigorous resistance to the assimilating and syncretistic influences of wider Hellenism.[46]

Putting the same point slightly differently, in the beginning 'Judaism' was essentially a term of differentiation not of self-identification. All four of our earliest sources reflect the perspective of Jews who lived in or wrote for the diaspora.[47] That is to say, 'Judaism' was not the self-reference of those who lived in a comfortable majority of fellow-religionists within the land of Israel, but a term whose function was precisely to distinguish those who used it of themselves from an environment which they found threatening.[48] Precisely the same is true of the term 'Jew': its very formation (*Ioudaios*, 'Judaean') betrays the perspective of the spectator, one who describes individuals by the land of their origin and by the religion centred there; its natural antonym is 'Gentile' and its content is in some measure determined by the antithesis 'Jews and Gentiles' – Jew being defined as non-Gentile; and its use in self-reference is again predominantly that of Hellenistic Jews (Philo, Josephus, Aristeas, Eupolemus, Artapanus,

---

45. See further my *Galatians*, Black's NT Commentary; London: A. & C. Black 1993, *ad loc.*

46. Similarly K.-W. Niebuhr, ' "Judentum" und "Christentum" bei Paulus und Ignatius von Antiochien', *ZNW* 85 (1994), pp. 218–33 (particularly, p. 221).

47. It is significant that the term occurs in 2 Maccabees, composed in Greek and a self-confessed 'epitome' of the five-volume work of Jason of Cyrene (2.26, 28), and not as a translation of some Hebrew term in 1 Maccabees.

48. K. G. Kuhn can find only one passage in rabbinic literature and perhaps Palestinian usage where *yhdwth* = *Ioudaismos* occurs, but, interestingly, in a description of the Jews in Babylon who did not change their God or their religious laws but held fast *byhdwthn* ('in their Judaism') (*Esther Rab.* 7.11) (Kuhn, *TDNT* 3.363 and 364 n. 49).

Hecataeus) in order to distinguish the people so designated from other peoples.[49]

The problem is compounded because something of the same process took place with the matching terms 'Christianity' and 'Christian'. For as 'Judaism' was coined to mark it off from 'Hellenism', so the term 'Christianity' appears to have been coined to mark it off from 'Judaism' (Ignatius, *Magn.* 10.3; *Philad.* 6.1). That is to say, 'Christianity' began as a linguistic phenomenon by being differentiated from and set in antithesis to 'Judaism' (cf. Eusebius, *dem. evang.* 1.2; Basil, *hom.* 24.1).[50] The history of the term 'Christians' appears to have been somewhat more convoluted. It began earlier, as a Latinism, *Christiani* (Acts 11.26), that is, once again, not as a term of self-definition, but, it would appear, as the attempt by Roman authorities in Antioch to make sense of what otherwise must have appeared as the rapid growth of a Jewish sect (the 'Herodians' is a similar Latinism – *Herodiani*). In this case, it is true that those so designated soon embraced the term for themselves as a very appropriate self-designation (1 Pet. 4.16).[51] What is also interesting for us, however, is the degree to which 'Christian' and 'Jew' continued to be confused in the thinking of others for some time to come, both in speaking of Gentile conversion (for Epictetus to be 'baptized', a Christian technical term(?), was to become a Jew),[52] and in the reuse of anti-Jewish vituperation against the Christians.[53] In other words, from an outsider's perspective the distinction 'Christian' meaning not-Jew evidently took some time to become established.

---

49. It could also be used of converts; see particularly R. S. Kraemer, 'On the Meaning of the Term "Jew" in Greco-Roman Inscriptions', *HTR* 82 (1989), pp. 35–53.

50. See further de Lange, pp. 29–33.

51. Lampe, *Christianos*.

52. 'When we see a man halting between two faiths, we are in the habit of saying, "He is not a Jew, he is only acting the part". But when he adopts the attitude of mind of the man who has been baptized and has made his choice, then he both is a Jew in fact and is also called one' (Epictetus 2.9.20). There is also a long-standing speculation that Flavius Clemens, cousin to Domitian, and his wife Flavia Domitilla, who were charged with atheism, along with 'many others who drifted into Jewish ways' (Cassius Dio 67.14.1–2) had in fact become Christians. Both inferences are questioned in *GLAJJ* §§254 and 435 (1.543 and 2.381), where the texts can be consulted.

53. Tacitus, writing early in the second century, designates the victims of Nero's persecution as 'Christians', but the very anti-Jewish character of his vituperation suggests that he saw them in the same frame as Jews (cf. *Ann.* 15.44.2–4 and 5.5.1 with *Hist.* 5.4.1). Likewise the accusation of ass-worship is a direct transfer of anti-Jewish to anti-Christian slander (details in *GLAJJ* 1.97). 'It is surely not coincidence that the popular imagination accused both Jews and Christians of exactly the same vices. It is quite probable that the Christians were the victims, in the first instance, of a kind of anti-Semitism' (Simon, *Verus Israel*, pp. 18–19).

Nevertheless, the point remains that both key terms, 'Judaism' and 'Christianity' had the function from the beginning of differentiating themselves not least from one another.[54] In other words, they embody the attitude of those early Christian writers illustrated above who thought it possible to define and defend Christianity only by distinguishing and distancing it from Judaism. Our very use of these terms in modern descriptions and discussions of the period is subtly influenced by this fact. Their very juxtaposition carries overtones of two well-defined, differentiated and developed religious systems set over against each other, where failure of particular individuals or groups to observe these differences became by very definition some kind of heretical departure from the system expressed in the terms themselves.[55] Of course, it was partly the purpose of those who developed the use of these terms to encourage such a sense of orthodoxy and heresy, as we have seen. But as we have also seen, the areas actually marked out by these terms were a good deal less well defined in reality and their boundaries in relation to each other a good deal more hazy.

Such reflections should also caution us against assuming that the problems of Jewish–Christian relations can be solved simply by recasting the definitions of the key terms 'Christianity' and 'Judaism'. This seems to be the logic behind the increasingly common talk today of Second Temple Judaism consisting latterly of many 'Judaisms', of which emerging Christianity was one. The motivation is to be applauded, but the result is a description of first-century 'Judaism' in the land of Israel which none of the 'sects' involved would have recognized – certainly not as a description of their mutual relationships. And if integral to the term 'Judaism' is the sense of ethnic identity with the people of the land of Judaea and of national religious identity over against the wider world, then perhaps we simply have to accept that a 'Christianity' which refused to count Jewish ethnic identity as integral to its own self-definition was bound to become something different from 'Judaism', so that to insist on speaking of Christianity as a kind of Judaism simply confuses the issues.

If therefore we want to make sense of what happened in the early centuries of the Christian era and to draw possible lessons for Jewish and Christian self-understanding and dialogue, we need to put the terms 'Jew/Christian' and 'Judaism/Christianity' themselves to one side. Their role as terms of mutual differentiation probably prevents their being used effectively in a more integrative way. From this

---

54. So also Niebuhr, pp. 224–33.

55. J. Lieu, 'History and Theology in Christian Views of Judaism', in *The Jews*, ed. Lieu *et al.*, pp. 79–96, notes that Simon does not escape the trap (p. 88).

perspective, the attempts made by the first Christians in effect to redefine the term 'Jew' (Rom. 2.28–9; Rev. 2.9; 3.9) must be counted a failure.

There is, however, another term which may serve our purposes, and serve them more effectively than 'Judaism' and 'Christianity' could – the term 'Israel'. For if we are right, the other terms expressed a spectator point of view, the perspective of one looking in from outside; whereas 'Israel' expresses the view of the insider, the view of the participant. As K. G. Kuhn notes in his survey of Jewish post-biblical usage, '"Israel" is the name which the people uses for itself, whereas "Jews" is the non-Jewish name for it.'[56] Or in the language used above, 'Jew' and 'Judaism' are terms of differentiation, whereas 'Israel' is a term of self-affirmation by reference to its own distinctively apprehended heritage. Thus, for example, the use of 'Jews' in I Maccabees where the context is official and the tone diplomatic, but of 'Israel' when it is a matter of self-designation;[57] in the Gospels 'king of the Jews' is Pilate's terminology, but 'king of Israel' that of the high priests (Mark 15.2, 9, 12, 26; 15.32 and parallels); Paul speaks regularly of 'Jew(s) and Greek(s)' as a way of categorizing the whole of humanity (e.g. Rom. 2.9–10; 3.9; 10.12; 1 Cor. 12.13; Gal. 3.28), while preferring to say of himself, 'I am an Israelite' (Rom. 11.1; 2 Cor. 11.22);[58] and in the rabbinic writings 'Israel' and not 'Jews' is the almost universal self-designation.[59] In short, 'Jews' naturally evokes the counterpart 'Gentiles', each defining itself by its exclusion of the other – 'Jew' = non-Gentile, 'Gentile' = non-Jew. In contrast, 'Israel' has no defining antonym; it is defined by the insider, not the outsider, and by reference to its internal history, not the history of nations and peoples.

This is not to deny that 'Israel' is also used in Christian polemic with similar effect to 'Jew' and 'Judaism'. For example, Barnabas uses 'Israel' as a term of differentiation: 'Israel' denotes the Jewish people, not 'us' (Barn. 5.2). And in the second half of his homily Melito regularly speaks harshly against Israel, as those who murdered Jesus, 'lawless Israel', 'ungrateful Israel' (72–99). Nevertheless, 'Israel' is

---

56. Kuhn, *TDNT* 3.360; see analysis and discussion on pp. 359–65; see further *Encyclopaedia Judaica* 10.22.

57. Kuhn, *TDNT*, 3.360–1.

58. In contrast it is the Gentile Luke who has Paul say of himself 'I am a Jew', not only to the Roman tribune but also to the Jerusalem crowd, speaking in Aramaic (Acts 21.39; 22.3).

59. S. Zeitlin, *The Jews: Race, Nation, or Religion?* Philadelphia: Dropsie College 1936, pp. 31–2, recalling that after the failure of the bar Kokhba revolt the Jews ceased to exist as a nation; de Lange, p. 29.

the term with the most positive potential for Jewish and Christian self-definition in relation to each other. For several reasons.

First, 'Israel' is a term of self-definition which both Jews and Christians wanted to use for themselves – both the rabbis[60] and the Christian fathers. For example, Justin, as we have seen, speaks of Christians as 'the true, spiritual Israel' (*Dial.* 11.5), and the *Apostolic Constitutions* likewise speaks of the Gentiles brought to God as 'the true Israel' (7.36.2).[61]

Second, its origin marks it as an essentially religious term, given according to tradition, as a mark of divine favour to Jacob ('he who strives with God'?) (Gen. 32.28), and frequently understood in our period as meaning 'he who sees God'.[62] As the name from which the people took its own self-designation, it signified for them their status as the people chosen by God, the people's own covenant name.[63] And though applicable primarily to the northern kingdom in the period of the divided kingdoms, it was too precious an expression of covenant self-identity not to be used by all who claimed to stand in the line of inheritance from the patriarchs.[64] It is thus a term defined, as Paul was subsequently able to argue, by divine grace and election, not by ethnic identity or religious praxis (Rom. 9.6–12). Jacob Neusner likewise argues that in rabbinic Judaism 'Israel' is not ethnically defined and so is capable of as universal an embrace as Christianity has usually claimed for itself alone in contrast to Judaism.[65]

Third, as the people's covenant name it was particularly cherished by the various sects of the late Second Temple Period who claimed it for themselves. But this posed something of a dilemma for such sects. Were only those 'Israel' who had remained true to the covenant, as understood by the group in focus, or would God restore the wholeness of disobedient and exiled Israel in the end (in eschatological fulfilment of the pattern in Deut. 30)? We see the ambivalence, for example, in CD 3.12–4.12, where 'Israel' appears on both sides of the equation – God's covenant with Israel, Israel has strayed, the 'sure house in Israel', 'the converts of Israel'. Again in the tension in *Jubilees* between

---

60. See again Zeitlin (n. 59 above).

61. See further Lampe, *Israël* 4.

62. *Philo* (LCL 10) 334; Lampe, *Israël* 1.

63. 'Israel implies the religious claim to be God's chosen people even when it is used in secular contexts, with no religious emphasis, as the accepted designation' (Kuhn, *TDNT* 3.362, with examples).

64. Zeitlin, p. 10, notes that the prophets of Judah (the southern kingdom) always delivered their messages in the name of the God of Israel, never of the God of Judah.

65. J. Neusner, 'Was Rabbinic Judaism Really "Ethnic"?', *CBQ* 57 (1995), pp. 281–305.

the condemnation of the sons of Israel for abandoning the covenant in 15.34 and the glorious blessing of Abraham for Jacob and all his sons in 22.23–31 – people of a renewed covenant, God's inheritance for ever. Or in the *Psalms of Solomon* between the sustained condemnation of Jewish 'sinners' and the final hope for Israel in 17.44–5 and 18.5.[66] Or in the famous *m. Sanhedrin* 10 between its opening confidence that 'All Israelites have a share in the world to come', and the subsequent qualification of those who will be excluded.[67]

What is particularly important about this third observation is that we see precisely the same ambivalence and tension in Christian claims to the heritage of Israel. In Paul between the affirmation that 'not all who are from Israel are Israel' and the assurance that 'all Israel will be saved' (Rom. 9.6; 11.26). In Paul's blessing on 'the Israel of God' (Gal. 6.16) and the claims of James 1.1 and 1 Peter 1.1 to be writing to 'the twelve tribes or exiles of the diaspora'; do these titles include or exclude ethnic Israel? And in the Fathers' readiness to use 'Israel' for both the old Israel and the new, as poignantly when Melito in the midst of his diatribe against Israel adds the charge, 'You did not turn out to be "Israel"; you did not "see God"' (*Peri Pascha* 82).[68] In other words, the Christian wrestling with its own self-understanding as Israel, in relation to Israel as a whole, is entirely of a piece with the wrestling which we see in the sectarian documents of second Temple Judaism. It is precisely in its claim to partake in Israel's heritage, to be Israel, that earliest Christianity most declares its Jewish character and its beginnings within second Temple Judaism. And if indeed for rabbinic Judaism too 'Israel' has a potential for inclusiveness[69] which is lacking in the term 'Judaism', then it is certainly worth exploring the implications for Jewish–Christian dialogue, rather than restricting discussion to the unavoidably more confrontational terms 'Judaism' and 'Christianity'.

In short, the very terms themselves, 'Judaism' and 'Christianity' reinforce the impression of two complete religious systems distinct in character from the beginning, where failure to observe the distinction was a form of nonconformity unacceptable to the great majority firmly inside each system. But that impression simply demonstrates

---

66. See further the sensitive discussion of E. P. Sanders, *Paul and Palestinian Judaism*, London: SCM 1977, pp. 240–57; also 361, 367–74, 378 (*Jubilees*) and 398–406, 408 (*Psalms of Solomon*).

67. Cf. the discussion in Schiffman, *Jew*, ch. 4. We may compare the continuing debate on 'Who is a Jew?' and who may be counted a citizen still raging within the state of Israel today.

68. See further Lampe, *Israël* 2 and 4.

69. Neusner (above, n. 65).

the effectiveness of those who in these early decades pressed for a clearer separation between the two and did so by the use of such clearly demarcated and mutually exclusive terms. If now we wish to explore the degree of commonality in the early centuries of the common era between what indeed did in due course become almost entirely separate systems, then we should do so using different terms of self-reference. And since 'Israel' is a term which both sides wish fully to embrace for themselves, while recognizing the tension between what is and what should be, between the Israel that is and what Israel hopefully shall be in the future, it certainly provides greater prospect of a more fruitful dialogue.

4. 'THE APOSTLE OF THE HERETICS'[70]

We turn finally to Paul as one of the most vital factors in this whole affair. For it is Paul, who was so characteristically representative of 'Judaism' (Gal. 1.13–14), who came to understand himself as quintessentially 'apostle of the Gentiles' (Rom. 11.13). It was Paul who, by questioning the function of the law in its role of defining his people, and by declaring that in Christ neither Jew nor Greek counted for anything (Gal. 3.28), made it virtually impossible for 'Christianity' to remain part of a 'Judaism' defined in ethnic terms. And it was Paul who was at one and the same time the hero of Marcion, who pushed the antithesis between old covenant and new to its extreme, and the *bête noire* of the Jewish Christians who stand behind the *pseudo-Clementines*, as being both traitor to his people and apostate from his ancestral religion.[71] Paul, in other words, stands at a point of still clear overlap between 'Christianity' and 'Judaism' where a crack between the two was just becoming visible and, in most reckoning, was responsible more than anyone else for expanding that crack into a rift.[72]

Such is the common perception of Paul. But in view of what we have seen earlier the question must now be posed: is this a fair understanding of Paul's role? Is Paul also a victim of the misreading of Jewish/Christian relations indicated above? Has Paul's reputation suffered unjustly by his becoming a *cause célèbre* among the extremists

---

70. The quotation is from Tertullian, *adv. Marc.* 3.5.

71. See also my *Unity and Diversity in the New Testament*, London: SCM/Philadelphia: TPI ²1990, pp. 241, 252–7, 288–96.

72. Cf. e.g. N. Elliott, *Liberating Paul: The Justice of God and the Politics of the Apostle*, Maryknoll, NY: Orbis 1994: 'Paul's dejudaization' began with Ephesians and Acts (p. 67).

on both sides? Above all, have Paul's own discussions relevant to our theme been misunderstood because read in terms of a 'Judaism' and 'Christianity' already clearly distinct from each other in substance and practice? To tackle such questions adequately would take a complete monograph. Here we can only indicate the lines which need to be followed up.

(a) First, we must recall and develop the point already made: that Paul does not speak in terms of Judaism and Christianity, but in terms of Israel (eleven times in Rom. 9–11 alone); and that his crucial discussion in Rom. 9–11 is very much of a piece with the tensions between the conflicting ideals of pure Israel and whole Israel which we noted elsewhere in Jewish writings. In addition now we need to note that the theme of Rom. 9–11 is not, as so many assume, the relation of Israel to the Church, but Israel itself.[73] In other words, we must not make the same mistake in talking of 'the Church' as we have in talking too quickly of 'Christianity'. In Rom. 9–11 what we now call 'the Church' is not yet seen as something distinct from Israel. On the contrary, in the paradigmatic imagery of the olive tree in Rom. 11.17–24, there is only one planting by God – Israel. God has not uprooted the olive tree Israel and planted another one. Gentiles have part in and prospect of salvation precisely by being grafted into the one olive tree, Israel. In short, Paul speaks as an Israelite, and the theme of Rom. 9–11, Paul's most mature treatment of the subject, is Israel – how Israel is constituted (by election of grace) and how God will remain true to his promises to Israel ('all Israel will be saved').

It is true that Paul can talk of 'the Jews' as a distancing formula. But the most severe statement, 1 Thess. 2.14–16, has in view the particular circumstances of Jesus' rejection and persecution of the churches in Judaea, probably as an expression of the eschatological tribulation expected for the end time.[74] On the other hand, in his most constructive treatment of the whole theme, Paul hastens to reaffirm the privileges and priority of the Jews (Rom. 3.1), as though to say, If you must think in terms of 'Jew and Greek' then remember that in God's purposes 'the Jew' comes first (Rom. 1.16; 2.9–10; 9.24). More to the present point, however, it is the nationalistic overtones implicit in the very term 'the Jews' itself which Paul more typically sets his face firmly against (Rom. 2.28; 3.29; Gal. 2.14–16), not least in the repeated formula, 'neither Jew nor Greek' (Gal. 3.28;

---

73. For detailed exegesis I may refer to my *Romans*, WBC 38; Dallas: Word 1988, *ad loc*.

74. 1 Thess. 2.14–16 much disputed; for details see above, p. 193, with bibliography.

also Col. 3.11; cf. Rom. 10.12; 1 Cor. 12.13). In other words, it is precisely Paul who pushes us towards a comprehensive theology of Israel rather than a theology which begins from the distinction 'Jew and Christian'.[75]

(b) Second, is it not the case, nevertheless, that Paul encourages a theology of two covenants – that ethnic Israel's relation to God continues to be governed by one covenant, while Christian Gentiles, or Gentiles and Jews, fall within a different covenant?[76] This impression could certainly be taken from the antitheses between law and promise in Galatians and Romans, and seems to be implied in the talk of a 'new covenant' now operative (1 Cor. 11.25), particularly in the sharp contrast between the new covenant and the old in 2 Cor. 3. Here too, however, impressions can be misleading, and not least when texts are read as speaking of two separate entities, Christianity and Judaism, and particularly in regard to Paul's use of the covenant concept.

It is a striking fact that in the two letters in which Paul discourses most fully on the theme of Israel (or Jew and Greek) he avoids speaking of the 'new covenant'. He does not say, as does the Epistle of Barnabas, that the covenant is ours and not theirs. He does not say, as does Hebrews, that the covenant with Israel is obsolete and finished. In Galatians the term itself carries none of that freight; it simply characterizes a relationship with God provided by God, whether with Abraham as promise, or as typified by Isaac and Ishmael respectively (Gal. 3.15, 17; 4.24). The fact that he can both contrast covenant with law in chapter 3, and yet in the very next chapter identify Sinai with the Ishmael covenant indicates clearly enough that the term is not for Paul a point of differentiation between Jew and Christian.[77] On the contrary, in the line of his argument in Galatians 'the Israel of God' (6.16), constituted as such by the promise to Abraham, must be the 'us' of 3.13–14, that is, those who inherit that promise, both Jews and Gentiles (3.8–9).[78]

In Romans it is even more striking that Paul limits his use of the term 'covenant' to one of the blessings originally bestowed on his

---

75. Cf. D. Boyarin, *A Radical Jew: Paul and the Politics of Identity*, Berkeley: University of California 1994.

76. So e.g. Gager, *Origins*, part IV; others cited in Pawlikowski (above, n. 3) and in my *Romans*, p. 683.

77. This point was first drawn to my attention by my doctoral postgraduate Ellen Juhl Christiansen. [See now her *The Covenant in Judaism and Paul: A Study of Ritual Boundaries as Identity Markers*, Leiden: Brill 1995; and my own 'Did Paul Have a Covenant Theology? Reflections on Romans 9.4 and 11.27', in S. E. Porter and J. C. R. de Roo (eds), *The Concept of the Covenant in the Second Temple Period*, JSJSupp 71; Leiden: Brill 2003, pp. 287–307.]

78. For detailed discussion again I must refer to my *Galatians, ad loc.*

own people (9.4)[79] and to the final hope of salvation for all Israel (11.27, citing Isa. 59.20–1). The covenant with Israel remains valid and in effect, and there is no thought of a separate or superseding covenant for Gentile (or Gentile and Jewish) believers. It would appear, then, that rather than confuse or compromise the covenant theology which had for so long characterized the relationship between God and his people, Paul limited it to his discussion of Israel's relationship with God, content in this case for the theological claim of a single people comprising both Jews and Gentiles (9.23–4; 15.8–9) to be carried by his imagery of promise (4.13–17; 9.8–9) and of the single olive tree (11.17–24).

What then of Paul's talk of the 'new covenant'? Here we need to recall that this language is almost certainly determined by allusion to Jer. 31.31–4.[80] That is to say, it belongs to the frequently recurring strand within Jewish writings which recognizes that outward obedience to the Torah is inadequate and only obedience from the heart will suffice, as in the familiar thought of the desirability of a circumcised heart (Deut. 10.16; Jer. 4.4; 9.25–6; Ezek. 44.9; 1QpHab 11.13; 1QS 5.5; 1QH 2.18; 18.20; Philo, *Spec. Leg.* 1.305). The hope of Jer. 31 is for the law to be written in the heart, in other words, not for a different covenant, but for a more effective version of the old one. This is reflected also in 'The Document of the New Covenant in the Land of Damascus' from Qumran, where the 'new covenant' made in the land of Damascus (CD 19.33–4; 20.12) is obviously a reaffirmation of the original 'covenant of the patriarchs' (1.4; 3.1–4; 6.2; 8.18; 19.31), the 'covenant of God' (3.11; 5.12; 7.5; 13.14; 20.17). So we should not be surprised that Paul also affirms that faith 'establishes the law', that he seeks to bring Gentiles to 'the obedience of faith', that those who walk according to the Spirit fulfil the requirement of the law, or that love of neighbour fulfils the whole law (Rom. 3.31; 1.5; 8.4; 13.8–10; Gal. 5.14). For Paul too the new covenant was all about a more effective way of fulfilling the old covenant.[81]

---

79. The plural, 'covenants', may simply denote the covenant with Abraham as renewed with Isaac and Jacob – the covenant(s) with the fathers (see further my *Romans*, p. 527).

80. For the allusion in 2 Cor. 3.3, 6, see particularly V. P. Furnish, *2 Corinthians*, AB 32A; New York: Doubleday 1984, pp. 181, 183–4, 196–7.

81. On Rom. 2.12–16 we may simply compare P. Stuhlmacher, *Der Brief an die Römer*, NTD 6; Göttingen: Vandenhoeck 1989, who argues effectively that Rom. 2.12–13 has to be understood in the light of 2.16 (42, 44–6), and A. F. Segal, 'Universalism in Judaism and Christianity', in *Paul in His Hellenistic Context*, ed. T. Engberg-Pedersen, Minneapolis: Fortress 1995, pp. 20–2: 'There is no separate covenant of law for the Jews' (p. 21). On 10.4 ('Christ is the end of the law'), note that it falls between the positive reference to the law in 9.31–2 and the identification of universal wisdom-law with the word of preaching

(c) There is, of course, third, a strong polemical note in much of Paul's writing in this area, particularly, once again, in Galatians and 2 Cor. 3. But here too the thrust and character of the polemic needs to be considered more carefully. In particular, it is simply not true that Paul denigrates the law in Gal. 3–4. On the contrary, he sees its role as essentially positive, as guarding and watching over Israel prior to the coming of Christ (3.23–5). It is true that he regards Israel still under the law as in the position of a child, not yet sufficiently mature to enter into its heritage as a son (4.1–7), but he regards believers too as still in a process of growth and transformation (2.19–20; 4.19), themselves not yet entered into their full heritage (5.21). So the picture is more one of a continuous spectrum, with those who live by the Spirit that much further along than those still living solely in terms of the law.[82]

Even in 2 Cor. 3 the polemic is not so stark as at first might appear. For the contrast is not between old covenant and new (3.6, 14) as complete and disparate entities. It is primarily between two modes of ministry (the key term is *diakonia* and its cognates – six times in 3.3–9); it is between one function of the law, that is its function of condemnation, and the *diakonia* of God's righteousness; it is between the law as *gramma* which kills, that is the law understood as something outward and visible, and the Spirit which makes alive (cf. Rom. 2.28–9).[83] In other words, the terms 'covenant', 'law' (which does not actually appear), *diakonia* and *gramma* are not to be taken as a sequence of synonyms. Alternatively expressed, the ministries contrasted both reflect divine glory, the one more fully and more lastingly than the other, but the same glory.[84] And Moses' turning to the Lord unveiled remains a type of the believer's reception of the Spirit (3.16–18). The continuity of covenants in function and purpose is still a fundamental part of Paul's presuppositions at this point.

(d) Finally, I might simply draw attention to a feature which

---

in 10.6–10 (citing Deut. 30.11–14), so that the negative thrust of 10.4 must be directed against the misunderstanding of the law explicit in 9.32 and implicit in 10.2–3; for detailed treatment again I must refer to my *Romans*.

82. See further my *Galatians*; also on the frequently misunderstood 3.19 and 21.

83. Even here the contrast is not so sharp as the contrast of 3.6 itself might seem to imply; Paul has already said that his *diakonia* is also 'from death to death' as well as 'from life to life' (2.16).

84. The most difficult exegetical question is over the significance of the repeated *katargeisthai* (3.7, 11, 13–14); is it the glory which 'fades', the veil which is 'taken away', or the old covenant which is 'transitory'? (see discussion in Furnish, *2 Corinthians, ad loc.*). If the last, it would be Paul's strongest statement of discontinuity between the two epochs of God's purpose, but in effect no stronger than the delimited role of the law in Gal. 3–4. On Rom. 10.4 see above, n. 81.

impressed me most strongly in my own study of Rom. 9–11. That is, the fact that Paul seems to go out of his way from the end of Rom. 10 to avoid anything distinctively Christian in terminology and in the hope he expresses – that is, 'Christian' as distinct from 'Jewish'. Even the final hope of 'the deliverer from zion' (11.26) is put in terms which all Jews of whatever persuasion would have been willing to acknowledge and affirm for themselves. And the final doxology is in praise of the one God alone. That is not to say, of course, that the hope and the faith expressed is not 'Christian'. Rather it is to recognize that Christian hope for the future consummation was one and the same as Israel's hope for itself; it was Israel's hope. Paul affirms his hope as a believer in Jesus Messiah as Israel's own hope for itself. Paul affirms his faith in the one God as one who also believes in Jesus as Lord. Had his intention been to drive a wedge between Jew and Christian, between Israel according to the flesh and Israel according to the Spirit, between old covenant and new, he could easily have done so by injecting specific reference to Jesus and some distinctively christological formulation. But he did not. This seems to me the action of a man who saw himself as both 'Jew' and 'Christian', who understood his faith as the faith of Israel, and who sought to retain and maintain the continuity and overlap between old covenant and new as strongly as possible, even at the cost of his own life.

The Paul who thus emerges from all this is a much more eirenic figure than he has usually been given credit for. However, because he stood at a crucial juncture in the process of earliest Christianity's self-definition his reputation has suffered probably unfairly in the subsequent process of Christianity's pulling apart from Judaism (and vice versa). Because he was such a significant figure he had to be claimed and claimed decisively by those who wished to establish Christianity's distinct identity over against Judaism if they were to have hope of success. His polemic against other Christian Jewish missionaries, in a context where distinct identities had not yet clearly emerged, could be too easily taken over and used to promote a much deeper split between Christianity and Judaism than Paul himself could ever have envisaged. Marcion simply represents the *reductio ad absurdum* of projecting one aspect of Paul's polemic in complete disregard for the circumstances of Paul's own writing and on into circumstances quite different from any that Paul would have conceived.

In contrast, when Paul is set more fully within the context of his own day he should be much less a stone of stumbling and symbol of offence in Jewish–Christian dialogue. Quite to the contrary, he has the potential to be a figure of rapprochement, less the apostate apostle to the Gentiles, less 'the apostle of the heretics', and more one who saw his mission as carrying forward Israel's calling to be 'a light to the nations' (Isa. 49.6).[85] It is Paul who most forceably answers our original question: not two covenants, two religions, two different peoples (Jews and Christians) but one covenant, one religion, one people, Israel.

5. CONCLUSION

When we put all these factors together we gain a different perspective from the traditional one on the character of relationships between Judaism and Christianity in the early centuries of the common era. If what has been said above is soundly based, then several conclusions should be drawn.

First, we should question the assumption that those who in the early centuries practised 'Judaism' as well as (or should we say as part of their) 'Christianity' were always mistaken. It is true that Paul warned the Christian Gentiles of Galatia against the adoption of the Jewish way of life and did so in the strongest terms. But that was because in those circumstances, in his view, the gospel itself was being put at risk. In different circumstances he hastened to defend and urge full acceptance of Christians who still observed Jewish scruples regarding food and festivals (Rom. 14.1–15.6). And in the still more different circumstances of Asia Minor two and a half centuries later, would he have been so quick to denounce those Christians who saw attendance at the synagogue as wholly of a piece with their baptismal faith? Certainly it must be questioned whether we can simply extrapolate Paul's disapproval of 'the weak' into the blanket condemnations of a Melito or a Chrysostom. And it needs to be appreciated that the negative tone of the term 'judaizer' owes more to F. C. Baur 150 years ago than to Paul or the Fathers. Perhaps, then, we should also be more open to the possibility that some of these early 'judaizing' believers were demonstrating a greater awareness of Christianity's integrally Jewish character than some of the writers whose writings have shaped Christian perception of Judaism. Alternatively expressed, Christians today may need to make amends to those who were dismissed as weak and heretical on this count in the early days, recognizing now that within the total sweep of the history of the people of God such individuals represented the Church's living (and necessary) connection with its Jewish heritage – an insight only fitfully sustained

---

85. See now my 'Paul: Apostate or Apostle of Israel?', *ZNW* 89 (1998), pp. 256–71.

in the intervening centuries, in individuals befriending particular rabbis in order to learn Hebrew or about Judaism, but of compelling and increasingly urgent importance today.

No doubt in that early period of self-definition both Judaism and Christianity had to find themselves in order to gain the self-confidence without which neither could have survived or flourished. But in retrospect it must be judged unfortunate that the process on both sides involved a greater degree of polemical defining-out than either's tradition validated. It is perhaps only now, at the end of the twentieth century, when the full cost of such self-definition has become clear, that the whole process of self-definition can be looked at afresh with more eirenic results.

If I am right, the importance and urgency of the present challenge consists simply in this: that neither Judaism nor Christianity can be true to itself without a fuller recognition of the other, and of the other's place within its own self-understanding. My thesis, stated at the beginning, is that Christianity cannot understand itself except as an expression of Judaism; that Judaism is not true to itself unless it recognizes Christianity as a legitimate expression of its own heritage; and that Christianity, equally, is not true to itself unless it recognizes Judaism as a legitimate expression of that same common heritage. But my plea in its developed form is that we go behind the differentiation and antitheses implicit in the very terms we use for each other (Judaism, Christianity) and return to the common ground given us in the term 'Israel'. 'What is Israel? Who is an Israelite?' are questions not simply for Jews and citizens, would-be citizens and potential citizens of the modern state of Israel. They are also questions for all Christians: what does it mean to be Israel? My thesis restated, then, is that these questions cannot be fully answered by one or other, but only by both. My thesis restated is that Israel cannot understand itself, cannot be Israel, unless the Christian recognizes that the Jew is also Israel and the Jew acknowledges that without the Christian Israel's destiny is incomplete.

Finally the role and function of Paul in all this needs to be reassessed. He surely deserves to be acquitted from the charge that he was the begetter of anti-Judaism, which comes no less strongly from some on the Christian side, and from the charge of apostasy which lies implicit in the attitude to him of many Jews still today. He was neither. In his own self-understanding and self-affirmation he was and remained an Israelite. He understood his mission to the Gentiles as a prophetic calling towards the fulfilment of the Servant of Yahweh's vocation to bring light to the nations. His emphasis on the Spirit's enabling and warnings against a superficial understanding of the covenant was wholly within the tradition of Israel's aspiration and exhortation. He willingly risked and in the event gave his life in order to reaffirm and cement afresh the spiritual ties between Gentile converts and Jerusalem. According to Acts he claimed and believed that his final imprisonment was 'for the sake of the hope of Israel' (Acts 28.20). And his own clearly stated hope was that 'all Israel will be saved' (Rom. 11.26). In the reassessment of Jewish–Christian relations both in the first three or four centuries and today, this Paul, Paul the Jew-become-apostle-to-the-nations is a resource and guide we cannot do without.

Bibliography

In a broad ranging study such as this, the bibliography could be endless. I therefore took the rather arbitrary decision to limit it to 300 titles, now supplemented by over 70 more recent items, which should be enough to make it of some use to those who consult it. I have excluded all commentaries and dictionary articles, and on particular points or passages further bibliography can be found in the notes. For those who would prefer an even more selective bibliography I have asterisked some three dozen titles.

P. J. Achtemeier, *The Quest for Unity in the New Testament Church*, Philadelphia: Fortress 1987

P. S. Alexander, 'Rabbinic Judaism and the New Testament', *ZNW* 74 (1983), pp. 237–46

P. S. Alexander, 'Jewish Law in the Time of Jesus: Towards a Clarification of the Problems', *Law and Religion. Essays on the Place of the Law in Israel and Early Christianity*, ed. B. Lindars, Cambridge: James Clarke 1988, pp. 44–58

P. S. Alexander, '"The Parting of the Ways" from the Perspective of Rabbinic Judaism', in *Jews and Christians: The Parting of the Ways AD 70 to 135*, ed. J. D. G. Dunn, Tübingen: Mohr Siebeck 1992; Grand Rapids: Eerdmans 1999, pp. 1–25

G. Alon, *The Jews in their Land in the Talmudic Age*, 2 vols, Jerusalem: Magnes 1980, 1984

Y. Amir, 'The Term *Ioudaismos*. A Study in Jewish-Hellenistic Self-Identification', *Immanuel* 14 (1982), pp. 34–41

J. Ashton, 'The Identity and Function of the *Ioudaioi* in the Fourth Gospel', *NovT* 27 (1985), pp. 40–75

M. Avi-Yonah and Z. Bavas, *Society and Religion in the Second Temple Period*, The World History of the Jewish People 1.8; Jerusalem: Massada, 1977

L. Baeck, *Judaism and Christianity*, Jewish Publication Society of America 1958

R. Banks, *Jesus and the Law in the Synoptic Tradition*, SNTSMS; Cambridge University 1975

J. M. G. Barclay, *Jews in the Mediterranean Diaspora from Alexander to Trajan (323 BCE–117 CE)*, Edinburgh: T. & T. Clark 1996

C. K. Barrett, 'Pauline Controversies in the Post-Pauline Period', *NTS* 20 (1973–74), pp. 229–45

C. K. Barrett, *The Gospel of John and Judaism*, London: SPCK 1975

M. Barth, *Jesus, Paulus und die Juden*, Zürch: EVZ 1967

M. Barth, 'St Paul – A Good Jew', *HBT* 1 (1979), pp. 7–45

M. Barth, *The People of God*, JSNTSupp 5; Sheffield: JSOT 1983

R. Bauckham, 'The Worship of Jesus in Apocalyptic Christianity', *NTS* 27 (1980–81), pp. 322–41

R. Bauckham, 'The Parting of the Ways: What Happened and Why', *Studia Theologica* 47 (1993), pp. 135–51

W. Bauer, *Orthodoxy and Heresy in Earliest Christianity*, Philadelphia: Fortress 1971

G. Baum, *Is the New Testament Anti-Semitic?*, New York: Paulist 1965

F. C. Baur, *Paul: the Apostle of Jesus Christ*, 2 vols, London: Williams & Norgate 1873, 1875

F. C. Baur, *The Church History of the First Three Centuries*, London: Williams & Norgate 1878

N. A. Beck, *Mature Christianity. The Recognition and Repudiation of the Anti-Jewish Polemic of the New Testament*, London/Toronto: Associated University Presses 1985

A. H. Becker, 'Beyond the Spatial and Temporal *Limes*', in Becker and Reed (eds), *The Ways that Never Parted*, pp. 373–92

A. H. Becker and A. Y. Reed (eds), *The Ways that Never Parted*, TSAJ 95; Tübingen: Mohr Siebeck 2003

S. Ben-Chorin, 'Antijüdische Elemente im Neuen Testament', *EvTh* 40 (1980), pp. 203–14

R. Bieringer *et al.* (eds), *Anti-Judaism and the Fourth Gospel*, Assen: Van Gorcum 2001

J. Blenkinsopp, 'Interpretation and the Tendency to Sectarianism: An Aspect of Second Temple History', *JCSD* 2.1–26

M. J. Borg, *Conflict, Holiness and Politics in the Teachings of Jesus*, New York/Toronto: Edwin Mellen 1984

W. Bousset, *Kyrios Christos: A History of the Belief in Christ from the Beginnings of Christianity to Irenaeus*, 1913, ²1921; Nashville: Abingdon 1970

W. Bousset and H. Gressmann, *Die Religion des Judentums im späthellenistischen Zeitalter*, HNT 21; Tübingen: Mohr 1925, ⁴1966

D. Boyarin, *A Radical Jew: Paul and the Politics of Identity*, Berkeley: University of California 1994

D. Boyarin, *Dying for God: Martyrdom and the Making of Judaism and Christianity*, Stanford: Stanford University 1999

D. Boyarin, 'Semantic Differences; or, "Judaism"/"Christianity"', in Becker and Reed (eds), *The Ways that Never Parted*, pp. 65–85

D. Boyarin, *Border Lines: The Partition of Judaeo-Christianity*, Philadelphia: University of Pennsylvania 2004

S. G. F. Brandon, *The Fall of Jerusalem and the Christian Church*, London: SPCK 1951

S. G. F. Brandon, *Jesus and the Zealots*, Manchester University 1967

R. L. Brawley, *Luke-Acts and the Jews. Conflict, Apology, and Conciliation*, SBLMS; Atlanta: Scholars 1987

M. Braybrooke, *Time to Meet: Towards a Deeper Relationship between Jews and Christians*, London: SCM Press 1990

M. Brett (ed), *Ethnicity and the Bible*, Leiden: Brill 1996

R. E. Brown, *The Community of the Beloved Disciple*, London: Chapman 1979

R. E. Brown, *The Churches the Apostles Left Behind*, London: Chapman 1984

R. E. Brown and J. P. Meier, *Antioch and Rome: New Testament Cradles of Catholic Christianity*, London: Chapman 1983

S. Brown, *The Origins of Christianity*, Oxford University 1984

F. F. Bruce, *New Testament History*, London: Nelson 1969

F. F. Bruce, *Men and Movements in the Primitive Church*, Exeter: Paternoster 1979

A. Büchler, *Types of Jewish-Palestinian Piety from 70 BCE to 70 CE*, London: Jews' College No. 8, 1922

J. A. Bühner, *Der Gesandte und sein Weg im 4. Evangelium*, Tübingen: Mohr-Siebeck 1977

R. Bultmann, *Theology of the New Testament*, 1948–53; 2 vols London: SCM Press 1952, 1955

P. M. van Buren, *A Theology of the Jewish-Christian Reality*, 4 vols, San Francisco: Harper & Row 1980–

F. C. Burkitt, *Christian Beginnings*, University of London 1924

J. Carleton Paget, 'Jewish Christianity', in W. Horbury *et al.*, *The Cambridge History of Judaism*, vol. 3: *The Early Roman Period*, Cambridge University 1999, pp. 731–75

S. J. Case, *The Evolution of Early Christianity*, University of Chicago 1914

M. Casey, *From Jewish Prophet to Gentile God*, Cambridge: James Clarke 1991

J. B. Chance, *Jerusalem, the Temple and the New Age in Luke-Acts*, Macon: Mercer 1988

R. H. Charles (ed.), *The Apocrypha and Pseudepigrapha of the Old Testament*, 2 vols, Oxford: Clarendon 1913

J. H. Charlesworth, *The Pseudepigrapha and Modern Research with a Supplement*, Chico: Scholars 1981

J. H. Charlesworth, *The Old Testament Pseudepigrapha*, 2 vols, New York: Doubleday/London: Darton, Longman & Todd 1983, 1985

J. H. Charlesworth, *Jesus within Judaism. New Light from Exciting Archaeological Discoveries*, London: SPCK 1988

J. H. Charlesworth (ed.), *Jews and Christians. Exploring the Past, Present and Future*, New York: Crossroad 1990

E. J. Christiansen, *The Covenant in Judaism and Paul: A Study of Ritual Boundaries as Identity Markers*, Leiden: Brill 1995

S. J. D. Cohen, 'Conversion to Judaism in Historical Perspective: From Biblical Israel to Postbiblical Judaism', *Conservative Judaism* 36 (1983), pp. 31–45

S. J. D. Cohen, 'The Political and Social History of the Jews in Greco-Roman Antiquity: the State of the Question', *EJMI*, pp. 33–56

**S. J. D. Cohen, *From Maccabees to the Mishnah*, Philadelphia: Westminster 1987

S. J. D. Cohen, 'Crossing the Boundary and Becoming a Jew', *HTR* 82 (1989), pp. 13–33

S. J. D. Cohen, *The Beginnings of Jewishness: Boundaries, Varieties, Uncertainties*, Berkeley: University of California 1999

**J. J. Collins, *Between Athens and Jerusalem. Jewish Identity in the Hellenistic Diaspora*, New York: Crossroad 1983

J. J. Collins, *The Apocalyptic Imagination. An Introduction to the Jewish Matrix of Christianity*, New York: Crossroad 1984

H. Conzelmann, *History of Primitive Christianity*, Nashville: Abingdon/London: Darton, Longman & Todd 1973

C. E. B. Cranfield, 'St Paul and the Law', *SJT* 17 (1964), pp. 43–68

A. D. Crown, 'Judaism and Christianity: The Parting of the Ways', in A. J. Avery-Peck *et al.*, (eds), *When Judaism and Christianity Began*, Leiden: Brill 2004, 2.545–62

O. Cullmann, *The Christology of the New Testament*, London: SCM Press/Philadelphia: Westminster 1959

O. Cullmann, *The Johannine Circle*, London: SCM Press/Philadelphia: Westminster 1976

G. Dalman, *The Words of Jesus*, Edinburgh: T. & T. Clark 1902

J. Danielou, *A History of Early Christian Doctrine. Vol. One: The Theology of Jewish Christianity*, London: Darton, Longman & Todd 1964

D. Daube, *The New Testament and Rabbinic Judaism*, London: Athlone 1956

A. T. Davies, (ed.), *AntiSemitism and the Foundations of Christianity*, New York: Paulist 1979

**W. D. Davies, *Paul and Rabbinic Judaism*, London: SPCK 1948, ⁴1981

W. D. Davies, *The Setting of the Sermon on the Mount*, Cambridge University 1964

W. D. Davies, *The Gospel and the Land. Early Christianity and Jewish Territorial Doctrine*, University of California 1974

W. D. Davies, *Jewish and Pauline Studies*, Philadelphia: Fortress 1983/London: SPCK: 1984

G. Dix, *Jew and Greek*, London: Dacre 1953

J. D. G. Dunn, *Jesus and the Spirit*, London: SCM Press/Philadelphia: Westminster 1975

J. D. G. Dunn, *Unity and Diversity in the New Testament*, London: SCM Press/Philadelphia: Westminster 1977, London: SCM Press/Philadelphia: TPI ²1990

**J. D. G. Dunn, *Christology in the Making: An Inquiry into the Origins of the Doctrine of the Incarnation* London: SCM Press/Philadelphia: Westminster 1980, ²1989

J. D. G. Dunn, 'Was Christianity a Monotheistic Faith from the Beginning?', *SJT* 35 (1982), pp. 303–36

J. D. G. Dunn, 'Let John be John. A Gospel for its Time', *Das Evangelium und die Evangelien*, hrsg. P. Stuhlmacher, WUNT 28; Tübingen: Mohr-Siebeck 1983, pp. 309–39 = *The Gospel and the Gospels*, Grand Rapids: Eerdmans 1991, pp. 293–322

**J. D. G. Dunn, *Jesus, Paul and the Law. Studies in Mark and Galatians*, London: SPCK/Louisville: Westminster 1990

J. D. G. Dunn (ed.), *Jews and Christians: The Parting of the Ways AD 70 to 135*, Tübingen: Mohr Siebeck 1992; Grand Rapids: Eerdmans 1999

J. D. G. Dunn, *The Theology of Paul the Apostle*, Grand Rapids: Eerdmans; Edinburgh: T. & T. Clark 1998

J. D. G. Dunn, 'Paul: Apostate or Apostle of Israel?', *Z N W* 89 (1998), pp. 256–71

J. D. G. Dunn, 'Was Judaism Particularist or Universalist?', in *Judaism in Late Antiquity*, part III: *Where We Stand: Issues and Debates in Ancient Judaism*, vol. 2, ed. J. Neusner and A. J. Avery-Peck, Handbuch der Orientalisk; Leiden: Brill 1999, pp. 57–73

J. D. G. Dunn, 'Who Did Paul Think He Was? A Study of Jewish Christian Identity', *NTS* 45 (1999), pp. 174–93

J. D. G. Dunn, 'The Jew Paul and his Meaning for Israel', in *Paulinische Christologie: Exegetische Beiträge*, ed. U. Schnelle and T. Söding, H. Hübner FS, Göttingen: Vandenhoeck & Ruprecht 2000, pp. 32–46, reprinted in *A Shadow of Glory: Reading the New Testament after the Holocaust*, ed. T. Linafelt, New York: Routledge 2002, pp. 201–15

J. D. G. Dunn, *Jesus Remembered*, Grand Rapids: Eerdmans 2003

J. D. G. Dunn, 'Did Paul Have a Covenant Theology? Reflections on Romans 9.4 and 11.27', in *The Concept of the Covenant in the Second Temple Period*, ed. S. E. Porter and J. C. R. de Roo, JSJSupp 71; Leiden: Brill 2003, pp. 287–307

J. D. G. Dunn, *The New Perspective on Paul*, WUNT 185; Tübingen: Mohr Siebeck 2005

J. D. G. Dunn (ed.), *The Parting of the Ways: AD 70–135*, Tübingen: Mohr-Siebeck 1992; Grand Rapids: Eerdmans 1999

A. Dupont-Sommer, *The Essene Writings from Qumran*, Oxford: Blackwell 1961

W. Eckert (ed.), *Antijudaismus im Neuen Testament*, München: Kaiser 1967

L. E. Elliott-Binns, *Galilean Christianity*, London: SCM Press 1956

P. F. Esler, *Community and Gospel in Luke-Acts. The Social and Political Motivations of Lucan Theology*, SNTSMS 57; Cambridge University 1987

C. A. Evans, 'Root Causes of the Jewish–Christian Rift from Jesus to Justin', in *Christian–Jewish Relations through the Centuries*, ed. S. E. Porter and B. W. R. Pearson, JSNTS 192; Sheffield Academic 2000, pp. 20–35

C. A. Evans and D. A. Hagner (eds), *Anti-Semitism and Early Christianity: Issues of Polemic and Faith*, Minneapolis: Fortress 1993

H. Falk, *Jesus the Pharisee. A New Look at the Jewishness of Jesus*, New York: Paulist 1979

L. H. Feldman, *Jew and Gentile in the Ancient World*, Princeton University 1993

E. S. Fiorenza, *In Memory of Her*, London: SCM Press/New York: Crossroad 1983

J. E. Fossum, *The Name of God and the Angel of the Lord*, WUNT 36; Tübingen: Mohr-Siebeck 1985

D. Frankfurter, 'Beyond "Jewish Christianity"', in Becker and Reed (eds), *The Ways that Never Parted*, pp. 131–43

P. Fredriksen, 'What "Parting of the Ways"?, in Becker and Reed (eds), *The Ways that never Parted*, pp. 35–63

S. Freyne, *Galilee from Alexander the Great to Hadrian 323 BCE to 135 CE*, Wilmington, Delaware: Glazier 1980

S. Freyne: 'Vilifying the Other and Defining the Self: Matthew's and John's Anti-Jewish Polemic in Focus', *To See Ourselves*, ed. J. Neusner, pp. 117–43

R. H. Fuller, *The Foundations of New Testament Christology*, London: Lutterworth 1965

B. Gärtner, *The Temple and the Community in Qumran and the New Testament*, SNTSMS; Cambridge University 1965

J. G. Gager, *Kingdom and Community: the Social World of Early Christianity*, Englewood Cliffs, New Jersey: Prentice-Hall 1975

J. G. Gager, *The Origins of Anti-Semitism. Attitudes toward Judaism in Pagan and Christian Antiquity*, New York: Oxford 1985

J. G. Gager, 'Judaism as Seen by Outsiders', *EJMI*, pp. 99–116

J. G. Gager, 'Did Jewish Christians See the Rise of Islam?', in Becker and Reed (eds), *The Ways that Never Parted*, pp. 361–72

D. Garlington, *'The Obedience of Faith'. A Pauline Phrase in Historical Context*, WUNT: Tübingen: Mohr-Siebeck 1991

L. Gaston, *No Stone on Another. Studies in the Significance of the Fall of Jerusalem in the Synoptic Gospels*, NovT Supp 23; Leiden: Brill 1970

L. Gaston, *Paul and the Torah*, Vancouver: University of British Columbia 1987

L. Gillet, *Communion in the Messiah. Studies in the Relationship between Judaism and Christianity*, London: Lutterworth 1942

M. Goguel, *The Birth of Christianity*, London: Allen & Unwin 1953

M. Goodman, 'Diaspora Reactions to the Destruction of the Temple', in *Jews and Christians: The Parting of the Ways AD 70 to 135*, ed. J. D. G. Dunn, Tübingen: Mohr Siebeck 1992; Grand Rapids: Eerdmans 1999, pp. 27–38

M. Goodman, 'Modeling the "Parting of the Ways"', in Becker and Reed (eds), *The Ways that Never Parted*, pp. 119–29

M. Goodman (ed), *Jews in a Graeco-Roman World*, Oxford: Clarendon 1998

L. Goppelt, *Jesus, Paul and Judaism*, New York: Nelson 1964

L. Goppelt, *Apostolic and Post-Apostolic Times*, London: Black 1970

L. Goppelt, *Theology of the New Testament*, Grand Rapids: Eerdmans 1982

D. E. Gowan, *Bridge Between the Testaments*, Pittsburg: Pickwick 1976

E. Grässer, *Der Alte Bund im Neuen. Exegetische Studien zur Israelfrage im Neuen Testament*, Tübingen: Mohr-Siebeck 1985

I. Gruenwald, *Apocalyptic and Merkabah Mysticism*, AGAJU 14; Leiden: Brill 1980

K. Haacker, 'Elemente des heidnischen Antijudaismus im Neuen Testament', *EvTh* 48 (1988), pp. 404–18

**D. A. Hagner, *The Jewish Reclamation of Jesus: An Analysis and Critique of the Modern Jewish Study of Jesus*, Grand Rapids: Zondervan 1984

F. Hahn, *Mission in the New Testament*, London: SCM Press 1965

F. Hahn, *The Titles of Jesus in Christology: their History in Early Christianity*, 1963; London: Lutterworth 1969

**F. Hahn, *The Worship of the Early Church*, Philadelphia: Fortress 1973

R. G. Hamerton-Kelly, *Pre-existence, Wisdom and the Son of Man*, SNTSMS; Cambridge University 1973

D. R. A. Hare, *The Theme of Jewish Persecution of Christians according to St Matthew*, SNTSMS 6; Cambridge University 1967

D. J. Harrington, *God's People in Christ. New Testament Perspectives on the Church and Judaism*, Philadelphia: Fortress 1980

A. Harnack, *What is Christianity?*, London: Putnam 1901

A. Harnack, *The Mission and Expansion of Christianity in the First Three Centuries* London: Williams & Norgate 1908

M. Hengel, *The Zealots* 1961, ²1976; Edinburgh; T. & T. Clark 1989

M. Hengel, *Judentum und Hellenismus*, 1969, ³1988; *Judaism and Hellenism*, 2 vols, London: SCM Press/Philadelphia: Fortress 1974

M. Hengel, *The Son of God: the Origin of Christology and the History of Jewish–Hellenistic Religion*, London: SCM Press/Philadelphia: Fortress 1974

M. Hengel, *Between Jesus and Paul*, London: SCM Press/Philadelphia: Fortress 1984

M. Hengel, *The 'Hellenization' of Judaea in the First Century after Christ*, London: SCM Press/Philadelphia: TPI 1990

R. T. Herford, *Judaism in the New Testament Period*, London: Lindsey 1928

R. T. Herford, *Christianity in Talmud and Midrash*, London: Williams & Norgate 1903

M. D. Hooker, *Continuity and Discontinuity: Early Christianity in its Jewish Setting*, London: Epworth 1986

W. Horbury, 'The Benediction of the *Minim* and Early Jewish-Christian Controversy', *JTS* 33 (1982), pp. 19–61

R. A. Horsley and J. S. Hanson, *Bandits, Prophets and Messiahs. Popular Movements at the Time of Jesus*, New York: Seabury 1985

R. A. Horsley, *Jesus and the Spiral of Violence. Popular Jewish Resistance in Roman Palestine*, San Francisco: Harper & Row 1987

F. J. A. Hort, *Judaistic Christianity*, 1894; Grand Rapids: Baker 1980

G. Howard, *Paul: Crisis in Galatia*, SNTSMS; Cambridge University 1979

H. Hübner, *Law in Paul's Thought*, 1978, ²1980; Edinburgh: T. & T. Clark/ Philadelphia: Fortress 1985

R. Hummel, *Die Auseinandersetzung zwischen Kirche und Judentum in Matthäusevangelium*, München: Kaiser 1966

**L. W. Hurtado, *One God, One Lord. Early Christian Devotion and Ancient Jewish Monotheism*, London: SCM Press/Philadelphia: Fortress 1988

L. W. Hurtado, *Lord Jesus Christ: Devotion to Jesus in Earliest Christianity*, Grand Rapids: Eerdmans 2003

A. Jaubert, *La notion d'alliance dans le Judaïsme*, Editions du Seuil 1963

J. Jeremias, *Jesus' Promise to the Nations*, London: SCM Press 1958

J. Jeremias, *Jerusalem at the Time of Jesus*, ³1962; London: SCM Press/Philadelphia: Fortress 1969

J. Jeremias, *The Prayers of Jesus*, London: SCM Press 1967

J. Jeremias, *New Testament Theology. Vol. 1. The Proclamation of Jesus*, London: SCM Press/New York: Scribners 1971

J. Jocz, *The Jewish People and Jesus Christ. A Study in the Controversy between Church and Synagogue*, London: SPCK 1954

M. de Jonge, *Christology in Context. The Earliest Christian Response to Jesus*, Philadelphia: Westminster 1988

E. A. Judge, 'Judaism and the Rise of Christianity: A Roman Perspective', *TynB* 45 (1994), pp. 355–68

D. Juel, *Messiah and Temple. The Trial of Jesus in the Gospel of Mark*, SBLDS; Missoula: Scholars 1977

S. T. Katz, 'Issues in the Separation of Judaism and Christianity after 70 CE. A Reconsideration', *JBL* 103 (1984), pp. 43–76

Y. Kaufmann, *Christianity and Judaism. Two Covenants*, Jerusalem: Magnes 1988

K. Kertelge, (ed.), *Das Gesetz im Neuen Testament*, QD; Freiburg: Herder 1986

G. D. Kilpatrick, *The Origins of the Gospel According to St Matthew*, Oxford: Clarendon 1946

S. Kim, *The Origin of Paul's Gospel*, WUNT, 2.4; Tübingen: Mohr-Siebeck 1981

W. Kinzig, ' "Non-separation": Closeness and Co-operation between Jews and Christians in the Fourth Century', *VC* 45 (1991), pp. 27–53

J. Klausner, *Jesus of Nazareth. His Life, Times and·Teaching*, London: George Allen & Unwin 1925

J. Klausner, *From Jesus to Paul*, London: George Allen & Unwin 1943

C. Klein, *Anti-Judaism in Christian Theology*, 1975; London: SPCK 1978

A. F. J. Klijn, *Jewish-Christian Gospel Tradition*, Leiden: Brill 1992

A. F. J. Klijn and G. J. Reinink, *Patristic Evidence for Jewish-Christian Sects*, NovTSupp 36; Leiden: Brill 1973

G. Klinzing, *Die Umdeutung des Kultus in der Qumrangemeinde und im NT*, SUNT 7; Göttingen: Vandenhoeck & Ruprecht 1971

K. Koch, *The Rediscovery of Apocalyptic*, 1970; London: SCM Press 1972

J. Koenig, *Jews and Christians in Dialogue. New Testament Foundations*, Philadelphia: Westminster 1979

H. Koester, *Introduction to the New Testament*, Berlin: de Gruyter 1984

A. T. Kraabel, 'The Roman Diaspora: Six Questionable Assumptions', *Essays in Honor of Y. Yadin*, ed. G. Vermes and J. Neusner, *JJS* 33 (1982), pp. 445–64

R. S. Kraemer, 'On the Meaning of the Term "Jew" in Greco-Roman Inscriptions', *HTR* 82 (1989), pp. 35–53

R. A. Kraft, 'The Multiform Jewish Heritage of Early Christianity', *Christianity, Judaism and Other Greco-Roman Cults. Studies for M. Smith*, ed. J. Neusner, *Part Three. Judaism before 70*, Leiden: Brill 1975, pp. 175–99

R. A. Kraft, 'The Weighing of the Parts', in Becker and Reed (eds), *The Ways that Never Parted*, pp. 87–94

R. A. Kraft and G. W. E. Nickelsburg, *Early Judaism and its Modern Interpreters*, Atlanta: Scholars 1986

L. J. Kreitzer, *Jesus and God in Paul's Eschatology*, JSNTSupp 19; Sheffield: JSOT 1987

N. de Lange, *Origen and the Jews: Studies in Jewish–Christian Relations in Third-Century Palestine*, Cambridge University 1976

P. Lapide, *Israelis, Jews and Jesus*, New York: Doubleday 1979

P. Lapide, *Paulus – Ketzer, Heiliger oder Rabbi?*, Gütersloh: Gütersloher 1989

P. Lapide and U. Luz, *Jesus in Two Perspectives. A Jewish-Christian Dialog*, Minneapolis: Augsburg 1985

A. R. C. Leaney, *The Jewish and Christian World 200 B.C. – A.D. 200*, Cambridge University 1985

S. Legasse, 'L'antijudaisme dans l'Evangile selon Matthieu', *L'Evangile selon*

Matthieu. Redaction et Theologie, par M. Didier, BETL 29; Leuven University 1972, pp. 417–28

R. Leivestad, *Jesus in his own Perspective*, Minneapolis: Augsburg 1987

J. Lieu, ' "The Parting of the Ways": Theological Construct or Historic Reality?', *JSNT* 56 (1994), pp. 101–19, reprinted in *Neither Jew nor Greek?*, pp. 11–29

J. Lieu, *Image and Reality: The Jews in the World of the Christians in the Second Century*, Edinburgh: T. & T. Clark 1996

J. Lieu, ' "Impregnable Ramparts and Walls of Iron': Boundary and Identity in Early "Judaism" and "Christianity" ', *NTS* 48 (2002), pp. 144–63

J. Lieu, *Neither Jew nor Greek? Constructing Christian Identity*, Edinburgh: T. & T. Clark 2003

J. Lieu, *Christian Identity in the Jewish and Graeco-Roman World*, Oxford University 2004

J. Lieu, J. North and T. Rajak (eds), *The Jews among Pagans and Christians in the Roman Empire*, London: Routledge 1992

J. B. Lightfoot, 'Paul and the Three', *Galatians*, London: Macmillan 1865

J. B. Lightfoot, 'The Christian Ministry', *St Paul's Epistle to the Philippians*, London: Macmillan 1868, pp. 179–267

J. N. Lightstone, *The Commerce of the Sacred. Mediation of the Divine among Jews in the Graeco-Roman Diaspora*, BJS 59; Chico: Scholars 1984

M. Limbeck, *Die Ordnung des Heils: Untersuchungen zum Gesetzesverständnis des Frühjudentums*, Düsseldorf: Patmos 1971

A. T. Lincoln, 'The Church and Israel in Ephesians 2', *CBQ* 49 (1987), pp. 605–24

G. Lohfink, *Die Sammlung Israels. Eine Untersuchung zur lukanischen Ekklesiologie*, SANT; München: Kösel 1975

A. F. Loisy, *The Birth of the Christian Religion*, New York: University 1962

B. Longenecker, *Eschatology and the Covenant. A Comparison of 4 Ezra and Romans 9–11*, JSNTSupp 57; Sheffield Academic Press 1991

R. N. Longenecker, *Paul: Apostle of Liberty*, Harper 1964

L. de Lorenzi, hrsg., *Die Israelfrage nach Römer 9–11*, Rome: Abtei von St Paul 1977

G. Lüdemann, *Paulus und das Judentum*, München: Kaiser 1983

H. Maccoby, *The Mythmaker. Paul and the Invention of Christianity*, London: Weidenfeld & Nicolson 1986

H. Maccoby, *Judaism in the First Century*, London: Sheldon 1989

**R. J. McKelvey, *The New Temple. The Church in the New Testament*, Oxford University 1969

**S. McKnight, *A Light Among the Gentiles. Jewish Missionary Activity in the Second Temple Period*, Minneapolis: Fortress 1991

R. S. MacLennan, *Early Christian Texts on Jews and Judaism*, Atlanta: Scholars 1990

J. Maier, *Jesus von Nazareth in der talmudischen Überlieferung*, Darmstadt: WB 1978

J. Maier, *Jüdische Auseinandersetzung mit dem Christentum in der Antike*, Darmstadt: WB 1982

C. Markschies, *Between Two Worlds: Structures of Earliest Christianity*, London: SCM Press 1999

J. L. Martyn, *History and Theology in the Fourth Gospel*, Nashville: Abingdon ²1979

J. L. Martyn, 'Glimpses into the History of the Johannine Community', *L'Evangile de Jean*, ed. M. de Jonge, BETL; Leuven University 1977, pp. 149–75

W. A. Meeks, ' "Am I a Jew?" Johannine Christianity and Judaism', *Christianity, Judaism and Other Greco-Roman Cults, Studies for M. Smith*, ed. J. Neusner, *Part One: New Testament*, Leiden: Brill 1975, pp. 163–86

W. A. Meeks, 'Breaking Away: Three New Testament Pictures of Christianity's Separation from the Jewish Communities', *To See Ourselves*, ed. J. Neusner, pp. 93–115

W. A. Meeks and R. L. Wilken, *Jews and Christians in Antioch in the First Four Centuries of the Common Era*, Missoula: Scholars 1978

P. H. Menoud, *L'Eglise naissante et le Judaïsme*, Montpelier: ETR 1952

B. Meyer, *The Aims of Jesus* London: SCM Press 1979

E. Meyer, *Ursprung und Anfänge des Christentums*, in 3 Bänden Stuttgart: Cotta'sche 1921–23

E. M. Meyers and J. F. Strange, *Archaeology, the Rabbis and Early Christianity*, London: SCM Press/Nashville: Abingdon 1981

C. G. Montefiore, *Judaism and St Paul*, London: Goschen 1914

C. G. Montefiore and H. Lowe, *A Rabbinic Anthology*, 1938; Schocken 1974

G. F. Moore, 'Christian Writers on Judaism', *HTR* 14 (1922), pp. 41–61

G. F. Moore, *Judaism in the First Three Centuries of the Christian Era. The Age of the Tannaim*, 3 vols, Cambridge, Mass. 1927–30

M. J. Mulder, *Mikra. Text, Translation, Reading and Interpretation of the Hebrew Bible in Ancient Judaism and Early Christianity*, Assen: Van Gorcum 1988

J. Munck, *Christ and Israel. An Interpretation of Romans 9–11*, Philadelphia: Fortress 1967

J. Munck, *Paul and the Salvation of Mankind*, London: SCM Press/Atlanta: John Knox 1959

J. Munck, 'Jewish Christianity in Post-Apostolic Times', *NTS* 6 (1959–60), pp. 103–16

**F. Mussner, *Tractate on the Jews: the Significance of Judaism for Christian Faith*, 1979; London: SPCK 1984

S. Neill & T. Wright, *The Interpretation of the New Testament 1861–1986*, Oxford University ²1988

J. Neusner, *The Rabbinic Traditions about the Pharisees before AD 70*, Leiden: Brill 1971

J. Neusner, *From Politics to Piety. The Emergence of Rabbinic Judaism*, Englewood Cliffs: Prentice Hall 1973

J. Neusner, *First Century Judaism in Crisis*, Nashville: Abingdon 1975

J. Neusner, 'The Formation of Rabbinic Judaism: Yavneh (Jamnia) from AD 70 to 100', *ANRW* II.19.2 (1979), pp. 3–42

J. Neusner, *Judaism: The Evidence of the Mishnah*, University of Chicago 1981

J. Neusner, 'Varieties of Judaism in the Formative Age', *Formative Judaism. Second Series*, BJS 41; Chico: Scholars 1983, pp. 59–89

**J. Neusner, *Judaism in the Beginning of Christianity*, London: SPCK 1984

J. Neusner, *Reading and Believing. Ancient Judaism and Contemporary Gullibil-ity*, BJS 113; Atlanta: Scholars 1986

J. Neusner, *Jews and Christians. The Myth of a Common Tradition*, London: SCM Press/Philadelphia: TPI 1991

J. Neusner, 'Was Rabbinic Judaism Really "Ethnic"?', *CBQ* 57 (1995), pp. 281–305

J. Neusner and E. S. Frerichs (ed.), *'To See Ourselves as Others See Us'. Christ-ians, Jews, 'Others' in Late Antiquity*, Chico: Scholars 1985

J. Neusner, et al. (ed.), *Judaisms and their Messiahs at the Turn of the Christian Era*, Cambridge University 1987

M. Newton, *The Concept of Purity at Qumran and in the Letters of Paul*, SNTSMS 53; Cambridge University 1985

G. W. E. Nickelsburg, *Resurrection, Immortality and Eternal Life in Inter-testamental Judaism*, Harvard Theological Studies 26; Cambridge: Harvard 1972

G. W. E. Nickelsburg and J. J. Collins (ed.), *Ideal Figures in Ancient Judaism*, Chico: Scholars 1980

G. W. E. Nickelsburg and G. W. Macrae (eds), *Christians among Jews and Gen-tiles*, K. Stendahl FS, Philadelphia: Fortress 1986

G. Nickelsburg and M. Stone, *Faith and Piety in Early Judaism*, Philadelphia: Fortress 1983

K. -W. Niebuhr, ' "Judentum" und "Christentum" bei Paulus und Ignatius von Antiochien', *ZNW* 85 (1994), pp. 218–33

D. Novak, *The Image of the non-Jew in Judaism. An Historical and Constructive Study of the Noahide Laws*, Lewiston/Queenston: Edwin Mellen 1983

**P. von der Osten-Sacken, *Christian-Jewish Dialogue. Theological Foundations*, 1982; Philadelphia: Fortress 1986

P. von der Osten-Sacken, *Die Heiligkeit der Tora. Studien zum Gesetz bei Paulus*, München: Kaiser 1989

J. A. Overman, *Matthew's Gospel and Formative Judaism. The Social World of the Matthean Community*, Minneapolis: Fortress 1990

J. Parkes, *The Conflict of the Church and the Synagogue*, Jewish Publication Society 1934; reprinted New York: Macmillan

J. Parkes, *Antisemitism*, Valentine Mitchell 1963

J. T. Pawlikowski, *Christ in the Light of the Christian–Jewish Dialogue*, New York: Paulist 1982

J. Pawlikowski, *Jesus and the Theology of Israel*, Wilmington: Glazier 1989

J. T. Pawlikowski, 'The Re-Judaization of Christianity: Its Impact on the Church and Its Implications for the Jewish People', in *People, Land and State of Israel: Jewish and Christian Perspectives, Immanuel* 22/23 (1994), pp. 60–74

S. E. Porter and B. W. R. Pearson, 'Ancient Understandings of the Christian–Jewish Split', in *Christian-Jewish Relations through the Centuries*, ed. S. E. Porter and B. W. R. Pearson, JSNTS 192; Sheffield Academic 2000, pp. 20–35

G. G. Porton, 'Diversity in Postbiblical Judaism', *EJMI*, pp. 57–80

H. Räisänen, *Paul and the Law*, WUNT; Tübingen: Mohr-Siebeck, 1984, Phila-delphia: Fortress 1986

H. Räisänen, *The Torah and Christ*, Helsinki: Finnish Exegetical Society 1986

A. Y. Reed, ' "Jewish Christianity" after the "Parting of the Ways" ', in Becker and Reed (eds), *The Ways that Never Parted*, pp. 189–231

**P. Richardson, *Israel in the Apostolic Church*, SNTSMS 10; Cambridge University 1969

P. Richardson (ed.), *Anti-Judaism in Early Christianity. Vol. I Paul and the Gospels*, Waterloo, Ontario: Wilfrid Laurier University 1986

J. Riches, *Jesus and the Transformation of Judaism*, London: Darton, Longman & Todd 1980

A. Ritschl, *Die Entstehung der altkatholischen Kirche*,²1857

E. Rivkin, *A Hidden Revolution. The Pharisees' Search for the Kingdom Within*, Nashville: Abingdon 1978

E. Rivkin, *What Crucified Jesus?*, Nashville: Abingdon 1984/London: SCM Press 1986

C. Rowland, *The Open Heaven. A Study of Apocalyptic in Judaism and Early Christianity*, London: SPCK/New York: Crossroad 1982

**C. Rowland, *Christian Origins*, London: SPCK/Minneapolis: Augsburg 1985

R. R. Ruether, *Faith and Fratricide. The Theological Roots of Anti-Semitism*, New York: Seabury 1974

D. S. Russell, *The Method and Message of Jewish Apocalyptic*, London: SCM Press/Philadelphia: Westminster 1964

L. Rutgers, 'Archaeological Evidence for the Interaction of Jews and non-Jews in Late Antiquity', *AJA* 96 (1992), pp. 101–18

S. Safrai, *The Literature of the Sages*, 2 vols, Assen: Van Gorcum 1987–

S. Safrai and M. Stern, *The Jewish People in the First Century* 2 vols, Assen: Van Gorcum 1974, 1976

A. J. Saldarini, 'Reconstructions of Rabbinic Judaism', *EJMI*, pp. 437–77

A. J. Saldarini, *Pharisees, Scribes and Sadducees in Palestinian Society*, Edinburgh: T. & T. Clark 1988

A. Salvesen, 'A Convergence of the Ways?', in Becker and Reed (eds.), *The Ways that Never Parted*, pp. 233–58

**E. P. Sanders, *Paul and Palestinian Judaism*, London: SCM Press/Philadelphia: Fortress 1977

E. P. Sanders (ed.), *Jewish and Christian Self-Definition*, 3 vols, London: SCM Press/Philadelphia: Fortress 1980, 1981, 1982

E. P. Sanders, *Paul, the Law and the Jewish People*, Philadelphia: Fortress 1984/London: SCM Press 1985

**E. P. Sanders, *Jesus and Judaism*, London: SCM Press/Philadelphia: Fortress 1985

E. P. Sanders, *Jewish Law from Jesus to the Mishnah. Five Studies*, London: SCM Press/Philadelphia: TPI 1990

J. T. Sanders, *The Jews in Luke-Acts*, London: SCM Press/Philadelphia: Fortress 1987

J. T. Sanders, *Schismatics, Sectarians, Dissidents, Deviants: The First One Hundred Years of Jewish-Christian Relations*, London: SCM Press 1993

S. Sandmel, *The Genius of Paul. A Study in History*, 1958; Philadelphia: Fortress 1979

S. Sandmel, *The First Century in Judaism and Christianity*, New York: Oxford University 1969

S. Sandmel, *Judaism and Christian Beginnings*, New York: Oxford University 1978

S. Sandmel, *AntiSemitism in the New Testament*, Philadelphia: Fortress 1978

P. Schäfer, 'Die Sogenannte Synode von Jabne. Zur Trennung von Juden und Christen im ersten/zweiten Jh. n. Chr.', *Studien zur Geschichte und Theologie des rabbinischen Judentums*, Leiden: Brill 1978, p. 45–64

S. Schechter, *Aspects of Rabbinic Theology*, Macmillan, 1909; Schocken 1961

L. H. Schiffman, 'At the Crossroads: Tannaitic Perspectives on the Jewish – Christian Schism', *JCSD* 2.115–56

**L. H. Schiffman, *Who Was a Jew? Rabbinic and Halakhic Perspectives on the Jewish – Christian Schism*, Hoboken: Ktav 1985

A. Schlatter, *Geschichte Israels von Alexander dem Grossen bis Hadrian*, ³1925; Darmstadt: WB 1977

A. Schlatter, *Synagoge und Kirtche bis zum Barkochba-Aufstand*, Stuttgart: Calwer 1966

W. Schmithals, *Paul and James*, 1963; London: SCM Press 1965

E. J. Schnabel, *Law and Wisdom from Ben Sira to Paul*, WUNT 2.16; Tübingen: Mohr-Siebeck 1985

H. J. Schoeps, *Theologie und Geschichte des Judenchristentums*, Tübingen: Mohr 1949

H. J. Schoeps, *Paul. The Theology of the Apostle in the Light of Jewish Religious History*, London: Lutterworth 1961

H. J. Schoeps, *Jewish Christianity. Factional Disputes in the Early Church*, 1964; Philadelphia: Fortress 1969

**E. Schürer, *The History of the Jewish People in the Age of Jesus Christ*, 4 vols, Edinburgh: T. & T. Clark 1973, 1978, 1986, 1987

A. Schweitzer, *The Quest of the Historical Jesus*, London: A. & C. Black 1910

R. Scroggs, *The Last Adam*, Oxford: Blackwell 1966

R. Scroggs, 'The Earliest Hellenistic Community', *Religions in Antiquity: Essays in Memory of E. R. Goodenough*, ed. J. Neusner Leiden: Brill 1969, pp. 176–206

**A. F. Segal, *Rebecca's Children. Judaism and Christianity in the Roman World*, Harvard University 1986

A. F. Segal, *The Other Judaisms of Late Antiquity*, BJS 127; Atlanta: Scholars 1987

A. F. Segal, *Paul the Convert. The Apostolate and Apostasy of Saul the Pharisee*, New Haven: Yale University 1990

A. F. Segal, 'Universalism in Judaism and Christianity', in *Paul in his Hellenistic Context*, ed. T. Engberg-Pedersen, Minneapolis: Fortress 1995, pp. 1–29

P. Sigal, *The Emergence of Contemporary Judaism. Vol. One. The Foundations of Judaism from Biblical Origins to the Sixth Century AD. Part One. From the Origins to the Separation of Christianity*, Pittsburgh: Pickwick 1980

P. Sigal, 'Aspects of Dual Convenant Theology: Salvation', *HBT* 5 (1983), pp. 1–48

M. Simon, *St Stephen and the Hellenists in the Primitive Church*, London: Longmans 1958

**M. Simon, *Verus Israel. A Study of the Relations Between Christians and Jews in the Roman Empire (AD 135–425)*, 1964; Oxford University 1986

E. M. Smallwood, *The Jews under Roman Rule*, Leiden: Brill 1976

M. Smith, 'Palestinian Judaism in the First Century', *Israel: Its Role in Civilization*, ed. M. Davis, New York: Jewish Theological Seminary of America 1956, pp. 67–81

H. F. D. Sparks (ed.), *The Apocryphal Old Testament* Oxford: Clarendon 1984

G. N. Stanton, 'The Gospel of Matthew and Judaism', *BJRL* 66 (1984), p. 264–84

G. N. Stanton, 'The Origin and Purpose of Matthew's Gospel. Matthean Scholarship from 1945 to 1980', *ANRW* II.25.3 (1985), pp. 890–1951

G. N. Stanton and G. G. Stroumsa (eds), *Tolerance and Intolerance in Early Judaism and Christianity*, Cambridge University 1998

**K. Stendahl, *Paul Among Jews and Gentiles*, London: SCM Press/Philadelphia: Fortress 1977

M. Stern, *Greek and Latin Authors on Jews and Judaism*, 3 vols, Jerusalem: Israel Academy of Sciences and Humanities, 1976, 1980, 1984

M. Stöhr, hrsg., *Jüdische Existenz und die Erneuerung der christlichen Theologie*, München, 1981

M. E. Stone, *Scriptures, Sects and Visions. A Profile of Judaism from Ezra to the Jewish Revolts*, Oxford: Blackwell 1982

M. E. Stone, (ed.), *Jewish Writings of the Second Temple Period*, Assen: Van Gorcum 1984

H. L. Strack and P. Billerbeck, *Kommentar zum Neuen Testament aus Talmud und Midrasch*, München: C. H. Beck, 4 vols, 1922–28

G. Strecker, 'On the Problem of Jewish Christianity', in Bauer, pp. 241–85

M. S. Taylor, *Anti-Judaisn and Early Christian Identity: A Critique of the Consensus*, Leiden: Brill 1995

V. Tcherikover, *Hellenistic Civilization and the Jews*, Jewish Publication Society of America 1959

G. Theissen, *The First Followers of Jesus*, London: SCM Press 1978 = *Sociology of Early Palestinian Christianity*, Philadelphia: Fortress 1978

**C. Thoma, *A Christian Theology of Judaism*, New York: Paulist 1980

P. J. Tomson and S. Schoon, in *The Image of the Judaeo-Christians in Ancient Jewish and Christian Literature*, ed. P. J. Tomson and D. Lambers-Petry, WUNT 158; Tübingen: Mohr Siebeck 2003

P. Trebilco, *Jewish Communities in Asia Minor*, SNTSMS 69; Cambridge University 1991

J. B. Tyson (ed.), *Luke-Acts and the Jewish People*, Minneapolis: Augsburg 1988

E. E. Urbach, *The Sages. Their Concepts and Beliefs*, 2 vols, Jerusalem: Magnes 1979

A. Vanhoye, *Old Testament Priests and the New Priest according to the New Testament*, Petersham, Mass.: St Bede's 1986

G. Vermes, *The Dead Sea Scrolls in English*, Harmondsworth: Penguin ³1987

G. Vermes, *Jesus the Jew*, London: Collins 1973; Philadelphia: Fortress/London: SCM Press ²1983

G. Vermes, *The Dead Sea Scrolls: Qumran in Perspective*, London: Collins 1977; London: SCM Press/Philadelphia: Fortress ²1982

G. Vermes, *Jesus and the World of Judaism*, London: SCM Press/Philadelphia: Fortress 1984

U. C. von Wahlde, 'The Johannine "Jews". A Critical Survey', *NTS* 28 (1982), pp. 33–60

B. Wander, *Trennungsprozesse zwischen frühen Christentum und Judentum im I. Jahrhundert n. Chr.*, Tübingen: Mohr Siebeck 1994

F. Watson, *Paul, Judaism and the Gentiles*, SNTSMS; Cambridge University 1986

A. J. M. Wedderburn, 'Paul and Jesus: the Problem of Continuity', *SJT* 38 (1985), pp. 189–203

J. Weiss, *Jesus' Proclamation of the Kingdom of God*, 1892; London: SCM Press/Philadelphia: Fortress 1971

J. Weiss, *The History of Primitive Christianity*, 1914; 1937; Harper 1959

S. Westerholm, *Jesus and Scribal Authority*, Lund: ConB 1978

**S. Westerholm, *Israel's Law and the Church's Faith. Paul and his Recent Interpreters*, Grand Rapids: Eerdmans 1988

M. Whittaker, *Jews and Christians: Graeco-Roman Views*, Cambridge University 1979

R. L. Wilken, *The Myth of Christian Beginnings*, London: SCM Press 1979

**M. R. Wilson, *Our Father Abraham. Jewish Roots of the Christian Faith*, Grand Rapids: Eerdmans 1989

S. G. Wilson, *The Gentiles and the Gentile Mission in Luke-Acts*, SNTSMS 23; Cambridge University 1973

S. G. Wilson, *Luke and the Law*, SNTSMS 50; Cambridge University 1983

S. G. Wilson, *Related Strangers: Jews and Christians 70–170 CE*, Minneapolis: Fortress 1995

S. G. Wilson (ed.), *Anti-Judaism in Early Christianity. Vol. 2. Separation and Polemic*, Waterloo, Ontario: Wilfrid Laurier University 1986

J. H. Yoder, *The Jewish–Christian Schism Revisited*, Grand Rapids: Eerdmans 2003

Y. K. Yu, *The New Covenant: the Promise and its Fulfilment*, PhD Diss., Durham University 1989

I. Zeitlin, *Jesus and the Judaism of his Time*, Oxford: Polity 1988

S. Zeitlin, *Who Crucified Jesus?*, New York: Bloch ⁵1964

D. Zeller, *Juden und Heiden in der Mission des Paulus: Studien zum Römerbrief*, Stuttgart: KBW 1973

M. Zetterholm, *The Formation of Christianity in Antioch: A Social-Scientific Approach to the Separation between Judaism and Christianity*, London: Routledge 2003

Index of Biblical and Ancient Writings

II JEWISH (OLD TESTAMENT) APOCRYPHA & PSEUDEPIGRAPHA
APOCRYPHA

PSEUDEPIGRAPHA

III DEAD SEA SCROLLS, PHILO, JOSEPHUS & RABBINIC TEXTS
DEAD SEA SCROLLS

PHILO

JOSEPHUS

RABBINIC TEXTS

V OTHER EARLY CHRISTIAN AND ANCIENT WRITINGS
OTHER EARLY CHRISTIAN TEXTS

OTHER ANCIENT WRITINGS

Index of Modern Authors

Index of Subjects

CPSIA information can be obtained at www.ICGtesting.com
Printed in the USA
BVOW08s1432020714

358031BV00009B/371/P